Of Grammatology

Of Grammatology

BY

Jacques Derrida

Translated by
Gayatri Chakravorty Spivak

MOTILAL BANARSIDASS PUBLISHERS
PRIVATE LIMITED • DELHI

First Indian Edition : Delhi, 1994
Reprint : Delhi, 2023

First Published : Maryland, 1976

ISBN: 978-81-208-1187-4 (Cloth)
ISBN: 978-93-917-5972-8 (Paper)

Also available at:
MOTILAL BANARSIDASS
41 U.A. Bungalow Road, Jawahar Nagar, Delhi 110 007
8 Mahalaxmi Chamber, 22 Bhulabhai Desai Road, Mumbai 400 026
236, 9th Main III Block, Jayanagar, Bangalore 560 011
120 Royapettah High Road, Mylapore, Chennai 600 004
Sanas Plaza, 1302 Baji Rao Road, Pune 411 002
8 Camac Street, Kolkata 700 017
Ashok Rajpath, Patna 800 004
Chowk, Varanasi 221 001

Printed in India

BY JAINENDRA PRAKASH JAIN AT SHRI JAINENDRA PRESS,
A-45 NARAINA, PHASE-I, NEW DELHI 110 028
AND PUBLISHED BY NARENDRA PRAKASH JAIN FOR
MOTILAL BANARSIDASS PUBLISHERS PRIVATE LIMITED,
BUNGALOW ROAD, DELHI 110 007

Contents

Acknowledgments

I thank Angelo Bertocci for having given me the idea for this translation. I thank Paul de Man for his patient and penetrating criticism of the Translator's Preface and the text, at a time when his own schedule was so thoroughly besieged. I thank J. Hillis Miller for his advice, his active encouragement, and his acute comments on the Translator's Preface. I owe him particular thanks for having introduced me to Derrida himself after I had been working on this book for a year. I am grateful to John Brenkmen, Leone Stein, and Paul M. Wright for their support during the early stages of the work. In the preparation of the translation, I have been particularly helped by four painstaking and indefatigable bilingual readers: Jessie L. Hornsby, Dori Katz, Richard Laden, Talbot Spivak. Pierre de Saint-Victor, the late Alexander Aspel, Jacques Bourgeacq and Donald Jackson untied occasional knots. To all of them, a considerable debt of gratitude is due. (The whole book is a gift for Talbot Spivak.) I thank also the Carver Foundation at the University of Iowa for making it possible for me to go to France in the summer of 1973 to discuss this book with Jacques Derrida. To Robert Scholes I am grateful for having made it possible for me to teach a seminar on Derrida at Brown University in the fall of 1974–75. At that seminar, especially through active exchange with Bella Brodzky and Tom Claire, I staked out the ground for my Preface.

I am grateful to Peter Bacon for typing the first half of the manuscript and the Preface from sometimes indecipherable copy. Pauline Grimson not only typed the rest, but always delivered material at very short notice without complaint, and conscientiously copy-edited my pages. I believe she came to feel a personal responsibility for the making of this book, and for that I am most grateful. I thank Timothy Shipe for his able assistance.

Without Dominick Franco, my research assistant, the manuscript would not have gone to press. Michael Ryan criticized each version of the Translator's Preface with a sharp and inspired eye and helped untiringly with library materials. I cannot thank him enough for his incredibly meticulous and informed reading of the final proofs. And Catty, indifferent yet devoted companion through a season of solitary labor.

I am grateful to *Grammatology* for having brought me the friendship of Marguerite and Jacques Derrida.

Gayatri Chakravorty Spivak

Translator's Preface

If you have been reading Derrida, you will know that a plausible gesture would be to begin with a consideration of "the question of the preface." But I write in the hope that for at least some of the readers of this volume Derrida is new; and therefore take it for granted that, for the moment, an introduction can be made.

Jacques Derrida is maître-assistant in philosophy at the Ecole Normale Supérieure in Paris. He was born forty-five years ago of Sephardic Jewish parents in Algiers.[1] At nineteen, he came to France as a student. He was at Harvard on a scholarship in 1956–57. In the sixties he was among the young intellectuals writing for the avant-garde journal *Tel Quel*.[2] He is now associated with GREPH (Groupe de Recherche de l'Enseignement Philosophique)—a student movement that engages itself with the problems of the institutional teaching of philosophy. He was for a time a visiting professor on a regular basis at the Johns Hopkins University, and now occupies a similar position at Yale. He has an affection for some of the intellectual centers of the Eastern seaboard—Cambridge, New York, Baltimore—in his vocabulary, "America." And it seems that at first these places and now more and more of the intellectual centers all over the United States are returning his affection.

Derrida's first book was a translation of Edmund Husserl's "Origin of Geometry," with a long critical introduction. This was followed by *La voix et le phénomène*, a critique of Husserl's theory of meaning. In between appeared a collection of essays entitled *L'écriture et la différence*. *De la grammatologie* came next, followed by two more collections—*La dissémination* and *Marges de la philosophie*. There was a little noticed introduction to the *Essai sur l'origine des connaissances humaines* by Condillac, entitled "L'archéologie du frivole," and *Positions*, a collection of interviews. This year his monumental *Glas* has appeared.[3]

Jacques Derrida is also this collection of texts.

In an essay on the "Preface" to Hegel's *Phenomenology of the Mind*, Jean Hyppolite writes:

When Hegel had finished the *Phenomenology* . . . he reflected retrospectively on his philosophic enterprise and wrote the "Preface." . . . It is a strange demonstration, for he says above all, "Don't take me seriously in a preface. The real philosophical work is what I have just written, the *Phenomenology of the Mind*. And if I speak to you outside of what I have written, these marginal comments cannot have the value of the work itself. . . . Don't take a preface seriously. The preface announces a project and a project is nothing until it is realized."[4]

It is clear that, as it is commonly understood, the preface harbors a lie. "Prae-fatio" is "a saying before-hand" (Oxford English Dictionary—OED). Yet it is accepted as natural by Hyppolite, as indeed by all of us, that "Hegel reflected *retrospectively* on his philosophic enterprise and wrote his 'Preface'." We may see this as no more than the tacit acceptance of a fiction. We think of the Preface, however, not as a literary, but as an expository exercise. It "involves a norm of truth," although it might well be the insertion of an obvious fiction into an ostensibly "true" discourse. (Of course, when the preface is being written by someone other than the author, the situation is yet further complicated. A pretense at writing *before* a text that one must have read *before* the preface can be written. Writing a postface would not really be different—but that argument can only be grasped at the end of this preface.)

Hegel's own objection to the Preface seems grave. The contrast between abstract generality and the self-moving *activity* of cognition appears to be structured like the contrast between preface and text. The method of philosophy is the structure of knowing, an activity of consciousness that moves of itself; this activity, the method of philosophical discourse, structures the philosophical text. The reader of the philosophical text will recognize this self-movement in his consciousness as he surrenders himself to and masters the text. Any prefatory gesture, abstracting so-called themes, robs philosophy of its self-moving structure. "In modern times," Hegel writes, "an individual finds the abstract form ready made."[5] Further,

let [modern man] read reviews of philosophical works, and even go to the length of reading the prefaces and first paragraphs of the works themselves; for the latter give the general principles on which everything turns, while the reviews along with the historical notice provide over and above the critical judgment and appreciation, which, being a judgment passed on the work, goes farther than the work that is judged. This common way a man can take in his dressing-gown. But spiritual elation in the eternal, the sacred, the infinite, moves along the high way of truth in the robes of the high priest.[6]

Yet, as Hyppolite points out, Hegel damns the preface in general even as he writes his own "Preface." And Derrida suggests that a very significant part of Hegel's work was but a play of prefaces (*Dis* 15f). Whereas Hegel's impatience with prefaces is based on philosophical grounds, his excuse for continuing to write them seems commonsensical: "Having in mind that the general idea of what is to be done, if it precedes the attempt to carry it out, facilitates the comprehension of this process, it is worth while to indicate here some rough idea of it, with the intention of eliminating at the same time certain forms whose habitual presence is a hindrance to philosophical knowledge [*in der Absicht zugleich, bei dieser Gelegenheit einige Formen zu entfernen, deren Gewohnheit ein Hindernis für das philosophische Erkennen ist*]."[7] Hegel's objection to prefaces reflects the following structure: preface/text = abstract generality/self-moving activity. His acceptance of prefaces reflects another structure: preface/text = signifier/signified. And the name of the "=" in this formula is the Hegelian *Aufhebung*.

Aufhebung is a relationship between two terms where the second at once annuls the first and lifts it up into a higher sphere of existence; it is a hierarchial concept generally translated "sublation" and now sometimes translated "sublimation." A successful preface is *aufgehoben* into the text it precedes, just as a word is *aufgehoben* into its meaning. It is as if, to use one of Derrida's structural metaphors, the son or seed (preface or word), caused or engendered by the father (text or meaning) is recovered by the father and thus justified.

But, within this structural metaphor, Derrida's cry is "dissemination," the seed that neither inseminates nor is recovered by the father, but is scattered abroad.[8] And he makes room for the prefatory gesture in quite another way:

The preface is a necessary gesture of homage and parricide, for the book (the father) makes a claim of authority or origin which is both true and false. (As regards parricide, I speak theoretically. The preface need make no overt claim—as this one does not—of destroying its pre-text. As a preface, it is already surrendered to that gesture. . . .) Humankind's common desire is for a stable center, and for the assurance of mastery—through knowing or possessing. And a book, with its ponderable shape and its beginning, middle, and end, stands to satisfy that desire. But what sovereign subject is the origin of the book? "I was not one man only," says Proust's narrator, "but the steady advance hour after hour of an army in close formation, in which there appeared, according to the moment, impassioned men, indifferent men, jealous men. . . . In a composite mass, these elements may, one by one, *without our noticing it*, be replaced by others, which others again eliminate or reinforce, until in the end a change has been brought about which it would be impossible to conceive if we were a single person."[9] What, then, is the book's identity? Ferdinand de Saussure had remarked that the "same" phoneme pronounced twice or by two different people is not identical with itself. Its only identity is in its difference from all other phonemes (77–78, **52–54***). So do the two readings of the "same" book show an identity that can only be defined as a difference. The book is not repeatable in its "identity": each reading of the book produces a simulacrum of an "original" that is itself the mark of the shifting and unstable subject that Proust describes, using and being used by a language that is also shifting and unstable. Any preface commemorates that difference in identity by inserting itself between two readings—in our case, my reading (given of course that my language and I are shifting and unstable), my rereading, my rearranging of the text—and your reading. As Hegel (and other defenders of the authority of the text) wrote preface on preface to match re-editions and revised versions, they unwittingly became a party to this identity in difference:

> From the moment that the circle turns, that the book is wound back upon itself, that the book repeats itself, its self-identity receives an imperceptible difference which allows us to step effectively, rigorously, and thus discreetly, out of the closure. Redoubling the closure, one splits it. Then one escapes it furtively, between two passages through the same book, through the same line, following the same bend. . . . This departure outside of the identical within the same remains very slight, it weighs nothing, it thinks and weighs the book *as such*. The return to the book is also the abandoning of the book. (*ED* 430)

The preface, by daring to repeat the book and reconstitute it in another register, merely enacts what is already the case: the book's repetitions are always other than the book. There is, in fact, no "book" other than these ever-different repetitions: the "book" in other words, is always already a "text," constituted by the play of identity and difference. A written preface provisionally localizes the place where, between reading and reading, book and book, the inter-inscribing of "reader(s)," "writer(s)," and language is forever at work. Hegel had closed the circle between father and son, text and preface. He had in fact suggested, as Derrida makes clear, that the fulfilled concept—the end of the self-acting method of the philosophical text—was the pre-dicate—pre-saying—pre-face, to the preface. In Derrida's reworking, the structure preface-text becomes open at both ends. The text has no stable identity, no stable origin, no stable end. Each act of reading the "text" is a preface to the next. The reading of a self-professed preface is no exception to this rule.

It is inaccurate yet necessary to say that something called *De la grammatologie* is (was) the provisional origin of my preface. And, even as I write, I project the moment, when you, reading, will find in my preface the provisional origin of your reading of *Of Grammatology*. There can be an indefinite number of variations on that theme.

*** Hereafter all page numbers in bold-face type refer to pages in this volume.**

Why must we worry over so simple a thing as preface-making? There is, of course, no real answer to questions of this sort. The most that can be said, and Derrida has reminded us to say it anew, is that a certain view of the world, of consciousness, and of language has been accepted as the correct one, and, if the minute particulars of that view are examined, a rather different picture (that is also a no-picture, as we shall see) emerges. That examination involves an enquiry into the "operation" of our most familiar gestures. To quote Hegel again:

> What is "familiarly known" is not properly known, just for the reason that it is "familiar." When engaged in the process of knowing, it is the commonest form of self-deception, and a deception of other people as well, to assume something to be familiar, and to let it pass [*gefallen zu lassen*] on that very account. Knowledge of that sort, with all its talking around it [*Hin- und Herreden*] never gets from the spot, but has no idea that this is the case. . . . To display [*auseinanderlegen*] an idea in its original [*ursprünglich*] elements means returning upon its moments, . . .[10]

When Derrida writes that, since Kant, philosophy has become aware of taking the responsibility for its discourse, it is this reexamination of the familiar that he is hinting at. And this is one of the reasons why he is so drawn to Mallarmé, "that exemplary poet," who invested every gesture of reading and writing—even the slitting of an uncut double page with a knife—with textual import.[11]

And if the assumption of responsibility for one's discourse leads to the conclusion that all conclusions are genuinely provisional and therefore inconclusive, that all origins are similarly unoriginal, that responsibility itself must cohabit with frivolity, this need not be cause for gloom. Derrida contrasts Rousseau's melancholy with Nietzsche's affirmative joy precisely from this angle: "Turned toward the presence, lost or impossible, of the absent origin, [the] structuralist thematic of broken immediateness is thus the sad, *negative*, nostalgic, guilty, Rousseauist aspect of the thought of play of which the Nietzschean *affirmation*—the joyous affirmation of the play of the world and of the innocence of becoming, the affirmation of a world of signs without fault, without truth, without origin, offered to an active interpretation—would be the other side." (*ED* 427, *SC* 264)

There is, then, always already a preface between two hands holding open a book. And the "prefacer," of the same or another proper name as the "author," need not apologize for "repeating" the text.

I

"It is inaccurate yet necessary to say," I have written above, "that something called *De la grammatologie* is (was) the provisional origin of my preface." Inaccurate yet necessary. My predicament is an analogue for a certain philosophical exigency that drives Derrida to writing "sous rature," which I translate as "under erasure." This is to write a word, cross it out, and then print both word and deletion. (Since the word is inaccurate, it is crossed out. Since it is necessary, it remains legible.) To take an example from Derrida that I shall cite again: ". . . the sign *is* that ill-named thing . . . which escapes the instituting question of philosophy . . ." (31, 19).

In examining familiar things we come to such unfamiliar conclusions that our very language is twisted and bent even as it guides us. Writing "under erasure" is the mark of this contortion.

Derrida directs us to Martin Heidegger's *Zur Seinsfrage* as the "authority" for this strategically important practice,[12] which we cannot understand without a look at Heidegger's formulation of it.

Zur Seinsfrage is ostensibly a letter to Ernst Jünger which seeks to establish a speculative definition of nihilism. Just as Hegel, writing a preface, philosophically confronted the problem of prefaces, so Heidegger, establishing a definition, philosophically confronts the problem of definitions: in order for the nature of anything in particular to be defined as an entity, the question of Being is general must always already be broached and answered in the affirmative. That something *is*, presupposes that *anything* can be.

What is this question of Being that is necessarily precomprehended in order that thinking itself occur? Since it is always anterior to thinking, it can never be formulated as an answer to the question "what is . . .:" "The 'goodness' of the rightfully demanded 'good definition' finds its confirmation in our giving up the wish to define in so far as this must be established on assertions in which thinking dies out. . . . No information can be given about nothingness and Being and nihilism, about their essence and about the (verbal) essence [it *is*] of the (nominal) essence [*it* is] which can be presented tangibly in the form of assertions [it is . . .]." (*QB* 80–81) This possibility of Being must be granted (or rather is already of itself granted) for the human being to say "I am," not to mention "you are," "she is." Even such negative concepts as "nothingness" or "nihilism" are held within this precomprehended question of Being which is asked and answered nonverbally, nonnominally, and without agency. This question, therefore, cannot be constructed to match an assertive answer. And the human being is the place or zone where this particular problem has its play; not the human being as an individual, but the human being as *Dasein*—simply being-there—as the principle that asks and posits: 'Man does not only stand *in* the critical zone. . . . He himself, but not he for himself and particularly not through himself alone, *is* this zone. . . ." (*QB* 82–83) But, Heidegger cautions us, this is not mysticism. It is the baffling result of an examination of the obvious, the lifting of the most natural forgetfulness.

"What if even the [propositional] language of metaphysics and metaphysics itself, whether it be that of the living or of the dead God, *as* metaphysics, formed that barrier which forbids a crossing over [*Übergehen*] the line [from the assertion, to the question, of Being]?" (Elsewhere Heidegger suggests, as does, of course, Nietzsche before him, that the propositional language of the sciences is just as forgetful of the question of Being.) "If that were the case, would not then the crossing [out] [diagonally—*Überqueren*] of the line necessarily become a transformation of language and demand a transformed relationship to the essence of language?" (QB 70–71)

As a move toward this transformation, Heidegger crosses out the word "Being," and lets both deletion and word stand. It is inaccurate to use the word "Being" here, for the differentiation of a "concept" of Being has already slipped away from that precomprehended question of Being. Yet it is necessary to use the word, since language cannot do more:

> A thoughtful glance ahead into this realm of "Being" can only write it as Being. The drawing of these crossed lines at first only wards off [*abwehrt*], especially the habit of conceiving "Being" as something standing by itself. . . . The sign of crossing through [*Zeichen der Durchkreuzung*] can, to be sure, . . . not be a merely negative sign of crossing out [*Zeichen der Durchstreichung*]. . . . Man in his essence is the memory [or "memorial," *Gedächtnis*] of Being, but of Being. This means that the essence of man is a part of that which in the crossed intersected lines of Being puts thinking under the claim of a more originary command [*anfänglichere Geheiss*]. (QB 80–81, 82–83)

Language is indeed straining here. The sentence "Man in his essence is the memory (memorial) of Being" avoids ascribing an agent to the unaskable question of Being. Heidegger is working with the resources of the old language, the language we already possess, and which possesses us. To make a new word is to run the risk of forgetting the problem or believing it solved: "That the transformation of the language which contemplates the essence of Being is subject to other demands than the exchanging of an old terminology for a new one, seems to be clear." This transformation should rather involve "crossing out" the relevant old terms and thus liberating them, exposing "the presumptuous demand that [thinking] know the solution of the riddles and bring salvation." (QB 72–73)

Now there is a certain difference between what Heidegger puts under erasure and what Derrida does. "Being" is the master-word that Heidegger crosses out. Derrida does not reject this. But his word is "trace" (the French word carries strong implications of track, footprint, imprint), a word that cannot be a master-word, that presents itself as the mark of an anterior presence, origin, master. For "trace" one can substitute "arche-writing" ("archi-écriture"), or "differance," or in fact quite a few other words that Derrida uses in the same way. But I shall begin with "trace/

track," for it is a simple word; and there also seems, I must admit, something ritually satisfying about beginning with the "trace."

To be sure, when Heidegger sets Being before all concepts, he is attempting to free language from the fallacy of a fixed origin, which is also a fixed end. But, *in a certain way*, he also sets up Being as what Derrida calls the "transcendental signified." For whatever a concept might "mean," anything that is conceived of in its being-present must lead us to the already-answered question of Being. In that sense, the sense of the final reference, Being is indeed the final signified to which all signifiers refer. But Heidegger makes it clear that Being cannot be contained by, is always prior to, indeed transcends, signification. It is therefore a situation where the signified commands, and is yet free of, all signifiers—a recognizably theological situation. The end of philosophy, according to Heidegger, is to restore the memory of that free and commanding signified, to discover *Urwörter* (originary words) in the languages of the world by learning to waylay the limiting logic of signification, a project that Derrida describes as "the other side of nostalgia, which I will call Heideggerian *hope*. . . . I . . . shall relate it to what seems to me to be retained of metaphysics in [Heidegger's] 'Spruch des Anaximander,' namely, the quest for the proper word and the unique name." (*MP* 29, *SP* 159–60)

Derrida seems to show no nostalgia for a lost presence. He sees in the traditional concept of the sign a hetereogeneity—"the other of the signified is never contemporary, is at best a subtly discrepant inverse or parallel—discrepant by the time of a breath—of the order of the signifier" (31, 18). It is indeed an ineluctable nostalgia for presence that makes of this heterogeneity a unity by declaring that a sign brings forth the presence of the signified. Otherwise it would seem clear that the sign is the place where "the completely other is announced as such—without any simplicity, any identity, any resemblance or continuity—in that which is not it" (69, 47). Word and thing or thought never in fact become one. We are reminded of, referred to, what the convention of words sets up as thing or thought, by a particular arrangement of words. The structure of reference works and can go on working not because of the identity between these two so-called component parts of the sign, but because of their relationship of difference. The sign marks a place of difference.

One way of satisfying the rage for unity is to say that, within the phonic sign (speech rather than writing) there is no structure of difference; and that this nondifference is felt as self-presence in the silent and solitary thought of the self. This is so familiar an argument that we would accept it readily if we did not stop to think about it. But if we did, we would notice that there is no necessary reason why a particular sound should be identical with a "thought or thing"; and that the argument applies even when one "speaks" silently to oneself. Saussure was accordingly obliged to point out that the phonic signifier is as conventional as the graphic (74, 51).

Armed with this simple yet powerful insight—powerful enough to "deconstruct the transcendental signified"—that the sign, phonic as well as graphic, is a structure of difference, Derrida suggests that what opens the possibility of thought is not merely the question of being, but also the never-annulled difference from "the completely other." Such is the strange "being" of the sign: half of it always "not there" and the other half always "not that." The structure of the sign is determined by the trace or track of that other which is forever absent. This other is of course never to be found in its full being. As even such empirical events as answering a child's question or consulting the dictionary proclaim, one sign leads to another and so on indefinitely. Derrida quotes Lambert and Peirce: " '[philosophy should] reduce the *theory of things* to the *theory of signs.*' . . . 'The idea of *manifestation* is the idea of a sign' " (72, 49), and contrasts them to Husserl and Heidegger. On the way to the trace/track, the word "sign" has to be put under erasure: "the sign is that ill-named thing, the only one, that escapes the instituting question of philosophy: 'What is . . . ?' "

Derrida, then, gives the name "trace" to the part played by the radically other within the structure of difference that is the sign. (I stick to "trace" in my translation, because it "looks the same" as Derrida's word; the reader must remind himself of at least the track, even the spoor, contained within the French word.) In spite of itself, Saussurean linguistics recognizes the structure of the sign to be a trace-structure. And Freud's psychoanalysis, to some extent in spite of itself, recognizes the structure of experience itself to be a trace-, not a presence-structure. Following an argument analogical to the argument on the sign, Derrida puts the word "experience" under erasure:

> As for the concept of experience, it is most unwieldy here. Like all the notions I am using, it belongs to the history of metaphysics and we can only use it under erasure. "Experience" has always designated the relationship with a presence, whether that relationship had the form of consciousness or not. Yet we must, by means of the sort of contortion and contention that discourse is obliged to undergo, exhaust the resources of the concept of experience before attaining and in order to attain, by deconstruction, its ultimate foundation. It is the only way to escape "empiricism" and the "naive" critiques of experience at the same time (89, 60).

Now we begin to see how Derrida's notion of "sous rature" differs from that of Heidegger's. Heidegger's Being might point at an inarticulable presence. Derrida's trace is the mark of the absence of a presence, an always already absent present, of the lack at the origin that is the condition of thought and experience. For somewhat different yet similar contingencies, both Heidegger and Derrida teach us to use language in terms of a trace-structure, effacing it even as it presents its legibility. We must remember this when we wish to attack Derrida or, for that matter, Heidegger, on certain sorts of straightforward logical grounds; for, one can always forget the invisible erasure, "act as though this makes no difference." (*MP* 3, *SP* 131)[13]

Derrida writes thus on the strategy of philosophizing about the trace:

The value of the transcendental arche [origin] must make its necessity felt before letting itself be erased. The concept of the arche-trace must comply with both that necessity and that erasure. It is in fact contradictory and not acceptable within the logic of identity. The trace is not only the disappearance of origin, . . . it means that the origin did not even disappear, that it was never constituted except reciprocally by a non-origin, the trace, which thus becomes the origin of the origin. From then on, to wrench the concept of the trace from the classical scheme which would derive it from a presence or from an originary non-trace and which would make of it an empirical mark, one must indeed speak of an originary trace or arche-trace (90, 61).

At once inside and outside a certain Hegelian and Heideggerian tradition, Derrida, then, is asking us to change certain habits of mind: the authority of the text is provisional, the origin is a trace; contradicting logic, we must learn to use and erase our language at the same time.

In the last few pages, we have seen Heidegger and Derrida engaged in the process of this curious practice. Derrida in particular is acutely aware that it is a question of strategy. It is the strategy of using the only available language while not subscribing to its premises, or "operat[ing] according to the vocabulary of the very thing that one delimits." (*MP* 18, *SP* 147) For Hegel, as Hyppolite remarks, "philosophical discourse" contains "its own criticism within itself." (*SC* 336, 158) And Derrida, describing the strategy "of a discourse which borrows from a heritage the resources necessary for the deconstruction of that heritage itself," remarks similarly, "language bears within itself the necessity of its own critique." (*ED* 416, *SC* 254) The remark becomes clearer in the light of writing "sous rature": "At each step I was obliged to proceed by ellipses, corrections and corrections of corrections, letting go of each concept at the very moment that I needed to use it, etc."[14]

There is some similarity between this strategy and what Lévi-Strauss calls *bricolage in La pensée sauvage*.[15] Derrida himself remarks:

Lévi-Strauss will always remain faithful to this double intention: to preserve as an instrument that whose truth-value he criticizes, conserving . . . all these old concepts, while at the same time exposing . . . their limits, treating them as tools which can still be of use. No longer is any truth-value [or rigorous meaning] attributed to them; there is a readiness to abandon them if necessary if other instruments should appear more useful. In the meantime, their relative efficacy is exploited, and they are employed to destroy the old machinery to which they belong and of which they themselves are pieces. Thus it is that the language of the human sciences criticizes *itself*. (*ED* 417; *SC* 255, 254)

One distinction between Lévi-Strauss and Derrida is clear enough. Lévi-Strauss's anthropologist seems free to pick his tool; Derrida's philosopher knows that there is no tool that does not belong to the metaphysical box, and proceeds from there. But there is yet another difference, a difference that we must mark as we outline Derridean strategy.

Lévi-Strauss contrasts the *bricoleur* to the engineer. ("The 'bricoleur' has no precise equivalent in English. He is a man who undertakes odd jobs and is a Jack of all trades or is a kind of professional do-it-yourself man, but . . he is of a different standing from, for instance, the English 'odd job man' or handyman."[16]) The discourse of anthropology and the other sciences of man must be *bricolage*: the discourses of formal logic, and the pure sciences, one presumes, can be those of engineering. The engineer's "instrument" is "specially adapted to a specific technical need"; the *bricoleur* makes do with things that were meant perhaps for other ends.[17] The anthropologist must tinker because, at least as Lévi-Strauss argues in *Le cru et le cuit*, it is in fact impossible for him to master the whole field. Derrida, by an important contrast, suggests that the field is *theoretically*, not merely empirically, unknowable. (*ED* 419 f., *SC* 259 f.) Not even in an ideal universe of an empirically reduced number of possibilities would the projected "end" of knowledge ever coincide with its "means." Such a coincidence—"engineering"—is an impossible dream of plenitude. The reason for *bricolage* is that there can be nothing else. No engineer can make the "means"—the sign—and the "end"—meaning—become self-identical. Sign will always lead to sign, one substituting the other (playfully, since "sign" is "under erasure") as signifier and signified in turn. Indeed, the notion of play is important here. Knowledge is not a systematic tracking down of a truth that is hidden but may be found. It is rather the field "of *freeplay*, that is to say, a field of infinite substitutions in the closure of a finite ensemble." (*ED* 423, *SC* 260)

For Derrida, then, the concept of the "engineer" "questioning the universe" is, like Hegel's father-text encompassing the son-preface, or Heidegger's Being as transcendental signified, "a theological idea," an idea that we *need* to fulfill our desire for plenitude and authority. He remarks that Lévi-Strauss, like Heidegger, is afflicted with nostalgia: "one . . . perceives in his work a sort of ethic of presence, an ethic of nostalgia for origins, an ethic of archaic and natural innocence, of a purity of presence and self-presence in speech—an ethic, nostalgia, and even remorse which he often presents as the motivation of the ethnological project when he moves toward archaic societies—exemplary societies in his eyes. These texts are well known." (*ED* 427, *SC* 264)

Derrida does not offer the obverse of this nostalgia. He does not see in the method of the so-called exact sciences an epistemological model of exactitude. All knowledge, whether one knows it or not, is a species of *bricolage*, with its eye on the myth of "engineering." But that myth is always totally other, leaving an originary trace within "bricolage." Like all "useful" words, "bricolage" must also be placed "under erasure." For it can only be defined by its difference from its opposite—"engineering." Yet that opposite, a metaphysical norm, can in fact never be present and thus, strictly speaking, there is no concept of "bricolage" (that which is not engineering). Yet the concept must be used—untenable but necessary. "From the moment that we cease to believe in such an engineer . . . as soon as it is admitted that every finite discourse is bound by a certain *bricolage*, . . . the very idea of *bricolage* is menaced and the difference in which it took on its meaning decomposes." (*ED* 418, *SC* 256) The possible and implicit hierarchical move, reminding us that *bricolage* as a model is "*pre*-scientific," low on a chain of teleologic development, here disappears. Derrida does not allow the possibility of seeing *bricolage* as a cruder, pre-scientific method of investigation, low on the evolutionary scale. One can now begin to understand a rather cryptic sentence in the *Grammatology*: "Without that track [of writing under erasure], . . . the ultra-transcendental text [*bricolage* under erasure] will so closely resemble the pre-critical text [*bricolage* plain and simple] as to be indistinguishable from it." (90, 61)

This undoing yet preserving of the opposition between *bricolage* and engineering is an analogue for Derrida's attitude toward all oppositions—an attitude that "erases" (in this special sense) all oppositions. I shall come back to this gesture again and again in this Preface.

(As he develops the notion of the joyful yet laborious strategy of rewriting the old language—a language, incidentally, we must know well—Derrida mentions the "clôture" of metaphysics. We must know that we are within the "clôture" of metaphysics, even as we attempt to undo it. It would be an historicist mistake to represent this "closure" of metaphysics as simply the temporal finishing-point of metaphysics. It is also the metaphysical desire to make the end coincide with the means, create an *en*-closure, make the definition coincide with the defined, the "father" with the "son"; within the logic of identity to balance the equation, close the circle. Our language reflects this desire. And so it is from within this language that we must attempt an "opening.")

II

Derrida uses the word "metaphysics" very simply as shorthand for any science of presence. (If he were to attempt a rigorous definition of metaphysics, the word would no doubt go "under erasure.") But it is this simple *bricoleur's* take on the word that permits Derrida to allow the possibility of a "Marxist" or "structuralist" metaphysics. He puts it succinctly in that early essay from which I have already quoted:

The history of metaphysics, like the history of the West, is the history of these metaphors and metonymies.[18] Its matrix—if you will pardon me for demonstrating so little and for being so elliptical in order to bring me more quickly to my principal theme—is the determination of being as *presence* in all the senses of this word. It would be possible to show that all the names related to fundamentals, to principles, or to the center have always designated the constant of a presence—*eidos, archè, telos, energeia, ousia* (essence, existence, substance, subject) *aletheia*, transcendentality, consciousness, or conscience, God, man, and so forth. (*ED* 410–11, *SC* 249)

I have lingered on the "question of the preface" and the pervasive Derridean practice of the "sous rature" to slip into the atmosphere of Derrida's thought. Now I speak of his acknowledged "precursors"—Nietzsche, Freud, Heidegger, Husserl.[19] I shall attend in greatest detail to Nietzsche because our received version of him is so different from Derrida's, and because Derrida's relationship to him is so inescapable. I shall then comment on Derrida's attitudes toward structuralism; on his own vocabulary and practice and on the structure of the *Grammatology*. A few words next about translation, and we are into the text.

Derrida has given us two lists of what we should look for in Nietzsche: "the systematic mistrust of metaphysics as a whole, the formal approach to philosophic discourse, the concept of the philosopher-artist, the rhetorical and philological question asked of the history of philosophy, the suspicion of the values of truth ('well applied convention'), of meaning and of being, of 'meaning of being', the attention to the economic phenomena of force and of difference of forces, and so forth." (*MP* 362–63) And, "Radicalizing the concepts of *interpretation, perspective, evaluation, difference* . . . Nietzsche, far from remaining *simply* (with Hegel and as Heidegger wished) *within* metaphysics, contributed a great deal to the liberation of the signifier from its dependence or derivation with respect to the logos, and the related concept of truth or the primary signified . . ." (31–32, 19).

It should by now be clear that Nietzsche's "suspicion of the value of truth . . . of meaning and of being, of 'meaning of being' " of the "concept of . . . the primary signified," is intimately shared by Derrida. The other items on the two lists can be brought under one head: philosophical discourse as formal, rhetorical, figurative discourse, a something to be deciphered. The end of this Preface will make clear how deeply Derrida is committed to such a notion. Here I shall comment on the implications of "the decipherment of figurative discourse" in Nietzsche.

As early as 1873, Nietzsche described metaphor as the originary process of what the intellect presents as "truth." "The intellect, as a means for the preservation of the individual, develops its chief power in dissimulation."[20] "A nerve-stimulus, first transcribed [*übertragen*] into an image [*Bild*]! First metaphor! The image again copied into a sound! Second metaphor! And each time he [the creator of language] leaps completely out of one sphere right into the midst of an entirely different one." (*NW* III. ii. 373, *TF* 178) In its simplest outline, Nietzsche's definition of metaphor seems to be the establishing of an identity between dissimilar things. Nietzsche's phrase is "Gleich machen" (make equal), calling to mind the German word "Gleichnis"—image, simile, similitude, comparison, allegory, parable—an unmistakable pointer to figurative practice in general. "Every idea originates through equating the unequal." (*NW* III. ii. 374, *TF* 179) "What, therefore, is truth? A mobile army of metaphors, metonymies, anthropomorphisms; . . . truths are illusions of which one has forgotten that they *are* illusions, . . . coins which have their obverse effaced and now are no longer of account as coins but merely as metal." (*NW* III. ii. 374–75, *TF* 180) I hold on here to the notions of a process of figuration and a process of forgetfulness.

In this early text, Nietzsche describes the figurative drive as "that impulse towards the formation of metaphors, that fundamental impulse of man, which we cannot reason away for one moment—for thereby we should reason away man himself. . . . (*NW* III. ii. 381, *TF* 188) Later he will give this drive the name "will to power." Our so-called will to truth is a will to power because "the so-called drive for knowledge can be traced back to a drive to appropriate and conquer."[21] Nietzsche's sense of the inevitable forcing of the issue, of exercising power, comes through in his italics: " 'Thinking' in primitive conditions (preorganic) is the crystallization of forms. . . . In our thought, the essential feature is fitting new material into old schemas, . . . *making* equal what is new."[22]

The human being has nothing more to go on than a collection of nerve stimuli. And, because he or she must be secure in the knowledge of, and therefore power over, the "world" (inside or outside), the nerve stimuli are explained and described through the categories of figuration that masquerade as the categories of "truth." These explanations and descriptions are "interpretations" and reflect a human inability to tolerate undescribed chaos—"that the collective character [*Gesamtcharakter*] of the world . . . is in all eternity chaos—in the sense not of a lack of necessity but of a lack of order, arrangement, form, beauty, wisdom, and whatever other names there are for our aesthetic anthropomorphisms [human weaknesses—*Menschlichkeiten*]."[23] As Nietzsche suggests, this need for power through anthropomorphic defining compels humanity to create an unending proliferation of interpretations whose only "origin," that shudder in the nerve strings, being a direct sign of nothing, leads to no primary signified. As Derrida writes, Nietzsche provides an "entire thematics of active interpretations, which substitutes an incessant deciphering for the disclosure of truth as a presentation of the thing itself." (*MP* 19, *SP* 149)

Interpretation is "the introduction of meaning" (or "deception through meaning"—*Sinnhineinlegen*), a making-sign that is a making-figure, for there is, in this thought, no possibility of a literal, true, self-identical meaning. Identification (*Gleich-machen*) constitutes the act of figuration. Therefore, "nothing is ever comprehended, but rather designated and distorted. . . ." This extends, of course, to the identity between an act (effect) and its purpose (cause): "Every single time something is done with a purpose in view, something fundamentally different and other occurs." (WM II. 59, 130; *WP* 301, 351) The will to power is a process of "incessant deciphering"—figurating, interpreting, sign-ifying through apparent identification. Thus, even supposing that an act could be isolated within its outlines, to gauge the relationship between it and its "originating" consciousness, the critical glance must reverse (necessarily nonidentically) this decipherment, follow the "*askew* path," read the act in its textuality. In this important respect, "without him [Nietzsche] the 'question' of the text would never have erupted, at least in the precise sense that it has taken today."[24]

In *The Genealogy of Morals*, Nietzsche reads the history of morality as a text. He interprets the successive *meanings* of systems of morality. "Purposes and utilities are only *signs* that a will to power has become master of something less powerful and has in turn imprinted the meaning of a function upon it [*ihm von sich aus den Sinn einer Funktion aufgeprägt hat*; this image of *Aufprägung*—imprinting—'figuration' in yet another sense, is most important in Nietzsche, and constantly recurs in this particular context]; and the entire history of a 'thing', an organ, a custom can in this way be a continuous sign-chain of ever new interpretations and makeshift excuses [*Zurechtmachungen*] whose causes do not even have to be related to one another in a purely chance fashion."[25] "All concepts in which an entire process is semiotically telescoped [*Zusammenfasst*] elude definition." (*NW*, VI. ii. 333, *GM* 80) Derrida would, of course, suspend the entire notion of semiosis, put the sign under erasure. It is possible to read such a suspension into Nietzsche's "continuous sign-chains," without origin and end in "truth." And thus it is possible to discover an affinity between Derrida's practice in *Of Grammatology* and Nietzsche's interpretation of value systems as infinite textuality; and to see in Derrida's decipherment of the negative valuation of writing within the speech-writing hierarchy the mark of a Nietzschean "genealogy."

But it is also possible to criticize Nietzsche's indefinite expansion of the notion of metaphoricity or figuration as a gesture that turns back upon itself. "Nietzsche stretches the limits of the metaphorical," Derrida writes:

> to such a point that he attributes metaphorical power to every use of sound in speaking: for does this not involve the transfer into the time of speaking of something that has a different nature in itself? . . . Strangely enough, this comes down to treating every signifier as a metaphor for the signified, while the classical concept of metaphor denotes only the substitution of one signified for another so that the one becomes the signifier of the other. Is not Nietzsche's procedure here precisely to extend to every element of discourse, under the name *metaphor*, what classical rhetoric no less strangely considered a quite specific figure of speech, *metonymy of the sign* [that the sign as "a part" *stood for* "the whole" meaning]?"[26]

We should, of course, note that Derrida's criticism is framed in two questions, rather than in a series of declarations. Yet, even if we were to take only the declarative sentence in our passage, it would be clear that Derrida criticizes Nietzsche precisely because what Nietzsche deciphers he holds decipherable and because metaphor (or figure) so vastly expanded could simply become the name of the process of signification rather than a critique of that process. It would be more acceptable if Nietzsche had put metaphor, or figure, or interpretation, or perspective, or, for that matter, truth, under erasure. I shall suggest that a move toward such an erasure may be traced through Nietzsche's critique of consciousness and the "subject." When the outlines of the "subject" are loosened, the concepts of figuration or metaphoricity—related to meaning-ful-ness,—are subsumed under the broader categories of appropriation and the play of resistant forces. The word "metaphor" is seen to be used "sous rature," as a methodological convenience, for it refers to a more encompassing structure not necessarily involved in meaning-making. Let us follow the unfolding of this pattern.

The "subject" is a unified concept and therefore the result of "interpretation." Nietzsche often stresses that it is a specifically linguistic figurative habit of immemorial standing: "that when it is thought [*wenn gedacht wird*] there must be something 'that thinks' is simply a formulation of our grammatical custom that adds a doer to every deed." (WM II. 13, WP 268) The "*insertion of a subject*" is "*fictitious*." (WM II. 110, WP 337) The will to power as the *subject*'s metaphorizing or figurating, or introduction of meaning, must therefore be questioned. And Nietzsche accordingly asks, pondering on the "making equal" of proximate sensations, a propos of how "*images* . . . then *words*, . . . finally *concepts* arise in the spirit": "Thus confusion of two sensations that are close neighbors, as we take note of these sensations; but *who* is taking note?" (*WM* II. 23, *WP* 275) Nietzsche accordingly entertains the notion of the will to power as an abstract and unlocalized figurative (interpretative) process: "One may not ask: 'who then interprets?' for the interpretation itself is a form of the will to power, exists (but not as a 'being' but as a process, a becoming) as an affect." (*WM* II. 61, *WP* 302)

Sometimes Nietzsche places this abstract will to power, an incessant figuration, not under the control of any knowing subject, but rather underground, in the unconscious. The Nietzschean unconscious is that vast arena of the mind of which the so-called "subject" knows nothing. As Derrida remarks: "both [Freud and Nietzsche] . . . often in a very similar way, questioned the self-assured certitude of consciousness. . . . For Nietzsche 'the important main activity is unconscious.'" (*MP* 18, *SP* 148)

If, however, we want to hold onto "the important main activity" we have to go further than the unconscious, we have to reach the body, the organism. If the "unconscious" is unknown to us, how much more so the body! Already in the early essay "On Truth and Falsity in their Ultramoral Sense," the connections are being established:

What indeed *does* man know about himself? . . . Does not nature keep secret from him most things, even about his body, *e.g.*, the convolutions of the intestines, the quick flow of the blood-currents, the intricate vibration of the fibres, so as to banish and lock him up in proud, delusive knowledge? Nature threw away the keys and woe to the fateful curiosity which might be able for a moment to look out and down through a crevice in the chamber of consciousness, and discover that man indifferent to his own ignorance, is resting on the pitiless, the greedy, the insatiable, the murderous, and, as it were, hanging in dreams on the back of a tiger. Whence, in the wide world, with this state of affairs, arise the impulse of truth? (*NW* III. ii, 371, TF 175–76)

Here is the early signal for a sweeping question like this one in *The Gay Science*: "The unconscious disguise of physiological needs under the cloaks of the objective, ideal, purely spiritual goes to frightening lengths—and often I have asked myself whether, taking a large view philosophy has not been merely an interpretation of the body and a *misunderstanding of the body*." (*NW* V. ii. 16, *GS* 34–35) A yet more sweeping declarative fragment: "Our most sacred convictions, the unchanging elements in our supreme values, are judgments of our muscles." (*WM* I. 370, *WP* 173) It is as if that controlling figurative practice that constitutes all our cognition is being handed over to the body. And indeed Nietzsche's speculation goes further. "Making equal" is seen as a symptom of being animate, rather than the "privilege" of being human; the will to power "appropriates" in the organism, before the "name of man" may be broached: "All thought, judgment, perception, as comparison [*Gleichnis*] has as its precondition a 'positing of equality' [*Gleichsetzen*], and earlier still a '*making* equal' [*Gleich-machen*]. The process of making equal is the same as the incorporation of appropriated material in the amoeba . . . [and] corresponds exactly to that external, mechanical process (which is its symbol) by which protoplasm continually makes what it appropriates equal to itself and arranges it into its own forms and ranks [*in seine Reihen und Formen einordnet*]." (*WM* II. 21, 25; *WP* 273–74, 276) Appropriation and its symbol, making equal, positing as equal—the process operates in the organic universe for its own preservation and constitution before the human consciousness appropriates it and declares it the process of the discovery of truth, the establishment of knowledge. The process differentiates itself into the mapping of the moral universe: "Is it virtuous when a cell transforms itself into a function of a stronger cell? It has to do so [*Sie muss es*]. And is it evil when the stronger cell assimilates the weaker? . . . Joy and desire appear together in the stronger that wants to transform something into its function, joy and the wish to be desired appear together in the weaker that wants to become a function." (*NW* V. ii. 154, *GS* 175–76) Here the relationship between figuration on the one hand, and appropriation, the play of forces, on the other, comes clear. Speaking of the human will to truth, linguistic figuration is the figure Nietzsche must employ. Moving "back" into the organism in general, differentiations among goodness, strength, truth begin to blur; appropriation comes to be a more embracing term than interpretation. Admittedly, this neutralizing rigor is not often *explicit* in Nietzsche. But when it is operative, the irreducible description of the will to power as a search for what is resistant to itself emerges. "The will to power can manifest itself only against resistances; therefore it seeks that which resists it. . . ." (*WM* II 123, *WP* 346) Consider also that curious series of notes, made between November 1887 and March 1888, where Nietzsche tries to bypass language to express what we can crudely call the will to power as the play of will and no-will. It is worth mediating upon the entire passage. Here I quote selectively to give a sense of the problem:

There are no durable ultimate units, no atoms, no monads; here, too, beings are only introduced by us. . . . "Value" is essentially the standpoint for the increase or decrease of these dominating centers ("multiplicities" in any case, but "units" are nowhere present in the nature of becoming). Linguistic means of expression are useless for expressing "becoming"; it accords with our inevitable need to preserve ourselves to posit a crude world of stability, of "things," etc. We may venture to speak of atoms and monads in a relative sense; and it is certain that the smallest world is most durable—There is no will: there are punctuations of will [*Willens-Punktationen*] that are constantly increasing or losing their power. (*WM* II. 171–72, *WP* 380–81)

Nietzsche uses the time-honored figure of the point (*stigmè*)[27] only as the relatively safest image of a unit, and even then not as a sign for durability or continuity, but rather as the participant in a disjunctive periodicity of (positive *or* negative) energizing, a punctuation perhaps also in the sense of the deployment of space as constituting what is usually taken to be a temporal or historical continuity. As we shall see later, the structural complicity here with Freud's psychic time-machine is striking. For the moment our argument is that in this strained and hedged image of the *Willens-Punktationen* (where it is not even clear if the topic is the restricted human will or the principle of the will to power—for who, after all, can "linguistically express" the will to power?), Nietzche's theory of metaphoricity or figuration explodes into "sous rature" and neutralizes into a play of resisting forces. This is how I must interpret Derrida's comment, made outside of the context of Nietzsche's theory of metaphor: ". . . the 'active' (in movement) discord of the different forces and of the differences between forces which Nietzsche opposes to the entire system of metaphysical grammar." (*MP* 19, *SP* 149)

Now if the "subject" is thus put in question, it is clear that the philosopher creating his system must distrust himself as none other. And indeed Nietzsche articulates this problem often. He couches his boldest insights in the form of questions that we cannot dismiss as a rhetorical ploy. Writing on "The Uses and Abuses of History" as early as 1874, he warns us: "And this present treatise, as I will not attempt to deny, shows the modern note of a weak personality in the intemperateness of its criticism, the unripeness of its humanity, in the too frequent transitions from irony to cynicism, from arrogance to scepticism."[28] The spirit of self-diagnosis is strong in every Nietzschean text. "Every society has the tendency to reduce its opponents to caricatures—at least in imagination— . . . Among immoralists it is the moralist: Plato, for example, becomes a caricature in my hands." (*WM* I. 410–11, *WP* 202) Quite in passing, he places a warning frame around all his philosophizing: "One seeks a picture of the world in *that* philosophy in which we feel freest; i.e., in which our most powerful drive feels free to function. This will also be the case with me!" (*WM* I. 410–11, *WP* 224–25) In a passage in *The Gay Science*, he spells out his version of the particular problem that leads Heidegger and Derrida to writing under erasure:

How far the perspective character of existence extends or indeed whether existence has any other character than this; whether existence without interpretation, without "sense," does not become "nonsense"; whether, on the other hand, all existence is not essentially an *interpreting* existence [*ein* auslegendes *Dasein*]—that cannot be decided even by the most industrious and most scrupulously conscientious analysis and self-examination of the intellect; for in the course of this analysis the human intellect cannot avoid seeing itself in its own perspective forms [*perspektivische Form*], and *only* in these. We cannot look around our own corner. (*NW* V. ii. 308, *GS* 336)

Instances can be multiplied. But we must not only record Nietzsche's awareness of this problem, but of some of his ways of coping with it. One of them might be Nietzsche's pervasive strategy of intersubstituting opposites. If one is always bound by one's perspective, one can at least deliberately reverse perspectives as often as possible, in the process undoing opposed perspectives, showing that the two terms of an opposition are merely accomplices of each other. It would take a detailed analysis of Nietzschean practice to demonstrate what I am merely going to suggest here: the notion that the setting up of unitary opposites is an instrument and a consequence of "making equal," and the dissolving of opposites is the philosopher's gesture against that will to power which would mystify her very self. Here let a representative remark suffice: "There are no opposites: only from those of logic do we derive the concept of opposites—and falsely transfer it to things." (*WM* II. 56, *WP* 298)

I have already dwelt on Nietzsche's problematizing of the opposition between "metaphor" and "concept," "body" and "mind." Any sampling of Nietzsche's writing would be crosshatched with such undoings. Here are a few provocative examples, which I append so that the reader may sense their implicit or explicit workings as she reads the *Grammatology*:

Subject and Object; both a matter of interpretation: "No, [objective] facts are precisely what there is not, only interpretations. We cannot establish any fact 'in itself' . . . 'Everything is subjective,' you say; but even this is interpretation. The subject is not something given, it is a superadded invention, stuck on to the tail [*etwas Hinzu-Erdichtetes, Dahinter-Gestecktes*]." (*WM* II. 11–12, *WP* 267)

Truth and error; no "truth" at the origin, but "truths" and "errors"—neither description more accurate than the other—cast up by the waves of control-preserving interpretations: "What are man's truths after all? They are man's *irrefutable* errors." (*NW* V. ii 196, *GS* 219) "Truth is the kind of error without which a certain species of living being could not live." (*WM* II. 19, *WP* 272)

Good and evil (morality and immorality): "An absurd presupposition . . . takes good and evil for realities that contradict one another (not as complementary value concepts). . . ." (*WM* I. 397, *WP* 192) "Morality itself is a special case of immorality." (*WM* I. 431, *WP* 217)

Theory and practice: "Dangerous distinction between 'theoretical' and 'practical' . . . as if pure spirituality produced [*vorlege*] . . . the problems of knowledge and metaphysics;— . . . as if practice must be judged by its own measure, whatever the answer of theory might turn out to be [*ausfalle*]." (*WM* I. 481, *WP* 251)

Purpose and accident, death and life: "Once you know that there are no purposes, you also know that there is no accident, for it is only beside a world of purposes that the word 'accident' has meaning. Let us beware of saying that death is opposed to life. The living is merely a type of what is dead, and a very rare type." (*NW* V. ii. 146, *GS* 168; again, the complicity with Freud's speculations about the individual, organic life, and inertia is striking.)[29]

Nietzsche's undoing of opposites is a version of Derrida's practice of undoing them through the concept of "differance" (deferment-difference), which I discuss later. Derrida himself notes the affinity:

> We could thus take up all the coupled oppositions on which philosophy is constructed, and from which our language lives, not in order to see opposition vanish but to see the emergence of a necessity such that one of the terms appears as the differance of the other, the other as "differed" within the systematic ordering [*l'économie*] of the same (e.g., the intelligible as differing from the sensible, as sensible differed; the concept as differed-differing intuition, life as differed-differing matter; mind as differed-differing life; culture as differed-differing nature. . . .). In Nietzsche, these are so many themes that can be related with the symptomatology that always diagnoses the evasions and ruses of anything disguised in its differance. (*MP* 18–19, *SP* 148–49)

One attempt at a holding action against the impossibility of breaking out of the enclosure of "interpretation" is a "plural style." In an essay translated as "The Ends of Man," Derrida writes: "As Nietzsche said, it is perhaps a change of style that we need; Nietzsche has reminded us that, if there is style, it must be *plural*."[30] And, much later, "the question of style can and must try its strength against the grand question of the interpretation, of, simply, interpretation, to resolve or disqualify it in its statement." (*QS* 253) The confounding of opposites, with the attendant switching of perspective, might be an example of that plural style. And so might Nietzsche's use of many registers of discourse in such works as *Thus Spoke Zarathustra, The Gay Science*, and *Ecce Homo*, or Derrida's shifts between commentary, interpretation, "fiction," in the works immediately following *Of Grammatology* and his typographical play with modes of discourse in *Marges* or *Glas*.

Perhaps Nietzsche's boldest insight in the face of the inescapable boundary is an exhortation to the will to ignorance: "It is not enough that you understand in what ignorance man and beast live; you must also have and acquire the *will* to ignorance." (*WM* II. 98, *WP* 328) What is more conventionally called "joyful unwisdom" (*NW* III. i. 252, *UA* 15) in an early text is later named "joyful *wisdom*"—the gay science—and seen as the greatest threat to the chain of self-preservative interpretations that accepts its own activity as "true" and "good": "The greatest danger that always hovered over humanity and still hovers over it is the eruption of *madness*—which means the eruption of arbitrariness in feeling, seeing, and hearing, the enjoyment of the mind's lack of discipline, the joy in human unreason. Not truth and certainty are the opposite of the world of the madman, but the universality and the universal binding force of a faith; in sum, the nonarbitrary character of judgments." (*NW* V. ii. 107–08, *GS* 130) The will to ignorance, the joyful wisdom, must also be prepared to rejoice in uncertainty, to rejoice in and even to will the reversal of all values that might have come to seem tenable: "No longer joy in certainty but in uncertainty . . . no longer will to preservation but to power. . . ." (*WM* II. 395, *WP* 545)

This continual risk-taking is the affirmative play in Nietzsche that Derrida will often comment on. "I do not know any other way," Nietzsche writes, "of associating with great tasks than *play*."[31] "Wisdom: that seems to the rabble to be a kind of flight, an artifice and means for getting oneself out of a dangerous game; but the genuine philosopher—as he seems to *us*, my friends?—lives 'unphilosophically' and 'unwisely,' above all *imprudently*, . . . he risks *himself* constantly, he plays the dangerous game."[32] This imprudence, constantly attempting to bypass the prudence of stabilizing through "interpretation," is *amor fati*, the love of what Derrida calls "the game of chance with necessity, of contingency with law." (*Dis* 309) This is the dance of the Over-man, a dance Nietzsche describes in terms of himself with a certain poignancy: "How wonderful and new and yet how gruesome and ironic I find my position vis-à-vis the whole of existence in the light of my insight! . . . I suddenly woke up in the midst of this dream, but only to the consciousness that I am dreaming and that I *must* go on dreaming lest I perish—. . . . Among all these dreamers, I, too, who 'know,' am dancing my dance." (*NW* V. ii. 90–91, *GS* 116)

The "knowledge" of the philosopher places him among the dreamers, for knowledge is a dream. But the philosopher "knowingly" agrees to dream, to dream of knowledge, agrees to "forget" the lesson of philosophy, only so as to "prove" that lesson. . . . It is a vertiginous movement that can go on indefinitely or, to use Nietzschean language, return eternally. This precarious "*forgetfulness*," "active *forgetfulness*," is what Derrida emphasizes in Nietzsche's Over-man. He writes, again in "The Ends of Man":

> His [the Over-man's] laughter will then break out towards a return which will no longer have the form of the metaphysical return of humanism any more than it will undoubtedly take the form, "beyond" metaphysics, of the memorial or of the guard of the sense of the being, or the form of the house and the truth

of Being. He will dance, outside of the house, that "aktive Vergeszlichkeit," that active forgetfulness ("oubliance") and that cruel (grausam) feast [which] is spoken of in *The Genealogy of Morals*. No doubt Nietzsche called upon an active forgetfulness ("oubliance") of Being which would not have had the metaphysical form which Heidegger ascribed to it. (*MP* 163, *EM* 57)

Like everything else in Nietzsche, this forgetfulness is at least double-edged. Even in his early writings "forgetfulness" makes its appearance in two opposed forms: as a limitation that protects the human being from the blinding light of an absolute historical memory (that will, among other things, reveal that "truths" spring from "interpretations"), as well as an attribute boldly chosen by the philosopher in order to avoid falling into the trap of "historical knowledge." In the work of the seventies, there are, on the one hand, passages such as the following (in which we must grasp the full irony of the word "truth"):

We do not yet know whence the impulse to truth comes, for up to now we have heard only about the obligation which society imposes in order to exist: to be truthful, that is, to use the usual metaphors, therefore expressed morally: we have heard only about the obligation to lie according to a fixed convention, to lie gregariously in a style binding for all. Now man of course forgets that matters are going thus with him; he therefore lies in that fashion pointed out unconsciously and according to habits of centuries' standing—and by *this very unconsciousness*, by this very forgetting, he arrives at a sense for truth. (*NW* III. ii. 375, *IF* 180–81)

If we appreciate the full irony of this passage, it becomes impossible for us to take a passage such as the following, also written in the seventies, at face value, with the "historical sense" as the unquestioned villain (although, admittedly, we must make a distinction between an academic and preservative [on the one hand] and a philosophic and destructive [on the other], sense of history): "The historical sense makes its servants passive and retrospective. Only in moments of forgetfulness, when that sense is intermittent [*intermittirt*; compare the discontinuous energizing of *Willens-Punktationen*], does the man who is sick of the historical fever ever act." (*NW* III. i. 301, *UA* 68) And through this network of shifting values, we begin to glimpse the complexity of the act of *choosing* forgetfulness, already advanced as a partial solution to the problem of history in the same early essay: ". . . the antidotes of history are the 'unhistorical' and the 'super-historical.' . . . By the word 'unhistorical' I mean the power, the art of *forgetting*, and of drawing a limited horizon round one's self." (*NW* III. i. 326, *UA* 95)

I am not going to comment extensively on Nietzsche's thought of forgetfulness, but simply remark that, even in the passage in *The Genealogy of Morals* to which Derrida expressly refers, this ambivalence is clearly marked. The joyous affirmative act of forgetfulness is also a deliberate repression:

Forgetting is no mere *vis inertiae* as the superficial imagine; it is rather an active and in the strictest sense positive faculty of repression [*Hemmungsvermögen*], that is responsible for the fact that what we experience and absorb enters our consciousness as little while we are digesting it (one might call the process "inpsychation") as does the thousandfold process, involved in physical nourishment—so-called "incorporation." To close the doors and windows of consciousness for a time; to remain undisturbed by the noise and struggle of our underworld of utility organs working with and against one another; a little quietness, a little tabula rasa of the consciousness, to make room for new thing, above all for the nobler functions and functionaries, for regulation, foresight, premeditation (for our organism is oligarchically directed [*oligarchisch eingerichtet*])—that is the purpose of active forgetfulness, which is like a doorkeeper, a preserver of psychic order, repose, and etiquette: so that it will be immediately obvious how there could be no happiness, no cheerfulness, no hope, no pride, no *present*, without forgetfulness. (*NW* VI. ii., 307–08; *GM* 57–58)

"Knowing" that there is nowhere an isolatable unit, not even an atomistic one, and that conceptions of a unified present are merely an interpretation, the philosopher, by an act of "forgetting" that knowledge, wins himself a "present." Within that created frame he, who has doubted the possibility of any stable morality, any possibility of truth, nonetheless speaks in one of the strongest polemical voices in European thought, not only taking sides but demolishing his opponents. Nietzsche's work is the unreconciled playground of this "knowledge" and this "forgetfulness," the establishment of the knowledge (that presents all knowing as mere symptom) as convincing as the voice of forgetfulness (that gives us the most memorable prophecy). The most common predicament in the reading of Nietzsche is to defeat oneself in the effort to establish a coherence between the two. But the sustaining of the incoherence, to make the two poles in a curious way interdependent,—that is Nietzsche's superb trick. What Nietzsche's *style* brings off here is, to borrow a Derridean pun, what the *stylus* performs when, in the gesture of "sous rature," it deletes and leaves legible at the same time. A hint is lodged in Nietzsche's own description of "the psychological problem in the type of Zarathustra:" "how he that says No and *does* No to an unheard-of degree, to everything to which one has so far said Yes, can nevertheless be the opposite of a No-saying spirit."[33]

Martin Heidegger, as we have seen, dreams of annulling a first forgetfulness of the question of Being. For him, "all fundamental-ontological construction [*fundamental-ontologische Konstruktion*] . . . must in its plan [*im Entwerfen*] wrest from forgetfulness that which is planned [*in den Entwurf Genommene*]. The basic, fundamental-ontological act of the metaphysics of *Dasein* is, therefore, a "remembering back [*Wiedererinnerung*]."[34] It is thus through the notion of an *active* forgetfulness that Nietzsche, Derrida believes, gives Heidegger the slip. To recall the passage from Derrida that I have already quoted, the "laughter" of the Over-man will not be a "memorial or . . . guard of the . . . form of the house and the truth of Being. He will dance, outside of the house, this . . . active forgetfulness."

Heidegger stands between Derrida and Nietzsche. Almost on every occasion that Derrida writes of Nietzsche, Heidegger's reading is invoked. It is as if Derrida discovers his Nietzsche through and against Heidegger. In the *Grammatology*, he writes: ". . . rather than protect Nietzsche from the Heideggerian reading, we should perhaps offer him up to it completely, underwriting that interpretation without reserve; in a *certain way* and up to the point where, the content of the Nietzschean discourse being almost lost for the question of being, its form regains its absolute strangeness, where his text finally invokes a different type of reading, more faithful to his type of writing." (32, 19)

Heidegger describes Nietzsche as the last metaphysician of the West. For Heidegger a metaphysician is one who asks the question "What is the being of the entity?" And, for Heidegger, Nietzsche's answer to this question is—the being of the entity is the will to power. And, as Heidegger has consistently pointed out, the place for the posing of the question of the being of the entity is man. Starting from this "metaphysical premise" Heidegger develops a thoroughly coherent reading of Nietzsche and reminds us again and again that to consider Nietzsche incoherent is simply not to grasp that his master-question is the same as that of all Western metaphysics: "What is the being of the entity?" It is as if Heidegger, philosopher of that special nostalgia for the original word, resolutely refuses to recognize that Nietzsche's consistency is established by virtue of an active forgetfulness the conditions for which are also inscribed in the Nietzschean text.

Heidegger often quotes a sentence from Nietzsche and declares "this means . . . ." Out of this highly didactic approach comes powerful formulae such as the following:

> We shall be able to determine the main thrust of Nietzche's metaphysical premise, when we consider the answer that he gives to the question of the *constitution* of the entity and its *mode of being*. . . . Nietzsche gives two answers: the entity in its totality is will to power, and the entity in its totality is the eternal return of the same. . . .In these two propositions . . . "is" means different things. The entity in totality "is" the will to power means: the entity as such is constituted as that which Nietzsche determines as the will to power. And the entity in totality "is" the eternal return of the same means the entity in totality *is* as entity in the mode of the eternal return of the same. The determination "will to power" answers the question of the entity *with ref-*

erence to its constitution; the determination "eternal return of the same" answers the question of the entity in totality *with reference to its mode of being.* However, constitution and mode of being belong together as determinations of the entity-ness of the entity.[35]

Everything is made to fall into place in terms of the question of being. That in Nietzsche concepts such as "entity" and "totality" are profoundly problematized (". . . there is no 'totality'; . . . no evaluation of human existence, of human aims, can be made in regard to something that does not exist . . ." [*WM* II. 169, *WP* 378]), that Nietzsche almost never speaks of the eternal return of the *same,* but simply of the eternal return—such massive details are set aside. Nietzsche's mockery of "making equal," "making same" (*Gleich*) is ignored in the energy of the Heideggerian copula that equates the will to power and the eternal return of the *same* (*Gleich*): "*Will to power is in essence and according to its inner possibility the eternal return of the same.*" (*HN* I. 467)

Because Heidegger does not acknowledge the plurality of Nietzsche's style, he does not allow Nietzsche the privilege of being a philosopher of the "sous rature." For him, Nietzsche remains a metaphysician who asks the question of being, but does not question the questioning itself! "Neither Nietzsche nor any thinker before him—also and exactly not Hegel, who before Nietzsche for the first time thought the *history* of philosophy philosophically—come to the commencing beginning, rather they see the beginning already and only in the light of what is already a falling off from the beginning and a quietening of the beginning: in the light of Platonic philosophy . . . Nietzsche himself already early on designates his philosophy as reversed Platonism. The reversal does not eliminate the Platonic premise, but rather solidifies it exactly through the appearance of elimination." (*HN* I. 469)

Within the encompassing and constricting frame of Nietzsche's metaphysics "*as the metaphysics of subjectivity*" (*HN* II. 199), Heidegger's reading of Nietzsche is superb. Unfortunately for my interests, and Derrida's, it matters more at this point that Heidegger feels compelled to bypass or explain away so much in Nietzsche. I reserve the occasion for a more thoroughgoing critique of the Heideggerian text on Nietzsche. Here let me indicate some sweeping instances. If Nietzsche speaks of the world and of our sensations as chaos, Heidegger explains chaos as "*the exclusive* [*eigentümlich*] *blueprint of the world in totality and its working.* . . . 'Chaos' cannot simply mean waste confusion, but the secrecy of the unsubdued domain of becoming." (*HN* I. 566) Art (whose status in Nietzsche is extremely elusive and problematic)[36] is then described as the supreme will to power, which, giving form to chaos, ("another sign-chain telescoped there," Nietzsche might mutter) is "the creative experience of becoming." (*HN* I. 568) If Nietzsche invokes the body and the organism in general as limits to consciousness, Heidegger brilliantly introduces the concept of "the bodying reason" and interprets Nietzsche's gesture as the extension of the concept of subjectivity to animality and the " 'body' . . . [as] the name for that form of the will to power in which the latter is immediately accessible to man as the distinct 'subject'." (*HN* II. 300) When Nietzsche writes: "To impose upon becoming the character of being —that is the supreme will to power" (*WM* II. 101, *WP* 330), Heidegger must read it without benefit of the pervasive irony of Nietzsche's double stance. He must even overlook the implications of the metaphor of imprinting (*aufzuprägen*) that is translated as "to impose" in the English version. He must often in practice overlook the fragmentary nature of *The Will to Power*, as he must overlook the interrogative form of many of Nietzsche's most aggressive insights. He must interpret the goal-lessness of the Over-man as "the unconditioned mastery of man on earth. The man of this mastery is the Over-man." (*HN* II. 125)

Derrida thinks there might be profit in pushing through a rigorously Heideggerian reading of Nietzsche—a reading that would develop into its ultimate coherence the Nietzsche who actively forgets the terrible text of his own "knowledge." At the limit such a reading would break open, "its form re-cover its absolute strangeness, and his text finally invoke another type of reading."

Derrida's own critique of Heidegger on Nietzsche—"La Question du style"—seems to move around an apparently unimportant moment in the Heideggerian text. The strategy of deconstruction, as we shall see later, often fastens upon such a small but tell-tale moment. In this particular essay, the moment is Heidegger's overlooking of the words "it *becomes a woman*" in the chapter entitled "How the 'True World' Ultimately Became a Fable: the History of An Error," in Nietzche's *The Twilight of the Idols*.[37]

Nietzsche's brief chapter gives the history of Western metaphysics in six formulaic paragraphs with accompanying "stage directions," written in a peculiarly Nietzschean tone of jest in earnest. At the moment when metaphysics changes from Platonism to Christianity, "the idea . . . *becomes a woman*." Heidegger takes no notice of this in his extended commentary on the chapter. At that omission Derrida fixes his glance, and in a bold and most surprising gesture, illuminates the "question of style" in Nietzsche through a discussion of the "question of woman."

A general reading of Nietzsche's text would see him as a raging misogynist. But Derrida's careful reading disengages a more complex collection of attitudes toward woman. Derrida breaks them into three and suggests that each Nietzschean attitude is contiguous with a psychoanalytical "position"—a modality of the subject's relationship with the object. Summarized, the "positions" would be as follows:

> The woman . . . condemned as . . . figure or power of lying. . . . He was, he feared such a castrated woman. . . .
>
> The woman . . . condemned as . . . figure or power of truth. . . . He was, he feared such a castrating woman. . . .
>
> The woman . . . recognized, beyond this double negation, affirmed as the affirmative, dissimulating, artistic, Dionysiac. . . . He was, he loved such an affirmative woman. (*QS* 265, 267)

By means of an elaborate argument on the question of style, Derrida cautions us that these three positions cannot be reconciled into a unity or even an "exhaustive code." (*QS* 266) But if, that warning heeded, we were to concentrate here on the tripartite schema, and glance again at the "History of An Error," we might distill a Derridean reading of Nietzsche.

According to Nietzsche, with the coming of Christianity, the period of castration began, and the idea, become a (castrating and castrated) woman, was pursued by the male type of the philosopher for possession and appropriation. Nietzsche is caught up within this scheme, speaks *for* men, proposes an Over-*man*. But his text is capable of pointing out that the woman undermines the act of masculine possession by "giving herself" (in the sense of playing a part, *playing* herself), even in the act of "giving herself" up to sexual mastery.[38] About this "truth as woman," one cannot then ask, "what is she?"—the ontological question—and expect an answer—the hermeneutic assumption: "Each time that the question of the proper [of the self-same, of appropriation, of knowledge as possession] emerges, . . . the onto-hermeneutic form of interrogation shows its limit." (QS 274) In the very act of surrender, woman dissimulates. Here we find a sexual description of that double register of knowledge-forgetfulness that forever ruptures Nietzsche's style. To possess the woman, one must *be* the woman ("the contemplative character . . . consists of male mothers" [*NW* V. ii. 106, GS 129]), and yet the being of the woman is unknown. The masculine style of possession through the stylus, the stiletto, the spurs, breaks down as protection against the enigmatic femininity of truth. "Perhaps truth is a woman who has reasons for not letting us see her reasons? Perhaps her name is—to speak Greek—Baubo [female genitals]?" (*NW* V. ii. 20, *GS* 38) "Even the compassionate curiosity of the wisest student of humanity is inadequate for guessing how this or that woman manages to accommodate herself to this solution of the [sexual] riddle . . . and how the ultimate philosophy and skepsis of woman casts anchor at this point!" (*NW* V. ii. 105, *GS* 128) Once we are put on the trail, the surprising passages appear, the text begins to open. Man must constantly attempt to *be* the truth as woman (articulate forgetfulness) in order to *know* her, which is impossible. "Man and woman change places, exchange their masks to infinity" (*QS* 273). Is Derrida suggesting that, in questioning a recoverable and possessable originary "truth," Nietzsche is symbolically questioning, as Freud did, the reality of a "primal scene," of things in general being taken to have begun with the castration of the phallus, with the distinct division into man and woman?

Is Nietzsche's desire (as Derrida sees it) to place the castrating idea *within* history akin to Freud's rewriting of the primal "scene" into the child's primal "fantasy?"[39] Is the Nietzschean text, in suggesting that in order to *have* (possess) the truth (woman) the philosopher must *be* the truth (woman), undoing Freud's incipient phallocentrism, which provides quite a different alternative: if the son (man) disavows sexual difference, he seeks to *be the phallus for* the mother (woman) and becomes "the lost object;" when the sexual difference is acknowledged, the son (man) *has* the phallus through identification with the father. Is Nietzsche seeking to undo that "repudiation of femininity" in the male—the other side of which is possession—that Freud posits as "nothing else than a biological fact" (GW XVI. 99, *SE* XXIII. 252), and describe a femininity that is not defined by a male desire to supply a lack?[40]

(Perhaps Derrida's Nietzsche goes "beyond" Derrida's Hegel. His consistent contraction for the Hegelian *savoir absolu* [absolute knowledge] in *Glas* is *Sa*. Not only is this a misspelling of "ça" [id, it], and the usual French contraction for "signifiant" [signifier], but also a possessive pronoun with a feminine object, which in this case is unnamed. Absolute knowledge as articulated by Hegel might be caught within the will to an unnamed [unnamable] "chose féminine" [female thing—in every sense].)

Derrida ends his essay with yet another long cautionary passage about the problem of reading Nietzsche,[41] of the fact that in his text in particular, as we have tried to explain, one consistent reading continually erases itself and invokes its opposite, and so on indefinitely: "Do not conclude from this that one must give up immediately the knowledge of what *it* means. . . . To be aware, as rigorously as possible, of that structural limit . . . one must push this deciphering as far as possible. . . . If Nietzsche meant [wanted to say] something, would it not be this limit of meaning [the will to say], as the effect of a will to power necessarily differential, therefore always divided, folded, multiplied? . . . As much as to say that there would no longer be a 'totality of Nietzsche's text,' even fragmentary or aphoristic." (*QS* 285)

And, inaugurating for us an attitude that I shall develop later in this Preface, Derrida writes: "The text can always remain at the same time open, proffered *and* indecipherable, even without our knowing that it is indecipherable." (*QS* 286)

I should note here that Derrida always makes a ritual (and undoubtedly correct) gesture of dismissal toward these fathers: "It was within concepts inherited from metaphysics that Nietzsche, Freud, and Heidegger worked." (*ED* 413, *SC* 251) Heidegger came close to undoing them, "destroying" them (Heidegger's word), but gave in to them as well. Freud nearly always believed that he worked within them. But Nietzsche cracked them apart and then advocated forgetting that fact! Perhaps this entire argument hangs on who *knew* how much of what he was doing. The will to knowledge is not easy to discard. When Derrida claims for himself that he is within yet without the clôture of metaphysics, is the difference not precisely that he *knows* it at least? It is difficult to imagine a solution to the problem that would go beyond Nietzsche's: to know and then actively to forget, convincingly to offer in his text his own misreading.

In *Cartesian Meditations,* Edmund Husserl differentiates between a "transcendental phenomenology of consciousness" and a "pure psychology of consciousness," the former a study where "'the psychic components of man . . . data belonging to the world . . . [are] not accepted as actuality, but only as an actuality-phenomenon," declaring them, however, an "exact parallel." Here is another distinction that a Nietzschean vision must undo.[42] And for Derrida, it is Freud who points toward a working of the psyche that "obliterates the transcendental distinction between the origin of the world and Being-in-the-world. Obliterates it while producing it."[43] Derrida does not look at psychoanalysis as a particular or "regional" discipline, but a way of reading that unscrambles "the founding concept-words of ontology, of being in its privilege" (35, 21). For his purposes, in other words, it is not a science that necessarily provides a correct picture of the psychic norm and prescribes cures for the abnormal, but rather teaches, through its own use thereof, a certain method of deciphering any text.

Whether he acknowledges it or not, Freud implies that the psyche is a sign-structure "sous rature," for, like the sign, it is inhabited by a radical alterity, what is totally other—"Freud gives it [this radical alterity] a metaphysical name, the unconscious" (*MP* 21, *SP* 151): "The unconscious is the true psychical reality; *in its innermost nature it is as much unknown to us as the reality of the external world, and it is as incompletely presented by the data of consciousness as is the external world by the communications of our sense-organs.*" (GW II–III. 617–18, *SE* V. 613) And, when he "substitutes" for "the antithesis between" "the conscious and the unconscious" that between the ego and the id (the it, the other), the notion of alterity remains undisturbed: "the id . . . is its [the ego's] other external world [*seine andere Aussenwelt*]." (GW XIII. 285, *SE* XIX. 55) This alterity can never be made present as such to the consciousness, which has dealings only with the preconscious, an area between itself and the unconscious. "To consciousness the whole sum of psychic processes presents itself as the realm of the preconscious." (*GW* X. 290, *SE* XIV. 191) Yet "unconscious wishes always remain active. . . . Indeed it is a prominent feature of unconscious processes that they are indestructible." (*GW* II–III. 583, *SE* V. 577)

Something that carries within itself the trace of a perennial alterity: the structure of the psyche, the structure of the sign. To this structure Derrida gives the name "writing." The sign cannot be taken as a homogeneous unit bridging an origin (referent) and an end (meaning), as "semiology," the study of signs, would have it. The sign must be studied "under erasure," always already inhabited by the trace of another sign which never appears as such. "Semiology" must give place to "grammatology." As I have suggested, this move relates closely to Nietzsche's "genealogical" study of morals as unending "sign-chains."

"Writing," then, is the name of the structure always already inhabited by the trace. This is a broader concept than the empirical concept of writing, which denotes an intelligible system of notations on a material substance. This broadening, Derrida feels, is accomplished by Freud's use of the metaphor of writing to describe both the content and the machinery of the psyche. In an essay translated as "Freud and the Scene of Writing," itself an example of the rhetorical analysis of "philosophical" texts that Nietzsche spoke of, Derrida traces the emergence of the metaphor of writing through three texts placed along a thirty-year span in Freud's career: "Project for A Scientific Psychology" (1895), *The Interpretation of Dreams* (1899) and "A Note Upon the 'Mystic Writing-Pad' " (1925). Through these three texts Freud had grappled with the problem of finding a description for the content as well as the apparatus of the psyche. With the 1925 "Note," Freud arrives at last at a description of the psyche as a "space of writing." This is indeed not our empirical concept of writing, for here "script . . . is never subject, extrinsic, and posterior to the spoken word." (*ED* 296, *FF* 75) Nor is it simply a metaphor for language. In the *Interpretation*, the dream-content—a paradigm of the entire memory-work of the psyche—"is expressed . . . in a pictographic [not phonetic] script." (*GW* II–III. 283, *SE* IV. 277) In the "Note," with its elaborate evocation of an actual writing toy, the question of the place of speech simply does not arise: "I do not think it is too far-fetched to compare the celluloid and waxed paper cover with the system *Pcpt.–Cs.* [perception-consciousness] and its protective shield, the wax slab with the unconscious behind them, and the appearance [becoming-visible; *Sichtbarwerden*] and disappearance of the writing with the flickering-up and passing away of consciousness in the process of perception." (*GW* XIV. 7, *SE* XIX. 230–31) In the last two chapters of the *Interpretation*, meditating in great detail upon "The Dream-Work" and "The Psychology of the Dream-Process," Freud is compelled, at the risk of some self-bafflement, to explode the idea of any unified agency for the psyche. By the time Freud comes to write the "Note," he has clearly established that the workings of the psychic apparatus are themselves not accessible to the psyche. It is this apparatus that "receives" the stimuli from the outside world. The psyche is "protected" from these stimuli. What we think of as "perception" is always already an inscription. If the stimuli lead to permanent "memory-traces"—marks which are *not* a part of conscious memory, and which will constitute the play of the psyche far removed from the time of the reception of the stimuli—there is no conscious perception. "The inexplicable phenomenon of consciousness arises [periodically and irregularly] in the perceptual system instead of the permanent traces." (*GW* XIV. 4–5, *SE* XIX. 228) There are periods, then, when the perceptual system is not activated and that is precisely when the lasting constitution of the psyche is being determined. It is only the periods of its actual activation that gives us the sense of time. "Our abstract idea of time seems to be wholly derived from the method of the working of the system *Pcpt.–Cs.* and to correspond to a perception on its own part [self-perception; *Selbstwahrnehmung*] of that method of working." (*GW* XIII. 28, *SE* XVIII 28) In the "Note," Freud undermines that primary bastion of selfhood—the continuity of time-perception—both more boldly and more tentatively; our sense of the continuity of time is a function of the discontinuous periodicity of the perceptual machine and, indeed, a perception of nothing more than the working of that machine: "this discontinuous method of functioning of the system *Pcpt.–Cs.* lies at the bottom of the formation [*Entstehung* rather than origin—*Ursprung*] of the concept of time." (*GW* XIV. 8, *SE* XIX. 231) Thus, within the Freudian thematics of the psyche, perception is an "originary inscription." And time, according to Kant the privileged and necessary "form of intuition," becomes a mark of "the economy of a writing" (*ED* 334, *FF* 112) on the mystic writing pad of the psyche.

Nietzsche had undone the sovereign self by criticizing causality and substance. He had indicated our ignorance of the minute particulars involved in a "single" human action. Freud undoes the sovereign self by meditating upon those minute particulars.

Freud's slow discovery of the metaphor of writing is so fascinating for Derrida because it does not have the usual strings attached. In the section "The Signifier and Truth" of the *Grammatology*, Derrida discusses one curious characteristic of the general usage of the metaphor of writing: even as it is used, it is contrasted to writing in the literal sense. "Writing in the common sense is the dead letter, it is the carrier of death [because it signifies the absence of the speaker]. . . . From another point of view, on the other face of the same proposition, writing in the metaphoric sense, natural, divine, and living writing, is venerated; it is equal in dignity to the origin of value, to the voice of conscience as divine law, to the heart, to sentiment and so forth." (29, 17) Because human beings need to comfort themselves with notions of presence, writing in the "literal" sense, signifying the absence of the actual author, must be "rejected," even when it is "accepted" as a metaphor. Freud's use of the metaphor of writing is uncontaminated by this double dealing. In fact, Freud speculates that the very mansion of presence, the perceiving self, is shaped by absence, and—writing.

The clôture of metaphysics found the origin and end of its study in presence. The questioners of that enclosure—among them Nietzsche, Freud, Heidegger—moved toward an articulation of the need for the strategy of "sous rature." Nietzsche puts "knowing" under erasure; Freud "the psyche," and Heidegger, explicitly, "Being." As I have argued, the name of this gesture effacing the presence of a thing and yet keeping it legible, in Derrida's lexicon, is "writing,"—the gesture that both frees us from and guards us within, the metaphysical enclosure.

Freud does not put the psyche under erasure merely by declaring it to be inhabited by a radical alterity; nor by declaring perception and temporality to be functions of a writing. He does it also by his many avowed questionings of that same topological fable of the mind that he constantly uses. It does not seem correct to unproblematize Freud's different models for the psychic system and call them "varying 'points of view' used by Freud to represent the psychic system."[44] The point is that Freud uses the dynamic (play of forces) or functional picture of the psyche almost to annul the topological one; yet gives the topological picture greatest usage; the typical sleight of hand of "sous rature." Not only does he write that he will "carefully avoid the temptation to determine psychical locality in any anatomical fashion" (*GW* II–III. 541, *SE* V. 536); but, he points out that, even within the "virtual" psychical topography

> an unconscious thought seeking to convey [translate] itself [*nach Ubersetzung*] into the preconscious so as to be able to force its way through into consciousness . . . is not the forming of a second thought situated in a new place, like a transcription that continues to exist alongside the original; and the notion of forcing a way through into consciousness must be kept carefully free from any idea of a change of locality. . . . What we are doing here is once again to replace a topological way of representing things by a dynamic one. . . . Nevertheless, I consider it expedient and justifiable to continue to make use of the figurative image of the two systems. (*GW* II–III. 614–15, *SE* V. 610–11)

Some fifteen years later, writing on the Unconscious, Freud assures us: "Study of the derivatives of the *Ucs.* will completely disappoint our expectations of a schematically clear-cut distinction between the two psychical systems." (*GW* X. 289, *SE* XIV. 190)

And yet the topographical fable continues to be used, to my mind precisely because it is a graphically representable one—a "structure" in that orthodox sense. Freud has dismantled the sovereignty of the self; his topographical description allows him to suggest the production of that self in the structuring of the text of the psyche. Derrida will say: "It is only necessary to reconsider the problem of the effect of subjectivity as it is produced by the structure of the text." (*Pos* F 122, *Pos* E 45)

"I propose that when we have succeeded in describing a psychical process in its dynamic, topographical and economic aspects," Freud writes, "we should speak of it as a *metapsychological* presentation." (GW X. 281, *SE* XIV. 181) The notion of an "economic" presentation of a mental process is pertinent to a reading of Derrida.

Economy is a metaphor of energy—where two opposed forces playing against each other constitute the so-called identity of a phenomenon. In Freud's "metapsychological presentations," the economic line of approach comes to modify the topographic and dynamic ones, although, as I suggest above, the other descriptions are never given up. "The ultimate things which psychological research can learn about [are] the behavior of the two primal instincts, their distribution, mingling and defusion—things which we cannot think of as being confined to a single province of the mental apparatus, the id, the ego or the super-ego. . . . Only by the concurrent or mutually opposing action"—in other words, economy—"of the two primal instincts—Eros and the death-instinct—, never by one or the other alone, can we explain the rich multiplicity [many-coloredness; *Buntheit*] of the phenomena [appearances, *Erscheinungen*] of life." (GW XVI. 88–89, *SE* XXIII, 242–43)

Economy is not a reconciliation of opposites, but rather a maintaining of disjunction. Identity constituted by difference is economy. In Freud's world, a train of thought is sustained by its opposite, a unit of meaning contains the possibility of its opposite: "Each train of thought is almost invariably accompanied by its contradictory counterpart, linked with it by antithetical association." (GW II–III, 316, *SE* IV. 312) Normality—an "ideal fiction" (GW XVI. 80, *SE* XXIII, 235)—and neurosis are accomplices: "Psycho-analytic research finds no fundamental, but only quantitative, distinctions between normal and neurotic life. . . . We must recognize that the psychical mechanism employed by neuroses is not created by the impact of a pathological disturbance upon the mind, but is present already in the normal structure of the mental apparatus." (GW II–III. 378, 613; *SE* V. 373, 607) Following a similar strategy, Freud will argue, after carefully developing a contrast between the pleasure principle and the death instinct: "The pleasure principle seems actually to serve the death instincts." (GW XIII. 69, *SE* XVIII. 63) The exposition of the death instinct itself is made in terms of a bold economy of life and inertia:

"The inertia inherent in organic life." (*GW* XIII. 38, *SE* XVIII. 36) We are not surprised when Freud proposes an economy of the body and the mind: ". . . the activity of thinking is also supplied from the sublimation of erotic motive forces." (*GW* XIII. 274, *SE* XIX. 45) Not only are we within the ambiance of that undoing-preserving of opposites that Derrida finds congenial also in Nietzsche; this last passage in fact advances what Nietzsche calls the "new psychology" as he points at the need for combining "philology" (the genealogy of language) and "physiology" (the field of the erotic).

I have cited above the Freudian argument that the establishment of permanent traces in the psychic apparatus precludes the possibility of immediate perception. Relating this delaying mechanism to the economy of opposites, Derrida writes: "Following a schema that continually guides Freud's thinking, the movement of the trace is described as an effort of life to protect itself *by deferring* the dangerous investment, by constituting a reserve (*Vorrat*). And all the conceptual oppositions that furrow Freudian thought relate each concept to the other like movements of a detour, within the economy of differance. The one is only the other deferred, the one differing from the other." (*MP* 19–20, *SP* 150)

This passage is taken from the essay "La différance." It emphasizes the presence of Freud in the articulation of what comes close to becoming Derrida's master-concept—"differance" spelled with an "a." Let us fasten on three moments in the quotation—"differing," "deferring," and "detour." I have spoken of the radically other, which is always different, nonidentical. Add to this the structure of the perennial postponement of that which is constituted only through postponement. The two together—"difference" and "deferment"—both senses present in the French verb "différer," and both "properties" of the sign under erasure—Derrida calls "différance." This differance—being the structure (a structure never quite there, never by us perceived, itself deferred and different) of our psyche—is also the structure of "presence," a term itself under erasure. For differance, producing the differential structure of our hold on "presence," never produces presence as such.

The structure of "presence" is thus constituted by difference and deferment. But since the "subject" that "perceives" presence is also constituted similarly, differance is neither active nor passive. The "-ance" ending is the mark of that suspended status. Since the difference between "difference" and "differance" is inaudible, this "neographism" reminds us of the importance of writing as a structure. The "a" serves to remind us that, even within the graphic structure, the perfectly spelled word is always absent, constituted through an endless series of spelling mistakes.

In "La différance," Derrida relates the thought of differance to Nietzsche, Freud, and Heidegger. But he seems most moved by the Freudian breakthrough. The disjunction between perception and the permanent trace seems to make thought itself a differance of perception. The complicity between the organism and the inertia of the inorganic state makes life a differance of death (*ED* 333 n., *FF* 112 n.). Through these Freudian insights, and Freud's notion that our perception of unconscious traces occur long "after the event," Derrida consolidates what he had spotted in Husserl's structuring of the Living Present in his Introduction to *The Origin of Geometry*: "the pure consciousness of delay." (p. 171)

Derrida quotes from *Beyond the Pleasure Principle*: "Under the influence of the ego's instincts of self-preservation, the pleasure principle is replaced by the reality principle. This latter principle does not abandon the intention of ultimately obtaining pleasure, but it nevertheless demands and carries into effect the postponement of satisfaction, the abandonment of a number of possibilities of gaining satisfaction and the temporary toleration of unpleasure as a step on the long indirect road (*Aufschub*) to pleasure." Within Freud's discourse, Derrida relates this postponement (deferment) and "the relation to the absolutely other [differance] that apparently breaks up any economy" by arguing as follows:

> The economic character of differance in no way implies that the deferred presence can always be recovered, that it simply amounts to an investment that only temporarily and without loss delays the presentation of presence. . . . The unconscious is not . . . a hidden, virtual, and potential self-presence. . . . There is no chance that the mandating subject "exists" somewhere, that it is present or is "itself," and still less chance that it will become conscious. . . . This radical alterity, removed from every possible mode of presence, is characterized by . . . delayed effects. In order to describe them, in order to read the traces of the "unconscious" traces (There are no "conscious" traces [since the traces are marked precisely when there is no *conscious* perception]), the language of presence or absence, the metaphysical speech of phenomenology, is in principle inadequate. (*MP* 21. *SP* 152)

Here I must repeat, with modifications, a question that I broached at the end of our discussion of Nietzsche, and perhaps attempt a partial answer to it: the question of mastery through knowledge in Derrida. Nietzsche had discovered the need to sustain disjunction, to love fate, cultivate *amor fati*. But his entire idiom of thought and action was to place the responsibility upon a self whose existence he argued against. His text became the violent and deliberate playground of differance. Freud allowed Derrida to think that the philosophic move did not necessarily require a Nietzschean violence. Simply to recognize that one is shaped by differance, to recognize that the "self" is constituted by its never-fully-to-be-recognized-ness, is enough. We do not have to cultivate forgetfulness or the love of chance; we *are* the play of chance and necessity. There is no harm in the will to knowledge; for the will to ignorance plays with it to constitute it—if we long to know we obviously long also to be duped, since knowledge is duping. Nietzsche on the other hand saw the "*active* forgetfulness of the question of being" as a gigantic ebullience. Perhaps it is after all a difference in metaphorical nuance. Derrida's understanding of such a forgetfulness—via Freud's research into memory—is that it is active in the shaping of our "selves" in spite of "ourselves." We are surrendered to its inscription. Perhaps, as I have argued, in the long run what sets "Derrida" apart is that he *knows* that he is always already surrendered to writing as he writes. His knowledge *is*, after all, his power. Nietzsche, paradoxically, *knew* even this, so that his affirmative and active (knowing) forgetfulness was a move against the inevitability of a knowledge symptomatically priding itself on remembering. It is curious that, speaking to Jean-Louis Houdebine about his strategy in an interview, Derrida remarks again and again, "But I knew what I was doing."[45] The will to power is not so easy to elude. It is also curious that, although Derrida speaks often of Nietzsche's explosive and affirmative and open play, he speaks rarely of Freud's own analysis of play as a restrictive gesture of power—most significantly in Freud's comments on the child's game of "*fort-da*," where the very economy of absence and presence is brought under control. (*GW* XIII. 11–15, *SE* XVIII. 14–17)

Yet, if we respect Derrida's discourse, we cannot catch him out so easily. What does it show but that he is after all caught and held by the metaphysical enclosure even as he questions it, that his text, as all others, is open to an interpretation that he has done a great deal to describe? He does not succeed in applying his own theory perfectly, for the successful application is forever deferred. Differance/writing/trace as a structure is no less than a prudent articulation of the Nietzschean play of knowledge and forgetfulness.

(After this writing, I heard Derrida's as yet unpublished lectures on Francis Ponge and Heidegger, delivered at Yale in the fall of 1975. He himself opens the question of differance and mastery there as the question of the desire of deconstruction. I present his argument briefly at the end of Section IV.)

Derrida receives from Freud an actual method of deciphering in the narrow sense as well. One important distinction between the Heideggerean method of "destruction" (see page xlviii), and Derrida's "de-construction" is the latter's attention to the minute detailing of a text, not only to the syntax but to the shapes of the words in it. Derrida is fascinated by Freud's notion that dreams may treat "words" as "things." The analytical method used in Part II of the *Grammatology* remains conservative from this point of view, and generally honors the outline of the word as such. Starting with

La dissémination, however, Derrida begins to notice the play of revelation and concealment lodged within *parts* of individual words. The tendency becomes pervasive in *Glas,* where the individual phonemes/graphemes constituting words are often evoked out into an independent dance. Derrida pushes through to an extreme Freud's own method of attending to the "syntax" of a dream text. I give below Freud's skeletal summary of the rich and complex method.

In *The Interpretation of Dreams,* he lists the four techniques employed by the dream-work of the psychic apparatus to distort or "refract" the dream-thought (psychic content) to produce the pictographic script of the dream: condensation, displacement, considerations of representability, and secondary revision. "Condensation" and "displacement" may be rhetorically translated as metaphor and metonymy.[46] The third item on the list points at the technique which distorts an idea so that it can be presented as an image. Freud's description of the fourth item recalls Nietzsche's words on the will to power seeking to preserve unification, as well as Derrida's description of the text in general: "A dream is a conglomerate which, for purposes of investigation, must be broken up once more into fragments. . . . A psychical force is at work [is displayed, *äussert*] in dreams which creates this apparent connectedness, which . . . submits the material produced by the dream-work to a 'secondary revision.'" (*GW* II–III. 451–52, *SE* V. 449) I reopen the question of Freud and textuality on page lxxvi.

This notion that the verbal text is constituted by concealment as much as revelation, that the concealment is itself a revelation and vice versa, brings Nietzsche and Freud together. Freud suggests further that where the subject is *not* in control of the text, where the text looks supersmooth or superclumsy, is where the reader should fix his gaze, so that he does not merely read but deciphers the text, and sees its play within the open textuality of thought, language, and so forth within which it has only a provisionally closed outline. He catches this notion thus: "There is often a passage in even the most thoroughly interpreted dream which has to be left obscure. . . . At that point there is a tangle of dream-thoughts which cannot be unravelled and which moreover adds nothing to our knowledge of the content of the dream." Derrida's "advance" on Freud here can be formulated thus: this tangle cannot be unravelled in terms of, and adds nothing to the contents of the dream-text within the limits set up by itself. If, however, we have nothing vested in the putative identity of the text or dream, that passage is where we can provisionally locate the text's moment of transgressing the laws it apparently sets up for itself, and thus unravel—deconstruct—the very text. This illuminates the lines in Freud that follow the passage above: "This is the dream's navel, the spot where it reaches down into the unknown. The dream-thoughts . . . cannot . . . have any definite endings: they are bound to branch out in every direction into the intricate network of our world of thought." (GW II–III. 530, *SE* V. 525)

It is difficult to bring out the close yet necessarily oblique relationship between Freud's and Derrida's methods of textual interpretation without going into extreme detail. However, as Derrida himself remarks, *Of Grammatology* and his earlier texts merely inaugurate the participation in a specifically Freudian intertextuality. The erotic investment of writing in children holds his interest in a long footnote on page 132 (333). The elaboration of the thematics of masturbation and writing, of the mark of supplementarity in the chain of mother-substitutions, as Derrida locates them in Rousseau's text, are psychoanalytical only in a very general sense. It should of course be abundantly clear that, even on so general a plane, Derrida would not use a psychoanalytical method to conduct us to "a psycho-biographical signified whose link with the literary signifier then becomes perfectly extrinsic and contingent" (228–29, 159). In fact, already in this early work, Derrida urges the importance, for grammatology, of a psychoanalysis that has freed itself from an attitude that sees all textuality as a dispensable source of substantive evidence. The use of the sexual structures of psychoanalysis as a tool of interpretation becomes steadily more marked in Derrida's later work. The essay on Nietzsche, commenting on "the question of style" as the "question of woman" is an example. And Derrida–Freud comes most disturbingly into his own in *Glas*. I shall deal with Derrida's modification of the theme of castration in connection with his reading of Jacques Lacan.

Derrida cautions us in a long headnote to "Freud and the Scene of Writing" that, the institution of grammatology through the recognition of systematic "repression" of writing throughout the history of the West cannot be taken as a psychoanalytic endeavor on a macrocosmic scale. For Freud's need to describe the coexistence of the (at least) double text of the psyche in terms of latent and manifest contents, or, indeed, repression and sublimation, is itself caught within that suspect terminology of binary oppositions; and further, the very pattern of repression in an individual can only be possible because of his need to reject all that is recognized to be inhabited by the structure of writing: castration (the loss of mastery), penis-envy (the fear of absence). I shall later present Derrida's counter-arguments—dissemination and the hymen. Yet Freud cannot be dismissed out of hand. Did he perhaps himself sense this need to reject writing? Derrida ends "Freud and the Scene of Writing" with this quotation from Freud's "Inhibitions, Symptoms and Anxiety": "As soon as writing, which entails making a liquid flow out of a tube on to a piece of white paper, assumes the significance of copulation, or as soon as walking becomes a symbolic substitute for treading upon the body of mother earth, both writing and walking are stopped because they represent the performance of a forbidden sexual act." (GW XIV. 116, *SE* XX. 90) Meanwhile, the word against Freud remains: "Necessity for an immense work of deconstruction of these concepts and the metaphysical phrases that condense and sediment there." (*ED* 294) This can indeed be the ever-sustained word against all gestures of surrender to precursors: As you follow, also deconstruct, for, as you deconstruct, you must follow.

I maintain . . . that Heidegger's text is of extreme importance, that it constitutes an unprecedented, irreversible advance and that we are still very far from having exploited all its critical resources. . . . [Yet there are] propositions whose disorder has . . . disconcerted me. To cite one example, 'Derridian grammatics are "modeled," in their broad outlines, on Heideggerian metaphors, which they attempt to "deconstruct" by substituting for the "presence of the logos" the anteriority of a trace; his grammatics become onto-theology relying upon the trace as their "basis," "foundation" or "origin."' (*Pos* F 73, 70, *Pos* EI 40, 39–40)

Taking issue against Elisabeth Roudinesco, whom he quotes above, Derrida states his relationship to Heidegger and warns against false descriptions of it. I have already considered his involvement in and rewriting of the Heideggerian "sous rature," and his use of Heidegger as a perspective on Nietzsche. Now I glance briefly at another aspect of Derrida's rewriting of Heidegger: the method of deconstruction as practised by Heideggerian metaphysics.

What Derrida balks at in Roudinesco's description is that a "grammatology"—science of the effacement of the trace—should be described as modeled on a "metaphysics"—science of presence; that it should be called an "onto-theology"—science of Being and of God as regulative presences, that the "trace," mark of radical anteriority, should be misnamed an "origin." We shall note and avoid these errors; and go on to say, as does Derrida of "differance": "By establishing this relation between a restricted [Heideggerian metaphysics] and a general system [grammatology]," Derrida "shifts and recommences the very project of philosophy." (*MP* 21, *SP* 151)

Heidegger already points toward the relationship between his own, and the grammatological methods, by ignoring, in his practice of reading, the absolute authority of the text. When Heidegger "reads" Hegel, or Kant, or Nietzsche, in the long run he "examine[s] not what [the author] says but" —note the passive construction, the withdrawal of authority from the sovereign author—"what is achieved." (*KPM* G 193, *KPM* E 221) He thinks of his own task as a "loosening up" of the "hardened tradition" of "ontology" by a "*positive* destruction,"[47] a "destructive retrospect of the history of ontology" which "lays bare the internal character or development" of a text. (*KPM* G 194, *KPM* E 222) (It is interesting to note that, in the first published version of *De la grammatologie*, Derrida uses the word "destruction" in place of "deconstruction.") Describing Derrida's own procedure, Paul de Man gives us something very close to these Heideggerian passages: "His text, as he puts it so well, is the unmaking of a construct. However negative it may sound, deconstruction implies the possibility of rebuilding."[48] Because the author fancies himself sovereign, there is a point, Heidegger suggests, where his own conception of the text blinds him: "Descartes had to neglect the question of Being altogether"; "the doctrine of the schematism . . . had to remain closed off to Kant."[49] Like the analyst moving with his patient in the seesaw of a "transference-relationship," the deconstructing critic must "free and . . . safeguard" the intrinsic powers "of a problem." (*KPM* G 185, *KPM* E 211) In Derrida's words:

> Reading must always aim at a certain relationship, unperceived by the writer, between what he commands and what he does not command of the schemata of the language that he uses. This relationship is not a certain quantitative distribution of shadow and light, of weakness and force, but a signifying structure that critical reading must *produce*. . . . [Without] all the instruments of traditional criticism, . . . critical production would risk developing in any direction and authorize itself to say almost anything. But this indispensable guard-rail has always only *protected*, never *opened*, a reading (227, 158).

To take apart, to produce a reading, to open the textuality of a text. Derrida shares these procedural guidelines with Heidegger. Freud has helped to push the procedure further—given him some means of locating the text's "navel," as it were, the moment that is undecidable in terms of the text's apparent system of meaning, the moment in the text that seems to transgress its own system of values. The desire for unity and order compels the author and the reader to balance the equation that is the text's system. The deconstructive reader exposes the grammatological structure of the text, that its "origin" and its "end" are given over to language in general (what Freud would call "the unknown world of thought"), by locating the moment in the text which harbors the unbalancing of the equation, the sleight of hand at the limit of a text which cannot be dismissed simply as a contradiction. In the *Grammatology*'s reading of Rousseau, this "moment" is the double-edged word "supplement." In *La pharmacie de Platon*, it is the double-edged word "*pharmakon*" as well as the absence of the word "*pharmakos*." In Derrida's brief reading of Aristotle's *Physics* IV, it is the unemphatic word "*ama*," carrying the burden of differance. (*Dis* 69–197, *MP* 31–78)

One important difference between Heidegger and Derrida lies in their concepts of time. Through a delicate analysis that I shall not attempt to reproduce here, Derrida demonstrates that, although Heidegger would purge Kant and Hegel—indeed what Heidegger sees as the entire Aristotelian tradition—of "the vulgar concept of time"—there can be no concept of time that is not caught within the metaphysical clôture: "wishing to produce that *other* concept, one quickly sees that it would be constructed with other metaphysical or onto-theological predicates." (*MP* 73)[50] Heidegger catches a glimpse of this through his crossing-out of "Being." At the stage of *Sein und Zeit*, however, Heidegger still thinks of "time" as that which "*needs to be explicated originarily* [einer ursprünglichen Explikation] *as the horizon for the understanding of Being*."[51] Time is still the model of pure auto-affection, where something ideal—*Being as such*—is produced without having to relate to an object. (Derrida puts auto-affection in question and suggests that it always already carries an irreducible element of hetero-affection, desiring and relating to an alterity, which in this case is the *question* of Being—or Being under erasure.) For the earlier Heidegger, then, the "question of Being," as Derrida points out in "Ousia et grammè," seem interchangeable. By the time of *Der Spruch des Anaximander*,[52] Heidegger himself sees Being as precomprehended and nonsignifiable, and the *presence* seemingly signified in a text is seen as the only means for language to point at the effaced *trace* (MP 76–77). Heidegger has by then arrived at the crossing-out of being, and does not find the meaning of being in temporality. But time itself seems more effectively crossed out for Derrida through the Freudian suggestion that time is the discontinuous perception of the psychic machinery.

Nietzsche, Freud, Heidegger. All three concerned with a problem that Heidegger would articulate thus: "*More originary* [ursprünglich] *than man is the finitude of the* Dasein *in him*." (*KPM* G 207, *KPM* E 237) All three proto-grammatologues. Nietzsche a philosopher who cut away the grounds of knowing. Freud a psychologist who put the psyche in question. Heidegger an ontologist who put Being under erasure. It was for Derrida to "produce" their intrinsic power and "discover" grammatology, the science of the "sous rature." That sleight of hand is contained in the name itself, "the logos of the grammè." The grammè is the written mark, the name of the sign "sous rature." "Logos" is at one extreme "law" and at the other "phonè"—the voice. As we have seen, the grammè would question the authority of the law, deconstruct the privilege of the spoken word. The word "Grammatology" thus appropriately *keeps alive* an unresolved contradiction. Derrida sets forth the meaning of this contradiction in the section of our book entitled "Of Grammatology as A Positive Science." And the texts of Nietzsche, Freud, and Heidegger are this contradiction's pre-text.

(The importance of the text of Edmund Husserl for Derrida lies precisely in its self-conflict. Husserl seems to Derrida to be a more than usually resolute suppressor of the more than usually astute grammatological suggestions implied by the Husserlian text.)

It is of course futile to trace the origin of a particular thought: "We know that the metaphor that would describe the genealogy of a text correctly is still *forbidden*" (149, 101). Yet one might wonder if the thought of "writing" in Derrida is not a sort of answer to the question of "geometry" in Husserl. As I have mentioned, Derrida's first book is a translation of and introduction to Husserl's "Origin of Geometry." The question asked by Husserl is precisely a question of the relationship between subjective and objective structures. How can the forms of an absolutely ideal objectivity—the essence of geometry (not actual systems of geometry) arise within the structures of the subject? At the end of his long introduction, Derrida suggests that Husserl's answer, if "produced" fully, would be that the possibility of objectivity is lodged within the subject's self-presence. The transcendental subject's ideal object is itself. In its contemplation of itself the self cannot remain within the "simple now-ness of a Living Present," it must give itself a history, differentiate itself from itself through a backward glance which also makes possible a forward glance: "An originary consciousness of delay can only have the pure form of anticipation. . . . Without this [consciousness] . . . discourse and history [and Geometry as the possibility of history] would not be possible."

Through these notions of self-differentiation and self-postponement, Husserl seems to be launching the idea of differance: "The originary Differance of the absolute Origin . . . is *perhaps* what has always been said through the concept of the '*transcendental*.' . . . This strange procession of a 'Rückfrage' [checking back], is the movement *sketched* in 'The Origin of Geometry.'[53] The idea is *perhaps* there in Husserl, and if so, it is only *sketched*. For, as we shall see later in my discussion of phonocentrism, Husserl surrounds this idea of differance with a constituting subject, a subject that generates and is therefore the absolute origin of the structure of difference. To win Husserl's thought, which unwillingly outlines the structures of grammatology, into grammatological discourse, a massive rewriting will have to be undertaken: "This determination of 'absolute subjectivity' would . . . have to be crossed out as soon as we conceive the present on the basis of differance, and not the reverse. The concept of *subjectivity* belongs *a priori* and *in general* to the order of the *constituted* [rather than the constituting]. . . . There is no constituting subjectivity. The very concept of constitution itself must be deconstructed." (*VP* 94 n., *SP* 84–85 n.)

Not only in the field of subjectivity, but also in the field of objective knowledge, Husserl seems to open as well as deliberately close the possibility of grammatology. If there is an "indeterminately general presumptive horizon" of the knowable, Husserl places it within the control of an infinitely synthesising directedness (intentionality) of the ego, an ego that can be uncovered for the philosopher only by bracketing, " 'putting out of play' of all positions taken toward the already-given Objective world."[54] If, almost in spite of himself, Husserl seems to suggest that expression can never be adequate to the sense which it expresses, he covers himself by giving to the "is" or to the predicative statement a privilege. Once again, Derrida must undertake a reversal. "It might then be thought [following Husserl] that the *sense of being* has been limited by the imposition of *form*—which . . . would, with the authority of the *is*, have assigned to the sense of being the closure of presence, the form-of-presence, presence-in-form, or form-presence. . . . [or] that [the] thought of form [*pensée de la forme*] has the power to extend itself beyond the thought of being [*pensée de l'être*]. . . . Our task is . . . to reflect on the circularity which makes the one pass into the other indefinitely." (*MP* 206–07, *SP* 127–28)

Freud had found in the mystic writing pad a model that would contain the problematics of the psyche—a virgin surface that still retained permanent traces. Husserl confronted a similar problem when he posited a "sense" that is anterior to the act of "expression" or "meaning." "How could we ever conceive," Derrida asks, "of the perpetual restoration of meaning in its virginal state [within the egological history]?" (*MP* 197, *SP* 118) Husserl does not stop to consider the question. He simply "betrays a certain uneasiness . . . and attributes the indecisiveness of his description to the incidentally metaphorical character of language." (*MP* 198, *SP* 119) Again it is Derrida who, through a careful consideration of precisely the metaphorics of Husserl's argument, must deliver the conclusion: "We must conclude that sense in general, the noematic [knowable] sense of every experience, is something which, by its very nature, must be already able to *be impressed* on a meaning, to leave or receive its formal determination in a meaning. Sense would therefore already be a kind of blank and mute writing which is reduplicated in meaning." (*MP* 197, *SP* 117)

One of Husserl's most original insights is that speech can be genuine without "knowledge," that the relation with the object that "animates the body of the signifier" need not be "known" by the speaker or hearer through direct intuition. Derrida, "following the logic and necessity of these [Husserl's] distinctions" (*VP* 102, *SP* 92), disengages a more radical suggestion:

> . . . . not only [does] meaning . . . . not essentially imply the intuition of the object but . . . it essentially excludes it. . . . My nonperception, my nonintuition, my *hic et nunc* absence are said by that very thing that I say, by *that* which I say and *because* I say it. . . . The absence of intuition—and therefore of the subject of the intuition—is not only *tolerated* by speech; it is *required* by the general structure of signification, when considered *in itself*. It is radically

requisite: the total absence of the subject and object of a statement—the death of the writer and/or the disappearance of the object he was able to describe—does not prevent a text from "meaning" something. On the contrary, this possibility gives birth to meaning as such, gives it out to be heard and read. (*VP* 102, 108; *SP* 92–93)

The structure of alterity (otherness and absence of meaning or self) must be operative within the sign for it to operate *as such*. But Husserl cannot fully articulate this trace-structure of expression, which his text suggests: "The theme of full 'presence,' the intuitionistic imperative [expression must be fulfilled through intuition], and the project of knowledge continue to command—at a distance, we said—the whole of the description. Husserl describes, and in one and the same movement effaces, the emancipation of speech as nonknowing." (*VP* 109, *SP* 97)

The intuitionistic imperative works curiously in the case of the word "I." Husserl will not grant it the possibility of being uttered without being known intuitively.

Husserl's premises should sanction our saying exactly the contrary. Just as I need not perceive in order to understand a statement about perception, so there is no need to inuit the object *I* in order to understand the word I. . . . Whether or not perception accompanies the statement of perception, whether or not life as self-presence accompanies the uttering of the *I*, is quite indifferent with regard to the functioning of meaning. My death is structurally necessary to the pronouncing of the I. . . . The anonymity of the written *I*, the impropriety [lack of property] of *I write, is*, contrary to what Husserl says, the "normal situation." (*VP* 107–08, *SP* 96–97)

Thus Derrida "produces" an ostensibly most anti-Husserlian reading of Husserl: for Husserl, as we have seen, the voice—not empirical speech but the phenomenological structure of the voice—is the most immediate evidence of self-presence. In that silent interior monologue, where no alien material signifier need be introduced, pure self-communication (auto-affection) is possible. Derrida shows that, if Husserlian theory is followed rigorously, a procedure Husserl himself seems unwilling to undertake, the structure of speech or voice is seen to be constituted by the necessary absence of both the object and the subject. It is constituted, in other words, by the structure of writing: "The autonomy of meaning with regard to intuitive cognition . . . [that] Husserl established . . . has its norm in writing." (*VP* 108, *SP* 96–97) (Derrida will argue, on p. 60 passim (40) of the *Grammatology*, that Saussure too is unable to accept non-intuition as a norm, but must see it as "crisis.")

Such is Derrida's intimate play with Husserl's text: always to produce the counter-reading out of the latter's protective hedging. Perhaps all texts are at least double, containing within themselves the seeds of their own destruction. In Husserl's case, the doubleness shows itself in an extraordinary transparency. "An underlying motif . . . disturb[s] and contest[s] the security of . . . [the] traditional distinctions [made in Husserl's text] *from within.*" (*VP* 92, *SP* 82; italics mine) (Although he had not made a theme of . . . the work of difference in the constitution of sense and signs, he *at bottom* recognized its necessity." (*VP* 114, *SP* 101; italics mine) No doubt the effort at helping Husserl's discourse dehisce sharpened Derrida's thoughts of grammatology. But the relationship between the two is interminably interpretive and has no place in a preface. *Speech and Phenomena*, Derrida's study of Husserl, is thus a philosophical companion-text to the study of Rousseau in Part II of the *Grammatology*.)

Hegel's shadow upon Derrida is diffuse and gigantic. We shall lose sight of the provisional outlines of the book *Grammatology* if we pursue indefinitely the remoter ancestors of the common noun "grammatology." Derrida's discussion of Hegel, "the first philosopher of writing," in the *Grammatology* and "Le puits et la pyramide: introduction à la sémiologie de Hegel" (MP 79–127) is explicit and clear. It prepares us for the joyous and magnificent unstitching of some Hegelian texts in *Glas*. It is an intimate intertextuality to which I direct your attention, and there make an end. I shall speak of Hegel a little toward the end of this Preface.

Let it finally be said that, within this framework, counting the proper names of predecessors must be recognized as a convenient fiction. Each proper name establishes a sovereign self against the anonymity of textuality. Each proper name pretends that it is the origin and end of a certain collocation of thoughts that may be unified: "The names of authors or of doctrines have here no substantial value. They indicate neither identities nor causes. It would be frivolous to think that 'Descartes,' 'Leibniz,' 'Rousseau,' etc. are names of authors, of the authors of movements or displacements that we thus designate. The indicative value that I attribute to them is first the name of a problem" (147–48, 99). Proper names are no more than serviceable "metonymic contractions."

III

"Structuralism" is the name of the problematics that we recognize most readily on the European scene of the sixties. What is Derrida's relationship to structuralism?

Definitions of movements of thought are always contingent and provisional. Here for the sake of exposition I shall use a shorthand definition:

structuralism is an attempt to isolate the general structures of human activity. Thus the structuralism I speak of is largely the study of literature, linguistics, anthropology, history, socio-ecnomics, psychology. A structure is a unit composed of a few elements that are invariably found in the same relationship within the "activity" being described. The unit cannot be broken down into its single elements, for the unity of the structure is defined not so much by the substantive nature of the elements as by their relationship. When Aristotle described tragedy as "the imitation of an action that is serious and also, as having magnitude, complete in itself . . . with incidents arousing pity and fear, wherewith to accomplish its catharsis of such emotions," he was describing the active structure of tragedy. We know Freud's psychic "description" in terms of the narcissistic and oedipal structures. In Roland Barthes's words: ". . . to find in it [the object] certain mobile fragments whose differential situation engenders a certain meaning; the fragment has no meaning in itself, but it is nonetheless such that the slightest variation wrought in its configuration produces a change in the whole."[55] Derrida, like Nietzsche, would find it merely symptomatic of the human desire for control to isolate such "units" in an "object" in any but the most provisional way: ". . . . a structural study of the historical ensemble—notions, institutions. . . . How are these elements in 'the historical ensemble' organized? What is a 'notion'? Do philosophical notions have a privilege? How do they relate to scientific concepts?" (*ED* 70)

The study of human activity in terms of the structure of the sign we might call semiotic or semiological structuralism. Can Derrida—substituting the structure of writing (the sign "sous rature") for the structure of the sign—simply be dubbed a grammatological structuralist historian of philosophy, and there an end? No doubt. But to grasp the implications of that formulaic description, we might launch, not only a shorthand definition, but a thumbnail "historical outline," that would be useful for the exigencies of the present discussion. It must of course be remembered that any such outline would have to be rigorously undone if "the direct object" of study were the movement "itself."

In the broad sense, structuralist descriptions have always been with us; it is customary to cite Aristotle and Plato. In the narrow sense, however, it is customary to locate the beginnings of modern structuralism in the following proper names: the Russian Formalists in literary criticism, Marcel Mauss in anthropology, Ferdinand de Saussure and N. S. Troubetzkoy in linguistics. The Formalists, reacting against what seemed like the fluid, rhapsodic style of Symbolist criticism (deconstructed, Symbolist criticism establishes its own variety of rigor), engaged in the isolation of objective categories descriptive of the "literariness" of the literary text.[56] Out of this enthusiasm came such significant texts as Vladimir Propp's codification of motif/structures in folk tales,[57] motif/structures that can be seen to inhabit the most sophisticated narratives. East European Structuralism has been developing the Formalists' investigative methods over the last few decades, but Derrida is most concerned with structuralism as it came to live in France.

For the study of the "laws" of the variations in the configuration of structures, the working analogies came from the study of linguistic structures. Troubetzkoy, studying the configuration of phonemes in the production of meaning, gave one analogy. Ferdinand de Saussure, describing the structure of the sign itself—"I mean by sign the whole that results from the associating of the signifier with the signified"[58]—gave another. Structuralist activity found its analogies in linguistics and semiotics. Claude Lévi-Strauss provides some acknowledgements. Abundantly to Marcel Mauss in his Introduction to *Sociologie et anthropologie*: ". . . . inspiring ourselves by Mauss's precept that all social phenomena may be assimilated into language, we see . . . [in them] the conscious expression of a semantic formation."[59] Here to Troubetzkoy (for Derrida's own discussion of this passage we should turn to pages 151 f. [102 f.] of *Of Grammatology*):

Structural linguistics will certainly play the same renovating role with respect to the social sciences that nuclear physics, for example, has played for the physical sciences. In what does this revolution consist . . . ? N. Troubetzkoy, the illustrious founder of structural linguistics, . . . reduced the structural method to four basic operations. First, structural linguistics shifts from the study of *conscious* linguistic phenomena to study of their *unconscious* infrastructure; second, it does not treat *terms* as independent entities, taking instead as its basis of analysis the *relations* between terms; third, it introduces the concept of *system*—". . . it shows concrete phonemic systems and elucidates their structure"—; finally, structuralist linguistics aims at discovering *general laws*. . . . In the study of kinship problems (and, no doubt, the study of other problems as well), the anthropologist finds himself in a situation which formally resembles that of the structural linguist. Like phonemes, kinship terms are elements of meaning; like phonemes, they acquire meaning only if they are integrated into systems. "Kinship systems," like "phonemic systems," are built by the mind on the level of unconscious thought. Finally, the recurrence of kinship patterns . . . in scattered regions of the globe and in fundamentally different societies, leads us to believe that, in the case of kinship as well as linguistics, the observable phenomena result from the action of laws which are general but implicit.[60]

Roman Jakobson, a member of the Prague School of Formalism, encountered Claude Lévi-Strauss in the United States in the 1950s. One account of the rise of "structuralism" is that what is recognized today as the mainstream structuralist method of the interpretation of texts arose out of this temporary conjunction.[61]

I indulge in this sort of sweeping historical fiction because, as I have suggested, Derrida's criticism of "structuralism," even as he inhabits it, would be a sweeping one. It would relate to the possibility of a general law. The law of differance is that any law is constituted by postponement and self-difference. The possibility of a general law is threatened on so general a level.

Derrida would also problematize the possibility of objective description. A structuralist statement of structuralist objectives bases itself on the distinction between subject and object. Structuralist conclusions are the object illuminated by the subject: "The goal of all structuralist activity, whether reflexive or poetic, is to reconstruct (*reconstituer*) an 'object' in such a way as to manifest thereby the rules of its functioning (the 'functions') of this object. Structure is therefore actually a *simulacrum* of the object, but a directed *interested* simulacrum, since the imitated object makes something appear which remained invisible or, . . . unintelligible in the natural object."[62] For Derrida, however, a text, as we recall, whether "literary," "psychic," "anthropological," or otherwise, is a play of presence and absence, a place of the effaced trace. ("If it is to be radically conceived, [the play] must be thought of before the alternative of presence and absence" [*ED* 426, *SC* 264].) And textuality is not only true of the "object" of study but also true of the "subject" that studies. It effaces the neat distinction between subject and object. The grammatological structure as a tool of description is that structure which forever eludes answering the question "what is . . . ?"—the basis of objective description. Even as it remains legible as a structure, it erases the aim of structuralism—to provide objective descriptions.

Speaking generally again, it may be said that the method of structuralism takes into account that its *objects of study* cannot have had simple origins in the sovereign subject of an "author." But the power of the *investigating subject*, which brings intelligibility to the natural object by imitating it as a structure, in spite of the many delicate argumentations around it, cannot ultimately be denied within the framework of structural study. A structure, it must be repeated, is the natural object plus the subjective intelligence of the structuralist: "the simulacrum is intellect added to object, and this addition has an anthropological value, in that it is man himself, his history, his situation, his freedom, and the very resistance which nature offers to his mind."[63]

The notion of "communication" (a "function" of human structures), important to structuralism as a tool of investigation, also carries with it the notion of unified subjects, of meaning as portable property: ". . . . *communication*, which, in fact, implies the *transmission charged with passing, from one subject to the other, the identity* of a *signified* object of a *meaning* or a *concept* in principle separable from the process of passage and of the signifying operation." (*Pos F* 34).

Derrida finds the concept of the binary sign itself, in its role as the guide of this objective enterprise, committed to a science of presence. Barthes writes eloquently: "The sign is not only the object of a particular knowledge, but also the object of a *vision*, analogous to the vision of the celestial spheres in Cicero's *Somnium Scipionis* or related to the molecular representations used by chemists; the semiologist *sees* the sign moving in the field of signification, he enumerates its valences, traces their configuration: the sign is, for him, a sensous idea."[64] And Derrida, diagnosing the symptoms of this longing for presence, writes: ". . . a semiology . . . whose . . . concepts and fundamental presuppositions are most precisely locatable from Plato to Husserl, passing by way of Aristotle, Rousseau, Hegel, etc." (*Pos* F 33)

Yet since, as I have argued, the structure of the grammè is the sign under erasure—both *conserving* and effacing the sign, Derrida must make use of the concept of the sign. His relationship to structuralism is therefore intimate. In an interview with Julia Kristeva, Derrida points out that Saussure's binary concept of the sign, questioning the separable primacy of meaning—the transcendental signified—pointed a way out of the metaphysics of presence:

> Saussurian semiology noted, against tradition, that the signified was inseparable from the signifier, that [they] are the two faces of one and the same production. . . . By showing that "it is impossible for sound alone, the material element, to belong to the language" and that "[in its essence the linguistic signifier] is in no way phonic" (p. 164)[65]; by desubstantializing at once the signified content and the "substance of expression"—which is therefore no longer exclusively the phonè—. . . . Saussure contributed greatly to turning against the metaphysical tradition the concept of the sign that he borrowed from it. (*Pos* F 28)

Derrida analyzes Saussure's *Cours de linguistique générale* and the linguistics of the first half of the present century in the chapter of this book entitled "Linguistics and Grammatology," and the argument about Saussure is best presented there. We might simply say that Saussure was not a grammatologist because, having launched the binary sign, he did not proceed to put it under erasure. The binary opposition within the Saussurian sign is in a sense paradigmatic of the structure of structuralist methodology. "We must doubtless resort to pairings like those of *signifier/signified* and *synchronic/diachronic* in order to approach what distinguishes structuralism from other modes of thought."[66]

In the passage where Lévi-Strauss acknowledges his debt to Troubetzkoy, for example, we notice the reference to a study of the *unconscious* infrastructure. In Derrida, via Freud, there would be a difficulty in setting up the opposition between the conscious and the unconscious within the subject as the founding principle of a systematic study. The unconscious is undecidable, either the always already other, out of reach of psychic descriptions, or else it is thoroughly and constitutively implicated in so-called conscious activity. Further, as I have pointed out, the opposition of the subject and the object, upon which the possibility of objective descriptions rests, is also questioned by the grammatological approach. The description of the object is as contaminated by the patterns of the subject's desire as is the subject constituted by that never-fulfilled desire. We can go yet further and repeat that the structure of binary oppositions in general is questioned by grammatology. Differance invites us to undo the need for balanced equations, to see if each term in an opposition is not after all an accomplice of the other: "At the point where the concept of differance intervenes . . . all the conceptual oppositions of metaphysics, to the extent that they have for ultimate reference the presence of a present, . . . (signifier/signified; sensible/intelligible; writing/speech; speech [*parole*]/language [*langue*]; diachrony/synchrony; space/time; passivity/activity etc.) become non-pertinent." (*Pos* 41)

It is therefore not too extravagant to say that "writing" or "differance" is the structure that would deconstruct structuralism—as indeed it would deconstruct all texts, being, as we shall see, the always already differentiated structure of deconstruction.

It should by now be clear where the structuralists have stopped short, or what they did not begin with. They have not thought the "sous rature."[67] It is as if they have grasped only Nietzsche's "knowledge," showing us the interpretive power working through human society, so that all its studies become "genealogical," an unending decipherment of sign-chains. How close to that aspect of Nietzsche this passage from Roland Barthes sounds!: ". . . structural man . . . too listens for the natural in culture, and constantly perceives in it not so much stable, finite, 'true' meanings as the shudder of an enormous machine which is humanity tirelessly undertaking to create meaning, without which it would no longer be human."[68] But it is also as if the gravest lesson of that knowledge, its need for abdication, has not been imagined by the structuralists. Nongrammatological structuralism cannot afford to cultivate the will to ignorance: "*Homo significans*: such would be the new man of structural inquiry."[69]

The solution is not merely to say "I shall not objectify." It is rather to recognize at once that there is no other language but that of "objectification" and that any distinction between "subjectification" and "objectification" is as provisional as the use of any set of hierarchized oppositions. Derrida sets this forth most energetically in two early essays where he deals with two structuralist critics who take elaborate precautions against objectification. I have already referred to one—"Structure, Sign, and Play in the Sciences of Man"—where Derrida interprets Lévi-Strauss's attempt at a mythomorphic criticism of myth. The other is "Cogito et l'histoire de la folie"—a critique of Michel Foucault's *Histoire de la folie à l'âge classique.*[70]

Foucault writes, writes Derrida, as if he "*knew* what madness meant" (*ED* 66). Foucault speaks thus for Reason, madness's other—if his own binary opposition is to be trusted. Yet he wishes to speak for "madness *itself*" (*ED* 56), write "the archaeology of [its] silence."[71] But how can this be more than merely rhetorical? For an archaeolgy is perpetrated through discourse, imposing reason's syntax upon folly's silence. Indeed Foucault recognizes the problem and on occasion articulates it.

But, "to say the difficulty, to say the difficulty of saying, is not yet to surmount it" (*ED* 61). Foucault sidesteps precisely this issue, says Derrida, by misreading Descartes.

Foucault sees in Descartes one of the exemplary separators of reason and madness. Derrida's reading of Descartes on folly is an elegant bit of deconstruction; he spots the moment of the forgetting of the trace in Descartes' text. Descartes, he argues, gives the name "folly" to the *pre*-reflexive cogito—*before* the "I think" can be reflected upon and pronounced. In the prereflexive cogito "folly" and "I think" are interchangeable, intersubstitutable. There the distinction between reason and folly does not appear. There the "cogito" cannot be communicated, made to appear to another self like my own. But when Descartes begins to speak and reflect upon the cogito, he gives it a temporal dimension, and distinguishes it from madness. The relationship between the prereflexive cogito (which is also madness) and the temporal cogito (which is distinct from madness) is thus analogous to that between the precomprehended question of Being and the propositional concept of Being. The possibility of discourse is lodged in the interminably repeated movement from the one to the other—from "excess" to a "closed structure." (*ED* 94) Foucault, not recognizing this, still remains confined within the structuralist science of investigation through oppositions.

This is a dated Foucault, the Foucault of the sixties. Even then he was violently unwilling to be called a structuralist, and he gets into this section of my preface because he diagnoses an age in terms of its *epistémè*, the self-defined structure of its knowing. This particular characteristic of Foucault's work has not disappeared. To diagnose the epistemic structure, he has had, with repeated protestations to the contrary, to step out of epistemic structures in general, assuming that were possible. To write his "archaeologies," he has had to analyze metaphors privileged by a particular age in what Derrida would call "meta-metaphorics." By describing grammatology as "a history of the possibility of history that would no longer be an archaeology," (43, 28), Derrida seems to declare an advance over Foucault. And by denying the status of a positive science to grammatology, he "erases" the advance. Perhaps there is an attempt to rewrite the Foucauldian method in "The White Mythology," Derrida's extended essay on metaphor:

Might we not dream . . . of some meta-philosophy, of a more general discourse which would still be of a philosophical kind, on metaphors of the "primary degree," on those non-true metaphors which set philosophy ajar [*entrouvert la philosophie*]? There would be some interest in work under the heading of a meta-metaphorics such as this. . . . First of all we shall direct interest upon a certain *usure* [both attrition through wear and tear and supplementation through usury] of metaphorical force in philosophical intercourse. It will become clear that this usure is not a supervenient factor modifying a kind of trope-decay which is *other-wise destined to remain intact*; on the contrary, it constitutes the very history and structure of philosophical metaphor. (*MP* 308, 249; "White Mythology" 61, 6; italics mine)

(It should be mentioned here that, at the end of the second edition of *Histoire de la folie,* which appeared eleven years after the first, Foucault includes a twenty-page rebuttal of Derrida's critique, entitled "Mon corps, ce papier, ce feu." Foucault's analysis of Derrida's misreading [as he thinks] of Descartes is thorough and often convincing, and should be examined carefully. For our purposes here, it suffices to note that Foucault does not address himself to the precomprehended cogito. His point is rather to prove that Descartes does indeed exclude madness as he does not exclude the dream. He takes Derrida's reading to be "a generalization of doubt," a taking away of the Cartesian certitude from Descartes. This reading is, of course, not altogether false, but it leaves untouched the configuration of Derrida's more interesting suggestion that the Cartesian certitude is grounded on a category that may just as easily be described as either certitude or doubt, neither certitude nor doubt. In fact when, speaking against Derrida, Foucault shows us that Descartes *disqualifies* [rather than excludes] madness from giving evidence, as an "excessive and impossible proof" [p. 596], we may suggest that Foucault's reading in this case is not very different from Derrida's.)

But the most interesting thing about Foucault's rebuttal is the virulence at the end. I shall make no attempt to defend Derrida here, but will extract a passage from Foucault to give you a taste of the hostility toward the threat of the "sous rature"—a concept that Foucault, in these lines, does not seem to have carefully attended—that is not necessarily confined to Michel Foucault:

Today Derrida is the most decisive representative of a [classical] system in its final glory; the reduction of discursive practice to textual traces; the elision of the events that are produced there in order to retain nothing but marks for a reading; the invention of voices behind texts in order not to have to analyse the modes of implication of the subject in discourse; assigning the spoken and the unspoken in the text to an originary place in order not to have to reinstate the discursive practises in the field of transformations where they are effectuated. . . . It is an historically sufficiently determined little pedagogy which manifests itself most visibly. A pedagogy that tells the pupil that there is nothing outside of the text, but that within it, in its interstices, in its white spaces and unspokennesses, the reserve of the origin reigns; it is not at all necessary to search elsewhere, for exactly here, to be sure not in the words, but in words as erasures, in their *grill*, "the meaning of being" speaks itself. A pedagogy that conversely gives to the voice of the teacher that unlimited sovereignty which permits them to read the text indefinitely [p. 602].

Derrida defends psychoanalysis against Foucault, who calls it "a monologue of reason *about* madness."[72] "It is not by chance that it is only today that such a project [as Foucault's] could be formed. . . . It must be supposed that . . . a certain liberation of madness has begun, that psychiatry, in however small a way, is open, that the concept of madness as unreason, if it ever had a unity, has been dislocated." (*ED* 61)

Jacques Lacan, the great contemporary interpreter of Freud, is an instigator of such a dislocation. Not only has he underwritten Freud's own denial of a difference in kind between the "normal" and the "abnormal" psyche, but he has also rejected the dogma, launched according to him by American ego psychologists,[73] that the ego is the primary determinant of the psyche. He works, rather, with a "subject" which can never be a "total personality," the "exercise of whose function" is to be forever divided from the object of its desire (Lacan computes the structural relationships among need, demand for love, and desire), and to constitute itself in the distortive play of metaphor and metonymy—displacement and condensation—that forever distances the other, the object of its desire, from itself. (*Ec* 692) Freud had not allowed verbality to lodge deeper than the Preconscious, thus protecting the metaphysical alterity of the Unconscious. Lacan extends Freud in a direction that Derrida would endorse. He defines the unconscious in terms of the structure of a language: "It is not only man who speaks, but . . . in man and by man it [id] speaks, . . . his nature becomes woven by the effects where the structure of language, whose material he becomes, is recovered." (*Ec* 688–89)

Derrida is aware of the affinity between Lacan's thought and his own: "In France, the 'literary criticism' marked by psychoanalysis had not asked the question of the text. . . . Although Lacan is not directly and systematically interested in the so-called 'literary' text, . . . the *general* question of the text is incessantly at work [in his discourse]." (*FV* 100–01)

Yet in spite of, perhaps because of, this proximity, the relationship between these two men is charged with unease. Dissociating himself from the "perversions" spawned by his own work between 1953 and 1967, Lacan finds it necessary to interject: ". . . my discourse . . . is a different kind of buoy in this rising tide of the signifier, of the signified, of the 'it speaks,' of trace, of *grammè*, of lure, of myth, from the circulation of which I have now withdrawn. Aphrodite of this foam, there has arisen from it latterly *differance*, with an *a*."[74] Derrida, in an uncharacteristically positivistic gesture, has settled the question of Lacan's influence upon himself in a long footnote to an interview. (*Pos* F 117 f., *Pos* E II. 43–44) But let us admit that, on occasion, Derrida will not allow Lacan the same playfulness with terms that he allows himself.[75]

The relationship between Jacques Lacan and Jacques Derrida has no apparent bearing upon the subject matter of the *Grammatology*. But the controlled and limited polemic between them does illuminate two issues important for an understanding of the *Grammatology* within the general framework of Derrida's thought: the place of "truth" in discourse and the place of the signifier in general.

First, then, a consideration of the place of "truth" in Lacanian discourse as Derrida interprets it.

The goal of Lacanian analysis is to draw out and establish the "truth" of the subject. It is not a simple question of objectification of a subjective situation. For "no language can speak the truth about truth, for the grounds of truth are that which it speaks, it cannot found itself in any other way." (*Ec* 867–68) "Language installs the dimension of truth (inconceivable outside of discourse or what is structured as discourse), even as it excludes all guarantee of this truth." Yet, just as, even while establishing the notion of "sous rature," Heidegger could not relinquish a nostalgia for undoing forgetfulness, so Lacan's thought must work in terms of a reference point that is the *primary truth*. The passage above continues: "In relation to this absence of guarantee, a primary affirmation is engendered that is also the *primary truth*." (*Sc* I. 98) As in Heidegger the answer to the precomprehended question of Being might be read as a self-sufficient signified of all signifiers, so Lacan's ineffable primary truth becomes its own guarantee. Derrida makes the Heideggerian connections explicit:

> Truth—cut off from [or adulterated with, *coupée de*] knowledge—is constantly determined as revelation, non-veiling, that is: necessarily as presence, presentation of the present, "Being of being" (*Anwesenheit*) or, in a more literally Heideggerian mode, as the unity of veiling and unveiling. The reference to the *results* of Heidegger's progress is often explicit in this form ("the radical ambiguity indicated by Heidegger to the extent that truth means revelation," [*Ec*] p. 166, "the passion for unveiling which has an object: the truth." [*Ec*] p. 193, etc.) (*Pos* F 117, *Pos* E II. 43)

Freud had given "a metaphysical name" to the radical alterity inhabiting the psyche—the unconscious. It appears to Derrida that, in spite of giving to the unconscious the structure of a language, Lacan has contrived to entrench Freud's metaphysical suggestions by making the unconscious the seat of verification and "truth." Lacan speaks often and at length about the "veritable subject of the unconscious" (*Ec* 417) and of "the truth" of the unconscious as the "cause" of the signifying symptomatology of the subject. The analyst interprets the distorted *énonciation* (speech event) of the subject's symptom into the true *énoncé* (narrated event) of the unconscious: ". . . to the extent that it [*the subject*] speaks, it is in the place of the Other that it begins to constitute that truthful lie [*mensonge veridique*] by way of which what partakes of desire on the level of the unconscious gets itself going."[76]

"Le mensonge veridique." This, Derrida feels, is too clearly Lacan's attitude toward fiction. Whereas Derrida sees "truth" (if one can risk that word) as being constituted by "fiction" (if one can risk *that* word), Lacan seems to use fiction as a clue to truth. There is a fairly detailed discussion of this in Derrida's "Le facteur de la vérité": "Once one had distinguished, as does the entire philosophical tradition, between truth and reality, it goes without saying that truth 'establishes itself in the structure of a fiction.' Lacan strongly insists upon the opposition truth/reality which he advances as a paradox. This opposition, as orthodox as possible, facilitates the passage of truth through fiction: common sense will always have made the division between reality and fiction." (*FV* 128) Here again, Lacan seems to Derrida to have carried forward Freud's less adventurous side—the side that solves puzzles--at the expense of the Freud who opens up the grammatology of the psyche. Lacan's misreading of the quotation from Crébillon at the end of Poe's "The Purloined Letter"—he substitutes "destin" (destiny) for the more problematic "dessein" (design)—is perhaps paradigmatic of this attitude.

Derrida's second point of disagreement with Lacan relates to the "transcendental signifier." In a note on page 32 (page 324) of the *Grammatology* Derrida cautions us that, when we teach ourselves to reject the notion of the primacy of the signified—of meaning over word—we should not satisfy our longing for transcendence by giving primacy to the signifier—word over meaning. And, Derrida feels that Lacan might have perpetrated precisely this.

The signifiers in Lacan are the symbols that relate the subject through the structure of desire to the unconscious. "So runs the signifier's answer [to the subject], above and beyond all significations: 'You think you act when I stir you at the mercy of the bonds through which I knot your desires. Thus do they grow and multiply in objects, bringing you back to the fragmentation of your shattered childhood." (*Ec* 40, *FF* 71–72) "You will grasp why the relationship of the subject to the signifier is the reference that we would place in the foreground of a general rectification of analytic theory, because it is as primary and constituting in the setting up of the analytical experience, as it is primary and constituting in the radical function of the unconscious."[77] It has "priority in relation to the signified." (*Ec* 29, *FF* 59) And "the signifier alone guarantees the theoretical coherence of the entirety [*ensemble*] [of the subject] as an entirety." (*Ec* 414) Each signifier in the subject is singular and indivisible. In this it shares, Derrida suggests, the uniqueness and unassailable presence traditionally accorded to the "idea." For the hallmark of a philosophically intelligible idea is that it can be infinitely repeated as the "same" idea: it is singular and indivisible. (*FV* 121, 126) To repeat our catechism: for Derrida, by contrast to all this, the signifier and signified are interchangeable; one is the differance of the other; the concept of the sign itself is no more than a legible yet effaced, unavoidable tool. Repetition leads to a simulacrum, not to the "same."

Lacan's radical description of the function of the signifier combines presence and absence. "For the signifier is a unit in its very uniqueness, being by nature *symbol only of an absence*." (*Ec* 24, *FF* 29) It signifies a desire for some thing that the subject has not, the other of the subject. And the master signifier of these signifiers of desire is the phallus, reflecting the powerful human passions, the fear of castration (of the mother) in the male and the envy of the penis in the female. This is not the phallus as an actual organ, penis or clitoris. It is the phallus as a *signifier*, that can come to take the place of all signifiers signifying all desires for all absences. "Its most profound relation: that by which the Ancients incarnated the *Nous* and the *Logos*." (*Ec* 695) "The phallus is a signifier, a signifier whose function . . . perhaps lifts the veil from that which it held in the mysteries. For it is the signifier destined to design in their entirety the effects of the signified, to the extent that the signifier conditions them by its signifier-presence [*présence de signifiant*]." (*Ec* 690) The position of the phallus "on the chain of signifiers to which it belongs even as it makes it possible" (*FV* 132) is, strictly speaking, *transcendental*. Heidegger's Being, even under erasure, could be a transcendental signified. Lacan's phallus, signifying an absence, is a transcendental signifier.

Within this sexual fable of the production of meaning, Derrida's term is dissemination. Exploiting a false etymological kinship between semantics and semen, Derrida offers this version of textuality: A sowing that does not produce plants, but is simply infinitely repeated. A semination that is not *in*semination but *dis*seminaton, seed spilled in vain, an emission that cannot return to its origin in the father. Not an exact and controlled polysemy, but a proliferation of always different, always postponed meanings. Speaking of the purloined letter as signifier, Lacan writes: ". . . a letter always arrives at its destination." (*Ec* 41, *FF* 72) It "always might not" (*FV* 115) is the mode of Derrida's answer. Castration, the lack of superintendence by phallic authority, is what transforms the "author" or the "book" into a "text." Presence can be articulated only if it is *fragmented* into discourse; "castration" and dismemberment being both a menace to and the condition of the possibility of discourse. Somewhat extravagantly, the phallus may itself be seen as the knife that severs itself to perpetuate its dissemination. One begins to suspect that a phallocentric fable of meaning simply will not suffice.

In what it seems satisfying to me to construe as a feminist gesture, Derrida offers us a hymeneal fable. The hymen is the always folded (therefore never single or simple) space in which the pen writes its dissemination. "Metaphorically" it means the consummation of marriage. "Literally" its presence signifies the absence of consummation. This and/or structure bodies forth the play of presence and absence. The hymen undoes oppositions because it acts as it suffers. This fabulous hymen, anagram of *hymme*, "always intact as it is always ravished, a screen, a tissue," undoes "the assurance of mastery" (*Dis* 260). I refer the reader to Derrida's "La double séance," where the hymen is lavishly (un)folded.

"If we imagine one hand writing upon the surface of the mystic writing-pad while another periodically raises its covering sheet from the wax slab, we shall have a concrete representation of the way in which I tried to picture the functioning of the perceptual apparatus of our mind" (*GW* XIV 11, *SE* XIX 234). Derrida's legend of meaning undoes Freud's phallocentrism through a double-jointed notion like the Freudian mystic writing-pad sketched above. No longer castration (the realization of sexual difference as the model for the difference between signifier and signified) as the origin of signification. Rather *involve* that sexual difference in the "concrete representation" (in the long run these words must be criticized, of course) of the making of meaning: dissemination into the hymen. Into the (n)ever-virgin, (n)ever-violated hymen of interpretation, always supplementing through its fold which is also an opening, is spilled the seed of meaning; a seed that scatters itself abroad rather than inseminates. Or, turning the terms around, the playfully disseminating rather than proprietorially hermeneutic gesture of interpretation (n)ever penetrates the hymen of the text. It is a sexual union forever deferred. In a triumph of colloquialism, Derrida writes what might be roughly translated as "It [dissemination] comes too soon." But in the French the play is more pronounced: "Elle—le [le sens] laisse d'avance tomber" (*Dis* 300)—"She lets it [the meaning] fall in advance." Derrida takes advantage of the simple grammatical fact that dissemination—the male act—being a noun ending in "tion," is feminine in French. The pronoun "elle" confuses sexual agency. And the "—" between subject and object-predicate commemorates the deferment inhabiting the hymeneal dissemination of meaning.

Derrida would see in Lacan's idiom of "good and bad faith," of "authenticity," of "truth," the remnants of a postwar "existentialist" ethic. He would see in Lacan many unacknowledged debts to the Hegelian and Husserlian phenomenology that the psychoanalyst ridicules (*Pos* F 117, *Pos* E II. 43). Lacan does abundantly present himself as the prophet who is energetically unveiling the "true" Freud. Such a vocation offends Derrida the deconstructor, for whom the critic's selfhood is as vulnerable with textuality as the text itself.

The previous section concerned itself with three magistral grammatologues: Friedrich Nietzsche, Sigmund Freud, Martin Heidegger. We come back to them in another way at the end of this section. For Derrida the provisionally locatable priming-point of structuralism, the awareness of the structurality of things, does not lie only in the discovery of the "objective" structures of language, providing "scientific" models for the study of "man." It lies also in the rigorous reopening of the question of the relationship between "subjective" and "objective" structures, a structure of desire that puts the status of the human being and of that very distinction in question:

> Where and how does this decentering, this notion of the structurality of structure, occur? It would be somewhat naive to refer to an event, a doctrine, or an author in order to designate this occurrence. It is no doubt part of the totality of an era[78] . . . . Nevertheless, if I wished to give some sort of indication by choosing one or two "names," and by recalling those authors in whose discourses this occurrence has most nearly maintained its most radical formulation, I would probably cite the Nietzschean critique of metaphysics, the critique of the concepts of being and truth, for which were substituted the concepts of play, interpretation, and sign (sign without truth present); the Freudian critique of self-presence, that is, the critique of consciousness, of the subject, of self-identity and self-proximity or self-possession; and, more radically, the Heideggerian destruction of metaphysics, of ontotheology, of the determination of being as presence. (*ED* 411–12, *SC* 249–50)

IV

The launching of the structural method meant an "inflation of the sign 'language'," and thus, as we have seen, an "inflation of the sign itself." (15, 6) And this, in fact, meant an inflation, not of the graphic, but of the phonic sign, of the rôle of the element of sound in the production of meaning, language as speech. Chapter 2 of the *Grammatology* describes how Saussure prescribed linguistics to be a study of speech alone, rather than speech and writing. The emphasis is shared by Jakobson, by Lévi-

Strauss, indeed by all semiological structuralism. Lacan, dealing ostensibly with the signifier alone, sees it as half of a "*phonematic* opposition" (*Ec* 414) and calls the subject's language, when it indicates the charge of the truth of the unconscious—a "full *speech*" [*parole pleine*].

In the *Grammatology* Derrida suggests that this rejection of writing as an appendage, a mere technique, and yet a menace built into speech—in effect, a scapegoat—is a symptom of a much broader tendency. He relates this *phono*centrism to *logo*centrism—the belief that the first and last things are the Logos, the Word, the Divine Mind, the infinite understanding of God, an infinitely creative subjectivity, and, closer to our time, the self-presence of full self-consciousness. In the *Grammatology* and elsewhere, Derrida argues that the evidence for this originary and teleologic presence has customarily been found in the voice, the *phonè*. This is most clearly presented in terms of Husserlian thought in Chapter 6, "The Voice that Keeps Silence," of *Speech and Phenomena*. We have seen how, according to Derrida, Husserl's text is tortured by a suppressed insight that the Living Present is always already inhabited by difference. What allows Husserl to operate this suppression is the evidence for self-presence that he finds in the voice—not the "real" voice, but the principle of the voice in our interior soliloquy: "Why is the phoneme the most 'ideal' of signs? . . . When I speak, it belongs to the phenomenological essence of this operation that *I hear myself* [je m'entende: *hear and understand*] *at the same time* that I speak. . . . As pure auto-affection, the operation of hearing oneself speak seems to reduce even the inward surface of one's own body. . . . This auto-affection is no doubt the possibility for what is called subjectivity." (*VP* 86–87, 88, 89; *SP* 77, 79)

The suggestion is, then, that this phonocentrism-logocentrism relates to centrism itself—the human desire to posit a "central" presence at beginning and end:

> The notion of the sign . . . remains within the heritage of that logocentrism which is also a phonocentrism: absolute proximity of voice and being, of voice and the meaning of being, of voice and the ideality of meaning. . . We already have a foreboding that phonocentrism merges with the historical determination of the meaning of being in general as *presence*, with all the subdeterminations which depend on this general form . . . (presence of the thing to the sight as *eidos*, presence as substance/essence/existence (*ousia*), temporal presence as point (*stigmè*) of the now or of the moment (*nun*), the self-presence of the cogito, consciousness, subjectivity, the co-presence of the other and of the self, intersubjectivity as the intentional phenomenon of the ego, and so forth). Logocentrism would thus support the determination of the being of the entity as presence. (23, 11–12)

Lacan's phallocentrism, extending, as Derrida sees it, Freud's metaphysical bondage, fits into this pattern: "Freud, like his followers, only *described* the necessity of phallogocentrism. . . . It is neither an ancient nor a speculative mistake. . . . It is an enormous and old root." (*FV* 145)

It is this longing for a center, an authorizing pressure, that spawns hierarchized oppositions. The superior term belongs to presence and the logos; the inferior serves to define its status and mark a fall. The oppositions between intelligible and sensible, soul and body seem to have lasted out "the history of Western philosophy," bequeathing their burden to modern linguistics' opposition between meaning and word. The opposition between writing and speech takes its place within this pattern.

In the spirit of interpretation rather than of commentary, I have described the structure of writing as the sign under erasure. It would now be appropriate to recall the opening pages of this Preface, and call the structure of writing "metaphysics under erasure." Trace-structure, everything always already inhabited by the track of something that is not itself, questions presence-structure. If "the present of self-presence . . . [seems] as indivisible as the blink of an eye" (*VP* 66, *SP* 59), we must recognize that "there is a duration to the blink, and it closes the eye." (*VP* 73, *SP* 65) This presence of the trace and trace of the presence Derrida names "archi-écriture."

You will participate in the slow unfolding of these arguments in the first part of *Of Grammatology*. I shall not "repeat" them at length here. But I shall point out again what I have pointed at before: the name "writing" is given here to an entire structure of investigation, not merely to "writing in the narrow sense," graphic notation on tangible material. Thus *Of Grammatology* is not a simple valorization of writing over speech, a simple reversal of the hierarchy, a sort of anti-McLuhan. The repression of writing in the narrow sense is a pervasive symptom of centrism and that is why much of our book concerns itself precisely with that. The usual notion of writing in the narrow sense does contain the elements of the structure of writing in general: the absence of the "author" and of the "subject-matter," interpretability, the deployment of a space and a time that is not "its own." We "recognize" all this in writing in the narrow sense and "repress" it; this allows us to ignore that everything else is also inhabited by the structure of writing in general, that "the thing itself always escapes." (*VP* 165, *SP* 104) Derrida's choice of the words "writing" or "arche-writing" is thus not fortuitous. Indeed, as Derrida repeatedly points out in the section on Lévi-Strauss, no rigorous distinction between writing in the narrow and the general senses can be made. One slips into the other, putting the distinction under erasure. Writing has had the negative privilege of being the scapegoat whose exclusion represents the definition of the metaphysical enclosure.

Yet the choice of "writing" is also polemical, against the manifest phonocentrism of structuralism. And this is precisely what has sometimes led to that general misunderstanding, to the hasty view that Derrida seems to be restoring priority to writing over speech in the study of language. But this is, of course, a very hasty view. A careful reading of the *Grammatology* shows quickly that Derrida points out, rather, that speech too—grafted within an empirical context, within the structure of speaker-listener, within the general context of the language, and the possibiliy of the absence of the speaker-listener (see page liii)—is structured as writing, that in this general sense, there is "writing in speech" (*ED* 294). The first part of the book is entitled "Writing *Before* the Letter"—writing before the fact of writing in the narrow sense. The second part, "Nature, Culture, Writing," shows how, in the texts of Jean-Jacques Rousseau and Claude Lévi-Strauss, the declared opposition between Nature and Culture is undone by both the empirical *fact* and the *structure* of writing.

But if there is no structural distinction between writing and speech, the choice of "writing" as an operative term is itself suspect, and a candidate for legible erasure. Derrida puts it this way: "This common root, which is not a root but the concealment of origin and which is not common because it does not come to the same thing except with the unmonotonous insistence of difference, the unnamable movement of *difference-itself* which I have strategically nicknamed *trace*, *reserve*, or *differance*, can be called writing only within the *historical* enclosure, that is to say within the boundaries of metaphysics." (142, 93).

If, in other words, the history of metaphysics could have been different, this problematic "common root" could have been named "speech." But, according to the only metaphysics and the only language we know or can know, the text of philosophy (of the so-called "sciences of man," of literature . . .) is always written (we read it in books, on tape, through the psychic machine); yet that text is always designated by philosophy (and so forth) to be speech ("Plato says . . . ," or at most, "it is as if Plato said . . ."). "Writing" is "immediate(ly) repressed." What is written is read as speech or the surrogate of speech. "Writing" is the name of what is never named. Given differance, however, it is a violence even to name it thus, or name it with a *proper* name. One can tolerate nothing more than the nicknaming of *bricolage*.

Derrida would not privilege a signifier into transcendence. The movement of "difference-itself," precariously saved by its resident "contradiction," has many nicknames: trace, differance, reserve, supplement, dissemination, hymen, greffe, pharmakon, parergon, and so on. They form a chain where each may be substituted for the other, but not exactly (of course, even two uses of the same word would not be exactly the same): "no concept overlaps with any other" (*Pos* F 109, *Pos* E 41). Each substitution is also a displacement, and carries a different metaphoric charge, as Derrida reminds us often. He is particularly careful in the case of "differance." It is not easy to coin a word without seeming to privilege it as a term of final reference. The essay "La différance" therefore spends a lot of energy on reminding us that "*Differance* is neither a *word* nor a *concept*," that it "is not theological, not even in the most negative order of negative theology. The latter . . . always hastens to remind us that, if we deny the predicate of existence to God, it is in order to recognize him as a superior, inconceivable, and ineffable mode of being." (*MP* 6, *SP* 134) Yet giving a definite name is a gesture of control as authorized by metaphysical practice. At the end of the essay he must therefore caution: "For us, differance remains a metaphysical name. . . . 'Older' than Being itself, our language has no name for such a differance. . . . Not even the name 'differance,' which . . . continually breaks up in a chain of differant [*différantes*] substitutions." (*MP* 28, *SP* 158–59) Of "hymen," he writes: "This word . . . is not indispensable. . . . If one replaced 'hymen' with 'marriage' or 'crime,' 'identity' or 'difference,' etc., the effect would be the same, except for a condensation or economic accumulation. . . ." (*ED* 149–50)

He practices this caution in an unemphatic way. He does not hold on to a single conceptual master-word for very long. "Arche-writing," "trace," "supplementarity," such important words in the *Grammatology*, do not remain consistently important conceptual master-words in subsequent texts. Derrida's vocabulary is forever on the move. He does not relinquish a term altogether. He simply reduces it to the lower case of a common noun, where each context establishes its provisional definition yet once again.

In the face of a textual energy that sets itself against congealment, I have already offered approximative descriptions of trace, differance, dissemination, hymen. Derrida's own remark to Jean-Louis Houdebine is not coy: "*Dissemination* ultimately has no meaning and cannot be channeled into a definition. I will make no attempt at that here and prefer to refer to the working of the texts." (*Pos* F 61, *Pos* E 37) Keeping that admonition in mind, let us say briefly that "Spacing . . . 'is' the index of an irreducible outside, and at the same time the index of a *movement*, of a displacement which indicates an irreducible alterity." (*Pos* F 107–08, *Pos* E II. 40) As such it reflects the structure of differance, as does a holding in "reserve," and the "*entame*"—both beginning something and breaking into something, both origin and trace. The supplement "is" an "*addition* [that] comes to *make up for* a deficiency, . . . to compensate for a primordial non-self-presence." (*VP* 97, *SP* 87) The structure of supplementarity is set forth in the second half of *Of Grammatology*. The *pharmakon* is a Greek word that includes among its meanings poison, medicine, magic potion. It is a word used to describe writing in Plato's *Phaedrus*. Plato describes Socrates as the *pharmakeus*—poisoner, medicine man, sorcerer. Yet neither of writing nor of Socrates does Plato use the related word *pharmakos*—scapegoat. Around this lacuna, Derrida recounts the fable of writing (and

Socrates) as scapegoat and welcomes *pharmakon* into this chain of substitutions for "écriture." *Greffe* is grafting-work, both horticultural and other wise (*Dis* 230). *Parergon*, a latecomer among these nicknames, is both a frame and a supplementary "addition."

Perhaps the definition of these nicknames should escape the form of mastery represented by the copula "is." In that spirit Derrida writes:

> The *pharmakon* is neither the cure nor the poison, neither good nor evil, neither the inside nor the outside, neither speech nor writing; the *supplément* is neither a plus nor a minus, neither an outside nor the complement of an inside, neither an accident nor an essence, etc.; the *hymen* is neither confusion nor distinction, neither identity nor difference, neither consummation nor virginity, neither the veil nor the unveiling, neither the inside nor the outside, etc.; the *gramme* is neither a signifier nor a signified, neither a sign nor a thing, neither a presence nor an absence, neither a position nor a negation, etc.; *l'espacement* [spacing] is neither space nor time; the *entame* is neither the [marred] integrity of a beginning or of a simple cut nor simply the secondary state. Neither/nor is at once *at once* or rather *or rather*. (*Pos* F 59, *Pos* E I. 36)

This might seem an attractively truant world of relativism. But the fearful pleasure of a truant world is the sense of an authority being defied. That absolute ground of authority Derrida would deny. It would be a spurious pleasure for the literary critic to feel that this is a more literary idiom than the austere propositional language we habitually associate with philosophy proper. Textuality inhabits both, and the distinction between them remains to be deconstructed. Once this is grasped, it may be noted that the awareness of the need for deconstruction seems more congenial to the "irresponsible" discourse of what is conventionally called literature. "The natural tendency of *theory*—of what unites philosophy and science in the *epistémè* [the accepted description of *how* one knows]—will push rather toward filling in the breach than toward forcing the enclosure. It was normal that the breakthrough was more secure and more penetrating in the areas of literature and poetry." (139, 92) The method of deconstruction has obvious interest for literary criticism. Problematizing the distinction between philosophy and literature, it would read "even philosophy" as "literature."

(It is not enough, however, simply to exclaim over the presence of two seemingly contradictory arguments within a text and declare a text satisfactorily disunified, and one's critical approach satisfactorily grammatological. If conventional criticism took pleasure in establishing the "unified" meaning of a text, this brand of criticism would derive a matching sense of mastery in disclosing a lack of unity. Such a critical method, relying heavily on polysemy, would not face the radical playfulness of dissemination. And the critical conclusions themselves, disclosing opposites, would imply their reconciliation in the text.)

Speaking of Derrida and Heidegger, I attempted a brief description of deconstructive procedure: to spot the point where a text covers, up its grammatological structure. Here let us expand that description a little.

"The desire for unity and order," I wrote, "compels the author and the reader to balance the equation that is the text's system." Derrida in fact relates this balancing of equations to the great circular project of all philosophy in the most general sense.[79] Hegel's concept of the interiorization [*Erinnerung*] of philosophy is, in this reading, one version of a colossal exigency. The related and powerful dogma in criticism, most recently underwritten by the critics of the Geneva School,[80] is the circle of hermeneutics (interpretation rather than exposition): criticism as a movement of identification between the "subjectivity" of the author as implied in the text, and the "subjectivity" of the critic:

> In fact, it is against the incessant reappropriation of this work of the simulacrum [as opposed to the identical repetition] in a Hegelian type of dialectics . . . that I am attempting to channel the critical enterprise, Hegelian idealism consisting precisely in *sublating* the binary oppositions of classical idealism, of resolving their contradiction in a third term which turns up to "aufheben," to deny while uplifting, while idealizing, while sublimating in an anamnestic interiority (*Erinnerung* [the German word also for memory]) while *interning* difference in a presence to itself. (*Pos* F 59, *Pos* E I. 36)

Hegel articulated the circle as his central theme (39–41, **25–26**), sublating the balanced binary oppositions of classical philosophy. But even in a classical philosophical text there seems to be a moment when the possibility of the indefinite loss of meaning (dissemination) is pulled back into the circuit of meaningfulness; the orderly oppositions functioning under the benign supervision of order as presence, presence as order. Such moments, too, operate in the interests of the circular project of philosophy. Derrida disengages them in such divergent texts as those of Aristotle and Descartes. When Aristotle declares Zeno's *aporia* (time both is and is not) and steps over it without deconstructing it (*MP* 57, Eng 73–74), or when Descartes proves God's existence by means of the natural light (of reason), which, "as something natural, . . . has its source in God, in the God whose existence has been put in doubt and then demonstrated *thanks to it*" (*MP* 319, *WM* 69–70), then Derrida points at that equation-balancing at work. Speaking of the metaphor of the house chosen again and again by philosophical practice, Derrida suggests the pervasiveness of the circular project, and its articulation in Hegel: ". . . . the borrowed dwelling [*demeure*] . . . expropriation, being-away-from-home, but still in a dwelling, away from home but in someone's home, a place of self-recovery, self-recognition, self-mustering, self-resemblance, outside of the self in itself [*hors de soi en soi*]. This is philosophical metaphor as a detour in (or in view of) the reappropriation, the second coming, the self-presence of the idea in its light. A metaphorical journey from the Platonic *eidos* to the Hegelian Idea." (*MP* 302, *WM* 55)

"Outside of the self—in itself." Derrida is doing more here than simply commenting on philosophy's circular project. He is describing one of the mainstays of this project—the opposition between metaphor and truth—metaphor as a detour to truth, truth as "outside itself" in the borrowed dwelling of a metaphor, but also "itself," since the metaphor points at its own truth.

Traditional textual interpretation founds itself on this particular understanding of metaphor: a detour to truth. Not only individual metaphors or systems of metaphors, but fiction in general is seen as a detour to a truth that the critic can deliver through her interpretation. We do not usually examine the premises of this familiar situation. If we did, we would find, of course, that not only is there no pure language that is free from metaphor—the metaphor "is therefore involved in the field it would be the purpose of a general 'metaphorology' to subsume" (*MP* 261, *WM* 18); we would find also that the idea that fiction begins in the truth of the author and ends in the uncovering of that truth by the critic is given the lie by our critical and pedagogical practice. Although we customarily say that the text is autonomous and self-sufficient, there would be no justification for our activity if we did not feel that the text *needed* interpretation. The so-called secondary material is not a simple adjunct to the so-called primary text. The latter inserts itself within the interstices of the former, filling holes that are always already there. Even as it adds itself to the text, criticism supplies a lack in the text and the gaps in the chain of criticism anterior to it. The text is not unique (the acknowledged presence of polysemy already challenges that uniqueness); the critic creates a substitute. The text belongs to language, not to the sovereign and generating author. (New Criticism, although it vigorously argued the self-enclosure and "organic unity" of the text, and indulged in practice in the adulation of the author, had a sense of this last insight in its critique of the "intentional fallacy.") Derrida, questioning the unity of language itself, and putting metaphor under erasure, radically opens up textuality.

Curiously enough, deconstructive criticism must take the "metaphoric" structure of a text very seriously. Since metaphors are not reducible to truth, their own structures "as such" are part of the textuality (or message) of the text.

And, as I have hinted before, deconstruction must also take into account the lack of sovereignty of the critic himself. Perhaps this "will to ignorance" is simply a matter of attitude, a realization that one's choice of "evidence" is provisional, a self-distrust, a distrust of one's own power, the control of one's vocabulary, a shift from the phallocentric to the hymeneal. Even so, it is an important enough lesson for the critic, that self-professed custodian of the public "meaning" of literature. The tone of the section entitled "The Exorbitant. Question of Method" where Derrida "justifies" his choice of subject, gives us a glimpse of that lesson learned. I quote a few sentences from it: "We must begin *wherever we are* and the thought of the trace . . . has already taught us that it is impossible to justify a point of departure absolutely. *Wherever we are*; in a text where we already believe ourselves to be" (232–33, 162).

But in the long run a critic cannot himself present his own vulnerability. We come back simply to that question of attitude. And to the awareness that both literature *and* its criticism must open itself to a deconstructive reading, that criticism does not reveal the "truth" of literature, just as literature reveals no "truth."

A reading that *produces* rather than *protects*. That description of deconstruction we have already entertained. Here is another: ". . . the task is . . . to dismantle [*déconstruire*] the metaphysical and rhetorical structures which are at work in [the text], not in order to reject or discard them, but to reinscribe them in another way." (*MP* 256, WM 13)

How to dismantle these structures? By using a signifier not as a transcendental key that will unlock the way to truth but as a *bricoleur*'s or tinker's tool—a "positive lever" (*Pos* F 109, *Pos* E II. 41). If in the process of deciphering a text in the traditional way we come across a word that seems to harbor an unresolvable contradiction, and by virtue of being *one* word is made sometimes to work in one way and sometimes in another and thus is made to point away from the absence of a unified meaning, we shall catch at that word. If a metaphor seems to suppress its implications, we shall catch at that metaphor. We shall follow its adventures through the text and see the text coming undone as a structure of concealment, revealing its self-transgression, its undecidability. It must be emphasized that I am not speaking simply of locating a moment of ambiguity or irony ultimately incorporated into the text's system of unified meaning but rather a moment that genuinely threatens to collapse that system. (It should also be repeated that, although in the *Grammatology* Derrida fastens upon the *word* [signifier, metaphor] "supplement" and related *words* in Rousseau's text as his lever, once the critic's glance is allowed to play upon parts of words and the spacing of a page, the prising-lever of undecidability may become much more elusive.) At any rate, the relationship between the reinscribed text and the so-called original text is not that of patency and latency, but rather the relationship between two palimpsests. The "original" text itself is that palimpsest on so-called "pre"-texts that the critic might or might not be able to disclose and any original inscription would still only be a trace: "Reading then resembles those X-ray pictures which discover, under the epidermis of the last painting, another hidden picture:

of the same painter or another painter, no matter, who would himself, for want of materials, or for a new effect, use the substance of an ancient canvas or conserve the fragment of a first sketch" (*Dis* 397).

I have suggested that Derrida implicates himself in the Freudian procedure of attending to the detail of a text. Here let me place, beside the metaphors of palimpsest and x-ray picture, Freud's own analogy—"though I know that in these matters analogies never carry us very far"—for the distortion of the psychic text:

> [there are] various methods . . . for making [an undesirable] book innocuous. [Derrida would transfer the analogy to the "undesirable" grammatological "threat" inhabiting every text.] One way would be for the offending passages to be thickly crossed through so that they were illegible. In that case they could not be transcribed, and the next copyist of the book would produce a text which was unexceptionable but which had gaps in certain passages, and so might be unintelligible in them. Another way . . . would be . . . to proceed to distort the text. Single words would be left out or replaced by others, and new sentences interpolated. *Best of all, the whole passage would be erased and a new one which said exactly the opposite put in its place.*" (GW XVI. 81–82, SE XXIII. 236; italics are mine)

(It is characteristic, of course, that Freud, who put the psyche under erasure, should, at the same time, use a thoroughly "centric" sentiment to close the passage: "It no longer contained what the author wanted to say.")

The sense of the horizon of indefinite meaning, with the provisional anchor of the text never given up, has led to a handful of spectacular readings. The two most adventurous are "La double séance" (a reading of Mallarmé's "Mimique"; *Dis* 199–317) and "La dissémination" (a reading of Philippe Sollers' *Nombres*; *Dis* 319–407). Those acts of controlled acrobatics are difficult to match. Yet the reading of *Phaedrus* in "La pharmacie de Platon" (*Dis* 69–197) and of *The Essay on the Origin of Languages* (235–445, 165–316), although less playful, seem equally impressive.

Speaking of the hymen, Derrida emphasizes the role of the blank spaces of the page in the play of meaning. Analogically, Derrida himself often devotes his attention to the text in its margins, so to speak. He examines the minute particulars of an undecidable moment, nearly imperceptible displacements, that might otherwise escape the reader's eye. Reading Foucault, he concentrates on three pages out of 673. Reading Rousseau, he chooses a text that is far from "central." Reading Heidegger, he proceeds to write a note on a note to *Sein und Zeit*.

His method, as he says to Jean-Louis Houdebine, perhaps a little too formulaically, is reversal and displacement. It is not enough "simply to *neutralize* the binary oppositions of metaphysics." We must recognize that, within the familiar philosophical oppositions, there is always "a violent hierarchy. One of the two terms controls the other (axiologically, logically, etc.), holds the superior position. To deconstruct the opposition is first . . . to overthrow [*renverser*] the hierarchy." (*Pos* F 57, *Pos* E. I. 36) To fight violence with violence. In the *Grammatology* this structural phase would be represented by all those pages where, all apologies to the contrary, the polemical energy seems clearly engaged in putting writing above speech. But in the next phase of deconstruction, this reversal must be displaced, the winning term put under erasure. The critic must make room for "the irruptive emergence of a new 'concept,' a concept which no longer allows itself to be understood in terms of the previous regime [system of oppositions]." In terms of our book, this would be the aspect that "allows for the dissonant emergence of a writing inside of speech, thus disorganizing all the received order and invading the whole sphere of speech" (*Pos* E I. 36).

To locate the promising marginal text, to disclose the undecidable moment, to pry it loose with the positive lever of the signifier; to reverse the resident hierarchy, only to displace it; to dismantle in order to reconstitute what is always already inscribed. Deconstruction in a nutshell. But take away the assurance of the text's authority, the critic's control, and the primacy of meaning, and the possession of this formula does not guarantee much.

Why should we undo and redo a text at all? Why not assume that words and the author "mean what they say?" It is a complex question. Here let us examine Derrida's most recent meditation upon the desire of deconstruction.

Derrida acknowledges that the desire of deconstruction may itself become a desire to reappropriate the text actively through mastery, to show the text what it "does not know." And as she deconstructs, all protestations to the contrary, the critic necessarily assumes that she at least, and for the time being, means what she says. Even the declaration of her vulnerability must come, after all, in the controlling language of demonstration and reference. In other words, the critic provisionally forgets that her own text is necessarily self-deconstructed, always already a palimpsest.

The desire of deconstruction has also the opposite allure. Deconstruction seems to offer a way out of the closure of knowledge. By inaugurating the open-ended indefiniteness of textuality—by thus "placing in the abyss" (*mettre en abîme*), as the French expression would literally have it—it shows us the lure of the abyss as freedom. The fall into the abyss of deconstruction inspires us with as much pleasure as fear. We are intoxicated with the prospect of never hitting bottom.

Thus a further deconstruction deconstructs deconstruction, both as the search for a foundation (the critic behaving as if she means what she says in her text), and as the pleasure of the bottomless. The tool for this, as indeed for any deconstruction, is our desire, itself a deconstructive and grammatological structure that forever differs from (we only desire what is not ourselves) and defers (desire is never fulfilled) the text of our selves. Deconstruction can therefore never be a positive science. For we are in a bind, in a "double (read abyssal) bind," Derrida's newest nickname for the schizophrenia of the "sous rature."[81] We *must* do a thing *and* its opposite, and indeed we desire to do both, and so on indefinitely. Deconstruction is a perpetually self-deconstructing movement that is inhabited by differance. No text is ever *fully* deconstructing or deconstructed. Yet the critic provisionally musters the metaphysical resources of criticism and performs what declares itself to be *one* (unitary) act of deconstruction. As I point out on pages **lxxxi–lxxxii**, the kinship with Freud's interminable and terminable analysis, involving both subject and analyst, is here not to be ignored.

Derrida is now ready to suggest that, in a certain sense, it is impossible "not to deconstruct/be deconstructed." All texts, whether written in the narrow sense or not, are rehearsing their grammatological structure, self-deconstructing as they constitute themselves. The single act of critical deconstruction is as necessary yet pointless, arrogant yet humble, as all human gestures. "In the deconstruction of the arche, one does not make a choice" (91, **62**).

These, then, are the lineaments of the Derridean double bind, deconstruction under erasure, the abyss placed in the abyss, active forgetfulness. (Here it may be pointed out that one of the traditional charges against writing is that it breeds passive forgetfulness (55, **37** and passim). In this respect also, deconstruction reinscribes the value of writing.) On page **xlv** I bring a charge of "prudence" against Derrida. The new Derrida shows us that this "prudence" is also the greatest "danger," the will to knowledge as will to ignorance and vice versa. "The 'knowledge' of the philosopher places him among the dreamers, for knowledge is a dream. But the philospher 'knowingly' agrees to dream, to dream of knowledge, agrees to 'forget' the lesson of philosophy, only so as to 'prove' that lesson. . . . It is a vertiginous movement."

As *Glas* will suggest, this philosophical agreement is the reader/writer's contract (*seing*) with the text. Let me add yet once again that this terrifying and exhilarating vertigo is not "mystical" or "theological." The abyss appears when Nietzsche, Freud, Heidegger, Derrida lift the lid of the most familiar and comforting notions about the possibility of knowledge.

V

Of Grammatology is the provisional origin of this Preface. But we have not kept track of the book's outline. We have considered instead the importance of erasure in Derrida; provided some ingredients for the computation of the intertextuality between Derrida, and Nietzsche, Heidegger, Freud, Husserl; given some indications of Derrida's view of Structuralism, especially of the metapsychological practice of Jacques Lacan; commented on the place of "writing" in Derrida's thought, hinted at the chain of its substitutions, given the recipe for deconstruction. Now that we begin the concluding movements of this repetitive preface, let us make *Of Grammatology* our provisional end.

Derrida situates *Of Grammatology* among his own texts thus:

> *Of Grammatology* can be taken as a long essay articulated in two parts . . . *between* which one can stitch in *L'écriture et la différence*. The *Grammatology* often refers to it. In that case, the interpretation of Rousseau [Part II of *Of Grammatology*] would be the twelfth item of the collection. Conversely, one can insert *Of Grammatology* in the middle of *L'écriture et la différence*. Since six texts of the latter are anterior, in fact and in principle, to the publication . . . in *Critique*, of the articles announcing *Of Grammatology*; the five last, beginning with "Freud and the Scene of Writing" are engaged in the grammatological overture. (*Pos* F 12–13)

Although Derrida continues ". . . things don't let themselves be reconstituted so simply," this fable of fragmentation is not without interest. There is a certain stitched-togetherness in *Of Grammatology*, and a decided disjunction between the sweeping, summarizing, theoretical breadth of the first part, and the interpretative, slow, reader's pace of the second.

Part I is an expanded version of a two-part review of Madeleine V-David's *Le débat sur les écritures et l'hiéroglyphe aux xvii°et xviii° siècles*, André Lerori-Gourhan's *Le geste et la parole*, and the papers of a colloquium entitled *L'écriture et la psychologie des peuples.*[82] Although the review articles contained most of the material of the entire Part I in their present order, it is in Chapter 3—"Of Grammatology as A Positive Science"—that their mark is most clearly felt. Each of the three books reviewed receives a section of the chapter. The first gives a summary of the moment when grammatology could historically have opened but did not, the moment of the decipherment of non-European scripts. The second investigates the possible physiological bases for the differentiation between writing and speech and genetic writing as the determinant of life. The third deals with the implications of varieties of "nonphonetic" writing. One cannot help wondering if all this overt interest in an account of writing in the narrow sense—rather than in the interpretation of texts—is not simply due to the regulating presence of books to be reviewed.

Indeed, in Part I and in the postscript to "Freud and the Scene of Writing," Derrida speaks most often of re-writing the "history of writing" in something suspiciously like the narrow sense—"an immense field where hitherto one has only done preparatory work" (*ED* 340). "Writing" so envisaged is on the brink of becoming a unique signifier, and Jacques Derrida's chief care. In his later work, the theoretical significance of the structure of writing and the grammatological opening remain intact. But he quietly drops the idea of being the authorized grammatological historian of writing in the narrow sense. "Writing" then takes its place on the chain of substitutions. In the *Grammatology*, then, we are at a specific and precarious moment in Derrida's career.

It is fascinating to study the changes and interpolations made in the text of the review articles as they were transformed into the book. (The text *is* genuinely enriched as the appropriate "difference"-s are changed to "differance"-s.) Most of the changes make the philosophical ground of the argument stronger. The superb discussion of the proper name (136–37, 89–90) is a case in point. So is the long footnote on the psychoanalysis of writing (132–34, 333–34), and the insertion of the remarks on the radical alterity necessarily inhabiting the sign. (69, 47) So is the cautionary addition on page 125 (84). (The original version ran: "It [genetic script] is a liberation which makes for the appearing of the *grammè* as such and no doubt makes possible the emergence of 'writing' in the narrow sense." [*Crit* II. 46] In the *Grammatology* Derrida annuls the possibility of the *grammè* ever appearing *as such*. He adds the following parenthesis after "as such": "[that is to say according to a new structure of nonpresence]," and goes on to add the following sentences: "But one cannot think them [the structurations of this *grammè*] without the most general concept of the *grammè*. That is irreducible and impregnable.")

From our point of view, what is most interesting is that the theme of "sous rature" is given its development almost entirely in the book rather than in the articles. As I have mentioned above, Derrida never discusses "sous rature" at great length. But in the articles all we have is a *mention* of the practice (*Crit* I. 1029) as it is to be found on page 38 (23) of *Of Grammatology*. The use of the crossed lines on page 31 (19), the discussion of Heidegger's notion of Being between pages 31 and 38 (19–23), the putting of "experience" under erasure on page 89 (60–61), of the "past" on page 97 (66–67), and the "originarity of the trace" on page 110 (75) are all passages only found in the book.

On the other hand, and curiously enough, the argument for historical necessity seems also to have been emphasized as the review articles were turned into the first part of the book. The first tiny change—from "the phoneticization of writing dissimulated its own history while producing it" (*Crit* I. 1017) to "the phoneticization of writing *must* dissimulate its own history while producing it" (11, 3)—sets the tone for all the small but weighty changes that will be made. They are not many, but they are unequivocal. Most of them, naturally enough, are confined to Chapter 1, "The End of the Book and the Beginning of Writing." The paragraph beginning "these disguises are not historical contingencies" (17, 7; the article had only the first two sentences) is a representative example. The repression of writing, and its recognition today, are seen as historically necessary events. In a text where he elaborately launches a theory against teleological patternings of history and thought, where he delivers the notion of the play of necessity and contingency, why does Derrida fabricate so strong an argument for historical necessity? Why is the opening chapter—"The End of the Book and the Beginning of Writing"—full of a slightly embarrassing messianic promise? If we really do not believe in "epistemological cut-off points," or in the possibility of stepping out of the metaphysical enclosure by simply deciding to, or in the linearity of time, then with what seriousness can we declare a different "world to come," a world where the "values of sign, speech, and writing," will be made to tremble? (14, 5) How reconcile ourselves with this break between the world of the past and the world of the future? It seems an empiricist betrayal of the structure of difference and postponement, and any deconstructive reading of Derrida will have to take this into account.

(We have seen that Derrida will not call grammatology a psychoanalysis of logocentrism. On page 20 [9–10] of the *Grammatology*, there is the merest hint of a psychoanalytical patterning of the history of writing that Derrida does not pursue: "This situation [the role of writing in the naming of the human element] has always already been announced. Why is it today in the process of making itself recognized *as such* and *after the fact* [*après coup*]"? Making itself recognized *as such*. Derrida makes an attempt on that page at answering that part of the question in terms of the development in ways and means of information retrieval, phonography, and cybernetics, all joining forces with anthropology and the history of writing—the sciences of man. But elsewhere in the book, as we have seen, he emphasizes that the situation can never be recognized *as such*, that we must surrender ourselves to being inscribed within the chain of future deconstructions and decipherings. It is therefore the *après coup* that seems more interesting here. That is the French word for Freud's "*Nachträglichkeit*"—translated into English as "deferred action." As we recall, at the time that a stimulus is received, it goes *either* into the perceptual system *or* into the Unconscious and produces a permanent trace. That particular trace might be energized into consciousness (as Freud reminds us over and over again, this topographical language must be used with caution) long afterward—*nachträglich, après coup*. But it never comes up *as such*; in fact, as Derrida argues, following Freud, the trace [*die Bahnung*] itself is primary. There is no "thing" there in the

Unconscious but simply the possibility for this particular path to be energized. When the track is opened up, and we have the *après coup* perception of the originary trace, the impulse in the Unconscious is not exhausted. Unconscious impulses are indestructible. Now before the remarks about theoretical mathematics, information retrieval *et alia* on page 20 [9–10], Derrida slips in, immediately after the sentences we are examining, the following words: "This question would call forth an interminable analysis." "Interminable analysis." The words themselves recall Freud's late essay "Analysis Terminable and Interminable."[83] The impulses in the Unconscious are indestructible, *après coup* they come up into consciousness interminably, and thus constitute the subject. A neurosis can never be analyzed to the full—the analysis would in fact, be interminable, if the practical analyst did not terminate it. Is the trace of the repression of writing in some indeterminate historical Unconscious "coming up" to our consciousness at the present historical moment, *après coup*? Derrida himself is clearly not willing to assume the responsibility for what might seem a psychoanalytic schema. This again is an undertaking for a future deconstructor. Yet there is, no doubt, a strong sympathy between Freud's notion of the theoretical impossibility of a full analysis and Derrida's polemic of the need for the perpetual renewal of the grammatological or deconstructive undertaking. In fact, that is what all of Derrida's work on "writing" has presented—although it seems to be receiving articulation today, variations of previous articulations have existed throughout history and the complex will have to be confronted perpetually as the language of confrontation, obeying our will to power, adapts to and is retrieved by logocentrism, or, as Freud would say, with a little help from Heidegger, as "the ego treats ~~recovery~~ itself as a new ~~danger~~." [GW XVI. 84, SE XXIII. 238; erasures mine] It seems quite plausible, then, to ask: if "the Freudian discourse—its syntax or . . . its work" were delivered from "his necessarily metaphysical and traditional concepts" [*ED* 294], would one be able to decipher a psychoanalytic schema in the obstinate historical pattern of *Of Grammatology*?)

There is also the shadow of a geographical pattern that falls upon the first part of the book. The relationship between logocentrism and ethnocentrism is indirectly invoked in the very first sentence of the "Exergue." Yet, paradoxically, and almost by a reverse ethnocentrism, Derrida insists that logocentrism is a property of the *West*. He does this so frequently that a quotation would be superfluous. Although something of the Chinese prejudice of the West is discussed in Part I, the *East* is never seriously studied or deconstructed in the Derridean text. Why then must it remain, recalling Hegel and Nietzsche in their most cartological humors, as the name of the limits of the text's knowledge?

The discussion of Lévi-Strauss in Part II, the only genuinely polemical and perhaps the least formally awkward section of the book, first appeared in 1966, as part of an issue on Lévi-Strauss of the *Cahiers pour l'analyse* (IV, September–October, 1966).

Derrida chooses Lévi-Strauss as his subject because, "at once conserving and annulling inherited conceptual oppositions, this thought, like Saussure's, stands on a borderline: sometimes within an uncriticized conceptuality, sometimes putting a strain on the boundaries, and working toward deconstruction" (154, 105). And he takes Lévi-Strauss to task for slackness of method, for sentimental ethnocentrism, for an oversimplified reading of Rousseau. He criticizes Lévi-Strauss for conceiving of writing only in the narrow sense, for seeing it as a scapegoat for all the exploitative evils of "civilization," and for conceiving of the violent Nambikwara as an innocent community "without writing." If the end of Part I seems too concerned with writing in the narrow sense, these chapters redeem themselves in that respect. For in them Derrida repeatedly moves us from writing in the narrow sense to writing in general—through such "systematic" statements as: "the genealogical relation and social classification are the stitched seam of arche-writing, condition of the (so-called oral) language, and of writing in the colloquial sense" (182, 125) to such "poetic" ones as: "the *silva* [forest] is savage, the *via rupta* [path cut through] is written . . . it is difficult to imagine that access to the possibility of road maps is not access to writing" (158, 108).

Perhaps the most interesting reason given for the impossibility of a community without writing is that the bestowing of the proper name, something no society can avoid, is itself inhabited by the structure of writing. For the phrase "proper name" signifies a classification, an institution carrying the trace of history, into which a certain sort of sign is made to fit. Thus the proper name, as soon as it is understood as such, is no longer fully unique and proper to the holder. The proper name is always already common by virtue of belonging to the category "proper." It is always already under erasure: "When within *consciousness*, the name *is called* proper, it is already classified and is obliterated in *being named*. It is already no more than a *so-called* proper name" (161, 109). Lévi-Strauss knows this, as his discussion of proper names in *The Savage Mind* (pp. 226f., Eng. pp. 172f.) demonstrates. But, having nothing but a restricted concept of writing, he cannot relate the proper name to writing: "The essence or the energy of the *graphein* . . . [is] the originary effacement of the proper name" (159, 108).

This argument does not only serve to undo the anthropoloigst's reverse ethnocentrism toward an "innocent community without writing." It points to the presence of writing in general in all the ramifications of the "proper"—the own, the distinguishing characteristic, the literal, the exclusively clean. It is so pervasive a Derridean theme that I can do no more than mention it here. In a way, Derrida's chief concern might be summarized thus: to problematize the proper name and proper (literal) meaning, the proper in general.

The argument points also to the theme of the play of desire around the proper name: The narcissistic desire to make one's own "proper" name "common," to make it enter and be at one with the body of the mother-tongue; and, at the same time, the oedipal desire to preserve one's proper name, to see it as the analogon of the *name* of the father. Much of Derrida's recent work meditates on this play. I shall quote the beginning of *Glas,* where Hegel (the "proper" name) is invoked as the eagle (the "common" name) that the French pronunciation of his name—"aigle"—turns him into:

Who, he?
His name is so strange. From the eagle he draws his imperial or historical power. Those who still pronounce it as French, and there are those, are silly only to a certain point: the restitution . . . of the magisterial cold . . . of the eagle caught in ice and frost [*gel*]. Let the emblemished philosopher be thus congealed. (p. 7)

Pages 145 to 151 (97–102) are a theoretical "justification" of what Derrida will come to call "intertextuality:" the interweaving of different texts (literally "web"-s) in an act of criticism that refuses to think of "influence" or "interrelationship" as simple historical phenomena. Intertextuality becomes the most striking conceptual and typographical signature in *Glas.* Pages 226 to 234 (157–64)—"The Exorbitant: Question of Method"—are, as I have suggested, a simple and moving exposition of the method of deconstruction as understood by the early Derrida.

Rousseau's place in Derrida's text is most importantly marked by the former's use of the word "supplement": "Writing will appear to me more and more," Derrida writes, "as another name for this structure of supplementarity. . . . It does not suffice to say that Rousseau thinks the supplement without thinking it, that he does not match his saying and his meaning, his descriptions and his declarations. . . . Using the word and describing the thing, Rousseau in a way displaces and deforms the sign 'supplement,' the unity of the signifier and the signified. . . . But these displacements and deformations are regulated by the contradictory unity —itself supplementary—of a desire" (348, 245). Of the issue of supplementarity itself, abundantly developed by Derrida in this book, there is no need to speak. Of more interest to me is the question, how does the word "supplement" signify Rousseau's desire? Before I attempt to gauge

Derrida's enigmatic answer to this question, I shall digress and point at the rather endearing conservatism of Chapter 3, Section I: "The Place of the Essay."

There is a certain mark of superior academic scholarship in that section that seems out of joint with the theoretical spirit of the book. Here the philosopher who has written "The outside is the inside" in Part I, speaks with perfect seriousness about internal and external evidence, and the thinker of "intertextuality" concerns himself with the relative dating of *The Essay on the Origin of Languages* and *The Discourse on Inequality*. This reader is happy that those marks of traditional scholarship were not unstitched. It is engrossing to watch the bold argument operating in the service of a conventional debate. For the burden of the proof lies on "the economy of pity"—the supplementarity of pity in both Rousseau texts—and intertextual practice does emerge as the two texts are woven together: "From one [text] to the other, an emphasis is displaced, a continuous sliding is in operation. . . . The Discourse wants to *mark the beginning*. . . . The Essay would make us *sense the beginnings*. . . . It seizes man . . . in that subtle transition from origin to genesis. . . . The description of pure nature in the *Discourse* made room within itself for such a transition. As always, it is the unseizable limit of the *almost*" (358, **253**). I do not believe that Derrida ever again devotes himself to this sort of textual scholarship. Here, too, the reading of *Of Grammatology* gives us the taste of a rather special early Derrida, the young scholar transforming the ground rules of scholarship.

The book ends with Rousseau's dream, the supplementary desire that I refer to above. Such an ending is a characteristic Derrida touch, criticism giving up the idiom of expository mastery in the end and taking on the idiom of the fabulist. "La pharmacie de Platon" ends with the scene of Plato in his pharmacy, "White Mythology" with the heliotrope stone. Examples can be multiplied.

Rousseau, that famous masturbator, has a philosophical wet dream: "Rousseau's dream consisted of making the supplement enter metaphysics by force" (444, **315**).

But is not that force precisely the energy of Derrida's own project? Is this not precisely the trick of writing, that dream-cum-truth, that breaches the metaphysical closure with an intrinsic yet supplementary violence? At the end of Derrida's book on Rousseau, Rousseau is set dreaming of Derrida. Perhaps the book does end with its author's signature.

It is customary at this point to say a few words about the problem of translation. Derrida's text certainly offers its share of "untranslatable" words. I have had my battles with "exergue" and "propre."[84] My special worry is "entamer." As we have seen, it is an important word in Derrida's vocabulary. It means both to break into and to begin. I have made do with "broach" or "breach," with the somewhat fanciful confidence that the shadow-word "breach" or "broach" will declare itself through it. With "entamer" as well as with other words and expressions, I have included the original in parenthesis whenever the wording and syntax of the French seemed to carry a special charge. To an extent, this particular problem informs the entire text. Denying the uniqueness of words, their substantiality, their transferability, their repeatability, *Of Grammatology* denies the possibility of translation. Not so paradoxically perhaps, each twist of phrase becomes at the same time "significant" and playful when language is manipulated for the purpose of putting signification into question, for deconstructing the binary opposition "signifier-signified." That playfulness I fear I have not been able remotely to capture. Even so simple a word as "de" carries a touch of play—hinting at both "of" and "from." (I have once resorted to "from/of," where the playfulness seemed to ask for special recognition [page **269**].) But that sort of heavy-handedness cannot punctuate an entire text where "penser" (to think) carries within itself and points at "panser" (to dress a wound); for does not thinking seek forever to clamp a dressing over the gaping and violent wound of the impossibility of thought? The translation of the title, suggesting "a piece of" as well as "about," I have retained against expert counsel.

I began this preface by informing my readers that Derrida's theory admitted—as it denied—a preface by questioning the absolute repeatability of the text. It is now time to acknowledge that his theory would likewise admit—as it denies—translation, by questioning the absolute privilege of the original. Any act of reading is besieged and delivered by the precariousness of intertextuality. And translation is, after all, one version of intertextuality.[85] If there are no unique words, if, as soon as a privileged concept-word emerges, it must be given over to the chain of substitutions and to the "common language," why should that act of substitution that is translation be suspect? If the proper name or sovereign status of the author is as much a barrier as a right of way, why should the translator's position be secondary? It must now be evident that, desiring to conserve the "original" (*De la grammatologie*) and seduced by the freedom of the absence of a sovereign text (not only is there no *Of Grammatology* before mine, but there have been as many translations of the text as readings, the text is infinitely translatable), translation itself is in a double bind (see pages **lxxvii–lxxviii**).

And, from quite another point of view, most practically and rigorously speaking, both Derrida and I being very roughly bilingual—his English a cut above my French—where does French end and English begin?

I shall not launch my philosophy of translation here. Instead I give you a glimpse of Derrida's:

> Within the limits of its possibility, or its *apparent* possibility, translation practices the difference between signified and signifier. But, if this difference is never pure, translation is even less so, and a notion of *transformation* must be substituted for the notion of translation: a regulated transformation of one language by another, of one text by another. We shall not have and never have had to deal with some "transfer" of pure signifieds that the signifying instrument—or "vehicle"—would leave virgin and intact, from one language to another, or within one and the same language. (*Pos* 31)

"From one language to another, *or* within one and the same language." Translation is a version of the intertexuality that comes to bear also within the "same" language. Ergo . . .

Heidegger's deconstructive (or "destructive") method is often based on consideration of how the so-called content of philosophy is affected by the exigencies of translation. Derrida writes of this in "La différance" and "Ousia et grammè." (*MP* 3–29, *SP* 129–60; *MP* 31–78) In the latter example there is a double play: Heidegger laments the loss for philosophy when the lone latin "presence" was pressed into service to translate the many nuanced Greek words signifying philosophical shadings of the idea of presence. Derrida engages in the parallel lament—how translate the many nuanced Heideggerian German words signifying philosophical shadings of the idea of presence through the lone Romance "présence?" Derrida goes on to use the business of "mistranslations" as an effective deconstructive lever of his own. The most sustained example is "La pharmacie de Platon," where he appropriately asks: why have translators obliterated the word "*pharmakon*" by providing a collection of different words as its translated substitute?

And all said and done, that is the sort of reader I would hope for. A reader who would fasten upon my mistranslations, and with that leverage deconstruct Derrida's text beyond what Derrida as controlling subject has directed in it.

VI

"The first part of this book, 'Writing before the Letter,' sketches in broad outlines *Now I insert my text within his and move you on, situating here* a theoretical matrix. It indicates certain significant historical moments, and proposes *My name*: certain critical concepts. *Gayatri Chakravorty Spivak*. These critical concepts are put to the test *the places of this work: Iowa City, (New Delhi–Dacca–Calcutta), Boston, Nice, Providence, Iowa City*, in the second part, 'Nature, Culture, Writing.' *Its time: July, 1970–October*, 1975. This part may be called illustrative . . .

Preface

The first part of this book, "Writing before the Letter,"[1] sketches in broad outlines a theoretical matrix. It indicates certain significant historical moments, and proposes certain critical concepts.

These critical concepts are put to the test in the second part, "Nature, Culture, Writing." This is the moment, as it were, of the example, although strictly speaking, that notion is not acceptable within my argument. I have tried to defend, patiently and at length, the choice of these examples (as I have called them for the sake of convenience) and the necessity for their presentation. It is a question of a reading of what may perhaps be called the "age" of Rousseau. A reading merely outlined; considering the need for such an analysis, the difficulty of the problems, and the nature of my project, I have felt justified in selecting a short and little-known text, the *Essay on the Origin of Languages.** I shall have to explain the privileged place I give to that work. There is yet another reason why my reading might be incomplete: although I have no ambition to illustrate a new method, I have attempted to produce, often embarrassing myself in the process, the problems of critical reading. These problems are at all times related to the guiding intention of this book. My interpretation of Rousseau's text follows implicitly the propositions ventured in Part I; propositions that demand that reading should free itself, at least in its axis, from the classical categories of history—not only from the categories of the history of ideas and the history of literature but also, and perhaps above all, from the categories of the history of philosophy.

It goes without saying that around that axis I have had to respect classical norms, or at least I have attempted to respect them. Although the word "age" or "epoch" can be given more than these determinations, I should mention that I have concerned myself with a *structural figure* as much as a *historical totality*. I have attempted to relate these two seemingly necessary approaches, thus repeating the question of the text, its historical status, its proper time and space. The age already in the *past* is in fact constituted in every respect as a *text*, in a sense of these words that I

* Derrida uses the 1817 Bélin edition of the *Essai*. My references, placed within brackets, as are all my interpolations, are to *On the Origin of Languages*, Jean Jacques Rousseau; *Essay on the Origin of Language*, Johann Gottfried Herder, tr. John H. Moran and Alexander Gode (New York, 1966).

Notes at the foot of the pages in this volume are translator's notes. Author's notes appear at the back of the book.

shall have to establish. As such the age conserves the values of legibility and the efficacy of a model and thus disturbs the time (tense) of the line or the line of time. I have tried to suggest this by calling upon and questioning the declared Rousseauism of a modern anthropologist.

I
Writing before the Letter

Exergue

1. The one who will shine in the science of writing will shine like the sun. A scribe (*EP*, p. 87)
O Samas (sun-god), by your light you scan the totality of lands as if they were cuneiform signs (ibid.).

2. These three ways of writing correspond almost exactly to three different stages according to which one can consider men gathered into a nation. The depicting of objects is appropriate to a savage people; signs of words and of propositions, to a barbaric people; and the alphabet to civilized people. J.-J. Rousseau, *Essai sur l'origine des langues.*

3. Alphabetic script is in itself and for itself the most intelligent. Hegel, *Enzyklopädie.*

This triple exergue is intended not only to focus attention on the *ethnocentrism* which, everywhere and always, had controlled the concept of writing. Nor merely to focus attention on what I shall call *logocentrism*: the metaphysics of phonetic writing (for example, of the alphabet) which was fundamentally—for enigmatic yet essential reasons that are inaccessible to a simple historical relativism—nothing but the most original and powerful ethnocentrism, in the process of imposing itself upon the world, controlling in one and the same *order*:

1. *the concept of writing* in a world where the phoneticization of writing must dissimulate its own history as it is produced;

2. *the history of* (the only) *metaphysics*, which has, in spite of all differences, not only from Plato to Hegel (even including Leibniz) but also, beyond these apparent limits, from the pre-Socratics to Heidegger, always assigned the origin of truth in general to the logos: the history of truth, of the truth of truth, has always been—except for a metaphysical diversion that we shall have to explain—the debasement of writing, and its repression outside "full" speech.

3. *the concept of science* or the scientificity of science—what has always been determined as *logic*—a concept that has always been a philosophical concept, even if the practice of science has constantly challenged its imperialism of the logos, by invoking, for example, from the beginning and ever increasingly, nonphonetic writing. No doubt this subversion has always been contained within a system of direct address [*système allocutoire*] which gave birth to the project of science and to the conventions of all nonphonetic characteristics.[1] It could not have been otherwise. None-

theless, it is a peculiarity of our epoch that, at the moment when the phoneticization of writing—the historical origin and structural possibility of philosophy as of science, the condition of the *epistémè*—begins to lay hold on world culture,[2] science, in its advancements, can no longer be satisfied with it. This inadequation had always already begun to make its presence felt. But today something lets it appear as such, allows it a kind of takeover without our being able to translate this novelty into clear cut notions of mutation, explicitation, accumulation, revolution, or tradition. These values belong no doubt to the system whose dislocation is today presented as such, they describe the styles of an historical movement which was meaningful—like the concept of history itself—only within a logocentric epoch.

By alluding to a science of writing reined in by metaphor, metaphysics, and theology,[3] this exergue must not only announce that the science of writing—*grammatology*[4]—shows signs of liberation all over the world, as a result of decisive efforts. These efforts are necessarily discreet, dispersed, almost imperceptible; that is a quality of their meaning and of the milieu within which they produce their operation. I would like to suggest above all that, however fecund and necessary the undertaking might be, and even if, given the most favorable hypothesis, it did overcome all technical and epistemological obstacles as well as all the theological and metaphysical impediments that have limited it hitherto, such a science of writing runs the risk of never being established as such and with that name. Of never being able to define the unity of its project or its object. Of not being able either to write its discourse on method or to describe the limits of its field. For essential reasons: the unity of all that allows itself to be attempted today through the most diverse concepts of science and of writing, is, in principle, more or less covertly yet always, determined by an historico-metaphysical epoch of which we merely glimpse the *closure*. I do not say the *end*. The idea of science and the idea of writing—therefore also of the science of writing—is meaningful for us only in terms of an origin and within a world to which a certain concept of the sign (later I shall call it *the* concept of sign) and a certain concept of the relationships between speech and writing, have *already* been assigned. A most determined relationship, in spite of its privilege, its necessity, and the field of vision that it has controlled for a few millennia, especially in the West, to the point of being now able to produce its own dislocation and itself proclaim its limits.

Perhaps patient meditation and painstaking investigation on and around what is still provisionally called writing, far from falling short of a science of writing or of hastily dismissing it by some obscurantist reaction, letting it rather develop its positivity as far as possible, are the wanderings of a way of thinking that is faithful and attentive to the ineluctable world of the future which proclaims itself at present, beyond the closure of knowledge.

The future can only be anticipated in the form of an absolute danger. It is that which breaks absolutely with constituted normality and can only be proclaimed, *presented*, as a sort of monstrosity. For that future world and for that within it which will have put into question the values of sign, word, and writing, for that which guides our future anterior, there is as yet no exergue.

1

The End of the Book and the Beginning of Writing

Socrates, he who does not write*—Nietzsche

However the topic is considered, the *problem of language* has never been simply one problem among others. But never as much as at present has it invaded, *as such*, the global horizon of the most diverse researches and the most heterogeneous discourses, diverse and heterogeneous in their intention, method, and ideology. The devaluation of the word "language" itself, and how, in the very hold it has upon us, it betrays a loose vocabulary, the temptation of a cheap seduction, the passive yielding to fashion, the consciousness of the avant-garde, in other words—ignorance—are evidences of this effect. This inflation of the sign "language" is the inflation of the sign itself, absolute inflation, inflation itself. Yet, by one of its aspects or shadows, it is itself still a sign: this crisis is also a symptom. It indicates, as if in spite of itself, that a historico-metaphysical epoch *must* finally determine as language the totality of its problematic horizon. It must do so not only because all that desire had wished to wrest from the play of language finds itself recaptured within that play but also because, for the same reason, language itself is menaced in its very life, helpless, adrift in the threat of limitlessness, brought back to its own finitude at the very moment when its limits seem to disappear, when it ceases to be self-assured, contained, and *guaranteed* by the infinite signified which seemed to exceed it.

The Program

By a slow movement whose necessity is hardly perceptible, everything that for at least some twenty centuries tended toward and finally succeeded in being gathered under the name of language is beginning to let itself be transferred to, or at least summarized under, the name of writing. By a hardly perceptible necessity, it seems as though the concept of writing

* "Aus dem Gedankenkreise der Geburt der Tragödie," I. 3. *Nietzsche Werke* (Leipzig, 1903), vol. 9, part 2, i, p. 66.

—no longer indicating a particular, derivative, auxiliary form of language in general (whether understood as communication, relation, expression, signification, constitution of meaning or thought, etc.), no longer designating the exterior surface, the insubstantial double of a major signifier, *the signifier of the signifier*—is beginning to go beyond the extension of language. In all senses of the word, writing thus *comprehends* language. Not that the word "writing" has ceased to designate the signifier of the signifier, but it appears, strange as it may seem, that "signifier of the signifier" no longer defines accidental doubling and fallen secondarity. "Signifier of the signifier" describes on the contrary the movement of language: in its origin, to be sure, but one can already suspect that an origin whose structure can be expressed as "signifier of the signifier" conceals and erases itself in its own production. There the signified always already functions as a signifier. The secondarity that it seemed possible to ascribe to writing alone affects all signifieds in general, affects them always already, the moment they *enter the game*. There is not a single signified that escapes, even if recaptured, the play of signifying references that constitute language. The advent of writing is the advent of this play; today such a play is coming into its own, effacing the limit starting from which one had thought to regulate the circulation of signs, drawing along with it all the reassuring signifieds, reducing all the strongholds, all the out-of-bounds shelters that watched over the field of language. This, strictly speaking, amounts to destroying the concept of "sign" and its entire logic. Undoubtedly it is not by chance that this *overwhelming* supervenes at the moment when the extension of the concept of language effaces all its limits. We shall see that this overwhelming and this effacement have the same meaning, are one and the same phenomenon. It is as if the Western concept of language (in terms of what, beyond its plurivocity and beyond the strict and problematic opposition of speech [*parole*] and language [*langue*], attaches it *in general* to phonematic or glossematic production, to language, to voice, to hearing, to sound and breadth, to speech) were revealed today as the guise or disguise of a primary writing:[1] more fundamental than that which, before this conversion, passed for the simple "supplement to the spoken word" (Rousseau). Either writing was never a simple "supplement," or it is urgently necessary to construct a new logic of the "supplement." It is this urgency which will guide us further in reading Rousseau.

These disguises are not historical contingencies that one might admire or regret. Their movement was absolutely necessary, with a necessity which cannot be judged by any other tribunal. The privilege of the *phonè* does not depend upon a choice that could have been avoided. It responds to a moment of *economy* (let us say of the "life" of "history" or of "being as self-relationship"). The system of "hearing (understanding)-oneself-speak" through the phonic substance—which *presents itself* as the nonexterior, nonmundane, therefore nonempirical or noncontingent signifier—has necessarily dominated the history of the world during an entire epoch, and has even produced the idea of the world, the idea of world-origin, that arises from the difference between the worldly and the non-worldly, the outside and the inside, ideality and nonideality, universal and nonuniversal, transcendental and empirical, etc.[2]

With an irregular and essentially precarious success, this movement would apparently have tended, as toward its *telos*, to confine writing to a secondary and instrumental function: translator of a full speech that was fully *present* (present to itself, to its signified, to the other, the very condition of the theme of presence in general), technics in the service of language, *spokesman*, interpreter of an originary speech itself shielded from interpretation.

Technics in the service of language: I am not invoking a general essence of technics which would be already familiar to us and would help us in *understanding* the narrow and historically determined concept of writing as an example. I believe on the contrary that a certain sort of question about the meaning and origin of writing precedes, or at least merges with, a certain type of question about the meaning and origin of technics. That is why the notion of technique can never simply clarify the notion of writing.

It is therefore as if what we call language could have been in its origin and in its end only a moment, an essential but determined mode, a phenomenon, an aspect, a species of writing. And as if it had succeeded in making us forget this, and *in wilfully misleading us*, only in the course of an adventure: as that adventure itself. All in all a short enough adventure. It merges with the history that has associated technics and logocentric metaphysics for nearly three millennia. And it now seems to be approaching what is really its own *exhaustion*; under the circumstances—and this is no more than one example among others—of this death of the civilization of the book, of which so much is said and which manifests itself particularly through a convulsive proliferation of libraries. All appearances to the contrary, this death of the book undoubtedly announces (and in a certain sense always has announced) nothing but a death of speech (of a *so-called* full speech) and a new mutation in the history of writing, in history as writing. Announces it at a distance of a few centuries. It is on that scale that we must reckon it here, being careful not to neglect the quality of a very heterogeneous historical duration: the acceleration is such, and such its qualitative meaning, that one would be equally wrong in making a careful evaluation according to past rhythms. "Death of speech" is of course a metaphor here: before we speak of disappearance, we must think of a new situation for speech, of its subordination within a structure of which it will no longer be the archon.

To affirm in this way that the concept of writing exceeds and comprehends that of language, presupposes of course a certain definition of language and of writing. If we do not attempt to justify it, we shall be giving in to the movement of inflation that we have just mentioned, which has also taken over the word "writing," and that not fortuitously. For some time now, as a matter of fact, here and there, by a gesture and for motives that are profoundly necessary, whose degradation is easier to denounce than it is to disclose their origin, one says "language" for action, movement, thought, reflection, consciousness, unconsciousness, experience, affectivity, etc. Now we tend to say "writing" for all that and more: to designate not only the physical gestures of literal pictographic or ideographic inscription, but also the totality of what makes it possible; and also, beyond the signifying face, the signified face itself. And thus we say "writing" for all that gives rise to an inscription in general, whether it is literal or not and even if what it distributes in space is alien to the order of the voice: cinematography, choreography, of course, but also pictorial, musical, sculptural "writing." One might also speak of athletic writing, and with even greater certainty of military or political writing in view of the techniques that govern those domains today. All this to describe not only the system of notation secondarily connected with these activities but the essence and the content of these activities themselves. It is also in this sense that the contemporary biologist speaks of writing and *pro-gram* in relation to the most elementary processes of information within the living cell. And, finally, whether it has essential limits or not, the entire field covered by the cybernetic *program* will be the field of writing. If the theory of cybernetics is by itself to oust all metaphysical concepts—including the concepts of soul, of life, of value, of choice, of memory—which until recently served to separate the machine from man,[8] it must conserve the notion of writing, trace, grammè [written mark], or grapheme, until its own historico-metaphysical character is also exposed. Even before being determined as human (with all the distinctive characteristics that have always been attributed to man and the entire system of significations that they imply) or nonhuman, the *grammè*—or the *grapheme*—would thus name the element. An element without simplicity. An element, whether it is understood as the medium or as the irreducible atom, of the arche-synthesis in general, of what one must forbid oneself to define within the system of oppositions of metaphysics, of what consequently one should not even call *experience* in general, that is to say the origin of *meaning* in general.

This situation has always already been announced. Why is it today in the process of making itself known *as such* and *after the fact*? This question would call forth an interminable analysis. Let us simply choose some points of departure in order to introduce the limited remarks to which I shall confine myself. I have already alluded to *theoretical* mathematics; its writing—whether understood as a sensible *graphie* [manner of writing] (and that already presupposes an identity, therefore an ideality, of its form, which in principle renders absurd the so easily admitted notion of the "sensible signifier"), or understood as the ideal synthesis of signifieds or a trace operative on another level, or whether it is understood, more profoundly, as the *passage* of the one to the other—has never been absolutely linked with a phonetic production. Within cultures practicing so-called phonetic writing, mathematics is not just an enclave. That is mentioned by all historians of writing; they recall at the same time the imperfections of alphabetic writing, which passed for so long as the most convenient and "the most intelligent"[4] writing. This enclave is also the place where the practice of scientific language challenges intrinsically and with increasing profundity the ideal of phonetic writing and all its implicit metaphysics (metaphysics *itself*), particularly, that is, the philosophical idea of the *epistémè*; also of *istoria*, a concept profoundly related to it in spite of the dissociation or opposition which has distinguished one from the other during one phase of their common progress. History and knowledge, *istoria* and *epistémè* have always been determined (and not only etymologically or philosophically) as detours *for the purpose of* the reappropriaton of presence.

But beyond theoretical mathematics, the development of the *practical methods* of information retrieval extends the possibilities of the "message" vastly, to the point where it is no longer the "written" translation of a language, the transporting of a signified which could remain spoken in its integrity. It goes hand in hand with an extension of phonography and of all the means of conserving the spoken language, of making it function without the presence of the speaking subject. This development, coupled with that of anthropology and of the history of writing, teaches us that phonetic writing, the medium of the great metaphysical, scientific, technical, and economic adventure of the West, is limited in space and time and limits itself even as it is in the process of imposing its laws upon the cultural areas that had escaped it. But this nonfortuitous conjunction of cybernetics and the "human sciences" of writing leads to a more profound reversal.

The Signifier and Truth

The "rationality"—but perhaps that word should be abandoned for reasons that will appear at the end of this sentence—which governs a writing thus enlarged and radicalized, no longer issues from a logos. Further, it inaugurates the destruction, not the demolition but the de-sedimentation, the de-construction, of all the significations that have their source in that of the logos. Particularly the signification of *truth*. All the metaphysical determinations of truth, and even the one beyond metaphysical onto-theology that Heidegger reminds us of, are more or less immediately inseparable from the instance of the logos, or of a reason thought within the lineage of the logos, in whatever sense it is understood: in the pre-

Socratic or the philosophical sense, in the sense of God's infinite understanding or in the anthropological sense, in the pre-Hegelian or the post-Hegelian sense. Within this logos, the original and essential link to the *phonè* has never been broken. It would be easy to demonstrate this and I shall attempt such a demonstration later. As has been more or less implicitly determined, the essence of the *phonè* would be immediately proximate to that which within "thought" as logos relates to "meaning," produces it, receives it, speaks it, "composes" it. If, for Aristotle, for example, "spoken words (ta en tē phonē) are the symbols of mental experience (pathēmata tes psychēs) and written words are the symbols of spoken words" (*De interpretatione*, 1, 16a 3) it is because the voice, producer of *the first symbols,* has a relationship of essential and immediate proximity with the mind. Producer of the first signifier, it is not just a simple signifier among others. It signifies "mental experiences" which themselves reflect or mirror things by natural resemblance. Between being and mind, things and feelings, there would be a relationship of translation or natural signification; between mind and logos, a relationship of conventional symbolization. And the *first* convention, which would relate immediately to the order of natural and universal signification, would be produced as spoken language. Written language would establish the conventions, interlinking other conventions with them.

Just as all men have not the same writing so all men have not the same speech sounds, but mental experiences, of which these are the *primary symbols* (*semeĩa prótos*), are the same for all, as also are those things of which our experiences are the images (*De interpretatione*, 1, 16a. Italics added).

The feelings of the mind, expressing things naturally, constitute a sort of universal language which can then efface itself. It is the stage of transparence. Aristotle can sometimes omit it without risk.[5] In every case, the voice is closest to the signified, whether it is determined strictly as sense (thought or lived) or more loosely as thing. All signifiers, and first and foremost the written signifier, are derivative with regard to what would wed the voice indissolubly to the mind or to the thought of the signified sense, indeed to the thing itself (whether it is done in the Aristotelian manner that we have just indicated or in the manner of medieval theology, determining the *res* as a thing created from its *eidos*, from its sense thought in the logos or in the infinite understanding of God). The written signifier is always technical and representative. It has no constitutive meaning. This derivation is the very origin of the notion of the "signifier." The notion of the sign always implies within itself the distinction between signifier and signified, even if, as Saussure argues, they are distinguished simply as the two faces of one and the same leaf. This notion remains therefore within the heritage of that logocentrism which is also a phonocentrism:

absolute proximity of voice and being, of voice and the meaning of being, of voice and the ideality of meaning. Hegel demonstrates very clearly the strange privilege of sound in idealization, the production of the concept and the self-presence of the subject.

> This ideal motion, in which through the sound what is as it were the simple subjectivity [*Subjektivität*], the soul of the material thing expresses itself, the ear receives also in a theoretical [*theoretisch*] way, just as the eye shape and colour, thus allowing the interiority of the object to become interiority itself [*läßt dadurch das Innere der Gegenstände für das Innere selbst werden*] (*Esthétique*, III. I tr. fr. p. 16).* . . . The ear, on the contrary, perceives [*vernimmt*] the result of that interior vibration of material substance without placing itself in a practical relation toward the objects, a result by means of which it is no longer the material form [*Gestalt*] in its repose, but the first, more ideal activity of the soul itself which is manifested [*zum Vorschein kommt*] (p. 296).†

What is said of sound in general is a fortiori valid for the *phonè* by which, by virtue of hearing (understanding)-oneself-speak—an indissociable system—the subject affects itself and is related to itself in the element of ideality.

We already have a foreboding that phonocentrism merges with the historical determination of the meaning of being in general as *presence*, with all the subdeterminations which depend on this general form and which organize within it their system and their historical sequence (presence of the thing to the sight as *eidos*, presence as substance/essence/existence [*ousia*], temporal presence as point [*stigmè*] of the now or of the moment [*nun*], the self-presence of the cogito, consciousness, subjectivity, the co-presence of the other and of the self, intersubjectivity as the intentional phenomenon of the ego, and so forth). Logocentrism would thus support the determination of the being of the entity as presence. To the extent that such a logocentrism is not totally absent from Heidegger's thought, perhaps it still holds that thought within the epoch of onto-theology, within the philosophy of presence, that is to say within philosophy *itself*. This would perhaps mean that one does not leave the epoch whose closure one can outline. The movements of belonging or not belonging to the epoch are too subtle, the illusions in that regard are too easy, for us to make a definite judgment.

The epoch of the logos thus debases writing considered as mediation of

* Georg Wilhelm Friedrich Hegel, *Werke*, Suhrkamp edition (Frankfurt am Main, 1970), vol. 14, p. 256; translated as *The Philosophy of Fine Art* by F. P. Osmaston (London, 1920), vol. 3, pp. 15–16.

† Hegel, p. 134; Osmaston, p. 341.

mediation and as a fall into the exteriority of meaning. To this epoch belongs the difference between signified and signifier, or at least the strange separation of their "parallelism," and the exteriority, however extenuated, of the one to the other. This appurtenance is organized and hierarchized in a history. The difference between signified and signifier belongs in a profound and implicit way to the totality of the great epoch covered by the history of metaphysics, and in a more explicit and more systematically articulated way to the narrower epoch of Christian creationism and infinitism when these appropriate the resources of Greek conceptuality. This appurtenance is essential and irreducible; one cannot retain the convenience or the "scientific truth" of the Stoic and later medieval opposition between *signans* and *signatum* without also bringing with it all its metaphysico-theological roots. To these roots adheres not only the distinction between the sensible and the intelligible—already a great deal—with all that it controls, namely, metaphysics in its totality. And this distinction is generally accepted as self-evident by the most careful linguists and semiologists, even by those who believe that the scientificity of their work begins where metaphysics ends. Thus, for example:

> As modern structural thought has clearly realized, language is a system of signs and linguistics is part and parcel of the science of signs, or *semiotics* (Saussure's *sémiologie*). The mediaeval definition of sign—"*aliquid stat pro aliquo*"—has been resurrected and put forward as still valid and productive. Thus the constitutive mark of any sign in general and of any linguistic sign in particular is its twofold character: every linguistic unit is bipartite and involves both aspects—one sensible and the other intelligible, or in other words, both the *signans* "signifier" (Saussure's *signifiant*) and the *signatum* "signified" (*signifié*). These two constituents of a linguistic sign (and of sign in general) necessarily suppose and require each other.[6]

But to these metaphysico-theological roots many other hidden sediments cling. The semiological or, more specifically, linguistic "science" cannot therefore hold on to the difference between signifier and signified—the very idea of the sign—without the difference between sensible and intelligible, certainly, but also not without retaining, more profoundly and more implicitly, and by the same token the reference to a signified able to "take place" in its intelligibility, before its "fall," before any expulsion into the exteriority of the sensible here below. As the face of pure intelligibility, it refers to an absolute logos to which it is immediately united. This absolute logos was an infinite creative subjectivity in medieval theology: the intelligible face of the sign remains turned toward the word and the face of God.

Of course, it is not a question of "rejecting" these notions; they are necessary and, at least at present, nothing is conceivable for us without them. It is a question at first of demonstrating the systematic and historical solidarity of the concepts and gestures of thought that one often believes can be innocently separated. The sign and divinity have the same place and time of birth. The age of the sign is essentially theological. Perhaps it will never *end*. Its historical *closure* is, however, outlined.

Since these concepts are indispensable for unsettling the heritage to which they belong, we should be even less prone to renounce them. Within the closure, by an oblique and always perilous movement, constantly risking falling back within what is being deconstructed, it is necessary to surround the critical concepts with a careful and thorough discourse—to mark the conditions, the medium, and the limits of their effectiveness and to designate rigorously their intimate relationship to the machine whose deconstruction they permit; and, in the same process, designate the crevice through which the yet unnameable glimmer beyond the closure can be glimpsed. The concept of the sign is here exemplary. We have just marked its metaphysical appurtenance. We know, however, that the thematics of the sign have been for about a century the agonized labor of a tradition that professed to withdraw meaning, truth, presence, being, etc., from the movement of signification. Treating as suspect, as I just have, the difference between signified and signifier, or the idea of the sign in general, I must state explicitly that it is not a question of doing so in terms of the instance of the present truth, anterior, exterior or superior to the sign, or in terms of the place of the effaced difference. Quite the contrary. We are disturbed by that which, in the concept of the sign—which has never existed or functioned outside the history of (the) philosophy (of presence)—remains systematically and genealogically determined by that history. It is there that the concept and above all the work of deconstruction, its "style," remain by nature exposed to misunderstanding and nonrecognition.

The exteriority of the signifier is the exteriority of writing in general, and I shall try to show later that there is no linguistic sign before writing. Without that exteriority, the very idea of the sign falls into decay. Since our entire world and language would collapse with it, and since its evidence and its value keep, to a certain point of derivation, an indestructible solidity, it would be silly to conclude from its placement within an epoch that it is necessary to "move on to something else," to dispose of the sign, of the term and the notion. For a proper understanding of the gesture that we are sketching here, one must understand the expressions "epoch," "closure of an epoch," "historical genealogy" in a new way; and must first remove them from all relativism.

Thus, within this epoch, reading and writing, the production or interpretation of signs, the text in general as fabric of signs, allow themselves to be confined within secondariness. They are preceded by a truth, or a meaning already constituted by and within the element of the logos. Even when the thing, the "referent," is not immediately related to the logos of a creator God where it began by being the spoken/thought sense, the signified has at any rate an immediate relationship with the logos in general (finite or infinite), and a mediated one with the signifier, that is to say with the exteriority of writing. When it seems to go otherwise, it is because a metaphoric mediation has insinuated itself into the relationship and has simulated immediacy; the writing of truth in the soul, opposed by *Phaedrus* (278a) to bad writing (writing in the "literal" [*propre*] and ordinary sense, "sensible" writing, "in space"), the book of Nature and God's writing, especially in the Middle Ages; all that functions as *metaphor* in these discourses confirms the privilege of the logos and founds the "literal" meaning then given to writing: a sign signifying a signifier itself signifying an eternal verity, eternally thought and spoken in the proximity of a present logos. The paradox to which attention must be paid is this: natural and universal writing, intelligible and nontemporal writing, is thus named by metaphor. A writing that is sensible, finite, and so on, is designated as writing in the literal sense; it is thus thought on the side of culture, technique, and artifice; a human procedure, the ruse of a being accidentally incarnated or of a finite creature. Of course, this metaphor remains enigmatic and refers to a "literal" meaning of writing as the first metaphor. This "literal" meaning is yet unthought by the adherents of this discourse. It is not, therefore, a matter of inverting the literal meaning and the figurative meaning but of determining the "literal" meaning of writing as metaphoricity itself.

In "The Symbolism of the Book," that excellent chapter of *European Literature and the Latin Middle Ages*, E. R. Curtius describes with great wealth of examples the evolution that led from the *Phaedrus* to Calderon, until it seemed to be "precisely the reverse" (tr. fr. p. 372)* by the "newly attained position of the book" (p. 374) [p. 306]. But it seems that this modification, however important in fact it might be, conceals a fundamental continuity. As was the case with the Platonic writing of the truth in the soul, in the Middle Ages too it is a writing understood in the metaphoric sense, that is to say a *natural*, eternal, and universal writing, the system of signified truth, which is recognized in its dignity. As in the *Phaedrus*, a certain fallen writing continues to be opposed to it. There remains to be written a history of this metaphor, a metaphor that systematically contrasts divine or natural writing and the human and laborious, finite and artificial inscription. It remains to articulate rigorously the stages of that history, as marked by the quotations below, and to follow the

* Ernst Robert Curtius, "Das Buch als Symbol," *Europäische Literatur und lateinisches Mittelalter* (Bern, 1948), p. 307. French translation by Jean Bréjoux (Paris, 1956): translated as *European Literature and the Latin Middle Ages*, by Willard R. Trask, Harper Torchbooks edition (New York, 1963), pp. 305, 306.

theme of God's book (nature or law, indeed natural law) through all its modifications.

Rabbi Eliezer said: "If all the seas were of ink, and all ponds planted with reeds, if the sky and the earth were parchments and if all human beings practised the art of writing—they would not exhaust the Torah I have learned, just as the Torah itself would not be diminished any more than is the sea by the water removed by a paint brush dipped in it."[7]

Galileo: "It [the book of Nature] is written in a mathematical language."*

Descartes: ". . . to read in the great book of Nature . . ."†

Demea, in the name of natural religion, in the *Dialogues*, . . . of Hume: "And this volume of nature contains a great and inexplicable riddle, more than any intelligible discourse or reasoning."††

Bonnet: "It would seem more philosophical to me to presume that our earth is a book that God has given to intelligences far superior to ours to read, and where they study in depth the infinitely multiplied and varied characters of His adorable wisdom."

G. H. von Schubert: "This language made of images and hieroglyphs, which supreme Wisdom uses in all its revelations to humanity—which is found in the inferior [*nieder*] language of poetry—and which, in the most inferior and imperfect way [*auf der allerniedrigsten und unvollkommensten*], is more like the metaphorical expression of the dream than the prose of wakefulness, . . . we may wonder if this language is not the true and wakeful language of the superior regions. If, when we consider ourselves awakened, we are not plunged in a millennial slumber, or at least in the echo of its dreams, where we only perceive a few isolated and obscure words of God's language, as a sleeper perceives the conversation of the people around him."§

Jaspers: "The world is the manuscript of an other, inaccessible to a universal reading, which only existence deciphers."||

Above all, the profound differences distinguishing all these treatments of the same metaphor must not be ignored. In the history of this treatment, the most decisive separation appears at the moment when, at the same time as the science of nature, the determination of absolute presence is constituted as self-presence, as subjectivity. It is the moment of the great rationalisms of the seventeenth century. From then on, the condemnation of fallen and finite writing will take another form, within which we still

* Quoted in Curtius, op. cit. (German), p. 326, (English), p. 324; Galileo's word is "philosophy" rather than "nature."

† Ibid. (German) p. 324, (English) p. 322.

†† David Hume, *Dialogues Concerning Natural Religion*, ed. Norman Kemp Smith (Oxford, 1935), p. 193.

§ Gotthilf Heinrich von Schubert, *Die Symbolik des Traumes* (Leipzig, 1862), pp. 23–24.

|| Quoted in Paul Ricoeur, *Gabriel Marcel et Karl Jaspers* (Paris, 1947), p. 45.

live: it is non-self-presence that will be denounced. Thus the exemplariness of the "Rousseauist" moment, which we shall deal with later, begins to be explained. Rousseau repeats the Platonic gesture by referring to another model of presence: self-presence in the senses, in the sensible cogito, which simultaneously carries in itself the inscription of divine law. On the one hand, *representative,* fallen, secondary, instituted writing, writing in the literal and strict sense, is condemned in *The Essay on the Origin of Languages* (it "enervates" speech; to "judge genius" from books is like "painting a man's portrait from his corpse," etc.). Writing in the common sense is the dead letter, it is the carrier of death. It exhausts life. On the other hand, on the other face of the same proposition, writing in the metaphoric sense, natural, divine, and living writing, is venerated; it is equal in dignity to the origin of value, to the voice of conscience as divine law, to the heart, to sentiment, and so forth.

The Bible is the most sublime of all books, . . . but it is after all a book. . . . It is not at all in a few sparse pages that one should look for God's law, but in the human heart where His hand deigned to write (*Lettre à Vernes*).*

If the natural law had been written only in the human reason, it would be little capable of directing most of our actions. But it is also engraved in the heart of man in ineffacable characters. . . . There it cries to him (*L'état de guerre.*) †

Natural writing is immediately united to the voice and to breath. Its nature is not grammatological but pneumatological. It is hieratic, very close to the interior holy voice of the *Profession of Faith,* to the voice one hears upon retreating into oneself: full and truthful presence of the divine voice to our inner sense: "The more I retreat into myself, the more I consult myself, the more plainly do I read these words written in my soul: be just and you will be happy. . . . I do not derive these rules from the principles of the higher philosophy, I find them in the depths of my heart written by nature in characters which nothing can efface." ††

There is much to say about the fact that the native unity of the voice and writing is *prescriptive.* Arche-speech is writing because it is a law. A natural law. The beginning word is understood, in the intimacy of self-presence, as the voice of the other and as commandment.

There is therefore a good and a bad writing: the good and natural is the divine inscription in the heart and the soul; the perverse and artful is technique, exiled in the exteriority of the body. A modification well within

* *Correspondance complète de Jean Jacques Rousseau,* ed. R. A. Leigh (Geneva, 1967), vol. V, pp. 65–66. The original reads "l'évangile" rather than "la Bible."

† Rousseau, *Oeuvres complètes,* Pléiade edition, vol. III, p. 602.

†† Derrida's reference is *Emile,* Pléiade edition, vol. 4, pp. 589, 594. My reference is *Emile,* tr. Barbara Foxley (London, 1911), pp. 245, 249. Subsequent references to this translation are placed within brackets.

the Platonic diagram: writing of the soul and of the body, writing of the interior and of the exterior, writing of conscience and of the passions, as there is a voice of the soul and a voice of the body. "Conscience is the voice of the soul, the passions are the voice of the body" [p. 249]. One must constantly go back toward the "voice of nature," the "holy voice of nature," that merges with the divine inscription and prescription; one must encounter oneself within it, enter into a dialogue within its signs, speak and respond to oneself in its pages.

It was as if nature had spread out all her magnificence in front of our eyes to offer its text for our consideration. . . . I have therefore closed all the books. Only one is open to all eyes. It is the book of Nature. In this great and sublime book I learn to serve and adore its author.

The good writing has therefore always been *comprehended*. Comprehended as that which had to be comprehended: within a nature or a natural law, created or not, but first thought within an eternal presence. Comprehended, therefore, within a totality, and enveloped in a volume or a book. The idea of the book is the idea of a totality, finite or infinite, of the signifier; this totality of the signifier cannot be a totality, unless a totality constituted by the signified preexists it, supervises its inscriptions and its signs, and is independent of it in its ideality. The idea of the book, which always refers to a natural totality, is profoundly alien to the sense of writing. It is the encyclopedic protection of theology and of logocentrism against the disruption of writing, against its aphoristic energy, and, as I shall specify later, against difference in general. If I distinguish the text from the book, I shall say that the destruction of the book, as it is now under way in all domains, denudes the surface of the text. That necessary violence responds to a violence that was no less necessary.

The Written Being/ The Being Written

The reassuring evidence within which Western tradition had to organize itself and must continue to live would therefore be as follows: the order of the signified is never contemporary, is at best the subtly discrepant inverse or parallel—discrepant by the time of a breath—from the order of the signifier. And the sign must be the unity of a heterogeneity, since the signified (sense or thing, noeme or reality) is not in itself a signifier, a *trace*: in any case is not constituted in its sense by its relationship with a possible trace. The formal essence of the signified is *presence*, and the privilege of its proximity to the logos as *phonè* is the privilege of presence. This is the inevitable response as soon as one asks: "what is the sign?," that is to say, when one submits the sign to the question of essence, to the "ti esti." The "formal essence" of the sign can only be determined in terms of presence.

One cannot get around that response, except by challenging the very form of the question and beginning to think that the sign is that ill-named thing, the only one, that escapes the instituting question of philosophy: "what is . . .?"[8]

Radicalizing the concepts of *interpretation, perspective, evaluation, difference,* and all the "empiricist" or nonphilosophical motifs that have constanty tormented philosophy throughout the history of the West, and besides, have had nothing but the inevitable weakness of being produced in the field of philosophy, Nietzsche, far from remaining *simply* (with Hegel and as Heidegger wished) *within* metaphysics, contributed a great deal to the liberation of the signifier from its dependence or derivation with respect to the logos and the related concept of truth or the primary signified, in whatever sense that is understood. Reading, and therefore writing, the text were for Nietzsche "originary"[9] operations (I put that word within quotation marks for reasons to appear later) with regard to a sense that they do not first have to transcribe or discover, which would not therefore be a truth signified in the original element and presence of the logos, as *topos noetos,* divine understanding, or the structure of a priori necessity. To save Nietzsche from a reading of the Heideggerian type, it seems that we must above all not attempt to restore or make explicit a less naive "ontology," composed of profound ontological intuitions acceding to some originary truth, an entire fundamentality hidden under the appearance of an empiricist or metaphysical text. The virulence of Nietzschean thought could not be more competely misunderstood. On the contrary, one must *accentuate* the "naiveté" of a breakthrough which cannot attempt a step outside of metaphysics, which cannot *criticize* metaphysics radically without still utilizing in a certain way, in a certain type or a certain style of *text,* propostions that, read within the philosophic corpus, that is to say according to Nietzsche ill-read or unread, have always been and will always be "naivetés," incoherent signs of an absolute appurtenance. Therefore, rather that protect Nietzsche from the Heideggerian reading, we should perhaps offer him up to it completely, underwriting that interpretation without reserve; in a *certain way* and up to the point where, the content of the Nietzschean discourse being almost lost for the question of being, its form regains its absolute strangeness, where his text finally invokes a different type of reading, more faithful to his type of writing: Nietzsche has *written what* he has written. He has written that writing—and first of all his own—is not originarily subordinate to the logos and to truth. And that this subordination has *come into being* during an epoch whose meaning we must deconstruct. Now in this direction (but only in this direction, for read otherwise, the Nietzschean demolition remains dogmatic and, like all reversals, a captive of that metaphysical edifice which it professes to overthrow. On that point and in that *order of reading,* the conclusions of

Heidegger and Fink are irrefutable), Heideggerian thought would reinstate rather than destroy the instance of the logos and of the truth of being as "primum signatum:" the "transcendental" signified ("transcendental" in a certain sense, as in the Middle Ages the transcendental—*ens, unum, verum, bonum*—was said to be the "primum cognitum") implied by all categories or all determined significations, by all lexicons and all syntax, and therefore by all linguistic signifiers, though not to be identified simply with any one of those signifiers, allowing itself to be precomprehended through each of them, remaining irreducible to all the epochal determinations that it nonetheless makes possible, thus opening the history of the logos, yet itself being only through the logos; that is, *being nothing* before the logos and outside of it. The logos *of* being, "Thought obeying the Voice of Being,"[10] is the first and the last resource of the sign, of the difference between *signans* and *signatum*. There has to be a transcendental signified for the difference between signifier and signified to be somewhere absolute and irreducible. It is not by chance that the thought of being, as the thought of this transcendental signified, is manifested above all in the voice: in a language of words [*mots*]. The voice *is heard* (understood)—that undoubtedly is what is called conscience—closest to the self as the absolute effacement of the signifier: pure auto-affection that necessarily has the form of time and which does not borrow from outside of itself, in the world or in "reality," any accessory signifier, any substance of expression foreign to its own spontaneity. It is the unique experience of the signified producing itself spontaneously, from within the self, and nevertheless, as signified concept, in the element of ideality or universality. The unworldly character of this substance of expression is constitutive of this ideality. This experience of the effacement of the signifier in the voice is not merely one illusion among many—since it is the condition of the very idea of truth—but I shall elsewhere show in what it does delude itself. This illusion is the history of truth and it cannot be dissipated so quickly. Within the closure of this experience, the word [*mot*] is lived as the elementary and undecomposable unity of the signified and the voice, of the concept and a transparent substance of expression. This experience is considered in its greatest purity—and at the same time in the condition of its possibility—as the experience of "being." The word "being," or at any rate the words designating the sense of being in different languages, is, with some others, an "originary word" ("*Urwort*"),[11] the transcendental word assuring the possibility of being-word to all other words. As such, it is precomprehended in all language and—this is the opening of *Being and Time*—only this precomprehension would permit the opening of the question of the sense of being in general, beyond all regional ontologies and all metaphysics: a question that broaches philosophy (for example, in the *Sophist*) and lets itself be taken over by philosophy, a question that Heidegger repeats by submitting the history of metaphysics to it. Heidegger reminds us constantly that the sense of being is neither the word "being" nor the concept of being. But as that sense is nothing outside of language and the language of words, it is tied, if not to a particular word or to a particular system of language (concesso non dato), at least to the possibility of the word in general. And to the possibility of its irreducible simplicity. One could thus think that it remains only to choose between two possibilities. (1) Does a modern linguistics, a science of signification breaking the unity of the word and breaking with its alleged irreducibility, still have anything to do with "language?" Heidegger would probably doubt it. (2) Conversely, is not all that is profoundly meditated as the thought or the question of being enclosed within an old linguistics of the word which one practices here unknowingly? Unknowingly because such a linguistics, whether spontaneous or systematic, has always had to share the presuppositions of metaphysics. The two operate on the same grounds.

It goes without saying that the alternatives cannot be so simple.

On the one hand, if modern linguistics remains completely enclosed within a classical conceptuality, if especially it naively uses the word *being* and all that it presupposes, that which, within this linguistics, deconstructs the unity of the word in general can no longer, according to the model of the Heideggerian question, as it functions powerfully from the very opening of *Being and Time,* be circumscribed as ontic science or regional ontology. In as much as the question of being unites indissolubly with the precomprehension of the *word being,* without being reduced to it, the linguistics that works for the deconstruction of the constituted unity of that word has only, in fact or in principle, to have the question of being posed in order to define its field and the order of its dependence.

Not only is its field no longer simply ontic, but the limits of ontology that correspond to it no longer have anything regional about them. And can what I say here of linguistics, or at least of a certain work that may be undertaken within it and thanks to it, not be said of all research *in as much as and to the strict extent that* it would finally deconstitute the founding concept-words of ontology, of being in its privilege? Outside of linguistics, it is in psychoanalytic research that this breakthrough seems at present to have the greatest likelihood of being expanded.

Within the strictly limited space of this breakthrough, these "sciences" are no longer *dominated* by the questions of a transcendental phenomenology or a fundamental ontology. One may perhaps say, following the order of questions inaugurated by *Being and Time* and radicalizing the questions of Husserlian phenomenology, that this breakthrough does not belong to science itself, that what thus seems to be produced within an ontic field or within a regional ontology, does not belong to them by rights and leads back to the question of being itself.

Because it is indeed the *question* of being that Heidegger asks metaphysics. And with it the question of truth, of sense, of the logos. The incessant meditation upon that question does not restore confidence. On the contrary, it dislodges the confidence at its own depth, which, being a matter of the meaning of being, is more difficult than is often believed. In examining the state just before all determinations of being, destroying the securities of onto-theology, such a meditation contributes, quite as much as the most contemporary linguistics, to the dislocation of the unity of the sense of being, that is, in the last instance, the unity of the word.

It is thus that, after evoking the "voice of being," Heidegger recalls that it is silent, mute, insonorous, wordless, originarily *a-phonic* (*die Gewähr der lautlosen Stimme verborgener Quellen* . . .). The voice of the sources is not heard. A rupture between the originary meaning of being and the word, between meaning and the voice, between "the voice of being" and the "*phonè*," between "the call of being," and articulated sound; such a rupture, which at once confirms a fundamental metaphor, and renders it suspect by accentuating its metaphoric discrepancy, translates the ambiguity of the Heideggerian situation with respect to the metaphysics of presence and logocentrism. It is at once contained within it and transgresses it. But it is impossible to separate the two. The very movement of transgression sometimes holds it back short of the limit. In opposition to what we suggested above, it must be remembered that, for Heidegger, the sense of being is never simply and rigorously a "signified." It is not by chance that that word is not used; that means that being escapes the movement of the sign, a proposition that can equally well be understood as a repetition of the classical tradition and as a caution with respect to a technical or metaphysical theory of signification. On the other hand, the sense of being is literally neither "primary," nor "fundamental," nor "transcendental," whether understood in the scholastic, Kantian, or Husserlian sense. The restoration of being as "transcending" the categories of the entity, the opening of the fundamental ontology, are nothing but necessary yet provisional moments. From *The Introduction to Metaphysics* onward, Heidegger renounces the project of and the word ontology.[12] The necessary, originary, and irreducible dissimulation of the meaning of being, its occultation within the very blossoming forth of presence, that retreat without which there would be no history of being which was completely *history* and history of *being*, Heidegger's insistence on noting that being is produced as history only through the logos, and is nothing outside of it, the difference between being and the entity—all this clearly indicates that fundamentally nothing escapes the movement of the signifier and that, in the last instance, the difference between signified and signifier *is nothing*. This proposition of transgression, not yet integrated into a careful discourse, runs the risk of formulating regression itself. One must therefore *go by way of* the question of being as it is directed by Heidegger and by him alone, at and beyond onto-theology, in order to reach the rigorous thought of that strange nondifference and in order to determine it correctly. Heidegger occasionally reminds us that "being," as it is fixed in its general syntactic and lexicological forms within linguistics and Western philosophy, is not a primary and absolutely irreducible signified, that it is still rooted in a system of languages and an historically determined "significance," although strangely privileged as the virtue of disclosure and dissimulation; particularly when he invites us to meditate on the "privilege" of the "third person singular of the present indicative" and the "infinitive." Western metaphysics, as the limitation of the sense of being within the field of presence, is produced as the domination of a linguistic form.[13] To question the origin of that domination does not amount to hypostatizing a transcendental signified, but to a questioning of what constitutes our history and what produced transcendentality itself. Heidegger brings it up also when in *Zur Seinsfrage*, for the same reason, he lets the word "being" be read only if it is crossed out (*kreuzweise Durchstreichung*). That mark of deletion is not, however, a "merely negative symbol" (p. 31) [p. 83]. That deletion is the final writing of an epoch. Under its strokes the presence of a transcendental signified is effaced while still remaining legible. Is effaced while still remaining legible, is destroyed while making visible the very idea of the sign. In as much as it de-limits onto-theology, the metaphysics of presence and logocentrism, this last writing is also the first writing.

To come to recognize, not within but on the horizon of the Heideggerian paths, and yet in them, that the sense of being is not a transcendental or trans-epochal signified (even if it was always dissimulated within the epoch) but already, in a truly *unheard of* sense, a determined signifying trace, is to affirm that within the decisive concept of ontico-ontological difference, *all is not to be thought at one go*; entity and being, ontic and ontological, "ontico-ontological," are, in an original style, *derivative* with regard to difference; and with respect to what I shall later call *differance*, an economic concept designating the production of differing/deferring. The ontico-ontological difference and its ground (*Grund*) in the "transcendence of Dasein" (*Vom Wesen des Grundes* [Frankfurt am Main, 1955], p. 16 [p. 29]) are not absolutely originary. Differance by itself would be more "originary," but one would no longer be able to call it "origin" or "ground," those notions belonging essentially to the history of onto-theology, to the system functioning as the effacing of difference. It can, however, be thought of in the closest proximity to itself only on one condition: that one begins by determining it as the ontico-ontological difference before erasing that determination. The necessity of passing through that erased determination, the necessity of that *trick of writing* is irreducible. An unemphatic and difficult thought that, through much unperceived mediation, must carry the entire burden of our question, a question that I shall provisionally call *historial* [*historiale*]. It is with its help that I shall later be able to attempt to relate differance and writing.

The hestitation of these thoughts (here Nietzsche's and Heidegger's) is not an "incoherence": it is a trembling proper to all post-Hegelian attempts and to this passage between two epochs. The movements of deconstruction do not destroy structures from the outside. They are not possible and effective, nor can they take accurate aim, except by inhabiting those structures. Inhabiting them *in a certain way*, because one always inhabits, and all the more when one does not suspect it. Operating necessarily from the inside, borrowing all the strategic and economic resources of subversion from the old structure, borrowing them structurally, that is to say without being able to isolate their elements and atoms, the enterprise of deconstruction always in a certain way falls prey to its own work. This is what the person who has begun the same work in another area of the same habitation does not fail to point out with zeal. No exercise is more widespread today and one should be able to formalize its rules.

Hegel was already caught up in this game. *On the one hand*, he undoubtedly *summed up* the entire philosophy of the logos. He determined ontology as absolute logic; he assembled all the delimitations of philosophy as presence; he assigned to presence the eschatology of parousia, of the self-proximity of infinite subjectivity. And for the same reason he had to debase or subordinate writing. When he criticizes the Leibnizian characteristic, the formalism of the understanding, and mathematical symbolism, he makes the same gesture: denouncing the being-outside-of-itself of the logos in the sensible or the intellectual abstraction. Writing is that forgetting of the self, that exteriorization, the contrary of the interiorizing memory, of the *Erinnerung* that opens the history of the spirit. It is this that the *Phaedrus* said: writing is at once mnemotechnique and the power of forgetting. Naturally, the Hegelian critique of writing stops at the alphabet. As phonetic writing, the alphabet is at the same time more servile, more contemptible, more secondary ("alphabetic writing expresses *sounds* which are themselves signs. It consists therefore of the signs of signs ['*aus Zeichen der Zeichen*'," *Enzyklopädie*, § 459])* but it is also the best writing, the mind's writing; its effacement before the voice, that in it which respects the ideal interiority of phonic signifiers, all that by which it sub-

* *Enzyklopädie der philosophischen Wissenschaften in Grundrisse*, Suhrkamp edition (Frankfurt am Main, 1970), pp. 273–76).

limates space and sight, all that makes of it the writing of history, the writing, that is, of the infinite spirit relating to itself in its discourse and its culture:

> It follows that to learn to read and write an alphabetic writing should be regarded as a means to infinite culture (*unendliches Bildungsmittel*) that is not enough appreciated; because thus the mind, distancing itself from the concrete sense-perceptible, directs its attention on the more formal moment, the sonorous word and its abstract elements, and contributes essentially to the founding and purifying of the ground of interiority within the subject.

In that sense it is the *Aufhebung* of other writings, particularly of hieroglyphic script and of the Leibnizian characteristic that had been criticized previously through one and the same gesture. (*Aufhebung* is, more or less implicitly, the dominant concept of nearly all histories of writing, even today. It is *the* concept of history and of teleology.) In fact, Hegel continues: "Acquired habit later also suppresses the specificity of alphabetic writing, which consists in seeming to be, in the interest of sight, a detour [*Umweg*] through hearing to arrive at representations, and makes it into a hieroglyphic script for us, such that in using it, we do not need to have present to our consciousness the mediation of sounds."

It is on this condition that Hegel subscribes to the Leibnizian praise of nonphonetic writing. It can be produced by deaf mutes, Leibniz had said. Hegel:

> Beside the fact that, by the practice which transforms this alphabetic script into hieroglyphics, the aptitude for abstraction acquired through such an exercise *is conserved* [italics added], the reading of hieroglyphs is for itself a deaf reading and a mute writing (*ein taubes Lesen und ein stummes Schreiben*). What is audible or temporal, visible or spatial, has each its proper basis and in the first place they are of equal value; but in alphabetic script there is only *one* basis and that following a specific relation, namely, that the visible language is related only as a sign to the audible language; intelligence expresses itself immediately and unconditionally through speech (ibid.).

What writing itself, in its nonphonetic moment, betrays, is life. It menaces at once the breath, the spirit, and history as the spirit's relationship with itself. It is their end, their finitude, their paralysis. Cutting breath short, sterilizing or immobilizing spiritual creation in the repetition of the letter, in the commentary or the *exegesis*, confined in a narrow space, reserved for a minority, it is the principle of death and of difference in the becoming of being. It is to speech what China is to Europe: "It is only to the exegeticism[14] of Chinese spiritual culture that their hieroglyphic writing is suited. This type of writing is, besides, the part reserved for a very small section of a people, the section that possesses the exclusive domain of spiritual culture. . . . A hieroglyphic script would require a philosophy as exegetical as Chinese culture generally is" (ibid.).

If the nonphonetic moment menaces the history and the life of the spirit as self-presence in the breath, it is because it menaces substantiality, that other metaphysical name of presence and of *ousia*. First in the form of the substantive. Nonphonetic writing breaks the noun apart. It describes relations and not apellations. The noun and the word, those unities of breath and concept, are effaced within pure writing. In that regard, Leibniz is as disturbing as the Chinese in Europe: "This situation, the analytic notation of representations in hieroglyphic script, which seduced Leibniz to the point of wrongly preferring this script to the alphabetic, rather contradicts the fundamental exigency of language in general, namely the noun. . . . All difference [*Abweichung*] in analysis would produce another formation of the written substantive."

The horizon of absolute knowledge is the effacement of writing in the logos, the retrieval of the trace in parousia, the reappropriation of difference, the accomplishment of what I have elsewhere called[15] the *metaphysics of the proper* [*le propre*—self-possession, propriety, property, cleanliness].

Yet, all that Hegel thought within this horizon, all, that is, except eschatology, may be reread as a meditation on writing. Hegel is *also* the thinker of irreducible difference. He rehabilitated thought as the *memory productive* of signs. And he reintroduced, as I shall try to show elsewhere, the essential necessity of the written trace in a philosophical—that is to say Socratic—discourse that had always believed it possible to do without it; the last philosopher of the book and the first thinker of writing.

2

Linguistics and Grammatology

Writing is nothing but the representation of speech; it is bizarre that one gives more care to the determining of the image than to the object.—
J.-J. Rousseau, Fragment inédit d'un essai sur les langues

The concept of writing should define the field of a science. But can it be determined by scholars outside of all the historico-metaphysical predeterminations that we have just situated so clinically? What can a science of writing begin to signify, if it is granted:

1) that the very idea of science was born in a certain epoch of writing;

2) that it was thought and formulated, as task, idea, project, in a language implying a certain kind of structurally and axiologically determined relationship between speech and writing;

3) that, to that extent, it was first related to the concept and the adventure of phonetic writing, valorized as the telos of all writing, even though what was always the exemplary model of scientificity—mathematics—constantly moved away from that goal;

4) that the strictest notion of a *general science of writing* was born, for nonfortuitous reasons, during a certain period of the world's history (beginning around the eighteenth century) and within a certain determined system of relationships between "living" speech and inscription;

5) that writing is not only an auxiliary means in the service of science—and possibly its object—but first, as Husserl in particular pointed out in *The Origin of Geometry,* the condition of the possibility of ideal objects and therefore of scientific objectivity. Before being its object, writing is the condition of the *epistémè.*

6) that historicity itself it tied to the possibility of writing; to the possibility of writing in general, beyond those particular forms of writing in the name of which we have long spoken of peoples without writing and without history. Before being the object of a history—of an historical science—writing opens the field of history—of historical becoming. And the former (*Historie* in German) presupposes the latter (*Geschichte*).

The science of writing should therefore look for its object at the roots of scientificity. The history of writing should turn back toward the origin of historicity. A science of the possibility of science? A science of science which would no longer have the form of *logic* but that of *grammatics*? A history of the possibility of history which would no longer be an archaeology, a philosophy of history or a history of philosophy?

The *positive* and the classical sciences of writing are obliged to repress this sort of question. Up to a certain point, such repression is even necessary to the progress of positive investigation. Beside the fact that it would still be held within a philosophizing logic, the ontophenomenological question of essence, that is to say of the origin of writing, could, by itself, only paralyze or sterilize the typological or historical research of *facts*.

My intention, therefore, is not to weigh that prejudicial question, that dry, necessary, and somewhat facile question of right, against the power and efficacy of the positive researches which we may witness today. The genesis and system of scripts had never led to such profound, extended, and assured explorations. It is not really a matter of weighing the question against the importance of the discovery; since the questions are imponderable, they cannot be weighed. If the issue is not quite that, it is perhaps because its repression has real consequences in the very content of the researches that, in the present case and in a privileged way, are always arranged around problems of definition and beginning.

The grammatologist least of all can avoid questioning himself about the essence of his object in the form of a question of origin: "What is writing?" means "where and when does writing begin?" The responses generally come very quickly. They circulate within concepts that are seldom criticized and move within evidence which always seems self-evident. It is around these responses that a typology of and a perspective on the growth of writing are always organized. All works dealing with the history of writing are composed along the same lines: a philosophical and teleological classification exhausts the critical problems in a few pages; one passes next to an exposition of facts. We have a contrast between the theoretical fragility of the reconstructions and the historical, archeological, ethnological, philosophical wealth of information.

The question of the origin of writing and the question of the origin of language are difficult to separate. Grammatologists, who are generally by training historians, epigraphists, and archeologists, seldom relate their researches to the modern science of language. It is all the more surprising that, among the "sciences of man," linguistics is the one science whose scientificity is given as an example with a zealous and insistent unanimity.

Has grammatology, then, the right to expect from linguistics an essential assistance that it has almost never looked for? On the contrary, does one not find efficaciously at work, in the very movement by which linguistics is instituted as a science, a metaphysical presupposition about the relationship between speech and writing? Would that presupposition not hinder the constitution of a general science of writing? Is not the lifting of that presupposition an overthrowing of the landscape upon which the science of language is peacefully installed? For better and for worse? For blindness as well as for productivity? This is the second type of question that I now wish to outline. To develop this question, I should like to approach, as a privileged example, the project and texts of Ferdinand de Saussure. That the particularity of the example does not interfere with the generality of my argument is a point which I shall occasionally try not merely to take for granted.

Linguistics thus wishes to be the science of language. Let us set aside all the implicit decisions that have established such a project and all the questions about its own origin that the fecundity of this science allows to remain dormant. Let us first simply consider that the scientificity of that science is often acknowledged because of its *phonological* foundations. Phonology, it is often said today, communicates its scientificity to linguistics, which in turn serves as the epistemological model for all the sciences of man. Since the deliberate and systematic phonological orientation of linguistics (Troubetzkoy, Jakobson, Martinet) carries out an intention which was originally Saussure's, I shall, at least provisionally, confine myself to the latter. Will my argument be equally applicable a fortiori to the most accentuated forms of phonologism? The problem will at least be stated.

The science of linguistics determines language—its field of objectivity—in the last instance and in the irreducible simplicity of its essence, as the unity of the *phonè*, the *glossa*, and the *logos*. This determination is by rights anterior to all the eventual differentiations that could arise within the systems of terminology of the different schools (language/speech [*langue/parole*]; code/message; scheme/usage; linguistic/logic; phonology/phonematics/phonetics/glossematics). And even if one wished to keep sonority on the side of the sensible and contingent signifier (which would be strictly speaking impossible, since formal identities isolated within a sensible mass are already idealities that are not purely sensible), it would have to be admitted that the immediate and privileged unity which founds significance and the acts of language is the articulated unity of sound and sense within the phonie. With regard to this unity, writing would always be derivative, accidental, particular, exterior, doubling the signifier: phonetic. "Sign of a sign," said Aristotle, Rousseau, and Hegel.

Yet, the intention that institutes general linguistics as a science remains in this respect within a contradiction. Its declared purpose indeed confirms, saying what goes without saying, the subordination of grammatology, the historico-metaphysical reduction of writing to the rank of an instrument enslaved to a full and originarily spoken language. But another gesture (not another statement of purpose, for here what does not go without saying is done without being said, written without being uttered) liberates the future of a general grammatology of which linguistics-phonology would be only a dependent and circumscribed area. Let us follow this tension between gesture and statement in Saussure.

*The Outside and the Inside**

On the one hand, true to the Western tradition that controls not only in theory but in practice (*in the principle of its practice*) the relationships between speech and writing, Saussure does not recognize in the latter more than a *narrow* and *derivative* function. Narrow because it is nothing but one modality among others, a modality of the events which can befall a language whose essence, as the facts seem to show, can remain forever uncontaminated by writing. "Language does have an . . . oral tradition that is independent of writing" (*Cours de linguistique générale*, p. 46). Derivative because *representative*: signifier of the first signifier, representation of the self-present voice, of the immediate, natural, and direct signification of the meaning (of the signified, of the concept, of the ideal object or what have you). Saussure takes up the traditional definition of writing which, already in Plato and Aristotle, was restricted to the model of phonetic script and the language of words. Let us recall the Aristotelian definition: "Spoken words are the symbols of mental experience and written words are the symbols of spoken words." Saussure: "Language and writing are two distinct systems of signs; the second *exists for the sole purpose of representing* the first" (p. 45; italics added) [p. 23†]. This representative determination, beside communicating without a doubt essentially with the idea of the sign, does not translate a choice or an evaluation, does not betray a psychological or metaphysical presupposition peculiar to Saussure; it describes or rather reflects the structure of a certain type of writing: phonetic writing, which we use and within whose element the *epistémè* in general (science and philosophy), and linguistics in particular, could be founded. One should, moreover, say *model* rather than *structure*; it is not a question of a system constructed and functioning perfectly, but of an ideal explicitly directing a functioning which *in fact* is never completely phonetic. In fact, but also for reasons of essence to which I shall frequently return.

To be sure this factum of phonetic writing is massive; it commands our entire culture and our entire science, and it is certainly not just one fact

* The title of the next section is "The Outside ✗ the Inside" (65, 44). In French, "is" (*est*) and "and" (*et*) "sound the same." For Derrida's discussion of the complicity between supplementation (and) and the copula (is), see particularly "Le Supplément de copule: la philosophie devant la linguistique," *MP*, pp. 209–46.

† Hereafter page numbers in parenthesis refer to the original work and those in brackets to the translation.

among others. Nevertheless it does not respond to any necessity of an absolute and universal essence. Using this as a point of departure, Saussure defines the project and object of general linguistics: "The linguistic object is not defined by the combination of the written word and the spoken word: *the spoken form alone constitutes the object*" (p. 45; italics added) [pp. 23–24].

The form of the question to which he responded thus entailed the response. It was a matter of knowing what sort of *word* is the object of linguistics and what the relationships are between the atomic unities that are the written and the spoken word. Now the word (*vox*) is already a unity of sense and sound, of concept and voice, or, to speak a more rigorously Saussurian language, of the signified and the signifier. This last terminology was moreover first proposed in the domain of spoken language alone, of linguistics in the narrow sense and not in the domain of semiology ("I propose to retain the word *sign* [*signe*] to designate the whole and to replace *concept* and *sound-image* respectively by *signified* [*signifié*] and *signifier* [*signifiant*]" p. 99 [p. 67]). The *word* is thus already a constituted unity, an effect of "the somewhat mysterious fact . . . that 'thought-sound' implies divisions" (p. 156) [p. 112]. Even if the word is in its turn articulated, even if it implies other divisions, as long as one poses the question of the relationships between speech and writing in the light of the indivisible units of the "thought-sound," there will always be the ready response. Writing will be "phonetic," it will be the outside, the exterior representation of language and of this "thought-sound." It must necessarily operate from already constituted units of signification, in the formation of which it has played no part.

Perhaps the objection will be made that writing up to the present has not only not contradicted, but indeed confirmed the linguistics of the word. Hitherto I seem to have maintained that only the fascination of the unit called *word* has prevented giving to writing the attention that it merited. By that I seemed to suppose that, by ceasing to accord an absolute privilege to the word, modern linguistics would become that much more attentive to writing and would finally cease to regard it with suspicion. André Martinet comes to the opposite conclusion. In his study "The Word,"[1] he describes the necessity that contemporary linguistics obeys when it is led, if not to dispense everywhere with the concept of the word, at least to make its usage more flexible, to associate it with the concepts of smaller or greater units (monemes or syntagms). In accrediting and consolidating the division of language into words in certain areas of linguistics, writing would thus have encouraged classical linguistics in its prejudices. Writing would have constructed or at least condensed the "screen of the word."

What a contemporary linguist can say of the word well illustrates the general revision of traditional concepts that the functionalist and structuralist research of the last thirty-five years had to undertake in order to give a scientific basis to the observation and description of languages. Certain applications of linguistics, like the researches relating to mechanical translation, by the emphasis they place on the written form of language, could make us believe in the fundamental importance of the divisions of the written text and make us forget that one must always start with the oral utterance in order to understand the real nature of human language. Also it is more than ever indispensable to insist on the necessity of pushing the examination beyond the immediate appearances and the structures most familiar to the researcher. It is behind the screen of the word that the truly fundamental characteristics of human language often appear.

One cannot but subscribe to this caution. Yet it must always be recognized that it throws suspicion only on a certain type of writing: phonetic writing conforming to the empirically determined and practiced divisions of ordinary oral language. The processes of mechanical translation to which it alludes conform similarly to that spontaneous practice. Beyond that model and that concept of writing, this entire demonstration must, it seems, be reconsidered. For it remains trapped in the Saussurian limitation that we are attempting to explore.

In effect Saussure limits the number of systems of writing to two, both defined as system of representation of the oral language, either representing *words* in a synthetic and global manner, or representing *phonetically* the elements of sounds constituting words:

There are only two systems of writing: 1) In an ideographic system each word is represented by a single sign that is unrelated to the component sounds of the word itself. Each written sign stands for a whole word and, indirectly, for the idea expressed by the word. The classic example of an ideographic system of writing is Chinese. 2) The system commonly known as "phonetic" tries to reproduce the succession of sounds that make up a word. Phonetic systems are sometimes syllabic, sometimes alphabetic, i.e., based on the irreducible elements of speech. Moreover, ideographic systems freely become mixtures when certain ideograms lose their original value and become symbols of isolated sounds. (p. 47) [pp. 25–26]

This limitation is at bottom justified, in Saussure's eyes, by the notion of the arbitrariness of the sign. Writing being defined as "a system of signs," there is no "symbolic" writing (in the Saussurian sense), no figurative writing; there is no *writing* as long as graphism keeps a relationship of natural figuration and of some resemblance to what is then not *signified* but represented, drawn, etc. The concept of pictographic or natural writing would therefore be contradictory for Saussure. If one considers the now recognized fragility of the notions of pictogram, ideogram etc., and the uncertainty of the frontiers between so-called pictographic, ideographic, and phonetic scripts, one realizes not only the unwiseness of the Saussurian limitation but the need for general linguistics to abandon an entire family of concepts inherited from metaphysics—often through the intermediary of a psychology—and clustering around the concept of arbitrariness. All this refers, beyond the nature/culture opposition, to a supervening opposition between *physis* and *nomos*, *physis* and *techné*, whose ultimate function is perhaps to *derive* historicity; and, paradoxically, not to recognize the rights of history, production, institutions etc., except in the form of the arbitrary and in the substance of naturalism. But let us keep that question provisionally open: perhaps this gesture, which in truth presides over metaphysics, is also inscribed in the concept of history and even in the concept of time.

In addition, Saussure introduces another massive limitation: "I shall limit discussion to the phonetic system and especially to the one used today, the system that stems from the Greek alphabet" (p. 48) [p. 26].

These two limitations are all the more reassuring because they are just what we need at a specific point to fulfill the most legitimate of exigencies; in fact, the condition for the scientificity of linguistics is that the field of linguistics have hard and fast frontiers, that it be a system regulated by an *internal* necessity, and that in a certain way its structure be closed. The representativist concept of writing facilitates things. If writing is nothing but the "figuration" (p. 44) [p. 23] of the language, one has the right to exclude it from the interiority of the system (for it must be believed that there is an *inside* of the language), as the image may be excluded without damage from the system of reality. Proposing as his theme "the representation of language by writing" Saussure thus begins by positing that writing is "unrelated to [the] . . . inner system" of language (p. 44), [p. 23]. External/internal, image/reality, representation/presence, such is the old grid to which is given the task of outlining the domain of a science. And of what science? Of a science that can no longer answer to the classical concept of the *epistémè* because the originality of its field—an originality that it inaugurates—is that the opening of the "image" within it appears as the condition of "reality;" a relationship that can no longer be thought within the simple difference and the uncompromising exteriority of "image" and "reality," of "outside" and "inside," of "appearance" and "essence," with the entire system of oppositions which necessarily follows from it. Plato, who said basically the same thing about the relationship between writing, speech, and being (or idea), had at least a more subtle, more critical, and less complacent theory of image, painting, and imitation than the one that presides over the birth of Saussurian linguistics.

It is not by chance that the exclusive consideration of phonetic writing permits a response to the exigencies of the "internal system." The basic functional principle of phonetic writing is precisely to respect and protect the integrity of the "internal system" of the language, even if in fact it does not succeed in doing so. *The Saussurian limitation does not respond, by a mere happy convenience, to the scientific exigency of the "internal system." That exigency is itself constituted, as the epistemological exigency in general, by the very possibility of phonetic writing and by the exteriority of the "notation" to internal logic.*

But let us not simplify: on that point Saussure too is not quite complacent. Why else would he give so much attention to that external phenomenon, that exiled figuration, that outside, that double? Why does he judge it impossible "to simply disregard" [literally "make abstraction of"] what is nevertheless designated as the abstract itself with respect to the inside of language? "Writing, though unrelated to its inner system, is used continually to represent language. We cannot simply disregard it. We must be acquainted with its usefulness, shortcomings, and dangers" (p. 44) [p. 23].

Writing would thus have the exteriority that one attributes to utensils; to what is even an imperfect tool and a dangerous, almost maleficent, technique. One understands better why, instead of treating this exterior figuration in an appendix or marginally, Saussure devotes so laborious a chapter to it almost at the beginning of the *Course*. It is less a question of outlining than of protecting, and even of restoring the internal system of the language in the purity of its concept against the gravest, most perfidious, most permanent contamination which has not ceased to menace, even to corrupt that system, in the course of what Saussure strongly wishes, in spite of all opposition, to consider as an external history, as a series of accidents affecting the language and befalling it *from without*, at the moment of "notation" (p. 45) [p. 24], as if writing began and ended with notation. Already in the *Phaedrus*, Plato says that the evil of writing comes from without (275a). The contamination by writing, the fact or the threat of it, are denounced in the accents of the moralist or preacher by the linguist from Geneva. The tone counts; it is as if, at the moment when the modern science of the logos would come into its autonomy and its scientificity, it became necessary again to attack a heresy. This tone began to make itself heard when, at the moment of already tying the *epistémè* and the *logos* within the same possibility, the *Phaedrus* denounced writing as the intrusion of an artful technique, a forced entry of a totally original sort, an archetypal violence: eruption of the *outside* within the *inside*, breaching into the interiority of the soul, the living self-presence of the soul within the true logos, the help that speech lends to itself. Thus incensed, Saussure's vehement argumentation aims at more than a theoretical error, more than a moral fault: at a sort of stain and primarily at a sin. Sin has been defined often—among others by Malebranche and by Kant—as the inversion of the natural relationship between the soul and the body through passion. Saussure here points at the inversion of the natural relationship between speech and writing. It is not a simple analogy: writing, the letter, the sensible inscription, has always been considered by Western tradition as the body and matter external to the spirit, to breath, to speech, and to the logos. And the problem of soul and body is no doubt derived from the problem of writing from which it seems—conversely—to borrow its metaphors.

Writing, sensible matter and artificial exteriority: a "clothing." It has sometimes been contested that speech clothed thought. Husserl, Saussure, Lavelle have all questioned it. But has it ever been doubted that writing was the clothing of speech? For Saussure it is even a garment of perversion and debauchery, a dress of corruption and disguise, a festival mask that must be exorcised, that is to say warded off, by the good word: "Writing veils the appearance of language; it is not a guise for language but a disguise" (p. 51) [p. 30]. Strange "image." One already suspects that if writing is "image" and exterior "figuration," this "representation" is not innocent. The outside bears with the inside a relationship that is, as usual, anything but simple exteriority. The meaning of the outside was always present within the inside, imprisoned outside the outside, and vice versa.

Thus a science of language must recover the *natural*—that is, the simple and original—relationships between speech and writing, that is, between an inside and an outside. It must restore its absolute youth, and the purity of its origin, short of a history and a fall which would have perverted the relationships between outside and inside. Therefore there would be a *natural order* of relationships between linguistic and graphic signs, and it is the theoretician of the arbitrariness of the sign who reminds us of it. According to the historico-metaphysical presuppositions evoked above, there would be first a *natural* bond of sense to the senses and it is this that passes from sense to sound: "the natural bond," Saussure says, "the only true bond, the bond of sound" (p. 46 [p. 25]. This natural bond of the signified (concept or sense) to the phonic signifier would condition the natural relationship subordinating writing (visible image) to speech. It is this natural relationship that would have been inverted by the original sin of writing: "The graphic form [*image*] manages to force itself upon them at the expense of sound . . . and the natural sequence is reversed" (p. 47) [p. 25]. Malebranche explained original sin as inattention, the temptation of ease and idleness, by that *nothing* that was Adam's "distraction," alone culpable before the innocence of the divine word: the latter exerted no force, no efficacy, since *nothing* had taken place. Here too, one gave in to *ease*, which is curiously, but as usual, on the side of technical artifice and not within the bent of the natural movement thus thwarted or deviated:

First, the graphic form [*image*] of words strikes us as being something permanent and stable, better suited than sound to constitute the unity of language throughout time. Though it creates a purely *fictitious* unity, the *superficial* bond of writing is much *easier* to grasp than the natural bond, the only true bond, the bond of sound (p. 46; italics added) [p. 25].

That "the graphic form of words strikes us as being something permanent and stable, better suited than sound to constitute the unity of language throughout time," is that not a natural phenomenon too? In fact a bad nature, "superficial" and "fictitious" and "easy," effaces a good nature by imposture; that which ties sense to sound, the "thought-sound." Saussure is faithful to the tradition that has always associated writing with the fatal violence of the political institution. It is clearly a matter, as with Rousseau for example, of a break with nature, of a usurpation that was coupled with the theoretical blindness to the natural essence of language, at any rate to the natural bond between the "instituted signs" of the voice and "the first language of man," the "cry of nature" (*Second Discourse*).* Saussure: "But the spoken word is so intimately bound to its written *image* that the latter manages to *usurp* the main role" (p. 45; italics added) [p. 24]. Rousseau: "Writing is nothing but the representation of speech; it is *bizarre* that one gives more care to the determining of the *image* than to the *object*." Saussure: "Whoever says that a certain letter must be pronounced a certain way is mistaking the written *image* of a sound for the sound itself. . . . [One] attribute[s] the oddity [*bizarrerie*] to an exceptional pronunciation" (p. 52) [p. 30].[2] What is intolerable and fascinating is indeed the intimacy intertwining image and thing, *graph, i.e.*, and phonè, to the point where by a mirroring, inverting, and perverting effect, speech seems in its turn the speculum of writing, which "manages to usurp the main role." Representation mingles with what it represents, to the point where one speaks as one writes, one thinks as if the represented were nothing more than the shadow or reflection of the representer. A dangerous promiscuity and a nefarious complicity between the reflection and the reflected which lets itself be seduced narcissistically. In this play of representation, the point of origin becomes ungraspable. There are things like reflecting pools, and images, an infinite reference from one to the other, but no longer a source, a spring. There is no longer a simple origin. For what is reflected is split *in itself* and not only as an addition to itself of its image. The reflection, the image, the double, splits what it doubles. The origin of the speculation becomes a difference. What can look at itself is not one; and the law of the addition of the origin to its representation, of the thing to its image, is that one plus one makes at least three. The

* "Discours sur l'origine et les fondements de l'inégalité." Derrida's references are to the Pléiade edition, vol. 3. Mine, placed within brackets, to "A Discourse on the Origin of Inequality," *The Social Contract and Discourses*, tr. G. D. H. Cole (London, 1913).

historical usurpation and theoretical oddity that install the image within the rights of reality are determined as the *forgetting* of a simple origin. By Rousseau but also for Saussure. The displacement is hardly anagrammatic: "The result is that people forget that they learn to speak before they learn to write and the natural sequence is reversed" (p. 47) [p. 25]. The violence of forgetting. Writing, a mnemotechnic means, supplanting good memory, spontaneous memory, signifies forgetfulness. It is exactly what Plato said in the *Phaedrus,* comparing writing to speech as *hypomnesis* to *mnémè,* the auxilliary aide-mémoire to the living memory. Forgetfulness because it is a mediation and the departure of the logos from itself. Without writing, the latter would remain in itself. Writing is the dissimulation of the natural, primary, and immediate presence of sense to the soul within the logos. Its violence befalls the soul as unconsciousness. Deconstructing this tradition will therefore not consist of reversing it, of making writing innocent. Rather of showing why the violence of writing does not *befall* an innocent language. There is an originary violence of writing because language is first, in a sense I shall gradually reveal, writing. "Usurpation" has always already begun. The sense of the right side appears in a mythological effect of return.

"The sciences and the arts" have elected to live within this violence, their "progress" has consecrated forgetfulness and "corrupted manners [*moeurs*]." Saussure again anagrammatizes Rousseau: "The literary language adds to the undeserved importance of writing. . . Thus writing assumes undeserved importance [*une importance à laquelle elle n'a pas droit*]" (p. 47) [p. 25]. When linguists become embroiled in a theoretical mistake in this subject, when they are taken in, they are *culpable,* their fault is above all *moral;* they have yielded to imagination, to sensibility, to passion, they have fallen into the "trap" (p. 46) [p. 25] of writing, have let themselves be fascinated by the "influence [*prestige*] of the written form" (ibid.), of that custom, that second nature. "The language does have a definite and stable oral tradition that is independent of writing, but the influence [*prestige*] of the written from prevents our seeing this." We are thus not blind to the visible, but blinded by the visible, dazzled by writing. "The first linguists confused language and writing, just as the humanists had done before them. Even Bopp. . . . His immediate successors fell into the same trap." Rousseau had already addressed the same reproach to the Grammarians: "For the Grammarians, the art of speech seems to be very little more than the art of writing."[3] As usual, the "trap" is artifice dissimulated in nature. This explains why *The Course in General Linguistics* treats *first* this strange external system that is writing. As necessary preamble to restoring the natural to itself, one must first disassemble the trap. We read a little further on:

To substitute immediately what is natural for what is artificial would be necessary; but this is impossible without first studying the sounds of what is language; detached from their graphic signs, sounds represent only vague notions, and the prop provided by writing, though deceptive, is still preferable. The first linguists, who knew nothing about the physiology of articulated sounds, were constantly falling into a trap; to let go of the letter was for them to lose their foothold; to me, it means a first step in the direction of truth (p. 55. Opening of the chapter on Phonology) [p. 32].

For Saussure, to give in to the "prestige of the written form" is, as I have just said, to give in to *passion*. It is passion—and I weigh my word—that Saussure analyzes and criticizes here, as a moralist and a psychologist of a very old tradition. As one knows, passion is tyrannical and enslaving: "Philological criticism is still deficient on one point: it follows the written language slavishly and neglects the living language" (p. 14) [pp. 1–2]. "The tyranny of writing," Saussure says elsewhere (p. 53) [p. 31]. That tyranny is at bottom the mastery of the body over the soul, and passion is a passivity and sickness of the soul, the moral perversion is *pathological*. The reciprocal effect of writing on speech is "wrong [*vicieuse*]," Saussure says, "such mistakes are really pathological" (p. 53) [p. 31]. The inversion of the natural relationships would thus have engendered the perverse cult of the letter-image: sin of idolatry, "superstition of the letter" Saussure says in the *Anagrams*[4] where he has difficulty in proving the existence of a "phoneme anterior to all writing." The perversion of artifice engenders monsters. Writing, like all artificial languages one would wish to fix and remove from the living history of the natural language, participates in the monstrosity. It is a deviation from nature. The characteristic of the Liebnizian type and Esperanto would be here in the same position. Saussure's irritation with such possibilities drives him to pedestrian comparisons: "A man proposing a fixed language that posterity would have to accept for what it is would be like a hen hatching a duck's egg" (p. 111) [p. 76]. And Saussure wishes to save not only the *natural life* of language, but the natural habits of writing. Spontaneous life must be protected. Thus, the introduction of scientific exigencies and the taste for exactitude into ordinary phonetic writing must be avoided. In this case, rationality would bring death, desolation, and monstrousness. That is why common orthography must be kept away from the notations of the linguist and *the multiplying of diacritical signs must be avoided*:

Are there grounds for substituting a phonologic alphabet for a system [*l'orthographe*] already in use? Here I can only broach this interesting subject. I think that phonological writing should be for the use of linguists only. First, how would it be possible to make the English, Germans, French, etc. adopt a uniform system! Next, an alphabet applicable to all languages would probably be weighed down by diacritical marks; and—to say nothing of the distressing appearance of a page of phonological writing—attempts to gain precision would obviously confuse the reader by obscuring what the writing was designed to express. The advantages would not be sufficient to compensate for the inconveniences. Phonological exactitude is not very desirable outside science (p. 57) [p. 34].

I hope my intention is clear. I think Saussure's reasons are good. I do not question, *on the level on which he says it,* the truth of *what Saussure says* in such a tone. And as long as an explicit problematics, a *critique* of the relationships between speech and writing, is not elaborated, what he denounces as the blind prejudice of classical linguists or of common experience indeed remains a blind prejudice, on the basis of a general presupposition which is no doubt common to the accused and the prosecutor.

I would rather announce the limits and the presuppositions of what seems here to be self-evident and what seems to me to retain the character and validity of evidence. The limits have already begun to appear: Why does a project of *general* linguistics, concerning the *internal system in general of language in general,* outline the limits of its field by excluding, as *exteriority in general,* a *particular* system of writing, however important it might be, even were it to be *in fact* universal?[5] A particular system which has precisely for its *principle* or at least for its *declared* project to be exterior to the spoken language. Declaration of principle, pious wish and historical violence of a speech dreaming its full self-presence, living itself as its own resumption; self-proclaimed language, auto-production of a speech declared alive, capable, Socrates said, of helping itself, a logos which believes itself to be its own father, being lifted thus above written discourse, *infans* (speechless) and infirm at not being able to respond when one questions it and which, since its "parent['s help] is [always] needed" (toū patrōs áeì deītai boīthoū—*Phaedrus* 275d) must therefore be born out of a primary gap and a primary *expatriation,* condemning it to wandering and blindness, to mourning. Self-proclaimed language but actually speech, deluded into believing itself completely alive, and violent, for it is not "capable of protect[ing] or defend[ing] [itself]" (dunatōs mēn amūnai éauto) except through expelling the other, and especially *its own* other, throwing it *outside* and *below,* under the name of writing. But however important it might be, and were it in fact universal or called upon to become so, that particular model which is phonetic writing *does not exist;* no practice is ever totally faithful to its principle. Even before speaking, as I shall do further on, of a radical and a priori necessary infidelity, one can already remark its massive phenomena in mathematical script or in punctuation, in *spacing* in general, which it is difficult to consider as simple accessories of writing. That a speech supposedly alive can lend itself to spacing in its own writing is what relates it originarily to its own death.

Finally, the "usurpation" of which Saussure speaks, the violence by which writing would substitute itself for its own origin, for that which ought not only to have engendered it but to have been engendered from itself—such a reversal of power cannot be an accidental aberration. Usurpation necessarily refers us to a profound possibility of essence. This is without a doubt inscribed within speech itself and he should have questioned it, perhaps even started from it.

Saussure confronts the system of the spoken language with the system of phonetic (and even alphabetic) writing as though with the telos of writing. This teleology leads to the interpretation of all eruptions of the nonphonetic within writing as transitory crisis and accident of passage, and it is right to consider this teleology to be a Western ethnocentrism, a premathematical primitivism, and a preformalist intuitionism. Even if this teleology responds to some absolute necessity, it should be problematized as such. The scandal of "usurpation" invites us expressly and intrinsically to do that. How was the trap and the usurpation possible? Saussure never replies to this question beyond a psychology of the passions or of the imagination; a psychology reduced to its most conventional diagrams. This best explains why all linguistics, a determined sector inside semiology, is placed under the authority and superiority of psychology: "To determine the exact place of semiology is the task of the psychologist" (p. 33) [p. 16]. The affirmation of the essential and "natural" bond between the *phonè* and the sense, the privilege accorded to an order of signifier (which then becomes the major signified of all other signifiers) depend expressly, and in contradiction to the other levels of the Saussurian discourse, upon a psychology of consciousness and of intuitive consciousness. What Saussure does not question here is the essential possibility of nonintuition. Like Husserl, Saussure determines this nonintuition teleologically as *crisis*. The *empty* symbolism of the written notation—in mathematical technique for example—is also for Husserlian intuitionism that which exiles us far from the *clear* evidence of the sense, that is to say from the full presence of the signified in its truth, and thus opens the possibility of crisis. This is indeed a crisis of the logos. Nevertheless, for Husserl, this possibility remains linked with the very moment of truth and the production of ideal objectivity: it has in fact an essential need for writing.[6] By one entire aspect of his text, Husserl makes us think that the negativity of the crisis is not a mere accident. But it is then the concept of crisis that should be suspect, by virtue of what ties it to a dialectical and teleological determination of negativity.

On the other hand, to account for "usurpation" and the origin of "passion," the classical and very superficial argument of the solid permanence of the written thing, not to be simply false, calls forth descriptions which are precisely no longer within the province of psychology. Psychology will never be able to accommodate within its space that which constitutes the absence of the signatory, to say nothing of the absence of the referent.

Writing is the name of these two absences. Besides, is it not contradictory to what is elsewhere affirmed about language having "a definite and [far more] stable oral tradition that is independent of writing" (p. 46) [p. 24], to explain the usurpation by means of writing's power of *duration*, by means of the *durability* of the substance of writing? If these two "stabilities" were of the same nature, and if the stability of the spoken language were superior and independent, the origin of writing, its "prestige" and its supposed harmfulness, would remain an inexplicable mystery. It seems then as if Saussure wishes *at the same time* to demonstrate the corruption of speech by writing, to denounce the harm that the latter does to the former, *and* to underline the inalterable and natural independence of language. "Languages are independent of writing" (p. 45) [p. 24]. Such is the truth of nature. And yet nature is affected—from without—by an overturning which modifies it in its interior, denatures it and obliges it to be separated from itself. Nature denaturing itself, being separated *from itself*, naturally gathering its outside into its inside, is *catastrophe*, a natural event that overthrows nature, or *monstrosity*, a natural deviation within nature. The function assumed in Rousseau's discourse by the catastrophe (as we shall see), is here delegated to monstrousness. Let us cite the entire conclusion of Chapter VI of the *Course* ("Graphic Representation of Language"), which must be compared to Rousseau's text on *Pronunciation*:

> But the tyranny of writing goes even further. By imposing itself upon the masses, spelling influences and modifies language. This happens only in highly literary languages where written texts play an important role. Then visual images lead to wrong [*vicieuses*] pronunciations; such mistakes are really pathological. Spelling practices cause mistakes in the pronunciation of many French words. For instance, there were two spellings for the surname Lefèvre (from latin *faber*), one popular and simple, the other learned and etymological: *Lefèvre* and *Lefèbvre*. Because *v* and *u* were not kept apart in the old system of writing, *Lefèbvre* was read as *Lefébure*, with a *b* that has never really existed and a *u* that was the result of ambiguity. Now, the latter form is actually pronounced (pp. 53–54) [p. 31].

Where is the evil? one will perhaps ask. And what has been invested in the "living word," that makes such "aggressions" of writing intolerable? What investment begins by determining the constant action of writing as a deformation and an aggression? What prohibition has thus been transgressed? Where is the sacrilege? Why should the mother tongue be protected from the operation of writing? Why determine that operation as a violence, and why should the transformation be only a deformation? Why should the mother tongue not have a history, or, what comes to the same thing, produce its own history in a perfectly natural, autistic, and domestic way, without ever being affected by any outside? Why wish to punish writing for a monstrous crime, to the point of wanting to reserve for it, even within scientific treatments, a "special compartment" that holds it at a distance? For it is indeed within a sort of intralinguistic leper colony that Saussure wants to contain and concentrate the problem of deformations through writing. And, in order to be convinced that he would take in very bad part the innocent questions that I have just asked—for after all *Lefébure is not a bad name* and we can love this play—let us read the following. The passage below explains to us that the "play" is not "natural," and its accents are pessimistic: "Mispronunciations due to spelling will probably appear more frequently and as time goes on, the number of useless letters pronounced by speakers will probably increase." As in Rousseau in the same context, the Capital is accused: "Some Parisians already pronounce the *t* in *sept femmes* 'seven women'." Strange example. The historical gap —for it is indeed history that one must stop in order to protect language from writing—will only widen:

> Darmsteter foresees the day when even the last two letters of *vingt* "twenty" will be pronounced—truly an orthographic *monstrosity*. Such phonic *deformations* belong to language but *do not stem from its natural functioning*. They are due to an *external* influence. Linguistics should put them into a *special compartment* for observation: they are *teratological* cases (p. 54; italics added) [pp. 31–32].

It is clear that the concepts of stability, permanence, and duration, which here assist thinking the relationships between speech and writing, are too lax and open to every uncritical investiture. They would require more attentive and minute analyses. The same is applicable to an explanation according to which "most people pay more attention to visual impressions simply because these are sharper and more lasting than aural impressions" (p. 46) [p. 25]. This explanation of "usurpation" is not only empirical in its form, it is problematic in its content, it refers to a metaphysics and to an old physiology of sensory faculties constantly disproved by science, as by the experience of language and by the body proper as language. It imprudently makes of visibility the tangible, simple, and essential element of writing. Above all, in considering the audible as the *natural* milieu within which language must *naturally* fragment and articulate its instituted signs, thus exercising its arbitrariness, this explanation excludes all possibility of some natural relationship between speech and writing at the very moment that it affirms it. Instead of deliberately dismissing the notions of nature and institution that it constantly uses, which ought to be done first, it thus confuses the two. It finally and most importantly contradicts the principal affirmation according to which "the thing that constitutes language [*l'essentiel de la langue*] *is* . . . unrelated to the phonic character of the linguistic sign" (p. 21) [p. 7]. This affirmation will soon occupy us; within it the other side of the Saussurian proposition denouncing the "illusions of script" comes to the fore.

What do these limits and presuppositions signify? First that a linguistics is not *general* as long as it defines its outside and inside in terms of *determined* linguistic models; as long as it does not rigorously distinguish essence from fact in their respective degrees of generality. The system of writing in general is not exterior to the system of language in general, unless it is granted that the division between exterior and interior passes through the interior of the interior or the exterior of the exterior, to the point where the immanence of language is essentially exposed to the intervention of forces that are apparently alien to its system. For the same reason, writing in general is not "image" or "figuration" of language in general, except if the nature, the logic, and the functioning of the image within the system from which one wishes to exclude it be reconsidered. Writing is not a sign of a sign, except if one says it of all signs, which would be more profoundly true. If every sign refers to a sign, and if "sign of a sign" signifies writing, certain conclusions—which I shall consider at the appropriate moment—will become inevitable. What Saussure saw without seeing, knew without being *able* to take into account, following in that the entire metaphysical tradition, is that a certain model of writing was necessarily but provisionally imposed (but for the inaccuracy in principle, insufficiency of fact, and the permanent usurpation) as instrument and technique of representation of a system of language. And that this movement, unique in style, was so profound that it permitted the thinking, *within language*, of concepts like those of the sign, technique, representation, language. The system of language associated with phonetic-alphabetic writing is that within which logocentric metaphysics, determining the sense of being as presence, has been produced. This logocentrism, this *epoch* of the full speech, has always placed in parenthesis, *suspended*, and suppressed for essential reasons, all free reflection on the origin and status of writing, all science of writing which was not *technology* and the *history of a technique*, itself leaning upon a mythology and a metaphor of a natural writing.* It is this logocentrism which, limiting the internal system of language in general by a bad abstraction, prevents Saussure and the majority of his successors[7] from determining fully and explicitly that which is called "the integral and concrete object of linguistics" (p. 23) [p. 7].

But conversely, as I announced above, it is when he is not expressly dealing with writing, when he feels he has closed the parentheses on that subject, that Saussure opens the field of a general grammatology. Which

* A play on "époque" (epoch) and "epoché," the Husserlian term for the "bracketting" or "putting out of play" that constitutes phenomenological reduction.

would not only no longer be excluded from general linguistics, but would dominate it and contain it within itself. Then one realizes that what was chased off limits, the wandering outcast of linguistics, has indeed never ceased to haunt language as its primary and most intimate possibility. Then something which was never spoken and which is nothing other than writing itself as the origin of language writes itself within Saussure's discourse. Then we glimpse the germ of a profound but indirect explanation of the usurpation and the traps condemned in Chapter VI. This explanation will overthrow even the form of the question to which it was a premature reply.

The Outside the Inside

The thesis of the *arbitrariness* of the sign (so grossly misnamed, and not only for the reasons Saussure himself recognizes)[8] must forbid a radical distinction between the linguistic and the graphic sign. No doubt this thesis concerns only the necessity of relationships between specific signifiers and signifieds *within* an allegedly natural relationship between the voice and sense in general, between the order of phonic signifiers and the content of the signifieds ("the only natural bond, the only true bond, the bond of sound"). Only these relationships between specific signifiers and signifieds would be regulated by arbitrariness. Within the "natural" relationship between phonic signifiers and their signifieds *in general*, the relationship between each determined signifier and its determined signified would be "arbitrary."

Now from the moment that one considers the totality of determined signs, spoken, and a fortiori written, as unmotivated institutions, one must exclude any relationship of natural subordination, any natural hierarchy among signifiers or orders of signifiers. If "writing" signifies inscription and especially the durable institution of a sign (and that is the only irreducible kernel of the concept of writing), writing in general covers the entire field of linguistic signs. In that field a certain sort of instituted signifiers may then appear, "graphic" in the narrow and derivative sense of the word, ordered by a certain relationship with other instituted—hence "written," even if they are "phonic"—signifiers. The very idea of institution—hence of the arbitrariness of the sign—is unthinkable before the possibility of writing and outside of its horizon. Quite simply, that is, outside of the horizon itself, outside the world as space of inscription, as the opening to the emission and to the spatial *distribution* of signs, to the *regulated play* of their differences, even if they are "phonic."

Let us now persist in using this opposition of nature and institution, of *physis* and *nomos* (which also means, of course, a distribution and division regulated in fact by *law*) which a meditation on writing should disturb although it functions everywhere as self-evident, particularly in the discourse of linguistics. We must then conclude that only the signs called *natural*, those that Hegel and Saussure call "symbols," escape semiology as grammatology. But they fall a fortiori outside the field of linguistics as the region of general semiology. The thesis of the arbitrariness of the sign thus indirectly but irrevocably contests Saussure's declared proposition when he chases writing to the outer darkness of language. This thesis successfully accounts for a conventional relationship between the phoneme and the grapheme (in phonetic writing, between the phoneme, signifier-signified, and the grapheme, pure signifier), but by the same token it forbids that the latter be an "image" of the former. Now it was indispensable to the exclusion of writing as "external system," that it come to impose an "image," a "representaton," or a "figuration," an exterior reflection of the reality of language.

It matters little, here at least, that there is in fact an ideographic filiation of the alphabet. This important question is much debated by historians of writing. What matters here is that in the synchronic structure and systematic principle of alphabetic writing—and phonetic writing in general—no relationship of "natural" representation, none of resemblance or participation, no "symbolic" relationship in the Hegelian–Saussurian sense, no "iconographic" relationship in the Peircian sense, be implied.

One must therefore challenge, in the very name of the arbitrariness of the sign, the Saussurian definition of writing as "image"—hence as natural symbol—of language. Not to mention the fact that the phoneme is the *unimaginable* itself, and no visibility can *resemble* it, it suffices to take into account what Saussure says about the difference between the symbol and the sign (p. 101) [pp. 68–69] in order to be completely baffled as to how he can at the same time say of writing that it is an "image" or "figuration" of language and define language and writing elsewhere as "two distinct systems of signs" (p. 45) [p. 23]. For the property of the sign is not to be an image. By a process exposed by Freud in *The Interpretation of Dreams*, Saussure thus accumulates contradictory arguments to bring about a satisfactory decision: the exclusion of writing. In fact, even within so-called phonetic writing, the "graphic" signifier refers to the phoneme through a web of many dimensions which binds it, like all signifiers, to other written and oral signifiers, within a "total" system open, let us say, to all possible investments of sense. We must begin with the possibility of that total system.

Saussure was thus never able to think that writing was truly an "image," a "figuration," a "representation" of the spoken language, a symbol. If one considers that he nonetheless needed these inadequate notions to decide upon the exteriority of writing, one must conclude that an entire stratum of his discourse, the intention of Chapter VI ("Graphic Representation of Language"), was not at all scientific. When I say this, my quarry is not primarily Ferdinand de Saussure's intention or motivation, but rather the entire uncritical tradition which he inherits. To what zone of discourse does this strange functioning of argumentation belong, this coherence of desire producing itself in a near-oneiric way—although it clarifies the dream rather than allow itself to be clarified by it—through a contradictory logic? How is this functioning articulated with the entirety of theoretical discourse, throughout the history of science? Better yet, how does it work from within the concept of science itself? It is only when this question is elaborated—if it *is* some day—when the concepts required by this functioning are defined outside of all psychology (as of all sciences of man), outside metaphysics (which can now be "Marxist" or "structuralist"); when one is able to respect all its levels of generality and articulation—it is only then that one will be able to state rigorously the problem of the articulated appurtenance of a text (theoretical or otherwise) to an entire set: I obviously treat the Saussurian text at the moment only as a telling example within a given situation, without professing to use the concepts required by the functioning of which I have just spoken. My justification would be as follows: this and some other indices (in a general way the treatment of the concept of writing) already give us the assured means of broaching the de-construction of *the greatest totality*—the concept of the *epistémè* and logocentric metaphysics—within which are produced, without ever posing the radical question of writing, all the Western methods of analysis, explication, reading, or interpretation.

Now we must think that writing is at the same time more exterior to speech, not being its "image" or its "symbol," and more interior to speech, which is already in itself a writing. Even before it is linked to incision, engraving, drawing, or the letter, to a signifier referring in general to a signifier signified by it, the concept of the *graphie* [unit of a possible graphic system] implies the framework of the *instituted trace*, as the possibility common to all systems of signification. My efforts will now be directed toward slowly detaching these two concepts from the classical discourse from which I necessarily borrow them. The effort will be laborious and we know a priori that its effectiveness will never be pure and absolute.

The instituted trace is "unmotivated" but not capricious. Like the word "arbitrary" according to Saussure, it "should not imply that the choice of the signifier is left entirely to the speaker" (p. 101) [pp. 68–69]. Simply, it has no "natural attachment" to the signified within reality. For us, the rupture of that "natural attachment" puts in question the idea of naturalness rather than that of attachment. That is why the word "institution" should not be too quickly interpreted within the classical system of oppositions.

The instituted trace cannot be thought without thinking the retention of difference within a structure of reference where difference appears *as such* and thus permits a certain liberty of variations among the full terms. The absence of *another* here-and-now, of another transcendental present, of *another* origin of the world appearing as such, presenting itself as irreducible absence within the presence of the trace, is not a metaphysical formula substituted for a scientific concept of writing. This formula, beside the fact that it is the questioning of metaphysics itself, describes the structure implied by the "arbitrariness of the sign," from the moment that one thinks of its possibility *short of* the derived opposition between nature and convention, symbol and sign, etc. These oppositions have meaning only after the possibility of the trace. The "unmotivatedness" of the sign requires a synthesis in which the completely other is announced as such—without any simplicity, any identity, any resemblance or continuity—within what is not it. *Is announced as such*: there we have all *history*, from what metaphysics has defined as "non-living" up to "consciousness," passing through all levels of animal organization. The trace, where the relationship with the other is marked, articulates its possibility in the entire field of the entity [*étant*], which metaphysics has defined as the being-present starting from the occulted movement of the trace. The trace must be thought before the entity. But the movement of the trace is necessarily occulted, it produces itself as self-occultation. When the other announces itself as such, it presents itsef in the dissimulation of itself. This formulation is not theological, as one might believe somewhat hastily. The "theological" is a determined moment in the total movement of the trace. The field of the entity, before being determined as the field of presence, is structured according to the diverse possibilities—genetic and structural—of the trace. The presentation of the other as such, that is to say the dissimulation of its "as such," has always already begun and no structure of the entity escapes it.

That is why the movement of "unmotivatedness" passes from one structure to the other when the "sign" crosses the stage of the "symbol." It is in a certain sense and according to a certain determined structure of the "as such" that one is authorized to say that there is yet no immotivation in what Saussure calls "symbol" and which, according to him, does not—at least provisionally—interest semiology. The general structure of the unmotivated trace connects within the same possibility, and they cannot be separated except by abstraction, the structure of the relationship with the other, the movement of temporalization, and language as writing. Without referring back to a "nature," the immotivation of the trace has always *become*. In fact, there is no unmotivated trace: the trace is indefinitely its own becoming-unmotivated. In Saussurian language, what Saussure does not say would have to be said: there is neither symbol nor sign but a becoming-sign of the symbol.

Thus, as it goes without saying, the trace whereof I speak is not more *natural* (it is not the mark, the natural sign, or the index in the Husserlian sense) than *cultural*, not more physical than psychic, biological than spiritual. It is that starting from which a becoming-unmotivated of the sign, and with it all the ulterior oppositions between *physis* and its other, is possible.

In his project of semiotics, Peirce seems to have been more attentive than Saussure to the irreducibility of this becoming-unmotivated. In his terminology, one must speak of a becoming-unmotivated of the *symbol*, the notion of the symbol playing here a role analogous to that of the sign which Saussure opposes precisely to the symbol:

> Symbols grow. They come into being by development out of other signs, particularly from icons, or from mixed signs partaking of the nature of icons and symbols. We think only in signs. These mental signs are of mixed nature; the symbol parts of them are called concepts. If a man makes a new symbol, it is by thoughts involving concepts. So it is only out of symbols that a new symbol can grow. Omne symbolum de symbolo.[9]

Peirce complies with two apparently incompatible exigencies. The mistake here would be to sacrifice one for the other. It must be recognized that the symbolic (in Peirce's sense: of "the arbitrariness of the sign") is rooted in the nonsymbolic, in an anterior and related order of signification: "Symbols grow. They come into being by development out of other signs, particularly from icons, or from mixed signs." But these roots must not compromise the structural originality of the field of symbols, the autonomy of a domain, a production, and a play: "So it is only out of symbols that a new symbol can grow. Omne symbolum de symbolo."

But in both cases, the genetic root-system refers from sign to sign. No ground of nonsignification—understood as insignificance or an intuition of a present truth—stretches out to give it foundation under the play and the coming into being of signs. Semiotics no longer depends on logic. Logic, according to Peirce, is only a semiotic: "Logic, in its general sense, is, as I believe I have shown, only another name for semiotics (*semeiotike*), the quasi-necessary, or formal, doctrine of signs." And logic in the classical sense, logic "properly speaking," nonformal logic commanded by the value of truth, occupies in that semiotics only a determined and not a fundamental level. As in Husserl (but the analogy, although it is most thought-provoking, would stop there and one must apply it carefully), the lowest level, the foundation of the possibility of logic (or semiotics) corresponds to the project of the *Grammatica speculativa* of Thomas d'Erfurt, falsely attributed to Duns Scotus. Like Husserl, Peirce expressly refers to it. It is a matter of elaborating, in both cases, a formal doctrine of conditions which a discourse must satisfy in order to have a sense, in order to "mean," even if it is false or contradictory. The general morphology of that meaning[10] (*Bedeutung, vouloir-dire*) is independent of all logic of truth.

The science of semiotic has three branches. The first is called by Duns Scotus *grammatica speculativa*. We may term it *pure grammar*. It has for its task to ascertain what must be true of the representamen used by every scientific intelligence in order that they may embody any *meaning*. The second is logic proper. It is the science of what is quasi-necessarily true of the representamina of any scientific intelligence in order that they may hold good of any *object*, that is, may be true. Or say, logic proper is the formal science of the conditions of the truth of representations. The third, in imitation of Kant's fashion of preserving old associations of words in finding nomenclature for new conceptions, I call *pure rhetoric*. Its task is to ascertain the laws by which in every scientific intelligence one sign gives birth to another, and especially one thought brings forth another.[11]

Peirce goes very far in the direction that I have called the de-construction of the transcendental signified, which, at one time or another, would place a reassuring end to the reference from sign to sign. I have identified logocentrism and the metaphysics of presence as the exigent, powerful, systematic, and irrepressible desire for such a signified. Now Peirce considers the indefiniteness of reference as the criterion that allows us to recognize that we are indeed dealing with a system of signs. *What broaches the movement of signification is what makes its interruption impossible. The thing itself is a sign.* An unacceptable proposition for Husserl, whose phenomenology remains therefore—in its "principle of principles"—the most radical and most critical restoration of the metaphysics of presence. The difference between Husserl's and Peirce's phenomenologies is fundamental since it concerns the concept of the sign and of the manifestation of presence, the relationships between the re-presentation and the originary presentation of the thing itself (truth). On this point Peirce is undoubtedly closer to the inventor of the word *phenomenology*: Lambert proposed in fact to "reduce *the theory of things* to the *theory of signs*." According to the "phaneoroscopy" or "phenomenology" of Peirce, *manifestation* itself does not reveal a presence, it makes a sign. One may read in the *Principle of Phenomenology* that "the idea of *manifestation* is the idea of a sign."[12] There is thus no phenomenality reducing the sign or the representer so that the thing signified may be allowed to glow finally in the luminosity of its presence. The so-called "thing itself" is always already a *representamen* shielded from the simplicity of intuitive evidence. The *representamen* functions only by giving rise to an *interpretant* that itself becomes a sign and so on to infinity. The self-identity of the signified conceals itself unceasingly and is always on the move. The property of the *representamen* is to be itself and another, to be produced as a structure of reference, to be separated from itself. The property of the *representamen* is not to be *proper* [*propre*], that is to say absolutely *proximate* to itself (*prope, proprius*). The *represented* is always already a *representamen.* Definition of the sign:

Anything which determines something else (its interpretant) to refer to an object to which itself refers (its object) in the same way, this interpretant becoming in turn a sign, and so on ad infinitum. . . . If the series of successive interpretants comes to an end, the sign is thereby rendered imperfect, at least.[13]

From the moment that there is meaning there are nothing but signs. We *think only in signs.* Which amounts to ruining the notion of the sign at the very moment when, as in Nietzsche, its exigency is recognized in the absoluteness of its right. One could call *play* the absence of the transcendental signified as limitlessness of play, that is to say as the destruction of ontotheology and the metaphysics of presence. It is not surprising that the shock, shaping and undermining metaphysics since its origin, lets itself *be named as such* in the period when, refusing to bind linguistics to semantics (which all European linguists, from Saussure to Hjemslev, still do), expelling the problem of *meaning* outside of their researches, certain American linguists constantly refer to the model of a game. Here one must think of writing as a game within language. (The *Phaedrus* (277e) condemned writing precisely as play—*paidia*—and opposed such childishness to the adult gravity [*spoudè*] of speech). This *play,* thought as absence of the transcendental signified, is not a play *in the world,* as it has always been defined, for the purposes of *containing* it, by the philosophical tradition and as the theoreticians of play also consider it (or those who, following and going beyond Bloomfield, refer semantics to psychology or some other local discipline). To think play radically the ontological and transcendental problematics must first be seriously *exhausted;* the question of the meaning of being, the being of the entity and of the transcendental origin of the world—of the world-ness of the world—must be patiently and rigorously worked through, the critical movement of the Husserlian and Heideggerian questions must be effectively followed to the very end, and their effectiveness and legibility must be conserved. Even if it were crossed out, without it the concepts of play and writing to which I shall have recourse will remain caught within regional limits and an empiricist, positivist, or metaphysical discourse. The counter-move that the holders of such a discourse would oppose to the precritical tradition and to metaphysical speculation would be nothing but the worldly representation of their own operation. It is therefore *the game of the world* that must be first thought; before attempting to understand all the forms of play in the world.[14]

From the very opening of the game, then, we are within the becoming-unmotivated of the symbol. With regard to this becoming, the opposition of diachronic and synchronic is also derived. It would not be able to command a grammatology pertinently. The immotivation of the trace ought now to be understood as an operation and not as a state, as an active movement, a demotivation, and not as a given structure. Science of "the arbitrariness of the sign," science of the immotivation of the trace, science of writing before speech and in speech, grammatology would thus cover a vast field within which linguistics would, by abstraction, delineate its own area, with the limits that Saussure prescribes to its internal system and which must be carefully reexamined in each speech/writing system in the world and history.

By a substitution which would be anything but verbal, one may replace *semiology* by *grammatology* in the program of the *Course in General Linguistics*:

> I shall call it [grammatology]. . . . Since the science does not yet exist, no one can say what it would be; but it has a right to existence, a place staked out in advance. Linguistics is only a part of [that] general science . . . ; the laws discovered by [grammatology] will be applicable to linguistics. (p. 33) [p. 16].

The advantage of this substitution will not only be to give to the theory of writing the scope needed to counter logocentric repression and the subordination to linguistics. It will liberate the semiological project itself from what, in spite of its greater theoretical extension, remained *governed* by linguistics, organized as if linguistics were at once its center and its telos. *Even though semiology was in fact more general and more comprehensive than linguistics, it continued to be regulated as if it were one of the areas of linguistics. The linguistic sign remained exemplary for semiology*, it dominated it as the master-sign and as the generative model: the pattern [*patron*].

> One could therefore say that signs that are wholly arbitrary realize better than the others the ideal of the semiological process; that is why language, the most complex and universal of all systems of expression, is also the most characteristic; in this sense linguistics can become *the master-pattern for all branches of semiology* although language is only one particular semiological system (p. 101; italics added) [p. 68].

Consequently, reconsidering the order of dependence prescribed by Saussure, apparently inverting the relationship of the part to the whole, Barthes in fact carries out the profoundest intention of the *Course*:

> From now on we must admit the possibility of reversing Saussure's proposition some day: linguistics is not a part, even if privileged, of the general science of signs, it is semiology that is a part of linguistics.[15]

This coherent reversal, submitting semiology to a "translinguistics," leads to its full explication a linguistics historically dominated by logocentric metaphysics, for which in fact there is not and there should not be "any meaning except as named" (ibid.). Dominated by the so-called "civilization of writing" that we inhabit, a civilization of so-called phonetic writing, that is to say of the logos where the sense of being is, in its telos, determined as parousia. The Barthesian reversal is fecund and indispensable for the description of the *fact and the vocation of signification* within the closure of this epoch and this civilization that is in the process of disappearing in its very globalization.

Let us now try to go beyond these formal and architectonic considerations. Let us ask in a more intrinsic and concrete way, how language is not merely a sort of writing, "comparable to a system of writing" (p. 33) [p. 16] —Saussure writes curiously—but a species *of* writing. Or rather, since writing no longer relates to language as an extension or frontier, let us ask how language is a possibility founded on the general possibility of writing. Demonstrating this, one would give at the same time an account of that alleged "usurpation" which could not be an unhappy accident. It supposes on the contrary a common root and thus excludes the resemblance of the "image," derivation, or representative reflexion. And thus one would bring back to its true meaning, to its primary possibility, the apparently innocent and didactic analogy which makes Saussure say:

> Language is [comparable to] a system of signs that express ideas, and is therefore *comparable to writing*, the alphabet of deaf-mutes, symbolic rites, polite formulas, military signals, etc. But it is the most important of all these systems (p. 33; italics added) [p. 16].

Further, it is not by chance that, a hundred and thirty pages later, at the moment of explaining *phonic difference* as the condition of linguistic *value* ("from a material viewpoint"),[16] he must again borrow all his pedagogic resources from the example of writing:

> Since an identical state of affairs is observable in writing, another system of signs, we shall use writing to draw some comparisons that will clarify the whole issue (p. 165) [p. 119].

Four demonstrative items, borrowing pattern and content from writing, follow.[17]

Once more, then, we definitely have to oppose Saussure to himself. Before being or not being "noted," "represented," "figured," in a "*graphie*," the linguistic sign implies an originary writing. Henceforth, it is not to the thesis of the arbitrariness of the sign that I shall appeal directly, but to what Saussure associates with it as an indispensable correlative and which would seem to me rather to lay the foundations for it: the thesis of *difference* as the source of linguistic value.[18]

What are, from the grammatological point of view, the consequences of this theme that is now so well-known (and upon which Plato already reflected in the *Sophist*)?

By definition, difference is never in itself a sensible plenitude. Therefore, its necessity contradicts the allegation of a naturally phonic essence of language. It contests by the same token the professed natural dependence of the graphic signifier. That is a consequence Saussure himself draws against the premises defining the internal system of language. He must now exclude the very thing which had permitted him to exclude writing: sound and its "natural bond" [*lien naturel*] with meaning. For example: "The thing that constitutes language is, as I shall show later, unrelated to the phonic character of the linguistic sign" (p. 21) [p. 7]. And in a paragraph on difference:

> It is impossible for sound alone, a material element, to belong to language. It is only a secondary thing, substance to be put to use. All our conventional values have the characteristic of not being confused with the tangible element which supports them. . . . The linguistic signifier . . . is not [in essence] phonic but incorporeal—constituted not by its material substance but the differences that separate its sound-image from all others (p. 164) [pp. 118–19]. The idea or phonic substance that a sign contains is of less importance than the other signs that surround it (p. 166) [p. 120]

Without this reduction of phonic matter, the distinction between language and speech, decisive for Saussure, would have no rigor. It would be the same for the oppositions that happened to descend from it: between code and message, pattern and usage, etc. Conclusion: "Phonology—this bears repeating—is only an auxiliary discipline [of the science of language] and belongs exclusively to speaking" (p. 56) [p. 33]. Speech thus draws from this stock of writing, noted or not, that language is, and it is here that one must meditate upon the complicity between the two "stabilities." The reduction of the *phonè* reveals this complicity. What Saussure says, for example, about the sign in general and what he "confirms" through the example of writing, applies also to language: "Signs are governed by a principle of general semiology: continuity in time is coupled to change in time; this is confirmed by orthrographic systems, the speech of deaf-mutes, etc." (p. 111) [p. 16].

The reduction of phonic substance thus does not only permit the distinction between phonetics on the one hand (and a fortiori accoustics or the physiology of the phonating organs) and phonology on the other. It also makes of phonology itself an "auxiliary discipline." Here the direction indicated by Saussure takes us beyond the phonologism of those who profess to follow him on this point: in fact, Jakobson believes indifference to the phonic substance of expression to be impossible and illegitimate. He thus criticizes the glossematics of Hjelmslev which requires and practices the neutralizing of sonorous substance. And in the text cited above, Jakobson and Halle maintain that the "theoretical requirement" of a research of invariables placing sonorous substance in parenthesis (as an empirical and contingent content) is:

1. *impracticable* since, as "Eli Fischer-Jorgensen exposes [it]," "the sonorous substance [is taken into account] at every step of the analysis."* But is that a "troubling discrepancy," as Jakobson and Halle would have it? Can one not account for it as a fact serving as an example, as do the phenomenologists who always need, keeping it always within sight, an exemplary empirical content in the reading of an essence which is independent of it by right?

2. *inadmissible in principle* since one cannot consider "that in language form is opposed to substance as a constant to a variable." It is in the course of this second demonstration that the literally Saussurian formulas reappear within the question of the relationships between speech and writing; the order of writing is the order of exteriority, of the "occasional," of the "accessory," of the "auxiliary," of the "*parasitic*" (pp. 116–17; italics added) [pp. 16–17]. The argument of Jakobson and Halle appeals to the factual genesis and invokes the secondariness of writing in the colloquial sense: "Only after having mastered speech does one graduate to reading and writing." Even if this commonsensical proposition were rigorously proved—something that I do not believe (since each of its concepts harbors an immense problem)—one would still have to receive assurance of its pertinence to the argument. Even if "after" were here a facile representation, if one knew perfectly well what one thought and stated while assuring that one learns to write *after* having learned to speak, would that suffice to conclude that what thus comes "after" is parasitic? And what is a parasite? And what if writing were precisely that which makes us reconsider our logic of the parasite?

In another moment of the critique, Jakobson and Halle recall the imperfection of graphic representation; that imperfection is due to "the cardinally dissimilar patterning of letters and phonemes:"

> Letters never, or only partially, reproduce the different distinctive features on which the phonemic pattern is based and unfailingly disregard the structural relationship of these features (p. 116) [p. 17].

I have suggested it above: does not the radical dissimilarity of the two elements—graphic and phonic—exclude derivation? Does not the inadequacy of graphic representation concern only common alphabetic writing, to which glossematic formalism does not essentially refer? Finally, if one

* Jakobson and Halle, *Fundamentals of Language*, loc. cit., p. 16.

accepts all the phonologist arguments thus presented, it must still be recognized that they oppose a "scientific" concept of the spoken word to a vulgar concept of writing. What I would wish to show is that one cannot exclude writing from the general experience of "the structural relationship of these features." Which amounts, of course, to reforming the concept of writing.

In short, if the Jakobsonian analysis is faithful to Saussure in this matter, is it not especially so to the Saussure of Chapter VI? Up to what point would Saussure have maintained the inseparability of matter and form, which remains the most important argument of Jakobson and Halle (p. 117), [p. 17]? The question may be repeated in the case of the position of André Martinet who, in this debate, follows Chapter VI of the *Course* to the letter.[19] And only Chapter VI, from which Martinet *expressly* dissociates the doctrine of what, in the *Course*, effaces the privilege of phonic substance. After having explained why "a dead language with a perfect ideography," that is to say a communication effective through the system of a generalized script, "could not have any real autonomy," and why *nevertheless*, "such a system would be something so particular that one can well understand why linguists *want to exclude it* from the domain of their science" (*La linguistique syncronique*, p. 18; italics added), Martinet criticizes those who, following a certain trend in Saussure, question the essentially phonic character of the linguistic sign: "Much will be attempted to prove that Saussure is right when he announces that 'the thing that constitutes language [*l'essentiel de la langue*] is . . . unrelated to the phonic character of the linguistic sign,' and, going beyond the teaching of the master, to declare that the linguistic sign does not necessarily have that phonic character" (p. 19).

On that precise point, it is not a question of "going beyond" the master's teaching but of following and extending it. Not to do it is to cling to what in Chapter VI greatly limits formal and structural research and contradicts the least contestable findings of Saussurian doctrine. To avoid "going beyond," one risks returning to a point that falls short.

I believe that generalized writing is not just the idea of a system to be invented, an hypothetical characteristic or a future possibility. I think on the contrary that oral language already belongs to this writing. But that presupposes a modification of the concept of writing that we for the moment merely anticipate. Even supposing that one is not given that modified concept, supposing that one is considering a system of pure writing as an hypothesis for the future or a working hypothesis, faced with that hypothesis, should a linguist refuse himself the means of thinking it and of integrating its formulation within his theoretical discourse? Does the fact that most linguists do so create a theoretical right? Martinet seems to be of that opinion. After having elaborated a purely "dactylological" hypothesis of language, he writes, in effect:

It must be recognized that the parallelism between this "dactylology" and phonology is complete as much in synchronic as in diachronic material, and that the terminology associated with the latter may be used for the former, except of course when the terms refer to the phonic substance. Clearly, if we do not *desire* to exclude from the domain of linguistics the systems of the type we have just imagined, it is most important to modify traditional terminology relative to the articulation of signifiers so as to eliminate all reference to phonic substance; as does Louis Hjelmslev when he uses "ceneme" and "cenematics" instead of "phoneme" and "phonematics." *Yet it is understandable that the majority of linguists hesitate to modify completely the traditional terminological edifice for the only theoretical advantages of being able to include in the field of their science some purely hypothetical systems. To make them agree to envisage such a revolution*, they must be persuaded that, in attested linguistic systems, they have no advantage in considering the phonic substance of units of expression as to be of direct interest (pp. 20–21; italics added).

Once again, we do not doubt the value of these phonological arguments, the presuppositions behind which I have attempted to expose above. Once one assumes these presuppositions, it would be absurd to reintroduce confusedly a derivative writing, in the area of oral language and within the system of this derivation. Not only would ethnocentrism not be avoided, but all the frontiers within the sphere of its legitimacy would then be confused. It is not a question of rehabilitating writing in the narrow sense, nor of reversing the order of dependence when it is evident. Phonologism does not brook any objections as long as one conserves the colloquial concepts of speech and writing which form the solid fabric of its argumentation. Colloquial and quotidian conceptions, inhabited besides—uncontradictorily enough—by an old history, limited by frontiers that are hardly visible yet all the more rigorous by that very fact.

I would wish rather to suggest that the alleged derivativeness of writing, however real and massive, was possible only on one condition: that the "original," "natural," etc. language had never existed, never been intact and untouched by writing, that it had itself always been a writing. An arche-writing whose necessity and new concept I wish to indicate and outline here; and which I continue to call writing only because it essentially communicates with the vulgar concept of writing. The latter could not have imposed itself historically except by the dissimulation of the arche-writing, by the desire for a speech displacing its other and its double and working to reduce its difference. If I persist in calling that difference writing, it is because, within the work of historical repression, writing was, by its situation, destined to signify the most formidable difference. It threatened the desire for the living speech from the closest proximity, it *breached* living speech from within and from the very beginning. And as we shall begin to see, difference cannot be thought without the *trace.*

This arche-writing, although its concept is *invoked* by the themes of "the arbitrariness of the sign" and of difference, cannot and can never be recognized as the *object of a science.* It is that very thing which cannot let itself be reduced to the form of *presence.* The latter orders all objectivity of the object and all relation of knowledge. That is why what I would be tempted to consider in the development of the *Course* as "progress," calling into question in return the uncritical positions of Chapter VI, never gives rise to a new "scientific" concept of writing.

Can one say as much of the algebraism of Hjelmslev, which undoubtedly drew the most rigorous conclusions from that progress?

The *Principes de grammaire générale* (1928) separated out within the doctrine of the *Course* the phonological principle and the principle of difference: It isolated a concept of *form* which permitted a distinction between formal difference and phonic difference, and this even within "spoken" language (p. 117). Grammar is independent of semantics and phonology (p. 118).

That independence is the very principle of glossematics as the formal science of language. Its formality supposes that "there is no necessary connexion between sounds and language."[20] That formality is itself the condition of a purely functional analysis. The idea of a linguistic function and of a purely linguistic unit—the glosseme—excludes then not only the consideration of the substance of expression (material substance) but also that of the substance of the content (immaterial substance). "Since language is a form and not a substance (Saussure), the glossemes are by definition independent of substance, immaterial (semantic, psychological and logical) and material (phonic, graphic, etc.)."[21] The study of the functioning of language, of its *play,* presupposes that the substance of *meaning* and, among other possible substances, that of *sound,* be placed in parenthesis. The unity of sound and of sense is indeed here, as I proposed above, the reassuring closing of play. Hjelmslev situates his concept of the *scheme* or *play* of language within Saussure's heritage—of Saussure's formalism and his theory of value. Although he prefers to compare linguistic value to the "value of exchange in the economic sciences" rather than to the "purely logico-mathematical value," he assigns a limit to this analogy.

> An economic value is by definition a value with two faces: not only does it play the role of a constant vis-à-vis the concrete units of money, but it also itself plays the role of a variable vis-à-vis a fixed quantity of merchandise which serves it as a standard. In linguistics on the other hand there is nothing that corresponds to a standard. That is why the game of chess and not economic fact remains for Saussure the most faithful image of a grammar. The scheme of language is in the last analysis *a game* and nothing more.[22]

In the *Prolegomera to a Theory of Language* (1943), setting forth the opposition *expression/content,* which he substitutes for the difference *signifier/signified,* and in which each term may be considered from the point of view of *form* or *substance,* Hjelmslev criticizes the idea of a language *naturally* bound to the substance of phonic expression. It is by mistake that it has hitherto been supposed "that the substance-expression of a spoken language should consist of 'sounds':"

Thus, as has been pointed out by the Zwirners in particular, the fact has been overlooked that speech is accompanied by, and that certain components of speech can be replaced by, gesture, and that in reality, as the Zwirners say, not only the so-called organs of speech (throat, mouth, and nose), but very nearly all the striate musculature cooperate in the exercise of "natural" language. Further, it is possible to replace the usual sound-and-gesture substance with any other that offers itself as appropriate under changed external circumstances. Thus the same linguistic form may also be manifested in writing, as happens with a phonetic or phonemic notation and with the so-called phonetic orthographies, as for example the Finnish. Here is a "graphic" substance which is addressed exclusively to the eye and which need not be transposed into a phonetic "substance" in order to be grasped or understood. And this graphic "substance" can, precisely from the point of view of the substance, be of quite various sorts.[23]

Refusing to presuppose a "derivation" of substances following from the substance of phonic expression, Hjelmslev places this problem outside the area of structural analysis and of linguistics.

Moreover it is not always certain what is derived and what not; we must not forget that the discovery of alphabetic writing is hidden in prehistory [n.: Bertrand Russell quite rightly calls attention to the fact that we have no means of deciding whether writing or speech is the older form of human expression (*An Outline of Philosophy* [London, 1927], p. 47)], so that the assertion that it rests on a phonetic analysis is only one of the possible diachronic hypotheses; it may also be rested on a formal analysis of linguistic structure. But in any case, as is recognized by modern linguistics, diachronic considerations are irrelevant for synchronic descriptions (pp. 104–05).

H. J. Uldall provides a remarkable formulation of the fact that glossematic criticism operates at the same time thanks to Saussure and against him; that, as I suggested above, the proper space of a grammatology is at the same time opened and closed by *The Course in General Linguistics.* To show that Saussure did not develop "all the theoretical consequences of his discovery," he writes:

It is even more curious when we consider that the practical consequences have been widely drawn, indeed had been drawn thousands of years before Saussure, for it is only through the concept of a difference between form and substance that we can explain the possibility of speech and writing existing at the same time as expressions of one and the same language. If either of these two substances, the stream of air or the stream of ink, were an integral part of the language itself, it would not be possible to go from one to the other without changing the language.[24]

Undoubtedly the Copenhagen School thus frees a field of research: it becomes possible to direct attention not only to the purity of a form freed from all "natural" bonds to a substance but also to everything that, in the stratification of language, depends on the substance of graphic expression. An original and rigorously delimited description of this may thus be promised. Hjelmslev recognizes that an "analysis of writing without regard to sound has not yet been undertaken" (p. 105). While regretting also that "the substance of ink has not received the same attention on the part of linguists that they have so lavishly bestowed on the substance of air," H. J. Uldall delimits these problems and emphasizes the mutual independence of the substances of expression. He illustrates it particularly by the fact that, in orthography, no grapheme corresponds to accents of pronunciation (for Rousseau this was the misery and the menace of writing) and that, reciprocally, in pronunciation, no phoneme corresponds to the spacing between written words (pp. 13–14).

Recognizing the specificity of *writing*, glossematics did not merely give itself the means of describing the *graphic* element. It showed how to reach the *literary* element, to what in literature passes through an irreducibly graphic text, tying the *play of form* to a determined substance of expression. If there is something in literature which does not allow itself to be reduced to the voice, to epos or to poetry, one cannot recapture it except by rigorously isolating the bond that links *the play of form* to the substance of graphic expression. (It will by the same token be seen that "pure literature," thus respected in its irreducibilty, also risks limiting the play, restricting it. The desire to restrict play is, moreover, irresistible.) This interest in literature is effectively manifested in the Copenhagen School.[25] It thus removes the Rousseauist and Saussurian caution with regard to literary arts. It radicalizes the efforts of the Russian formalists, specifically of the O.PO.IAZ, who, in their attention to the being-literary of literature, perhaps favored the phonological instance and the literary models that it dominates. Notably poetry. That which, within the history of literature and in the structure of a literary text in general, escapes that framework, merits a type of description whose norms and conditions of possibility glossematics has perhaps better isolated. It has perhaps thus better prepared itself to study the purely graphic stratum within the structure of the literary text within the history of the becoming-literary of literality, notably in its "modernity."

Undoubtedly a new domain is thus opened to new and fecund researches. But I am not primarily interested in such a parallelism or such a recaptured parity of substances of expression. It is clear that if the phonic substance lost its privilege, it was not to the advantage of the graphic substance, which lends itself to the same substitutions. To the extent that it liberates and is irrefutable, glossematics still operates with a popular concept of writing. However original and irreducible it might be, the "form of expression" linked by correlation to the *graphic* "substance of expression" remains very determined. It is very dependent and very derivative with regard to the arche-writing of which I speak. This arche-writing would be at work not only in the form and substance of graphic expression but also in those of nongraphic expression. It would constitute not only the pattern uniting form to all substance, graphic or otherwise, but the movement of the *sign-function* linking a content to an expression, whether it be graphic or not. This theme could not have a place in Hjelmslev's system.

It is because arche-writing, movement of differance, irreducible arche-synthesis, opening in one and the same possibility, temporalization as well as relationship with the other and language, cannot, as the condition of all linguistic systems, form a part of the linguistic system itself and be situated as an object in its field. (Which does not mean it has a real field *elsewhere, another* assignable *site*.) Its concept could in no way enrich the scientific, positive, and "immanent" (in the Hjelmslevian sense) description of the system itself. Therefore, the founder of glossematics would no doubt have questioned its necessity, as he rejects, en bloc and legitimately, all the extra-linguistic theories which do not arise from the irreducible immanence of the linguistic system.[26] He would have seen in that notion one of those appeals to experience which a theory should dispense with.[27] He would not have understood why the name writing continued to be used for that X which becomes so different from what has always been called "writing."

I have already begun to justify this word, and especially the necessity of the communication between the concept of arche-writing and the vulgar concept of writing submitted to deconstruction by it. I shall continue to do so below. As for the concept of experience, it is most unwieldy here. Like all the notions I am using here, it belongs to the history of metaphysics and we can only use it under erasure [*sous rature*]. "Experience" has always designated the relationship with a presence, whether that relationship had the form of consciousness or not. At any rate, we must, according to this sort of contortion and contention which the discourse is obliged to undergo, exhaust the resources of the concept of experience before attaining and in order to attain, by deconstruction, its ultimate foundation. It is the only way to escape "empiricism" and the "naive" critiques of experience at the same time. Thus, for example, the experience whose "theory," Hjelmslev says, "must be independent" is not the whole of experience. It always corresponds to a certain type of factual or regional experience (historical, psychological, physiological, sociological, etc.), giving rise to a science that is itself regional and, as such, rigorously outside linguistics. That is not so at all in the case of experience as arche-writing. The parenthesizing of regions of experience or of the totality of natural experience must discover a field of transcendental experience. This experience is only accessible in so far as, after having, like Hjelmslev, isolated the specificity of the linguistic system and excluded all the extrinsic sciences and metaphysical speculations, one asks the question of the transcendental origin of the system itself, as a system of the objects of a science, and, correlatively, of the theoretical system which studies it: here of the objective and "deductive" system which glossematics wishes to be. Without that, the decisive progress accomplished by a formalism respectful of the originality of its object, of "the immanent system of its objects," is plagued by a scientificist objectivism, that is to say by another unperceived or unconfessed metaphysics. This is often noticeable in the work of the Copenhagen School. It is to escape falling back into this naive objectivism that I refer here to a transcendentality that I elsewhere put into question. It is because I believe that there is a short-of and a beyond of transcendental criticism. To see to it that the beyond does not return to the within is to recognize in the contortion the necessity of a pathway [*parcours*]. That pathway must leave a track in the text. Without that track, abandoned to the simple content of its conclusions, the ultra-transcendental text will so closely resemble the precritical text as to be indistingiushable from it. We must now form and meditate upon the law of this resemblance. What I call the erasure of concepts ought to mark the places of that future meditation. For example, the value of the transcendental arche [*archie*] must make its necessity felt before letting itself be erased. The concept of arche-trace must comply with both that necessity and that erasure. It is in fact contradictory and not acceptable within the logic of identity. The trace is not only the disappearance of origin—within the discourse that we sustain and according to the path that we follow it means that the origin did not even disappear, that it was never constituted except reciprocally by a nonorigin, the trace, which thus becomes the origin of the origin. From then on, to wrench the concept of the trace from the classical scheme, which would derive it from a presence or from an originary nontrace and which would make of it an empirical mark, one must indeed speak of an originary trace or arche-trace. Yet we know that that concept destroys its name and that, if all begins with the trace, there is above all no originary trace.[28] We must then *situate*, as a simple *moment of the discourse*, the phenomenological reduction and the Husserlian reference to a transcendental experience. To the extent that the concept of experience in general—and of transcendental experience, in Husserl in particular—remains governed by the theme of presence, it participates in the movement of the reduction of the trace. The Living Present (*lebendige Gegenwart*) is the universal and absolute form of transcendental experience to which Husserl refers us. In the descriptions of the movements of temporalization, all that does not torment the simplicity and the domination of that form seems to indicate to us how much transcendental phenomenology belongs to metaphysics. But that must come to terms with the forces of rupture. In the originary temporalization and the movement of relationship with the outside, as Husserl actually describes them, non-presentation or depresentation is as "originary" as presentation. *That is why a thought of the trace can no more break with a transcendental phenomenology than be reduced to it.* Here as elsewhere, to pose the problem in terms of choice, to oblige or to believe oneself obliged to answer it by a *yes* or *no*, to conceive of appurtenance as an allegiance or nonappurtenance as plain speaking, is to confuse very different levels, paths, and styles. In the deconstruction of the arche, one does not make a choice.

Therefore I admit the necessity of going through the concept of the arche-trace. How does that necessity direct us from the interior of the linguistic system? How does the path that leads from Saussure to Hjelmslev forbid us to avoid the originary trace?

In that its passage through *form* is a passage through the *imprint*. And the meaning of differance in general would be more accsessible to us if the unity of that double passage appeared more clearly.

In both cases, one must begin from the possibility of neutralizing the phonic substance.

On the one hand, the phonic element, the term, the plenitude that is called sensible, would not appear as such without the difference or opposition which gives them *form*. Such is the most evident significance of the appeal to difference as the reduction of phonic substance. Here the appearing and functioning of difference presupposes an originary synthesis not preceded by any absolute simplicity. Such would be the originary trace. Without a retention in the minimal unit of temporal experience, without a trace retaining the other as other in the same, no difference would do its work and no meaning would appear. It is not the question of a constituted difference here, but rather, before all determination of the content, of the *pure* movement which produces difference. *The (pure) trace is differance.* It does not depend on any sensible plentitude, audible or visible, phonic or graphic. It is, on the contrary, the condition of such a plenitude. Although it *does not exist,* although it is never a *being-present* outside of all plenitude, its possibility is by rights anterior to all that one calls sign (signified/signifier, content/expression, etc.), concept or opeartion, motor or sensory. This differance is therefore not more sensible than intelligible and it permits the articulation of signs among themselves within the same abstract order—a phonic or graphic text for example—or between two orders of expression. It permits the articulation of speech and writing—in the colloquial sense—as it founds the metaphysical opposition between the sensible and the intelligible, then between signifier and signified, expression and content, etc. If language were not already, in that sense, a writing, no derived "notation" would be possible; and the classical problem of relationships between speech and writing could not arise. Of course, the positive *sciences* of signification can only describe the *work* and the *fact* of differance, the determined differences and the determined presences that they make possible. There cannot be a science of differance itself in its operation, as it is impossible to have a science of the origin of presence itself, that is to say of a certain nonorigin.

Differance is therefore the formation of form. But it is *on the other hand* the being-imprinted of the imprint. It is well-known that Saussure distinguishes between the "sound-image" and the objective sound (p. 98) [p. 66]. He thus gives himself the right to "reduce," in the phenomenological sense, the sciences of accoustics and physiology at the moment that he institutes the science of language. The sound-image is the structure of the appearing of the sound [*l'apparaître du son*] which is anything but the sound appearing [*le son apparaissant*]. It is the sound-image that he calls *signifier*, reserving the name *signified* not for the thing, to be sure (it is reduced by the act and the very ideality of language), but for the "concept," undoubtedly an unhappy notion here; let us say for the ideality of the sense. "I propose to retain the word *sign* [*signe*] to designate the whole and to replace *concept* and *sound-image* respectively by *signified* [*signifié*] and *signifier* [*signifiant*]." The sound-image is what is *heard*; not the *sound* heard but the being-heard of the sound. Being-heard is structurally phenomenal and belongs to an order radically dissimilar to that of the real sound in the world. One can only divide this subtle but absolutely decisive heterogeneity by a phenomenological reduction. The latter is therefore indispensable to all analyses of being-heard, whether they be inspired by linguistic, psychoanalytic, or other preoccupations.

Now the "sound-image," the structured appearing [*l'apparaître*] of the sound, the "sensory matter" *lived* and *informed* by differance, what Husserl would name the *hylè/morphé* structure, distinct from all mundane reality, is called the "psychic image" by Saussure: "The latter [the sound-image] is not the material sound, a purely physical thing, but the psychic imprint of the sound, the impression that it makes on our senses [*la représentation que nous en donne le témoignage de nos sens*]. The sound-image is sensory, and if I happen to call it 'material,' it is only in that sense, and by way of opposing it, to the other term of the association, the concept, which is generally more abstract" (p. 98) [p. 66]. Although the word "psychic" is not perhaps convenient, except for exercising in this matter a phenomenological caution, the originality of a certain place is well marked.

Before specifying it, let us note that this is not necessarily what Jakobson and other linguists could criticize as "the mentalist point of view":

In the oldest of these approaches, going back to Baudouin de Courtenay and still surviving, the phoneme is a sound imagined or intended, opposed to the emitted sound as a "psychophonetic" phenomenon to the "physiophonetic" fact. It is the psychic equivalent of an exteriorized sound.[29]

Although the notion of the "psychic image" thus defined (that is to say according to a prephenomenological psychology of the imagination) is indeed of this mentalist inspiration, it could be defended against Jakobson's criticism by specifying: (1) that it could be conserved without necessarily affirming that "our internal speech . . . is confined to the distinctive features to the exclusion of the configurative, or redundant features;" (2) that the qualification *psychic* is not retained if it designates exclusively *another natural reality, internal and not external.* Here the Husserlian correction is indispensable and transforms even the premises of the debate. Real (*reell* and not *real*) component of lived experience, the *hylè/morphé* structure is not a reality (*Realität*). As to the intentional object, for example, the content of the image, it does not really (*reall*) belong either to the world or to lived experience: the nonreal component of lived experience. The psychic image of which Saussure speaks must not be an internal reality copying an external one. Husserl, who criticizes this concept of "portrait" in *Ideen* I* shows also in the *Krisis* (pp. 63 f.)† how phenomenology should overcome the naturalist opposition—whereby psychology and the other sciences of man survive—between "internal" and "external" experience. It is therefore indispensable to preserve the distinction between the appearing sound [*le son apparaissant*] and the appearing of the sound [*l'apparaître du son*] in order to escape the worst and the most prevalent of confusions; and it is in principle possible to do it without "attempt[ing] to overcome the antinomy between invariance and variability by assigning the former to the internal and the latter to the external experience" (Jakobson, op. cit., p. 112) [p. 12]. The difference between invariance and variability does not separate the two domains from each other, it divides each of them within itself. That gives enough indication that the essence of the *phonè* cannot be read di-

* *Ideen zu einer reinen Phänomenologie und phänomenologischen Philosophie.* I. Buch, *Gesammelte Werke* (The Hague, 1950), Band 3; *Ideas: General Introduction to Pure Phenomenology*, tr. W. R. Boyce (New York, 1931).

† *Husserliana. Gesammelte Werke*, ed. H. L. van Breda (The Hague, 1950–73), vol. 6.

rectly and primarily in the text of a mundane science, of a psycho-physiophonetics.

These precautions taken, it should be recognized that it is in the specific zone of this imprint and this trace, in the temporalization of a *lived experience* which is neither *in* the world nor in "another world," which is not more sonorous than luminous, not more *in* time than *in* space, that differences appear among the elements or rather produce them, make them emerge as such and constitute the *texts,* the chains, and the systems of traces. These chains and systems cannot be outlined except in the fabric of this trace or imprint. The unheard difference between the appearing and the appearance [*l'apparaissant et l'apparaître*] (between the "world" and "lived experience") is the condition of all other differences, of all other traces, and *it is already a trace.* This last concept is thus absolutely and by rights "anterior" to all *physiological* problematics concerning the nature of the *engramme* [the unit of engraving], or *metaphysical* problematics concerning the meaning of absolute presence whose trace is thus opened to deciphering. *The trace is in fact the absolute origin of sense in general. Which amounts to saying once again that there is no absolute origin of sense in general. The trace is the differance* which opens appearance [*l'apparaître*] and signification. Articulating the living upon the nonliving in general, origin of all repetition, origin of ideality, the trace is not more ideal than real, not more intelligible than sensible, not more a transparent signification than an opaque energy and *no concept of metaphysics can describe it.* And as it is *a fortiori* anterior to the distinction between regions of sensibility, anterior to sound as much as to light, is there a sense in establishing a "natural" hierarchy between the sound-imprint, for example, and the visual (graphic) imprint? The graphic image is not seen; and the acoustic image is not heard. The difference between the full unities of the voice remains unheard. And, the difference in the body of the inscription is also invisible.

The Hinge [La Brisure]

You have, I suppose, dreamt of finding a single word for designating difference and articulation. I have perhaps located it by chance in Robert[*'s Dictionary*] *if I play on the word, or rather indicate its double meaning. This word is* brisure [*joint, break*] *"—broken, cracked part. Cf. breach, crack, fracture, fault, split, fragment,* [brèche, cassure, fracture, faille, fente, fragment.]*—Hinged articulation of two parts of wood- or metal-work. The hinge, the* brisure [*folding-joint*] *of a shutter. Cf.* joint."*—Roger Laporte* (letter)

Origin of the experience of space and time, this writing of difference, this fabric of the trace, permits the difference between space and time to be articulated, to appear as such, in the unity of an experience (of a "same" lived out of a "same" body proper [*corps propre*]). This articulation therefore permits a graphic ("visual" or "tactile," "spatial") chain to be adapted, on occasion in a linear fashion, to a spoken ("phonic," "temporal") chain. It is from the primary possibility of this articulation that one must begin. Difference is articulation.

This is, indeed, what Saussure says, contradicting Chapter VI:

> The question of the vocal apparatus obviously takes a secondary place in the problem of language. One definition of *articulated* language might confirm that conclusion. In Latin, *articulus* means a member, part, or subdivision of a sequence; applied to speech [*langage*], articulation designates either the subdivision of a spoken chain into syllables or the subdivision of the chain of meanings into significant units. . . . Using the second definition, we can say that *what is natural to mankind is not spoken language* but the faculty of constructing a language; i.e., a system of distinct signs corresponding to distinct ideas (p. 26; italics added) [p. 10].

The idea of the "psychic imprint" therefore relates essentially to the idea of articulation. Without the difference between the sensory appearing [*apparaissant*] and its lived appearing [*apparaître*] ("mental imprint"), the temporalizing synthesis, which permits differences to appear in a chain of significations, could not operate. That the "imprint" is irreducible means also that speech is originarily passive, but in a sense of passivity that all intramundane metaphors would only betray. This passivity is also the relationship to a past, to an always-already-there that no reactivation of the origin could fully master and awaken to presence. This impossibility of reanimating absolutely the manifest evidence of an originary presence refers us therefore to an absolute past. That is what authorized us to call *trace* that which does not let itself be summed up in the simplicity of a present. It could in fact have been objected that, in the indecomposable synthesis of temporalization, protection is as indispensable as retention. And their two dimensions are not added up but the one implies the other in a strange fashion. To be sure, what is anticipated in protention does not sever the present any less from its self-identity than does that which is retained in the trace. But if anticipation were privileged, the irreducibility of the always-already-there and the fundamental passivity that is called time would risk effacement. On the other hand, if the trace refers to an absolute past, it is because it obliges us to think a past that can no longer be understood in the form of a modified presence, as a present-past. Since past has always signified present-past, the absolute past that is retained in the trace no longer rigorously merits the name "past." Another name to erase, especially since the strange movement of the trace proclaims as much as it recalls: differance defers-differs [*diffère*]. With the same precaution and under the same erasure, it may be said that its passivity is also its relationship with the "future." The concepts of *present, past,* and *future,* everything in the concepts of time and history which implies evidence of them—the metaphysical concept of time in general—cannot adequately describe the structure of the trace. And deconstructing the simplicity of presence does not amount only to accounting for the horizons of potential presence, indeed of a "dialectic" of protention and retention that one would install in the heart of the present instead of surrounding it with it. It is not a matter of complicating the structure of time while conserving its homogeneity and its fundamental successivity, by demonstrating for example that the past present and the future present constitute originarily, by dividing it, the form of the living present. Such a complication, which is in effect the same that Husserl described, abides, in spite of an audacious phenomenological reduction, by the evidence and presence of a linear, objective, and mundane model. *Now* B would be as such constituted by the retention of *Now* A and the protention of *Now* C; in spite of all the play that would follow from it, from the fact that each one of the three *Now-s* reproduces that structure in itself, this model of successivity would prohibit a *Now* X from taking the place of *Now* A, for example, and would prohibit that, by a delay that is inadmissible to consciousness, an experience be determined, in its very present, by a present which would not have preceded it immediately but would be considerably "anterior" to it. It is the problem of the deferred effect (*Nachträglichkeit*) of which Freud speaks. The temporality to which he refers cannot be that which lends itself to a phenomenology of consciousness or of presence and one may indeed wonder by what right all that is in question here should still be called time, now, anterior present, delay, etc.

In its greatest formality, this immense problem would be formulated thus: is the temporality described by a transcendental phenomenology as "dialectical" as possible, a ground which the structures, let us say the unconscious structures, of temporality would simply modify? Or is the phenomenological model itself constituted, as a warp of language, logic, evidence, fundamental security, upon a woof that is not its own? And which—such is the most difficult problem—is no longer at all mundane? For it is not by chance that the transcendental phenomenology of the internal time-*consciousness*, so careful to place cosmic time within brackets, must, as consciousness and even as internal consciousness, live a time that is an accomplice of the time of the world. Between consciousness, perception (internal or external), and the "world," the rupture, even in the subtle form of the reduction, is perhaps not possible.

It is in a certain "unheard" sense, then, that speech is in the world, rooted in that passivity which metaphysics calls sensibility in general. Since there is no nonmetaphoric language to oppose to metaphors here, one must, as Bergson wished, multiply antagonistic metaphors. "Wish sensibilized," is how Maine de Biran, with a slightly different intention, named the vocalic word. That the logos is first imprinted and that that imprint is the writing-resource of language, signifies, to be sure, that the logos is not a creative activity, the continuous full element of the divine word, etc. But it would not mean a single step outside of metaphysics if nothing more than a new motif of "return to finitude," of "God's death," etc., were the result of this move. It is that conceptuality and that problematics that must be deconstructed. They belong to the onto-theology they fight against. Differance is also something other than finitude.

According to Saussure, the passivity of speech is first its relationship with language. The relationship between passivity and difference cannot be distinguished from the relationship between the fundamental *unconsciousness* of language (as rootedness within the language) and the *spacing* (pause, blank, punctuation, interval in general, etc.) which constitutes the origin of signification. It is because "language is a form and not a substance" (p. 169) [p. 122] that, paradoxically, the activity of speech can and must always draw from it. But if it is a form, it is because "in language there are only differences" (p. 166) [p. 120]. *Spacing* (notice that this word speaks the articulation of space and time, the becoming-space of time and the becoming-time of space) is always the unperceived, the nonpresent, and the nonconscious. *As such*, if one can still use that expression in a nonphenomenological way; for here we pass the very limits of phenomenology. Arche-writing as spacing cannot occur *as such* within the phenomenological experience of a *presence*. It marks *the dead time* within the presence of the living present, within the general form of all presence. The dead time is at work. That is why, once again, in spite of all the discursive resources that the former may borrow from the latter, the concept of the trace will never be merged with a phenomenology of writing. As the phenomenology of the sign in general, a phenomenology of writing is impossible. No intuition can be realized in the place where "the 'whites' indeed take on an importance" (Preface to *Coup de dés*).*

Perhaps it is now easier to understand why Freud says of the dreamwork that it is comparable rather to a writing than to a language, and to a hieroglyphic rather than to a phonetic writing.[30] And to understand why Saussure says of language that it "is not a function of the speaker" (p. 30) [p. 14]. With or without the complicity of their authors, all these propositions must be understood as more than the simple *reversals* of a metaphysics of presence or of conscious subjectivity. Constituting and dislocating it at the same time, writing is other than the subject, in whatever sense the latter is understood. Writing can never be thought under the category of the subject; however it is modified, however it is endowed with consciousness or unconsciousness, it will refer, by the entire thread of its

* *Mallarmé*, tr. Anthony Hartley (Harmondsworth, 1965), p. 209.

history, to the substantiality of a presence unperturbed by accidents, or to the identity of the selfsame [*le propre*] in the presence of self-relationship. And the thread of that history clearly does not run within the borders of metaphysics. To determine an X as a subject is never an operation of a pure convention, it is never an indifferent gesture in relation to writing.

Spacing as writing is the becoming-absent and the becoming-unconscious of the subject. By the movement of its drift/derivation [*dérive*] the emancipation of the sign constitutes in return the desire of presence. That becoming—or that drift/derivation—does not befall the subject which would choose it or would passively let itself be drawn along by it. As the subject's relationship with its own death, this becoming is the constitution of subjectivity. On all levels of life's organization, that is to say, of *the economy of death*. All graphemes are of a testamentary essence.[31] And the original absence of the subject of writing is also the absence of the thing or the referent.

Within the horizontality of spacing, which is in fact the precise dimension I have been speaking of so far, and which is not opposed to it as surface opposes depth, it is not even necessary to say that spacing cuts, drops, and causes to drop within the unconscious: the unconscious is nothing without this cadence and before this caesura. This signification is formed only within the hollow of differance: of discontinuity and of discreteness, of the diversion and the reserve of what does not appear. This hinge [*brisure*] of language as writing, this discontinuity, could have, at a given moment within linguistics, run up against a rather precious *continuist* prejudice. Renouncing it, phonology must indeed renounce all distinctions between writing and the spoken word, and thus renounce not itself, phonology, but rather phonologism. What Jakobson recognizes in this respect is most important for us:

> The stream of oral speech, physically continuous, originally confronted the mathematical theory of communication with a situation "considerably more involved" ([C.E.] Shannon and [W.] Weaver [*The Mathematical Theory of Communication* (Urbana, 1949), pp. 74 f., 112 f.]) than in the case of a finite set of discrete constituents, as presented by written speech. Linguistic analysis, however, came to resolve oral speech into a finite series of elementary informational units. These ultimate discrete units, the so-called "distinctive features," are aligned into simultaneous bundles termed "phonemes," which in turn are concatenated into sequences. Thus form in language has a manifestly granular structure and is subject to a quantal description.[32]

The hinge [*brisure*] marks the impossibility that a sign, the unity of a signifier and a signified, be produced within the plenitude of a present and an absolute presence. That is why there is no full speech, however much one might wish to restore it by means or without benefit of psychoanalysis. Before thinking to reduce it or to restore the meaning of the full speech which claims to be truth, one must ask the question of meaning and of its origin in difference. Such is the place of a problematic of the *trace*.

Why of the *trace*? What led us to the choice of this word? I have begun to answer this question. But this question is such, and such the nature of my answer, that the place of the one and of the other must constantly be in movement. If words and concepts receive meaning only in sequences of differences, one can justify one's language, and one's choice of terms, only within a topic [an orientation in space] and an historical strategy. The justification can therefore never be absolute and definitive. It corresponds to a condition of forces and translates an historical calculation. Thus, over and above those that I have already defined, a certain number of givens belonging to the discourse of our time have progressively imposed this choice upon me. The word *trace* must refer to itself to a certain number of contemporary discourses whose force I intend to take into account. Not that I accept them totally. But the word *trace* establishes the clearest connections with them and thus permits me to dispense with certain developments which have already demonstrated their effectiveness in those fields. Thus, I relate this concept of *trace* to what is at the center of the latest work of Emmanuel Levinas and his critique of ontology:[33] relationship to the illeity as to the alterity of a past that never was and can never be lived in the originary or modified form of presence. Reconciled here to a Heideggerian intention,—as it is not in Levinas's thought—this notion signifies, sometimes beyond Heideggerian discourse, the undermining of an ontology which, in its innermost course, has determined the meaning of being as presence and the meaning of language as the full continuity of speech. To make enigmatic what one thinks one understands by the words "proximity," "immediacy," "presence" (the proximate [*proche*], the own [*propre*], and the pre- of presence), is my final intention in this book. This deconstruction of presence accomplishes itself through the deconstruction of consciousness, and therefore through the irreducible notion of the trace (*Spur*), as it appears in both Nietzschean and Freudian discourse. And finally, in all scientific fields, notably in biology, this notion seems currently to be dominant and irreducible.

If the trace, arche-phenomenon of "memory," which must be thought before the opposition of nature and culture, animality and humanity, etc., belongs to the very movement of signification, then signification is a priori written, whether inscribed or not, in one form or another, in a "sensible" and "spatial" element that is called "exterior." Arche-writing, at first the possibility of the spoken word, then of the "*graphie*" in the narrow sense, the birthplace of "usurpation," denounced from Plato to Saussure, this trace is the opening of the first exteriority in general, the enigmatic relationship of the living to its other and of an inside to an outside: spacing. The outside, "spatial" and "objective" exteriority which we believe we know as the most familiar thing in the world, as familiarity itself, would not appear without the grammè, without differance as temporalization, without the nonpresense of the other inscribed within the sense of the present, without the relationship with death as the concrete structure of the living present. Metaphor would be forbidden. The presence-absence of the trace, which one should not even call its ambiguity but rather its play (for the word "ambiguity" requires the logic of presence, even when it begins to disobey that logic), carries in itself the problems of the letter and the spirit, of body and soul, and of all the problems whose primary affinity I have recalled. All dualisms, all theories of the immortality of the soul or of the spirit, as well as all monisms, spiritualist or materialist, dialectical or vulgar, are the unique theme of a metaphysics whose entire history was compelled to strive toward the reduction of the trace. The subordination of the trace to the full presence summed up in the logos, the humbling of writing beneath a speech dreaming its plenitude, such are the gestures required by an onto-theology determining the archeological and eschatological meaning of being as presence, as parousia, as life without differance: another name for death, historical metonymy where God's name holds death in check. That is why, if this movement begins its era in the form of Platonism, it ends in infinitist metaphysics. Only infinite being can reduce the difference in presence. In that sense, the name of God, at least as it is pronounced within classical rationalism, is the name of indifference itself. Only a positive infinity can lift the trace, "sublimate" it (it has recently been proposed that the Hegelian *Aufhebung* be translated as sublimation; this translation may be of dubious worth as translation, but the juxtaposition is of interest here). We must not therefore speak of a "theological prejudice," functioning sporadically when it is a question of the plenitude of the logos; the logos as the sublimation of the trace is *theological*. Infinitist theologies are always logocentrisms, whether they are creationisms or not. Spinoza himself said of the understanding—or logos—that it was the *immediate* infinite mode of the divine substance, even calling it its eternal son in the *Short Treatise*.* It is also to this epoch, "reaching completion" with Hegel, with a theology of the absolute concept as logos, that all the noncritical concepts accredited by linguistics belong, at least to the extent that linguistics must confirm—and how can a *science* avoid it?—the Saussurian decree marking out "the internal system of language."

It is precisely these concepts that permitted the exclusion of writing: image or representation, sensible and intelligible, nature and culture, nature and technics, etc. They are solidary with all metaphysical conceptuality and particularly with a naturalist, objectivist, and derivative determination of the difference between outside and inside.

* Spinoza, *Short Treatise on God, Man and His Well Being*, tr. A. Wolf (New York, 1967).

And above all with a "vulgar concept of time." I borrow this expression from Heidegger. It designates, at the end of *Being and Time*, a concept of time thought in terms of spatial movement or of the now, and dominating all philosophy from Aristotle's *Physics* to Hegel's *Logic*.[34] This concept, which determines all of classical ontology, was not born out of a philosopher's carelessness or from a theoretical lapse. It is intrinsic to the totality of the history of the Occident, of what unites its metaphysics and its technics. And we shall see it later associated with the linearization of writing, and with the linearist concept of speech. This linearism is undoubtedly inseparable from phonologism; it can raise its voice to the same extent that a linear writing can seem to submit to it. Saussure's entire theory of the "linearity of the signifier" could be interpreted from this point of view.

Auditory signifiers have at their command only the dimension of time. Their elements are presented in succession; they form a chain. This feature becomes readily apparent when they are represented in writing. . . . The signifier, being auditory, is unfolded solely in time from which it gets the following characteristics: (a) it represents a span, and (b) the span is measurable in a single dimension; it is a line.[35]

It is a point on which Jakobson disagrees with Saussure decisively by substituting for the homogeneousness of the line the structure of the musical staff, "the chord in music."[36] What is here in question is not Saussure's affirmation of the temporal essence of discourse but the concept of time that guides this affirmation and analysis: time conceived as linear successivity, as "consecutivity." This model works by itself and all through the *Course*, but Saussure is seemingly less sure of it in the *Anagrams*. At any rate, its value seems problematic to him and an interesting paragraph elaborates a question left suspended:

That the elements forming a word *follow one another* is a truth that it would be better for linguistics not to consider uninteresting because evident, but rather as the truth which gives in advance the central principle of all useful reflections on words. In a domain as infinitely special as the one I am about to enter, it is always by virtue of the fundamental law of the human word in general that a question like that of consecutiveness or nonconsecutiveness may be posed.[37]

This linearist concept of time is therefore one of the deepest adherences of the modern concept of the sign to its own history. For at the limit, it is indeed the concept of the sign itself, and the distinction, however tenuous, between the signifying and signified faces, that remain committed to the history of classical ontology. The parallelism and correspondence of the faces or the planes change nothing. That this distinction, first appearing in Stoic logic, was necessary for the coherence of a scholastic thematics dominated by infinitist theology, forbids us to treat today's debt to it as a contingency or a convenience. I suggested this at the outset, and perhaps the reasons are clearer now. The *signatum* always referred, as to its referent, to a *res*, to an entity created or at any rate first thought and spoken, thinkable and speakable, in the eternal present of the divine logos and specifically in its breath. If it came to relate to the speech of a finite being (created or not; in any case of an intracosmic entity) through the *intermediary* of a *signans*, the *signatum* had an *immediate* relationship with the divine logos which thought it within presence and for which it was not a trace. And for modern linguistics, if the signifier is a trace, the signified is a meaning thinkable in principle within the full presence of an intuitive consciousness. The signfied face, to the extent that it is still originarily distinguished from the signifying face, is not considered a trace; by rights, it has no need of the signifier to be what it is. It is at the depth of this affirmation that the problem of relationships between linguistics and semantics must be posed. This reference to the meaning of a signified thinkable and possible outside of all signifiers remains dependent upon the onto-theo-teleology that I have just evoked. It is thus the idea of the sign that must be deconstructed through a meditation upon writing which would merge, as it must, with the undoing [*sollicitation*]* of onto-theology, faithfully repeating it in its *totality* and *making* it *insecure* in its most assured evidences.[38] One is necessarily led to this from the moment that the trace affects the totality of the sign in both its faces. That the signified is originarily and essentially (and not only for a finite and created spirit) trace, that it is *always already in the position of the signifier*, is the apparently innocent proposition within which the metaphysics of the logos, of presence and consciousness, must reflect upon writing as its death and its resource.

* Derrida comments on this Latinate use of "sollicitation" in "Force et signification," *ED*, p. 13.

3

Of Grammatology as a Positive Science

On what conditions is a grammatology possible? Its fundamental condition is certainly the undoing [*sollicitation*] of logocentrism. But this condition of possibility turns into a condition of impossibility. In fact it risks destroying the concept of science as well. Graphematics or grammatography ought no longer to be presented as sciences; their goal should be exorbitant when compared to grammato*logical knowledge.*

Without venturing up to that perilous necessity, and within the traditional norms of scientificity upon which we fall back provisionally, let us repeat the question; on what conditions is grammatology possible?

On the condition of knowing what writing is and how the plurivocity of this concept is formed. Where does writing begin? When does writing begin? Where and when does the trace, writing in general, common root of speech and writing, narrow itself down into "writing" in the colloquial sense? Where and when does one pass from one writing to another, from writing in general to writing in the narrow sense, from the trace to the *graphie*, from one graphic system to another, and, in the field of a graphic code, from one graphic discourse to another, etc.?

Where and how does it begin . . . ? A question of origin. But a meditation upon the trace should undoubtedly teach us that there is no origin, that is to say simple origin; that the questions of origin carry with them a metaphysics of presence. Without venturing here up to that perilous necessity, continuing to ask questions of origin, we must recognize its two levels. "Where" and "when" may open empirical questions: what, within history and within the world, are the places and the determined moments of the first phenomena of writing? These questions the investigation and research of facts must answer; history in the colloquial sense, what has hitherto been practiced by nearly all archeologists, epigraphists, and prehistorians who have interrogated the world's scripts.

But the question of origin is at first confounded with the question of essence. It may just as well be said that it presupposes an onto-phenomenological question in the strict sense of that term. One must know *what* writing *is* in order to ask—knowing what one is talking about and what *the question is*—where and when writing begins. What is writing? How can it be identified? What certitude of essence must guide the empirical investigation? Guide it in principle, for it is a necessary fact that empirical investigation quickly activates reflexion upon essence.[1] It must operate through "examples," and it can be shown how this impossibility of beginning at the beginning of the straight line, as it is assigned by the logic of transcendental reflexion, refers to the originarity (under erasure) of the trace, to the root of writing. What the thought of the trace has already taught us is that it could not be simply submitted to the onto-phenomenological question of essence. The trace *is nothing*, it is not an entity, it exceeds the question *What is?* and contingently makes it possible. Here one may no longer trust even the opposition of fact and principle, which, in all its metaphysical, ontological, and transcendental forms, has always functioned within the system of *what is*. Without venturing up to the perilous necessity of the question on the arche-question "what is," let us take shelter in the field of grammatological knowledge.

Writing being thoroughly historical, it is at once natural and surprising that the scientific interest in writing has always taken the form of a history of writing. But science also required that a theory of writing should guide the pure description of facts, taking for granted that this last expression has a sense.

Algebra: Arcanum and Transparence

The extent to which the eighteenth century, here marking a break-off point, attempted to comply with these two exigencies, is too often ignored or underestimated. If for profound and systematic reasons, the nineteenth century has left us a heavy heritage of illusions or misunderstandings, all that concerns the theory of the written sign at the end of the seventeenth and during the eighteenth centuries has suffered the consequences.[2]

We must learn to reread what has been thus confused for us. Madeleine V.-David, one of those scholars who, in France, have untiringly kept alive the historical investigations of writing by watching over the philosophical question,[3] has just collected in a valuable work the pieces essential for a dossier: of a debate exciting the passions of all European minds at the end of the seventeenth and all through the eighteenth centuries. A blinding and misunderstood symptom of the crisis of European consciousness. The first plans for a "general history of writing" (Warburton's expression, dating from 1742)[4] were born in a milieu of thought where proper scientific work had constantly to overcome the very thing that moved it: speculative prejudice and ideological presumption. Critical work progresses by stages and its entire strategy can be reconstructed after the fact. It first sweeps away the "*theological*" prejudice; it is thus that Fréret qualifies the myth of a primitive and natural writing given by God, as Hebrew script was for Blaise de Vigenère; in his *Traité des chiffres ou secrètes manières d'escrire* (1586), he says of these characters that they are "the most ancient of all, formed indeed by the Lord God's own finger."* In all its forms, overt or covert, this theologism, which is actually something other and more than prejudice, constituted the major obstacle to all grammatology. No history of writing could come to terms with it. And especially no history of the very script of those whom this theologism blinded: the alphabet, whether Greek or Hebrew. The element of the science of writing had to remain invisible within its history, and especially to those who could perceive the history of other scripts. Thus there is nothing surprising in the fact that the necessary decentering followed the becoming-legible of nonoccidental scripts. The history of the alphabet is accepted only after recognizing the multiplicity of the *systems* of script and after assigning a history to them, whether or not one is in the position to determine it scientifically.

This first decentering is, itself, limited. It is recentered upon ahistorical grounds which, in an analogous way, reconcile the logico-philosophical (blindness to the condition of the logico-philosophical: phonetic writing) and the theological points of view.[5] It is the "*Chinese*" prejudice; all the philosophical projects of a universal script and of a universal language, pasilaly, polygraphy, invoked by Descrates, outlined by Father Kircher, Wilkes,[6] Leibniz, etc., encouraged seeing in the recently discovered Chinese script a model of the philosophical language thus removed from history. Such at any rate is the *function* of the Chinese model in Leibniz's projects. For him what liberates Chinese script from the voice is also that which, arbitrarily and by the artifice of invention, wrenches it from history and gives it to philosophy.

The philosophical exigency that guided Leibniz had been formulated quite a few times before him. Among all who inspired him, Descartes himself comes first. Replying to Mersenne, who had sent him (from a publication unknown to us) an advertisement boasting a system of six propositions for a universal language, Descartes begins by declaring all his distrust.[7] He considers with disdain certain propositions which were, according to him, no more than "sales talk" and "sales pitch." And he has a "bad opinion of the word 'arcanum':" "as soon as I see the word *arcanum* (mystery) in any proposition I begin to suspect it." To this project he opposes arguments that are, one will recall,[8] those of Saussure:

> . . . [the] discordant combinations of letters which would often make the sounds unpleasant and intolerable to the ear. It is to remedy this defect that all the differences in inflexions of words have been introduced by usage; and it is

* Quoted in M. V.-David, op cit., p. 28n.

impossible for your author to have avoided the difficulty while making his grammar universal among different nations; for what is easy and pleasant in our language is coarse and intolerable to Germans, and so on.

This language would, in addition, require that the "primitive words" of all languages be learnt; "this is too burdensome."

Except for communicating them "through writing." And it is an advantage that Descartes does not fail to recognize:

> It is true that if each man uses as primitive words the words of his own language, he will not have much difficulty, but in that case he will be understood only by the people of his own country unless he writes down what he wants to say and the person who wants to understand him takes the trouble to look up all the words in the dictionary; and this is too burdensome to become a regular practice. . . . So the only possible benefit that I see from his invention would be in the case of the written word. Suppose he had a big dictionary printed of all the languages in which he wanted to make himself understood and put for each word a symbol corresponding to the meaning and not to the syllables, a single symbol, for instance, for *aimer*, *amare*, and *philein*: then those who had the dictionary and knew his grammar could translate what was written into their own language by looking up each symbol in turn. But this would be no good except for reading mysteries and revelations; in other cases no-one who had anything better to do would take the trouble to look up all these words in a dictionary. So I do not see that all this has much use. Perhaps I am wrong.

And with a profound irony, more profound perhaps than ironical, Descartes opines that error may also result through a possible cause other than non-self-evidence, failure of attention, or an over-hasty will: a *fault of reading*. The value of a system of language or writing is not measured by the yardstick of intuition, of the clarity or the distinction of the idea, or of the presence of the object as evidence. The system must itself be *deciphered*:

> Perhaps I am wrong; I just wanted to write to you all I could conjecture on the basis of the six propositions which you sent me. When you have seen the system, you will be able to say if I worked it out correctly [*déchiffrée*].

The profundity draws the irony further than it would go if it merely *followed its author*. Further perhaps than the foundation of Cartesian certitude.

After which, in the form of note and postscript, Descartes defines the Leibnizian project very simply. It is true that he sees the story of philosophy there; only philosophy may write it, for philosophy depends on it totally, but by the same token, it can never hope "to see such a language in use."

The discovery of such a language depends upon the true philosophy. For without that philosophy it is impossible to number and order all the thoughts of men or even to separate them out into clear and simple thoughts, which in my opinion is the great secret for acquiring true scientific knowledge. . . . I think it is possible to invent such a language and to discover the science on which it depends: it would make [even] peasants better judges of the truth about the world than philosophers are now. But do not hope ever to see such a language in use. For that, the order of nature would have to change so that the world turned into a terrestial paradise; and that is too much to suggest outside of fairyland.[9]

Leibniz expressly refers to this letter and to the *analytical* principle it formulates. The entire project implies the decomposition into simple ideas. It is the only way to substitute calculation for reasoning. In that sense, the universal characteristic depends on philosophy for its principle but it may be undertaken without waiting for the completion of philosophy:

However, although this language depends on the true philosophy, it does not depend on its perfection. In other words, this language can be established even if philosophy is not perfect; and as man's knowledge grows, this language will grow as well. Meanwhile it will be a great help—for using what we know, for finding out what we lack, for inventing ways of redeeming the lack, but especially for settling controversies in matters that depend on reasoning. For then reasoning and calculating will be the same thing.[10]

To be sure, these are not the only corrections of the Cartesian tradition. Descartes's analyticism is intuitionist, that of Leibniz points beyond manifest evidence, toward order, relation, point of view.[11]

The characteristic economizes on the spirit and the imagination, whose expense must always be husbanded. It is the principal goal of this great science that I am used to calling *Characteristic*, of which what we call Algebra, or Analysis, is only a small branch; for it is this science that gives speech to languages, letters to speech, numbers to arithmetic, notes to music; it teaches us the secret of stabilizing reasoning, and of obliging it to leave visible marks on the paper in a little volume, to be examined at leisure: finally, it makes us reason at little cost, putting characters in the place of things in order to ease the imagination.[12]

In spite of all the differences that separate the projects of universal language or writing at this time (notably with respect to history and language),[13] the concept of the simple absolute is always necessarily and indispensably involved. It would be easy to show that it always leads to an infinitist theology and to the logos or the infinite understanding of God.[14] That is why, appearances to the contrary, and in spite of all the seduction that it can legitimately exercise on our epoch, the Leibnizian project of a universal characteristic that is not essentially phonetic does not interrupt logocentrism in any way. On the contrary, universal logic confirms logocentrism, is produced within it and with its help, exactly like the Hegelian critique to which it will be subjected. I emphasize the complicity of these two contradictory movements. Within a certain historical epoch, there is a profound unity among infinitist theology, logocentrism, and a certain technicism. The originary and pre- or meta-phonetic writing that I am attempting to conceive of here leads to nothing less than an "overtaking" of speech by the machine.

In an original and non-"relativist" sense, logocentrism is an ethnocentric metaphysics. It is related to the history of the West. The Chinese model only apparently interrupts it when Leibniz refers to it to teach the Characteristic. Not only does this model remain a domestic representation,[15] but also, it is praised only for the purpose of designating a lack and to define the necessary corrections. What Leibniz is eager to borrow from Chinese writing is its arbitrariness and therefore its independence with regard to history. This arbitrariness has an essential link with the nonphonetic essence which Leibniz believes he can attribute to Chinese writing. The latter seems to have been "invented by a deaf man" (*New Essays*):

Loqui est voce articulata signum dare cogitationis suae. *Scribere* est id facere permanentibus, in charta ductibus. Quos ad vocem referri non est necesse, ut apparet ex Sinensium characteribus (*Opuscules*, p. 497).*

Elsewhere:

There are perhaps some artificial languages which are wholly of choice and entirely arbitrary, as that of China is believed to have been, or as those of George Dalgarno and the late Mr. Wilkins, bishop of Chester.[16]

In a letter to Father Bouvet (1703), Leibniz is bent on distinguishing the Egyptian, popular, sensory, allegorical writing from the Chinese, philosophical, and intellectual writing:

. . . Chinese characters are perhaps more philosophical and seem to be built upon more intellectual considerations, such as are given by numbers, orders, and relations; thus there are only detached strokes that do not culminate in some resemblances to a sort of body.

This does not prevent Leibniz from promising a script for which the Chinese would be only a blueprint:

This sort of plan would at the same time yield a sort of universal script, which would have the advantages of the Chinese script, for each person would understand it in his own language, but which would infinitely surpass the Chinese,

* Speech is to give the sign of one's thought with an articulated voice. Writing is to do it with permanent characters on paper. The latter need not be referred back to the voice, as is obvious from the characters of the Chinese script.

in that it would be teachable in a few weeks, having characters perfectly linked according to the order and connection of things, whereas, since Chinese script has an infinite number of characters according to the variety of things, it takes the Chinese a lifetime to learn their script adequately.[17]

The concept of Chinese writing thus functioned as a sort of European hallucination. This implied nothing fortuitous: this functioning obeyed a rigorous necessity. And the hallucination translated less an ignorance than a misunderstanding. It was not disturbed by the knowledge of Chinese script, limited but real, which was then available.

At the same time as the "Chinese prejudice," a "*hieroglyphist prejudice*" had produced the same effect of interested blindness. The occultation, far from proceeding, as it would seem, from ethnocentric scorn, takes the form of an hyperbolical admiration. We have not finished verifying the necessity of this pattern. Our century is not free from it; each time that ethnocentrism is precipitately and ostentatiously reversed, some effort silently hides behind all the spectacular effects to consolidate an inside and to draw from it some domestic benefit. The astonishing Father Kircher thus devoted his entire genius to opening the West to Egyptology,[18] but the very excellence that he recognized in a "sublime" script forbade any scientific deciphering of it. Evoking the *Prodromus coptus sive aegyptiacus* (1636), M. V.-David writes:

This work is, in some of its parts, the first manifesto of Egyptological research, since in it the author determines the *nature of the ancient Egyptian language* —the instrument of discovery having been furnished him from elsewhere.* The same book however pushes aside all projects of deciphering the hieroglyphs. * cf. *Lingua aegyptiaca restituta*.[19]

Here the process of nonrecognition through assimilation is not, as in Leibniz, of a rationalistic and calculating kind. It is mystical:

According to the *Prodromus*, hieroglyphs are indeed a script, but not a script composed of letters, words, and determined parts of speech that we generally use. They are a far finer and more sublime script, closer to abstractions, which, by an ingenious linking of symbols, or its equivalent, proposes *at once* (*uno intuitu*) to the intelligence of the scholar a complex reasoning, elevated notions, or some mysterious insignia hidden in the breast of nature or the Divinity.[20]

Between rationalism and mysticism there is, then, a certain complicity. The writing of the other is each time invested with a domestic outline. What one might, following Bachelard, call an "epistemological breach," is brought about above all by Fréret and Warburton. One can make out the laborious process of disentanglement by which both prepared their decision, the former using the Chinese and the latter the Egyptian example.

With much respect for Leibniz and the project for a universal script, Fréret cuts to pieces the representation of the Chinese script that is implied therein: "Chinese script is indeed not a philosophical language which leaves nothing to be desired. . . . The Chinese have never had anything like it."[21]

But, for all that, Fréret is not free of the hieroglyphist prejudice, which Warburton destroys by violently criticizing Father Kircher.[23] The apologetic purpose that animates this critique does not make it ineffectual.

It is in the theoretical field thus liberated that the scientific techniques of deciphering were perfected by the Abbé Barthélemey and then by Champollion. Then a systematic reflection upon the correspondence between writing and speech could be born. The greatest difficulty was already to conceive, in a manner at once historical and systematic, the organized cohabitation, within the same graphic code, of figurative, symbolic, abstract, and phonetic elements.[24]

Science and the Name of Man

Had grammatology entered upon the assured path of a science? To be sure, techniques of deciphering went on progressing at an accelerated pace.[25] But the general histories of writing, wherein devotion to systematic classification always oriented simple description, were to be governed for a long time by theoretical concepts that are clearly not commensurate with the great discoveries—discoveries that should have shaken the most assured foundations of our philosophical conceptuality, entirely commanded by a situation determined by the relationships between logos and writing. All the great histories of writing open with an exposition of a classificatory and systematic project. But today one could transpose to the domain of writing what Jakobson says of languages since Schlegel's typological attempts:

> . . . questions of typology retained a speculative, pre-scientific character for a long time. While genetic grouping of languages made amazing progress, the time was not yet ripe for their typological classification. (op. cit. p. 69) *

A systematic critique of the concepts used by historians of writing can seriously blame the rigidity or the insufficient differentiation of a theoretical apparatus only if it first locates the false evidence that guides the work. Evidence all the more efficacious because it belongs to the deepest, the oldest, and apparently the most natural, the least historical layer of our conceptuality, that which best eludes criticism, and especially because it

* English original, "Typological Studies and Their Contribution to Historical Comparative Linguistics," *Proceedings of the Eighth International Congress of Linguists* (Oslo, 1958), p. 18.

supports that criticism, nourishes it, and informs it; our historical ground itself.

In all histories or general typologies of writing may be encountered a concession analogous to the one that made Father Berger, author, in France, of the first big *Histoire de l'écriture dans l'antiquité* (1892), say: "Most often the facts do not conform to the distinctions which . . . are only exact in theory" (p. XX). Yet, the issue was nothing less than the distinctions between phonetic and ideographic, syllabic and alphabetic, scripts, between image and symbol, etc. The same may be said of the instrumentalist and technicist concepts of writing, inspired by the phonetic model which it does not conform to except through a teleological illusion, and which the first contact with nonoccidental scripts ought to have demolished. This instrumentalism is implicit everywhere. Nowhere is it as systematically formulated, with all the attendant consequences, as by Marcel Cohen: Language being an "instrument," writing is the "extension to an instrument."[26] The exteriority of writing to speech, of speech to thought, of the signifier to the signified in general, could not be described better. There is much food for thought in the matter of the price thus paid by a linguistics—or by a grammatology—which, in this case, professes to be Marxist, to the metaphysical tradition. But the same tribute may be identified everywhere: logocentric teleology (a pleonastic expression); opposition between nature and institution; play of differences between symbol, sign, image, etc., a naive concept of representation; an uncritical opposition between sensible and intelligible, between soul and body; an objectivist concept of the body proper [*corps propre*] and of the diversity of sensory functions (the "five senses" considered as so many apparatuses at the disposition of the speaker or writer); opposition between analysis and synthesis, abstract and concrete, which plays a decisive role in the classifications proposed by Février and Cohen and in the debate that opposes them; a concept of the concept upon which the most classical philosophic reflection has left little mark; a reference to consciousness and to the unconscious which would necessarily invoke a more vigilant use of these notions and some consideration for those studies that make these notions their theme;[27] a notion of the sign that philosophy, linguistics, and semiology illuminate rarely and feebly. The competition between the history of writing and the science of language is sometimes experienced in terms of hostility rather than collaboration. Supposing, of course, that the competition is admitted. Thus, a propos of the great distinction operated by Février between "synthetic writing" and "analytic writing," as also a propos of the "word" which plays for him a central role, the author notes: "The problem is of the order of linguistics, we shall not deal with it here" (op. cit., p. 49). Elsewhere, the noncommunication with linguistics is justified by Février in these terms:

[Mathematics] is a special language which no longer has any relationship with language, it is a sort of universal language, that is to say we ascertain through mathematics that language—vengeance upon linguists—is absolutely incapable of accommodating certain forms of modern thought. And at present it is writing, so badly misunderstood, that takes the place of language, after having been its servant (*EP*, p. 349).

It can be shown that these presuppositions and all the oppositions thus accredited form a system: we circulate from one to the other within the same structure.

Not only does the theory of writing need an intrascientific and epistemological liberation, analogous to the one brought about by Fréret and Warburton, without touching the layers of which we speak there. Now a reflection must clearly be undertaken, within which the "positive" discovery and the "deconstruction" of the history of metaphysics, in all its concepts, are controlled reciprocally, minutely, laboriously. Without this, any epistemological liberation would risk being illusory or limited, proposing merely practical conveniences or notional simplifications on bases that are untouched by criticism. Such is undoubtedly the limitation of the remarkable enterprise of I. J. Gelb (op. cit.); in spite of immense progress and the project of erecting a grammatological scientificity and creating a unified system of simple, supple, and manageable notions, in spite of the exclusion of inadequate concepts—such as of the ideogram—most of the conceptual oppositions that I have just cited continue to function there securely.

Through all the recent work in the area, one glimpses the future extensions of a grammatology called upon to stop receiving its guiding concepts from other human sciences or, what nearly always amounts to the same thing, from traditional metaphysics. A grammatology may be surmised through the wealth and novelty of information, as well as through the treatment of this information, even if, in these pioneering works, the conceptualization often falls short of a bold and confident thrust.

What seems to announce itself now is, on the one hand, that grammatology must not be one of the *sciences of man* and, on the other hand, that it must not be just one *regional science* among others.

It ought not to be *one of the sciences of man*, because it asks first, as its characteristic question, the question of the *name of man*. To free unity from the concept of man is undoubtedly to renounce the old notion of peoples said to be "without writing" and "without history." André Leroi-Gourhan shows it well; to refuse the name of man and the ability to write beyond its own proper community, is one and the same gesture. Actually, the peoples said to be "without writing" lack only a certain type of writing. To refuse the name of writing to this or that technique of consignment is the "ethnocentrism that best defines the prescientific vision of man" and at the same time results in the fact that "in many human groups, the only word by which the members designate their ethnic group is the word 'man'." (*GP* 11, pp. 32 and passim)

But it is not enough to denounce ethnocentrism and to define anthropological unity by the disposition of writing. Leroi-Gourhan no longer describes the unity of man and the human adventure thus by the simple possibility of the *graphie* in general; rather as a stage or an articulation in the history of life—of what I have called differance—as the history of the *grammè*. Instead of having recourse to the concepts that habitually serve to distinguish man from other living beings (instinct and intelligence, absence or presence of speech, of society, of economy, etc. etc.), the notion of *program* is invoked. It must of course be understood in the cybernetic sense, but cybernetics is itself intelligible only in terms of a history of the possibilities of the trace as the unity of a double movement of protention and retention. This movement goes far beyond the possibilities of the "intentional consciousness." It is an emergence that makes the *grammè* appear *as such* (that is to say according to a new structure of nonpresence) and undoubtedly makes possible the emergence of the systems of writing in the narrow sense. Since "genetic inscription" and the "short programmatic chains" regulating the behavior of the amoeba or the annelid up to the passage beyond alphabetic writing to the orders of the logos and of a certain *homo sapiens*, the possibility of the *grammè* structures the movement of its history according to rigorously original levels, types, and rhythms.[28] But one cannot think them without the most general concept of the *grammè*. That is irreducible and impregnable. If the expression ventured by Leroi-Gourhan is accepted, one could speak of a "liberation of memory," of an exteriorization always already begun but always larger than the trace which, beginning from the elementary programs of so-called "instinctive" behavior up to the constitution of electronic card-indexes and reading machines, enlarges differance and the possibility of putting in reserve: it at once and in the same movement constitutes and effaces so-called conscious subjectivity, its logos, and its theological attributes.

The history of writing is erected on the base of the history of the *grammè* as an adventure of relationships between the face and the hand. Here, by a precaution whose schema we must constantly repeat, let us specify that the history of writing is not explained by what we believe we know of the face and the hand, of the glance, of the spoken word, and of the gesture. We must, on the contrary, disturb this familiar knowledge, and awaken a meaning of hand and face in terms of that history. Leroi-Gourhan describes the slow transformation of manual motricity which frees the audio-phonic system for speech, and the glance and the hand for writing.[29] In all these descriptions, it is difficult to avoid the mechanist, technicist, and teleological language at the very moment when it is precisely a question of retrieving the origin and the possibility of movement, of the machine, of the *technè*, of orientation in general. In fact, it is not difficult, it is essentially impossible. And this is true of all discourse. From one discourse to another, the difference lies only in the mode of inhabiting the interior of a conceptuality destined, or already submitted, to decay. Within that conceptuality or already without it, we must attempt to recapture the unity of gesture and speech, of body and language, of tool and thought, before the originality of the one and the other is articulated and without letting this profound unity give rise to confusionism. These original significations must not be confused *within the orbit* of the system where they are opposed. But to think the history of the system, its meaning and value must, in an *exorbitant* way, be somewhere exceeded.

This representation of the *anthropos* is then granted: a precarious balance linked to manual-visual script.[30] This balance is slowly threatened. It is at least known that "no major change" giving birth to "a man of the future" who will no longer be a "man," "can be easily produced without the loss of the hand, the teeth, and therefore of the upright position. A toothless humanity that would exist in a prone position using what limbs it had left to push buttons with, is not completely inconceivable."[31]

What always threatens this balance is confused with the very thing that broaches the *linearity* of the symbol. We have seen that the traditional concept of time, an entire organization of the world and of language, was bound up with it. Writing in the narrow sense—and phonetic writing above all—is rooted in a past of nonlinear writing. It had to be defeated, and here one can speak, if one wishes, of technical success; it assured a greater security and greater possibilities of capitalization in a dangerous and anguishing world. But that was not done *one single time*. A war was declared, and a suppression of all that resisted linearization was installed. And first of what Leroi-Gourhan calls the "mythogram," a writing that spells its symbols pluri-dimensionally; there the meaning is not subjected to successivity, to the order of a logical time, or to the irreversible temporality of sound. This pluri-dimensionality does not paralyze history within simultaneity, it corresponds to another level of historical experience, and one may just as well consider, conversely, linear thought as a reduction of history. It is true that another word ought perhaps to be used; the word history has no doubt always been associated with a linear scheme of the unfolding of presence, where the line relates the final presence to the orignary presence according to the straight line or the circle. For the same reason, the pluri-dimensional symbolic structure is not given within the category of the simultaneous. Simultaneity coordinates two absolute presents, two points or instants of presence, and it remains a linearist concept.

The concept of *linearization* is much more effective, faithful, and intrinsic than those that are habitually used for classifying scripts and describing their history (pictogram, ideogram, letter, etc.). Exposing more than one prejudice, particularly about the relationship between ideogram and pictogram, about so-called graphic "realism," Leroi-Gourhan recalls the unity, within the mythogram, of all the elements of which linear writing marks the disruption: technics (particularly graphics), art, religion, economy. To recover the access to this unity, to this other structure of unity, we must de-sediment "four thousand years of linear writing."[32]

The linear norm was never able to impose itself absolutely for the very reasons that intrinsically circumscribed graphic phoneticism. We now know them; these limits came into being at the same time as the possibility of what they limited, they opened what they finished and we have already named them: discreteness, differance, spacing. The production of the linear norm thus emphasized these limits and marked the concepts of symbol and language. The process of linearization, as Leroi-Gourhan describes it on a very vast historical scale, and the Jakobsonian critique of Saussure's linearist concept, must be thought of together. The "line" represents only a particular model, whatever might be its privilege. This model *has become* a model and, as a model, it remains inaccessible. If one allows that the linearity of language entails this vulgar and mundane concept of temporality (homogeneous, dominated by the form of the now and the ideal of continuous movement, straight or circular) which Heidegger shows to be the intrinsic determining concept of all ontology from Aristotle to Hegel, the meditation upon writing and the deconstruction of the history of philosophy become inseparable.

The enigmatic model of the *line* is thus the very thing that philosophy could not see when it had its eyes open on the interior of its own history. This night begins to lighten a little at the moment when linearity—which is not loss or absence but the repression of pluri-dimensional[33] symbolic thought—relaxes its oppression because it begins to sterilize the technical and scientific economy that it has long favored. In fact for a long time its possibility has been structurally bound up with that of economy, of technics, and of ideology. This solidarity appears in the process of thesaurization, capitalization, sedentarization, hierarchization, of the formation of ideology by the class that writes or rather commands the scribes.[34] Not that the massive reappearance of nonlinear writing interrupts this structural solidarity; quite the contrary. But it transforms its nature profoundly.

The end of linear writing is indeed the end of the book,[35] even if, even today, it is within the form of a book that new writings—literary or theoretical—allow themselves to be, for better or for worse, encased. It is less a question of confiding new writings to the envelope of a book than of finally reading what wrote itself between the lines in the volumes. That is why, beginning to write without the line, one begins also to reread past writing according to a different organization of space. If today the problem of reading occupies the forefront of science, it is because of this suspense between two ages of writing. Because we are beginning to write, to write differently, we must reread differently.

For over a century, this uneasiness has been evident in philosophy, in science, in literature. All the revolutions in these fields can be interpreted as shocks that are gradually destroying the linear model. Which is to say the *epic* model. What is thought today cannot be written according to the line and the book, except by imitating the operation implicit in teaching modern mathematics with an abacus. This inadequation is not *modern*, but it is exposed today better than ever before. The access to pluridimensionality and to a delinearized temporality is not a simple regression toward the "mythogram;" on the contrary, it makes all the rationality subjected to the linear model appear as another form and another age of mythography. The meta-rationality or the meta-scientificity which are thus announced within the meditation upon writing can therefore be no more shut up within a science of man than conform to the traditional idea of science. In one and the same gesture, they leave *man*, *science*, and the *line* behind.

Even less can this meditation be contained within the limits of a *regional science*.

The Rebus and the Complicity of Origins

Were it a graphology. And even a graphology renewed and fertilized by sociology, history, ethnography, and psychoanalysis.

> Since individual markings reveal the particularities of the mind of those who write, the national markings should permit to a certain extent researches into the particularities of the collective mind of peoples.[36]

Such a cultural graphology, however legitimate its project might be, can come into being and proceed with some certitude only when the more general and fundamental problems have been elucidated; as to the articulation of an individual and a collective *graphie*, of the graphic "discourse"—so to speak—and the graphic "code," considered not from the point of view of the intention of signification or of denotation, but of style and connotation; problems of the articulation of graphic forms and of diverse substances, of the diverse forms of graphic substances (materials: wood, wax, skin, stone, ink, metal, vegetable) or instruments (point, brush, etc., etc.); as to the articulation of the technical, economic, or historical levels (for example, at the moment when a graphic *system* is constituted and at the moment, which is not necessarily the same, when a graphic *style* is fixed); as to the limit and the sense of variations in style within the system; as to all the investitures to which a *graphie*, in form and substance, is submitted.

From this latter point of view, a certain privilege should be given to research of the psychoanalytic type. In as much as it touches the originary constitution of objectivity and of the value of the object—the constitution of *good* and *bad* objects as categories that do not allow themselves to be derived from a *theoretical* formal ontology and from a science of the objectivity of the object in general—psychoanalysis is not a simple regional science, although, as its name indicates, it is presented under the heading of psychology. That it adheres to this title is certainly not a matter of indifference and hints at a certain state of criticism and epistemology. Nevertheless, even if psychoanalysis did not achieve the transcendentality—under erasure—of the arche-trace, even if it remained a mundane science, its generality would have a controlling meaning with regard to all local science. Here I am quite obviously thinking of researches of the type undertaken by Melanie Klein. An example of it may be found in the essay on "*The Role of the School in the Libidinal Development of the Child*"[37] which evokes, from the clinical point of view, all the investments with which the operations of reading and writing, the production and management of the number, etc., are charged. To the extent that the constitution of ideal objectivity must essentially pass through the written signifier,[38] no theory of this constitution has the right to neglect the investments of writing. These investments not only retain an opacity in the ideality of the object, but permit the liberation of that ideality. It gives the force without which an objectivity in general would not be possible. I do not dissimulate the gravity of such an affirmation and the immense difficulty of the task thus assigned to both the theory of objectivity and psychoanalysis. But the necessity is commensurate with the difficulty.

It is in his very work that the historian of writing encounters this necessity. His problems cannot be grasped except at the root of all sciences. Reflection on the essence of mathematics, politics, economics, religion, technology, law, etc., communicates most intimately with the reflection upon and the information surrounding the history of writing. The continuous vein that circulates through all these fields of reflection and constitutes their fundamental unity is the problem of the phoneticization of writing. This phoneticization has a history, no script is absolutely exempt from it, and the enigma of this evolution does not allow itself to be dominated by the concept of history. To be sure, the latter appears at a determined moment in the phoneticization of script and it presupposes phoneticization in an essential way.

On this subject, what does the most massive, most recent, and least contestable information teach us? First, that for structural or essential reasons, a purely phonetic writing is impossible and has never finished reducing the nonphonetic. The distinction between phonetic and nonphonetic writing, although completely indispensable and legitimate, remains very derivative with regard to what may be called a synergy and a fundamental synesthesia. It follows that not only has phoneticization never been omnipotent but also that it has always already begun to undermine the mute signifier. "Phonetic" and "nonphonetic" are therefore never pure qualities of certain systems of writing, they are the abstract characteristics of typical elements, more or less numerous and dominant within all systems of signification in general. Their importance owes less to their quantitative distribution than to their structural organization. The cuneiform, for example, is at the same time ideogrammatic and phonetic. And, indeed, one cannot say that each graphic signifier belongs to such and such a class, the cuneiform code playing alternately on two registers. In fact, each graphic form may have a *double value*—ideographic and phonetic. And its phonetic value can be simple or complex. The same signifier may have one or various phonic values, it may be *homophonic* or *polyphonic*. To this general complexity of the system is added yet another subtle recourse to categorical determinatives, to phonetic complements useless in reading, to a very irregular punctuation. And Labat shows that it is impossible to understand the system without going through its history.[39]

This is true of all systems of writing and does not depend upon what is sometimes hastily considered to be levels of elaboration. Within the structure of a pictographic tale for example, a representation-of-a-thing, such as a totemic blazon, may take the symbolic value of a proper name. From that moment on, it can function as apellation within other series with a phonetic value.[40] Its stratification may thus become very complex and go beyond the empirical *consciousness* linked to their immediate usage. Going beyond this real consciousness, the structure of this signifier may continue to operate not only on the fringes of the potential consciousness but according to the causality of the unconscious.

Thus the name, especially the so-called proper name, is always caught in a chain or a system of differences. It becomes an appellation only to the extent that it may inscribe itself within a figuration. Whether it be linked by its origin to the representations of things in space or whether it remains caught in a system of phonic differences or social classifications apparently released from ordinary space, the proper-ness of the name does not escape spacing. Metaphor shapes and undermines the proper name. The literal [*propre*] meaning does not exist, its "appearance" is a necessary function—and must be analyzed as such—in the system of differences and metaphors. The absolute parousia of the literal meaning, as the presence to the self of the logos within its voice, in the absolute hearing-itself-speak, should be *situated* as a function responding to an indestructible but relative necessity, within a system that encompasses it. That amounts to *situating* the metaphysics or the ontotheology of the logos.

The problem of the picture-puzzle (*rébus à transfert*) brings together all the difficulties. As pictogram, a representation of the thing may find itself endowed with a phonetic value. This does not efface the "pictographic" reference which, moreover, has never been simply "realistic." The signifier is broken or constellated into a system: it refers at once, and at least, to a thing and to a sound. The thing is itself a collection of things or a chain of differences "in space;" the sound, which is also inscribed within a chain, may be a word; the inscription is then ideogrammatical or synthetic, it cannot be decomposed; but the sound may also be an atomic element itself entering into the composition: we are dealing then with a script apparently pictographic and in fact phonetico-analytical in the same way as the alphabet. What is now known of the writing of the Aztecs of Mexico seems to cover all these possibilities.

Thus the proper name *Teocaltitlan* is broken into several syllables, rendered by the following images: lips (*tentli*), road (*otlim*), house (*calli*), and finally tooth (*tlanti*). The procedure is closely bound up with that . . . of suggesting the name of a person by images of the beings or things that go into the making of his name. The Aztecs achieved a greater degree of phoneticism. By having recourse to a truly phonetic analysis, they succeeded in rendering separate sounds through images.[41]

The work of Barthel and Knorosov* on the Mayan glyphs do not lead to harmonious results, their progress remains very slow, but the presence of phonetic elements now seems almost certain. And the same is true of the writing of the Easter Islands.[42] Not only is the latter picto-ideo-phonographic, but in the very interior of its non-phonetic structures, equivocity and overdetermination can give rise to metaphors taken over by a true *graphic rhetoric*, if this absurd expression may be risked.

We shall now discover the complexity of this structure in the so-called "primitive" scripts and in cultures believed "without writing." But we have known for a long time that largely nonphonetic scripts like Chinese or Japanese included phonetic elements very early. They remained structurally dominated by the ideogram or algebra and we thus have the testimony of a powerful movement of civilization developing outside of all logocentrism. Writing did not reduce the voice to itself, it incorporated it into a system:

This script had more or less recourse to phonetic borrowings, certain signs being used for their sound independently of their original meaning. But this phonetic

* For Thomas S. Barthel, see note 42. Among the many works by Ju. V. Knorozov on the Maya script are Kratkie itogi izucenija dervnej pis'-mennosti Majja v Sovetskom sojuze: . . ./ *A Short Survey of the Study of the Ancient Maya script of the Soviet Union/ Ceskoslavenska* Etnografie (Praha) IV, 1956, 309 C. Loukotka; "New Data on the Mayan Written Language," *Journal de la Société des Americanistes*, Nouvelle série (Paris, 1956), pp. 209–17; "Le Problème du déchiffrement de l'écriture maya," *Diogène* 40 (1962): 121–28.

use of signs could never become extensive enough to corrupt Chinese writing in principle and lead it onto the path of phonetic notation. . . . Writing in China, never having *reached* a phonetic analysis of language, was never felt to be a more or less faithful transference [*décalque*] of speech, and that is why the graphic sign, symbol of a reality singular and unique like itself, has retained much of its primitive prestige. There is no reason for believing that *in antiquity* speech in China had not the same efficaciousness as writing, but it was possible for its power to have been partly *eclipsed* by writing. On the contrary, in civilizations where writing evolved toward syllabification and the alphabet early enough, it is the word which concentrated in itself, definitively, all the powers of religious and magical creation. And in fact it is remarkable that in China this strange valorization of speech, word, syllable, or vowel, attested in all great ancient civilizations from the Mediterranean basin to India, is not encountered.[43]

It is difficult not to subscribe to this analysis globally. Let us note, however, that it seems to consider "the phonetic analysis of language" and phonetic writing as a normal "outcome," as an historical telos *within sight* of which, like a ship steering to port, Chinese script had to an extent run aground. Can it be thought that the system of Chinese script is thus a sort of unfulfilled alphabet? On the other hand, Gernet seems to explain the "primitive prestige" of Chinese graphism by its "symbolic" relationship with a "reality singular and unique like itself." Is it not evident that no signifier, whatever its substance and form, has a "unique and singular reality?" A signifier is from the very beginning the possibility of its own repetition, of its own image or resemblance. It is the condition of its ideality, what identifies it as signifier, and makes it function as such, relating it to a signified which, for the same reasons, could never be a "unique and singular reality." From the moment that the sign appears, that is to say from the very beginning, there is no chance of encountering anywhere the purity of "reality," "unicity," "singularity." So by what right can it be supposed that speech could have had, "in antiquity," before the birth of Chinese writing, the sense and value that we know in the West? Why would speech in China have had to be "eclipsed" by writing? If one wishes really to penetrate to the thing that, under the name of writing, separates much more than techniques of notation, should one not get rid, among other ethnocentric presuppositions, also of a sort of graphic monogenetism that transforms all differences into divergences or delays, accidents or deviations? And examine this heliocentric concept of speech? As well as the resemblance of the logos to the sun (to the good or to the death that one cannot look at face to face), to the king or to the father (the good or the intelligible sun are compared to the father in the *Republic*, 508 c)? What must writing be in order to threaten this analogical system in its vulnerable and secret center? What must it be in order to signify the *eclipse* of what is *good* and of the *father?* Should one not stop considering writing as the eclipse that comes to surprise and obscure the glory of the word? And if there is some necessity of eclipse, the relationship of shadow and light, of writing and speech, should it not itself appear in a different way?

In a different way: the necessary decentering cannot be a philosophic or scientific act as such, since it is a question of dislocating, through access to another system linking speech and writing, the founding categories of language and the grammar of the *epistémè*. The natural tendency of *theory*—of what unites philosophy and science in the *epistémè*—will push rather toward filling in the breach than toward forcing the closure. It was normal that the breakthrough was more secure and more penetrating on the side of literature and poetic writing: normal also that it, like Nietzsche, at first destroyed and caused to vacillate the transcendental authority and dominant category of the *epistémè*: being. This is the meaning of the work of Fenellosa[44] whose influence upon Ezra Pound and his poetics is well-known: this irreducibly graphic poetics was, with that of Mallarmé, the first break in the most entrenched Western tradition. The fascination that the Chinese ideogram exercised on Pound's writing may thus be given all its historical significance.

Ever since phoneticization has allowed itself to be questioned in its origin, its history and its adventures, its movement is seen to mingle with that of science, religion, politics, economy, technics, law, art. The origins of these movements and these historical regions dissociate themselves, as they must for the rigorous delimitation of each science, only by an abstraction that one must constantly be aware of and use with vigilance. This complicity of origins may be called arche-writing. What is lost in that complicity is therefore the myth of the simplicity of origin. This myth is linked to the very concept of origin; to speech reciting the origin, to the myth of the origin and not only to myths of origin.

The fact that access to the written sign assures the sacred power of keeping existence operative within the trace and of knowing the general structure of the universe; that all clergies, exercising political power or not, were constituted at the same time as writing and by the disposition of graphic power; that strategy, ballistics, diplomacy, agriculture, fiscality, and penal law are linked in their history and in their structure to the constitution of writing; that the origin assigned to writing had been—according to the chains and mythemes—always analogous in the most diverse cultures and that it communicated in a complex but regulated manner with the distribution of political power as with familial structure; that the possibility of capitalization and of politico-administrative organization had always passed through the hands of scribes who laid down the terms of many wars and whose function was always irreducible, whoever the contending parties might be; that through discrepancies, inequalities of development, the play of permanencies, of delays, of diffusions, etc., the solidarity among ideological, religious, scientific-technical systems, and the systems of writing which were therefore more and other than "means of communication" or vehicles of the signified, remains indestructible; that the very sense of power and effectiveness in general, which could appear as such, as meaning and mastery (by idealization), only with so-called "symbolic" power, was always linked with the disposition of writing; that economy, monetary or pre-monetary, and graphic calculation were co-originary, that there could be no law without the possibility of trace (if not, as H. Lévy-Bruhl shows, of notation in the narrow sense), all this refers to a common and radical possibility that no determined science, no abstract discipline, can think as such.[45]

Indeed, one must understand this *incompetence* of science which is also the incompetence of philosophy, the *closure* of the *epistémè*. Above all it does not invoke a return to a prescientific or infra-philosophic form of discourse. Quite the contrary. This common root, which is not a root but the concealment of the origin and which is not common because it does not amount to the same thing except with the unmonotonous insistence of difference, this unnameable movement of *difference-itself*, that I have strategically nicknamed *trace, reserve,* or *differance,* could be called writing only within the *historical* closure, that is to say within the limits of science and philosophy.

The constitution of a science or a philosophy of writing is a necessary and difficult task. But, a *thought* of the trace, of differance or of reserve, having arrived at these limits and repeating them ceaselessly, must also point beyond the field of the *epistémè*. Outside of the economic and strategic reference to the name that Heidegger justifies himself in giving to an analogous but not identical transgression of all philosophemes, *thought* is here for me a perfectly neutral name, the blank part of the text, the necessarily indeterminate index of a future epoch of differance. *In a certain sense, "thought" means nothing.* Like all openings, this index belongs within a past epoch by the face that is open to view. This thought has no weight. It is, in the play of the system, that very thing which never has weight. Thinking is what we already know we have not yet begun; measured against the shape of writing, it *is broached* only in the *epistémè*.

Grammato*logy*, this thought, would still be walled-in within presence.

II
Nature, Culture, Writing

I felt as if I had been guilty of incest.—The Confessions of Jean Jacques Rousseau

Introduction to the "Age of Rousseau"

In the voice we have an organ answering to hearing; we have no such organ answering to sight, and we do not repeat colours as we repeat sounds. This supplies an additional means of cultivating the ear by practising the active and passive organs one with the other.—Emile

If one had faith in the organization of a classical reading, one would perhaps say that I had just proposed a double grid: *historical* and *systematic*. Let us pretend to believe in this opposition. Let us do it for the sake of convenience, for I hope that the reasons for my suspicion are by now clear enough. Since I am about to deal with what, using the same language and with as much caution, I call an "*example*," I must now justify my choice.

Why accord an "exemplary" value to the "age of Rousseau"? What privileged place does Jean-Jacques Rousseau occupy in the history of logocentrism? What is meant by that proper name? And what are the relationships between that proper name and the texts to which it was underwritten? I do not profess to bring to these questions anything more than the beginning of an answer, perhaps only the beginning of an elaboration, limited to the preliminary organization of the question. This work will present itself gradually. I cannot therefore justify it by way of anticipation and preface. Let us nevertheless attempt an overture.

If the history of metaphysics is the history of a determination of being as presence, if its adventure merges with that of logocentrism, and if it is produced wholly as the reduction of the trace, Rousseau's work seems to me to occupy, between Plato's *Phaedrus* and Hegel's *Encyclopaedia*, a singular position. What do these three landmarks signify?

Between the overture and the philosophical accomplishment of phonologism (or logocentrism), the motif of presence was decisively articulated. It underwent an internal modification whose most conspicuous index was the moment of certitude in the Cartesian cogito. Before that, the identity of presence offered to the mastery of repetition was constituted under the "objective" form of the ideality of the *eidos* or the substantiality of *ousia*. Thereafter, this objectivity takes the form of *representation*, of the *idea* as the modification of a self-present substance, conscious and certain of itself at the moment of its relationship to itself. Within its most general form, the mastery of presence acquires a sort of infinite assurance. The power of repetition that the *eidos* and *ousia* made available seems to acquire an absolute independence. Ideality and substantiality relate to themselves, in the element of the *res cogitans*, by a movement of pure auto-affection. Consciousness is the experience of pure auto-affection. It calls itself infallible and if the axioms of *natural reason* give it this certitude, overcome the provocation of the Evil Spirit, and prove the existence of God, it is because they constitute the very element of thought and of self-presence. Self-presence is not disturbed by the divine origin of these axioms. The infinite alterity of the divine substance does not interpose itself as an element of mediation or opacity in the transparence of self-relationship and the purity of auto-affection. God is the name and the element of that which makes possible an absolutely pure and absolutely self-present self-knowledge. From Descartes to Hegel and in spite of all the differences that separate the different places and moments in the structure of that epoch, God's infinite understanding is the other name for the logos as self-presence. The logos can be infinite and self-present, it can be *produced as auto-affection*, only through the *voice*: an order of the signifier by which the subject takes from itself into itself, does not borrow outside of itself the signifier that it emits and that affects it at the same time. Such is at least the experience—or consciousness—of the voice: of hearing (understanding)-oneself-speak [*s'entendre-parler*]. That experience lives and proclaims itself as the exclusion of writing, that is to say of the invoking of an "exterior," "sensible," "spatial" signifier interrupting self-presence.

Within this age of metaphysics, between Descartes and Hegel, Rousseau is undoubtedly the only one or the first one to make a theme or a system of the reduction of writing profoundly implied by the entire age. He repeats the inaugural movement of the *Phaedrus* and of *De interpretatione* but starts from a new model of presence: the subject's self-presence within *consciousness* or *feeling*. What he excluded more violently than others must, of course, have fascinated and tormented him more than it did others. Descartes had driven out the sign—and particularly the written sign—from the cogito and from clear and distinct evidence; the latter being the very presence of the idea to the soul, the sign was an accessory abandoned in the region of the senses and of the imagination. Hegel reappropriates the sensible sign to the movement of the Idea. He criticizes Leibniz and praises phonetic writing within the horizon of an absolutely self-present logos, remaining close to itself within the unity of its speech and its concept. But neither Descartes nor Hegel grappled with the problem of writing. The place of this combat and crisis is called the eighteenth century. Not only because it restores the rights of sensibility, the imagination, and the sign, but because attempts of the Leibnizian type had opened a breach within logocentric security. We must bring to light what it was that, right from the start, within these attempts at a universal characteristic, limited the power and extent of the breakthrough. Before Hegel and in explicit terms, Rousseau condemned the universal characteristic; not because of the theological foundation which ordained its possibility for the infinite understanding or logos of God, but because it seemed to suspend the voice. "Through" this condemnation can be read the most energetic eighteenth-century *reaction* organizing the defense of phonologism and of logocentric metaphysics. What threatens is indeed writing. It is not an accidental and haphazard threat; it reconciles within a single historical system the projects of *pasigraphy*, the discovery of non-European scripts, or at any rate the massive progress of the techniques of *deciphering*, and finally the idea of a *general science of language and writing*. Against all these pressures, a battle is then declared. "Hegelianism" will be its finest scar.

The names of authors or of doctrines have here no substantial value. They indicate neither identities nor causes. It would be frivolous to think that "Descartes," "Leibniz," "Rousseau," "Hegel," etc., are names of authors, of the authors of movements or displacements that we thus designate. The indicative value that I attribute to them is first the name of a problem. If I provisionally authorize myself to treat this historical structure by fixing my attention on philosophical or literary texts, it is not for the sake of identifying in them the origin, cause, or equilibrium of the structure. But as I also do not think that these texts are the simple *effects* of structure, in any sense of the word; as I think that *all concepts hitherto proposed in order to think the articulation of a discourse and of an historical totality are caught within the metaphysical closure that I question here*, as we do not know of any other concepts and cannot produce any others, and indeed shall not produce so long as this closure limits our discourse; as the primordial and indispensable phase, in fact and in principle, of the development of this problematic, consists in questioning the internal structure of these texts as symptoms; as that is the only condition for determining these symptoms *themselves* in the totality of their metaphysical appurtenance; I draw my argument from them in order to isolate Rousseau, and, in Rousseauism, the theory of writing. Besides, this abstraction is partial and it remains, in my view, provisional. Further on, I shall directly approach the problem within a "question of method."

Beyond these broad and preliminary justifications, other urgencies should be invoked. In Western and notably French thought, the dominant discourse—let us call it "structuralism"—remains caught, by an entire layer, sometimes the most fecund, of its stratification, within the metaphysics—logocentrism—which at the same time one claims rather precipitately to have "gone beyond." If I have chosen the example of the texts of Claude Lévi-Strauss, as points of departure and as a springboard for a reading of

Rousseau, it is for more than one reason; for the theoretical wealth and interest of those texts, for the animating role that they currently play, but also for the place occupied in them by the theory of writing and the theme of fidelity to Rousseau. They will, therefore, in this study, be somewhat more than an exergue.

1

The Violence of the Letter: From Lévi-Strauss to Rousseau

Shall I proceed to the teaching of writing? No, I am ashamed to toy with these trifles in a treatise on education.—*Emile*

It [writing] seems to favor rather the exploitation than the enlightenment of mankind. . . . Writing, on this its first appearance in their midst, had allied itself with falsehood.—"A Writing Lesson," *Tristes Tropiques.**

Metaphysics has constituted an exemplary system of defense against the threat of writing. What links writing to violence? What must violence be in order for something in it to be equivalent to the operation of the trace?

And why bring this question into play within the affinity or filiation that binds Lévi-Strauss to Rousseau? Another difficulty is added to the problem of the justification of this historical contraction; what is a lineage in the order of discourse and text? If in a rather conventional way I call by the name of *discourse* the present, living, conscious *representation* of a *text* within the experience of the person who writes or reads it, and if the text constantly goes beyond this representation by the entire system of its resources and its own laws, then the question of genealogy exceeds by far the possibilities that are at present given for its elaboration. We know that the metaphor that would describe the genealogy of a text correctly is still *forbidden*. In its syntax and its lexicon, in its spacing, by its punctuation, its lacunae, its margins, the historical appurtenance of a text is never a straight line. It is neither causality by contagion, nor the simple accumulation of layers. Nor even the pure juxtaposition of borrowed pieces. And if a text always gives itself a certain representation of its own roots, those roots live only by that representation, by never touching the soil, so to speak. Which undoubtedly destroys their *radical essence*, but not the necessity of their *racinating function*. To say that one always interweaves roots endlessly, bending them to send down roots among the roots, to pass through the

* Claude Lévi-Strauss, *Tristes Tropiques* (Paris, 1955), pp. 344, 345, translated as *Tristes Tropiques* by John Russell (New York, 1961), pp. 292, 293.

same points again, to redouble old adherences, to circulate among their differences, to coil around themselves or to be enveloped one in the other, to say that a text is never anything but a *system of roots*, is undoubtedly to contradict at once the concept of system and the pattern of the root. But in order not to be pure appearance, this contradiction takes on the meaning of a contradiction, and receives its "illogicality," only through being thought within a finite configuration—the history of metaphysics—and caught within a root system which does not end there and which as yet has no name.

The text's self-consciousness, the circumscribed discourse where genealogical representation is articulated (what Lévi-Strauss, for example, makes of a certain "eighteenth century," by quoting it as the source of his thought), without being confused with genealogy itself, plays, precisely by virtue of this divergence, an organizing role in the structure of the text. Even if one did have the right to speak of retrospective illusion, it would not be an accident or a theoretical falling off; one would have to account for its necessity and its positive effects. A text always has several epochs and reading must resign itself to that fact. And this genealogical self-representation is itself already the representation of a self-representation; what, for example, "the French eighteenth century," if such a thing existed, already constructed as its own source and its own presence.

Is the play of these appurtenances, so manifest in texts of anthropology and the "sciences of man," produced totally within a "history of metaphysics?" Does it somewhere force the closure? Such is perhaps the widest horizon of the questions which will be supported by a few examples here. To which proper names may be assigned: the sustainers of the discourse, Condillac, Rousseau, Lévi-Strauss; or common names: concepts of analysis, of genesis, of origin, of nature, of culture, of sign, of speech, of writing, etc.; in short, the common name of the proper name.

In linguistics as well as in metaphysics, *phonologism* is undoubtedly the exclusion or abasement of writing. But it is also the granting of authority to a science which is held to be the model for all the so-called sciences of man. In both these senses Lévi-Strauss's structuralism is a phonologism. As for the "models" of linguistics and phonology, what I have already brought up will not let me skirt around a structural anthropology upon which phonological science exercises so *declared* a fascination, as for instance in "Language and Kinship";[1] it must be questioned line by line.

> The advent of structural linguistics [*phonologie*] completely changed this situation. Not only did it renew linguistic perspectives; a transformation of this

magnitude is not limited to a single discipline. Structural linguistics will certainly play the same renovating role with respect to the social sciences that nuclear physics, for example, has played for the physical sciences [*l'ensemble des sciences exactes*] (p. 39) [p. 31].

If we wished to elaborate the question of the *model*, we would have to examine all the "as"-s and "likewise"-s that punctuate the argument, ordering and authorizing the analogy between phonology and sociology, between phonemes and the terms of kinship. "A striking analogy," we are told, but the functioning of its "as" shows us quickly enough that this is a very infallible but very impoverished generality of structural laws, no doubt governing the systems considered, but also dominating many other systems without privilege; a phonology exemplary as the example in a series and not as the regulative model. But on this terrain questions have been asked, objections articulated; and as the *epistemological* phonologism establishing a science as a master-model presupposes a *linguistic* and *metaphysical* phonologism that raises speech above writing, it is this last that I shall first try to identify.

For Lévi-Strauss has written of writing. Only a few pages, to be sure[2] but in many respects remarkable; very fine pages, calculated to amaze, enunciating in the form of paradox and modernity the anathema that the Western world has obstinately mulled over, the exclusion by which it has constituted and recognized itself, from the *Phaedrus* to the *Course in General Linguistics*.

Another reason for rereading Lévi-Strauss: if, as I have shown, writing cannot be felt without an unquestioning faith in the entire system of differences between *physis* and its other (the series of its "others:" art, technology, law, institution, society, immotivation, arbitrariness, etc.), and in all the conceptuality disposed within it, then one should follow with the closest attention the troubled path of a thinker who sometimes, at a certain stage in his reflections, bases himself on this difference, and sometimes leads us to its point of effacement: "The opposition between nature and culture to which I attached much importance at one time . . . now seems to be of primarily methodological importance."[3] Undoubtedly Lévi-Strauss has only traveled from one point of effacement to another. *Les structures élémentaires de la parenté* (1949),* dominated by the problem of the prohibition of incest, already credited difference only around a suture. As a result both the one and the other became all the more enigmatic. And it would be risky to decide if the seam—the prohibition of incest—is a strange exception that one happened to encounter within the

* *Les structures élémentaires de la parenté*, 2d edition (Paris, 1967); translated as *The Elementary Structures of Kinship*, Rodney Needham et al. (Boston, 1969).

transparent system of difference, a "fact," as Lévi-Strauss says, with which "we are then confronted" (p. 9) [p. 8]; or is rather the origin of the difference between nature and culture, the condition—outside of the system—of the system of difference. The condition would be a "scandal" only if one wished to comprehend it *within* the system whose condition it precisely is.

> Let us suppose then that everything universal in man relates to the natural order, and is characterized by spontaneity, and that everything subject to a norm is cultural and is both relative and particular. We are then confronted with a fact, or rather, a group of facts, which, in the light of previous definitions, are not far removed from a scandal: . . . [for] the prohibition of incest . . . presents, without the slightest ambiguity, and inseparably combines, the two characteristics in which we recognize the conflicting features of two mutually exclusive orders. It constitutes a rule, but a rule which, alone among all the social rules, possesses at the same time a universal character (p. 9) [pp. 8–9].

But the "scandal" appeared only at a certain moment of the analysis; the moment when, giving up a "real analysis" which will never reveal any difference between nature and culture, one passed to an "ideal analysis" permitting the definition of "the double criterion of norm and universality." It is thus from the confidence placed in the difference between the two analyses that the scandal took its scandalous meaning. What did this confidence signify? It appeared to itself as the scholar's right to employ "methodological tools" whose "logical value" is anticipated, and in a state of precipitation, with regard to the "object," to "truth," etc., with regard, in other words, to what science works toward. These are the first words—or nearly so—of *Structures*:

> It is beginning to emerge that this distinction between the state of nature and the state of society (today I would rather say state of nature and state of culture) while of no acceptable historical significance, does contain a logic, fully justifying its use by modern sociology as a methodological tool (p. 1) [p. 3].

This is clear: in regard to the "chiefly methodological value" of the concepts of nature and culture, there is no evolution and even less retraction from *Structures* to *The Savage Mind*. Nor is there either evolution or retraction with regard to this concept of methodogical tool; *Structures* announces most precisely what, more than a decade later, will be said of "*bricolage*," of tools such as "means" "collected or retained on the principle that 'they may always come in handy.'" "Like '*bricolage*' on the technical plane, mythical reflection can reach brilliant unforeseen results on the intellectual plane. Conversely, attention has often been drawn to the mytho-poetical nature of '*bricolage*'" (pp. 26 f.) [pp. 17–18]. To be sure, it would still remain to be asked if the anthropologist considers himself "engineer" or "*bricoleur.*" *Le cru et le cuit* [Paris, 1964] is presented as "the myth of mythology" ("Preface," p. 20).*

Nevertheless, the effacement of the frontier between nature and culture is not produced by the same gesture from *Structures* to *The Savage Mind.* In the first case, it is rather a question of respecting the originality of a scandalous suture. In the second case, of a reduction, however careful it might be not to "dissolve" the specificity of what it analyzes:

> . . . it would not be enough to reabsorb particular humanities into a general one. This first enterprise opens the way for others which Rousseau [whose "usual acumen" Lévi-Strauss has just praised] would not have been so ready to accept and which are incumbent on the exact natural sciences: the reintegration of culture in nature and finally of life within the whole of its physio-chemical conditions (p. 327) [p. 247].

At once conserving and annulling inherited conceptual oppositions, this thought, like Saussure's, stands on a borderline: sometimes within an uncriticized conceptuality, sometimes putting a strain on the boundaries, and working toward deconstruction.

Finally, why Lévi-Strauss *and* Rousseau? The quotation above necessarily leads us to this question. This conjunction must be justified gradually and intrinsically. But it is already known that Lévi-Strauss not only feels himself to be *in agreement* with Jean-Jacques, to be his heir at heart and in what might be called theoretical affect. He also often presents himself as Rousseau's modern disciple; he reads Rousseau as the *founder,* not only the prophet, of modern anthropology. A hundred texts glorifying Rousseau may be cited. Nevertheless, let us recall, at the end of *Totémisme aujourd'hui,*† the chapter on "Totemism from Within:" "a . . . militant fervor for ethnography," the "astonishing insight" of Rousseau who, "more prudent . . . than Bergson" and "before even the 'discovery' of totemism "penetrate[d]" (p. 147) that which opens the possibility of totemism in general, namely:

1. *Pity,* that fundamental affection, as primitive as the love of self, which unites us to others naturally: to other human beings, certainly, but also to all living beings.

2. The *originarily metaphoric*—because it belongs to the passions, says Rousseau—essence of our *language.* What authorizes Lévi-Strauss's interpretation is the *Essay on the Origin of Languages,* which we shall try to read closely later: "As man's first motives for speaking were of the passions

* Tr. John and Doreen Weightman, *The Raw and the Cooked,* (Harper Torchbooks edition New York, 1970), p. 12.

† *Totémisme aujourd'hui,* 2d edition (Paris, 1965); translated as *Totemism,* Rodney Needham (Boston, 1963).

[and not of needs], his first expressions were tropes. Figurative language was the first to be born" [p. 12]. It is again in "Totemism from Within" that the second *Discourse* is defined as "the first treatise of general anthropology in French literature. In almost modern terms, Rousseau poses the central problem of anthropology, viz., the passage from nature to culture" (p. 142) [p. 99]. And here is the most systematic homage: "Rousseau did not merely foresee anthropology; he founded it. First in a practical way, in writing that *Discours sur l'origine et les fondements de l'inégalité parmi les hommes* which poses the problem of the relationships between nature and culture, and which is the first treatise of general anthropology; and later on the theoretical plane, by distinguishing, with admirable clarity and concision, the proper object of the anthropologist from that of the moralist and the historian: 'When one wants to study men, one must consider those around one. But to study man, one must extend the range of one's vision. One must first observe the differences in order to discover the properties' (*Essay on the Origin of Languages*, Chapter VIII) [pp. 30–31]."[4]

It is therefore a declared and militant Rousseauism. Already it imposes on us a very general question that will orient all our readings more or less directly: to what extent does Rousseau's appurtenance to logocentric metaphysics and within the philosophy of presence—an appurtenance that we have already been able to recognize and whose exemplary figure we must delineate—to what extent does it limit a scientific discourse? Does it necessarily retain within its boundaries the Rousseauist discipline and fidelity of an anthropologist and of a theorist of modern anthropology?

If this question is not sufficient to link the development which will follow with my initial proposition, I should perhaps recapitulate:

1. that digression about the violence that *does not supervene* from without upon an innocent language in order to surprise it, a language that suffers the aggression of writing as the accident of its disease, its defeat and its fall; but is the originary violence of a language which is always already a writing. Rousseau and Lévi-Strauss are not for a moment to be challenged when they relate the power of writing to the exercise of violence. But radicalizing this theme, no longer considering this violence as *derivative* with respect to a naturally innocent speech, one reverses the entire sense of a proposition—the unity of violence and writing—which one must therefore be careful not to abstract and isolate.

2. that other ellipsis of the metaphysics or onto-theology of the logos (par excellence in its Hegelian moment) as the powerless and oneiric effort to master absence by reducing the metaphor within the absolute parousia of sense. Ellipsis of the originary writing within language as the irreducibility of metaphor, which it is necessary here to think in its possibility and short of its rhetorical repetition. The irremediable absence of the

proper name. Rousseau no doubt believed in the figurative initiation of language, but he believed no less, as we shall see, in a progress toward literal (proper) meaning. "Figurative language was the first to be born," he says, only to add, "proper meaning was discovered last" (*Essay*).[5] It is to this eschatology of the *proper* (*prope*, *proprius*, self-proximity, self-presence, property, own-ness) that we ask the question of the *graphein*.

The Battle of Proper Names

But how is one to distinguish, in writing, between a man one mentions and a man one addresses. There really is an equivocation which would be eliminated by a vocative mark.—Essay on the Origin of Languages

Back now from *Tristes Tropiques* to the *Essay on the Origin of Languages*, from "A Writing Lesson" given to the writing lesson refused by the person who was "ashamed to toy" with the "trifl[ing]" matter of writing in a treatise on education. My question is perhaps better stated thus: do they say the same thing? Do they do the same thing?

In that *Tristes Tropiques* which is at the same time *The Confessions* and a sort of supplement to the *Supplément au voyage de Bougainville,** the "Writing Lesson" marks an episode of what may be called the anthropological war, the essential confrontation that opens communication between peoples and cultures, even when that communication is not practiced under the banner of colonial or missionary oppression. The entire "Writing Lesson" is recounted in the tones of violence repressed or deferred, a violence sometimes veiled, but always oppressive and heavy. Its weight is felt in various places and various moments of the *narrative*: in Lévi-Strauss's account as in the relationship among individuals and among groups, among cultures or within the same community. What can a relationship to writing signify in these diverse instances of violence?

Penetration in the case of the Nambikwara. The anthropologist's affection for those to whom he devoted one of his dissertations, *La vie familiale et sociale des Indiens Nambikwara* (1948). Penetration, therefore, into "the lost world" of the Nambikwara, "the little bands of nomads, who are among the most genuinely 'primitive' of the world's peoples" on "a territory the size of France," traversed by a *picada* (a crude trail whose "track" is "not easily distinguished from the bush" [p. 262]; one should meditate upon all of the following together: writing as the possibility of the road and of difference, the history of writing and the history of the road, of the rupture, of the *via rupta*, of the path that is broken, beaten, *fracta*, of the space of reversibility and of repetition traced by the opening, the divergence from, and

* Denis Diderot, *Oeuvres complètes*, Pléiade edition (Paris, 1935), pp. 993–1032; "Supplement to Bougainville's 'Voyage'," *Rameau's Nephew and Other Works*, ed. Jacques Barzun and Ralph H. Bowen (Garden City, 1956), pp. 187–239.

the violent spacing, of nature, of the natural, savage, salvage, forest. The *silva* is savage, the *via rupta* is written, discerned, and inscribed violently as difference, as form imposed on the *hylè*, in the forest, in wood as matter; it is difficult to imagine that access to the possibility of a road-map is not at the same time access to writing). The territory of the Nambikwara is crossed by the line of an autochthonic picada. But also by another *line*, this time imported:

[An abandoned telephone line] obsolete from the day of its completion [which] hung down from poles never replaced when they go to rot and tumble to the ground. (Sometimes the termites attack them, and sometimes the Indians, who mistake the humming of the telegraph wires for the noise of bees on their way to the hive.) [p. 262]

The Nambikwara, whose tormenting and cruelty—presumed or not—are much feared by the personnel of the line, "brought the observer back to what he might readily, though mistakenly, suppose to be the childhood of our race" [p. 265]. Lévi-Strauss describes the biological and cultural type of this population whose technology, economy, institutions, and structures of kinship, however primitive, give them of course a rightful place within humankind, so-called human society and the "state of culture." They speak and prohibit incest. "All were interrelated, for the Nambikwara prefer to marry a niece (their sister's daughter), or a kinswoman of the kind which anthropologists call 'cross-cousin': the daughter of their father's sister, or of their mother's brother" [p. 269]. Yet another reason for not allowing oneself to be taken in by appearances and for not believing that one sees here the "childhood of our race:" the structure of the language. And above all its *usage*. The Nambikwara use several dialects and several systems according to situations. And here intervenes a phenomenon which may be crudely called "linguistic" and which will be of central interest to us. It has to do with a *fact* that we have not the means of interpreting beyond its general conditions of possibility, its a priori; whose factual and empirical causes—as they open within this determined situation—will escape us, and, moreover, call forth no question on the part of Lévi-Strauss, who merely notes them. This fact bears on what we have proposed about the essence or the energy of the *graphein* as the originary effacement of the proper name. From the moment that the proper name is erased in a system, there is writing, there is a "subject" from the moment that this obliteration of the proper is produced, that is to say from the first appearing of the proper and from the first dawn of language. This proposition is universal in essence and can be produced *a priori*. How one passes from this *a priori* to the determination of empirical facts is a question that one cannot answer in general here. First because, by definition, there is no general answer to a question of this form.

It is therefore such a *fact* that we encounter here. It does not involve the structural effacement of what we believe to be our proper names; it does not involve the obliteration that, paradoxically, constitutes the originary legibility of the very thing it erases, but of a prohibition heavily superimposed, in certain societies, upon the use of the proper name: "They are not allowed . . . to use proper names" [p. 270], Lévi-Strauss observes.

Before we consider this, let us note that this prohibition is necessarily derivative with regard to the constitutive erasure of the proper name in what I have called arche-writing, within, that is, the play of difference. It is because the proper names are already no longer proper names, because their production is their obliteration, because the erasure and the imposition of the letter are originary, because they do not supervene upon a proper inscription; it is because the proper name has never been, as the unique appellation reserved for the presence of a unique being, anything but the original myth of a transparent legibility present under the obliteration; it is because the proper name was never possible except through its functioning within a classification and therefore within a system of differences, within a writing retaining the traces of difference, that the interdict was possible, could come into play, and, when the time came, as we shall see, could be transgressed; transgressed, that is to say restored to the obliteration and the non-self-sameness [*non-propriété*] at the origin.

This is strictly in accord with one of Lévi-Strauss's intentions. In "Universalization and Particularization" (*The Savage Mind*, Chapter VI) it will be demonstrated that "one . . . never names: one classes someone else . . . [or] one classes oneself."[6] A demonstration anchored in some examples of prohibitions that affect the use of proper names here and there. Undoubtedly one should carefully distinguish between the essential necessity of the disappearance of the proper name and the determined prohibition which can, contingently and ulteriorly, be added to it or articulated within it. Nonprohibition, as much as prohibition, presupposes fundamental obliteration. Nonprohibition, the *consciousness* or exhibition of the proper name, only makes up for or uncovers an essential and irremediable impropriety. When within *consciousness*, the name *is called* proper, it is already classified and is obliterated in *being named*. It is already no more than a *so-called* proper name.

If writing is no longer understood in the narrow sense of linear and phonetic notation, it should be possible to say that all societies capable of producing, that is to say of obliterating, their proper names, and of bringing classificatory difference into play, practice writing in general. No reality or concept would therefore correspond to the expression "society without writing." This expression is dependent on ethnocentric oneirism, upon the vulgar, that is to say ethnocentric, misconception of writing. The scorn for writing, let us note in passing, accords quite happily with this ethnocentrism. The paradox is only apparent, one of those contradictions where a perfectly coherent desire is uttered and accomplished. By one and the same gesture, (alphabetic) writing, servile instrument of a speech dreaming of its plenitude and its self-presence, is scorned and the dignity of writing is refused to nonalphabetic signs. We have perceived this gesture in Rousseau and in Saussure.

The Nambikwara—the *subject* of "A Writing Lesson"—would therefore be one of these peoples without writing. They do not make use of what *we* commonly call writing. At least that is what Lévi-Strauss tells us: "That the Nambikwara could not write goes without saying" [p. 288]. This incapacity will be presently thought, within the ethico-political order, as an innocence and a non-violence interrupted by the forced entry of the West and the "Writing Lesson." We shall be present at that scene in a little while.

How can access to writing in general be refused to the Nambikwara except by determining writing according to a model? Later on we shall ask, confronting many passages in Lévi-Strauss, up to what point it is legitimate not to call by the name of writing those "few dots" and "zigzags" on their calabashes, so briefly evoked in *Tristes Tropiques*. But above all, how can we deny the practice of writing in general to a society capable of obliterating the proper, that is to say a violent society? For writing, obliteration of the proper classed in the play of difference, is the originary violence itself: pure impossibility of the "vocative mark," impossible purity of the mark of vocation. This "equivocation," which Rousseau hoped would be "eliminated" by a "vocative mark," cannot be effaced. For the existence of such a mark in any code of punctuation would not change the problem. The death of absolutely proper naming, recognizing in a language the other as pure other, invoking it as what it is, is the death of the pure idiom reserved for the unique. Anterior to the possibility of violence in the current and derivative sense, the sense used in "A Writing Lesson," there is, as the space of its possibility, the violence of the arche-writing, the violence of difference, of classification, and of the system of appellations. Before outlining the structure of this implication, let us read the scene of proper names; with another scene, that we shall shortly read, it is an indispensable preparation for the "Writing Lesson." This scene is separated from the "Writing Lesson" by one chapter and another scene: "Family Life." And it is described in Chapter 26 [23] "On the Line."

The Nambikwara make no difficulties and are quite indifferent to the presence of the anthropologist with his notebooks and camera. But certain problems of language complicated matters. They are not allowed, for instance, to use proper names. To tell one from another we had to do as the men of the line do and agree with the Nambikwara on a set of nicknames which would serve for identification. Either Portuguese names, like Julio, Jose-Maria, Luisa; or sobriquets such as *Lebre*, hare, or *Assucar*, sugar. I even knew one whom Rondon or one of his companions had nicknamed Cavaignac on account of his little pointed beard—a rarity among Indians, most of whom have no hair on their faces. One day, when I was playing with a group of children, a little girl was struck by one of her comrades. She ran to me for protection and began to whisper something, a "great secret," in my ear. As I did not understand I had to ask her to repeat it over and over again. Eventually her adversary found out what was going on, came up to me in a rage, and tried in her turn to tell me what seemed to be another secret. After a little while I was able to get to the bottom of the incident. The first little girl was trying to tell me her enemy's name, and when the enemy found out what was going on she decided to tell me the other girl's name, by way of reprisal. Thenceforward it was easy enough, though not very scrupulous, to egg the children on, one against the other, till in time I knew all of their names. When this was completed and we were all, in a sense, one another's accomplices, I soon got them to give me the adults' names too. When this [cabal] was discovered the children were reprimanded and my sources of information dried up.[7]

We cannot enter here into the difficulties of an empirical deduction of this prohibition, but we know a priori that the "proper names" whose interdiction and revelation Lévi-Strauss describes here are not proper names. The expression "proper name" is improper, for the very reasons that *The Savage Mind* will recall. What the interdict is laid upon is the uttering of what *functions* as the proper name. And this function is *consciousness* itself. The proper name in the colloquial sense, in the sense of consciousness, is (I should say "in truth" were it not necessary to be wary of that phrase)[8] only a designation of appurtenance and a linguistico-social classification. The lifting of the interdict, the great game of denunciation and the great exhibition of the "proper" (let us note that we speak here of an act of war and there is much to say about the fact that it is little girls who open themselves to this game and these hostilities) does not consist in revealing proper names, but in tearing the veil hiding a classification and an appurtenance, the inscription within a system of linguistico-social differences.

What the Nambikwara hid and the young girls lay bare through transgression, is no longer the absolute idioms, but already varieties of invested common names, "abstracts" if, as we read in *The Savage Mind* (p. 242) [p. 182], "systems of appellations also have their 'abstracts.' "

The concept of the proper name, unproblematized as Lévi-Strauss uses it in *Tristes Tropiques*, is therefore far from being simple and manageable. Consequently, the same may be said of the concepts of violence, ruse, perfidy, or oppression, that punctuate "A Writing Lesson" a little further on. We have already noted that violence here does not unexpectedly break in all at once, starting from an original innocence whose nakedness is *surprised* at the very moment that the secret of the *so-called* proper names is violated. The structure of violence is complex and its possibility—writing—no less so.

There was in fact a first violence to be named. To name, to give names that it will on occasion be forbidden to pronounce, such is the originary violence of language which consists in inscribing within a difference, in classifying, in suspending the vocative absolute. To think the unique *within* the system, to inscribe it there, such is the gesture of the arche-writing: arche-violence, loss of the proper, of absolute proximity, of self-presence, in truth the loss of what has never taken place, of a self-presence which has never been given but only dreamed of and always already split, repeated, incapable of appearing to itself except in its own disappearance. Out of this arche-violence, forbidden and therefore confirmed by a second violence that is reparatory, protective, instituting the "moral," prescribing the concealment of writing and the effacement and obliteration of the so-called proper name which was already dividing the proper, a third violence can *possibly* emerge or not (an empirical possibility) within what is commonly called evil, war, indiscretion, rape; which consists of revealing by effraction the so-called proper name, the originary violence which has severed the proper from its property and its self-sameness [*propreté*]. We could name a third violence of reflection, which denudes the native non-identity, classification as denaturation of the proper, and identity as the abstract moment of the concept. It is on this tertiary level, that of the empirical consciousness, that the common concept of violence (the system of the moral law and of transgression) whose possibility remains yet unthought, should no doubt be situated. The scene of proper names is written on this level; as will be later the writing lesson.

This last violence is all the more complex in its structure because it refers at the same time to the two inferior levels of arche-violence and of law. In effect, it reveals the first nomination which was already an expropriation, but it denudes also that which since then functioned as the proper, the so-called proper, substitute of the deferred proper, *perceived* by the *social* and *moral consciousness* as the proper, the reassuring seal of self-identity, the secret.

Empirical violence, war in the colloquial sense (ruse and perfidy of little girls, *apparent* ruse and perfidy of little girls, for the anthropologist will prove them innocent by showing himself as the true and only culprit; ruse and perfidy of the Indian chief playing at the comedy of writing, *apparent* ruse and perfidy of the Indian chief borrowing all his resources from the Occidental intrusion), which Lévi-Strauss always thinks of as an *accident*. An accident occurring, in his view, upon a terrain of innocence, in a "state of culture" whose *natural* goodness had not yet been degraded.[9]

Two pointers, seemingly anecdotal and belonging to the decor of the representation to come, support this hypothesis that the "Writing Lesson" will confirm. They announce the great staging of the "lesson" and show to advantage the art of the composition of this travelogue. In accordance with eighteenth-century tradition, the anecdote, the page of confessions, the fragment from a journal are knowledgeably put in place, calculated for the purposes of a philosophical demonstration of the relationships between nature and society, ideal society and real society, most often between the *other* society and our *society*.

What is the first pointer? The battle of proper names follows the arrival of the foreigner and that is not surprising. It is born in the presence and even from the presence of the anthropologist who comes to disturb order and natural peace, the complicity which peacefully binds the good society to itself in its play. Not only have the people of the Line imposed ridiculous sobriquets on the natives, obliging them to assume these intrinsically (hare, sugar, Cavaignac), but it is the anthropological eruption which breaks the secret of the proper names and the innocent complicity governing the play of young girls. It is the anthropologist who violates a virginal space so accurately connoted by the scene of a game and a game played by little girls. The mere presence of the foreigner, the mere fact of his having his eyes open, cannot not provoke a violation: the *aside*, the secret murmured in the ear, the successive movements of the "stratagem," the acceleration, the precipitation, a certain increasing jubilation in the movement before the falling back which follows the consummated fault, when the "sources" have "dried up," makes us think of a dance and a fête as much as of war.

The mere presence of a spectator, then, is a violation. First a pure violation: a silent and immobile foreigner attends a game of young girls. That one of them should have "struck" a "comrade" is not yet true violence. No integrity has been breached. Violence appears only at the moment when the intimacy of proper names can be opened to forced entry. And that is possible only at the moment when the space is shaped and reoriented by the glance of the foreigner. The eye of the other calls out the proper names, spells them out, and removes the prohibition that covered them.

At first the anthropologist is satisfied merely to see. A fixed glance and a mute presence. Then things get complicated, become more tortuous and labyrinthine, when he becomes a party to the play of the rupture of play, as he lends an ear and broaches a first complicity with the victim who is also the trickster. Finally, for what counts is the names of the adults (one could say the eponyms and the secret is violated only in the place where the names are attributed), the ultimate denunciation can no longer do without the active intervention of the foreigner. Who, moreover, claims to have intervened and accuses himself of it. He has seen, then heard; but, passive in the face of what he already knew he was provoking, he still waited to hear the master-names. The violation was not consummated, the naked base of the proper was still reserved. As one cannot or rather must not incriminate the innocent young girls, the violation will be accomplished by the thenceforward active, perfidious, and rusing intrusion of the foreigner who, having seen and heard, is now going to "excite" the young girls, loosen their tongues, and get them to divulge the precious names: those of the adults (the dissertation tells us that only "the adults possessed names that were proper to them," p. 39). With a bad conscience, to be sure, and with that pity which Rousseau said unites us with the most foreign of foreigners. Let us now reread the *mea culpa*, the confession of the anthropologist who assumes entire responsibility for a violation that has satisfied him. After *giving* one another *away*, the young girls *gave away* the adults.

> The first little girl was trying to tell me her enemy's name, and when the enemy found out what was going on she decided to tell me the other girl's name, by way of reprisal. Thenceforward it was easy enough, though not very scrupulous, to egg the children on, one against the other, till in time I knew all their names. When this was completed and we were all, in a sense, one another's accomplices, I soon got them to give me the adults' names too [p. 270].

The true culprit will not be punished, and this gives to his fault the stamp of the irremediable: "When this [cabal] was discovered the children were reprimanded and my sources of information dried up."

One already suspects—and all Lévi-Strauss's writings would confirm it—that the critique of ethnocentrism, a theme so dear to the author of *Tristes Tropiques*, has most often the sole function of constituting the other as a model of original and natural goodness, of accusing and humiliating oneself, of exhibiting its being-unacceptable in an anti-ethnocentric mirror. Rousseau would have taught the modern anthropologist this humility of one who knows he is "unacceptable," this remorse that produces anthropology.[10] That is at least what we are told in the Geneva lecture:

> In truth, I am not "I," but the feeblest and humblest of "others." Such is the discovery of the *Confessions*. Does the anthropologist write anything other than confessions? First in his own name, as I have shown, since it is the moving force of his vocation and his work; and in that very work, in the name of the society, which, through the activities of its emissary, the anthropologist, chooses for itself other societies, other civilizations, and precisely the weakest and most humble; but only to verify to what extent that first society is itself "unacceptable" (p. 245).

Without speaking of the point of mastery thus gained by the person who conducts this operation at home, one rediscovers here a gesture inherited from the eighteenth century, from a certain eighteenth century at any rate, for even in that century a certain sporadic suspicion of such an exercise had already commenced. Non-European peoples were not only studied as the index to a hidden good Nature, as a native soil recovered, of a "zero degree" with reference to which one could outline the structure, the growth, and above all the degradation of our society and our culture. As always, this archeology is also a teleology and an eschatology; the dream of a full and immediate presence closing history, the transparence and indivision of a parousia, the suppression of contradiction and difference. The anthropologist's mission, as Rousseau would have assigned it, is to work toward such an end. Possibly against the philosophy which "alone" would have sought to "excite" "antagonisms" between the "self and the other."[11] Let us not be accused here of forcing words and things. Let us rather read. It is again the Geneva lecture, but a hundred similar passages may be found:

The Rousseauist revolution, pre-forming and initiating the anthropological revolution, consists in refusing the expected identifications, whether that of a culture with that culture, or that of an individual, member of one culture, with a personage or a social function that the same culture wishes to impose upon him. In both cases the culture or the individual insists on the right to a free identification which can only be realized *beyond* man: an identification with all that lives and therefore suffers; and an identification which can also be realized *short of* the function or the person; with a yet unfashioned, but given, being. Then the self and the other, freed of an antagonism that only philosophy seeks to excite, recover their unity. An original alliance, at last renewed, permits them to found together the *we* against the *him*, against a society inimical to man, and which man finds himself all the more ready to challenge because Rousseau, by his example, teaches him how to elude the intolerable contradictions of civilized life. For if it is true that Nature has expelled man, and that society persists in oppressing him, man can at least reverse the horns of the dilemma to his own advantage, *and seek out the society of nature in order to meditate there upon the nature of society*. This, it seems to me, is the indissoluble message of *The Social Contract*, the *Lettres sur la botanique*, and the *Reveries*.[12]

"A Little Glass of Rum," which is a severe criticism of Diderot and a glorification of Rousseau ("[who] of all the *philosophes*, came nearest to being an anthropologist . . . our master . . . our brother, great as has been our ingratitude toward him; and every page of this book could have been dedicated to him, had the object thus proffered not been unworthy of his great memory") concludes thus: ". . . the question to be solved is whether or not these evils are themselves inherent in that state [of society]. We must go beyond the evidence of the injustices or abuses to which the social order gives rise and discover the unshakeable basis of human society."[13]

The diversified thinking of Lévi-Strauss would be impoverished if it were not emphatically recalled here that this goal and this motivation do not exhaust, though they do more than connote, the task of science. They mark it profoundly in its very content. I had promised a second pointer. The Nambikwara, around whom the "Writing Lesson" will unfold its scene, among whom evil will insinuate itself with the intrusion of writing come from *without* (*exothen*, as the *Phaedrus* says)—the Nambikwara, who do not know how to write, are *good*, we are told. The Jesuits, the Protestant missionaries, the American anthropologists, the technicians on the Line, who believed they perceived violence or hatred among the Nambikwara are not only mistaken, they have probably projected their own wickedness upon them. And even provoked the evil that they then believed they saw or wished to perceive. Let us reread the end of Chapter 17 [24], entitled, always with the same skill, "Family Life." This passage immediately precedes "A Writing Lesson" and is, in a certain way, indespensable to it. Let us first confirm what goes without saying: if we subscribe to Lévi-Strauss's declarations about their innocence and goodness, their "great sweetness of nature," "the most . . . authentic manifestations of human tenderness," etc. only by assigning them a totally derived, relative, and empirical place of legitimacy, regarding them as descriptions of the empirical affections of the *subject* of this chapter—the Nambikwara as well as the author—if then we subscribe to these descriptions only as *empirical relation*, it does not follow that we give credence to the moralizing descriptions of the American anthropologist's converse deploring of the hatred, surliness, and lack of civility of the natives. In fact these two accounts are symmetrically opposed, they have the same dimensions, and arrange themselves around one and the same axis. After having cited a foreign colleague's publication, which is very severe toward the Nambikwara for their complacency in the face of disease, their filthiness, wretchedness, and rudeness, their rancorous and distrustful character, Lévi-Strauss argues:

When I myself had known them, the diseases introduced by white men had already decimated them; but there had not been, since Rondon's always humane endeavors, any attempt to enforce their submission. I should prefer to forget Mr. Oberg's harrowing description and remember the Nambikwara as they appear in a page from my notebooks. I wrote it one night by the light of my pocket-lamp: "The camp-fires shine out in the darkened savannah. Around the hearth which is their only protection from the cold, behind the flimsy screen of foliage and palm-leaves which had been stuck into the ground where it will best break the force of wind and rain, beside the baskets filled with the pitiable objects which comprise all their earthly belongings, the Nambikwara lie on the bare earth. Always they are haunted by the thought of other groups, as fearful and hostile as they are themselves, and when they lie entwined together, couple by couple, each looks to his mate for support and comfort and finds in the other a bulwark, the only one he knows, against the difficulties of every day and the meditative melancholia which from time to time overwhelms the Nambikwara. The visitor who camps among the Indians for the first time cannot but feel anguish and pity at the sight of a people so totally dis-provided for; beaten down into the hostile earth, it would seem, by an implacable cataclysm; naked and shivering beside their guttering fires. He gropes his way among the bushes, avoiding where he can the hand, or the arm, or the torso that lies gleaming in the firelight. But this misery is enlivened by laughing whispers. Their embraces are those of couples possessed by a longing for a lost oneness; their caresses are in no wise disturbed by the footfall of a stranger. In one and all there may be glimpsed a great sweetness of nature, a profound nonchalance, an animal satisfaction as ingenuous as it is charming, and, beneath all this, something that can be recognized as one of the most moving and authentic manifestations of human tenderness" [p. 285].

The "Writing Lesson" follows this description, which one may indeed read for what it claims, at the outset, to be: a page "from my notebooks" scribbled one night in the light of a pocket lamp. It would be different if this moving painting were to belong to an anthropological discourse. However, it certainly sets up a premise—the goodness or innocence of the Nambikwara—indispensable to the subsequent demonstration of the conjoint intrusion of violence and writing. Here a strict separation of the anthropological confession and the theoretical discussion of the anthropologist must be observed. The difference between empirical and essential must continue to assert its rights.

We know that Lévi-Strauss has very harsh words for the philosophies that have made the mind aware of this distinction, and which are, for the most part, philosophies of consciousness, of the cogito in the Cartesian or Husserlian sense. Very harsh words also for *L'Essai sur les données immédiates de la conscience,** which Lévi-Strauss reproaches his old teachers for having pondered too much instead of studying Saussure's *Course in General Linguistics.*[14] Now whatever one may finally think of philosophies thus incriminated or ridiculed (and of which I shall say nothing here except to note that only their ghosts, which sometimes haunt school manuals, selected extracts, or popular opinion, are evoked here), it should be recognized that the difference between empirical affect and the structure of essence was for them a major rule. Neither Descartes nor Husserl would ever have suggested that they considered an empirical modification of their relationship with the world or with others as scientific truth, nor the quality of an emotion as the premise of a syllogism. Never in the *Regulae* does one pass from the phenomenologically irrefutable truth of "I see yellow" to the judgment "the world is yellow." Let us not pursue this direction. Never, at any rate, would a rigorous philosopher of consciousness have been so quickly persuaded of the fundamental goodness and virginal innocence of the Nambikwara merely on the strength of an empirical account. From the point of view of anthropological science, this conclusion is

* Henri Bergson (Paris, 1889); translated as *Time and Free Will*, by F. L. Pogson (London and New York, 1910).

as surprising as the wicked American anthropologist's might be "distressing" (Lévi-Strauss's word). Surprising, indeed, that this unconditional affirmation of the radical goodness of the Nambikwara comes from the pen of an anthropologist who sets against the bloodless phantoms of the philosophers of consciousness and intuition, those who have been, if the beginning of *Tristes Tropiques* is to be believed, his only true masters: Marx and Freud.

The thinkers assembled hastily at the beginning of that book under the banner of metaphysics, phenomenology, and existentialism, would not be recognized in the lineaments ascribed to them. But it would be wrong to conclude that, conversely, Marx and Freud would have been satisfied by the theses written in their name—and notably the chapters that interest us. They generally demanded to see proof when one spoke of "great sweetness of nature," "profound nonchalance," "animal satisfaction as ingenuous as it is charming," and "something that can be recognized as one of the most moving and authentic manifestations of human tenderness." They wanted to see proof and would undoubtedly not have understood what could possibly be referred to as "the original alliance, later renewed," permitting "the found[ing] together of the *we* against the *him*" (already quoted), or as "that regular and, as it were crystalline structure which the best-preserved of primitive societies teach us is not antagonistic to the human condition" (*Leçon inaugurale au Collège de France*, p. 49).*

Within this entire system of philosophical kinship and claims of genealogical filiations, not the least surprised might well be Rousseau. Had he not asked that he be allowed to live in peace with the philosophers of consciousness and of interior sentiment, in peace with that sensible cogito,[15] with that interior voice which, he believed, never lied? To reconcile Rousseau, Marx, and Freud is a difficult task. Is it possible to make them agree among themselves in the systematic rigor of conceptuality?

Writing and Man's Exploitation by Man

The "bricoleur" may not ever complete his purpose but he always puts something of himself into it.*—*The Savage Mind

Perhaps his system is false; but developing it, he has painted himself truly.*—*J.-J. Rousseau, Dialogues

Let us finally open "A Writing Lesson." If I give so much attention to the chapter, it is not in order to take unfair advantage of a travel journal,

* *The Scope of Anthropology*, tr. Sherry Ortner Paul and Robert A. Paul (London, 1967), p. 49.

something that could be considered the least scientific expression of a thought. On the one hand, all the themes of the systematic theory of writing presented for the first time in *Tristes Tropiques* may be found in other writings,[16] in another form and more or less dispersed. On the other hand, the theoretical content is itself expounded at length in this work, at greater length than anywhere else, by way of comment on an "extraordinary incident." This incident is also reported in the same terms at the beginning of the dissertation on the Nambikwara, seven years earlier than *Tristes Tropiques*. Finally, it is only in *Tristes Tropiques* that the system is articulated in the most rigorous and complete way. The indispensable premises, namely the nature of the organism submitted to the aggression of writing, are nowhere more explicit. That is why I have followed the description of the innocence of the Nambikwara at length. Only an innocent community, and a community of reduced dimensions (a Rousseauist theme that will soon become clearer), only a micro-society of non-violence and freedom, all the members of which can by rights remain within range of an immediate and transparent, a "crystalline" address, fully self-present in its living speech, only such a community can suffer, as the surprise of an aggression coming *from without*, the insinuation of writing, the infiltration of its "ruse" and of its "perfidy." Only such a community can import *from abroad* "the exploitation of man by man." "The Lesson" is therefore complete; in subsequent texts, the theoretical conclusions of the incident will be presented without the concrete premises, original innocence will be *implied but not expounded*. In the previous text, the dissertation on the Nambikwara, the incident is reported but it does not lead, as in *Tristes Tropiques*, to a long meditation on the historical meaning, origin, and function of the written. On the other hand, I shall draw from the dissertation information that will be valuable as annotations to *Tristes Tropiques*.

Writing, the exploitation of man by man: I do not impose these words upon Lévi-Strauss. Let us recall the *Conversations* by way of precaution: ". . . writing itself, in that first instance, seemed to be associated in any permanent way only with societies which were based on the exploitation of man by man" (p. 36) [p. 30]. In *Tristes Tropiques*, Lévi-Strauss is aware of proposing a Marxist theory of writing. He says it in a letter of 1955 (the year the book appeared) to the *Nouvelle critique*. Criticized by M. Rodinson in the name of Marxism, he complains:

> If he [M. Rodinson] had read my book, instead of confining himself to the extracts published a few months ago, he would have discovered—in addition to a Marxist hypothesis on the origins of writing—two studies dedicated to Brazilian tribes (the Caduveo and the Bororo), which are efforts to interpret native superstructures based upon dialectical materialism. The novelty of this approach in the Western anthropological literature perhaps deserves more attention and sympathy.[17]

Our question is therefore no longer only "how to reconcile Rousseau and Marx" but also: "Is it sufficient to speak of superstructure and to denounce in an hypothesis an exploitation of man by man in order to confer a Marxian pertinence upon this hypothesis?" A question that has meaning only through implying an original rigor in Marxist criticism and distinguish it from all other criticism of suffering, of violence, of exploitation, etc.; for example, from Buddhist criticism. Our question has clearly no meaning at the point where one can say "between Marxist criticism . . . and Buddhist criticism . . . there is neither opposition nor contradiction."[18]

Another precaution is necessary before the "Lesson." I have earlier emphasized the ambiguity of the ideology which governs the Saussurian exclusion of writing: a profound ethnocentrism privileging the model of phonetic writing, a model that makes the exclusion of the *graphie* easier and more legitimate. It is, however, an ethnocentrism *thinking itself* as anti-ethnocentrism, an ethnocentrism in the consciousness of a liberating progressivism. By radically separating language from writing, by placing the latter below and outside, believing at least that it is possible to do so, by giving oneself the illusion of liberating linguistics from all involvement with written evidence, one thinks in fact to restore the status of authentic language, human and fully signifying language, to all languages practiced by *peoples whom one nevertheless continues to describe as "without writing."* It is not fortuitous that the same ambiguity affects Lévi-Strauss's intentions.

On the one hand, the colloquial difference between language and writing, the rigorous exteriority of one with respect to the other, is admitted. This permits the distinction between peoples using writing and peoples without writing. Lévi-Strauss is never suspicious of the value of such a distinction. This above all allows him to consider the passage from speech to writing as a *leap,* as the instantaneous crossing of a line of discontinuity: passage from a fully oral language, pure of all writing—*pure,* innocent—to a language appending to itself its graphic "representation" as an accessory signifier of a new type, opening a technique of oppression. Lévi-Strauss needed this "epigenetist" concept of writing in order that the theme of evil and of exploitation suddenly coming about with the *graphie* could indeed be the theme of a surprise and an accident affecting the purity of an innocent language from without. Affecting it *as if by chance.*[19] At any rate the epigenetist thesis repeats, in connection with writing this time, an affirmation that we could have encountered five years previously in the *Introduction à l'oeuvre de Marcel Mauss* (p. 47): "Language could only have been born suddenly." We might well find numerous questions to raise about this paragraph, which ties sense to signification and more narrowly to linguistic signification in the *spoken* language. Let us simply read these few lines:

Whatever might have been the moment and the circumstances of its appearance on the scale of animal life, language could only have been born suddenly. Things could not have begun to signify progressively. Following a transformation whose study does not belong to the social sciences, but to biology and psychology, a passage was effected from a stage where nothing had sense to another where everything did.

(That biology and psychology could account for this rupture would seem to us more than problematic. There follows a fertile distinction between *signifying* discourse and *knowing* discourse, which, some fifty years previously, a philosopher of consciousness, more neglected than others, had articulated rigorously in logical investigations.) *

This epigenetism is, nevertheless, not the most Rousseauist aspect of a thought which so often gives as its authority the *Essay on the Origin of Languages* and the second *Discourse*—where however it is also a question of "the infinite space of time that the first invention of languages must have cost" [p. 189].

The traditional and fundamental ethnocentrism which, inspired by the model of phonetic writing, separates writing from speech with an ax, is thus handled and thought of as anti-ethnocentrism. It supports an ethico-political accusation: man's exploitation by man is the fact of writing cultures of the Western type. Communities of innocent and unoppressive speech are free from this accusation.

On the other hand—it is the other side of the same gesture—if Lévi-Strauss constantly recognizes the pertinence of the division between peoples with and peoples without writing, this division is effaced by him from the moment that one might ethnocentrically wish to make it play a role in the reflection on history and on the respective value of cultures. The difference between peoples with and peoples without writing is accepted, but writing as the criterion of historicity or cultural value is not taken into account; ethnocentrism will apparently be avoided at the very moment when it will have already profoundly operated, silently imposing its standard concepts of speech and writing. This was exactly the pattern of the Saussurian gesture. In other words, all the liberating criticisms and legitimate denunciations with which Lévi-Strauss has harried the presupposed distinctions between historical societies and societies without history, remain dependent on the concept of writing I problematize here.

What is the "Writing Lesson?"

Lesson in a double sense. The title effectively preserves both senses. Writing lesson since it is a question of the learning of writing. The Nambikwara chief learns writing from the anthropologist, at first without

* Edmund Husserl, *Logische Untersuchungen, Husserliana*, Nijhoff edition (1950–), vol. 18; *Logical Investigations*, tr. J. N. Findley (New York).

comprehension, he mimics writing before he understands its function as language; or rather he understands its profoundly enslaving function before understanding its function, here accessory, of communication, signification, of the tradition of a signified. But the writing lesson is also a lesson learned from writing; instruction that the anthropologist believes he can induce from the incident in the course of a long meditation, when, fighting against insomnia, he reflects on the origin, function, and meaning of writing. Having taught the gesture of writing to a Nambikwara chief who learned without comprehension, the anthropologist understands what he has taught and induces the lesson of writing.

Thus, two moments:

A. The empirical relation of a perception: the scene of the "extraordinary incident."

B. After the vicissitudes of the day, sleepless in the watches of the night, a historico-philosophical reflection on the scene of writing and the profound meaning of the incident, of the closed history of writing.

A. *The extraordinary incident.* From the very first lines, the decor reminds us of that anthropological violence of which I spoke above. The two parts are well engaged here, and that restores the true meaning of the remarks on "a great sweetness of nature," "an animal satisfaction as ingenuous as it is charming," the "profound nonchalance," "the most moving and authentic manifestations of human tenderness." For example:

> . . . their more than dubious welcome combined with their leader's extreme nervousness seemed to suggest that he had forced their hand, somewhat, in the whole matter. Neither we nor the Indians felt at all at our ease, the night promised to be cold, and, as there were no trees, we had to lie, like the Nambikwara, on the bare ground. No one slept: we kept, all night long, a polite watch upon one another. It would have been rash to prolong the adventure, and I suggested to the leader that we should get down to our exchanges without further delay. It was then that there occurred an extraordinary incident which forces me to go back a little in time. That the Nambikwara could not write goes without saying. But they were also unable to draw, except for a few dots and zigzags on their calabashes. I distributed pencils and paper among them, none the less, as I had done with the Caduveo. At first they made no use of them. Then, one day, I saw that they were all busy drawing wavy horizontal lines on the paper. What were they trying to do? I could only conclude that they were writing—or, more exactly, they were trying to do as I did with my pencils. As I had never tried to amuse them with drawings, they could not conceive of any other use for this implement. With most of them, that was as far as they got: but their leader saw further into the problem. Doubtless he was the only one among them to have understood what writing was for [p. 288].

Let us mark a first pause here. Among many others, this fragment comes superimposed upon a passage from the thesis on the Nambikwara. The incident was already related there and it may be useful to refer to it. Three specific points omitted from *Tristes Tropiques* can be found in the thesis. They are not without interest.

1. This small group of Nambikwara[20] nevertheless uses a word to designate the act of writing, at least a word that may serve that end. There is no linguistic surprise in the face of the supposed irruption of a new power. This detail, omitted from *Tristes Tropiques,* was indicated in the thesis:

> The Nambikwara of group (a) do not know anything about design, if one excepts some geometric sketches on their calabashes. For many days, they did not know what to do with the paper and the pencils that we distributed to them. Some time later, we saw them very busily drawing wavy lines. In that they imitated the only use that they had seen us make of our notebooks, namely writing, but without understanding its meaning or its end. They called the act of writing iekariukedjutu, namely: "drawing lines."

It is quite evident that a literal translation of the words that mean "to write" in the languages of peoples with writing would also reduce that word to a rather poor gestural signification. It is as if one said that such a language has no word designating writing—and that therefore those who practice it do not know how to write—just because they use a word meaning "to scratch," "to engrave," "to scribble," "to scrape," "to incise," "to trace," "to imprint," etc. As if "to write" in its metaphoric kernel, meant something else. Is not ethnocentrism always betrayed by the haste with which it is satisfied by certain translations or certain domestic equivalents? To say that a people do not know how to write because one can translate the word which they use to designate the act of inscribing as "drawing lines," is that not as if one should refuse them "speech" by translating the equivalent word by "to cry," "to sing," "to sigh?" Indeed "to stammer." By way of simple analogy with respect to the mechanisms of ethnocentric assimilation/exclusion, let us recall with Renan that, "in the most ancient languages, the words used to designate foreign peoples are drawn from two sources: either words that signify 'to stammer,' 'to mumble,' or words that signify 'mute.' "[21] And ought one to conclude that the Chinese are a people without writing because the word *wen* designates many things besides writing in the narrow sense? As in fact J. Gernet notes:

> The word *wen* signifies a conglomeration of marks, the simple symbol in writing. It applies to the veins in stones and wood, to constellations, represented by the strokes connecting the stars, to the tracks of birds and quadrupeds on the ground (Chinese tradition would have it that the observation of these tracks suggested the invention of writing), to tattoo and even, for example, to the designs that decorate the turtle's shell ("The turtle is wise," an ancient text says—gifted with magico-religious powers—"for it carries designs on its back"). The term *wen* has designated, by extension, literature and social courtesy. Its

antonyms are the words *wu* (warrior, military) and *zhi* (brute matter not yet polished or ornamented).[22]

2. In this operation, which consists of "drawing lines" and which is thus incorporated into the dialect of this subgroup, Lévi-Strauss finds an exclusively "aesthetic" signification: "They called the act of writing iekariukedjutu, namely 'drawing lines,' which had an aesthetic interest for them." One wonders what the import of such a conclusion could be and what the specificity of the aesthetic category could signify here. Lévi-Strauss seems not only to presume that one can isolate aesthetic value (which is clearly most problematic, and in fact it is the anthropologists more than anyone else who have put us on guard against this abstraction), but also to suppose that in writing "properly speaking," to which the Nambikwara would not have access, the aesthetic quality is extrinsic. Let us merely mention this problem. Moreover, even if one did not wish to treat the meaning of such a conclusion with suspicion, one could still be troubled by the paths that lead to it. The anthropologist has arrived at this conclusion through a sentence noted in *another* subgroup: "Kihikagnere mũ\iene" translated by "drawing lines, that's pretty." To conclude from this proposition thus translated and recorded within another group (bl), that drawing lines held for group (al) an "aesthetic interest," which implies *only* an aesthetic interest, is what poses problems of logic that once again we are content simply to mention.

3. When, in *Tristes Tropiques*, Lévi-Strauss remarks that "the Nambikwara could not write . . . they were also unable to draw, except for a few dots and zigzags on their calabashes," because, helped by instruments furnished by them, they trace only "wavy horizontal lines" and that "with most of them, that was as far as they got," these notations are brief. Not only are they not to be found in the thesis, but, in fact, eighty pages further on (p. 123), the thesis presents the results at which certain Nambikwara very quickly arrived and which Lévi-Strauss treats as "a cultural innovation inspired by our own designs." It is not merely a question of representational designs (cf. Figure 19, p. 123) showing a man or a monkey, but of diagrams describing, explaining, writing, a genealogy and a social structure. And that is a decisive phenomenon. It is now known, thanks to unquestionable and abundant information, that the birth of writing (in the colloquial sense) was nearly everywhere and most often linked to genealogical anxiety. The memory and oral tradition of generations, which sometimes goes back very far with peoples supposedly "without writing," are often cited in this connection. Lévi-Strauss himself does it in the *Conversations* (p. 29) [p. 26]:

I know, of course, that the societies we call primitive often have a quite staggering capacity for remembering, and we have been told about Polynesian communities who can recite straight off family trees involving dozens of generations; but that kind of feat obviously has its limits.

Now it is this limit which is crossed more or less everywhere when writing—in the colloquial sense—appears. Here its function is to conserve and give to a genealogical classification, with all that that might imply, a supplementary objectification of another order. So that a people who accede to the genealogical pattern accede also to writing in the colloquial sense, understand its function and go much farther than *Tristes Tropiques* gives it to be understood ("that was as far as they got"). Here one passes from arche-writing to writing in the colloquial sense. This passage, whose difficulty I do not wish to underestimate, is not a passage from speech to writing, it operates within writing in general. The genealogical relation and social classification are the stitched seam of arche-writing, condition of the (so-called oral) language, and of writing in the colloquial sense.

"But their leader saw further into the problem." The dissertation tells us that this leader is "remarkably intelligent, aware of his responsibilities, active, enterprising, and ingenious." "He was a man of about thirty-five, married to three women." "His attitude to writing is most revealing. He immediately understood its role as sign, and the social superiority that it confers." Lévi-Strauss follows up with an account which is reproduced in nearly the same terms in *Tristes Tropiques*:

> Doubtless he was the only one among them who understood what writing was for. So he asked me for one of my note pads and thus we were similarly equipped when we were working together; he did not give me his answers in words, but traced a wavy line or two on the paper and gave it to me, as if I could read what he had to say. He himself was all but deceived by his own play-acting. Each time he drew a line he examined it with great care, as if its meaning must suddenly leap to the eye; and every time a look of disappointment came over his face. But he would never give up trying, and there was an unspoken agreement between us that his scribblings had a meaning that I pretended to decipher; his own verbal commentary was so prompt in coming that I had no need to ask him to explain what he had written [pp. 288–89].

What immediately follows this passage corresponds to a passage in the thesis which comes more than forty pages (p. 89) after the above and concerns the function of the commandment, a significant fact to which I shall return.

> And now, no sooner was everyone assembled than he drew forth from a basket a piece of paper covered with scribbled lines and pretended to read from it. With a show of hesitation he looked up and down his "list" for the objects to be given in exchange for his people's presents. To so and so a bow and arrows, a machete! and another a string of beads! for his necklaces—and so on for

two solid hours. What was he hoping for? To deceive himself, perhaps: but, even more, to amaze his companions and persuade them that *his* intermediacy was responsible for the exchanges, that he had allied himself with the white man, and that he could now share in his secrets. We were in a hurry to get away, since there would obviously be a moment of real danger at which all the marvels I had brought would have been handed over. . . . So I did not go further into the matter and we set off on the return journey, still guided by the Indians [p. 289].

The story is very beautiful. It is in fact tempting to read it as a parable in which each element, each semanteme, refers to a recognized function of writing: hierarchization, the economic function of mediation and of capitalization, participation in a quasi-religious secret; all this, verified in any phenomenon of writing, is here assembled, concentrated, organized in the structure of an exemplary event or a very brief sequence of fact and gestures. All the organic complexity of writing is here collected within the simple focus of a parable.

B. *The rememoration of the scene*. Let us now pass on to the lesson of the lesson. It is longer than the relation of the incident, covers three very dense pages, and the text of the *Conversations*, which reproduces the essential parts of it, is considerably briefer. It is therefore in the thesis that the incident is reported without theoretical commentary and in the anthropologist's confession that the theory is most abundantly developed.

Let us follow the thread of the demonstration through the evocation of apparently unquestionable historical facts. It is the split between the factual certainty and its interpretative reconsideration that will be of special interest to us. The most serious split appears first, but not only, between the meager fact of the "extraordinary incident" and the general philosophy of writing. The point of the incident in effect supports an enormous theoretical edifice.

After the "extraordinary incident," the anthropologist's situation remains precarious. Certain words dominate the description: "abortive meeting," "mystifications," "something irritating," the anthropologist "suddenly . . . found . . . [himself] alone, and lost, in the middle of the bush," "in despair," "demoralized," he "was no longer armed" in a "hostile zone" and he is agitated by "dark thoughts." Then the threat subsides, the hostility disappears. It is night, the incident is closed, the exchanges have taken place; it is time to reflect upon the story, it is the moment of wakefulness and rememoration. "Still tormented by this absurd incident, I slept badly. To while away the hours I went back, in my mind, to the scene of the previous morning."

Two significances are quickly drawn from the incident itself.

1. The appearance of writing is *instantaneous*. It is not prepared for. Such a leap would prove that the possibility of writing does not inhabit

speech, but the outside of speech. "So writing had made its appearance among the Nambikwara! But not at all, as one might have supposed, as the result of a laborious apprenticeship." From what does Lévi-Strauss arrive at this epigenetism that is indispensable if one wishes to safeguard the exteriority of writing to speech? From the incident? But the scene was not the scene of the *origin*, but only that of the *imitation* of writing. Even if it were a question of writing, what has the character of suddenness here is not the passage to writing, the invention of writing, but the importation of an already constituted writing. It is a borrowing and an artificial borrowing. As Lévi-Strauss himself says: "The symbol had been borrowed, but the reality remained quite foreign to them" [p. 290]. Besides, this character of suddenness obviously belongs to all the phenomena of the diffusion or transmission of writing. It could never describe the appearance of writing, which has, on the contrary, been laborious, progressive, and differentiated in its stages. And the rapidity of the borrowing, when it happens, presupposes the previous presence of the structures that make it possible.

2. The second significance that Lévi-Strauss believes he can read in the very text of the scene is connected to the first. Since they learned without understanding, since the Chief used writing effectively without knowing either the way it functioned or the content signified by it, the end of writing is political and not theoretical, "*sociological, rather than . . . intellectual*" [p. 290]. This opens and covers the entire space within which Lévi-Strauss is now going to think writing.

> The symbol had been borrowed, but the reality remained quite foreign to them. Even the borrowing had had a sociological, rather than an intellectual object: for it was not a question of knowing specific things, or understanding them, or keeping them in mind, but merely of enhancing the prestige and authority of one individual—or one function—at the expense of the rest of the party. A native, still in the period of the stone age, had realized that even if he could not himself understand the great instrument of understanding he could at least make it serve other ends [p. 290].

Distinguishing thus "the sociological" from the "intellectual end," attributing the former and not the latter to writing, one credits a very problematic difference between intersubjective relationship and knowledge. If it is true, as I in fact believe, that writing cannot be thought outside of the horizon of intersubjective violence, is there anything, even science, that radically escapes it? Is there a knowledge, and, above all, a language, scientific or not, that one can call alien at once to writing and to violence? If one answers in the negative, as I do, the use of these concepts to discern the specific character of writing is not pertinent. So much so that all the examples[28] by which Lévi-Strauss next illustrates this proposition are of course true and probing, but too much so. The conclusion that they sustain goes far beyond the field of what is here called "writing" ("writing" in the usual sense). It also covers the field of unwritten speech. In other words, if writing is to be related to violence, writing appears well before writing in the narrow sense; already in the differance or the arche-writing that opens speech itself.

Thus suggesting what he will later confirm, that the essential function of writing is to favor the enslaving power rather than "disinterested" science, according to the distinction he seems to hold, Lévi-Strauss now can, in a second wave of meditation, neutralize the frontier between peoples without and with writing; not with regard to the use of writing, but with regard to what is supposed to be deducible from it, with regard to their historicity or nonhistoricity. This neutralization is very valuable; it authorizes the themes (a) of the essential and irreducible relativity in the perception of historical movement (cf. *Race et Histoire*), (b) of the differences between "warm" and "cold" in the "historical temperature" of societies (*Conversations*, p. 43 [pp. 38–39] and passim), (c) of the relationships between anthropology and history.[24]

Thus, given this trust in the presumed difference between knowledge and power, it is a matter of showing that writing is not at all pertinent to the appreciation of historical rhythms and types; the age of the wholesale creation of social, economic, technical, political, and other structures, upon which we still subsist—the neolithic age—did not know writing.[25] What does this imply?

In the text that follows, I shall isolate three potentially controversial propositions. I shall not engage in the controversy, because I want to proceed more quickly to the end of the argument that interests Lévi-Strauss and to situate the debate there.

First Proposition.

> After eliminating all the criteria by which people habitually distinguish civilization from barbarism, this one should at least be retained: that certain peoples write and others do not. The first group can accumulate a body of knowledge [earlier acquisitions—*acquisitions anciennes*] that helps it to move ever faster toward the goal that it has assigned to itself; the second is confined within limits that the memory of individuals can never hope to extend, and it must remain the prisoner of a history worked out from day to day, with neither an origin nor the lasting consciousness of a plan. Yet nothing of what we know of writing, or of its role in evolution, can be said to justify this conception [p. 291].

This proposition has meaning only on two conditions:

1. That one take no notice of the idea and the project of science, of the idea, that is, of truth as a theoretically infinite transmissibility; this has an historical possibility only with writing. Faced with the Husserlian analyses (*Krisis* and *The Origin of Geometry*) which remind us of this evidence, Lévi-Strauss's proposal can be sustained only by denying all spec-

ificity to the scientific project and to the value of truth in general. This last position does not lack force, but it cannot show the worth and coherence of that force except by relinquishing its claim to be a scientific discourse. A well-known pattern. It is in *fact* what seems to be happening here.

2. That the Neolithic, to which in fact may be attributed the creation of the deep structures upon which we still live, did not know anything like writing. It is here that the concept of writing, as it is used by a modern anthropologist, would seem singularly narrow. Anthropology today gives us a great deal of information about scripts that preceded the alphabet, about other systems of phonetic writing or systems quite ready to be phoneticized. The weight of this information makes it unnecessary for us to insist.

Second Proposition. Supposing every thing was acquired before writing, Lévi-Strauss has only to argue:

> Conversely, between the invention of writing and the birth of modern science, the western world has lived through some five thousand years, during which time the sum of its knowledge has rather *gone up and down* than known *a steady increase* [p. 292] (italics added).

One could be shocked by this affirmation, but I shall avoid that. I do not believe that such an affirmation is *false*. But no more do I believe that it is *true*. It is rather an answer, suiting a particular purpose, to a meaningless question.[26] Is not the notion of the quantity of knowledge suspect? What is a quantity of knowledge? How is it modified? Without speaking of the science of order or of quality, we may wonder what the quantity of the science of pure quantity signifies. How can it be evaluated in quantity? Such questions can only be answered in the style of pure empiricity. Unless one attempts to respect the very complex laws of the capitalization of learning, something that cannot be done without considering writing more attentively. One can say the opposite of what Lévi-Strauss says and it would be neither truer nor more false. One can say that during such and such a half-century, even before "modern science," and today every minute, the accretion of knowledge has gone infinitely beyond what it was for millennia. So much for accretion. As for the notion of fluctuation, it presents itself as perfectly empirical. In any case, propositions of essence can never be made to fit a scale.

Third Proposition. It is the most disconcerting step in the development of this paragraph. Let us suppose that the advent of writing three or four thousand years ago had brought nothing decisive in the domain of knowledge. Lévi-Strauss concedes nevertheless that it has not at all been the same thing for the last two centuries. However, according to his own scale, it is not clear what justifies this cut-off point. Yet it is there: "Doubtless the scientific expansion of the nineteenth and twentieth centuries could hardly have occurred, had writing not existed. But this condition, however necessary, cannot in itself explain that expansion" [p. 292]

Not only is the cut-off point surprising, but one also wonders what particular objection Lévi-Strauss seems to reject here. No one has ever thought that writing—the written notation, since that is at issue here—was the sufficient condition of science; and that it would suffice to know how to write in order to be learned. Much has been written that would suffice to rid us of this illusion if we possessed it. But to recognize that writing is the "necessary condition" of science, that there is no science without writing, is what is important, and Lévi-Strauss knows this. And as it is difficult in any rigorous way to place the beginnings of science in the nineteenth century, his entire argument founders on or is contaminated by the gross mark of empirical approximation.

In truth this depends—and that is why I pass over this argument quickly—on the fact that Lévi-Strauss is determined to abandon this terrain, to explain very quickly why the problem of science is not the best access to the origin and function of writing: "If we want to correlate the appearance of writing with certain other characteristics of civilization, we must look elsewhere" [p. 292]. Thus it must rather be domonstrated that, according to the dissociation which had perplexed us, the origin of writing responded to a more "sociological" than "intellectual" necessity. The following page must therefore not only make clear this sociological necessity—which would be a poor truism and would have little enough to do with the sociological specificity of writing—but also that this social necessity is that of "domination," "exploitation," "enslavement," and "perfidy."

To read this page appropriately, one must differentiate it into its strata. The author presents here what he calls his "hypothesis:" "If my hypothesis is correct, the primary function of writing, as a means of communication, is to facilitate[27] the enslavement of other human beings." On a first level, this hypothesis is so quickly confirmed that it hardly merits its name. These facts are well known. It has long been known that the power of writing in the hands of a small number, caste, or class, is always contemporaneous with hierarchization, let us say with political differance; it is at the same time distinction into groups, classes, and levels of economico-politico-technical power, and delegation of authority, power deferred and abandoned to an organ of capitalization. This phenomenon is produced from the very onset of sedentarization; with the constitution of stocks at the origin of agricultural societies. Here things are so patent[28] that the empirical illustration that Lévi-Strauss sketches could be infinitely enriched. This entire structure appears as soon as a society begins to live as a society, that is to say from the origin of life in general, when, at very heterogeneous levels of organization and complexity, it is possible to *defer presence*, that is to say *expense* or consumption, and to organize production, that is to say *reserve* in general. This is produced well before the appearance of writing in the narrow sense, but it is true, and one cannot ignore it, that the appearance of certain systems of writing three or four thousand years ago was an extraordinary leap in the history of life. All the more extraordinary because a prodigious expansion of the power of differance was not accompanied, at least during these millennia, by any notable transformation of the organism. It is precisely the property of the power of differance to modify life less and less as it spreads out more and more. If it should grow *infinite*—and its essence excludes this a priori—life itself would be made into an impassive, intangible, and eternal presence: infinite differance, God or death.

This leads us to a second level of reading. It will show, at the same time, Lévi-Strauss's final intention, toward which the demonstration orients the factual evidence, as well as the political ideology that, in the name of a Marxist hypothesis, is articulated with the finest example of what I have called the "metaphysics of presence."

Previously the empirical character of the analyses concerning the status of science and the accumulation of knowledge removed all rigor from each of the propositions advanced and permitted their consideration with an equal pertinence as true or false. It is the pertinence of the question which appeared doubtful. The same thing happens here again. What is going to be called *enslavement* can equally legitimately be called *liberation*. And it is at the moment that this oscillation is *stopped* on the signification of enslavement that the discourse is frozen into a determined ideology that we would judge disturbing if such were our first preoccupation here.

In this text, Lévi-Strauss does not distinguish between hierarchization and domination, between political authority and exploitation. The tone that pervades these reflections is of an anarchism that deliberately confounds law and oppression. The idea of law and positive right, although it is difficult to think them in their formality—where it is so general that ignorance of the law is no defense—before the possibility of writing, is determined by Lévi-Strauss as constraint and enslavement. Political power can only be the custodian of an unjust power. A classical and coherent thesis, but here advanced as self-evident, without opening the least bit of critical dialogue with the holders of the other thesis, according to which the generality of the law is on the contrary the condition of liberty in the city. No dialogue, for example, with Rousseau who would no doubt have shuddered to see a self-proclaimed disciple define law as follows:

> Writing may not have sufficed to consolidate human knowledge, but it may well have been indispensable to the consolidation of dominions. To bring the matter nearer to our own time: the European-wide movement towards compulsory education in the nineteenth century went hand in hand with the extension of military service and with proletarization. The struggle against illiteracy is thus indistinguishable from the increased powers exerted over the individual

citizen by the central authority. For it is only when everyone can read that Authority can decree that "ignorance of law is no defence."[29]

One must be careful in order to appreciate these grave declarations. One must above all avoid reversing them and taking the opposite view. In a certain given historical structure—for example, in the age of which Lévi-Strauss speaks—it is undoubtedly true that the progress of formal legality, the struggle against illiteracy, and the like, could have functioned as a mystifying force and an instrument consolidating the power of a class or a state whose formal-universal significance was confiscated by a particular empirical force. Perhaps this necessity is indispensable and impossible to supersede. But to derive from it the authority to define the law and the state in a simple and univocal manner, to condemn them from an ethical point of view, and with them the extension of writing, compulsory military service and proletarization, the generality of political obligation and the idea that "ignorance of the law is no defense," is a consequence that cannot be rigorously deduced from these premises. If they are nevertheless deduced, as here, it must also be concluded that nonexploitation, liberty and the like "go hand in hand" (to utilize this most equivocal concept) with illiteracy and the absence of compulsory military service, public instruction or law in general. I shall not belabor the obvious.

Let us beware of opposing Lévi-Strauss to the system of classical argumen's, or of opposing him to himself (on the preceding page, he had linked the violence of writing to the fact that it was reserved for a minority, confiscated by the scribes in the service of a caste. Now, an enslaving violence is assigned to total literacy.) The incoherence is only apparent; universality is always monopolized as empirical force by a determined empirical force, such is the unique affirmation that is common to both these propositions.

In order to tackle this problem, should one wonder what the meaning of enslavement to a law of universal form can be? One could do it, but it is better to give up that classical course; it would soon enough show us that the access to writing is the constitution of a free subject in the violent movement of its own effacement and of its own bondage. A movement unthinkable within the classical concepts of ethics, psychology, political philospohy, and metaphysics. Let us leave that proposition up in the air, for we have not yet finished reading the writing "Lesson."

For Lévi-Strauss goes further under the auspices of this libertarian ideology, whose anticolonialist and antiethnocentric hue is rather specific:

All this moved rapidly from the national to the international level, thanks to the mutual complicity which sprang up between new-born states—confronted as these were with the problems that had been our own, a century or two ago—

and an international society of peoples long privileged. These latter recognize that their stability may well be endangered by nations whose knowledge of the written word has not, as yet, empowered them to think in formulae which can be modified at will. Such nations are not yet ready to be "edified;" and when they are first given the freedom of the library shelves [*au savoir* entassé *dans les bibliothèques*] they are perilously vulnerable to the ever more deliberately misleading (mendacious—*mensonges*] effects of the printed word (italics added).

Taking the same precautions that we took a moment ago with respect to the possible truthfulness of such statements, let us paraphrase this text. It is, in the name of the liberty of formerly colonized peoples, a critique of the young states that side with the old states so recently denounced ("complicity . . . between young states . . . and an international society of peoples long privileged"). Critique of an "enterprise:" the propagation of writing is presented through the concepts of a voluntarist psychology, the international political phenomenon that it constitutes is described in terms of a deliberately and consciously organized plot. A critique of the State in general and of the young States that extend writing for propagandistic ends, to assure the legibility and effectiveness of their tracts, to protect themselves from "nations whose knowledge of the written word has not, as yet, empowered them to think in formulae which can be modified at will." Which implies that oral formulae are not modifiable, not more modifiable at will than written formulae. This is not the least of the paradoxes. Yet once again, I do not profess that writing may not and does not in fact play this role, but from that to attribute to writing the specificity of this role and to conclude that speech is exempt from it, is an abyss that one must not leap over so lightly. I shall not comment on what is said about access to "[knowledge *piled up on*] library shelves," determined in an unequivocal way as vulnerability to the "mendacious effects of the printed word" and so on. The ideological atmosphere within which such formulae breathe *today* could be described. Suffice it to recognize here the heritage of the second *Discourse* ("throwing aside, therefore, all those scientific books . . . and contemplating the first and most simple operations of the human soul . . ." [p. 157] "O man, . . . behold your history, such as I have thought to read it, not in books written by your fellow-creatures, who are liars, but in nature, which never lies" [p. 176]), of *Emile* ("The misuse of books is the death of learning . . ." ". . . so many books lead us to neglect the book of the world . . ." ". . . we should not read, but rather look." "I get rid of the chief cause of their sorrows, namely their books. Reading is the curse of childhood." "The child who reads ceases to think," etc.), of *A Savoyard Priest* ("So I closed all my books . . ."), (pp. 574, 575, 186, 378) [pp. 414, 415, 131, 270] of the *Lettre à Christophe de Beaumont*

("I looked for truth in books: I found in them nothing but lies and error").*

After this nocturnal meditation, Lévi-Strauss returns to the "extraordinary incident." And it is to give praise, now justified by history, to those wise Nambikwara who had the courage to resist writing as well as the mystification of their leader. Praise to those who knew to interrupt—only for a time, alas—the fatal course of evolution and who "[won] themselves a respite." In this respect and with regard to what concerns Nambikwara society, the anthropologist is resolutely conservative. As he will note about a hundred pages later, "at home, the anthropologist may be a natural subversive, a convinced opponent of traditional usage: but no sooner has he in focus a society different from his own than he becomes respectful of even the most conservative practices" [p. 380].

Two motifs in the concluding lines: on the one hand, as with Rousseau, the theme of a necessary or rather fatal degradation, as the very form of progress; on the other hand, nostalgia for what preceded this degradation, an affective impulse toward the islets of resistance, the small communities that have provisionally protected themselves from corruption (cf. *Conversations*, p. 49 [p. 41] on this subject), a corruption linked, as in Rousseau, to writing and to the dislocation of a unanimous people assembled in the self-presence of its speech. We shall return to this. Let us read: "Doubtless the die is already cast" (the question here is the fatal evolution into which peoples who were hitherto protected from writing are already seduced; a more fatalistic than determinable proposition. The historical concatenation is thought under the concept of play and chance. The frequent metaphor of the player in Lévi-Strauss's texts must be studied). "But in *my* Nambikwara village people [in the original "*fortes têtes*," "strong-minded people"] were not so easily taken in" (italics added).

These strong-minded people are the resisters, those whom their leader could not trick, and who have more character than subtlety, more heart and traditional pride than openness of mind.

> Those who moved away from him, after he had tried to play the civilized man (after my visit he was abandoned by most of his followers), must have had a confused understanding of the fact that writing, on this its first appearance in their midst, had allied itself with falsehood; and so they had taken refuge, deeper in the bush, to win themselves a respite [p. 293].

(The episode of this resistance is also given in the thesis, p. 89.)

1.—If words have a meaning, and if "writing, on this its first appearance in their midst, had allied itself with falsehood," one should think that deception and all the associated values and nonvalues were absent in societies

* *Oeuvres complètes* (Paris, 1835), p. 775.

without writing. To doubt this it is not necessary to cover a lot of ground; only an empirical detour by the evocation of facts, the aprioric or transcendental regression that we followed by way of introduction. Recalling in this introduction that violence did not wait for the appearance of writing in the narrow sense, that writing has always begun in language, we, like Lévi-Strauss, conclude that violence is writing. But, coming at it another way, this proposition has a radically different meaning. It ceases to be supported by the myth of myth, by the myth of a speech originally good, and of a violence which would come to pounce upon it as a fatal accident. A fatal accident which is nothing but history itself. Not that, by this more or less overt reference to the idea of a fall into evil from the innocence of the word, Lévi-Strauss makes this classical and implicit theology his own. It is just that his anthropological discourse is produced through concepts, schemata, and values that are, systematically and genealogically, accomplices of this theology and this metaphysics.

Therefore I shall not make the long empirical or aprioric disgression here. I shall merely compare different moments in the description of Nambikwara society. If the "Lesson" is to be believed, the Nambikwara did not know violence before writing; nor hierarchization, since that is quickly assimilated into exploitation. Round about the "Lesson," it suffices to open *Tristes Tropiques* and the thesis at any page to find striking evidence to the contrary. We are dealing here not only with a strongly hierarchized society, but with a society where relationships are marked with a spectacular violence. As spectacular as the innocent and tender frolics evoked at the beginning of the "Lesson," and that we were thus justified in considering as the calculated premises of a loaded argument.

Among many analogous passages that we cannot cite here, let us look at page 87 of the dissertation. The subject is clearly the Nambikwara before writing:

And the leader must display an unfailing talent, related more to electoral politics than to the exercise of power, to maintain his group, and, if possible, enlarge it through new memberships. The nomadic band represents in fact a fragile unity. If the leader's authority is too exacting, if he monopolizes too great a number of women, if he is not capable—during periods of dearth—of resolving problems of food, discontent arises, individuals or families break away and conglomerate into a kindred group whose affairs seem better conducted; better nourished due to the discovery of hunting- or fruit-and-berry-picking grounds, or richer through exchange with neighboring groups, or more powerful after victorious battles. The leader then finds himself at the head of too limited a group, incapable of facing daily difficulties, or whose women are open to rape by stronger neighbors. He is then obliged to abdicate, and with his last faithful friends, to throw in his lot with a more fortunate faction; Nambikwara society is thus in a perpetual state of flux; groups form and unform, enlarge and disappear and, sometimes at intervals of a few months, the composition, number, and regrouping of the bands become unrecognizable. All these transformations are accompanied by intrigues and conflicts, rises and falls, all being produced at an extremely fast pace.

One could also cite entire chapters of the thesis entitled "War and Commerce," and "From Birth to Death." Also everything concerning the use of poisons, in the thesis and in *Tristes Tropiques;* just as there is a battle of proper names, there is a battle of poisons in which the anthropologist is himself embroiled:

A delegation of four men came to me and, in a quite threatening tone, asked me to mix poison (which they brought me at the same time) with the next dish that I should offer to A6; it was considered indispensable to suppress him rapidly, because, I was told, he was "very wicked" (kakore) "and totally worthless" (aidotiene) (p. 124).

I shall cite only one more passage, happy complement of an idyllic description:

I have described the tender comradeship which presides over the relationship between the sexes, and the general harmony which reigns in the bosom of the groups. But as soon as these change for the worse, it is to make room for the most extreme solutions: poisonings and assassinations. . . . No South American group, to our knowledge, conveys in so sincere and spontaneous a manner . . . violent and opposed sentiments, whose individual expression seems indissociable from a social stylization that never betrays them (p. 126).

(Is this final formula not applicable to all social groups in general?)

2.—Thus we are led back to Rousseau. The ideal profoundly underlying this philosophy of writing is therefore the image of a community immediately present to itsef, without difference, a community of speech where all the members are within earshot. To confirm this, I shall refer neither to *Tristes Tropiques* nor to its theoretical echo (the *Conversations*), but to a text included in *Structural Anthropology* and completed in 1958 with allusions to *Tristes Tropiques.* Writing is here defined as the condition of *social inauthenticity*:

In this respect it is, rather, modern societies that should be defined by a privative character. Our relations with one another are now only occasionally and fragmentarily based upon global experience, *the concrete "apprehension" of one person by another*. They are largely the result of a [indirect] construction, through written documents. We are no longer linked to our past by an oral tradition which implies *direct* [*vécu*] *contact* with others (storytellers, priests, wise men, or elders), but by books *amassed* in libraries, books from which criticism endeavors—with extreme difficulty—to form a picture of their authors. And we communicate with the immense majority of our contemporaries by all kinds of intermediaries—written documents or administrative machinery—which undoubtedly vastly extend our contacts but at the same time make those contacts somewhat "*unauthentic.*" This has become typical of the relationship between the citizen and the public authorities. We should like to avoid describing negatively the tremendous revolution brought about by the invention of writing. But it is essential to realize that writing, while it conferred vast benefits on humanity, did in fact deprive it of something fundamental. (pp. 400–02; italics added) [pp. 363–64]

From then on, the anthropologist's mission carries an ethical significance: to find and fix on that terrain the "levels of authenticity." The criterion of authenticity is the "neighborliness" in the small communities where "everyone knows everyone else."

On the contrary, if we carefully consider the points on which anthropological investigations have been brought to bear, we note that in its increasingly intensive study of modern societies, anthropology has endeavored to identify *levels of authenticity* within them. When the ethnologist studies a village, an enterprise, or the neighborhood of a large town, his task is facilitated by the fact that almost everyone knows everyone else. . . . In the future, it will no doubt be recognized that anthropology's most important contribution to social sciences is to have introduced, if unknowingly, this fundamental distinction between two types of social existence: a way of life recognized at the outset as traditional and archaic and characteristic of "authentic" societies and a more modern form of existence, from which the first-named type is not absent but where groups that are not completely, or are imperfectly, "authentic" are organized within a much larger and specifically "unauthentic" system (pp. 402–03) [pp. 364–65].

The clarity of this text is sufficient unto itself. "In the future, it may be recognized" if this is in fact "anthropology's most important contribution to social science." This model of a small community with a "crystalline" structure, completely self-present, assembled in its own neighborhood, is undoubtedly Rousseauistic.

We shall have to examine this very closely in more than one text. For the moment, and always for the same reasons, let us rather turn to the *Essay*. Rousseau shows there that social *distance*, the dispersion of the neighborhood, is the condition of oppression, arbitrariness, and vice. The governments of oppression all make the same gesture: to break presence, the co-presence of citizens, the unanimity of "assembled peoples," to create a situation of dispersion, holding subjects so far apart as to be incapable of feeling themselves together in the space of one and the same speech, one and the same persuasive exchange. This phenomenon is described in the last chapter of the *Essay*. The now recognized ambiguity of this structure is such that one can equally well reverse its direction and show that this co-presence is sometimes also that of the crowd subjected to a demagogic harangue. We must attend to the signs of Rousseau's vigilance when confronted by the possibility of such a reversal. Nevertheless, the *Essay* first puts us on guard against the structures of social life and of information within the modern political machine. It is a praise of eloquence or rather of the elocution of the full speech, a condemnation of mute and impersonal signs: money, tracts ("placards"), weapons and soldiers in uniform:

The languages develop naturally on the basis of men's needs, changing and varying as those needs change. In ancient times, when persuasion played the role of public force, eloquence was necessary. Of what use would it be today, when public force has replaced persuasion. One needs neither art nor metaphor to say *such is my pleasure*. What sort of public discourses remain then? Sermons. And why should those who preach them be concerned to persuade the people, since it is not they who dispose of benefices. Our popular tongues have become just as completely useless as eloquence. Societies have assumed their final form: no longer is anything changed except by arms and cash. And since there is nothing to say to people besides *give money*, it is said with placards on street corners or by soldiers in their homes. It is not necessary to assemble anyone for that. On the contrary, the subjects must be kept apart. That is the first maxim of modern politics. . . . It was easy for the ancients to make themselves understood by people in public. They could speak all day with no discomfort. . . . If a man were to harangue the people of Paris in the Place Vendôme in French, if he shouted at the top of his voice, people would hear him shouting, but they would not be able to distinguish a word. . . . If charlatans are less common in the public squares of France than in those of Italy, it is not because they would be less well heard [*écoutés*] in France, but only because they would not be as well understood [*entendus*]. . . . But I say that any tongue with which one cannot make oneself understood to the people assembled is a slavish tongue. It is impossible for a people to remain free and speak the tongue (Chap. 10, "Relationship of Langauges to Government") [pp. 72–73].

Self-presence, transparent proximity in the face-to-face of countenances and the immediate range of the voice, this determination of social authenticity is therefore classic: Rousseauistic but already the inheritor of Platonism, it relates, we recall, to the Anarchistic and Libertarian protestations against Law, the Powers, and the State in general, and also with the dream of the nineteenth-century Utopian Socialisms, most specifically with the dream of Fourierism. In his laboratory, or rather in his studio, the anthropologist too uses this dream, as one weapon or instrument among others. Serving the same obstinate desire within which the anthropologist "always puts something of himself," this tool must come to terms with other "means to hand." For the anthropologist also desires to be Freudian, Marxist (with a "Marxism," as we recall, whose work of criticism would be neither in "opposition" nor in "contradiction" with "Buddhist criticism") and he even confesses to being tempted by "vulgar materialism."[30]

The only weakness of *bricolage*—but, seen as a weakness is it not irremediable?—is a total inability to justify itself in its own discourse. The already-there-ness of instruments and of concepts cannot be undone or reinvented. In that sense, the passage from desire to discourse always loses itself in *bricolage*, it builds its castles with debris ("Mythical thought . . . builds ideological castles out of the debris of what was once a social discourse." *The Savage Mind*, p. 32 [p. 21]). In the best of cases, the discourse of *bricolage* can confess itself, confess in itself its desire and its defeat, provoke the thought of the essence and the necessity of the already-there, recognize that the most radical discourse, the most inventive and systematic engineer are surprised and circumvented by a history, a language, etc., a *world* (for "world" means nothing else) from which they must borrow their tools, if only to destroy the former machine (the strop-catapult [*bricole*] seems originally to have been a machine of war or the hunt, constructed to destroy. And who can believe the image of the peaceful *bricoleur*?). The idea of the engineer breaking with all *bricolage* is dependent on a creationist theology. Only such a theology can sanction an essential and rigorous difference between the engineer and the *bricoleur*. But that the engineer should always be a sort of *bricoleur* should not ruin all criticism of *bricolage*; quite the contrary. Criticism in what sense? First of all, if the difference between *bricoleur* and engineer is basically theological, the very concept of *bricolage* implies a fall and an accidental finitude. This techno-theological significance must be abandoned in order to think the originary appurtenance of desire to discourse, of discourse to the history of the world, and the already-three-ness of the language in which desire deludes itself. Then, even supposing that, by *bricolage*, one conserves the idea of *bricolage*, one must know that all *bricolages* are not equally worthwhile. *Bricolage* criticizes itself.

Finally, the value of "social authenticity" is one of the two indispensable poles of the structure of morality in general. The ethic of the living word would be perfectly respectable, completely utopian and a-topic [*utopique et atopique*] as it is (unconnected to *spacing* and to differance as writing), it would be as respectable as respect itself if it did not live on a delusion and a nonrespect for its own condition of origin, if it did not dream in speech of a presence denied to writing, denied by writing. The ethic of speech is the *delusion* of presence mastered. Like the *bricole*, the delusion or lure designates first a hunter's stratagem. It is a term of falconry: "a piece of red feather," says Littré, "in the form of a bird, which serves to recall the bird of prey when it does not return straight to the fist." Example: ". . . the master called, made a feint,/Held fist and lure toward what seemed turned to stone, . . ." (La Fontaine) [*Fables*, XII, 12; *The Fables of La Fontaine*, tr. Marianne Moore (New York, 1952), p. 294].

To recognize writing in speech, that is to say differance and the absence of speech, is to begin to think the lure. There is no ethics without the presence *of the other* but also, and consequently, without absence, dissimulation, detour, differance, writing. The arche-writing is the origin of morality as of immorality. The nonethical opening of ethics. A violent opening. As in the case of the vulgar concept of writing, the ethical instance of violence must be rigorously suspended in order to repeat the genealogy of morals.

Since they both scorn writing, Rousseau and Lévi-Strauss both praise the range of the voice. Nevertheless, in the texts that we must now read, Rousseau is suspicious also of the illusion of full and present speech, of the illusion of presence within a speech believed to be transparent and innocent. It is toward the praise of silence that the myth of a full presence wrenched from differance and from the violence of the word is then deviated. Nevertheless, in a certain way, "public force" has already begun to "compensate for [*suppléer*] persuasion."

It is perhaps time to reread the *Essay on the Origin of Languages*.

2

"... *That Dangerous Supplement*..."

How people will cry out against me! I hear from afar the shouts of that false wisdom which is ever dragging us onwards, counting the present as nothing, and pursuing without a pause a future which flies as we pursue, that false wisdom which removes us from our place and never brings us to any other.—Emile

All the papers which I have collected to fill the gaps in my memory and to guide me in my undertaking, have passed into other hands, and will never return to mine.—Confessions

I have implied it repeatedly: the praise of living speech, as it *preoccupies* Lévi-Strauss's discourse, is faithful to only one particular motif in Rousseau. This motif comes to terms with and is organized by its contrary: a perpetually reanimated mistrust with regard to the so-called full speech. In the spoken address, presence is at once promised and refused. The speech that Rousseau raised above writing is speech as it should be or rather as it *should have been*. And we must pay attention to that mode, to that tense which relates us to presence within living colloquy. *In fact*, Rousseau had tested the concealment within speech itself, in the mirage of its immediacy. He had recognized and analyzed it with incomparable acumen. We are dispossessed of the longed-for presence in the gesture of language by which we attempt to seize it. To the experience of the "robber robbed" that Starobinski admirably describes in *L'oeil vivant* [Paris, 1961]. Jean Jacques is subjected not only in the play of the mirror image which "captures his reflection and exposes his presence" (p. 109). It lies in wait for us from the first word. The speculary dispossession which at the same time institutes and deconstitutes me is also a law of language. It operates as a power of death in the heart of living speech: a power all the more redoubtable because it opens as much as it threatens the possibility of the spoken word.

Having in a certain way recognized this power which, inaugurating speech, dislocates the subject that it constructs, prevents it from being present to its signs, torments its language with a complete writing, Rousseau is nevertheless more pressed to exorcise it than to assume its necessity. That is why, straining toward the reconstruction of presence, he valorizes and disqualifies writing at the same time. At the same time; that is to say, in one divided but coherent movement. We must try not to lose sight of its strange unity. Rousseau condemns writing as destruction of presence and as disease of speech. He rehabilitates it to the extent that it promises the reappropriation of that of which speech allowed itself to be dispossessed. But by what, if not already a writing older than speech and already installed in that place?

The first movement of this desire is formulated as a theory of language. The other governs the experience of the writer. In the *Confessions,* when Jean-Jacques tries to explain how he became a writer, he describes the passage to writing as the restoration, by a certain absence and by a sort of calculated effacement, of presence disappointed of itself in speech. To write is indeed the only way of keeping or recapturing speech since speech denies itself as it gives itself. Thus an *economy of signs* is organized. It will be equally disappointing, closer yet to the very essence and to the necessity of disappointment. One cannot help wishing to master absence and yet we must always let go. Starobinski describes the profound law that commands the space within which Rousseau must move:

> How will he overcome the misunderstanding that prevents him from expressing himself according to his true value? How escape the risks of improvised speech? To what other mode of communication can he turn? By what other means manifest himself? Jean-Jacques chooses to be *absent* and to *write*. Paradoxically, he will hide himself to show himself better, and he will confide in written speech: "I would love society like others, if I were not sure of showing myself not only at a disadvantage, but as completely different from what I am. The part that I have taken of *writing and hiding myself* is precisely the one that suits me. If I were present, one would never know what I was worth" (*Confessions*). The admission is singular and merits emphasis: Jean-Jacques breaks with others, only to present himself to them in written speech. Protected by solitude, he will turn and re-turn his sentences at leisure.[1]

Let us note that the economy is perhaps indicated in the following: the operation that substitutes writing for speech also replaces presence by value: to the *I am* or to the *I am present* thus sacrificed, a *what* I am or a *what I am worth* is *preferred*. "If I were present, one would never know what I was worth." I renounce my present life, my present and concrete existence in order to make myself known in the ideality of truth and value. A well-known schema. The battle by which I wish to raise myself above my life even while I retain it, in order to enjoy recognition, is in this case within myself, and writing is indeed the phenomenon of this battle.

Such would be the writing lesson in Jean-Jacque's existence. The act of writing would be essentially—and here in an exemplary fashion—the greatest sacrifice aiming at the greatest symbolic reappropriation of presence. From this point of view, Rousseau knew that death is not the simple outside of life. Death by writing also inaugurates life. "I can certainly say that I never began to live, until I looked upon myself as a dead man" (*Confessions*, Book 6 [p. 236]). As soon as one determines it within the system of this economy, is not the sacrifice—the "literary suicide"—dissipated in the *appearance*? Is it anything but a symbolic reappropriation? Does it not renounce the *present* and the *proper* in order to master them better in their meaning, in the ideal form of truth, of the presence of the present and of the proximity or property of the proper? We would be obliged to decide that a ruse and an appearance are necessary if in fact we were to abide by these concepts (sacrifice, expenditure, renunciation, symbol, appearance, truth, etc.) which determine what we here call economy in terms of truth and appearance, starting from the opposition presence/absence.

But the work of writing and the economy of differance will not be dominated by this classical conceptuality, this ontology, or this epistemology. On the contrary, these furnish its hidden premises. Differance does not *resist* appropriation, it does not impose an exterior limit upon it. Differance began by *broaching* alienation and it ends by leaving reappropriation *breached*. Until death. Death is the movement of differance to the extent that that movement is necessarily finite. This means that differance makes the opposition of presence and absence possible. Without the possibility of differance, the desire of presence as such would not find its breathing-space. That means by the same token that this desire carries in itself the destiny of its non-satisfaction. Differance produces what it forbids, makes possible the very thing that it makes impossible.

If differance is recognized as the obliterated origin of absence and presence, major forms of the disappearing and the appearing of the entity, it would still remain to be known if being, before its determination into absence or presence, is already implicated in the thought of differance. And it differance as the project of the mastery of the entity should be understood with reference to the sense of being. Can one not think the converse? Since the sense of being is never produced as history outside of its determination as presence, has it not always already been caught within the history of metaphysics as the epoch of presence? This is perhaps what Nietzsche wanted to write and what resists the Heideggerian reading of Nietzsche; *differance* in its *active* movement—*what* is comprehended in the concept of *differance* without exhausting it—is what not only precedes metaphysics but also extends beyond the thought of being. The latter speaks *nothing other than* metaphysics, even if it exceeds it and thinks it as what it is within its closure.

From/Of Blindness to the Supplement

In terms of this problematical scheme, we must therefore think Rousseau's experience and his theory of writing together, the accord and the discord that, under the name of writing, relate Jean-Jacques to Rousseau, uniting and dividing his proper name. On the side of experience, a recourse to literature as reappropriation of presence, that is to say, as we shall see, of Nature; on the side of theory, an indictment against the negativity of the letter, in which must be read the degeneracy of culture and the disruption of the community.

If indeed one wishes to surround it with the entire constellation of concepts that shares its system, the word *supplement* seems to account for the strange unity of these two gestures.

In both cases, in fact, Rousseau considers writing as a dangerous means, a menacing aid, the critical response to a situation of distress. When Nature, as self-proximity, comes to be forbidden or interrupted, when speech fails to protect presence, writing becomes necessary. It must *be added* to the word urgently. I have identified in advance one of the forms of this *addition*; speech being natural or at least the natural expression of thought, the most natural form of institution or convention for signifying thought, writing is added to it, is adjoined, as an image or representation. In that sense, it is not natural. It diverts the immediate presence of thought to speech into representation and the imagination. This recourse is not only "bizarre," but dangerous. It is the addition of a technique, a sort of artificial and artful ruse to make speech present when it is actually absent. It is a violence done to the natural destiny of the language:

> Languages are made to be spoken, writing serves only as a supplement to speech. . . . Speech represents thought by conventional signs, and writing represents the same with regard to speech. Thus the art of writing is nothing but a mediated representation of thought.

Writing is dangerous from the moment that representation there claims to be presence and the sign of the thing itself. And there is a fatal necessity, inscribed in the very functioning of the sign, that the substitute make one forget the vicariousness of its own function and make itself pass for the plenitude of a speech whose deficiency and infirmity it nevertheless only *supplements*. For the concept of the supplement—which here determines that of the representative image—harbors within itself two significations whose cohabitation is as strange as it is necessary. The supplement adds itself, it is a surplus, a plenitude enriching another plenitude, the *fullest measure* of presence. It cumulates and accumulates presence. It is thus that art, *technè*, image, representation, convention, etc., come as supplements to nature and are rich with this entire cumulating function. This kind of supplementarity determines in a certain way all the conceptual oppositions within which Rousseau inscribes the notion of Nature to the extent that it *should* be self-sufficient.

But the supplement supplements. It adds only to replace. It intervenes or insinuates itself *in-the-place-of*; if it fills, it is as if one fills a void. If it represents and makes an image, it is by the anterior default of a presence. Compensatory [*suppléant*] and vicarious, the supplement is an adjunct, a subaltern instance which *takes-(the)-place* [*tient-lieu*]. As substitute, it is not simply added to the positivity of a presence, it produces no relief, its place is assigned in the structure by the mark of an emptiness. Somewhere, something can be filled up *of itself*, can accomplish itself, only by allowing itself to be filled through sign and proxy. The sign is always the supplement of the thing itself.

This second signification of the supplement cannot be separated from the first. We shall constantly have to confirm that both operate within Rousseau's texts. But the inflexion varies from moment to moment. Each of the two significations is by turns effaced or becomes discreetly vague in the presence of the other. But their common function is shown in this: whether it adds or substitutes itself, the supplement is *exterior*, outside of the positivity to which it is super-added, alien to that which, in order to be replaced by it, must be other than it. Unlike the *complement*, dictionaries tell us, the supplement is an "*exterior* addition" (Robert's *French Dictionary*).

According to Rousseau, the negativity of evil will always have the form of supplementarity. Evil is exterior to nature, to what is by nature innocent and good. It supervenes upon nature. But always by way of compensation for [*sous l'espèce de la suppléance*] what *ought to* lack nothing at all in itself.

Thus presence, always natural, which for Rousseau more than for others means maternal, *ought to be* self-sufficient. Its *essence*, another name for presence, may be read through the grid of this ought to be [*ce conditionnel*]. Like Nature's love, "there is no substitute for a mother's love," says *Emile*.[2] It is in no way *supplemented*, that is to say it does not have to be supplemented, it suffices and is self-sufficient; but that also means that it is irreplacable; what one would substitute for it would not equal it, would be only a mediocre makeshift. Finally it means that Nature does not supplement *itself* at all; Nature's supplement does not proceed from Nature, it is not only inferior to but other than Nature.

Yet all education, the keystone of Rousseauist thought, will be described or presented as a system of substitution [*suppléance*] destined to reconstitute Nature's edifice in the most natural way possible. The first chapter of *Emile* announces the function of this pedagogy. Although there is no substitute for a mother's love, "it is better that the child should suck the breast of a healthy nurse rather than of a petted mother, if he has any further evil to fear from her who has given him birth" (ibid.) [p. 12]. It is indeed culture or cultivation that must supplement a deficient nature, a deficiency that cannot by definition be anything but an accident and a deviation from Nature. Culture or cultivation is here called habit; it is necessary and insufficient from the moment when the substitution of mothers is no longer envisaged only "from the physiological point of view":

Other women, or even other animals, may give him the milk she denies him, but there is no substitute for a mother's love. The woman who nurses another's child in place of her own is a bad mother; how can she be a good nurse? She may become one in time; use [habit] will overcome nature . . . (ibid.).

Here the problems of natural right, of the relationship between Nature and Society, the concepts of alienation, alterity, and corruption, are adapted most spontaneously to the pedagogic problem of the substitution of mothers and children:

And this affection when developed has its drawbacks, which should make every sensible woman afraid to put her child out to nurse. Is she prepared to divide her mother's rights, or rather to abdicate them in favor of a stranger; to see her child loving another as much as and more than herself . . . (ibid.).

If, premeditating the theme of writing, I began by speaking of the substitution of mothers, it is because, as Rousseau will himself say, "more depends on this than you realize."

How emphatically would I speak if it were not so hopeless to keep struggling in vain on behalf of a real reform. More depends on this than you realize. Would you restore all men to their primal duties, begin with the mothers; the results will surprise you. Every evil follows in the train of this first sin; the whole moral order is disturbed, nature is quenched in every breast . . . (p. 18) [p. 13].

Childhood is the first manifestation of the deficiency which, in Nature, calls for substitution [*suppléance*]. Pedagogy illuminates perhaps more crudely the paradoxes of the supplement. How is a natural weakness possible? How can Nature ask for forces that it does not furnish? How is a child possible in general?

First Maxim.—Far from being too strong, children are not strong enough for all the claims of nature. Give them full use of such strength as they have and which they will not abuse. *Second Maxim.*—Help them and supply what they lack, in intelligence or in strength, whenever the need is of the body (p. 50) [p. 35].

All the organization of, and all the time spent in, education will be regulated by this necessary evil: "supply [*suppléer*] . . . [what] . . . is lacking" and to replace Nature. It must be done as little and as late as possible. "One of the best rules of good farming [*culture*] is to ***keep things back*** as much as possible" (p. 274) [p. 193]. "Give nature time to work before you ***take over her business*** [act in her place—***agir à sa place***]" (p. 102; italics added) [p. 71].

Without childhood, no supplement would ever appear in Nature. The supplement is here both humanity's good fortune and the origin of its perversion. The health of the human race:

> Plants are fashioned by cultivation, and men by education. If man were born big and strong, his size and strength would be useless to him until he had learned to use them; they would create a prejudice against him, by not allowing others to think of assisting him; and, left to himself, he would die miserably before knowing his needs. We complain of the state of infancy; we do not see that, if man had not begun by being a child, the human race would have perished (p. 67).

The threat of perversion:

> While the Author of nature has given children the active principle, He takes care that it shall do little harm by giving them small power to use it. But as soon as they can think of people as tools that they are responsible for activating, they use them to carry out their wishes and to ***supplement*** their own weakness. This is how they become tiresome, masterful, imperious, naughty, and unmanageable; a development which does not spring from a natural love of power, but one which gives it to them, for it does not need much experience to realize how pleasant it is to act through the hands of others and to move the world by simply moving the tongue (p. 49; italics added) [p. 34].

The supplement will always be the moving of the tongue or acting through the hands of others. In it everything is brought together: progress as the possibility of perversion, regression toward an evil that is not natural and that adheres to the power of substitution that permits us to asbent ourselves and act by proxy, through representation, through the hands of others. Through the written [*par écrit*]. This substitution always has the form of the sign. The scandal is that the sign, the image, or the representer, become forces and make "the world move."

This scandal is such, and its evil effects are sometimes so irreparable, that the world seems to turn the wrong way (and we shall see later what such a *catastrophe* can signify for Rousseau); then Nature becomes the supplement of art and society. It is the moment when evil seems incurable: "As the child does not know how to be cured, let him know how to be ill. The one art takes the place of [*supplée*] the other and is often more successful; it is the art of nature" (p. 31) [p. 22]. It is also the moment when maternal nature, ceasing to be loved, as she ought to be, for herself and in an immediate proximity ("O Nature! O my mother! behold me under thy protection alone! Here there is no cunning or knavish mortal to thrust himself between me and thee." [*Confession*, Book 12] [p. 669]) becomes the substitute for another love and for another attachment:

The contemplation of Nature always had a very great attraction for his heart; he found there a supplement to the attachments that he needed; but he would have left the supplement for the thing, if he had had the choice, and he was reduced to converse with the plants only after vain efforts to converse with human beings (*Dialogues*, p. 794).

That botany becomes the supplement of society is more than a catastrophe. It is the catastrophe of the catastrophe. For in Nature, the plant is the most *natural* thing. It is natural *life*. The mineral is distinguished from the vegetable in that it is a dead and useful Nature, servile to man's industry. When man has lost the sense and the taste of true natural riches—plants—he rummages in the entrails of his mother and risks his health:

The Mineral Kingdom has nothing in itself either amiable or attractive; its riches, enclosed in the breast [womb—*sein*] of the earth, seem to have been removed from the gaze of man in order not to tempt his cupidity; they are there like a reserve to serve one day as a *supplement* to the true wealth which is more within his grasp, and for which he loses taste according to the extent of his corruption. Then he is compelled to call in industry, to struggle, and to labor to alleviate his miseries; he searches the entrails of earth; he goes seeking to its center, at the risk of his life and at the expense of his health, for imaginary goods in place of the real good which the earth offers of herself if he knew how to enjoy it. *He flies from the sun and the day, which he is no longer worthy to see.*[3]

Man has thus put out his eyes, he blinds himself by the desire to rummage in these entrails. Here is the horrible spectacle of the punishment that follows the crime, in sum a simple substitution:

He buries himself alive, and does well, not being worthy of living in the light of day. There quarries, pits, forges, furnaces, a battery of anvils, hammers, smoke and fire, succeed to the fair images of his rustic labors. The wan faces of the unhappy people who languish in the poisonous vapors of mines, of black forgemen, of hideous cyclops, are the spectacle which the working of the mine substitutes, in the heart [womb] of the earth for that of green fields and flowers, the azure sky, amorous shepherds and robust laborers upon its surface.[4]

Such is the scandal, such the catastrophe. The supplement is what neither Nature nor Reason can tolerate. Neither Nature, our "common mother" (*Reveries*, p. 1066) [p. 143], nor the reason which is reasonable, if not reasoning (*De l'état de nature*, [*Pléiade*, vol. 3], p. 478). And had they not done everything to avoid this catastrophe, to protect themselves from this violence and to guard and keep us from this fatal crime? "so that," says the second *Discourse* precisely of mines, "it looks as if nature had taken pains to keep the fatal secret from us" (p. 172) [p. 200]. And let us not forget that the violence that takes us toward the entrails of the earth, the moment of mine-blindness, that is, of metallurgy, is the origin of society. For according to Rousseau, as we shall often confirm, agriculture, marking the organization of civil society, assumes the beginning of metallurgy. Blindness thus produces that which is born at the same time as society: the languages, the regulated substitution of signs for things, the order of the supplement. One goes *from blindness to the supplement*. But the blind person cannot see, in its origin, the very thing he produces to supplement his sight. *Blindness to the supplement* is the law. And especially blindess to its concept. Moreover, it does not suffice to locate its functioning in order to *see* its meaning. The supplement has no sense and is given to no intuition. We do not therefore make it emerge out of its strange pneumbra. We speak its reserve.

Reason is incapable of thinking this double infringement upon Nature: that there is *lack* in Nature and that *because of that very fact* something *is added* to it. Yet one should not say that Reason is *powerless to think this*; it is constituted by that lack of power. It is the principle of identity. It is the thought of the self-identity of the natural being. It cannot even determine the supplement as its other, as the irrational and the non-natural, for the supplement comes *naturally* to put itself in Nature's place. The supplement is the image and the representation of Nature. The image is neither in nor out of Nature. The supplement is therefore equally dangerous for Reason, the natural health of Reason.

Dangerous supplement. These are the words that Rousseau uses in the *Confessions*. He uses them in a context which is only apparently different, and in order to explain, precisely, a "condition almost unintelligible and inconceivable [to reason]": "In a word, between myself and the most passionate lover there was only one, but that an essential, point of distinction, which makes my condition almost unintelligible and inconceivable" (*Pléiade*, vol. 1, [p. 111]).

If we lend to the text below a paradigmatic value, it is only provisional and does not prejudge what the discipline of a future reading might rigorously determine. No model of reading seems to me at the moment ready to measure up to this text—which I would like to read as a *text* and not as a document. Measure up to it fully and rigorously, that is, beyond what already makes the text most legible, and more legible than has been so far thought. My only ambition will be to draw out of it a signification which that presumed future reading will not be able to dispense with [*faire économie*]; the economy of a written text, circulating through other texts, leading back to it constantly, conforming to the element of a language and to its regulated functioning. For example, what unites the word "supplement" to its concept was not invented by Rousseau and the originality of its functioning is neither fully mastered by Rousseau nor simply imposed by history and the language, by the history of the language. To speak of the writing of Rousseau is to try to recognize what escapes these categories of passivity and activity, blindness and responsibility. And one cannot abstract from the written text to rush to the signified it *would mean*, since the signified is here the text itself. It is so little a matter of looking for a *truth signified* by these writings (metaphysical or psychological truth: Jean-Jacque's life behind his work) that if the texts that interest us *mean* something, it is the engagement and the appurtenance that encompass existence and writing in the same *tissue*, the same *text*. The same is here called supplement, another name for differance.

Here is the irruption of the dangerous supplement in Nature, between nature and nature, between natural innocence as *virginity* and natural innocence as *pucelage**: "In a word, between myself and the most passionate lover there was only one, but that an essential, point of distinction, which makes my condition almost unintelligible and inconceivable." Here, the lineation should not hide the fact that the following paragraph is destined to explain the "only one point of distinction" and the "almost unintelligible and inconceivable" "condition." Rousseau elaborates:

> I had returned from Italy not quite the same as I had entered it, but as, perhaps, no one of my age had ever returned from it. I had brought back, not my virginity but my *pucelage*. I had felt the progress of years; my restless temperament had at last made itself felt, and its first outbreak, quite involuntary, had caused me alarm about my health in a manner which shows better than anything else the innocence in which I had lived up to that time. Soon reassured, I learned that dangerous means of assisting it [*ce dangereux supplément*], which cheats Nature and saves up for young men of my temperment many forms of excess at the expense of their health, strength, and, sometimes, their life (*Pléiade*, I, pp. 108–09 [p. 111].

We read in *Emile* (Book IV): "If once he acquires this dangerous habit [*supplément*] he is ruined" [p. 299]. In the same book, it is also a question of "mak[ing] up . . . by trading on . . . inexperience" [*suppléer en gagnant de vitesse sur l'experience*; literally "supplementing by out-distancing experience"] (p. 437) [p. 315], and of the "mind, which reinforces [*supplée*] . . . the bodily strength" (p. 183) [p. 129].

The experience of auto-eroticism is lived in anguish. Masturbation reassures ("soon reassured") only through that culpability traditionally attached to the practice, obliging children to assume the fault and to

* "*Pucelage*" is the more earthy French word for the actual physical fact of sexual intactness, in the female the membrane itself. Rousseau applies the word to his own case with some derision, contrasting it to the spiritual innocence of true "virginity."

interiorize the threat of castration that always accompanies it. Pleasure is thus lived as the irremediable loss of the vital substance, as exposure to madness and death. It is produced "at the expense of their health, strength, and, sometimes, their life." In the same way, the *Reveries* will say, the man who "searches the entrails of earth . . . goes seeking to its center, at the risk of his life and at the expense of his health, for imaginary goods in place of the real good which the earth offers of herself if he knew how to enjoy it." (*Pléiade*, vol. 1, 1067 [p. 145]).

And indeed it is a question of the imaginary. The supplement that "cheats" maternal "nature" operates as writing, and as writing it is dangerous to life. This danger is that of the image. Just as writing opens the crisis of the living speech in terms of its "image," its painting or its representation, so onanism announces the ruin of vitality in terms of imaginary seductions:

This vice, which shame and timidity find so convenient, possesses, besides a great attraction for lively imaginations—that of being able to dispose of the whole sex as they desire, and to make the beauty which tempts them minister to their pleasures, without being obliged to obtain its consent [*Confessions*, p. 111].

The dangerous supplement, which Rousseau also calls a "fatal advantage," is properly *seductive*; it leads desire away from the good path, makes it err far from natural ways, guides it toward its loss or fall and therefore it is a sort of lapse or scandal (*scandalon*). It thus destroys Nature. But the scandal of Reason is that nothing seems more natural than this destruction of Nature. It is myself who exerts myself to separate myself from the force that Nature has entrusted to me: "Seduced by this fatal advantage, I did my best to destroy the good constitution which Nature had restored to me, and [to] which I had allowed time to strengthen itself." We know what importance *Emile* gives to time, to the slow maturation of natural forces. The entire art of pedagogy is a calculated patience, allowing the work of Nature time to come to fruition, respecting its rhythm and the order of its stages. The dangerous supplement destroys very quickly the forces that Nature has slowly constituted and accumulated. In "out-distancing" natural experience, it runs non-stop [*brûle les étapes*—literally "burns the halting-points"] and consumes energy without possibility of recovery. As I shall confirm, like the sign it bypasses the presence of the thing and the duration of being.

The dangerous supplement breaks with Nature. The entire description of this moving away from Nature has a *scene* [*théâtre*]. The *Confessions* stage the evocation of the dangerous supplement at the moment when it is a question of making visible a distancing which is neither the same nor an other; Nature draws away at the same time as the Mother, or rather

"Mamma," who already signified the disappearance of the true mother and has substituted herself in the well-known ambiguous manner. It is therefore now a question of the distance between Mamma and the person she called "Little one."[5] As *Emile* says, all evil comes from the fact that "women have ceased to be mothers, they do not and will not return to their duty" (p. 18) [p. 14]. A certain absence, then, of a certain sort of mother. And the experience of which we speak is such as to reduce that absence as much as to maintain it. A *furtive* experience, that of a thief who needs invisibility: that the mother be invisible and not see. These lines are often quoted:

> I should never have done, if I were to enter into the details of all the follies which the remembrance of this dear mamma caused me to commit when I was no longer in her presence. How often have I kissed my bed, since she had slept in it; my curtains, all the furniture of my room, since they belonged to her, and her beautiful hand had touched them; even the floor, on which I prostrated myself, since she had walked upon it! Sometimes, even in her presence, I was guilty of extravagances, which only the most violent love seemed capable of inspiring. At table one day, just when she had put a piece of food into her mouth, I exclaimed that I saw a hair in it; she put back the morsel on her plate, and I eagerly seized and swallowed it.[6] In a word, between myself and the most passionate lover there was only one, but that an essential, point of distinction, which makes my condition almost unintelligible and inconceivable . . . [A little above, we read] I only felt the full strength of my attachment when I no longer saw her (p. 107) [pp. 110–11]

The Chain of Supplements

The discovery of the dangerous supplement will be next cited *among* these "follies," but it will still retain a privilege; Rousseau evokes it after the others and as a sort of explanation of the state inconceivable to reason. For it is not the question of diverting total enjoyment toward a particular substitute, but now of experiencing it or miming it *directly and in its totality*. It is no longer a question of kissing the bed, the floor, the curtains, the furniture, etc., not even of "swallowing" the "piece . . . [that] she had put into her mouth," but of "dispos[ing] of the whole sex as . . . [one] desire[s]."

I remarked that the stage of this theater was not only a setting in the generally understood sense: an ensemble of accessories. The topographic disposition of the experience is not unimportant. Jean-Jacques is in the house of Madame de Warens; close enough to *Mamma* to see her and to nourish his imagination upon her but with the possibility of a partition. It is at the moment when the mother disappears that substitution becomes possible and necessary. The play of maternal presence or absence, this alteration of perception and imagination must correspond to an organization of space; the text argues as follows:

Add to this habit the circumstances of my position, living as I was with a beautiful woman, caressing her image in the bottom of my heart, seeing her continually throughout the day, surrounded in the evening by objects which reminded me of her, sleeping in the bed in which I knew she had slept! What causes for excitement! Many a reader, who reflects upon them, no doubt already considers me as half-dead! Quite the contrary; that which ought to have destroyed me was just the thing that saved me, at least for a time. Intoxicated with the charm of living with her, with the ardent desire of spending my life with her, I always saw in her, whether she were absent or present, a tender mother, a beloved sister, a delightful friend, and nothing more. . . . She was for me the only woman in the world; and the extreme sweetness of the feelings with which she inspired me did not allow my senses time to awake for others, and protected me against her and all her sex.

This experience was not an event marking an archaic or adolescent period. Not only did it construct or sustain a particular hidden foundation, an edifice of significations. It remained an active obsession whose "present" is constantly reactivated and constituted in its turn, until the end of Jean-Jacques Rousseau's "life" and "text." A little later, a little further on in the text of the *Confessions* (Book IV),[7] "a little incident, which I find some difficulty in relating," [p. 150] is related to us. The encounter with a man "addicted to the same vice." Terrified, Jean-Jacques runs away, "trembling as if" he had just "committed a crime." "The recollection of this incident cured me of it for a long time" [p. 151].

For a long time? Rouseeau will never stop having recourse to, and accusing himself of, this onanism that permits one to be himself affected by providing himself with presences, by summoning absent beauties. In his eyes it will remain the model of vice and perversion. Affecting oneself by another presence, one *corrupts* oneself [makes oneself other] by oneself [*on s'altère soi-même*]. Rousseau neither wishes to think nor can think that this alteration does not simply happen to the self, that it is the self's very origin. He must consider it a contingent evil coming from without to affect the integrity of the subject. But he cannot give up what immediately restores to him the other desired presence; no more than one can give up language. This is why, in this respect as well, as he says in the *Dialogues* [*Pléiade*, vol. 1] (p. 800), "to the end of his life he will remain an aged child."

The restitution of presence by language, restitution at the same time symbolic and immediate. This contradiction must be thought. Immediate experience of restitution because as experience, as consciousness or conscience, *it dispenses with passage through the world*. What is touching is touched, auto-affection gives itself as pure autarchy. If the presence that it then gives itself is the substitutive symbol of another presence, it has never been possible to desire that presence "in person" before this play of substitution and this symbolic experience of auto-affection. The thing itself does not appear outside of the symbolic system that does not exist without the possibility of auto-affection. Experience of *immediate* restitution, also because it *does not wait*. It is satisfied then and there and in the moment. If it waits, it is not because the other makes it wait. Pleasure seems no longer to be deferred. "Why give oneself so much trouble in a hope remote from so poor and uncertain a success, when one can, from the very instant . . ." (*Dialogues*).

But what is no longer deferred is also absolutely deferred. The presence that is thus delivered to us in the present is a chimera. Auto-affection is a pure speculation. The sign, the image, the representation, which come to supplement the absent presence are the illusions that sidetrack us. To culpability, to the anguish of death and castration, is added or rather is assimilated the experience of frustration. *Donner le change* ["sidetracking" or, "giving money"]: in whatever sense it is understood, this expression describes the recourse to the supplement admirably. In order to explain his "dislike" for "common prostitutes," Rousseau tells us that in Venice, at thirty-one, the "propensity which had modified all my passions" (*Confessions*, p. 41) [p. 35][8] has not disappeared: "I had not lost the pernicious habit of satisfying my wants [*donner le change*]" (p. 316) [p. 289].

The enjoyment of the *thing itself* is thus undermined, in its act and in its essence, by frustration. One cannot therefore say that it has an essence or an act (*eidos, ousia, energeia*, etc.). Something promises itself as it escapes, gives itself as it moves away, and strictly speaking it cannot even be called presence. Such is the constraint of the supplement, such, exceeding all the language of metaphysics, is this structure "almost inconceivable to reason." *Almost* inconceivable: simple irrationality, the opposite of reason, are less irritating and waylaying for classical logic. The supplement is maddening because it is neither presence nor absence and because it consequently breaches both our pleasure and our viriginity. ". . . abstinence and enjoyment, pleasure and wisdom, escaped me in equal measure" (*Confessions*, p. 12).

Are things not complicated enough? The symbolic is the immediate, presence is absence, the nondeferred is deferred, pleasure is the menace of death. But one stroke must still be added to this system, to this strange economy of the supplement. In a certain way, it was already legible. A terrifying menace, the supplement is also the first and surest protection; against that very menace. This is why it cannot be given up. And sexual auto-affection, that is auto-affection in general, neither begins nor ends with what one thinks can be circumscribed by the name of masturbation. The supplement has not only the power of *procuring* an absent presence through its image; procuring it for us through the proxy [*procuration*] of the sign, it holds it at a distance and masters it. For this presence is at the same time desired and feared. The supplement transgresses and at the same time respects the interdict. This is what also permits writing as the supplement of speech; but already also the spoken word as writing in general. Its economy exposes and protects us at the same time according to the play of forces and of the differences of forces. Thus, the supplement is dangerous in that it threatens us with death, but Rousseau thinks that it is not at all as dangerous as "cohabitation with women." Pleasure *itself*, without symbol or suppletory, that which would accord us (to) pure presence itself, if such a thing were possible, would be only another name for death. Rousseau says it:

Enjoyment! Is such a thing made for man? Ah! If I had ever in my life tasted the delights of love even once in their plenitude, I do not imagine that my frail existence would have been sufficient for them, I would have been dead in the act (*Confessions*, Book VIII).

If one abides by the universal evidence, by the necessary and a priori value of this proposition in the form of a sigh, one must immediately recognize that "cohabitation with women," hetero-eroticism, can be lived (effectively, really, as one believes it can be said) only through the ability to reserve within itself its own supplementary protection. In other words, between auto-eroticism and hetero-eroticism, there is not a frontier but an economic distribution. It is within this general rule that the differences are mapped out. This is Rousseau's general rule. And before trying—what I do not pretend to be doing here—to encompass the pure singularity of Rousseau's economy or his writing, we must carefully raise and articulate between them all the structural or essential necessities on their different levels of generality.

It is from a certain determined representation of "cohabitation with women" that Rousseau had to have recourse throughout his life to that type of dangerous supplement that is called masturbation and that cannot be separated from his activity as a writer. To the end. Thérèse—the Thérèse of whom we can speak, Thérèse in the text, whose name and "life" belong to the writing we read—experienced it at her cost. In Book XII of the *Confessions*, at the moment when "I must speak without reserve," the "two reasons combined" of certain "resolutions" is confided to us:

I must speak without reserve. I have never concealed either my poor mamma's faults or my own. I must not show greater favor to Thérèse either; and, pleased as I am to render honor to one who is so dear to me, neither do I wish to conceal her faults, if so be that an involuntary change in the heart's affections is really a fault. I had long since observed that her affection for me had cooled. . . . I was conscious again of an unpleasantness, the effects of which I had formerly felt when with mamma; and the effect was the same with Thérèse. Let us not look for perfections which are not to be found in nature; it would be the same with any other woman whatsoever. . . . My situation, however, was at that time the same, and even aggravated by the animosity of my enemies, who only sought to find me at fault. I was afraid of a repetition; and, not desiring to run the risk of it, I preferred to condemn myself to strict continence, than to expose Thérèse to the risk of finding herself in the same condition again. Besides, I had observed that intercourse with women distinctly aggravated my ill-health. . . . These two reasons combined caused me to form resolutions which I had sometimes been very inconsistent in keeping, but in which I had persevered with greater firmness for the last three or four years (p. 595) [pp. 616–17].

In the *Manuscrit de Paris*, after "distinctly aggravated my ill-health!" we read: "the corresponding vice, of which I have never been able to cure myself completely, appeared to me to produce less injurious results. These two reasons combined . . ."[9]

This perversion consists of preferring the sign and protects me from mortal expenditure. To be sure. But this apparently egotistical economy also functions within an entire system of moral representation. Egotism is redeemed by a culpability, which determines auto-eroticism as a fatal waste and a wounding of the self by the self. But as I thus harm only myself, this perversion is not truly condemnable. Rousseau explains it in more than one letter. Thus: "With that exception and [the exception of] vices that have always done harm to me alone, I can expose to all eyes a life irreproachable in all the secrets of my heart" (to M. de Saint-Germain, 2–26–70). "I have great vices, but they have never harmed anyone but me" (to M. Le Noir, 1–15–72).[10]

Jean-Jacques could thus look for a supplement to Thérèse only on one condition: that the system of supplementarity in general be already open in its possibility, that the play of substitutions be already operative for a long time and that *in a certain way Thérèse herself be already a supplement.* As Mamma was already the supplement of an unknown mother, and as the "true mother" herself, at whom the known "psychoanalyses" of the case of Jean-Jacques Rousseau stop, was also in a certain way a supplement, from the first trace, and even if she had not "truly" died in giving birth. Here is the chain of supplements. The name Mamma already designates one:

Ah, my Thérèse! I am only too happy to possess you, modest and healthy, and not to find what I never looked for. [The question is of "maidenhood" [*pucelage*] which Thérèse has just confessed to have lost in innocence and by accident.] At first I had only sought amusement; I now saw that I had found more and gained a companion. A little intimacy with this excellent girl, a little reflection upon my situation, made me feel that, while thinking only of my pleasures, I had done much to promote my happiness. *To supply the place of* my extinguished ambition, I needed a lively sentiment which should *take complete possession of* [literally "fill"—*remplit*] my heart. In a word, I needed a successor to mamma. As I should never live with her again, I wanted someone to live with her pupil, in whom I might find the simplicity and docility of heart which she had found in me. I felt it neecssary that the gentle tranquillity of private and domestic life *should make up* to me for the loss of the brilliant career which I was renouncing. When I was quite alone, I felt a void in my heart, which it only needed another heart *to fill*. Destiny had deprived me of, or, at least in part, alienated me from, that heart for which Nature had formed me. From that moment I was alone; for *with me it has always been everything or nothing. I found in Thérèse the substitute* [*supplément*] *that I needed.*[11]

Through this sequence of supplements a necessity is announced: that of an infinite chain, ineluctably multiplying the supplementary mediations that produce the sense of the very thing they defer: the mirage of the thing itself, of immediate presence, of originary perception. Immediacy is derived. That all begins through the intermediary is what is indeed "inconceivable [to reason]."

The Exorbitant. Question of Method

"For me there has never been an intermediary between everything or nothing." The intermediary is the mid-point and the mediation, the middle term between total absence and the absolute plenitude of presence. It is clear that mediacy is the name of all that Rousseau wanted opinionatedly to efface. This wish is expressed in a deliberate, sharp, thematic way. It does not have to be deciphered. Jean-Jacques recalls it here at the very moment when he is spelling out the supplements that are linked together to replace a mother or a Nature. And here the supplement occupies the middle point between total absence and total presence. The play of substitution fills and marks a determined lack. But Rousseau argues as if the recourse to the supplement—here to Thérèse—was going to appease his impatience when confronted with the intermediary: "From that moment I was alone; for me there has never been an intermediary between everything and nothing. I found in Thérèse the substitute that I needed." The virulence of this concept is thus appeased, as if one were able to *arrest it,* domesticate it, tame it.

This brings up the question of the usage of the word "supplement": of Rousseau's situation within the language and the logic that assures to this word or this concept sufficiently *surprising* resources so that the presumed subject of the sentence might always say, through using the "supplement," more, less, or something other than what he *would mean* [*voudrait dire*]. This question is therefore not only of Rousseau's writing but also of our reading. We should begin by taking rigorous account of this *being held within* [*prise*] or this *surprise*: the writer writes *in* a language and *in* a logic whose proper system, laws, and life his discourse by definition cannot dominate absolutely. He uses them only by letting himself, after a fashion and up to a point, be governed by the system. And the reading must always aim at a certain relationship, unperceived by the writer, between what he commands and what he does not command of the patterns of the language that he uses. This relationship is not a certain quantitative distribution of shadow and light, of weakness or of force, but a signifying structure that critical reading should *produce*.

What does produce mean here? In my attempt to explain that, I would initiate a justification of my principles of reading. A justification, as we shall see, entirely negative, outlining by exclusion a space of reading that I shall not fill here: a task of reading.

To produce this signifying structure obviously cannot consist of reproducing, by the effaced and respectful doubling of commentary, the conscious, voluntary, intentional relationship that the writer institutes in his exchanges with the history to which he belongs thanks to the element of language. This moment of doubling commentary should no doubt have its place in a critical reading. To recognize and respect all its classical exigencies is not easy and requires all the instruments of traditional criticism. Without this recognition and this respect, critical production would risk developing in any direction at all and authorize itself to say almost anything. But this indispensable guardrail has always only *protected*, it has never *opened*, a reading.

Yet if reading must not be content with doubling the text, it cannot legitimately transgress the text toward something other than it, toward a referent (a reality that is metaphysical, historical, psychobiographical, etc.) or toward a signified outside the text whose content could take place, could have taken place outside of language, that is to say, in the sense that we give here to that word, outside of writing in general. That is why the methodological considerations that we risk applying here to an example are closely dependent on general propositions that we have elaborated above; as regards the absence of the referent or the transcendental signified. *There is nothing outside of the text* [there is no outside-text; *il n'y a pas de hors-texte*]. And that is neither because Jean-Jacques' life, or the existence of Mamma or Thérèse *themselves*, is not of prime interest to us, nor because we have access to their so-called "real" existence only in the text and we have neither any means of altering this, nor any right to neglect this limitation. All reasons of this type would already be sufficient, to be sure, but there are more radical reasons. What we have tried to show by following the guiding line of the "dangerous supplement," is that in what one calls the real life of these existences "of flesh and bone," beyond and behind what one believes can be circumscribed as Rousseau's text, there has never been anything but writing; there have never been anything but supplements, substitutive significations which could only come forth in a chain of differential references, the "real" supervening, and being added only while taking on meaning from a trace and from an invocation of the supplement, etc. And thus to infinity, for we have read, *in the text*, that the absolute present, Nature, that which words like "real mother" name, have always already escaped, have never existed; that what opens meaning and language is writing as the disappearance of natural presence.

Although it is not commentary, our reading must be intrinsic and remain within the text. That is why, in spite of certain appearances, the locating of the word *supplement* is here not at all psychoanalytical, if by that we understand an interpretation that takes us outside of the writing toward a psychobiographical signified, or even toward a general psychological structure that could rightly be separated from the signifier. This method has occasionally been opposed to the traditional doubling commentary; it could be shown that it actually comes to terms with it quite easily. *The security with which the commentary considers the self-identity of the text, the confidence with which it carves out its contour, goes hand in hand with the tranquil assurance that leaps over the text toward its presumed content, in the direction of the pure signified*. And in effect, in Rousseau's case, psychoanalytical studies like those of Dr. Laforgue transgress the text only after having read it according to the most current methods. The reading of the literary "symptom" is most banal, most academic, most naive. And once one has thus blinded oneself to the very tissue of the "symptom," to its proper texture, one cheerfully exceeds it toward a psychobiographical signified whose link with the literary signifier then becomes perfectly extrinsic and contingent. One recognizes the other aspect of the same gesture when, in general works on Rousseau, in a package of classical shape that gives itself out to be a synthesis that faithfully restores, through commentary and compilation of themes, the totality of the work and the thought, one encounters a chapter of biographical and psychoanalytical cast on the "problem of sexuality in Rousseau," with a reference in an Appendix to the author's medical case-history.

If it seems to us in principle impossible to separate, through interpretation or commentary, the signified from the signifier, and thus to destroy writing by the writing that is yet reading, we nevertheless believe that this impossibility is historically articulated. It does not limit attempts at deciphering in the same way, to the same degree, and according to the same rules. Here we must take into account the history of the text in general. When we speak of the writer and of the encompassing power of the language to which he is subject, we are not only thinking of the writer in literature. The philosopher, the chronicler, the theoretician in general, and at the limit everyone writing, is thus taken by surprise. But, in each case, the person writing is inscribed in a determined textual system. Even if there is never a pure signified, there are different relationships as to that which, from the signifier, *is presented* as the irreducible stratum of the signified. For example, the philosophical text, although it is in fact always written, includes, precisely as its philosophical specificity, the project of effacing itself in the face of the signified content which it transports and in general teaches. Reading should be aware of this project, even if, in the last analysis, it intends to expose the project's failure. The entire history of texts, and within it the history of literary forms in the West, should be studied from this point of view. With the exception of a thrust or a point of resistance which has only been very lately recognized as such, literary writing has, almost always and almost everywhere, according to some fashions and across very diverse ages, lent itself to this *transcendent* reading, in that search for the signified which we here put in question, not to annull it but to understand it within a system to which such a reading is blind. Philosophical literature is only one example within this history but it is among the most significant. And it interests us particularly in Rousseau's case. Who at the same time and for profound reasons produced a philosophical literature to which belong *The Social Contract* and *La nouvelle Héloise*, and chose to live by literary writing; by a writing which would not be exhausted by the message—philosophical or otherwise—which it could, so to speak, deliver. And what Rousseau has said, as philosopher or as psychologist, of writing in general, cannot be separated from the system of his own writing. We should be aware of this.

This poses formidable problems. Problems of outlining in particular. Let me give three examples.

1. If the course I have followed in the reading of the "supplement" is not merely psychoanalytical, it is undoubtedly because the habitual psychoanalysis of literature begins by putting the literary signifier as such within parentheses. It is no doubt also because psychoanalytic theory itself is for me a collection of texts belonging to my history and my culture. To that extent, if it marks my reading and the writing of my interpretation, it does not do so as a principle or a truth that one could abstract from the textual system that I inhabit in order to illuminate it with complete neutrality. In a certain way, I am *within* the history of psychoanalysis as I am *within* Rousseau's text. Just as Rousseau drew upon a language that was already there—and which is found to be somewhat our own, thus assuring us a certain minimal readability of French literature—in the same way we operate today within a certain network of significations marked by psycho-

analytic theory, even if we do not master it and even if we are assured of never being able to master it perfectly.

But it is for another reason that this is not even a somewhat inarticulate psychoanalysis of Jean-Jacques Rousseau. Such a psychoanalysis is already obliged to have located all the structures of appurtenance within Rousseau's text, all that is not unique to it—by reason of the encompassing power and the already-thereness of the language or of the culture—all that could be inhabited rather than produced by writing. Around the irreducible point of originality of this writing an immense series of structures, of historical totalities of all orders, are organized, enveloped, and blended. Supposing that psychoanalysis can by rights succeed in outlining them and their interpretations, supposing that it takes into account the entire history of metaphysics—the history of that Western metaphysics that entertains relationships of cohabitation with Rousseau's text, it would still be necessary for this psychoanalysis to elucidate the law of its own appurtenance to metaphysics and Western culture. Let us not pursue this any further. We have already measured the difficulty of the task and the element of frustration in our interpretation of the supplement. We are sure that something irreducibly Rousseauist is captured there but we have carried off, at the same time, a yet quite unformed mass of roots, soil, and sediments of all sorts.

2. Even supposing that Rousseau's text can be rigorously isolated and articulated within history in general, and then within the history of the sign "supplement," one must still take into consideration many other possibilities. Following the appearances of the word "supplement" and of the corresponding concept or concepts, we traverse a certain path within Rousseau's text. To be sure, this particular path will assure us the economy of a synopsis. But are other paths not possible? And as long as the totality of paths is not effectively exhausted, how shall we justify this one?

3. In Rousseau's text, after having indicated—by anticipation and as a prelude—the function of the sign "supplement," I now prepare myself to give special privilege, in a manner that some might consider exorbitant, to certain texts like the *Essay on the Origin of Languages* and other fragments on the theory of language and writing. By what right? And why these short texts, published for the most part after the author's death, difficult to classify, of uncertain date and inspiration?

To all these questions and within the logic of their system, there is no satisfying response. In a certain measure and in spite of the theoretical precautions that I formulate, my choice is in fact *exorbitant*.

But what is the exorbitant?

I wished to reach the point of a certain exteriority in relation to the totality of the age of logocentrism. Starting from this point of exteriority, a certain deconstruction of that totality which is also a traced path, of that orb (*orbis*) which is also orbitary (*orbita*), might be broached. The first gesture of this departure and this deconstruction, although subject to a certain historical necessity, cannot be given methodological or logical intra-orbitary assurances. Within the closure, one can only judge its style in terms of the accepted oppositions. It may be said that this style is empiricist and in a certain way that would be correct. The *departure* is radically empiricist. It proceeds like a wandering thought on the possibility of itinerary and of method. It is affected by nonknowledge as by its future and it *ventures out* deliberately. I have myself defined the form and the vulnerability of this empiricism. But here the very concept of empiricism destroys itself. To *exceed* the metaphysical orb is an attempt to get out of the orbit (*orbita*), to think the entirety of the classical conceptual oppositions, particularly the one within which the value of empiricism is held: the opposition of philosophy and nonphilosophy, another name for empiricism, for this incapability to sustain on one's own and to the limit the coherence of one's own discourse, for being produced as truth at the moment when the value of truth is shattered, for escaping the internal contradictions of skepticism, etc. *The thought of this historical opposition between philosophy and empiricism is not simply empirical and it cannot be thus qualified without abuse and misunderstanding.*

Let us make the diagram more specific. What is exorbitant in the reading of Rousseau? No doubt Rousseau, as I have already suggested, has only a very relative privilege in the history that interests us. If we merely wished to situate him within this history, the attention that we accord him would be clearly disproportionate. But that is not our intention. We wish to identify a decisive articulation of the logocentric epoch. For purposes of this identification Rousseau seems to us to be most revealing. That obviously supposes that we have already prepared the exit, determined the repression of writing as the fundamental operation of the epoch, read a certain number of texts but not all of them, a certain number of Rousseau's texts but not all of them. This avowal of empiricism can sustain itself only by the strength of the question. The opening of the question, the departure from the closure of a self-evidence, the putting into doubt of a system of oppositions, all these movements necessarily have the form of empiricism and of errancy. At any rate, they cannot be described, *as to past norms*, except in this form. No other trace is available, and as these errant questions are not absolute beginnings in every way, they allow themselves to be effectively reached, on one entire surface, by this description which is also a criticism. We must begin *wherever we are* and the thought of the trace, which cannot not take the scent into account, has already taught us that it was impossible to justify a point of departure absolutely. *Wherever we are*: in a text where we already believe ourselves to be.

Let us narrow the arguments down further. In certain respects, the theme of supplementarity is certainly no more than one theme among others. It is in a chain, carried by it. Perhaps one could substitute something else for it. *But it happens that this theme describes the chain itself, the being-chain of a textual chain, the structure of substitution, the articulation of desire and of language, the logic of all conceptual oppositions taken over by Rousseau,* and particularly the role and the function, in his system, of the concept of Nature. It tells us in a text what a text is, it tells us in writing what writing it, in Rousseau's writing it tells us Jean-Jacque's desire, etc. If we consider, according to the axial proposition of this essay, that there is nothing outside the text, our ultimate justification would be the following: the concept of the supplement and the theory of writing designate textuality itself in Rousseau's text in an indefinitely multiplied structure—*en abyme* [*in an abyss*]—to employ the current phrase. And we shall see that this abyss is not a happy or unhappy accident. An entire theory of the structural necessity of the abyss will be gradually constituted in our reading; the indefinite process of supplementarity has always already *infiltrated* presence, always already inscribed there the space of repetition and the splitting of the self. Representation *in the abyss* of presence is not an accident of presence; the desire of presence is, on the contrary, born from the abyss (the indefinite multiplication) of representation, from the representation of representation, etc. The supplement itself is quite exorbitant, in every sense of the word.

Thus Rousseau inscribes textuality in the text. But its operation is not simple. It tricks with a gesture of effacement, and strategic relations like the relationships of force among the two movements form a complex design. This design seems to us to be represented in the handling of the concept of the supplement. Rousseau cannot utilize it at the same time in all the virtualities of its meaning. The way in which he determines the concept and, in so doing, lets himself be determined by that very thing that he excludes from it, the direction in which he bends it, here as addition, there as substitute, now as the positivity and exteriority of evil, now as a happy auxiliary, all this conveys neither a passivity nor an activity, neither an unconsciousness nor a lucidity on the part of the author. Reading should not only abandon these categories—which are also, let us recall in passing, the founding categories of metaphysics—but should produce the law of this relationship to the concept of the supplement. It it certainly a production, because I do not simply duplicate what Rousseau thought of this relationship. The concept of the supplement is a sort of blind spot in Rousseau's text, the not-seen that opens and limits visibility. But the production, if it attempts to make the not-seen accessible to sight, does not leave the text. It has moreover only believed it was doing so by illusion. It is contained in the transformation of the language it designates, in the regulated exchanges between Rousseau and history. We know that these exchanges only take place by way of the language and the text, in the infrastructural sense that we now give to that word. And what we call production is necessarily a text, the system of a writing and of a reading which we know is ordered around its own blind spot. We know this a priori, but only now and with a knowledge that is not a knowledge at all.

3

Genesis and Structure of the Essay on the Origin of Languages

I. The Place of the "Essay"

What about the voice within the logic of the supplement? within that which should perhaps be called the "graphic" of the supplement?

Within the chain of supplements, it was difficult to separate writing from onanism. Those two supplements have in common at least the fact that they are dangerous. They transgress a prohibition and are experienced within culpability. But, by the economy of differance, they confirm the interdict they transgress, get around a danger, and reserve an expenditure. In spite of them but also thanks to them, we are authorized to see the sun, to deserve the light that keeps us on the surface of the mine.

What culpability attaches to these two experiences? What fundamental culpability is found fixed or deflected there? These questions may be elaborated in their proper place only if we first describe the structural and "phenomenological" superficies of these two experiences, especially the area they have in common.

In both cases, the possibility of auto-affection manifests itself as such: it leaves a trace of itself in the world. The worldly residence of a signifier becomes impregnable. That which is written remains, and the experience of touching-touched admits the world as a third party. The exteriority of space is irreducible there. Within the general structure of auto-affection, within the giving-oneself-a-presence or a pleasure, the operation of touching-touched receives the other within the narrow gulf that separates doing from suffering. And the outside, the exposed surface of the body, signifies and marks forever the division that shapes auto-affection.

Auto-affection is a universal structure of experience. All living things are capable of auto-affection. And only a being capable of symbolizing, that is to say of auto-affecting, may let itself be affected by the other in general. Auto-affection is the condition of an experience in general. This possibility —another name for "life"—is a general structure articulated by the history of life, and leading to complex and hierarchical operations. Auto-affection, the as-for-itself or for-itself—subjectivity—gains in power and in its mastery of the other to the extent that its power of repetition *idealizes itself*. Here idealization is the movement by which sensory exteriority, that which affects me or serves me as signifier, submits itself to my power of repetition, to what thenceforward appears to me as my spontaneity and escapes me less and less.

One must understand speech in terms of this diagram. Its system requires that it be heard and understood immediately by whoever emits it. It produces a signifier which seems not to fall into the world, outside the ideality of the signified, but to remain sheltered—even at the moment that it attains the audiophonic system of the other—within the pure interiority of auto-affection. It does not fall into the exteriority of space, into what one calls the world, which is nothing but the outside of speech. Within so-called "living" speech, the spatial exteriority of the signifier seems absolutely reduced.[1] It is in the context of this possibility that one must pose the problem of the cry—of that which one has always excluded, pushing it into the area of animality or of madness, like the myth of the inarticulate cry—and the problem of speech (voice) within the history of life.

Conversation is, then, a communication between two absolute origins that, if one may venture the formula, auto-affect reciprocally, repeating as immediate echo the auto-affection produced by the other. Immediacy is here the myth of consciousness. Speech and the consciousness of speech—that is to say consciousness simply as self-presence—are the phenomenon of an auto-affection lived as suppression of differance. That *phenomenon*, that presumed suppression of differance, that lived reduction of the opacity of the signifier, are the origin of what is called presence. That which is not subjected to the process of differance is *present*. The present is that from which we believe we are able to think time, effacing the inverse necessity: to think the present from time as differance.

This very formal structure is implied by all analyses of the investments of the system of orality and of the audiophonic system in general, however rich and diverse the field might be.

From the moment that nonpresence comes to be felt within speech itself —and there is at least a foreboding of it from the very threshold of articulation and diacriticity—writing is somehow fissured in its value. On the one hand, as we have seen, it is the effort of symbolically reappropriating presence. On the other, it consecrates the dispossession that had already dislocated the spoken word. In both senses, one may say that in one way or another, it had already begun to undermine and shape "living" speech, exposing it to the death within the sign. But the supplementary sign does not expose to death by affecting a self-presence that is already possible. *Auto*-affection constitutes the same (*auto*) as it divides the same. Privation of presence is the condition of experience, that is to say of presence.

In as much as it *puts into play* the presence of the present and·the life of the living, the movement of language does not, one suspects, have only an analogical relationship with "sexual" auto-affection. It is totally indistinguishable from it, even if that totality is severely articulated and differentiated. The logocentric longing par excellence is to distinguish one from the other. Its last resort would be to dissolve sexuality within the transcendental generality of the structure "touching-touched," as a certain phenomenology might describe it. That dissociation is the very one by which one wishes to distinguish speech from writing. In the same way that the "fatal advantage" of sexual auto-affection begins well before what is thought to be circumscribed by the name of masturbation (organization of so-called wrong and pathological gestures, confined to some children or adolescents), the supplementary menace of writing is older than what some think to exalt by the name of "speech."

From then on, metaphysics consists of excluding non-presence by determining the supplement as *simple exteriority*, pure addition or pure absence. The work of exclusion operates within the structure of supplementarity. The paradox is that one annuls addition by considering it a pure addition. *What is added is nothing because it is added to a full presence to which it is exterior.* Speech comes to be added to intuitive presence (of the entity, of *essence,* of the *eidos,* of *ousia,* and so forth); writing comes to be added to living self-present speech; masturbation comes to be added to so-called normal sexual experience; culture to nature, evil to innocence, history to origin, and so on.

The concept of origin or nature is nothing but the myth of addition, of supplementarity annulled by being purely additive. It is the myth of the effacement of the trace, that is to say of an originary differance that is neither absence nor presence, neither negative nor positive. Originary differance is supplementarity as *structure.* Here structure means the irreducible complexity within which one can only shape or shift the play of presence or absence: that within which metaphysics can be produced but which metaphysics cannot think.

This movement of the effacement of the trace has been, from Plato to Rousseau to Hegel, imposed upon writing in the narrow sense; the necessity of such a displacement may now be apparent. Writing is one of the representatives of the trace in general, it is not the trace itself. *The trace itself does not exist.* (To exist is to be, to be an entity, a being-present, *to on.*) In a way, this displacement leaves the place of the decision hidden, but it also indicates it unmistakably.

Writing, Political Evil, and Linguistic Evil. Desire desires the exteriority of presence and nonpresence. This exterority is a matrix. Among all its representations (exteriority of nature and its others, of good and of evil, of innocence and perversity, of consciousness and nonconsciousness, of life and death, etc.), one in particular requires our special notice. It will introduce us to *The Essay on the Origin of Languages*. It is the exterioirty of mastery and servitude or of liberty and nonliberty. Among all these representations, the exteriority of liberty and nonliberty is perhaps privileged. More clearly than others, it brings together the historical (political, economic, technological) and the metaphysical. Heidegger has summarized the history of metaphysics by repeating that which made of liberty the condition of presence, that is to say, of truth.[2] And speech always presents itself as the best expression of liberty. It is by itself language at liberty and the liberty of language, the freedom of a speech which need not borrow its signifiers from the exteriority of the world, and which therefore seems incapable of being dispossessed. Do the most imprisoned and deprived beings not make use of that interior spontaneity which is speech? What is true of the citizen is in the first place true of those naked beings exposed to the power of others: the newborn. "Your first gifts are fetters, your first treatment, torture. *Their voice alone is free*; why should they not raise it in complaint?" (*Emile*, p. 15 [p. 11]; italics added).

The Essay on the Origin of Languages opposes speech to writing as presence to absence and liberty to servitude. These are almost the final words of the *Essay*: "But I say that any tongue with which one cannot make oneself understood to the people assembled is a slavish tongue. It is impossible for a people to remain free and speak that tongue" (Chap. XX). With this sentence, through the detour of the Lévi-Straussian ideology of the "neighborhood," of a "small community where everybody knew everybody else" and where nobody went beyond earshot we have set foot again upon a Rousseauist ground that we had hardly left: a classical ideology according to which writing takes the status of a tragic fatality come to prey upon natural innocence, interrupting the golden age of the present and full speech.

Rousseau concludes thus:

> These superficial reflections, which hopefully might give birth to more profound ones, I shall conclude with the passage that suggested them to me:
> "*To observe in fact and to show by examples, the degree to which the character, customs and interests of a people influence their language, would provide material for a sufficiently philosophical investigation.*" (*Remarks on a General and Reasoned Grammar*, by M. Duclos, p. 2 [pp. 73–74]).

In fact, the *Commentary*[3] of Duclos, with the *Essai sur l'origine des connaissances humaines** of Condillac (1746), seems to have been one of the

* I have used the facsimile reproduction of the translation by Thomas Nugent, with an introduction by Robert G. Weyant (Gainesville, Florida, 1971), and placed page references within brackets. Derrida's source is given in note 57.

major "sources" of *The Essay on the Origin of Languages.* One might even be tempted to consider Rousseau's *Essay* as the accomplishment of the "philsophic" program charted by Duclos. The latter regrets

the penchant we have of making our language soft, effeminate and monotonous. We have reason to avoid roughness in pronunciation, but I think we go too far into the opposite fault. Formerly we pronounced many more diphthongs than we do today; in the tenses, as J'avois [jhavwa], j'aurois [jhorwa], and in many nouns, such as François [Franswa], Anglois [Anglwa], Polonois [Polonwa], whereas today we say j'avais [jhavay], Fransay, Anglay, Polonay. Those diphthongs, however, gave force and variety to pronunciation, and saved it from a monotony that partly arises from our multitude of mute e-s.[4]

The degradation of the language is the symptom of a social and political degradation (a theme that will become most frequent in the second half of the eighteenth century); it has its origins in the aristocracy and in the capital city. Duclos announces the Rousseauist themes most precisely when he holds forth thus: "What we call *society,* and what our ancestors would merely have called a *coterie,* decides the nature of language and manners [*moeurs*] today. When a word has been for a time in use *in these social circles,* its pronunciation softens."[5] Duclos finds equally intolerable similar multilations inflicted upon words, their corruptions, and above all their abridgements; one must on no account *shorten* [*couper*] words:

This nonchalance in pronunciation, which is not incompatible with an impatience in expression, makes us corrupt even the nature of words, by chopping them up in such a way that the meaning is no longer recognizable. Today, for example, one pronounces the proverb as, in spite of him and his teeth [*ses dens*], rather than in spite of him and his helpers [*ses aidans*]. We have more of these words shortened or corrupted by usage than one would credit. Our language will become imperceptibly more proper for conversations than for the tribune, and conversation sets the tone for the Chair, the Bar, and for the Theater; whereas with the Greeks and Romans, the tribune did not submit to it. A sustained pronunciation and a fixed and distinct prosody must be maintained in particular by peoples who are obliged to treat publicly matters that are of interest to all the auditors, for, other things being equal, an orator whose pronunciation is firm and varied would be understood at a greater distance than another . . .

Deterioration in the language and in pronounciation is thus inseparable from political corruption. The political model that inspires Duclos is Athenian or Roman democracy. The language is the property of the people. Each derives its unity from the other. For if language has a body and a system, they inhere in the people assembled and "bodily" united: "It is a people in a body that makes a language. . . . A people is thus the absolute master of the *spoken* language, and it is an empire they possess unawares."[6] To dispossess the people of their mastery of the language and thus of their self-mastery, one must suspend the *spoken* element in language. Writing is the very process of the dispersal of peoples unified as bodies and the beginning of their enslavement: "The body of a nation alone has authority over the *spoken language*, and the writers have the right over the *written* language: *The people, Varro said, are not masters of writing as they are of speech*" (p. 420).

This unity of political and linguistic evil calls for a "philosophical examination." Rousseau already responds to this appeal by means of the *Essay*. But we shall, very much later, recognize Duclos's problematics in a much sharper form. The difficulty of the pedagogy of language and of the teaching of foreign languages is, *Emile* will say, that one cannot separate the signifier from the signified, and, changing words, one changes ideas in such a way that the teaching of a language transmits at the same time an entire national culture over which the pedagogue has no control, which resists him like the already-there preceding the formation, the institution preceding instruction.

> You will be surprised to find that I reckon the study of languages among the useless lumber of education. . . . If the study of languages were merely the study of words, that is, of the symbols by which language expresses itself, then this might be a suitable study for children; but languages, as they change the symbols, also modify the ideas which the symbols express. Minds are formed by language, thoughts take their color from its ideas. Reason alone is common to all. Every language has its own form, a difference which may be partly cause and partly effect of difference in national character; this conjecture appears to be confirmed by the fact that in every nation under the sun speech follows the changes of manners, and is preserved or altered along with them (p. 105 [p. 73]).

And this entire theory of the teaching of languages rests on rigorous distinctions separating thing, meaning (or idea), and sign; today we would speak of the referent, the signified, and the signifier. If the representer may have an effect, sometimes pernicious, on the represented, and if the child must not and cannot "learn to speak more than one language," it is that "each thing may have a thousand different signs for him; but each idea may have only one form" (ibid.)

Launched by Duclos, the invitation to the "philosophic examination" occupied Rousseau for a long time. In 1754 it had been formulated in the *Commentary*. It is cited at the conclusion of the *Essay*; elsewhere other passages of the *Commentary* are evoked, notably in Chapter VII. Do these citations, which could not have been anterior to the publication of the second *Discourse* (*Discourse on the Origin and Foundations of Inequality Among Men*), also dated 1754, lead us to some certainty about the date of the composition of the *Essay?* And to what extent can one connect this chronological problem with the systematic problem of what is called the author's thought? The importance that we assign to this work compels us to consider the question.

On the date of the composition of this little known and posthumously published text, the most authoritative interpreters and historians rarely agree. And when they do, it is generally for different reasons. The ultimate question at stake within this problem is evident: can one speak of this as a work of maturity? does its content accord with the second *Discourse* and the later works?

In this debate, external arguments always mingle with internal ones. The debate has continued for more than seventy years and has gone through two phases. If we begin by remembering the most recent, it is primarily because it has developed a little as if the first phase had not brought the external aspect of the problem to what I would consider to be a definite conclusion. But it is also because, in a certain way, it has renewed the form of the internal problem.

The Present Debate: The Economy of Pity. The passages cited from Duclos are not the sole indications that allow modern commentators to conclude that the *Essay* comes after the second *Discourse* or that it is at the most its contemporary. B. Gagnebin and M. Raymond recall in their edition of the *Confessions*[7] that "the *Essay on the Origin of Languages* appeared for the first time in a volume of *Treatises on Music* by J.-J. Rousseau which De Peyrou published in Geneva in 1781, based on the manuscript which he possessed and which he bequeathed to the Library of Neuchâtel (No. 7835)." The editors of the *Confessions* draw attention to "this most remarkable little work, too little read" and use the citations from Duclos as evidence for placing it after the second *Discourse*. "In short," they add, "the very material of the *Essay* presupposes a knowledge and a maturity of thought that Rousseau had not acquired in 1750." This is also the opinion of R. Derathé,[8] at least on Chapter IX and X, which are among the most important and which, explaining the "Formation of the Languages of the South" and the "Formation of the Languages of the North," develop the themes most akin to those of the second *Discourse*.

Is it not plausible—and tempting to imagine—that Rousseau might have spread out the composition of this text over many years? Can one not isolate in it many strata of his reflections? Could the passages from Duclos not have been introduced later? Could certain of the important chapters not have been composed, completed, or revised at the same time as the second *Discourse* or even after? That would reconcile the interpretations and would give a certain authority to the hypothesis of those who now place the conception, if not the entire execution, of the *Essay* well before

1754. Thus Vaughan thinks, for external reasons, that the *Essay* was planned before the second *Discourse*, and even before the first *Discourse* (1750).[9] Indeed it relates very closely to the writings on music. Its full title says it well: *Essay on the Origin of Languages, which treats of Melody, and Musical Imitation*. It is known that the writings on music follow from a very precocious inspiration. In 1742 Rousseau read at the Academy of Sciences his *Projet concernant les nouveaux signes pour la musique*. In 1743 the *Dissertation sur la musique moderne* appeared. In 1749, year of the composition of the first *Discourse*, Rousseau wrote, at D'Alembert's behest, the articles on music for the *Encyclopaedia*. It is in the context of these articles that he will write the *Dictionnaire de musique** to which the *Essay* was joined at the time of its first publication. Can one not imagine that the *Essay* was projected at this time, even if its execution stretched out over many years, Rousseau modifying till 1754 certain intentions and certain chapters until he thought to make of the *Essay*, as he says in a "Preface,"[10] a piece of the second *Discourse*?

However, in spite of the convenience and plausibility of this reconciling conjecture; there is one point at which, for internal and systematic reasons, it is difficult to get rid of the disagreement by assigning a period and a part of the truth to each hypothesis. Here one must choose sides.

The moment comes with respect to the philosophical content of Chapter IX, "Formation of the Southern Languages." It is over the subject of this fundamental chapter that Derathé and Starobinski differ. To be sure, they are never directly opposed on this point. But both give a note[11] to it, and their confrontation may illuminate our problem.

That the essay was an intended part of the second *Discourse* is, according to Derathé, "the most plausible hypothesis, at least with respect to Chapters IX and X . . . which show the same preoccupations as *The Discourse on Inequality*."

Now, it is precisely in Chapter IX that Starobinski locates an affirmation which seems incompatible to him with the intention of the second *Discourse*. From it he concludes that Rousseau's thought had evolved. And it could only have evolved from the *Essay* to the *Discourse*, since the doctrine will seemingly no longer vary on this point after 1754. Thus, systematically and historically, the *Essay* is anterior to the second *Discourse*. And that would appear from an examination of the status given by him to that fundamental sentiment which according to him is *pity*. Briefly, the *Discourse* makes of it a *natural* feeling or virtue, coming before the use of reflection, while in the *Essay*, Rousseau seems to think that it is previously *aroused* [*éveillée*]—let us conserve all the indeterminacy of the word for the moment—by judgment.

*(Paris, 1768). Translated as *A Dictionary of Music* by William Waring (London, 1779).

Since it gives rise to no disagreement, let us first recall the doctrine of the *Discourse*. Rousseau affirms there unambiguously that pity is more primitive than the work of reason and reflection. That is a condition of its universality. And the argument could not help but aim at Hobbes:

I think I need not fear contradiction in holding man to be possessed of the only *natural* virtue, which could not be denied him by the most violent detractor of human virtue.[12] I am speaking of compassion [*pitié*], which is a disposition suitable to creatures so weak and subject to so many evils as we certainly are: by so much the more universal and useful to mankind, *as it comes before any kind of reflection*; and at the same time so natural, that the very brutes themselves sometimes give evident proofs of it.

And after giving examples of it within the human and the animal order, but referring almost always to the mother-child relationship, Rousseau continues:

Such is the pure emotion of nature, *prior to all kinds of reflection*! Such is the force of natural compassion [*la pitié naturelle*], which the greatest depravity of morals has as yet hardly been able to destroy! . . . Mandeville well knew that, in spite of all their morality, men would have never been better than monsters, had not nature bestowed on them a sense of compassion [*pitié*], to aid their reason. . . . It is then certain that compassion [*pitié*] is a natural feeling, which, by moderating the violence of love of self in each individual, contributes to the preservation of the whole species. It is this compassion [*pitié*] that hurries us *without reflection* to the relief of those who are in distress: it is this which in a state of nature *supplies the place* of laws, morals, and virtues, with the advantage that none are tempted to disobey its *gentle voice* [pp. 183–84].[13]

Let us pause before we take up the thread of the debate. Let us reconsider the system of metaphors. Natural pity, which is illustrated archetypically by the relationship between mother and child, and generally by the relationship between life and death, commands like a gentle voice. In the metaphor of that soft voice the presence of the mother as well as of Nature is at once brought in. That the soft voice must be the mother's as well as Nature's is clear from the fact that it is, as the metaphor of the voice clearly always indicates in Rousseau, a law. "No one is tempted to disobey it" at the same time because it is soft and because, being natural, and absolutely original, it is also inexorable. That maternal law is a voice. Pity is a voice. As opposed to writing, which is *without pity*, the voice is always, in its essence, the passage of virtue and good passion. The order of pity "takes the place of law," it supplements law, that is to say instituted law. But as institutional law is also the supplement of natural law when the latter is lacking, it is clear that only the concept of the supplement allows us to think the relationship between nature and law here. These two terms have no meaning except within the structure of supplementarity. The authority of nonmaternal law has no sense except as it is substituted for the authority of natural law, for the "gentle voice" which it was clearly necessary to be "tempted to disobey." The order without pity to which one accedes when the gentle voice stops making itself heard, is it quite simply, as we let it be imagined a moment ago, the order of writing? Yes and no. Yes, to the extent that writing is read literally, or is tied to the letter [*on lit écriture à la lettre, ou on la lie à la lettre*]. No, as long as writing is understood in its metaphor. One might then say that the natural law, the gentle voice of pity, is not only uttered by a maternal solicitude, it is inscribed in our hearts by God. It concerns the natural writing, the writing of the heart, which Rousseau opposes to the writing of reason. Only the latter is without pity, it alone transgresses the interdict that, under the name of natural affection, links the child to the mother and protects life from death. To transgress the law and the voice of pity is to replace natural affection by perverse passion. The first is good because it is inscribed in our hearts by God. It is here that we encounter that divine or natural writing whose metaphoric displacement we have already situated. In *Emile*, describing what he calls the "second birth," Rousseau will write:

> Our passions are the chief means of self-preservation; to try to destroy them is therefore as absurd as it is useless; this would be to overcome nature, to reshape God's handiwork. If God bade man annihilate the passions he has given him, He would and would not do so; He would contradict himself. He has never given such a foolish commandment, there is nothing like it written on the heart of man, and what God will have a man do, He does not leave to the words of another man, He speaks Himself; His words are written in the secret heart (pp. 246–47) [p. 173].

The absolutely primitive passion, which God may not ask us to deny without contradicting Himself, is the love of self [*l'amour de soi*]. It is well-known that Rousseau distinguishes it from that self-love [*l'amour-propre*] which is its corrupt form. Now, if the source of all passions is natural, all the passions are not so. "A thousand strange channels have swollen it" (ibid.). What concerns us here about the status of pity, the root of the love of others, is that it is neither the source itself, nor a secondary stream of passion, one acquired passion among others. It is *the first diversion* of the love of self. It is *almost* primitive, and it is in the difference between absolute proximity and absolute identity that all the problematics of pity are lodged. "The child's first sentiment is love of self [*l'amour de soi*]; and his second, which is derived from it, is love of those about him" (p. 248) [p. 174]. That diversion/derivation is next demonstrated: it is less an estrangement and an interruption of the love of self than its first and most necessary consequence. If pity moderates "the violenec [*l'activité*] of love of self" (second *Discourse*, p. 156) [p. 184], it is perhaps less by opposing itself to it[14] than by expressing it in an indirect way, by defering it, since such moderation "contributes to the preservation of the whole species" (ibid.).

It must further be understood how and why pity, itself supplanted by law and society, may also play the role of that which supplants. Why at a given time or all the time does it take the place of culture, being that which "in a state of nature supplies the place of laws, morals, and virtues?" [*Discourse*, p. 184]. Against what analogue of itself, against what depravity does it guard us, which resembles and yet differs from it enough so that a substitution may take place?

Is it by chance that, like many another supplement, the natural and prereflexive sentiment of pity, which "contributes to the preservation of the whole species," protects us from, among other deadly menaces, love? Is it by chance that pity protects man (*homo*) from destruction through the fury of love, to the extent that it protects man (*vir*) from his destruction through the fury of woman? What God's inscription means is that pity—which ties the child to the mother and life to nature—must protect us from the amorous passion which ties the child's becoming-man (the "second birth") to the mother's becoming-woman. That becoming is the great substitution. Pity protects the humanity of man, and the life of the living, to the extent that it saves, as we shall go on to see, the virility of man and the masculinity of the male.

In fact, if pity is natural, if that which brings us to identify with others is an innate movement, love or the amorous passion is, on the contrary, not natural at all. It is a product of history and society.

> Of the passions that stir the heart of man, there is one which makes the sexes necessary to each other, and is extremely ardent and impetuous; a terrible passion that braves danger, surmounts all obstacles, and in its transports seems calculated to bring destruction on the human race which it is really destined to preserve. What must become of men who are left to this brutal and boundless rage, without modesty, without shame, and daily upholding their amours at the price of their blood? (*Discourse*, p. 157) [p. 185]

Under this bloody picture one must read, as in a palimpsest, *the other scene*: that which, a moment ago and in the same colors, exhibited a world of dead horses, ferocious animals, and children torn from the mother's breast.

The amorous passion is thus the perversion of natural pity. Unlike the latter, it limits our attachment to a single person. As always in Rousseau, evil here has the form of determination, of comparison and of *preference*. That is to say of difference. This invention of culture denatures pity, deflects its spontaneous movement, which would carry it instinctively and indistinctly toward everything living, whatever may be its species and sex. Jealousy, which marks the gap between pity and love, is not only a creation of culture in our society. As a ruse of comparison, it is a stratagem of femininity, an arresting of nature by woman. What is cultural and historical in love is at the service of femininity: made to enslave man to woman. It is "a factitious sentiment; born of social usage, super-subtly celebrated by women, with care for the establishment of their empire, and rendering dominant the sex that ought to obey" (p. 158). *Emile* will say that "the law of nature bids the woman obey the man" (p. 517) [p. 370]. And Rousseau describes here the battle between man and woman according to the pattern and in the very terms of the Hegelian dialectic of master and slave, which illuminates not only his text but also *The Phenomenology of the Mind*:

> If he takes a wife from a lower class, natural and civil law are in accordance and all goes well. When he marries a woman of higher rank it is just the opposite case; the man must choose between diminished rights or imperfect gratitude; he must be ungrateful or despised. Then the wife, laying claim to authority, makes herself a tyrant over her lawful head; and the master, who has become a slave, is the most ridiculous and miserable of creatures. Such are the unhappy favorites whom the sovereigns of Asia honor and torment with their alliance; people tell us that if they desire to sleep with their wife they must enter by the foot of the bed (ibid.).

The historical perversion[15] is introduced through a double substitution: substitution of a political command for domestic government, and of moral for physical love. It is natural that the woman govern the home and Rousseau recognizes her "natural talent" for it; but she must do it under the husband's authority, "as a minister reigns in the State, by contriving to be ordered to do what she wants":

> I expect that many of my readers will remember that I think women have a natural gift for managing men, and will accuse me of contradicting myself; yet they are mistaken. There is a vast difference between claiming the right to command, and managing him who commands. Women's reign is a reign of *gentleness*, tact, and kindness; *her commands are caresses*, her threats are tears. She should reign in the home as a minister reigns in the state, by contriving to be ordered to do what she wants. In this sense, I grant you, that the best managed homes are those where the wife has most power. But when she despises the *voice* of her head, when she desires to usurp his rights and take the command upon herself, this inversion of the proper order of things leads only to misery, scandal, and dishonor (ibid.; italics added).

In modern society, then, order has been reversed by woman and that is the very form of usurpation. That substitution is not one abuse among others. It is the paradigm of violence and political anomaly. Like the linguistic evil of which we spoke above—and we shall soon see the two directly linked—that substitution is a political evil. The *Letter to M. d'Alembert* says it well:

. . . and, no longer wishing to tolerate separation, unable to make themselves into men, the women make us into women. This disadvantageous result which degrades man is very important everywhere; but it is especially so in states like ours, whose interest it is to prevent it. Whether a monarch governs men or women ought to be rather indifferent to him, provided that he be obeyed; but in a republic, men are needed.[16]

The morality of this proposition is that women themselves would gain if the republic restored the natural order, for in a perverse society man scorns the woman he must obey: "Cowardly devoted to the will of the sex that we ought to protect rather than serve, we have learnt to scorn them while we obey, to outrage them by our railing concern." And Paris, guilty of the degradations of language, is again incriminated: "And each Parisian woman in her apartment assembles a seraglio of men more feminine than herself, who know how to render all kinds of homage to beauty, except for that of the heart which she deserves" (ibid.).

The "natural" image of woman, as Rousseau reconstitutes it, emerges slowly: exalted by man but submissive to him, she must govern without being mistress. One must *respect* her, that is to say love her, from a sufficient distance so that the forces—our own and those of the body politic —are not breached through it. For we risk our *constitution* not only by "cohabiting with women" (instead of containing them within domestic government) but also by regulating our society according to theirs. "They [men] are affected as much as and more than, women by commerce that is too intimate: they lose only their morals, but we lose our morals and our constitution" (p. 204) [p. 100]. The contest is not equal; perhaps that is the most profound signification of the play of supplementarity.

This takes us directly to the other form of substitutive perversion: that which adds moral to physical love. There is a naturalness in love: it serves procreation and the conservation of the species. That which Rousseau calls "the physicalness of Love" is, as its name indicates, natural, and thus joined to the movement of pity. Desire is not pity, to be sure, but, according to Rousseau, it is prereflexive like pity. Now one must "distinguish . . . between what is moral and what is physical in the passion called love" (second *Discourse*, p. 157) [p. 196]. Within the "moral" that substitutes itself for the natural, within the institution, history, and culture, female perfidy, thanks to social usage, works to arrest natural desire in order to capture its energy so that it may be directed to a single person. It thus makes sure of an usurping of control:

The physical part of love is that general desire which urges the sexes to union with each other. The moral part is that which determines and fixes this desire exclusively upon one particular object; or at least gives it a greater degree of energy toward the object thus preferred. (*Discourse*, pp. 157–58) [p. 186]

The operation of femininity—and that femininity, the feminine principle, may be at work among women just as much as among those whom society calls men and whom, Rousseau says, "women turn to women"—consists therefore in capturing energy to attach it to a single theme, a sole representation.

Such is the history of love. In it is reflected nothing but history as denaturalization: that which adds itself to nature, the moral supplement, displaces the force of nature by substitution. In that sense the supplement is nothing, it has no energy of its own, no spontaneous movement. It is a parasitic organism, an imagination or representation which determines and orients the force of desire. One can never explain, in terms of nature and natural force, the fact that something like the difference of a *preference* might, without any force of its own, force force. Such an inexplicability gives all its style and all its form to Rousseau's thought.

This pattern is already an interpretation of history by Rousseau. But this interpretation lends itself in its turn to a second interpretation where we notice a certain hesitation. Rousseau seems to oscillate between two readings of this history. And the sense of that oscillation should be recognized here. It will illuminate our analysis yet further. Sometimes the perverse substitution is described as the origin of history, as historicity itself and the first deviation with respect to natural desire. Sometimes it is described as an historical depravity *within* history, not just a corruption within the form of supplementarity but a supplementary corruption. It is thus that one may read descriptions of an historical society within which woman takes her place, remains in her place, occupies her natural place, as an object of uncorrupted love:

The ancients spent almost their whole lives *in the open air*, either dispatching their business or taking care of the state's in the public place, or walking in the country, in gardens, on the seashore, in the rain or under the sun, and almost always bareheaded. In all of this, no women; but they were quite able to find them in case of need, and we do not find from their writings and the samples of their conversation which are left to us that intelligence, taste, or even love, lost anything by this reserve. (*Letter to M. d'Alembert*, p. 204 [p. 101]. Italics added.)

But is there a difference between corruption in the form of supplementarity and supplementary corruption? Perhaps it is the concept of supplementarity itself that allows us to think these two interpretations of interpretation at the same time. From the first departure from nature, the play of history—as supplementarity—carries within itself the principle of its own degradation, of the supplementary degradation, of the degradation of degradation. The acceleration, the precipitation of perversion within history, is implied from the very start by the historical perversion itself.

But the concept of the supplement, considered, as we have already done, as an *economic* concept, should allow us to say the contrary at the same time without contradiction. The logic of the supplement—which is not the logic of identity—allows the acceleration of evil to find at once its historical compensation and its historical guardrail. History precipitates history, society corrupts society, but the evil that links both in an indefinite chain [*qui les abîme*] has its natural supplement as well: history and society produce their own resistance to the abyss [*l'abîme*].

Thus, for example, the "moral part" of love is immoral: captor and destroyer. But just as one may guard presence through defering it, just as one may defer the expense, put off the mortal "cohabitation" with woman by that other power of death which is auto-eroticism, so also, according to this economy of life or death, society may place a moral guardrail over the abyss of "moral love." The morality of society can in fact defer or weaken the capturing of energy by imposing on woman the virtue of *modesty*. Within modesty, that product of social refinement, it is in fact natural wisdom, the economy of life, that controls culture by culture. (Rousseau's entire discourse, let us note in passing, finds here its proper field of exercise.) As women betray the natural morality of physical desire, society invents—but it is a ruse of nature—the moral imperative of modesty which limits immorality; limits morality in fact, for "moral love" was never immoral except as it menaced man's life. The theme of modesty has a greater importance in *The Letter to M. d'Alembert* than is generally thought. But it is central in *Emile*, especially in that Fifth Book which one must follow here line by line. Modesty is clearly defined there as a supplement of natural virtue. It has to do with knowing if men wish to allow themselves to be "dragged to their death" (p. 447 [p. 322]), by the number and intemperance of women. Their "boundless desire" does not in fact have that sort of natural restraint that one encounters in female animals. With the latter,

when the need is satisfied, the desire ceases; they no longer make a feint of repulsing the male, they do it in earnest. They do exactly the opposite of what Augustus' daughter did; they receive no more passengers when the ship has its cargo. . . . Instinct both drives and stops them. *But what would take the place of* [supplement] *this negative instinct in women if you rob them of their modesty?* To wait for them not to concern themselves with men, is to wait for them to be good for nothing. (Italics added.) [And this supplement is indeed the economy of men's lives]:* Their natural intemperance would lead them to death; because it contains their desires, modesty is the true morality of women.

It is clearly confirmed that the concept of nature and the entire system it commands may not be thought except under the irreducible category of the supplement. Although modesty comes to fill the lack of a natural and instinctive restraint, it is, nonetheless, as a supplement, and moral as it certainly is, natural. This product of culture has a natural origin and a natural end. God Himself has inscribed it in His creatures: "The Most High has deigned to do honor to mankind; he has endowed man with boundless passions, together with a law to guide them, so that man may be alike free and self-controlled; though swayed by these passions man is endowed with reason by which to control them. Woman is also endowed with boundless passions; God has given her modesty to restrain them" [p. 323]. Thus God gives *reason* to supplement natural inclinations. Reason is thus at once within nature and in a supplementary role to nature; it is a supplementary ration. Which supposes that nature might sometimes lack something within itself or, what is the same thing, might sometimes exceed itself. And God even adds a bonus (*praemium*), a recompense, a supplement to the supplement: "Moreover," Rousseau continues, "he has given to both a present reward for the right use of their powers, in the delight which springs from that right use of them, i.e., the taste for right conduct established as the law of our behavior. To my mind this is far higher than the instinct of the beasts" [p. 323].

Guided by this pattern, one would have to reread all the texts describing culture as the corruption of nature: in the sciences, the arts, spectacles, masques, literature, writing. One would have to take them up again within the network of this structure of "moral love," as the war of the sexes and as the chaining of the force of desire by the feminine principle. Setting not only men against women but also men against men, this war is historic. It is not a natural or biological phenomenon. As in Hegel, it is a war of consciousness and desires, not of needs or natural desires. How does one identify it? In particular by what cannot be explained by the scarcity of females or by "the exclusive intervals, during which the females constantly refuse the addresses of the male, which," Rousseau notes,

> amounts to the first cause, for if each female admits the male but during two months in the year, it is the same as if the number of females were five-sixths less. Now, neither of these two cases is applicable to the human species, in which the number of females usually exceeds that of males, and among whom it has never been observed, even among savages, that the females have, like those of other animals, their stated times of passion and indifference.[17]

* Interpolation Derrida's.

"Moral love," not having any biological foundation, is born of the power of the imagination. All the depravity of culture, as the movement of difference and preference, is therefore related to the possession of *women.* One must know who will have the women but also what the women will have. And what price will be paid within that calculation of forces. Now according to the principle of acceleration or of capitalization that we have just defined, what opens evil is also that which precipitates toward the worst. Rousseau might say like Montaigne "Our morals bend with a marvelous inclination toward worsening" (*Essais* II.82).* Thus writing, here literary, conspires with moral love. The first appears at the same time as the second. But moral love degrades even writing. It enervates writing as it enervates man. It provokes

> these throngs of ephemeral works which come to light every day, made only to amuse women and having neither strength nor depth, [and which] fly from the dressing table to the counter. This is the way to rewrite ever again the same things and to make them always new. Two or three will be cited which will serve as exceptions; but I will cite a hundred thousand which will confirm the rule. It is for this reason that most of the productions of our age will pass with it, and posterity will think that very few books were written in this age which produced so many.[18]

Has this detour taken us far from our initial preoccupation? How will it help us to situate the *Essay* more precisely?

We have just verified that, comprehended by the entire system of oppositions that it sustains, the concept of natural pity is fundamental. Yet, according to Starobinski, it is absent, indeed excluded, from the *Essay on the Origin of Languages*. And one cannot ignore this fact when assigning it a place within the history and architechtonics of Rousseau's thought:

> The importance of the spontaneous outburst of pity, the unreasoned foundation of morality, has been indicated by Rousseau since the Preface to the *Discourse;* cf. p .126 and n. 1. In this part of the *Discourse*, and later in *Emile*, Rousseau does not cease affirming that pity is a virtue that "precedes the usage of all reflexion." This is the definitive state of Rousseau's thought on this subject. Now the *Essay on the Origin of Languages*, ch. IX, formulates on this point many quite different ideas, which will perhaps allow us to attribute to this text (or at least to this chapter) a date anterior to the final draft of the *Discourse on the Origin of Inequality*. In the *Essay*, Rousseau does not admit the possibility of an unpremeditated burst of sympathy, and seems more inclined to sustain the Hobbesian idea of the war of all against all: "They were not bound by any idea of common brotherhood and, having no rule but that of force, they believed themselves each other's enemies. . . . An individual isolated on the face of the earth, at the mercy of mankind, is bound to be a ferocious

* Garnier edition (Paris, 1958), vol. 2, p. 376.

animal. . . . We develop social feeling only as we become enlightened. Although pity is native to the human heart, it would remain eternally quiescent unless it were activated by imagination. How are we moved to pity? By getting outside ourselves and identifying with a being who suffers. We suffer only as much as we believe him to suffer. . . . He who has never been reflective is incapable of being merciful or just or pitying. He is just as incapable of being malicious and vindictive" [pp. 31–32].

This more intellectualist conception of pity agrees with the thought of Wollaston.

Are these affirmations, extracted from the *Essay* and quoted by Starobinski, incompatible with the theses of the *Discourse* and *Emile*? It seems not. At least for three sorts of reasons:

A. First, Rousseau makes a concession in the *Essay* which assures its place within the entire theory—supposedly "later"—of pity. He writes: "Although pity is native to the human heart . . ." He thus recognizes that pity is an innate, spontaneous, and prereflexive virtue. That will be the thesis of the *Discourse* and of *Emile*.

B. It is "imagination," not "reason," without which this pity "natural to man's heart" would remain unawakened and "inactive." According to the second *Discourse*, natural pity is in danger of being strangled or corrupted by reason and reflection. Reflective reason is not contemporaneous with pity. The *Essay* does not say the contrary. Pity does not awaken with reason but with imagination which wrenches it from its slumbering inactuality. Not only does Rousseau take for granted the distinction between imagination and reason, but he makes this difference the strength of his entire thought.

Certainly imagination here has a value whose ambiguity is often recognized. If it is able to corrupt us, it is first because it opens the possibility of progress. It *broaches* history. Without it perfectibility, which, as one knows, constitutes the absolute distinguishing trait of humanity for Rousseau, would be impossible. Although the concept of reason is very complex in Rousseau,[19] it may be said that, in certain regards, reason, in as much as it is the understanding and the faculty of forming ideas, is less proper to humanity than imagination and perfectibility. We have already noticed in what sense reason may be called natural. One may also remark that from another point of view animals, although they are gifted with intelligence, are not perfectible. They are deprived of the imagination, of that power of anticipation that exceeds the givens of the senses and takes us toward the unperceived:

Every animal has ideas, since it has senses; it even combines those ideas in a certain degree; and it is only in degree that man differs, in this respect, from the brute. Some philosophers have even maintained that there is a greater difference between one man and another than between some men and some beasts. It is not, therefore, so much the understanding that constitutes the specific difference between the man and the brute, as the human quality of free agency. (Second *Discourse*, p. 141 [p. 170])

Liberty is therefore perfectibility. "There is another very specific quality which distinguishes them [man and animal], and which will admit of no dispute. This is the faculty of self-improvement [*se perfectionner*] (p. 142) [p. 171].

The imagination is at the same time the condition of perfectibility—liberty—and that without which pity would neither awaken nor exercise itself within the human order. It activates and excites a potential power.

1. Imagination inaugurates liberty and perfectibility because sensibility, as well as intellectual reason, filled and satiated by the presence of the perceived, is exhausted by a fixist concept. Animality has no history because feeling and understanding are, at root, functions of passivity. "As reason has little force, interest alone does not have as much force as one believes. Only imagination is active and one excites the passions only by imagination" (*Letter to the Prince of* Würtemberg. 11.10.63).* Immediate consequence: reason, a function of interest and need, the technical and calculating faculty, is not the origin of language, which is also a human property and without which there would be no perfectibility. Language is born of the imagination which arouses or at any rate excites sentiment or passion. This affirmation, which will be repeated ceaselessly, is already there at the opening of the *Essay*: "Speech distinguishes man among animals." The first words of Chapter II: "It seems then that need dictated the first gestures, while the passions wrung forth the first words" [p. 11].

We thus see two series working themselves out: (1) animality, need, interest, gesture, sensibility, understanding, reason, etc. (2) humanity, passion, imagination, speech, liberty, perfectibility, etc.

It will gradually appear that, under the complexity of strands tangled in Rousseau's texts among these terms, requiring the minutest and most careful analyses, these two series always relate to each other according to the structure of supplementarity. All the names of the second series are metaphysical determinations—and therefore inherited, arranged with a laborious and interrelating coherence—of *supplementary differance*.

A dangerous differance, of course. For we have omitted the master-name of the supplementary series: death. Or rather, for death is nothing, the relationship to death, the anguished anticipation of death. All the possibilities of the supplementary series, which have the relationships of metonymic substitutions among themselves, indirectly name the danger itself, the horizon and source of all determined dangers, the abyss from which all menaces announce themselves. We should not be surprised when, in the second *Dis-*

* *Correspondance complète*, vol. 18, p. 118.

course, the notion of perfectibility or liberty is set forth at the same time as the knowledge of death. The property of man is announced from the double possibility of liberty and of the express anticipation of death. The difference between human desire and animal need, between relationship with the woman and relationship with the female, is the fear of death:

> The only goods he [the animal] recognizes in the universe are food, a female, and sleep: the only evils he fears are pain and hunger. I say pain, and not death: for no animal can know what it is to die; the knowledge of death and its terror being one of the first acquisitions made by man in departing from an animal state. (Second *Discourse,* p. 143 [p. 171]) So does the *child* become man when he opens himself to "the consciousness of death." (*Emile,* p. 20) [p. 15]

If one moves along the course of the supplementary series, he sees that imagination belongs to the same chain of significations as the anticipation of death. Imagination is at bottom the relationship with death. The image is death. A proposition that one may define or make indefinite thus: *the* image is *a* death or (*the*) death is *an* image. Imagination is the power that allows life to affect itself with its own re-presentation. The image cannot represent and add the representer to the represented, except in so far as the presence of the re-presented is already folded back upon itself in the world, in so far as life refers to itself as to its own lack, to its own wish for a supplement. The presence of the represented is constituted with the help of the addition to itself of that nothing which is the image, announcement of its dispossession within its own representer and within its death. The property [*le propre*] of the subject is merely the movement of that representative expropriation. In that sense imagination, like death, is *representative and supplementary.* Let us not forget that these are the qualities Rousseau expressly recognizes in writing.

Imagination, liberty, and speech belong then to the same structure as the relationship with death (let us rather say relationship than anticipation; to suppose that there is a being-faced-with death is not necessarily to suppose that there is a relationship established with a more or less distanced point on a horizon of time. It is a structure of presence). How do pity and the identification with others' suffering intervene there?

2. I have said that the imagination is the only thing which can excite natural pity. Rousseau says this clearly in the *Essay,* but, contrary to what Starobinski's most careful formulation would seem to imply, he also invariably says it elsewhere. For him, pity never stops being a natural sentiment or an inner virtue that only imagination has the power to awaken or reveal. Let us note in passing that Rousseau's entire theory of the theatre also establishes a connection, within representation, between the power of identification—pity—and the faculty of the imagination. If now it is remembered that Rousseau gives the name terror to the fear of death (*Discourse,*

p. 143) [p. 171], one perceives together the entire system which organizes the concepts of terror and pity on the one hand, and of the tragic scene, representation, the imagination, and death on the other. This example makes the ambivalence of the power of imagining understandable: it surmounts animality and arouses human passion only by opening the scene and the space of theatrical representation. It inaugurates the perversion whose possibility is itself inscribed in the notion of perfectibility.

The scheme upon which Rousseau's thought has never varied would therefore be the following: pity is innate, but in its natural purity it is not the property of man in particular, it belongs to all living beings in general. It is "so natural, that the very brutes themselves sometimes give eivdent proofs of it" [p. 182]. Without imagination, this pity does not awaken of itself in humanity, is not accessible to passion, language, and representation, does not produce identification with the other as with another me. Imagination is the becoming-human of pity.

That is indeed the thesis of the *Essay*: "Although pity is native to the human heart, it would remain eternally quiescent unless it were activated by imagination" [p. 32]. This appeal to activation and to actualization by the imagination is so little in contradiction with other texts that one can follow everywhere in Rousseau's work a theory of *innateness* as *virtuality* or of naturality as sleeping potentiality.[20] Not a very original theory to be sure, but one whose organizing role is indispensable. It asks us to think of nature not as a given, as a real presence, but as a *reserve*. This concept is itself confusing: one may determine it as a hidden actuality, dissimulated deposit, but also as a reserve of indeterminate power. Such that the imagination, which makes the power of that reserve come forth, is at once beneficent and maleficent. "In fact such is the empire of the imagination among us and such is its influence, that from it are born not only the virtues and the vices, but also good and evil" (*Dialogues, Pléiade* I, pp. 815–16). And if "certain people pervert the usage of this consoling faculty" (ibid.), it is once more by the power of the imagination. Escaping all real and exterior influence, the imagination, faculty of signs and appearances, perverts itself. It is the subject of perversion. It awakens the potential faculty but just as quickly transgresses it. It brings forth the power which was held back but, by showing that power what lies beyond it, by "superseding" it, imagination signifies for it its powerlessness. It animates the faculty of enjoyment but inscribes a difference between desire and power. If we desire beyond our power of satisfaction, the origin of that surplus and of that difference is named imagination. This permits us to determine a function of the concept of nature or of primitiveness: it is the equilibrium between reserve and desire. An impossible equilibrium, for desire cannot awaken and move out of its reserve except by the imagination, which also breaks the equilibrium. This impossible thing—another name for nature— therefore remains a limit. According to Rousseau, ethics, "human wisdom," "the path of true happiness," consists, then, in staying as close as possible to that limit, and in "decreasing the difference between our desires and our powers [*l'excès des désirs sur les facultés*]."

> In this condition, nature, who does everything for the best, has placed him from the first. To begin with, she gives him only such desires as are necessary for self-preservation and such powers as are sufficient for their satisfaction. All the rest she has stored in his mind as a sort of reserve, to be drawn upon at need. It is only in this primitive condition that we find the equilibrium between desire and power, and then alone man is not unhappy. *As soon as his potential powers of mind begin to function, imagination, more powerful than all the rest, awakes, and precedes all the rest.* It is imagination which enlarges the bounds of possibility for us, whether for good or ill, and therefore stimulates and feeds desires by the hope of satisfying them. But the object which seemed within our grasp flies quicker than we can follow. . . . Thus we exhaust our strength, yet never reach our goal, and the nearer we are to pleasure, the further we are from happiness. On the other hand, the more nearly a man's condition approximates to this state of nature *the more the difference between his desires and his powers is small*, and he is therefore less remote from happiness. . . . The world of reality has its bounds, the world of imagination is boundless; as we cannot enlarge the one, let us restrict the other; for all the sufferings which really make us miserable arise from the difference between the real and the imaginary. (*Emile*, p. 64 [pp. 44–45]. Italics added.)

Thus we note:

1. that imagination, origin of the difference between power and desire, is determined as *differance*: of or within presence or pleasure [*jouissance*];
2. that the relationship to nature is defined in terms of negative distance. It is not a question of departing from nature, or of rejoining it, but of reducing its "distance."
3. that imagination, which excites other virtual faculties, is none the less itself a virtual faculty: "the most active of all." So much so that the power of transgressing nature is itself within nature. It belongs to nature's resources. Better: we shall see that the power of transgression holds the reserve in reserve. This being-in-nature has thus the strange mode of being of the supplement. Designating at once the excess and lack of nature *within* nature. Here we shall locate the unsteadying of a classical logic through the signification of *being-within*, as through one example among others.

In as much as it is "the most active of all" the faculties, imagination cannot be awakened by any faculty. When Rousseau says it "awakens itself," he means it in a very strictly reflexive sense. Imagination alone has the power of *giving birth to itself*. It creates nothing because it is imagination. But it receives nothing that is alien or anterior to it. It is not affected by the "real." It is pure auto-affection. It is the other name of differance as auto-affection.[21]

Rousseau delineates man out of this possibility. Imagination inscribes the animal within human society. It makes the animal accessible to humankind. The paragraph of the *Essay* which we are considering ends thus: "He who imagines nothing senses no-one but himself; he is alone in the midst of humankind." This solitude or this nonbelonging to humankind is due to the fact that suffering remains mute and closed in upon itself. Which signifies on the one hand that it cannot open itself, by the awakening of pity, to the suffering of the other as other; and on the other hand that it cannot exceed itself toward death. Indeed, the animal does have a potential faculty of pity, but it imagines neither the suffering of the other *as such* nor the passage from suffering *to death*. Indeed, that is one and the same limit. The relation with the other and the relation with death are one and the same opening. That which is lacking in what Rousseau calls the animal is the ability to live its suffering as the suffering of another and as the threat of death.

Thought within its concealed relation to the logic of the supplement, the concept of virtuality or potentiality (like the entire problematic of power and the act) undoubtedly has for its function, for Rousseau in particular and within metaphysics in general, the systematic predetermining of becoming as production and development, evolution or history, through the substitution of the accomplishment of a *dynamis* for the substitution of a trace, of pure history for pure play, and, as I noted above, of a welding together for a break. The movement of supplementarity seems to escape this alternative and to permit us to think it.

C. Rousseau thus comes to evoke the awakening of pity by the imagination—that is to say by representation and reflection—in the double but actually in the single sense of those words. In the same chapter, he forbids us to think that before the actualization of pity through imagination, man is wicked and bellicose. Let us recall Starobinski's interpretation: "In the *Essay*, Rousseau does not admit the possibility of an unpremeditated burst of sympathy, and seems more inclined to sustain the Hobbesian idea of the war of all against all":

> They were not bound by an idea of common brotherhood and, having no rule but that of force, they believed themselves each other's enemies. . . . An individual isolated on the face of the earth, at the mercy of mankind, is bound to be a ferocious animal. [*Essay*, pp. 31–32]

Rousseau does not say "they were each other's enemies" but "they believed themselves each other's enemies." It seems to be that we have the right to, and indeed should, consider that nuance. Primitive hostility comes out of a primitive illusion. This first *opinion* is due to a misguided belief, born of isolation, feebleness, dereliction. That it is only a simple opinion and already an illusion appears clearly in these three sentences that must not be overlooked:

> . . . they believed themselves each other's enemies. *This belief was due to their weakness and ignorance. Knowing nothing, they feared everything. They attacked in self-defense.* An individual isolated on the face of the earth . . . [*Essay*, p. 32. Italics added.]

Ferocity is thus not bellicose but fearful. Above all, it is incapable of declaring war. It is the animal's characteristic ("ferocious animal"), the characteristic of the isolated being who, not having been awakened to pity by the imagination, does not yet participate in sociality or in humankind. That animal, let us emphasize, "would be *ready* to do unto others all the evil that he *feared* from them. *Fear and weakness are the sources of cruelty*" [*Essay*, p. 32. Italics added]. Cruelty is not positive wickedness. The disposition to do evil finds its resource only in the other, in the illusory representation of evil that the other *seems* disposed to do to me.

Is this not already sufficient reason for setting aside the resemblance with the Hobbesian theory of a natural war that imagination and reason would merely organize into a sort of economy of aggressivity? But Rousseau's text is even clearer. In the *Essay*, the paragraph that occupies us comprises another proposition which forbids us to consider the moment of slumbering pity as the moment of bellicose wickedness, as a "Hobbesian" moment. How in fact does Rousseau describe that moment (here at least it does not matter if it is real or mythic), the structural instance of slumbering pity? What, according to him, is that moment when language, imagination, relation to death, etc., are still *reserved?*

At that moment, he says, "he who has never been reflective is incapable of being merciful or just or pitying" [p. 32]. To be sure. But that is not to say that he would be unjust and pitiless. He is simply held short of that opposition of values. For Rousseau follows up immediately: "He is just as incapable of being malicious and vindictive. He who imagines nothing is aware only of himself; he is isolated in the midst of mankind" (ibid.).

In that "state," the oppositions available in Hobbes have neither sense nor value. The system of appreciation within which political philosophy moves, has as yet no chance to function. And one thus sees more clearly within what (neutral, naked, and bare) element that system enters into play. Here one may speak with indifference of goodness or badness, of peace or war: each time it will be as true as false, always irrelevant. What Rousseau thus reveals is the neutral origin of all ethico-political conceptuality, its field of objectivity, and its axiological system. All the oppositions that follow in the wake of the classical philosophy of history, culture, and society must therefore be neutralized. Before this neutraliaztion, or this reduction, political philosophy proceeds within the naiveté of acquired and accidental evidence. And it incessantly risks "the blunder made by those who, in reasoning on the state of nature, always import into it ideas gathered in a state of society" (Second *Discourse*, p. 146) [p. 174].

The reduction that the *Essay* operates has a particular style. Rousseau neutralizes oppositions by erasing them; and he erases them by affirming contradictory values at the same time. The procedure is used with coherence and firmness, precisely in Chapter 9:

> This accounts for the apparent contradictions seen in the fathers of nations: so natural, and so inhuman; such ferocious behavior and such tender hearts. . . . These barbaric times were a golden age, not because men were united, but because they were separated. . . . If you wish, men would attack each other when they met, but they rarely met. A state of war prevailed universally, and the entire earth was at peace [p. 33].[22]

To privilege one of the two terms, to believe that only a state of war actually existed, was the Hobbesian error that strangely "redoubles" the illusory "opinion" of the first "men" who "believed they were enemies of each other." Again no difference between *Essay* and *Discourse*. The reduction operating within the *Essay* will be confirmed in the *Discourse*, precisely in the course of a critique of Hobbes. What is reproached in Hobbes is precisely that he concludes too quickly that men were neither naturally awakened to pity, nor "bound by any idea of common fraternity," that they were therefore wicked and bellicose. We cannot read the *Essay* as Hobbes might have hastily interpreted it. We cannot conclude wickedness from nongoodness. The *Essay* says it and the *Discourse* confirms it, if we assume that the latter comes after the former:

> Above all, let us not conclude, with Hobbes, that because man has no idea of goodness, he must be naturally wicked; that he is vicious because he does not know virtue. . . . Hobbes did not reflect that the same cause, which prevents a savage from making use of his reason, as our jurists hold, prevents him also from abusing his faculties, as Hobbes himself allows: so that it may be justly said that savages are not bad merely because they do not know what it is to be good: for it is neither the development of the understanding nor the restraint of law that hinders them from doing ill; but the peacefulness of their passions, and their ignorance of vice: *tanto plus in illis proficit vitiorum ignoratio, quam in his cognitio virtutis*.[23]

One knows also from other indications that the economy of pity does not vary from the *Essay* to the great works. When pity is awakened itself by imagination and reflection, when sensible presence is exceeded by its image, we can imagine and judge that the other feels and suffers. Yet, we neither can nor should *simply experience* the suffering of others *by itself*.

According to Rousseau pity does not allow the movement of identification to be simple and entire. Apparently for two reasons, actually for a single profound reason. It is a question yet again of a certain *economy*.

1. We neither can nor should feel the pain of others immediately and absolutely, for such an interiorization or identification would be dangerous and destructive. That is why the imagination, the reflection, and the judgment that arouse pity also limit its power and hold the suffering of the other at a certain distance. One knows this suffering for what it is, one pities others, but one protects oneself, and holds the evil at arm's length. This doctrine—which could further be related to the theory of dramatic representation—is formulated in both the *Essay* and *Emile*. The paradox of the relation to the other is clearly articulated in those two texts: the more you identify with the other, the better you feel his suffering as *his*: our own suffering is that of the other. That of the other, as itself, must remain the other's. There is no authentic identification except in a certain non-identification, etc. The *Essay*:

How are we moved to pity? By getting outside ourselves and identifying with a being who suffers. We suffer only as much as we believe him to suffer. It is not in ourselves, but in him that we suffer [p. 32].

Emile:

He shares the suffering of his fellow-creatures, but he shares it of his own free will and finds pleasure in it. He enjoys at once the pity he feels for their woes and the joy of being exempt from them; he feels in himself that state of vigor which projects us beyond ourselves, and bids us carry elsewhere the superfluous activity of our well-being. To pity another's woes we must indeed know them, but we need not feel them (p. 270) [p. 190].

We must therefore not let ourselves be destroyed by identification with others. The economy of pity and of morality must always let itself be contained within the limits of the love of self, all the more because it alone can illuminate the good of others for us. That is why the maxim of natural goodness: "*Do to others as you would have them do unto you*" should be tempered by this other maxim, "much less perfect indeed, but perhaps more useful; *do good to yourself with as little evil as possible to others*" (Second *Discourse*, p. 156) [p. 185]. The latter is put "*in place*" of the former.

2. Further, identification by interiorization would not be moral.

a) It would not recognize suffering as the suffering of the other. Morality, respect for the other, therefore supposes a certain nonidentification. This paradox of pity as relation to the other is presented by Rousseau also as the paradox of the imagination and of time, that is to say of *comparison*. This concept, so important in Rousseau's thought, is at the center of the *Essay's* Chapter IX and it intervenes in the explication of pity.

In the experience of suffering as the suffering of the other, the imagination, as it opens us to a certain nonpresence within presence, is indispensable: the suffering of others is lived by comparison, as our nonpresent, past or future suffering. Pity would be impossible outside of this structure, which links imagination, time, and the other as one and the same opening into nonpresence:

To pity another's woes we must indeed know them, but we need not feel them. When we have suffered, when we are in fear of suffering, we pity those who suffer; but when we suffer ourselves, we pity none but ourselves. (*Emile*, p. 270) [p. 190]

Just before this, Rousseau had explained this unity of pity and the experience of time in memory or anticipation, in imagination and nonperception in general:

The bodily effect of our sufferings is less than one would suppose; it is memory that prolongs the pain, imagination which projects it into the future, and makes us really to be pitied. This is, I think, one of the reasons why we are more callous to the sufferings of animals than of men, although a fellow-feeling ought to make us identify ourselves equally with either. We scarcely pity the carthorse in his shed, for we do not suppose that while he is eating his hay he is thinking of the blows he has received and the labors in store for him. [*Emile*] (p. 264) [p. 186]

b) Identification pure and simple would be immoral because it would remain empirical and would not be produced in the element of the concept, of universality, and formality. The condition of morality is that through the unique suffering of a unique being, through his presence and his empirical existence, humanity gives itself up to pity. As long as this condition is not fulfilled, pity risks becoming unjust. Imagination and temporality therefore open the reign of concept and law. One may say that already for Rousseau, the concept—which he also calls comparison—*exists* as time. It is for him, as Hegel will say—*Dasein*. Pity is contemporary with speech and representation:

To prevent pity degenerating into weakness we must generalize it and extend it to mankind. Then we only yield to it when it is in accordance with justice, since justice is of all the virtues that which contributes most to the common good. Reason and self-love compel us to love mankind even more than our neighbor, and to pity the wicked is to be very cruel to other men. (pp. 303–04) [*Emile*, p. 215][24]

On this point there is no development in Rousseau's thought. It seems to me that one cannot draw an *internal* argument out of this in order to conclude a precociousness or a philosophical anteriority for the *Essay*. For the moment, the field of external hypotheses is thus opened, even if we reserve the possibility of raising other internal problems when the time comes.

The Initial Debate and the Composition of the Essay. To treat the external problem, we shall deal with some declarations by Rousseau himself in addition to the quotations from Duclos. First an important passage from the *Confessions*. From it one may at least conclude that the *Essay*, originally conceived as an appendix to the second *Discourse*, was, in Rousseau's mind, quite separate from his first writings on music. The time is 1761:

Besides these two works and my "Dictionnaire de Musique," at which I worked from time to time, I had some other writings of less importance, all ready for publication, which I intended to bring out, either separately or in a general collection of my works, if I ever undertook to produce one. The most important of these, most of which are still in manuscript in the hands of Du Peyrou, was an "Essai sur l'Origine des Langues," which I had read to M. de Malesherbes and the Chevalier de Lorenzi, who expressed his approval of it. I calculated that all these works together, after all expenses, would be worth to me at least 8,000 or 10,000 francs, which I intended to sink in a life-annuity for myself and Therese. After this, we would go and live together in the corner of some province (p. 560) [pp. 580–81].

Malesherbes advised him to publish the *Essay* separately.[25] All this happened in 1761, at the time of the publication of *Emile*.

From the external point of view, the problem thus seems simple, and we can consider it as closed more than fifty years ago by Masson in an article of 1913.[26] The polemic had been opened by Espinas.[27] Fastening upon what he considered to be contradictions in Rousseau's thought, he was already stressing what in the *Essay* and even in the article *Economie politique* in the *Encyclopaedia* (an article that poses analogous problems of dating and of internal relationships with the *Discourse*) seemed to him to oppose the Second *Discourse*. Thus, for example, the *Discourse*, which begins by "setting aside all facts" in order to describe an ideal structure or an ideal genesis, is in his view incompatible with the *Essay*, which calls to some extent upon Genesis, alludes to names like Adam, Cain, Noah, and deals with a certain factual content which belongs to history as well as to myth. One must of course study carefully Rousseau's usage of this factual content, and examine if, by using it as a guide to reading or to pivotal examples, Rousseau does not neutralize it as fact—a step which he permits himself to take in the *Discourse* as well; notably in those notes to the *Discourse* among which, as we know, the *Essay* was perhaps supposed to be included.

Whatever the case may be, unlike Starobinski, Espinas does not conclude from this supposed contradiction that the *Essay* came before the *Discourse*.

Considering the quotations from Duclos, he draws the opposite conclusion: the *Essay* came after the *Discourse*.[28]

Lanson then contests this interpretation.[29] But always on the same grounds: the *discrepancy* between the *Essay* and the major works. For the sake of the philosophical reasons which constitute the real stakes of this debate and indeed animate it, Lanson wishes at all costs to preserve the unity of Rousseau's thought as it was to fulfill itself in its "maturity."[30]

He must therefore relegate the *Essay* to a place among the works of Rousseau's youth:

> The *Essay on the Origin of Languages* is certainly in contradiction with the *Discourse on Inequality*. But what proof does M. Espinas have for placing the former chronologically after the latter, and very close to it? Some passages quoted by Rousseau from a work by Duclos that appeared in 1754. What value does this argument have, since it is known moreover that the text of the *Essay* was revised by Rousseau at least once or twice? The quotations from Duclos could have entered the text at one of those revisions. For my part, I have reason to believe through certain positive indications that the *Essay on the Origin of Languages* dates from an epoch when Rousseau's systematic views were not yet formed, and that under its original title (*Essai sur le principe de la mélodie*), it was a reply to Rameau's *Démonstration du principe de l'harmonie* (1749–1750). By its matter and tenor, the *Essay* comes out of the same current of thought which exists in Condillac's *An Essay on the Origin of Human Knowledge* (1746) and in Diderot's *Lettre sur les sourds et muets* (1750–1751). I should be much inclined to place the composition of Rousseau's *Essay* at the latest in 1750, between the composition and the success of the first *Discourse*.

It is difficult to consider the quotations from Duclos as late insertions. Even if in fact they were, as quotations, late, the reading of the *Commentary on General Grammar* seems to have deeply marked, indeed inspired, the entire *Essay*. As for affinities with Condillac and Diderot, they are far from limited to this work alone.

That is why, on this problem of chronology whose external aspect is so difficult to delimit, Masson's response to Lanson seems eminently convincing to me.[31] Here I extract a long fragment of it.

Recalling Lanson's argument, Masson writes:

> These arguments are very skillful and almost convincing; but perhaps they presented themselves to M. Lanson only because he did not wish to find Rousseau in "contradiction" with himself. If the *Essay* had not seemed to "contradict" the second *Discourse*, who knows if M. Lanson would have pushed the original version so far back? I do not wish to examine here the internal relationships between the *Essay* and *Inequality*; in my opinion, the "contradiction" between the two works is not as "certain" as M. Lanson judges. I shall limit myself to two external remarks that seem decisive to me. 1) The

manuscript of the *Essay on the Origin of Languages* is still at the Library of Neuchâtel, No. 7835 (5 paperbound books, 150 x 230mm., bound, with a blue silk ribbon). Very beautifully written, obviously intended for the press, it carries on the first page: by J.-J. Rousseau, Citizen of Geneva. It is without a doubt the copy that Jean-Jacques transcribed in 1761, when he thought for a while of using this work in reply to "that Rameau who continued to mistreat him so villainously" (letter to Malesherbes, 9.25.61). Later, very likely at Motiers, as we shall see, he took the copy up again for revision, additions, or corrections, easily recognizable, for the ink and the writing are quite different. If I were studying the *Essay* itself,[32] these variants would be worth noting; but I have kept only those corrections which are of chronological significance. In the copy of 1761, the text forms a whole: it is one dissertation; the division into chapters was introduced in Motiers' revision. Thus it is not only to Chapter 20, but to the entire *Essay* that the last lines of the work apply: "These superficial reflections, which hopefully might give birth to more profound ones, I shall conclude with the passage that suggested them to me: *To observe in fact and to show by examples, the degree to which the character, customs and interests of a people influence their language, would provide material for a sufficiently philosophical investigation*" [pp. 73–74]. This "passage" is extracted from Duclos' books, *Remarques sur la grammaire génerale et raisonnée*, p. 11, which appeared in the first half of 1754. 2) We have also a more formal testimony given by Rousseau himself. About 1763, he wished to bring together in one small volume three short works that he had in hand: *L'imitation théâtrale, Essay on the Origin of Languages, Le Lévite d'Ephraim*. The collection was never published, but a projected preface remains in one of his notebooks of rough drafts (Mss of Neuchâtel, No. 7887 F[os] 104–05). From that preface I omit what concerns *Theatrical Imitation* and *The Levite*, and publish the paragraph concerning the *Essay*[33]: "the second part was at first nothing but a part of the *Discourse on Inequality*, that I cut off from it as too long and out of place. I took it up again [Rousseau had at first written: I completed it]—provoked by *M. Rameau's Errors on Music*—that title which is perfectly fulfilled by the work which bears it—but for two words that I had struck off [in the *Encyclopaedia*]. However, restrained by the ridiculousness of holding forth upon languages when one hardly knows one, and, furthermore, discontented with that fragment, I had resolved to suppress it as unworthy of public attention. But an illustrious magistrate, who cultivates and protects letters [Malesherbes], thought of it more favorably than I; I defer with pleasure, as one may well believe, my judgment to his, and with the help of other writings, I attempt to pass off a piece that I might not have risked by itself." It does not seem that any internal evidence can stand against this testimony by Rousseau himself. In 1754, then, the *Essay* on languages was a long note to the second *Discourse*; in 1761, it became an independent dissertation, augmented and corrected to make it a riposte to Rameau. Finally, in 1763, this dissertation, revised for one last time, was divided into chapters.

II. Imitation

We have now been brought quite naturally to the problem of the *composition* of the *Essay*: not only of the time of its writing, but of the space of its structure. Rousseau divided it into chapters belatedly. What scheme guided him? The architecture must find its justification in the deep intention of the *Essay*. It is for that reason that it interests us. Yet we must not confound the meaning of the architecture with the declared intention of the work.

Twenty chapters of most unequal length. A disquiet *seems* to animate all Rousseau's reflections and to give them their vehemence: they are concerned *at first* with the origin and degeneration of music. The chapters that concern music, its emergence and its decadence, are contained between Chapter 12, "The Origin of Music and its Relations," and Chapter 19, "How Music Has Degenerated." If one wants to maintain that the destiny of music is the major preoccupation of the *Essay*, it must be explained that the chapters that directly concern that subject occupy hardly a third of the work (a little more if you consider the number of chapters, a little less if you consider the number of pages) and that the rest of the essay does not deal with it at all. Whatever may be the history of its writing, its unity of composition is not the less evident and no development is out of alignment.

The Interval and the Supplement. The themes of the first eleven chapters are the genesis and degeneration of language, the relationships between speech and writing, the difference between the formation of the languages of the north and the languages of the south. Why is it necessary to treat these problems before proposing a theory of music? For several types of reasons.

1. There is no music before language. Music is born of voice and not of sound. No prelinguistic sonority can, according to Rousseau, open the time of music. In the beginning is the song.

This proposition is absolutely necessary within Rousseau's systematics. If music awakens in song, if it is initially uttered, *vociferated*, it is because, like all speech, it is born in passion. That is to say in the transgression of need by desire and the awakening of pity by imagination. Everything proceeds from this inaugural distinction: "It seems then that need dictated the first gestures, while the passions wrung forth the first words."

If music presupposes voice, it comes into being at the same time as human society. As speech, it requires that the other be present to me as other through compassion. Animals, whose pity is not awakened by the imagination, have no affinity with the other as such. That is why there is no animal music. One speaks of animal music only by looseness of vocabulary and by anthropomorphic projection. The difference between the glance and the voice is the difference between animality and humanity. Transgressing space, mastering the outside, placing souls in communication, voice transcends natural animality. That is to say a certain death signified by space. Exteriority is inanimate. The arts of space carry death within themselves and *animality* remains the *inanimate* face of *life*. The song presents life to itself. In that sense, it is more *natural* to man but more foreign to a nature which is in itself dead nature [still life]. One sees here what difference—at the same time interior and exterior—divides the significations of nature, life, animality, humanity, art, speech, and song. The animal who, as we have seen, has no relationship to death, is on the side of death. Speech, on the other hand, is *living* speech even while it institutes a relation to death, and so on. It is presence in general that is thus divided. "From this it is evident that painting is closer to nature and that music is more dependent on human art. It is evident also that the one is more interesting than the other precisely because it does more to relate man to man, and gives us some idea of our kind. Painting is often dead and inanimate. It can carry you to the depth of the desert; but as soon as vocal signs strike your ear, they announce to you a being like yourself. They are, so to speak, the organs of the soul. If they also paint solitude for you [*s'ils vous peignent aussi la solitude*], they tell you you are not there alone. Birds whistle; man alone sings. And one cannot hear either singing or a symphony without immediately acknowledging the presence of another intelligent being" (Chap. XVI) [pp. 63–64].

Song is at the orient of music but it does not reduce itself to voice any more than voice reduces itself to noise. In the *Dictionary of Music*, Rousseau confesses his embarrassment in the article *Song* [*chant; tune* in the contemporary English translation]. If the song is indeed "a kind of modification of the human voice" it is difficult to assign to it an absolutely characteristic [*propre*] modality. After having proposed the "*calcula* [*tions*] *of intervals,*" Rousseau advances the most equivocal criterion of "*permanence,*" and then of melody as "*imitation* of the accents of the speaking or passionate voice." The difficulty is that the concepts of an intrinsic and systematic description must be found. No more than the voice[34] does the song disclose its essence in an anatomical description. But vocal intervals are also alien to the system of musical intervals. Rousseau therefore hesitates, in the *Dictionary* as much as in the *Essay*, between two necessities: of marking the difference between the systems of vocal and musical intervals, but also of reserving all the resources of song in the original voice. The notion of *imitation* reconciles these two exigencies within ambiguity. The first chapter of the *Essay* corresponds in part to this passage in the article *Song*:

It is very difficult to determine in what the voice which forms the words, differs from that which forms the *song*. This difference is sensible, but we cannot very clearly perceive in what it consists, and when we seek to find it, we find it not. Mons. Dodart has made anatomic observations, by favor of which he thinks really to discover, in the different situations of the larynx, the cause of two kinds of voice. But I do not know if these observations or the consequences drawn from them, are to be depended on. There seems to be wanting to the sounds which form the discourse, no more than *permanence*, to form a real *song*: It appears also, that the different inflexions which we give to the voice in speaking, form intervals which are not at all harmonic, *which form no parts of the system in our music*, and which consequently not being expressed in notes, are not properly a *song* for us. *The song does not seem natural to mankind*. Tho' the savages of America sing, because they speak, yet *a true savage never sung*. The dumb don't sing, they form only accents without permanence, a disgustful [*sourds*—muted] bellowing which their wants draw from them. I should doubt, if the Sieur Pereyre, with all his ingenuity, could ever draw from them any musical air. Children scream, cry, but they don't sing. The first expressions of nature have nothing in them melodious or sonorous, and they [children] learn to sing, as to speak, from our example. The melodious and appreciable tune, is only an artificial imitation of the accents in the speaking or passionate voice. *We cry, we complain, without singing; but, in song, we imitate cries and laments; and as, of all imitations, the most interesting is that of the human passions, so of all the methods of imitating, the most agreeable is the song*. (Only the word song [*chant*] is italicized by Rousseau.)

Through that example one may analyze the subtle functioning of the notions of nature and imitation. On several levels, nature is the ground, the inferior step: it must be crossed, exceeded, but also rejoined. We must return to it, but without annulling the difference. This difference, separating the imitation from what it imitates, must be *almost nil*. Through the voice one must transgress the nature that is animal, savage, mute, infant or crying; by singing transgress or modify the voice. But the song must imitate cries and laments. This leads to a second polar determination of nature: it becomes the unity—as ideal limit—of the imitation and what is imitated, of voice and song. If that unity were accomplished, imitation would become useless: the unity of unity and difference would be lived in immediacy. Such, according to Rousseau, is the archeo-teleologic definition of nature. *Elsewhere* is the name and the place, the name of the non-place of that nature. Elsewhere in time, *in illo tempore*; elsewhere in space, *alibi*. The natural unity of the cry, the voice, and the song, is the proto-Greek or the Chinese experience. The article *Voice* analyses and amplifies the same debate around the theses of Dodart and of Duclos (in the article *Déclamation des anciens* in the *Encyclopaedia*). The differences among languages are measured by the distance which, in the system of each language, separates the voice of speech from the voice of song, "for as there are languages more or less harmonious, whose accents are more or less musical, we take notice also, in these languages, that the speaking and singing *voices* are connected or removed in the same proportion. So, as the Italian language is more musical than the French, its speaking is less distant from song; and in that language it is easier to recognize a man singing if we have heard him speak. In a language which would be completely harmonious, as was the Greek at the beginning, the difference between the speaking and singing voices would be nil. We should have the same voice for speaking and singing. Perhaps that may be at present the case of the Chinese" [p. 464].

2. We have just accepted two pieces of evidence: the unity of nature or the identity of origin is shaped and undermined by a strange difference which constitutes it by breaching it; we must account for the origin of the *voice of speech*—therefore of society—*before* assigning, and *in order to assign*, its possibility to music, that is to say to the *voice of song*. But since in the *beginning* of the *all-harmonious* voice, word and song are (were) identified, *before and in order to* have perhaps a juridical or methodological meaning; they have no structural or genetic value. One might have been tempted to accord a structural value to the difference between speech and song, since Rousseau recognized that the latter comes to "modify" the former. But the archeoteleological concept of nature also annuls the structural point of view. In the beginning or in the ideal of the all-harmonious voice, the modification becomes one with the substance that it modifies. (This scheme has a general value and governs all discourses, from the moment that they make the smallest appeal to any of these notions, no matter which one: nature and its other, archeology and eschatology, substance and mode, origin and genesis.)

Of course, the methodological or juridical point of view has no rigorous value the moment the difference of value between the structural and genetic points of view is annulled. Rousseau does not notice this consequence but we should recognize that it would wreak havoc to more than one discourse.

We must now study the consequence. It is a matter of presenting, with reference to the origin of language and society, a certain number of oppositions of concepts indispensable for understanding at the same time the possibility of both speech and song. And above all for understanding the tension or the difference that, in language as in music, operates at once as opening and menace, principle of life and of death. Since *the first* speech must be *good*, since the archeo-teleology of the nature of the language and the language of nature dictate to us, as does "the voice of nature," that the original and ideal essence of speech is song itself, one cannot treat the two origins separately. But as the method of the discourse must retrace its path and take into account the historical regression or degradation, it must separate the two questions provisionally and, in a certain manner, begin with the end.

This then is the story. For the history that follows the origin and is added to it is nothing but the story of the separation between song and speech. If we consider the difference which fractured the origin, it must be said that this history, which is decadence and degeneracy through and through, had no prehistory. Degeneration as separation, severing of voice and song, has always already begun. We shall see that Roussau's entire text *describes* origin as the beginning of the end, as the inaugural decadence. Yet, in spite of that description, the text twists about in a sort of oblique effort to act *as if* degeneration were not prescribed in the genesis and as if evil *supervened upon* a good origin. As if song and speech, which have the same act and the same birthpangs, had not always already begun to separate themselves.

Here one reencounters the advantages and dangers of the concept of the supplement, and also of the concept of "fatal advantage" and "dangerous supplement."

The growth of music, the desolating separation of song and speech, has the form of writing as "dangerous supplement": calculation and grammaticality, *loss of energy and substitution*. The history of music is parallel to the history of the language, its evil is in essense graphic. When he undertakes to explain *how music has degenerated* (Chapter 19), Rousseau recalls the unhappy history of the language and of its disastrous "perfecting": "To the degree that the language improved, melody, being governed by new rules, imperceptibly *lost* its *former energy*, and the *calculus of intervals was substituted for nicety of inflection*" (italics added) [p. 68].

Substitution distances from birth, from the natural or maternal origin. Forgetfulness of the beginning is a calculation that puts harmony in the place of melody, the science of intervals in the place of the warmth of accent. In this weaning of the voice of speech, a "new object" comes at once to usurp and compensate for the "maternal traits." What suffers then from this is the "oral accent." Music thus finds itself "deprived of its" proper, that is to say natural and moral, "effects": "Melody being *forgotten*, and the attention of musicians being completely turned toward harmony, everything gradually came to be governed according to this *new object*. The genres, the modes, the scale, all received new faces. Harmonic successions came to dictate the sequence of parts. This sequence having *usurped the name* of melody, it was, in effect, impossible to recognize the *traits of its mother* in this new melody. And our musical system having thus *gradually* become purely harmonic, it is not surprising that its *oral tone* [*accent*] has *suffered*, and that our music has lost almost all its *energy*. Thus we see how singing *gradually* became an art entirely *separate* from speech, from which it takes its origin; how the harmonics of sounds resulted in the *forgetting* of vocal inflections; and finally, how music, restricted to purely physical concurrences of vibrations, found itself *deprived* of the moral power it had yielded when it was the *twofold voice of nature*" (italics added) [p. 71].

The points italicized in the passage should guide a subreading of this text and of many analogous texts. On each occasion one would notice:

1. That Rousseau weaves his text with heterogeneous threads: the instanteous *displacement* that *substitutes* a "*new object*," which institutes a substitutive supplement, must constitute a history, a progressive becoming *gradually* producing the *forgetting* of the voice of nature. The violent and irruptive movement that *usurps, separates* and *deprives* is simultaneously described as a progressive implicating of, and a gradual distancing from, the origin, a slow growth of a disease of language. Weaving together the two significations of supplementarity—substitution and accretion—Rousseau describes the replacement of an *object* as a deficit in *energy*, the production of a re-placement as effacement by forgetting.

2. The adverb "doubly" [twofold] summons up in its own condition of possibility the metaphor of the voice of nature: "gentle voice," maternal voice, song as original voice, sung speech conforms to the prescriptions of natural law. In every sense of this word, nature speaks. And to hear and understand the laws formed by her gentle voice—which, as we recall, "no one is tempted to disobey," but which one must have been tempted to disobey—it is necessary to find again the "oral accent" of sung speech, take possession again of our own lost voice, the voice which, uttering and hearing, understanding-itself-signifying a melodious law, "was the twofold voice of nature."

The Engraving and the Ambiguities of Formalism. How was this supplementary substitution fatal? How *is* it fatal? How *was it to be*—for such is the time of its *quiddity*—what it necessarily is? What is the fissure that, within the origin itself, destines its appearance?

This fissure is not one among others. It is *the* fissure: the necessity of interval, the harsh law of spacing. It could not endanger song except by being inscribed in it from its birth and in its essence. Spacing is not the accident of song. Or rather, as accident and accessory, fall and supplement, it is also that without which, strictly speaking, the song would not have come into being. In the *Dictionary*, the interval is a part of the definition of song. It is therefore, so to speak, an originary accessory and an essential accident. Like writing.

Rousseau says it without wishing to say it.* What he wishes to say is:

* For the relationship between "wishing to say" and "meaning," see "La forme et le vouloir-dire," *MP*, pp. 185–207, *SP*, pp. 107–28.

accessory accessory, accidental accident, the exterior outside, the supplementary evil or the accessory supplement. And space exterior to time. Spacing alien to the time of melody. As we shall see, even while saying that spacing assures the possibility of speech and song. Rousseau *wishes* to think of space as a simple outside by way of which disease and death in general, and especially the disease and death of sung speech, make their entry. He wishes to pretend that the "fineness of infections" and of the "oral accent" did not already and always lend itself to spatialization, geometricization, grammaticalization, regularization, prescription; or to reason. As he wishes to efface this *always-already*, he determines spacing as an event and as a catastrophic event. We shall have to come back more than once to that concept of catastrophe. Let us note here that this catastrophe has indeed the form of philosophic reason. That is why the birth of philosophy during the epoch of Greek tragedy constitutes the best example of such a catastrophe:

When the theaters had taken a regular form, all singing was according to prescribed modes. And, to the degree that the rules of imitation proliferated, imitative language was enfeebled. The study of philosophy and the progress of reasoning, while having perfected grammar, deprived language of its vital, passionate quality which made it so singable. Composers, who originally were engaged by poets and worked only for them, under their direction so to speak, were becoming independent as early as the time of Melanippides and Philoxenus. This is the license of which Music complains so bitterly in a comedy of Pherecrates, according to the passage preserved by Plutarch. Thus melody, originally an aspect of discourse, imperceptibly assumes a separate existence and music becomes more independent of speech. That is also when it stopped producing the marvels it had produced when it was merely the accent and harmony of poetry and gave to it the power over the passions that speech subsequently exercised only on reason. Thus, as soon as Greece became full of sophists and philosophers, she no longer had any famous musicians or poets. In cultivating the art of convincing, that of arousing the emotions was lost. Plato himself, envious of Homer and Euripides, decried the one and was unable to imitate the other. [*Essay*, pp. 68–69]

Further, according to the law of supplementary acceleration that we noticed above and that we could call the law of *geometric regression*, another catastrophe necessarily adds itself to the first. Almost all the significations that will constantly define the figure of evil and the process of its degeneration are recorded there: a simultaneously violent and progressive substitution of servitude for political freedom as freedom of the living word, dissolution of the small democratic and autarchic city, preponderance of articulation over accentuation, of consonant over vowel, of northern over southern, of the capital over the province. Going necessarily in the direction of the first catastrophe, the supplementary catastrophe nevertheless destroys its positive or compensating effects. Let us italicize:

Servitude soon *joined* forces with philosophy. In fetters, Greece lost the fire that warms only free spirits, and in praising her tyrants, she never recovered the style [*ton*] in which she had sung her heroes. The intermingling of the Romans further weakened whatever harmony and accent remained to the language. Latin, a less musical, more *surded* [*mute*] tongue, did harm to the music in adopting it. The singing employed in the *capital* gradually corrupted that of the provinces. The Roman theaters harmed [*nuisirent à*] those of Athens. When Nero carried off the prize, Greece had ceased to merit any. And the same melodiousness, parceled between two tongues, had become less well suited to either. Finally came the *catastrophe that disrupted the progress of the human spirit without removing the faults that were its product*. Europe, flooded with *barbarians, enslaved* by ignoramuses, lost at the same time her sciences, her arts, and that universal instrument of both: that is, *harmoniously perfected language*. Imperceptibly, these coarse men engendered by the *North* made every ear accustomed to their rude voices. Their harsh, *expressionless* [*dénuée d'accent*] voices were noisy without being sonorous. The Emperor Julian compared Gallic speech to the croaking of frogs. All their *articulations*, like their voices, being nasal and *muffled*, they could give only some kind of distinctness to their singing, augmenting the vowel sounds to cover up *the abundance and harshness of the consonants*. (Chap. 19) [*Essay*, p. 69]

In addition to the system of oppositions that controls the entire *Essay* (servitude/politico-linguistic liberty, North/South, articulation/accent, consonant/vowel, capital/province//autarchic and democratic city), we may perceive here the strange workings of the historical process according to Rousseau. It never varies: beginning with an origin or a center that divides itself and leaves itself, an historical circle is described, which is degenerative in direction but progressive and compensatory in effect. On the circumference of that circle are new origins for new circles that accelerate the degeneration by annulling the compensatory effects of the preceding circle, and thereby also making its truth and beneficence appear. It is thus, by destroying the "progress of the human spirit" that the anterior cycle had produced, that the invasion of the northern barbarians ushered in a new cycle of historical degeneration. The harmful and dissolving effects of philosophy had in fact been limited by themselves. Their system comprised, in some way, its own curb. Within the following system or circle, that curb will have disappeared. Follows an acceleration of evil, which nevertheless will find a new internal regulation, a new organ of equilibrium, a new supplementary compensation (which will consist for example of "reinforcing vowel sounds to cover the abundance and harshness of consonants"), and thus to infinity. But this infinity is still not that of a horizon or an abyss, of a progress or a fall. It is the infinity of a repetition following a strange course. For the preceding diagram must be complicated further: each new cycle begins a progression-regression which, destroying the effects of the preceding one, brings us back to a nature yet more secret, more ancient, more archaic. Progress consists always of taking us closer to animality while annulling the progress through which we have transgressed animality. I shall confirm it often. In any case, it would be difficult to represent the "thus to infinity" of this movement by the tracing of a line, however complicated that line might be.

What cannot be thus represented by a line is the turn (trick/trope) of the re-turn when it has the bearing of re-presentation. What one cannot represent is the relationship of representation to so-called originary presence. The re-presentation is also a de-presentation. It is tied to the work of spacing.

Spacing insinuates into presence an interval which not only separates the different times of speech and of song but also the represented from the representer. Such an interval is prescribed by the origin of art as determined by Rousseau. According to a tradition that remains imperturbable here, Rousseau is sure that the essence of art is *mimesis*. Imitation redoubles presence, adds itself to it by supplementing it. Thus it makes the present pass into its outside. In the inanimate arts, the outside is split and it is the reproduction of the outside in the outside. The presence of the thing itself is already exposed in exteriority, it must therefore be depresented and represented in an outside of the outside. In the living arts, and preeminently in song, the outside imitates the inside. It is *expressive*. It "paints" passions. The metaphor which makes the song a painting is possible, it can wrest from itself and drag outside into space the intimacy of its virtue, only under the common authority of the concept of imitation. Painting and song are reproductions, whatever might be their differences; the inside and the outside share them equally, expression has already begun to make passion go outside itself, it has begun to set it forth and to paint it.

That confirms what we proposed above: imitation cannot allow itself to be appreciated by a simple act. Rousseau has need of imitation, he advances it as the possibility of song and the emergence out of animality, but he exalts it only as a reproduction adding itself to the represented though it *adds nothing*, simply supplements it. In that sense he praises art or *mimesis* as a supplement. But by the same token praise may instantly turn to criticism. Since the supplementary mimesis adds *nothing*, is it not useless? And if nevertheless, adding itself to the represented, it is not nothing, is that imitative supplement not dangerous to the integrity of what is represented and to the original purity of nature?

This is why, travelling along the system of supplementarity with a blind infallibility, and the sure foot of the sleepwalker, Rousseau must at once denounce *mimesis* and art as supplements (supplements that are dangerous when they are not useless, superfluous when they are not disastrous, in truth both at the same time) and recognize in them man's good fortune, the expression of passion, the emergence from the inanimate.

It is the status of the *sign* that is marked by the same ambiguity. Signifier imitates signified. Art is woven with signs. In so far as signification seems to be, at first glance at least, nothing but an instance of imitation, let us turn to *Emile*. The ambiguity of the treatment reserved for imitation in that book will clarify those passages in the *Essay* that deal with the sign, art, and imitation.

Pedagogy cannot help but encounter the problem of imitation. What is example? Should one educate by example or explanation? Should the teacher make an example of himself and not interfere any further, or pile lesson upon exhortation? And is there virtue in being virtuous by imitation? All these questions are asked in the second book of *Emile*.

The problem at first is knowing how to teach generosity or "liberality" to the child. Even before the word and the theme of imitation occupy the front of the stage, the problem of the sign is posed. To teach the child true generosity is to make sure that he is not content only to imitate it. What does it mean to imitate generosity? It is to give signs in the place of things, words in the place of sentiments, money in the place of real goods. Therefore the child must be taught not to imitate liberality, and this teaching must combat resistance. The child spontaneously wants to guard his goods and put one off the scent [literally, give away the coin]: "Observe that the only things children are set to give are things of which they do not know the value, bits of metal carried in their pockets for which they have no further use. A child would rather give a hundred coins than one cake" [*Emile*, p. 67]. What one gives easily is not signifiers inseparable from signifieds or things, it is the devalued signifiers. The child would not give away money so easily if he knew how to, or could, do something with it. "But get this prodigal giver to distribute what is dear to him, his toys, his sweets, his own lunch, and we shall soon see if you have made him really generous" (*Emile*, pp. 97–99) [p. 67].

Not that the child is naturally greedy. He desires naturally to keep what he desires. It is normal and natural. Here vice or perversity would consist of not attaching oneself to things that are naturally desirable but to their substitutive signifiers. If a child loved money for money's sake, he would be perverse; he would no longer be a child. *For Rousseau the concept of the child is always related to the sign. More precisely, childhood is the non-relation to the sign as such.* But what is a sign as such? There is no sign as such. Either the sign is considered a thing, and it is not a sign. Or it is a reference, and thus not itself. According to Rousseau, the child is the name of that which should not relate in any way to a separated signifier, loved in some way for itself, like a fetish. This perverse use of the signifier is in a certain way at once forbidden and tolerated by the structure of imitation.

As soon as a signifier is no longer imitative, undoubtedly the threat of perversion becomes acute. But already within imitation, the gap between the thing and its double, that is to say between the sense and its image, assures a lodging for falsehood, falsification, and vice.

Hence the hesitation in *Emile*. On the one hand, everything begins with imitation and the child learns only by example. Here *imitation is good*, it is more human, it has nothing to do with aping. Those who, following Locke's argument, give children reasons for the advantage of being liberal rather than examples of liberality, would in fact be the deceptive ones. One will never pass from that "usurious liberality" to the true generosity that is transmitted only by example and *good imitation*: "Teachers, have done with these shams; be good and kind; let your example sink into your scholars' memories until they can enter their hearts" [*Emile*, p. 68].

But this good imitation already carries within itself the premises of its corruption [*altération*]. And all the problems of pedagogy in *Emile* may be summarized in this fact. The child is at first passive, the example engraves itself within the memory, "*waiting*" to enter the heart. It may remain in the memory without entering the heart; and conversely, because of the resemblance between the heart and memory, the child may feign feeling from the heart when he actually contents himself with imitating according to the signs of memory. He may always content himself with *giving signs*. A first time, good imitation may be impossible, a second time, it may be turned away from its good usage. "Rather than hasten to demand deeds of charity from my pupil I prefer to perform such deeds in his presence, even depriving him of the means of imitating me, as an honor beyond his years" [*Emile*, p. 68]. "I know that all these imitative virtues are only the virtues of a monkey, and that a good action is only morally good when it is done as such and not because others do it. But at an age when the heart does not yet feel anything, you must make children copy the deeds you wish to grow into habits, until they can do them with understanding and for the love of what is good" [*Emile*, p. 68].[35]

The possibility of imitation seems thus to interrupt natural simplicity. With imitation, is it not duplicity that insinuates itself within presence? And yet, according to a scheme that we have already identified, Rousseau wished that good imitation should regulate itself according to a natural imitation. The taste for and power of imitation are inscribed within nature. Like pretense, if they are a corruption *of* imitation, vice and duplicity are not daughters of but diseases of imitation, are not its natural effect but a monstrous anomaly. Evil is a result of a sort of perversion of imitation, of the imitation within imitation. And that evil has a social origin.

Man imitates, as do the beasts. The love of imitating comes from well-regulated nature; in society it becomes a vice. The monkey imitates man, whom he fears, and not the other beasts, which he scorns; he thinks what is done by his betters must be good. Amongst us, on the other hand, our harlequins imitate all that is good to degrade it and bring it into ridicule; knowing their own baseness they try to equal what is better than they are, or if they strive to imitate what they admire, their bad taste appears in their choice of models, they would rather deceive others or win applause for their own talents than become wiser or better. [*Emile*, p. 68]

Here the relationships among childhood, animality, and man in society order themselves according to the structure and problematics which we had such difficulty in outlining in the analysis of pity. And it is not by chance: the same paradox—of the alteration of identity and of identification with the other—is here at work. Imitation and pity have the same foundation: a sort of metaphorical ecstacy: "Imitation has its roots in our perpetual desire to transport ourselves outside of ourselves (ibid.).

Let us return to the *Essay*. The ruses of metaphor now appear in the mimetology of all the arts. If art is imitation, it is essential to remember that everything in it *signifies*. In the aesthetic experience, we are affected not by things but by signs:

No one doubts that man is changed by his senses. But instead of distinguishing the changes, we confuse them with their causes. We attach too much and too little importance to sensations. We do not see that frequently they affect us not merely as sensations, but as signs or images, and that their moral effects also have moral causes. Just as the feelings that a painting excites in us are not at all due to colors, the power of music over our souls is not at all the work of sounds. Beautiful, subtly shaded colors are a pleasing sight; but this is purely a pleasure of the sense. It is the drawing, the imitation, which gives life and spirit to these colors. The passions they express are what stir ours; the objects they represent are what affect us. Colors entail no interest or feeling at all. The strokes of a touching picture affect us even in a print. Without these strokes in the picture, the colors would do nothing more (Chap. XIII) [p. 53].

If art operates through the sign and is effective through imitation, it can only take place within the system of a culture, and the theory of art is a theory of mores. A "moral" impression, contrary to a " 'sensible' impression," is recognized through the fact that it places its force in a sign. Aesthetics passes through a semiology and even through an ethnology. The effects of aesthetic signs are only determined within a cultural system. "Unless the influence of sensations upon us is due mainly to moral causes, why are we so sensitive to impressions that mean nothing to the uncivilized? Why is our most touching music only a pointless noise to the ear of a West Indian? Are his nerves of a different nature from ours?" (Chap. XV) [*Essay*, p. 59].

Medicine itself must take account of the semiological culture within which it must heal. As with the therapeutic art, the therapeutic effects of art are not natural in as much as they work through signs; and if the cure is a language, the remedies must make themselves understood to the sick through the code of his culture:

The healing of tarantula bites is cited as proof of the physical power of sounds. But in fact this evidence proves quite the opposite. What is needed for curing those bitten by this insect are neither isolated sounds, nor even the same tunes. Rather, each needs tunes with familiar melodies and understandable lyrics. Italian tunes are needed for Italians; for Turks, Turkish tunes. Each is affected only by accents familiar to him. His nerves yield only to what his spirit predisposes [for] them. One must speak to him in a language he understands, if he is to be moved by what he is told. The cantatas of Bernier are said to have cured the fever of a French musician. They would have given one to a musician of any other nation. (Chap. 15) [*Essay*, p. 60]

Rousseau does not go so far as to consider that the symptoms themselves belong to a culture and that the bite of a tarantula might have different effects in different places. But the principle of such a conclusion is clearly indicated in his explication. There is a single exception, which is more than simply strange, within this ethno-semiotics: cooking, or rather taste. Rousseau condemns gluttony without mercy. One might wonder why: "I know of only one affective sense in which there is no moral element: that is taste. And, accordingly, gluttony is the main vice only of those who have no sense of taste" (ibid.). "Who have no sense of taste" means here, of course, "who do nothing but taste," who have nothing but uneducated and uncultivated sensations.

As the value of *virtuality* or potentiality further introduces here an element of transition and confusion, of graduality and of shifts within the rigor of distinctions and within the functioning of concepts—limits of animality, childhood, savagery, etc.—one must admit that "moral impressions" through signs and a system of differences can always be already discerned, although confusedly, in the animal. "Something of this moral effect is perceivable even in animals." We realized the need for this hesitation in connection with pity, and at the same time with imitation:

So long as one insists on considering sounds only in terms of the shock that they excite in our nerves, one will not attain the true principle of music, nor its power over men's hearts. The sounds of a melody do not affect us merely as sounds, but as signs of our affections, of our feelings. It is thus that they excite in us the emotions that they express, whose image we recognize in it. Something of this moral effect is perceivable even in animals. The barking of one dog will attract another. When my cat hears me imitate a mewing, I see it become immediately attentive, alert, agitated. When it discovers that I am just counterfeiting the voice of its species, it relaxes and resumes its rest. Since there is nothing at all different in the stimulation of the sense organ, and the cat had initially been deceived, what accounts for the difference? (ibid.)

From this irreducibility of the semiotic order, Rousseau also draws conclusions against the sensationalism and materialism of his own century: "Colors and sounds can do much, as representations and signs, very little simply as objects of sense" [*Essay*, p. 61]. The argument for art as signifying text is at the service of metaphysics and of spiritualist ethics: "I believe that had these ideas been better developed, we should have been spared many stupid arguments about ancient music. But in this century when all the operations of the soul have to be materialized, and even human feeling deprived of all morality, I am deluded if the new philosophy does not become as destructive of good taste as of virtue" (ibid.).

We must be attentive to the ultimate finality of the esteem which the sign enjoys. According to a general rule which is important for us, attention to the signifier has the paradoxical effect of reducing it. Unlike the concept of the supplement which, of course, *signifies* nothing, simply replaces a lack, the signifier, as it is indicated in the grammatical form of this word and the logical form of the concept, signifies a signified. One cannot separate its effectiveness from the signified to which it is tied. It is not the body of the sign that acts, for that is all sensation, but rather the signified that it expresses, imitates, or transports. It would be wrong to conclude that, in Rousseau's critique of sensationalism, it is the sign itself that exhausts the operation of art. We are moved, "excited," by the represented and not by the representer, by the expressed and not by the expression, by the inside which is exposed and not by the outside of the exposition. Even in painting, representation comes alive and touches us only if it imitates an object, and, better, if it expresses a passion: "It is the drawing, the imitation, which gives life and spirit to these colors. The passions they express are what stir ours. . . . The strokes of a touching picture affect us even in a print" [*Essay*, p. 53].

The engraving: art being born of imitation, only belongs to the work proper as far as it can be retained in an engraving, in the reproductive impression of its *outline*. If the beautiful loses nothing by being reproduced, if one recognizes it in its sign, in the sign of the sign which a copy must be, then in the "first time" of its production there was already a reproductive essence. The engraving, which copies the models of art, is nonetheless the model for art. If the origin of art is the possibility of the engraving, the death of art and art as death are prescribed from the very birth of the work. The principle of life, once again, is confounded with the principle of death. Once again, Rousseau desires to separate them but once again, he accedes within his description and within his text to that which limits or contradicts his desire.

On the one hand, in fact, Rousseau does not doubt that imitation and formal outline are the property of art and he inherits, as a matter of course, the traditional concept of *mimesis*; a concept that was first that of the philosophers whom Rousseau, one must remember, accused of having killed song. This accusation could not be radical, since it moved within the conceptuality inherited from this philosophy and of the metaphysical conception of art. The outline that lends itself to the print or engraving, the line which *is imitated,* belongs to all the arts, to the arts of space as much as to the arts of duration, to music no less than to painting. In both it outlines the space of imitation and the imitation of space.

> Music is no more the art of combining sounds to please the ear than painting is the art of combining colors to please the eye. If there were no more to it than that, they would both be natural sciences rather than fine arts. Imitation alone raises them to this level. But what makes painting an imitative art? Drawing. What makes music another? Melody. (Chap. 13) [*Essay*, p. 55]

The *outline* (design or melodic line) is not only what permits imitation and the recognition of the represented in the representer. It is the element of formal difference which permits the contents (colored or sonorous substance) to appear. By the same token, it cannot *give rise* to [literally *provide space* for] art (techné) as *mimesis* without constituting it forthwith as a *technique of imitation.* If art lives from an originary reproduction, the outline that permits this reproduction, opens in the same stroke the space of calculation, of grammaticality, of the rational science of intervals, and of those "rules of imitation" that are fatal to energy. Let us recall: "And, to the degree that the rules of imitation proliferated, imitative language was enfeebled" [*Essay*, p. 68]. Imitation is therefore at the same time the life and the death of art. Art and death, art and its death are comprised in the space of the *alteration* of the originary *iteration* (*iterum*, anew, does it not come from Sanskrit *itara*, other?); of repetition, reproduction, representation; or also in space as the possibility of iteration and the exit from life placed outside of itself.

For the outline is spacing itself, and marking figures, it shapes the surfaces of painting as much as the time of music:

> The role of melody in music is precisely that of drawing in a painting. This is what constitutes the strokes and figures, of which the harmony and the sounds are merely the colors. But, it is said, melody is merely a succession of sounds. No doubt. And drawing is only an arrangement of colors. An orator uses ink to write out his compositions: does that mean ink is a very eloquent liquid? (Chap. 13) [*Essay*, p. 53]

Thus disengaging a concept of formal difference, criticizing with vigor an aesthetic that one might call substantialist rather than materialist, more attentive to sensory content than to formal composition, Rousseau yet places a great deal of the burden of art—here music—upon the *outline.* That is to say to what can give rise to cold calculation and the rules of imitation. According to a logic with which we are now familiar, Rousseau confronts that danger *by opposing good form to bad form*, the form of life to the form of death, *melodic* to *harmonic* form, form with imitative content to form without content, form full of sense to empty abstraction. *Rousseau reacts against formalism. In his eyes formalism is also a materialism and a sensationalism.*

It is difficult to understand what is at stake in Chapters 13—"On Melody"—and 14—"On Harmony"—if one does not perceive its immediate context: the polemic with Rameau. These chapters assemble and stylize a discussion developed in the corresponding articles of the *Dictionary of Music* and in the *Examen des deux principes avancés par M. Rameau dans sa brochure intitulé* "Erreurs sur la musique," *dans* l'Encyclopedie" (1755). But this context serves only to reveal a systematic and permanent necessity.

For Rousseau the difference between the melodic and harmonic form has a decisive importance. By all the features that distinguish them, they are opposed, as the life to the death of the song. Yet, if one thinks of the origin of the word ("originally a proper name") and of "the ancient treatises that we have remaining," "*harmony* would be very difficult to distingiush from melody, unless one adds to the latter the ideas of ryhthm and measure, without which, in effect, no melody can have a determined character; whereas *harmony* has its own by itself, independent of every other quantity" [*Dictionary*, pp. 286–87]. The difference proper to harmony must thus be looked for in the moderns, for whom it is "a succession of concords according to the laws of modulation." The principles of this harmony have been assembled into systems only by the moderns. Examining that of Rameau, Rousseau reproaches him first for passing off as natural what is purely conventional: "I ought however to declare, that this system, as ingenious as it may appear, is not in any way founded on nature, as he incessantly repeats it; that it is established only on analogies and conveniencies, which one, who is tolerable at invention, might over throw tomorrow, by others much more natural" (*Dictionary* [p. 187]). Rameau's fault is twofold: an artificialist exuberance and an illusory or abusive recourse to nature, an excess of arbitrariness which claims to be grounded solely in the physics of sound. One cannot deduce a science of series and intervals from simple physics; Rousseau's argument is noteworthy in many ways:

The physical principle of the resonance presents to us the solitary concords and establishes not the succession. A regular succession is however necessary. A dictionary of chosen words is not an harangue, nor a collection of good concords a piece of music. A *sense is wanting; an union in the music as well as language is necessary: Something of what precedes must be transmitted to what follows, that the whole may form a concinnity* [skillful congruity] *and may be truly one.* Moreover, the composed sensation, which results from a perfect concord, is resolved in the absolute sensation of each of the sounds which compose it; and in the compared sensation of each of these intervals which these same sounds form between themselves, *there is nothing beyond the sensible in this concord; from whence it follows, that it is only by the connection of the sounds, and the analogy of the intervals, that the union in question can be established: There lies the true and only principle, whence flow all the laws of harmony and modulation.* If then, the whole of *harmony* was formed only by a succession of perfect major concords, it would be sufficient to proceed to them by intervals similar to those which compose such a concord; for then, some sound of the preceding concord being necessarily prolonged on the following, all the concords would be found sufficiently united, and the *harmony* would be *one*, at least, in this sense. But besides that such successions would exclude the whole melody, by excluding the diatonic genus, which forms its bass, they would not reach the true aim of the art, since *music, being a discourse, ought, like it, to have its periods, its phrases, suspensions, stops, and punctuation of every kind*; and as the uniformity of the harmonic courses presents nothing of these properties, the diatonic course required the major and minor concords to be intermixt, and we have felt the necessity of dissonances to mark the stops and phrases. Moreover, the united succession of perfect major concords, neither gives the perfect minor concord, the dissonance, or any kind of phrase, and its punctuation appears entirely erroneous. Mons. Rameau, insisting absolutely, in his system, that all our *harmony* should be drawn from nature, has had recourse, for this purpose, to another experiment of his own invention. (Ibid. The author italicizes only the word *harmony*.)

Rameau's mistake corresponds to the model of all mistakes and all historical perversions as they *take shape* under Rousseau's eyes: according to the circle, the ellipse, or the unrepresentable figure of the movement of history, cold rationality and abstract convention there join dead nature, the reign of physicality; a certain rationalism there mingles with materialism or sensationalism. Or empiricism: false empiricism, empiricism falsifying the immediate givens of experience. And this falsification that misleads reason is primarily a fault of the heart. If Rameau is mistaken,[36] his errings are moral faults before being theoretical errors. One may read in the *Examination*: "I shall not pretend to avow that the work entitled *Errors on Music* seems to me in fact to crawl with mistakes, and that I see nothing more just in it than the title. But those errors are not in M. Rameau's reason; they have their source nowhere but in the heart: and when passion does not blind him, he will judge better than anyone the good rules of his art." The aberration of the heart which drives him to persecute[37] Rousseau can become a theoretical error only by making him deaf to the soul of music: melody and not harmony; by making him deaf—a more serious accusation—as musician as much as musicographer: "I notice in the *Errors on Music* two of these important principles. The first, which guided M.

Rameau in all his writings, and, what is worse, in all his music, is that harmony is the unique foundation of art, that melody derives from it, and that all the grand effects of music are born of harmony alone (ibid.)."

Rameau's aberration is a symptom. It betrays the sickness both of the history of the West and of European ethnocentrism. For harmony according to Rousseau is a musical perversion that dominates Europe (Northern Europe) alone, and ethnocentrism consists of considering it a natural and universal principle of music. The harmony that destroys the *energy* of music and shackles its *imitative* force—melody—is absent in the beginning of music (*in illo tempore*) and in non-European music (*alibi*). One wonders if Rousseau, conforming to a schema that we now know well, does not criticize ethnocentrism by a symmetrical counter-ethnocentrism and a profound Western ethnocentrism: notably by claiming that harmony is the evil and the science proper to Europe.[38]

The good form of music, which, through representative imitation, produces sense while exceeding the senses, would be melody. One must, according to the same principle of dichotomy which is repeated endlessly, distinguish within melody itself a principle of life and a principle of death, and hold them carefully separated one from the other. Just as there is a good musical form (melody) and a bad musical form (harmony), there is a good and a bad melodic form. By a dichotomous operation that one must ever begin anew and carry further, Rousseau exhausts himself in trying to separate, as two exterior and heterogeneous forces, a positive and a negative principle. Of course, the malign element in melody communicates with the malign element of music in general, that is to say with harmony. This second dissociation between good and bad melodic form puts the first exteriority into question: there is harmony already within melody:

> *Melody* has reference to two different principles, according to the manner in which we consider it. Taken in the connection of sounds, and by the rules of the mode, *it has its principle in harmony;* since it is an harmonic analysis which gives the degrees of the gamut [scale], the chords of the mode, and the laws of the modulation, the only elements of singing. According to this principle, the whole force of *melody* is bounded to flattering the ear by agreeable sounds, as one flatters the eye by agreeable concords of colors; but when taken as an art of imitation, by which the mind may be affected with different images, the heart moved by different sentiments, the passions excited or calmed, in a word, moral effect be operated, which surpass the immediate empire of the sense, another principle must be sought for it, for we see no hold, by which the harmony alone, and whatever comes from it, can affect us thus. [*Dictionary*, p. 227]

What is there to say about this second principle? It must undoubtedly permit imitation: imitation alone can *interest* us in art, concern us by representing nature and by expressing the passions. But what is it within melody that imitates and expresses? It is the *accent.* If we have lingered long in the debate with Rameau, it is also in order to delimit this notion of accent better. It will be indispensable for us when we come to it in the theory of the relationships between speech and writing.

What is this second principle It is *in nature* as well as the first [I italicize: Rousseau recognizes that harmony, the principle against nature, principle of death and of barbarism, is also in nature], but to discover it therein, a more nice observation is necessary, tho' more simple, and a greater sensibility in the observer. This principle is the same which makes the tone of the voice vary when we speak, according to the things we say, and the movements we use in speaking. It is the *accent* of the language which determines the *melody* in each nation; it is the *accent* which makes us speak while singing, and speak with *more or less energy,* according as the language has more or less accent. That, whose accent is most expressed, should produce a *melody* more lively and more passionate. That which has little or no accent, can have only a cold and languishing *melody,* without character or expression. Herein are the true principles. [*Dictionary,* p. 228] (Italics added.)

The *Essay,* and notably the three chapters on the origin of music, on melody, and on harmony, which thus follow the order of growth, may be read according to the same pattern. But the concept of the supplement is this time present in the text, *named* even though it is never (as it nowhere is) *expounded.* It is indeed this difference between implication, nominal presence, and thematic exposition that interests us here.

The chapter on melody proposes the same definitions but it is not without significance that the pedagogic argumentation that introduces them is totally derived from an analogy with an art of space, painting. The point is first to show by this example that the science of relations is cold, without imitative energy (like the calculation of intervals within harmony), while the imitative expression of meaning (of passion, of the thing as it interests us) is the true living content of the work. Let us not be surprised to see Rousseau place design on the side of art, and colors on the side of science and the calculation of relationships. The paradox is apparent. By design, one must understand condition of imitation; by color, natural substance, whose physical play can be explained by physical causes and can become the object of a quantitative science of relationships, of a science of space and of the analogical disposition of intervals. The analogy between the two arts—music and painting—appears thus: *it is analogy itself.* These two arts carry a corruptive principle, which strangely enough is also in nature, and in both cases, that corruptive principle is linked to spacing, to the calculable and analogical regularity of intervals. Thus, in both cases, whether music or painting, whether it is the scales of music or the scales of color, the harmony of tone as visible or audible nuance, the rational calculation of harmonics is a *chromatic*, if one understands that word in the larger sense, beyond what one specifies with respect to the fact of the scale and the bass part in music. Rousseau does not use the word in the *Essay*, but the analogy does not escape him in the *Dictionary*: "*Chromatic*, [adjective sometimes taken substantively]. A kind of music which proceeds in several consecutive semi-tones. This word is derived from the Greek *chroma* which signifies color, either because the Greeks marked these notes with red characters, or differently colored; or, according to authors, because the chromatic kind is a medium between the two others, as color is between black and white; or according to others, because this kind varies and embellishes the diatonic by its semi-tones, which, in music, produces the same effect as the colors in painting" [p. 61]. The chromatic, the *scale* [*gamme*], is to the origin of art what writing is to speech. (And one will reflect on the fact that *gamma* is also the name of a Greek letter introduced into the system of literal musical notation.) Rousseau wishes to restore a natural degree of art within which chromatics, harmonics, and interval would be unknown. He wishes to efface what he had *furthermore* (and *elsewhere*) already recognized, that there is harmony within melody, etc. But the *origin must* (*should*) *have been* (such is, here and elsewhere, the grammar and the lexicon of the relationship to the origin) *pure* melody: "The first tales, the first speeches, the first laws, were in verse. Poetry was devised before prose. That *was bound to be*, since feelings speak before reason. And so it was bound to be the same with music. At first, there was no music but melody and no other melody than the varied sounds of speech. Accents constituted singing." (Italics added.) [*Essay*, pp. 50–51]

But just as in painting the art of design is degraded when the physics of color is substituted for it,[39] so in the song melody is originally corrupted by harmony. Harmony is the originary supplement of melody. But Rousseau never makes explicit the originarity of the lack that makes necessary the addition of the supplement—the quantity and the differences of quantity that always already shape melody. He does not make it explicit, or rather he says it without saying it, in an oblique and clandestine manner. And reading it, it must be surprised at "this work of contraband," if I may add a passage from the *Confessions* here.[40] In the passage of the *Essay* that we have just cited, the definition of the origin of music was developed in this way, without the contradiction or the impurity becoming its themes. "Accents constituted singing, quantity constituted measure, and one spoke as much by sounds and rhythm as by articulations and words. To speak and to sing were formerly one, says Strabo, which shows that in his opinion poetry is the source of eloquence. *It should be said that both had the same source*, not that they were initially the same thing. Considering the way in which the earliest societies were bound together, is it surprising that the first stories were in verse and the first laws were sung? Is it surprising that the first grammarians suboridnated their art to music and were professors of both?" [Italics added; p. 51]

We shall have to relate these propositions to analogous ones, those of Vico for example. For the moment I am interested in the logic proper to Rousseau's discourse: instead of concluding from this simultaneity that the song broached itself in grammar, that difference had already begun to corrupt melody, to make both it and its laws possible at the same time, Rousseau prefers to believe that grammar *must* (*should*) *have* been comprised, in the sense of being confused with; within melody. There *must* (*should*) *have* been plenitude and not lack, presence without difference. From then on the dangerous supplement, scale or harmony, *adds itself from the outside as evil and lack* to happy and innocent plenitude. It would come from an outside which would be simply the outside. This conforms to the logic of identity and to the principle of classical ontology (the outside is outside, being is, etc.) but not to the logic of supplementarity, which would have it that the outside be inside, that the other and the lack come to add themselves as a plus that replaces a minus, that what adds itself to something takes the place of a default in the thing, that the default, as the outside of the inside, should be already within the inside, etc. What Rousseau in fact describes is that the lack, adding itself as a plus to a plus, cuts into an energy which *must (should) have* been and remain intact. And indeed it breaks in as a dangerous supplement, as a *substitute* that *enfeebles, enslaves, effaces, separates,* and *falsifies*: "Even if one spent a thousand years calculating the relations of sounds and the laws of harmony, how would one ever make of that art an imitative art? Where is the principle of this supposed imitation? Of what harmony is it the sign? And what do chords have in common with our passions? . . . But in the process it also shackles melody, *draining it* of *energy* and expressiveness. It *wipes out* [*efface*] *passionate accent, replacing* [*substituer*] it with the harmonic interval. It is restricted to only two types of songs, within which its possibilities are determined by the number of oral tones. It *eliminates* [*efface et détruit*] many sounds or intervals which do not fit into its system. Thus in brief, it *separates* singing from speech, setting these two languages against each other to their *mutual deprivation of all authenticity* [*vérité*], so that it is absurd for them to occur together in a pathetic subject." (Italics added; yet once again, I emphasize particularly the strange association of the values of effacement and substitution) [*Essay*, pp. 57–58].

What does Rousseau say without saying, see without seeing? That substitution has always already begun; that imitation, principle of art, has always already interrupted natural plenitude; that, having to be a *discourse*, it has always already broached presence in differance; that in Nature it is always that which supplies Nature's lack, a voice that is substituted for the voice of Nature. But he says it without drawing any conclusions:

By itself, harmony is insufficient even for those expressions that seem to depend uniquely on it. Thunder, murmuring waters, winds, tempests, are but poorly rendered by simple chords. Whatever one does, noise alone does not speak to the spirit at all. The objects must speak in order to be understood. *In all imitation, some form of discourse must substitute for the voice of nature.* The musician who would represent noise by noise deceives himself. *He knows nothing of either the weakness or the strength of his art,* concerning which his judgment is tasteless and unenlightened. Let him realize that he will have to render noise in song; that to produce the croaking of frogs, he will have to have them sing. *For it is not enough to imitate them;* he must do so touchingly and pleasantly. Otherwise, his tedious imitation is nothing, and will neither interest nor impress anyone. (Italics added) [*Essay*, p. 58]

The Turn of Writing.* We are thus brought back to discourse as supplement. And to the structure of the *Essay* (origin of langauge, origin and degeneracy of music, degeneracy of language) which reflects the structure of language not only in its becoming but also in its space, in its disposition, in what may literally be called its *geography*.

Language is a *structure*—a system of oppositions of places and values—and an *oriented* structure. Let us rather say, only half in jest, that *its orientation is a disorientation.* One will be able to call it a *polarization.* Orientation gives direction to movement by relating it to its origin as to its dawning. And it is starting from the light of origin that one thinks of the West, the end and the fall, cadence or check, death or night. According to Rousseau, who appropriates here a most banal opposition from the seventeenth century,[41] language *turns,* so to speak, as the earth turns. Here neither the orient nor the occident is privileged. The references are to the extremities of the axis around which the globe *turns* (*polos, polein*) and which is called the *rational* axis: the South Pole and the North Pole.

There will be neither an historical line nor an immobile picture of languages. There will be a *turn* (trope) of language. And this movement of culture will be both ordered and rhythmed according to the most natural thing in nature: the earth and the seasons. Languages are *sown*. And they themselves pass from one season to another. The division between languages, the apportionment in the formation of languages, between the systems turned toward the North and the systems turned toward the South—that interior limit—already leaves its furrow in language in general and each language in particular. Such at least is our interpretation. Rousseau *would wish* the opposition between southern and northern in order to place a natural frontier between different types of languages. However, what he *describes* forbids us to think it. That description shows that the

* "Trope" in its root is "turn"; the other meaning of the French "tour" is "trick." The title could thus read "The Turning/Trope/Trick of Writing."

opposition north/south being rational and not natural, structural and not factual, relational and not substantial, traces an axis of reference *inside* each language. No language is from the south or the north, no real element of the language has an absolute situation, only a differential one. That is why the polar opposition does not divide a set of already existing languages; it is described, though not declared, by Rousseau to be the origin of languages. We must measure this gap between the description and the declaration.

What I shall loosely call the polarization of languages repeats within each linguistic system the opposition that permits us to think the emergence of language from nonlanguage: the opposition of passion and need and the entire series of connotative significations. Whether from north or south, all language in general springs forth when passionate desire exceeds physical need, when imagination *is awakened*, which awakens pity and gives movement to the supplementary chain. But once languages are constituted, the polarity need/passion, and the entire supplementary structure, remain operative within each linguistic system: languages are more or less close to pure passion, that is to say more or less distant from pure need, more or less close to pure language or pure nonlanguage. And the measure of that proximity furnishes the structural principle of a classification of languages. Thus the languages of the north are *on the whole* languages of need, the languages of the south, to which Rousseau devotes ten times the space in his description, are *on the whole* languages of passion. But this *description* does not prevent Rousseau from *declaring* that the one group is born of passion, the other of need: the one group expresses *first* passion, the other expresses *first* need. In southern countries, the first discourses were songs of love, in northern countries "the first words . . . were not *love me* [*aimez-moi*] but *help me* [*aidez-moi*]." If one took this declaration literally, one would have to judge it contradictory both to the descriptions and to other declarations: notably to that which excludes the possibility of a language arising out of pure need. But in order to be not merely apparent, these contradictions are regulated by the desire of considering the functional or polar origin as the real and natural origin. Not being able simply to accept the fact that the concept of origin has merely a relative function within a system situating a multitude of origins in itself, each origin capable of being the effect or the offshoot of another origin, the north capable of becoming the south for a more northern site, etc., Rousseau would like the absolute origin to be an absolute south. It is in terms of this diagram that the questions of fact and principle, of real and ideal origin, of genesis and structure in Rousseau's discourse must be asked anew. The diagram is undoubtedly more complex than one generally thinks.

One must here take into account the following necessities: the south is the place of origin or the cradle of languages. Thus the southern languages are closer to childhood, nonlanguage, and nature. But at the same time, being closer to the origin, they are purer, more alive, more animated. On the other hand, the northern languages are distant from the origin, less pure, less alive, less warm. In them one can follow the progress of death and coldness. But even here, the fact that this distance takes us closer to the origin is not representable. The northern languages lead back to that need, to that physicality, to that nature to which the southern languages, which had just left it, were in the closest possible proximity. It is always the impossible design, the unbelievable line of the supplementary structure. Although the difference between south and north, passion and need, explains the origin of languages, it persists in the constitued languages, and at the extreme, the north amounts to the south of the south, which puts the south to the north of the north. Passion animates need more or less, and from the inside. Need constrains passion more or less, and from the inside. This polar difference should rigorously prevent the distinction of two series simply exterior to one another. But one now knows why Rousseau was anxious to maintain that impossible exteriority. His text moves, then, between what we have called *description* and *declaration*, which are themselves structural poles rather than natural and fixed points of reference.

According to the pressing force of need persisting in passion, we shall have different types of passion and therefore different types of languages. The pressure of need varies with place. Place is at the same time geographical situation and seasonal period. Since the difference in the pressure of needs depends upon a local difference, one will not be able to distinguish the question of the morphological classification of languages, which takes into account the effects of need on the form of a language, from the question of the place of origin of the language, *typology* from *topology*. One must consider *together* the origin of languages and the difference among languages. Such that, continuing our reflection on the organization of the Essay, we see Rousseau approaching this double question as one and the same question; and doing so after having spoken of the definition of language in general or of primitive languages in general. Chapter 8, "General and Local Difference in the Origin of Languages," presents itself thus: "All that I have said so far applies to primitive tongues in general, and to such development as is due merely to the passage of time. But it does not explain either their origin or their differences" [p. 30].

How does the place of origin of a language immediately mark the difference proper to the language? What is here the privilege of the place? The locale signifies first the nature of the soil and of the climate: "The principal cause that distinguishes them is local, deriving from the various climates in which they are born, and the way in which they take form. It is necessary to go back to this cause in order to understand the general and characteristic differences between the tongues of the south and those of the north" [*Essay*, p. 30]. A proposition which conforms to the promise that opens the *Essay*: one must furnish a *natural*, nonmetaphysical, nontheological explanation of the origin of languages:

Speech distinguishes man among the animals; language distinguishes nations from each other; one does not know where a man comes from until he has spoken. Out of usage and necessity, each learns the language of his own country. But what determines that this language is that of his country and not of another? In order to tell, it is necessary to go back to some principle that belongs to the locality itself and antedates its customs, for speech, being the first social institution, owes its form to natural causes alone [p. 5].

To return to these natural causes is, then, to avoid the theologico-moral *usteron proteron*, that of Condillac for example. One knows that in the second *Discourse*, Rousseau, while recognizing his debt fully, still reproaches Condillac for allowing himself mores and a society to explain the origin of languages, especially at the moment when he professes to give a purely natural explanation of what nevertheless remains in his eyes a gift of God. Rousseau regrets that Condillac supposes precisely that which one must question from the beginning, namely " a sort of society already established among the inventors of language." It is "the blunder made by those who, in reasoning on the state of nature, always import into it ideas gathered in a state of society" [*Discourse*, pp. 174–75]. On this point also, the *Essay* agrees with the *Discourse*. There is no social institution before language, it is not one cultural element among others, it is the element of institutions in general, it includes and constructs the entire social structure. Since nothing precedes it in society, its cause can only be precultural or natural. Although its essence is in the passions, its cause, which is not its essence, arises out of nature, that is to say from need. And if one wants to find a precise point of juncture between the second *Discourse* and the four chapters of the *Essay* dealing with the origin and the differences of languages, notably in that factual content from which we have drawn the argument, one should reread, in Part One of the *Discourse*, the page on the relationships between instincts and society, between passion and need, north and south. There one would see (1) that supplementarity is the structural rule ("Savage man, left by nature solely to the direction of instinct, *or rather indemnified for what he may lack by faculties capable at first of supplying its place, and afterwards of raising him much above it*, must accordingly begin with purely animal functions" (italics added) [p. 171]; (2) that in spite of the essential heterogeneity of passion and need, the former is added to the latter as an effect to a cause, a product to an origin: "Whatever moralists may hold, the human understanding is greatly indebted to the passions. . . . The passions, again, originate in our wants" [*Discourse*, p. 171]; (3) that Rousseau then *makes room* for a geographical explanation: a structural explanation which he says can be sustained by facts; and that this explanation amounts to a difference between the peoples of the north and those of the south, the former receiving a supplement to fulfill a lack that the latter do not suffer. And when Chapter 8 of the *Essay* announces its considerations of the differences in this way: "Let us try to follow the order of nature in our investigations. I shall enter now upon a long digression on a subject so hackneyed it is trivial, but one to which it is nonetheless always necessary to return, in order to find the origin of human institutions" [p. 31], one can imagine the placing of a long footnote to this passage of the *Discourse* (Rousseau is explaining that "the passions in their turn draw their origin from our needs"):

It would be easy, were it necessary, to support this opinion by facts, and to show that, in all the nations of the world, the progress of the understanding has been exactly proportionate to the wants which the peoples had received from nature, or been subjected to by circumstances, and in consequence to the passions that induced them to provide for those necessities. I might instance the arts, rising up in Egypt and expanding with the inundation of the Nile. I might follow their progress into Greece, where they took root afresh, grew up and towered to the skies, among the rocks and sands of Attica, without being able to germinate on the fertile banks of the Eurotas: I might observe that in general, the people of the North are more industrious than those of the South, because they cannot get on so well without being so: *as if nature wanted to equalize matters by giving their understandings the fertility she had refused to their soil* (pp. 143–44 [171–72]; italics added).

There is, then, an economy of nature which attends to the regulating of faculties according to needs, and distributes supplements and compensations. This supposes that the sphere of necessity is itself complex, hierarchized, differentiated. It is in this sense that we should relate to all such texts Chapter 8 of Book III of *The Social Contract*;* the influence of *De l'esprit des Loix*† upon the chapter has been noticed; an entire theory of the *excess* of the production of work according to need systematically dovetails with a typology of the forms of government (according to "the distance between people and government") and with an explanation by climate (according to whether one goes away from or "nearer . . . to the equator"): "We find then, in every climate, natural causes according to which the form of government which it requires can be assigned, and we can even say what sort of inhabitants it should have" [*Social Contract*, p. 65].

* I have used the version of the *Social Contract* to be found in Cole, op. cit., and included my references within brackets.

† Charles Louis de Secondat, baron de Montesquieu, *Oeuvres complètes* (Paris, 1748), vol. I; translated as *The Spirit of the Laws* by Thomas Nugent, new edition (London, 1878).

But the theory of needs that underlies the *Essay* is set forth, perhaps better than elsewhere, in a fragment of five pages, whose inspiration is undeniably that of the chapters that interest us and undoubtedly also that of the project of the *Political Institutions.*[42] Three sorts of needs are distingiushed there: those that "deal with subsistence" and "with preservation" (nourishment, sleep); those that deal with "well-being," which are "properly speaking no more than appetites, but sometimes so violent that they torment more than true needs" ("luxury of sensuality, of softness, the union of sexes and all that flatter our senses"): "a third order of needs which, born after the others, do not allow them to take precedence, are those that arise from public opinion." The first two must be satisfied for the last to appear, Rousseau notes, but we have observed that *the second or secondary need supplants each time, by force or urgency, the first need. There is already a perversion of needs, an inversion of their natural order.* And we have just seen included among needs what is elsewhere named passion. Need is thus permanently present within passion. But if one wants to be aware of the first origin of passion, society, and language, one must return to the profundity of the needs of the first order. Our fragment thus defines the program of the *Essay*, which it proceeds to flesh out in a few pages:

> Thus all reduces itself at first to subsistence, and in that respect man is a function of his environment. He depends on everything and he becomes what everything he depends upon forces him to be. Climate, soil, air, water, productions of the earth and sea, form his temperament, his character, determine his tastes, his passions, his work, his actions of all kinds. [The natural explanation is not good for the atoms of culture but for the total social fact:] If that is not exactly true of individuals, it is undeniably true of peoples. . . . Thus before one broaches the history of our species, one must begin by examining its habitation and all its varieties (p. 530).

The explanation by the natural locale is not a static one. It takes into account the natural revolutions: seasons and migrations. Rousseau's dynamic is a strange system within which the critique of ethnocentrism organically comes to terms with a Europeocentrism. It is better understood by carefully weaving together a piece of *Emile* and a piece of the *Essay*. It is then seen how the concept of *culture*, in a very rare usage, unites nature and society by virtue of its metaphoricity. In the *Essay* as in *Emile*, the changes of place and seasons, the displacements of man and terrestrial revolutions are taken care of by the natural explanation. But if that explanation is preceded, in the *Essay*, by a protestation against European prejudice, it is followed, in *Emile*, by a Europeocentric profession of faith. As the protestation and the profession of faith have not the same function and are not on the same level, and as they do not contradict each other, we will profit by recomposing their system. Let us first place the texts side by side:

The *Essay*:
The great shortcoming of Europeans is always to philosophize on the origins of things exclusively in terms of what happens within their own milieu. They never fail to show us primitive men inhabiting a barren and harsh world, dying of cold and hunger, desperate for shelter and clothing, with nothing in sight but Europe's ice and snow. But they fail to realize that, just like all life, the human race originated in warm climes, and that on two-thirds of the globe, winter is hardly known. When one wants to study men, one must consider those around one. But to study man, one must extend the range of one's vision. One must first observe the differences in order to discover the properties. The human race, born in warm lands, spread itself into cold areas where it multiplied, and then coursed back into the warm lands. From this action and reaction come the revolutions of the earth and the continual agitation of its inhabitants (Chap. 8) [pp. 30–31].

Emile:
The birthplace is not a matter of indifference in the *education* [*culture*] of man; *it is only in temperate climes that he comes to his full growth*. The disadvantages of extremes are easily seen. A *man is not planted in one place like a tree, to stay there the rest of his life*, and to pass from one extreme to another you must travel twice as far as he who starts half-way. . . . A Frenchman can live in New Guinea or in Lapland, but a negro cannot live in Tornea nor a Samoyed in Benin. It seems also as if the brain were less perfectly organized in the two extremes. Neither the negroes nor the Laps are as wise as Europeans. So if I want my pupil to be a citizen of the world I will choose him in the temperate zone, in France for example, rather than elsewhere.
In the north with its barren soil men devour much food, in the fertile south they eat little. This produces another difference: the one is industrious, the other contemplative (p. 27; italics added) [p. 20].

How do these two apparently contradictory texts complement each other? We shall see below how culture is linked to agriculture. It appears here that man, in as much as he depends upon a soil and a climate, *is cultivated*: he sprouts, he forms a society and "The birthplace is not a matter of indifference in the education [*culture*] of man." But this culture is also the power of changing terrain, of opening oneself to another culture: man may look far, "he is not planted in one place like a tree," he is engaged, both texts say, in migrations and revolutions. From that perspective, one may criticize ethnocentrism in as much as it shuts us in within a locality and an empirical culture: the European makes the mistake of not traveling, of deeming himself the immobile center of the world, of resting planted like a tree in his own country. But this criticism of the empirical Europe should not prevent us from recognizing, Rousseau seems to think, that the European, by his natural locality, occupying the middle between extremes, has a greater facility for traveling, for opening himself to the horizon and diversity of universal culture. At the center of the world, the European has the luck or power to be European and everything else at the same time. ("It is only in temperate climates that he [man] comes to his full growth—") He is simply wrong in not using this universal opening *in fact*.

All this argumentation circulates between the two Europes; it has remained or become classic. We shall not examine it here for its own sake: let us only consider that it is the condition of all Rousseau's discourse. If, in his eyes, there were no unlocking of a determined culture, no opening into all other cultures in general, no mobility and possibility of imaginary variations, these questions would remain closed. Better, it would be impossible to determine difference. Difference only appears starting from a certain middle point, a certain median, mobile and temperate, between north and south, need and passion, consonant and accent, etc. Under the factual determination of this temperate zone (Europe, "in France, for example, rather than elsewhere"), birthplace of the anthropologist and of the citizen of the world, an essential necessity is concealed: it is *between* different things that one can think difference. But this difference-between may be understood in two ways: as another difference or as access to nondifference. It is not at all doubtful for Rousseau that the inhabitant of the temperate zone *should* make of his difference, effacing it or surmounting it in an interested in-difference, an opening to the humanity of man. Pedagogical success and ethnological humanism would have the good fortune of producing itself in Europe, "in France, for example, rather than elsewhere," in that happy region of the world where man is neither warm nor cold.

From this privileged place of observation, one will better dominate the play of oppositions, order, and the predominance of extremes. One will better understand the natural causes of culture. Since language is not an element but the element of culture, one must first locate, both in the language and in nature, the oppositions of corresponding and interarticulated values. What, within language, must correspond to the predominance of need, that is to say the north? Consonant or articulation. To the predominance of passion, that is to say of the south? Accent or inflection.

The play of predominances would be inexplicable if one held to the simple proposition according to which languages are born of passion (Chapter 3). In order that need may come to dominate passion in the north, an inversion or perversion must already be possible within the order of need and of a need that is forever related to passion, arousing it, persevering in it, submitting to it or controlling it. The appeal to the second *Discourse* and to the *Fragment* was thus indispensable. It permits us to explain this affirmation of the *Essay*: "Eventually all men became similar, but the order of their progress is different. In southern climes, where nature is bountiful, needs are born of passion. In cold countries, where she is miserly, passions are born of need, and the languages, sad daughters of necessity, reflect their austere origin" (Chap. 10) [*Essay*, p. 46].

Now if the predominance of the North Pole over the South, of need over passion, of articulation over accent, is in fact *gradual*, it nonetheless has the sense of *substitution*. As we have often shown, progressive effacement is also the installation of a supplementary substitute. The man of the North substituted *help-me* [*aidez-moi*] for *love-me* [*aimez-moi*], clarity for energy, articulation for accent, reason for heart. Formal substitution undoubtedly conveys a weakening of energy, of warmth, of life, of passion, but it remains a transformation, a revolution in form and not only a diminishing of force. An explanation of this substitution in terms of a simple degradation is most inadequate; it so strongly implies a displacement and an inversion that it refers us to a completely different function of need. In the *normal* order of origin (in the South), the proposition of Chapter 2 (*That the first invention of speech is due not to need but to passions* and "the natural effect of the first needs was to separate men, and not to reunite them") has an absolutely general value. But this normal order of origin is reversed in the North. The North is not simply the distanced other of the South, it is not the limit that one reaches if he starts out from the unique southern origin. Rousseau is in a way compelled to recognize that the North is also *another origin*. It is to death that he accords this status, because the absolute North is death. Normally need isolates men instead of bringing them closer; in the North, it is the origin of society:

> The idleness that nurtures passion *is replaced by work, which represses it*. Before being concerned with living happily, one had to be concerned with living. Mutual need uniting men to a greater extent when sentiment has not done so, society would be formed only through industry. The ever-present danger of perishing would not permit a language restricted to gesture. And, the first words among them were not *love me* [*aimez-moi*] but *help me* [*aidez-moi*].
> These two expressions, although similar enough, are pronounced in a very *different* tone. The whole point was not to make someone *feel* something, but to make him *understand*. Thus what was needed was not *vigor* [*énergie*] but *clarity*. For the *accents* which the heart does not provide, distinct *articulation* is *substituted*. And if some trace of nature remains in the form of the language, this too contributes to its austerity. (Italics added.)

In the north, the passions do not disappear: there is substitution, not effacement. The passions are not extenuated but *repressed* by what takes the place of desire: work. Work represses more than it lessens the force of desire. It displaces it. That is why "Northern men are not passionless, but their passions are, in effect, of another kind" [*Essay*, p. 48]: anger, irritation, fury, disquietude are the displacements of southern passion. In the south, passion is not repressed, whence a certain softness, a certain intemperance for which people in tempered regions do not have an unreserved indulgence:

The passions of the warm countries are voluptuous, relating to love and tenderness. Nature does so much for people there that they have almost nothing to do. Provided that an Asiatic has women and repose, he is contented. But in the north, where people consume a great deal, on barren soil, men are easily irritated, being subject to so many needs. Anything happening near them disturbs them. As they subsist only through effort, the poorer they are the more firmly they hold to the little they have. To approach them is to threaten their lives. This is what accounts for their irascible temper, their quickness to attack anyone who offends them. Thus too their most natural tone of voice is angry and menacing, and their words are always accompanied by *emphatic articulation*, which makes them harsh and loud. . . . These, in my opinion are the most general physical causes of the characteristic differences of the primitive tongues. Those of the south are bound to be *lively, sonorous, accented, eloquent*, and frequently *obscure because of their power*. Those of the north are bound to be *dull, harsh, articulated, shrill, monotonous*, and to have a *clarity due more to vocabulary than to good construction*. The modern tongues, with all their intermingling and recasting, still retain something of these differences. (Chap. 10, 11. Italics added.) [pp. 48–49]

The pole of linguistic articulation is in the north. Articulation (difference within language) is thus not a simple effacement; it does not tone down the energy either of desire or of the accent. It displaces and represses desire by work. It is not the sign of a weakening of force, in spite of what Rousseau sometimes seems to make us think, but it conveys, on the contrary, a conflict of antagonistic forces, a difference within the force. The force of need, its own economy, that which makes work necessary, works precisely against the force of desire and represses it, breaking its song into articulation.

This conflict of forces responds to an economy that is no longer simply that of need, but the system of the relations of force between desire and need. Here two forces that one may indifferently consider forces of life or of death are opposed. Responding to the urgency of need, the man of the north protects his life not only against penury but against the death that would follow the unrestrained liberation of southern desire. He protects himself against the menace of voluptuousness. But conversely, he fights against this force of death with another force of death. From this point of view, it appears that life, energy, desire, etc., are of the South. The northern language is less alive, less animated, less song-like, colder. To fight against death, the man of the North dies a little earlier and "it is known . . . that northern peoples do not die singing any more than swans do" (Chap. 14) [p. 58].

Writing is at the North: cold, necessitous, reasoning, turned toward death, to be sure, but by that *tour de force*, by that detour of force which forces it to hold on to life. In fact, the more a language is articulated, the more articulation extends its domain, and thus gains in rigor and in vigor, the more it yields to writing, the more it calls writing forth. This is the central thesis of the *Essay*. The progress of history, the degradation which unites with it according to the strange graphic of supplementarity, goes toward the North and toward death: history effaces vowel accent, or rather represses it, hollows out articulation, extends the power of writing. That is why the ravages of writing are more felt in the modern languages:

> The modern tongues, with all their intermingling and recasting, still retain something of these differences. French, English, German: each is a language private to a group of men who help each other, reason together calmly, or who become angry. But the ministers of the gods proclaiming sacred mysteries, sages giving laws to their people, leaders swaying the multitude, have to speak Arabic or Persian.[43] *Our tongues are better suited to writing than speaking,* and there is more pleasure in reading us than in listening to us. Oriental tongues, on the other hand, lose their life and warmth when they are written. The words do not convey half the meaning: all the effectiveness is in the tone of voice [*accents*]. Judging the genius of the Orientals from their books is like painting a man's portrait from his corpse (Chap. 11; italics added) [p. 49].

The oriental corpse is in the book. Ours is already in our speech. Our language, even if we are pleased to speak it, has already substituted too many articulations for too many accents, it has lost life and warmth, it is already eaten by writing. Its accentuated features have been gnawed through by the consonants.

Although it was not the only degree of articulation for Rousseau, the fragmentation of language into words had already cancelled the energy of the accent (by using that verb—"to cancel" [*biffer*]—we leave the values of effacement and erasure, of extenuation and repression, in their ambiguity, as Rousseau proposes them simultaneously). The languages of the North are "clear because of the power of words"; in the languages of the South, "the meaning is only half in the words, all the force is in the accents."

Cancellation amounts to producing a supplement. But as always, the supplement is incomplete, unequal to the task, it lacks something in order for the lack to be filled, it participates in the evil that it should repair. The loss of accent is inadequately compensated for by articulation: the latter is "strong," "hard," and "noisy," it does not sing. And when writing tries to supplement accent by accents, it is nothing but make-up dissimulating the corpse of the accent. Writing—here the inscribing of accents—not only hides language under its artifice, it masks the already decomposed corpse of language. "We [moderns] have no idea of a sonorous and harmonious language, spoken as much according to sounds as it is according to words. It is mistaken to think that accent marks can *make up for* [*suppléer*] oral intonation [*l'accent*]. One invents accent signs [*accens*] only when intonation [*l'accent*] has already been lost"[44] (Chap. 7; italics added) [*Essay*, pp. 24–25]. Accents are, like punctuation, an evil of writing: not only an invention of *copyists* but of copyists who are *strangers* to the language which they transcribe; the copyist or his reader is by definition a stranger to the living use of language. They always deal with a moribund speech in order to camouflage it: "When the Romans began to study Greek, the copyists invented signs for accent marks, aspiration marks, and marks of prosody, to indicate their pronunciation. But by no means does it follow that these signs were in use among the Greeks, who would not need them" [*Essay*, pp. 29–30 n.]. For obvious reasons, Rousseau was of necessity fascinated by the person of the copyist. Especially but not only within the musical order, the moment of transcription is the dangerous moment, as is the moment of writing, which in a way is already a transcription, the imitation of other signs; reproducing the signs, producing the signs of signs, the copyist is always tempted to add *supplementary* signs to improve the restitution of the original. The good copyist must resist the temptation of the supplementary sign. He must rather show himself economical in the use of signs. In the admirable article "copyist" in the *Dictionary of Music*, with the minuteness and volubility of an artisan explaining his craft to the apprentice, Rousseau advises "never to write useless notes," "not to multiply signs in a useless way."[45]

Punctuation is the best example of a nonphonetic mark within writing. Its impotence in transcribing accent and inflexion isolates or analyses the misery of writing reduced to its proper means. Unlike Duclos,[46] who yet inspires him, here Rousseau accuses, rather than the essence of punctuation, the imperfect state in which it has been left: a vocative mark must be invented to "distingiush a man named from a man called." And even a mark of irony. For while distrusting writing, and indeed because of that distrust, Rousseau wants to exhaust all its univocity, clarity, precision. These values are negative when they chill the expression of passion; but they are positive when they avoid trouble, ambiguity, hypocrisy, and the dissimulation of the original spoken word or song. The *Dictionary of Music* recommends "exactness of the connections" and "a neatness in our signs" (article on copyist) [*copiste*; p. 96].

The difference between accent or intonation on the one hand and accents on the other thus separates speech and writing as quality and quantity, force and spacing. "Our professed accents are nothing but vowels, or signs of quantity; they mark no variety of sound." Quantity is linked to articulation. Here to the articulation into sounds and not, as immediately above, to articulation into words. Rousseau is aware of what André Martinet calls the *double articulation* of language: into sounds and into words. The opposition of "vowels" or "voice" to accent or "diversity of sounds" evidently presupposes that the vowel is not pure voice, but a voice that has already undergone the differential work of articulation. Voice and vowel are not opposed here, to the consonant, as they are in another context.

The entire Chapter 7, "On Modern Prosody," which criticizes French grammarians and plays a decisive role in the *Essay*, is strongly inspired by Duclos. The borrowings are declared, massive, determining. Given the architectonic importance of this chapter, it is difficult to believe that the borrowings from Duclos were inserted after the fact.

But, furthermore, is it a matter of borrowing? As usual, Rousseau makes the borrowed pieces play within an absolutely original organization. Of course he cites and recites such and such a passage from the "Commentary" (Chapter 4) here and there. Even when he is not actually quoting, he draws from passages like the following, which, with many others, would anticipate a similar Saussurian development (supra, p. 57, 38–39).

> The superstition of etymology gives rise to as many inconsistencies in its small domain, as superstition properly speaking does in graver matters. Our orthography is an assemblage of bizarrerie and contradictions. . . . Yet, whatever care one took in noting our prosody, beside the unpleasantness of seeing print bristling with signs, I have strong doubts that that would be of much use. There are things which can only be learnt through usage; they are purely organic and give so little foothold to reason, that it would be impossible to grasp them by theory alone, which is faulty even in the authors who expressly deal with them. I sense even that what I write here is very difficult to make comprehensible, and that it would be very clear, if I explained it in my person (pp. 414–15).

But Rousseau keeps an eye on his borrowings, reinterprets them, and applies himself to enhancing their value in a manner to which we must pay heed. He insists, for example, upon the notion that the accent is *cancelled* by the sign and the use of the spoken word by the artifice of writing. Cancelled by a work of erasure and replacement, obliterated rather than forgotten, toned down, devalued. "According to M. Duclos, 'all the ancient prosodic signs supposed a quite fixed function, not yet bowing to usage.' I would add that they substituted for it" [*Essay*, p. 27]. And Rousseau's entire argument follows the history of the accentuation or of the punctuation superadded to the primitive Hebraic language.

The conflict then is between the force of accentuation and the force of articulation. This concept of articulation must stop us here. It had served to define arche-writing as it is already at work within speech. And Saussure, in contradiction to his phonologist thesis, recognized, we recall, that the power of articulation alone—and not spoken language—was "natural to man." Being the condition of speech, does articulation itself not remain a-phasic?

Rousseau introduces the concept of articulation in Chapter 4, "On the Distinctive Characteristics of the First Language and the Changes It Had to Undergo." The first three chapters deal with the origin of languages. Chapter 5 will be entitled "On Script." *Articulation is the becoming-writing of language.* Rousseau, *who would like to say* that this becoming-writing *comes upon the origin unexpectedly,* takes it as his premise, and according to it *describes in fact* the way in which that *becoming-writing encroaches upon the origin,* and arises from the origin. The becoming-writing of language is the becoming-language of language. He *declares* what he *wishes to say,* that is to say that articulation and writing are a post-originary malady of language; he says or *describes* that which he *does not wish to say*: articulation and therefore the space of writing operates at the origin of language.

Like those of imitation—and for the same profound reasons—the value and operation of articulation are ambiguous: principles of life *and* principles of death, and therefore the motive forces of progress in the sense that Rousseau gives to that word. He *would like to say* that progress, however ambivalent, occurs *either* toward the worse, *or* toward the better, either for better or for worse. The first chapter of the *Essay* shows in effect, according to a concept of animal language which some hold even today, that the *natural* languages of the animals exclude progress. "Conventional language is characteristic of man alone. That is why man makes progress, whether for good or ill, and animals do not" [*Essay,* p. 10].

But Rousseau *describes what he does not wish to say*: that "progress" takes place *both* for the worse *and* for the better. At the same time. Which annuls eschatology and teleology, just as difference—or originary articulation—annuls archeology.

III. *Articulation*

All this appears in the handling of the concept of articulation. To demonstrate it we must make a long detour. To understand how "articulations, which are conventional" (Chapter 4), operate, we must once again go through the problem of the concept of nature. To avoid rushing directly into the center of the difficulty which many commentators on Rousseau have already well defined, we shall try, in a limited and prefatory way, to locate it in the *Essay.* Already there it is formidable.

"That Movement of the Wand . . ." Let us begin with some simple certainties and choose some propositions whose literal clarity leaves little in doubt. We read them in the first chapter.

First propostion. "Speech distinguishes man among the animals." These are the first words of the *Essay*. Speech is also "the first social institution." It is therefore not natural. It is natural to man, it belongs to his nature, to his essence, which is not, unlike that of animals, natural.

Speech belongs to man, to the humanity of man. But Rousseau distinguishes between language [*langue*] and speech [*parole*]. The usage of speech is universally human but languages are diverse. "Language distinguishes nations from each other; one does not know where a man comes from until he has spoken. Out of usage and necessity, each learns the language of his own country. But what determines that this language is that of his country and not of another? In order to tell, it is necessary to go back to some principle that belongs to the locality itself and antedates its customs, for speech, being the first social institution, owes its form to natural causes alone" [*Essay*, p. 5]. Thus the natural causality of language splits itself in two.

1. Speech, the possibility of discourse in general, must have, as the first institution, only *general* natural causes (relationships between need and passion, etc.).

2. But beyond the general existence of speech, one must account, by equally natural causes, for its *forms* ("speech, being the first social institution, owes its form to natural causes alone"). It is the explication of the diversity of languages by physicality, geography, climate, etc. This double natural explanation announces the division of the *Essay* in its first part, into what concerns language and what concerns languages. The first seven chapters explain by natural causes language in general (or the primitive language), its origin, and its decadence. With the eighth chapter, we pass from language to languages. General and local differences are explained by natural causes.

How should this natural explanation be analyzed?

Second proposition: "As soon as one man was recognized by another as a sentient, thinking being similar to himself, the desire or need to communicate his feelings and thoughts made him seek the means to do so" [*Essay*, p. 5]. Desire *or* need; the home of two origins, southern or northern, is already assured. And Rousseau refuses, as he also does in the second *Discourse*, to wonder if the language preceded the society as its condition, or conversely. He sees no solution, and no doubt no sense, to such a question. In the second *Discourse*, confronted by the immense difficulty of the genealogy of language, almost giving up a natural and purely human explanation, Rousseau writes what is also implied in the *Essay*: "For myself, I am so aghast at the increasing difficulties which present themselves, and so well convinced of the almost demonstrable impossibility that languages should owe their original institution to merely human means, that I leave, to any one who will undertake it, the discussion of the difficult problem, which was most necessary, the existence of society to the invention of language, or the invention of language to the establishment of society" (p. 151) [p. 179].

Same gesture in the *Essay*: one is given language and society at the same time, at the moment when the pure state of nature is crossed, when absolute dispersion is overcome for the first time. One attempts to seize the origin of language at the moment of this first crossing over. In the second *Discourse*, we can still locate a footnote reference: a place is indicated for that long digression which would have been the *Essay*. It is in the first part, immediately after the critique of Condillac and of those who, "reasoning from the state of nature, transport there ideas taken from society." Rousseau knows that it is very difficult to find the resource of an explanation for the birth of languages in the pure state of nature and in the original dispersion. And he proposes a leap: "We will suppose, however, that this first difficulty is obviated. Let us for a moment then take ourselves as being on this side of the vast space which must lie between a pure state of nature and that in which languages had become necessary, and, admitting their necessity, let us inquire how they could first be established. Here we have a new and worse difficulty to grapple with" (p. 14) [p. 175].

"Let us for a moment then take ourselves as being on this side of the vast space." Up to what point? Not up to constituted society but up to the moment when the conditions for its birth are united. Between the pure state of nature and that moment—"a multitude of centuries," rhythmed by distinct steps.[47] But it is difficult to discern the stages. The difference among all Rousseau's texts is subtle, perhaps unstable, always problematic on this point. To the distinctions already located, we must, at the risk of complicating the debate, add the following specification, which concerns precisely the *Essay* in its relationship to the *Discourse*. Between the pure state of nature and society, Rousseau describes, both in the *Discourse* and in the *Essay*, an age of huts. And since that age is presented in Chapter 9 of the *Essay* as the "primitive times," one might be tempted to think that the pure state of nature is radically situated only in the second *Discourse* (first part), the age of huts of the *Essay* corresponding to the one that appeared after the pure state of nature in the second part of the *Discourse*. Even though this hypothesis does not seem simply false and is in fact confirmed by many descriptive elements, it must be nuanced or complicated. As it is evoked in the *Essay*, the age of huts is much closer to the pure state of nature. Speaking of "primitive times," when "the sparse human population had no more social structure than the family, no laws but those of nature, no language but that of gesture and some inarticulate sounds," Rousseau adds in a note: "I consider primitive the period of time from the dispersion of men to any period of the human race that might be taken as determining an epoch" [*Essay*, p. 31, n. 1]. And certainly familial societies do not have the same status here as in the second part of the *Discourse*.[48] The two accounts become similar, it seems, only at the moment when, after a revolution that we shall examine later, ties of another family are constituted, making possible love, morality, speech. It is only the close of Chapter 9 of the *Essay* that one may compare to the second part of the *Discourse*.

"Let us for a moment then take ourselves as being on this side of the vast space . . ." and give ourselves the following hypothesis: starting from the state of pure nature, thanks to a certain reversal that we shall discuss later, man encounters man and recognizes him. Pity awakens and becomes active, he wishes to communicate. But at that moment man has just left nature. It is still by natural causes that the means of communication must be explained. Man can at first use only natural dispositions or "instruments": the senses.

Third proposition. Man must therefore act by his senses upon the senses of others. "Hence the institution of sensate signs for the expression of thought. The inventors of language did not proceed rationally in this way; rather their instinct suggested the consequence of them" [*Essay*, p. 5]. We have two ways of working on the senses of others: movement and voice. Naturally, Rousseau does not wonder what "means" or "instrument" might mean, nor, as he does in *Emile* (p. 160), if voice is not itself a sort of movement. "The action of movement is immediate through touching, or mediate through gesture. The first can function only within arm's length, while the other extends as far as the visual ray. Thus vision and hearing are the only passive organs of language among *distinct* [*dispersés*] individuals" (*Essay*, p. 6) (italics added).

The analysis of the "instruments" of language is therefore governed by the situation of pure dispersion which characterizes the state of nature. Language could have emerged only out of dispersion. The "natural causes" by which one explains it are not recognized as natural except in so far as they accord with the state of nature, which is determined by dispersion. This dispersion should no doubt be overcome by language but, for that very reason, it determines the *natural condition* of language.

The natural condition: it is remarkable that the original dispersion out of which language began continues to mark its milieu and essence. That language must traverse space, be obliged to be spaced, is not an accidental trait but the mark of its origin. In truth, dispersion will never be a past, a prelinguistic situation in which language would certainly have been born only to break with it. The original dispersion leaves its mark within language. We shall have to verify it: articulation, which seemingly introduces difference as an institution, has for ground and space the dispersion that is natural: space itself.

At this point, the concept of nature becomes even more enigmatic and if one does not want Rousseau to contradict himself at all, one must use a great deal of analysis and sympathy.

The natural is first valorized and then disqualified: the original is also the inferior retained within the superior. The language of gesture and the language of voice, sight and hearing, are "equally natural." Nevertheless, one is more natural than the other and because of this it is first and better. It is the language of gesture, which is "more easy and depends less on conventions." Of course there can be conventions of the language of gestures. Rousseau alludes later to a gestural code. But that code is less remote from nature than is the spoken language. For that reason, Rousseau begins with praise for the language of gestures although, further on, wishing to show the superiority of passion over need, he will place speech above gesture. This contradiction is only apparent. Natural immediacy is at once origin and end, but in the double sense of these words: birth and death, unfinished sketch and finished perfection. From then on, all value is determined according to its proximity to an absolute nature. But as this concept is that of a polarized structure, proximity is a distancing. All the contradictions of the discourse are *regulated*, rendered necessary yet resolved, by this structure of the concept of nature. *Before all determinations of a natural law, there is, effectively constraining the discourse, a law of the concept of nature.*

A contradiction regulated in this way appears in a flagrant manner when, praising the language of gesture, Rousseau speaks of love. Further on, he will say of this passion that it is at the origin of sung speech; here, he makes drawing its best interpreter. To appeal to the eye in order to declare love is more natural, more expressive, more *alive*: at once more immediate and more alive, therefore more energetic, more present, more free. Thus *resolving* the entire contradiction, summing it up into its two poles, the *Essay* begins with praise and concludes with condemnation of the mute sign. The first chapter exalts language without voice, that of glance and gesture (which Rousseau distinguishes from our gesticulation): "Thus one speaks more effectively to the eye than to the ear" [*Essay*, p. 8]. The last chapter depicts, at the other pole of history, the ultimate servitude of a society organized by the circulation of silent signs: "Societies have assumed their final form: no longer is anything changed except by arms and cash. And since there is nothing to say to people besides *give money*, it is said with placards on street corners or by soldiers in their homes" [*Essay*, p. 72].

The mute sign is a sign of liberty when it expresses within immediacy; then, what it expresses and he who expresses himself through it are *properly* present. There is neither detour nor anonymity. The mute sign signifies slavery when re-presentative mediacy has invaded the entire system of signification: then, through infinite circulation and references, from sign to sign and from representer to representer, the selfsameness [*propre*] of presense has no longer a place: no one is there for anyone, not even for himself; one can no longer dispose of meaning; one can no longer stop it, it is carried into an endless movement of signification. The system of the sign has no outside. As it is speech that has opened this endless movement [*l'abîme*] of signification—thus constantly risking the loss of signification—it is tempting to return to an archeological moment, a first moment of sign without speech, when passion, beyond need but short of articulation and difference, expresses itself in an unheard of way: an *immediate sign*:

> Although the language of gesture and spoken language are equally natural, still the first is easier[49] and depends less upon conventions. For more things affect our eyes than our ears. Also, visual forms are more varied than sounds, and more expressive, saying more in less time. Love, it is said, was the inventor of drawing. It might also have invented speech, though less happily. Not being very well pleased with it, it disdains it; it has livelier ways of expressing itself. How she could say things to her beloved, who traced his shadow with such pleasure! What sounds might she use to render this movement of the magic wand? [*Essay*, p. 6]

The movement of the magic wand that traces with so much pleasure does not fall outside of the body. Unlike the spoken or written sign, it does not cut itself off from the desiring body of the person who traces or from the immediately perceived image of the other. It is of course still an image which is traced at the tip of the wand, but an image that is not completely separated from the person it represents; what the drawing draws is almost present in person in his *shadow*. The distance from the shadow or from the wand is almost nothing. She who traces, holding, handling, now, the wand, is very close to touching what is very close to being the other *itself*, close by a minute difference; that small difference—visibility, spacing, death—is undoubtedly the origin of the sign and the breaking of immediacy; but it is in reducing it as much as possible that one marks the contours of signification. One thinks the sign beginning from its limit, which belongs neither to nature nor to convention. Now this limit—of an impossible sign, of a sign giving the signified, indeed the thing, *in person*, immediately—is necessarily closer to gesture or glance than to speech. A certain ideality of the sound behaves essentially as the power of abstraction and mediation. The movement of the wand is rich with all possible discourses but no discourse can reproduce it without impoverishing and deforming it. The written sign is absent from the body but this absence is already announced within the invisible and ethereal element of the spoken word, powerless to imitate the contact and the movement of the bodies. The gesture, that of passion rather than that of need, considered in its purity of origin, guards us against an already alienating speech, a speech already carrying in itself death and absence. That is why, when it does not precede the spoken word, it supplements it, corrects its fault and fills its lack. The movement of the wand is a substitute for all discourse that, at a greater distance, would substitute itself for it. This relationship of mutual and incessant supplementarity or substitution is the order of language. It is the origin of language, as it is described without being declared, in the *Essay on the Origin of Languages,* which is here also in agreement with the second *Discourse*: in both texts, the visible gesture, more natural and more expressive, can join itself as a supplement to speech, which is itself a substitute for gesture. This graphic of supplementarity is the origin of languages: it separates gesture and speech primitively united in the mythic purity, absolutely immediate and therefore natural, of the cry:

> The first language of mankind, the most universal and vivid, in a word the only language man needed, before he had occasion to exert his eloquence to persuade assembled multitudes, was the simple cry of nature. . . . When the ideas of men began to expand and multiply, and closer communication took place among them, they strove to invent more numerous signs and a more copious language. *They multiplied the inflexions of the voice, and added gestures, which are in their nature more expressive, and depend less for their meaning on a prior determination* (p. 148; italics added) [p. 176].

Gesture is here an adjunct of speech, but this *adjunct* is not a supplementing by artifice, it is a re-course to a more natural, more expressive, more immediate sign. It is the more universal the less it depends on conventions.[50] But if gesture supposes a distance and a spacing, a milieu of visibility, it ceases being effective when the excess of distance or mediation interrupts visibility: then speech supplements gesture. Everything in language is substitute, and this concept of substitute precedes the opposition of nature and culture: the supplement can equally well be natural (gesture) as artificial (speech).

> But, as hardly anything can be indicated by gestures, except *objects actually present* or easily described, and *visible actions*; as they are not universally in use—for darkness or the interposition of a material object destroys their efficacy—*and as besides they rather request than secure our attention*; men at length bethought themselves of *substituting* for them the articulate sounds of the voice, which, without bearing the same relation to any particular ideas, are better calculated to express them all, as conventional [*institués*] signs. *Such a substitution* could only be made by common consent, and must have been effected in a manner not very easy for men whose gross organs had not been accustomed to any such exercise. It is also in itself still more difficult to conceive, since such a common agreement must have been motivated, and speech seems to have been highly necessary to establish the use of it (pp. 148–49; italics added) [pp. 176–77].

Speech excites attention, the visible exacts it: is it because the ear is always open and offered to provocation, more passive than sight? One can *more naturally* close one's eyes or distract his glance than avoid listening. Let us not forget that this natural situation is primarily that of the child at the breast.

This structure of supplementarity, reflexive, mutual, speculative, infinite, alone permits an explanation of the fact that the language of space, sight, and muteness (Rousseau knew also[51] that it signified death) sometimes takes the place of speech when the latter is attended by a *greater* threat of absence and cuts into life's energy. In that case, the language of visible gestures is more alive. Love "might also have invented speech, though less happily. Not being very well pleased with it, it disdains it; it has livelier ways of expressing itself. How she could say things to her beloved, who traced his shadow with such pleasure! What sounds might she use to work such magic?" [*Essay*, p. 6].

It is therefore after the invention of language and the birth of passion that desire, in order to recapture presence and according to the pattern I have identified, returns to the movement of the magic wand, to the finger and the eye, to a mutism charged with discourse. It is the question of a supplementary return toward a greater naturalness, not of an origin of language. Rousseau clarifies it further on by distinguishing gesture from gesticulation: the former, which sketches the shadow of presence, silently governs the first metaphor; the latter is an indiscreet and cumbersome adjunct of speech. It is a bad supplement. The silent language of love is not a prelinguistic gesture, it is a "mute eloquence."

Our [European] gestures merely indicate our natural unrest. It is not of those that I wish to speak. Only Europeans gesticulate when speaking; one might say that all their power of speech is in their arms. Their lungs are powerful too, but to nearly no avail. Where a Frenchman would strain and torture his body, emitting a great verbal torrent, a Turk will momentarily remove his pipe from his mouth to utter a few words softly, crushing one with a single sentence. [Here the Turk is no longer, like his language, from the North, but from the Orient. We are at once from the North and from the Occident.] [*Essay*, p. 6]

The value of the mute sign is also that of sobriety and discretion *within speech*: the economy of speech.

Since learning to gesticulate, we have forgotten the art of pantomime, for the same reason that with all our beautiful systems of grammar we no longer understand the symbols of the Egyptians. What the ancients said in the liveliest way, they did not express in words but by means of signs. They did not say it, they showed it. [*Essay*, p. 6]

What they showed was clearly not the thing but its hieroglyphic metaphor, the visible sign. This praise of Egyptian symbolism may surprise us: it is a praise of writing and a praise of savagery, more precisely of that writing of which we are told further along that it suits savages. Savagery does not characterize the primitive state of man, the state of pure nature, but rather the state of society being born, of the first language and the first passions. A state structurally anterior to the state of barbarism, itself anterior to civil society. In fact, in the chapter "On Script" (5), Egyptian hieroglyphs are defined as the most crude and most antique script. It would suit people assembled as a nation under the form of savagery:

> The cruder the writing, the more ancient the langauge. The primitive way of writing was not to represent sounds, but objects themselves whether directly, as with the Mexicans, or by allegorical imagery, or as the Egyptians did in still other ways. This stage corresponds to passionate language, and already supposes some society and some needs to which the passions have given birth. . . . The depicting of objects is appropriate to a savage people. [*Essay*, pp. 16–17]

The hieroglyphic language is an impassioned language. Savagery holds itself closest to this passional origin of language. The paradox is that thus it also holds itself closer to writing than to speech. Because gesture, which elsewhere expresses need, here represents passion. It is writing not only because it traces, like the movement of the wand, a design in space, but because the signifier first signifies a signifier, and not the thing itself or a directly presented signified. The hieroglyphic *graphie* is already allegorical. The gesture which speaks before words [*dit la parole avant les mots*] and which "argues with the eyes," is the moment of savage writing.

> Consider ancient history; it is full of such ways of appealing to the eye, each of them more effective than all the discourse that might have *replaced it*. An object held up before speaking will arouse the imagination, excite curiosity, hold the mind in suspense, in expectation of what will be said. I have noticed that Italians and Provencals, among whom gesture ordinarily precedes discourse, use this as a way of drawing attention and of pleasing their listeners. *But in the most vigorous language, everything is said symbolically, before one actually speaks*. Tarquin, or Thrasybulus lopping off poppies; Alexander applying his seal to the mouth of his favorite, Diogenes promenading in front of Zeno: do they not speak more effectively than with words? What verbal circumlocution would express the same idea as well?[52] (Italics added.) [*Essay*, pp. 6–7]

How can the language of gesture or sight express passion here, and need elsewhere? The "contradiction" between these different texts responds to the unity of an intention and the necessity of a constraint.

1. Rousseau speaks the desire of immediate presence. When the latter is *better represented* by the range of the voice and reduces dispersion, he praises living speech, which is the language of the passions. When the immediacy of presence is *better represented* by the proximity and rapidity of the gesture and the glance, he praises the most savage writing, which does not represent oral representation: the hieroglyph.

2. This concept of writing designates the place of unease, of the regu-

lated incoherence within conceptuality, both beyond the *Essay* and beyond Rousseau. This incoherence would apply to the fact that the unity of need and passion (with the entire system of associated significations) constantly effaces the limit that Rousseau obstinately sketches and recalls. Rousseau *declares* this backbone, without which the entire conceptual organism would break up, and *wishes to think it* as a distinction; he *describes* it as a supplementary differance. This constrains in its graphics the strange unity of passion and need.

How does writing reveal it? How is writing, like pity, for example, both in nature and outside of it? Like the awakening of imagination before this, what does the awakening of writing signify here, if it belongs neither to nature nor to its other?

Writing precedes and follows speech, it comprehends it. This is already true from the only point of view that concerns us here: that of the structure of the *Essay*. On the one hand, the theory of writing follows the genealogy of speech and is proposed as a sort of supplementary appendix. Once one has described the passional origin of speech, one can accessorily consider that accessory which is writing, in order to draw from it some supplementary information about the state of languages. The entire chapter "On Script" is opened and governed by this declared project. After having summarized the progress of languages and the movement of supplementarity and substitution which holds it to its law ("one substitutes" new articulations for accents that efface themselves, "one substitutes ideas for sentiments," etc.), Rousseau introduces a new development: "Another way of comparing languages and determining their relative antiquity is to consider their script, and reason inversely from the degree of perfection of this art" [p. 16].

Yet writing had to appear even before there was a question of speech and its passional origin. The movement of the magic wand and the hieroglyph expressed a passion before the passion that draws out "the primitive voices"; and as writing will also be recognized as the language of need, it will have stated need before need. The first allusion to writing holds itself out of reach of all *distinction*, if not of all differance of need from passion. The *advantage* of writing requires a new conceptuality.

The metaphoric origin of speech opens an eye, one might say, at the center of language. And the passion that draws out the first voices relates to the image. The visibility inscribed on the act of birth of the voice is not purely perceptive, it signifies. Writing is the eve of speech. That appears also from the first chapter.

Darius, engaged with his army in Scythia, receives from the King of Scythia a frog, a bird, a mouse, and five arrows. The herald makes the presentation in silence and departs. That terrible harangue was understood; and Darius returned to his own country as quickly as he could. *Substitute a letter* [namely, a phonetic script] for this sign: the more menancing it is, the less frightening will it be. It will be no more than a boast, which would draw merely a smile from Darius.[53] [*Essay*, p. 7]

And after another series of Biblical and Greek examples,

Thus one speaks more effectively to the eye than to the ear. There is no one who does not feel the truth of Horace's judgment in this regard. Clearly the most eloquent speeches are those containing the most imagery; and sounds are never more *forceful* than when they produce the effects of colors. (Italics added.) [*Essay*, p. 8]

Decisive consequence: eloquence depends upon the image. What is already announced is "That the First Language Had to Be Figurative" (title of Chapter 3). The metaphor within spoken language draws its *energy* from the visible and from a sort of oral picto-hieroglyphics. Now if one considers that Rousseau elsewhere associates visibility, space, painting, writing, etc., with the loss of passional energy, with need and sometimes with death, one must surely decide within, the *advantage of writing*, in favor of the unity of heterogeneous or so-declared values. But Rousseau cannot declare this unity of the advantage of writing. He can only describe it clandestinely as he plays with the different parts of his discourse. Even though he contradicts himself, he places writing on the side of need and speech on the side of passion. In the passage that we have just cited, it is clear that it is a question of passional signs. That will be confirmed further along when hieroglyphic script will be defined as "impassioned language." Yet if "sounds never have more energy than when they make the effect of colors," it is not that color or that space as such which speaks to passion. Rousseau unexpectedly reverses the order of the demonstration: only the spoken word has the power of expressing or exciting passion.

But when it is a question of stirring the heart and inflaming the passions, it is an altogether different matter. The successive impressions of discourse, which strike a redoubled blow, produce *a different feeling from that of the continuous presence of the same object*, which can be taken in at a single glance. Imagine someone in a painful situation that is fully known; as you watch the afflicted person, you are not likely to weep. But give him time to tell you what he feels and soon you will burst into tears. It is solely in this way that the scenes of a tragedy produce their effect.* Pantomime without discourse will leave you nearly tranquil; discourse without gesture will bring tears from you. *The passions have*

* I have said elsewhere why *feigned misfortunes touch us more than real ones*. There is a type that weeps at a tragedy, yet has never had any pity for the suffering. The invention of theater is remarkable for inflating our pride with all the virtues in which we are entirely lacking. [*Essay*, pp. 8–9] [Rousseau's footnote.]

their gestures, but they also have their accents; and these accents, which thrill us, *these tones of voice that cannot fail to be heard, penetrate to the very depths of the heart, carrying there the emotions they wring from us, forcing us in spite of ourselves* to feel what we hear. *We conclude that while visible signs can render a more exact imitation, sounds more effectively arouse interest.*

In this argument I have emphasized the two controlling strands.

Right at first the sound touches us, interests us, impassions us all the more because *it penetrates us*. It is the element of interiority because its essence, its own energy, implies that its reception is obligatory. As we noted above, I can close my eyes, I can avoid being touched by that which I see and that which is perceptible at a distance. But my passivity and my passion are totally open to "accents to which one may not conceal one's organ," which "penetrate through it to the bottom of one's heart, and carry there in spite of us the movements which draw them forth." Voice penetrates into me violently, it is the privileged route for forced entry and interiorization, whose reciprocity produecs itself in the "hearing-oneself-speak," in the structure of the voice and of interlocution.[54]

This violence obliges Rousseau to temper the praise of passion and to suspect this complicity between voice and heart. But another violence complicates this scheme even more. Within the voice, the presence of the object already disappears. The self-presence of the voice and of the heading-oneself speak conceals the very thing that visible space allows to be placed before us. The thing disappearing, the voice substitutes an acoustic sign for it which can, in the place of the object taken away, penetrate profoundly into me, to lodge there "in the depth of the heart." It is the only way of interiorizing the phenomenon; by transforming it into *akoumène*; which supposes an originary synergy and an originary synesthesia; but which also supposes that the disappearance of presence in the form of the object, the being-before-the-eyes or being-at-hand, installs a sort of fiction, if not a lie, at the very origin of speech. Speech never gives the thing itself, but a simulacrum that touches us more profoundly than the truth, "strikes" us more effectively. Another ambiguity in the appreciation of speech. It is not the presence of the object which moves us but its phonic sign: "The successive impressions of discourse, which strike a redoubled blow, produce a different feeling from that of the continuous presence of the same object. . . . I have said elsewhere why feigned misfortunes touch us more than real ones." If the theater is condemned, it is thus not because it is, as its name implies, a place of spectacle; it is because it makes us hear and understand.

Thus is explained the nostalgia for a society of need that Rousseau disqualifies so harshly elsewhere. Dream of a mute society, of a society before the origin of languages, that is to say, strictly speaking, a society before society.

This leads me to think that if the only needs we ever experienced were physical, we should most likely never have been able to speak; we would fully express our meanings by the language of gesture alone. We would have been able to establish societies little different from those we have, or such as would have been better able to achieve their goals. We would have been able to institute laws, to choose leaders, to invent arts, to establish commerce, and to do, in a word, almost as many things as we do with the help of speech. Without fear of jealousy, the secrets of oriental gallantry are passed across the more strictly guarded harems in the epistolary language of salaams. The mutes of great nobles understand each other, and understand everything that is said to them by means of signs, just as well as one can understand anything said in discourse. [*Essay*, p. 9]

With reference to this society of mute writing, the advent of speech resembles a catastrophe, an unpredictable misfortune. Nothing made it necessary. At the end of the *Essay*, this pattern is exactly inverted.

Things are further complicated if one considers that the language of needs is a natural language and that it would be difficult to find a sure criterion for distinguishing between this mute society and animal society. One does then perceive that the only difference between what Rousseau wished to consider the fixity of animal language and the progressiveness of human languages is not dependent on any one organ, any one sense, is not to be found in either the visible or the audible order. It is once again the *power of substituting one organ for another, of articulating space and time,* sight and voice, hand and spirit, it is this *faculty of supplementarity* which is the true "origin"—or nonorigin—of languages: articulation in general, as articulation of nature and of convention, of nature and all its others. This is what one must emphasize right from the close of Chapter I:

It appears again, by the same observations, that the invention of the art of communicating our ideas depends less upon the organs we use in such communication than it does upon a power proper to man, according to which he uses his organs in this way, and which, *if he lacked these, would lead him to use others to the same end.* Give man a structure [organically] as crude as you please: doubtless he will acquire fewer ideas, but if only he has some means of contact with his fellow men, by means of which one can act and another can sense, he will finally succeed in communicating whatever ideas he might have. Animals have a more than sufficient structure for such communication, but none of them has ever made use of it. This seems to me a quite characteristic difference. That those animals which *live and work in common, such as beavers, ants, bees, have some natural language for communicating among themselves, I would not question.* There is even reason to think that the speech of beavers and ants is *by gesture; i.e., it is only visual.* If so, such languages are natural, not acquired. The animals that speak them possess them a-borning: they all have them, and they are everywhere the same. They are entirely unchanging and make not the slightest progress. Conventional language is characteristic of man alone. (Italics added.) [*Essay*, p. 10]

Animal language—and animality in general—represents here the still living myth of fixity, of symbolic incapacity, of nonsupplementarity. If we consider the *concept* of animality not in its content of understanding or misunderstanding but in its specific *function*, we shall see that it must locate a moment of *life* which knows nothing of symbol, substitution, lack and supplementary addition, etc.—everything, in fact, whose appearance and play I wish to describe here. A life that has not yet broached the play of supplementarity and which at the same time has not yet let itself be violated by it: a life without differance and without articulation.

The Inscription of the Origin. This detour was necessary for recapturing the function of the concept of *articulation*. It broaches language: it opens speech as institution born of passion but it threatens song as original speech. It pulls language toward need and reason—accomplices—and therefore lends itself to writing more easily. The more articulated a language is, the less accentuated it is, the more rational it is, the less musical it is, and the less it loses by being written, the better it expresses need. It becomes Nordic.

Rousseau wants us to think of this movement as an accident. He describes it however in its originary necessity. This unhappy accident is also a "natural progress." It does not come unexpectedly upon a constituted song, nor does it surprise a full music. Before articulation, therefore, we now know, there is no speech, no song, and thus no music. Passion could not be expressed or imitated without articulation. The "cry of nature" (second *Discourse*), the "simple sounds [that] emerge naturally from the throat" (*Essay* 4), do not make a language because articulation has not yet played there. "Natural sounds are inarticulate" (*Essay* 4). Convention has its hold only upon articulation, which pulls language out of the cry, and increases itself with consonants, tenses, and quantity. *Thus language is born out of the process of its own degeneration.* That is why, in order to convey Rousseau's *descriptive* procedure, which does not wish to restore the facts but merely to measure a deviation, it is perhaps imprudent to call by the name of zero degree or simple origin that out of which the deviation is measured or the structure outlined. Zero degree or origin implies that the commencement be simple, that it not be at the same time the beginning of a degeneration, that it be possible to think it in the form of presence in general, whether it be a modified presence or not, whether it be past event or permanent essence. To speak of simple origin, it must also be possible to measure deviation according to a simple axis and in a single direction. Is it still necessary to recall that nothing in Rousseau's description authorizes us to do so?

To speak of origin and zero degree in fact comments on Rousseau's declared intention and it corrects on that point more than one classical or hasty reading. But in spite of that declared intention, Rousseau's discourse lets itself be constrained by a complexity which always has the form of the supplement of or from the origin. His declared intention is not annulled by this but rather *inscribed* within a system which it no longer dominates. The desire for the origin becomes an indispensable and indestructible function situated within a syntax without origin. Rousseau would like to separate originarity from supplementarity. All the rights constituted by our logos are on his side: it is unthinkable and intolerable that what has the name *origin* should be no more than a point situated within the system of supplementarity. The latter in fact wrenches language from its condition of origin, from its conditional or its future of origin, from that which it must (ought to) have been and what it has never been; it could only have been born by suspending its relation to all origin. Its history is that of the supplement of (from) origin: of the originary substitute and the substitute of the origin. Let us observe the play of the tenses and modes at the end of Chapter 4 which describes the ideal of the language of origin:

Since natural sounds are inarticulate, words *would have* few articulations. Interposing some consonants to fill the gaps between vowels *would suffice* to make them fluid and easy to pronounce. On the other hand, the sounds would be very varied, and the diversity of accents for each sound *would further multiply* them. Quantity and rhythm *would account for* still further combinations. Since sounds, accents, and number, which are natural, would leave little to articulation, which is conventional, it *would be sung* rather than spoken. Most of the root words would be imitative sounds or accents of passion, or effects of sense objects. It *would contain* many onomatopoeic expressions. This language *would have* many synonyms for expressing the same thing according to various relationships.* It *would have* few adverbs and abstract names for expressing these same relationships. It *would have* many augmentatives, diminutives, composite words, expletive particles to indicate the cadence of sentences and fullness of phrases. It *would have* many irregularities and anomalies. It *would deemphasize* grammatical analogy for euphony, number, harmony, and beauty of sounds. Instead of arguments, it *would have* aphorisms. It *would persuade* without convincing, and *would represent* without reasoning. [Follows the customary extrinsic or archaeological reference.] It *would resemble* Chinese in certain respects, Greek and Arabic in others. If you understand these ideas in all their ramifications, you will find that Plato's *Cratylus* is not as ridiculous as it appears to be (italics added) [pp. 15–16].

* It is said that the Arabs have more than a thousand different words for *camel* and more than a hundred for *sword*, etc. [Rousseau's footnote.]

The stage thus described in the conditional is *already* that of a language that has broken with gesture, need, animality, etc. But of a language that *has not yet* been corrupted by articulation, convention, supplementarity. The time of that language is the unstable, inaccessible, mythic limit between that *already* and this *not-yet*: time of a language *being born*, just as there was a time for "society being born." Neither before nor after the origin.

After having observed this play of the temporal mode, let us continue with our reading. The chapter "On Script" follows immediately. The title alone separates the quotation above from the one following. I stress the sense of certain verbs and the mode of all the verbs:

Anyone who studies the history and progress of the tongues will see that the more the words become monotonous, the more the consonants multiply; that, as accents fall into disuse and quantities are neutralized, they are *replaced* [*supplée*] by grammatical combinations and new articulations. But only the pressure of time brings these changes about. To the degree that needs multiply, that affairs become complicated, that light is shed [knowledge is increased], language changes its character. It becomes more regular and less passionate. It *substitutes* ideas for feelings. It no longer speaks to the heart but to reason. For that very reason, accent diminishes, articulation increases. Language becomes more exact and clearer, but more prolix, duller and colder. This progression seems to me entirely natural [p. 16].

Thus supplementarity makes possible all that constitutes the property of man: speech, society, passion, etc. But what is this property [*propre*] of man? On the one hand, it is that of which the possibility must be thought before man, and outside of him. Man allows himself to be announced to himself after the fact of supplementarity, which is thus not an attribute—accidental or essential—of man. For on the other hand, supplementarity, which *is nothing*, neither a presence nor an absence, is neither a substance nor an essence of man. It is precisely the play of presence and absence, the opening of this play that no metaphysical or ontological concept can comprehend. Therefore this property [*propre*] of man is not a property of man: it is the very dislocation of the proper in general: it is the dislocation of the characteristic, the proper in general, the impossibility—and therefore the desire—of self-proximity; the impossibility and therefore the desire of pure presence. That supplementarity is not a characteristic or property of man does not mean only, and in an equally radical manner, that it is not a characteristic or property; but also that its play precedes what one calls man and extends outside of him. Man *calls himself* man only by drawing limits excluding his other from the play of supplementarity: the purity of nature, of animality, primitivism, childhood, madness, divinity. The approach to these limits is at once feared as a threat of death, and desired as access to a life without differance. The history of man *calling himself* man is the articulation of *all* these limits among themselves. All concepts determining a non-supplementarity (nature, animality, primitivism, childhood, madness, divinity, etc.) have evidently no truth-value. They belong—moreover, with the idea of truth itself—to an epoch of supplementarity. They have meaning only within a closure of the game.

Writing will appear to us more and more as another name for this structure of supplementarity. If one takes into account that, according to Rousseau himself, articulation makes possible both speech and writing (a language is necessarily articulated and the more articulated it is, the more it lends itself to writing) one should be assured of what Saussure hesitated to say in what we know of the *Anagrams*, namely, that there are no phonemes before the grapheme. That is, before that which operates as a principle of death within speech.

Perhaps now one will better grasp the situation of Rousseau's discourse with reference to this concept of the supplement, and by the same token, the status of the analysis that I am attempting here. It does not suffice to say that Rousseau thinks the supplement without thinking it, that he does not match his saying and his meaning, his descriptions and his declarations. One must still organize this separation and this contradiction. Rousseau uses the word and describes the thing. But now we know that what concerns us here belongs neither to word nor to thing. Word and thing are referential limits that only the supplementary structure can produce and mark.

Using the word and describing the thing, Rousseau in a way displaces and deforms the sign "supplement," the unity of the signifier and the signified, as it is articulated among nouns (supplement, substitute [*supplément, suppléant*]), verbs (to supply, to be substituted [*suppléer, se substituer*], etc.) and adjectives (supplementary, suppletory [*supplémentaire, supplétif*]) and makes the signifieds play on the register of plus or minus. But these displacements and deformations are regulated by the contradictory unity—itself supplementary—of a desire. As in the dream, as Freud analyzes it, incompatibles are simultaneously admitted as soon as it is a matter of satisfying a desire, in spite of the principle of identity, or of the excluded third party—the logical time of consciousness. Using a word other than dream, inaugurating a conceptuality which would no longer belong to the metaphysics of presence or consciousness (opposing wakefulness and dream even within Freud's discourse), it would be necessary to define a space in which this regulated "contradiction" has been possible and can be described. What is called "history of ideas" would have to begin by disengaging this space before articulating its field in terms of other fields. These are, of course, questions that can only be asked.

What are the two contradictory possibilities that Rousseau wishes to retain simultaneously? And how does he do it? He wishes on the one hand to *affirm*, by giving it a positive value, everything of which articulation is the principle or everything with which it constructs a system (passion, language, society, man, etc.). But he intends to affirm simultaneously all that is cancelled by articulation (accent, life, energy, passion yet again, and so on). The supplement being the articulated structure of these two possibilities, Rousseau can only decompose them and dissociate them into two simple units, logically contradictory yet allowing an intact purity to both the negative and the positive. And yet Rousseau, caught, like the logic of identity, *within* the graphic of supplementarity, says what he does not wish to say, describes what he does not wish to conclude: that the positive (is) the negative, life (is) death, presence (is) absence and that this repetitive supplementarity is not comprised in any dialectic, at least if that concept is governed, as it always has been, by a horizon of presence. Moreover, Rousseau is not alone in being caught in the graphic of supplementarity. All meaning and therefore all discourse is caught there, particularly and by a singular turn, the discourse of the metaphysics within which Rousseau's concepts move. And when Hegel will proclaim the unity of absence and presence, of nonbeing and being, dialectics or history will continue to be, at least on the level of discourse that we have called Rousseau's wishing-to-say, a movement of mediation between two full presences. Eschatological parousia is also the presence of the full speech, bringing together all its differences and its articulations within the consciousness (of) self of the logos. Consequently, before asking the necessary questions about the historical situation of Rousseau's text, we must locate all the signs of its appurtenance to the metaphysics of presence, from Plato to Hegel, rhythmed by the articulation of presence upon self-presence. The unity of this metaphysical tradition should be respected in its general permanence through all the marks of appurtenance, the genealogical sequences, the stricter routes of causality that organize Rousseau's text. We must recognize, prudently and as a preliminary, what this historicity amounts to; without this, what one would inscribe within a narrower structure would not be a text and above all not Rousseau's text. It does not suffice to understand Rousseau's text within that implication of the epochs of metaphysics or of the West—what I only diffidently sketch here. We must also know that this history of metaphysics, to which the concept of history itself returns, belongs to an ensemble for which the name history is no longer suitable. All this interplay of implications is so complex that it would be more than imprudent to wish to assure oneself as to how much of it is proper to a text [*revient en propre à un texte*], for example, Rousseau's. That is not only difficult, it is in fact impossible; the question which one professes to answer here has undoubtedly no meaning outside of the metaphysics of presence, of the proper [*propre*] and of the subject. There is not, strictly speaking, a text whose author or subject is Jean-Jacques Rousseau.

From this principal proposition, it remains to draw the rigorous consequences, without confusing all the subordinate propositions under the pretext that their meaning and their limits are already contested at their root.

The Neume. We shall, then, examine how Rousseau operates when, for example, he attempts to define the limit of possibility of the thing whose impossibility he describes: the natural voice or the inarticulate language. No longer the animal cry before the birth of language; but not yet the articulated language, already shaped and undermined by absence and death. Between the prelinguistic and the linguistic, between cry and speech, animal and man, nature and society, Rousseau looks for a limit "being born," and he gives it several determinations. There are at least two of them that have the same function. They relate to childhood and to God. In each, two contradictory predicates are united: it is a matter of language uncontaminated by supplementarity.

The model of this impossible "natural voice" is first that of childhood. Described in the conditional in the *Essay*—let us recall the analysis of the "natural voices" that "are not articulated"—consider it now in *Emile*. The *alibi* and the *in illo tempore* are no longer Chinese or Greek, but the child:

> *All our languages are the result of art.* It has long been a subject of inquiry whether there ever was a *natural language* common to all; no doubt there is, *and it is the language of children before they begin* [*have learned*] *to speak. This language is inarticulate, but it has tone, stress, and meaning. The use of our own language has led us to neglect it so far as to forget it altogether.* Let us study children and we shall soon learn it afresh from them. Nurses can teach us this language; they understand all their nurslings say to them, they answer them, and keep up long conversations with them; and though they use words, these words are quite useless. *It is not the sense of the word, but its accompanying intonation* [*accent*] *that is understood* (p. 45; italics added) [p. 32].

To speak before knowing how to speak, such is the limit toward which Rousseau obstinately guides his repetition of origin. This limit is indeed that of nonsupplementarity but as there must already be language there, the supplement must announce itself without having been produced, lack and absence must have begun without beginning. Without the summons of the supplement, the child would not speak at all: if he did not suffer, if he lacked nothing, he would not call, he would not speak. But if supplementarity had simply been produced, if it had really begun, the child would speak knowing how to speak. *The child speaks before knowing how to speak.* He has language, but what is lacking in it is the power of *replacing itself,* of substituting one sign for another, one organ of expression for another; what he lacks is, as the *Essay* said, let us recall, "a power proper to man, according to which he uses his organs in this way, and which, if he lacked these, would lead him to use others to the same end" [p. 10]. The child—the concept of the child—is the concept of one who has no more than one language because he has only one organ. And that signifies that his lack, his unease itself, is unique and uniform, not countenancing any substitution or any operation of supplementing. Such is Rousseau's child. He has no language because he has only one:

> He has only one language because he has, so to say, only one kind of discomfort. In the imperfect state of his sense organs he does not distingiush their several impressions; all ills produce one feeling of sorrow. (p. 46) [*Emile*, p. 32]

The child will know how to speak when one form of his unease can be substituted for another; then he will be able to slip from one language to another, slide one sign under another, play with the signifying substance; he will enter into the order of the supplement, here determined as the human order: he will no longer weep, he will know how to say "I hurt."

> When children begin to talk they cry less. This progress is quite natural; one language supplants another. . . . When once Emile has said, "It hurts me," it will take a very sharp pain to make him cry. (p. 59) [*Emile*, p. 41]

To speak before knowing how: childhood is good because speech is good, the property [*propre*] of man. The child speaks. Childhood is good because the knowledge of speech comes only with the evil of articulation. The child does not know how to speak. But childhood is not good since already it speaks; and it is not good because it does not have the property and the good of man: knowledge of speech. Whence the regulated instability of the judgments on childhood: for better and for worse, it is sometimes on the side of animality, sometimes on the side of humanity. That the child speaks without knowing how to speak, that may be to his credit; but he also speaks without knowing how to sing: which is why he is no longer an animal that neither speaks nor sings, and not yet a man who both speaks and sings:

> Man has three kinds of voice, the speaking or articulate voice, the singing or melodious voice, and the pathetic or accented voice, which serves as the language of the passions, and gives life to song and speech. The child has these three voices, just as the man has them, but he does not know how to use them in combination. Like us, he laughs, cries, laments, shrieks, and groans, but he does not know how to combine these inflections with speech or song. These three voices find their best expression in perfect music. Children are incapable of such music, and their singing lacks feeling. In the same way their spoken language lacks expression; they shout, but they do not speak with emphasis, and there is as little power in their voice as there is emphasis in their speech. (*Emile*, pp. 161–62) [p. 113]

Articulation, wherever one finds it, is indeed articulation: that of the members and the organs, differance (in the) (self-same) [*propre*] body. Is not breath seemingly the most appropriate thing for effacing this differance in natural expression? A speaking and singing breath, breath of language which is nonetheless inarticulate.

Such a breath cannot have a human origin and a human destination. It is no longer on the way to humanity like the language of the child, but is rather on the way to superhumanity. Its principle and its end are theological, as the voice and providence of nature. It is on this onto-theological model that Rousseau regulates his repetitions of origin. With this exemplary model of a pure breath (*pneuma*) and of an intact life, of a song and an inarticulate language, of speech without spacing, we have, even if it is placeless [*atopique*] or utopian, a paradigm suitable to our measure. We can name and define it. It is the *neume*: pure vocalization, form of an inarticulate song without speech, whose name means breath, which is inspired in us by God and may address only Him. The *Dictionary of Music* defines it as such:

NEUME. s.f. A term in church-music. The neume is a kind of short recapitulation of the air in a mode, which is made at the end of an antiphon, by a simple variety of sounds, and without joining to them any words. The Catholics authorize this singular custom on a passage of St. Augustine, who says, that no words being possible to be worthy of pleasing God, it is laudable to address him in a confused music of jubilation. "For to whom is such a jubilation suitable, unless to an ineffable Being? and how can we celebrate this ineffable Being, *since we cannot be silent, or find any thing in our transports which can express them, unless unarticulated sounds?*" (Italics added.) [pp. 270–71]

To speak before knowing how to speak, not to be able either to be silent or to speak, this limit of origin is indeed that of a pure presence, present enough to be living, to be felt in pleasure [*jouissance*] but pure enough to have remained unblemished by the work of difference, inarticulate enough for self-delight [*jouissance de soi*] not to be corrupted by interval, discontinuity, alterity. Indeed, Rousseau thinks that this experience of a continual present is *accorded* only to God: given to God or to those whose hearts accord and agree with God's. It is indeed this accord, this resemblance of the divine and the human that inspires him when he dreams, in the *Reveries*, of that experience of a time reduced to presence, "*where the present lasts forever, without marking its duration in any way, and without any trace of succession*" [p. 113].

Let us reread all these pages: they speak the sorrow of time torn in its presence by memory and anticipation. The pleasure [*jouissance*] of a continuous and inarticulate presence is a *nearly* impossible experience: "scarcely is there, in our most living delights, a moment where the heart can truly say to us: *I wish that this moment should last forever*" [pp. 112–13]. The heart is not on organ because it is not inscribed with a system of differences and articulations. It is not an organ because it is the organ of pure presence. Rousseau experienced this nearly impossible state on the Island of St. Pierre. Much has been written[55] of that description on the themes of nature, water, flowing, etc. Comparing it to pure vocalization, to the pure vowels of the natural language and of the neume, I shall extract from it only the system of four significations.

The pleasure [*jouissance*] of self-presence, pure auto-affection, uncorrupted by any outside, is *accorded* to God:

> What is the nature of pleasure in such a situation? Nothing external to oneself, nothing except oneself and one's own [*propre*] existence; so long as this state lasts, one suffices to oneself, like God [pp. 113–14].

There must be *movement*, life, [*jouissance*] delight in time, self-presence there. But that movement should be *without intervals*, without difference, without discontinuity:

> There should be neither an absolute repose nor too much agitation, but a uniform and moderate movement which should have neither shocks nor intervals. Without movement, life is only a lethargy. If the movement is unequal or too strong, it awakens. . . . The movement which does not come from without, then, is made within us.

This movement is an *inarticulate speech*, a speech before words, alive enough to speak, pure, interior and homogeneous enough to relate to no object, to gather into itself no mortal difference, no negativity; it is a charm and therefore a song:

> If the movement is unequal or too strong, it awakens; in recalling us to environing objects, it destroys the charm of the reverie and draws us out of ourselves to put us in an instant under the yoke of fortune and man and to bring us back to the feeling of our unhappiness. An absolute silence leads to sadness; it offers us an image of death [p. 115].

Yet, if our hearts are pure enough for it, we live this almost impossible experience, that is almost alien to the constraints of supplementarity, already as a supplement, as a *compensation* [*dédommagement*]. And it is the difference between our experience and that of God Himself:

> But an unfortunate who has been withdrawn from human society, and who can do nothing here below that is useful or good for himself or for others, can find in that state consolations [*dédommagements*] for all human enjoyments which fortune and man cannot remove from him. It is true that these consolations cannot be felt by all souls, nor in all situations. It is necessary that the heart should be at peace and that no passion should come to trouble the calm [p. 114].

The difference between God and ourselves is that God distributes, and we receive, compensations. Rousseau's entire moral theology implies, and the *Vicar* often uses this word, that divine solicitude can always procure just *compensations*. God alone may dispense with the supplement that He dispenses. He is the dispensation of (exemption from) the supplement.

The neume, the spell of self-presence, inarticulate experience of time, tantamount to saying: *utopia*. Such a language—since a language must be involved—does not, properly speaking, take place. It does not know articulation, which cannot take place without spacing and without organization of spaces. There is no language before differences of locale.

The four chapters on "General and Local Difference in the Origin of Languages" (8), "Formation of the Southern Languages" (9), "Formation of the Languages of the North" (10) and "Reflections on these Differences" (11) give the lie by their description to what seems required by the declared organization of the *Essay*. What they describe is that before articulation, that is to say before local difference, there is nothing that one may call language. For we shall see that local differences between the two poles of language always amount to an articulatory play. One cannot therefore describe the structure or the general essence of the language without taking topography into account. Yet that is what Rousseau wanted to do by dealing with language in general before beginning the chapter on the general and local difference in the origin of languages. In doing so, he had believed it possible to dissociate structure from origin, or structural origin from local origin: "All that I have said so far applies to primitive tongues in general, and to such development as is due merely to the passage of time. But it does not explain either their origin or their differences" [*Essay*, p. 30]. Thus opens the eighth chapter.

If it is true that hereafter articulation measures local difference and that nothing precedes it within language, can one conclude from it that in the classification of languages, in their local or geographic distribution, in the structure of their development, there is no more than a play of correspondences, situations, relations? Can one conclude from it that there is no absolute, immobile, and natural center? There again, we must distinguish between description and declaration.

Rousseau *declares* the center: there is one single origin, one single zero point in the history of languages. It is the South, the warmth of life, the energy of passion. In spite of the apparent symmetry of the two chapters, in spite of that *description* of a double origin of which we have spoken above, Rousseau *does not wish* to speak of the two poles of formation: only of a formation and a deformation. Language truly forms itself only in the South. The originary center of language is well reflected in the center of the *Essay*, in that Chapter 9, which is by far the longest and richest of all.

In spite of appearances, and contrary to what one might think, Rousseau does not here simply stop putting aside all the facts. No doubt the factual content is richer than in the second *Discourse*. But it functions as a structural index, with the "consciousness of example" which regulates the phenomenological intuition of essence. The first lines, the first note, already authorize this interpretation:

In primitive times* the sparse human population had no more social structure than the family, no laws but those of nature, no language, but that of gesture and some inarticulate sounds.

* *I consider primitive the period of time from the dispersion of men to any period of the human race that might be taken as determining an epoch.* [Essay, p. 31]

The expression "primitive times," and all the evidence which will be used to describe them, refer to no date, no event, no chronology. One can vary the facts without modifying the structural invariant. It is a time before time. In every possible historical structure, there seemingly would be a prehistoric, presocial, and also prelinguistic stratum, that one ought always to be able to lay bare. Dispersion, absolute solitude, mutism, experience irrevocably destined to a prereflexive sensation, immediate, without memory, without anticipation, without imagination, without the power of reason or comparison, such would be the virgin soil of any social, historic, or linguistic adventure. Recourse to factual illustration, even to events distant from the origin, is purely fictive. Rousseau is sure of that. And when we make objections to him on historical grounds, or when he seems to make similar objections to himself, in the name of verisimilitude or the compossibility of facts, he wheels around, reminds us that he could not care less about facts when he describes the origin and that he has given a definition of "primitive times."

I am told that Cain was a farmer and Noah planted grapes. Why not? They were solitaries. What did they have to fear? Besides, this does not conflict with my thesis. I have said what I understand by primitive times. [*Essay*, p. 34]

We have here another way into the problem of the relationships between the *Essay* and the second *Discourse* from the point of view of the state of pure nature. There is nothing before the "primitive times" and therefore no rigorously determinable discrepancy between the two texts. We suggested it above in connection with the age of huts. Now we must be more precise.

At first reading, the discrepancy seems incontestable. The "savage" of the *Discourse* wanders in the forests "without industry, without speech, and without home" [p. 188]. The barbarian of the *Essay* has a family, a cabin and a language, even if he is reduced to "gesture and some inarticulate sounds" [p. 31].

But these discordancies do not seem pertinent from the point of view that interests us. Rousseau is not describing two different and successive states. The family, in the *Essay*, is not a society. It does not limit the primitive dispersion. "In primitive times the *sparse* human population had no more social structure than the family." Which signifies that this family was not a society. It was, as J. Mosconi has called it (cf. supra), a preinstitutional phenomenon, purely natural and biological. It was the indispensable condition of that process of generations that the *Discourse* also recognized ("the generations multiplied uselessly"). This natural milieu, entailing no institution, had no *true language*. And after having attributed "gesture and some inarticulate sounds" to them as language, Rousseau is more precise in a note:

> Genuine languages are not at all of domestic origin. They can be established only under a more general, more durable covenant. The American savages hardly speak at all except outside their homes. Each keeps silent in his hut, speaking to his family by signs. And these signs are used infrequently, for a savage is less disquieted, less impatient than a European; he has fewer needs and he is careful to meet them himself.

But to efface the contradiction or rigorous discrepancy between the two texts, one does not have to reduce them to repetitions or overlappings of each other. From one to the other, an emphasis is displaced, a continuous sliding is in operation. Or rather, without imputing any order of succession there, we may say that from the *Discourse* to the *Essay* the sliding movement is toward continuity. The *Discourse* wants to *mark the beginning*: it therefore sharpens and radicalizes the characteristics of virginity within the state of pure nature. The *Essay* would make us *sense the beginnings,* the movement by which "men sparsely placed on the face of the earth," continuously wrench themselves away, within a society *being born,* from the state of pure nature. It captures man as he *passes* into birth, in that subtle transition from origin to genesis. These two projects do not contradict each other, one does not even have priority over the other, and, as I have noted above, the description of pure nature in the *Discourse* made room within itself for such a transition.

As always, it is the ungraspable limit of the *almost.* Neither nature nor society, but *almost* society. Society in the process of birth. The moment when man, no longer belonging, or almost not belonging, to the state of pure nature (which, the *Discourse* clearly says, "no longer exists, perhaps never did exist, and probably will never exist; and of which it is, nevertheless, necessary to have true ideas, in order to form a proper judgment of our present state," "Preface") [p. 155], holds himself still short of society, or almost so. It is the only means of restoring the becoming-culture of nature. The family, which Hegel too will call prehistoric, the hut, the language of gestures and inarticulate sounds, are the indications of that *almost.* The "savage" life of hunters, the "barbaric" and pre-agricultural life of shepherds, correspond to this state of almost-society. As in the *Discourse,* so in the *Essay* society depends upon agriculture and agriculture upon metallurgy.[56]

Rousseau encounters here the problem of references to Holy Writ. One can in fact object that "there was already a great deal of agriculture in the time of the patriarchs." The response further clarifies the status of factual history. The facts reported by the Scriptures do not concern the state of pure nature. But instead of bluntly distinguishing between structural origin and empirical origin, a conciliatory Rousseau hides behind a Biblical authority which furnishes him with a structural pattern, by admitting that the patriarchal age is much removed from the origins:

> All this is true. But the ages should not be confused. The patriarchal period that we know is very remote from primitive times. Scripture lists ten intervening generations at a time when men were very long-lived. What did they do during these ten generations? We know nothing about it. *Living almost without society, widely scattered, hardly speaking at all, how could they write?* And given the uniformity of their isolated life, what events would they have transmitted to us? (Italics added.) [*Essay*, pp. 35–36]

Rousseau adds another resource to this Biblical one: the decadence or the re-decline into barbarism after passing through agriculture. Thanks to a catastrophic event annulling progress and compelling repetition, structural analysis can recommence from zero. This confirms that the structural account does not follow a linear genesis but indicates permanent possibilities which may at any moment reappear in the course of a cycle. The nearly-social state of barbarism may *in fact* exist before or after, indeed during and under the state of society.

> Adam spoke, Noah spoke; but it is known that Adam was taught by God himself. In scattering, the children of Noah abandoned agriculture, and the common tongue perished with the first society. That had happened before there was any Tower of Babel. [*Essay*, p. 36]

Because there may always be a resurgence of dispersion, because its threat belongs to the essence of society, the analysis of the state of pure nature and the recourse to natural explanations is always possible. On that point Rousseau's procedure is reminiscent of Condillac's: who, while admitting that language was given by God as a finished product to Adam and Eve, supposes "that some time after the deluge two children, one male, and the other female, wandered about in the deserts, before they understood the use of any sign." "Let me then be permitted to make the supposition, and the question will be to know, in what manner this nation first invented language."[57] This discourse, this detour, had already been practiced by Warburton—Condillac cites him—and what Kant will borrow in

*Die Religion innerhalb der Grenzen der blossen Vernunft** will at least be analogous.

If there was then a slight shift from the *Discourse* to the *Essay*, it is the result of that continuous sliding, that slow transition from pure nature to the birth of society. But this evidence is not so simple. For no continuity from inarticulate to articulate, from pure nature to culture, from plenitude to the play of supplementarity, is possible. The *Essay*, having to describe the *birth*, the being-born of the supplement, must reconcile the two times. *The departure from nature is at once progressive and brutal, instantaneous and interminable*. The structural caesura is trenchant but the historical separation is slow, laborious, progressive, imperceptible. On the issue of that double temporality, the *Essay* again agrees with the *Discourse*.[58]

That "Simple Movement of the Finger." Writing and the Prohibition of Incest. Society at birth is effectively subjected, according to the *Essay*, to a sort of law of three conditions. But, among the "three conditions of man considered in relation to society" (Chap. 9) or "the three different stages according to which one can consider man assembled into a nation" (Chap. 5), only the last marks man's access to himself within society. It is the condition of civil and ploughing man. The two preceding states (savage hunter and barbaric shepherd) still belong to a sort of prehistory. That which primarily interests Rousseau is therefore the passage from the second into the third condition.

This passage was in fact extremely slow, uncertain, and precarious, but since nothing in the previous state contained the structural ingredient to produce the subsequent one, the genealogy must describe a rupture or a reversal, a revolution or a catastrophe.

The second *Discourse* often speaks of revolution. If the word "catastrophe" is pronounced only once in the *Essay*, the concept is ever-present there. And it is not, as has been said, a weakness of the system; it is prescribed by the chain of all the other concepts.

Why is the origin of civil man, the origin of languages, etc., the origin, in a word, of the supplementary structure, and, as we shall see, the origin of writing also, catastrophic? Why does it follow an upheaval in the form of reversal, of return, of revolution, of a progressive movement in the form of a regression?

If we follow the anthropo-geographic theme and the schema of the natural explanation that orient the chapters on the formation of languages, it is indeed necessary that such a catastrophe appear there first as

* Translated as *Religion within the Limits of Reason Alone* by Theodore M. Greene and Hoyt H. Hudson (New York, 1960).

a terrestrial revolution. Without it, man would never have left the "golden centuries" of "barbarism." Nothing within the system of barbarism could produce a force of rupture or a reason for leaving it. The causality of the rupture had therefore to be at once natural and exterior to the system of the precivil state. The terrestrial revolution responds to these two exigencies. It is evoked at a point which is strictly the center of the *Essay*:

> The gentle climates, the fat and fertile lands, have been the first to be inhabited and the last in which nations formed, because in them men could do without one another more easily than elsewhere and because there the needs which give rise to social structures make themselves felt later.
>
> Supposing eternal spring on the earth; supposing plenty of water, livestock, and pasture, and supposing that men, as they leave the hands of nature, were once spread out in the midst of all that, I cannot imagine how they would ever be induced to give up their primitive liberty, abandoning the isloated pastoral life so fitted to their natural indolence,[59] to impose upon themselves unnecessarily the labors and the inevitable misery of a social mode of life.
>
> He who willed man to be social, by the touch of a finger shifted the globe's axis into line with the axis of the universe. I see such a *slight movement* changing the face of the earth and deciding the vocation of mankind: in the distance I hear the joyous cries of an insane multitude; I see the building of castles and cities; I see the birth of the arts; I see nations forming, expanding, and dissolving, following each other like ocean waves; I see men gathered together at certain points of their homeland for their mutual development, turning the rest of the world into a hideous desert: fitting monument to social union and the usefulness of the arts. [*Essay*, pp. 38–39; italics added]

The natural indolence of the barbarian is not one empirical characteristic among others. It is an originary determination indispensable to the natural system. It explains that man could not leave barbarism and its golden century spontaneously; he did not have within himself the motion for going further. Rest is natural. The origin and the end are inertia. Since disturbance cannot be born out of rest, it could not encroach upon the state of man and the corresponding terrestrial state, upon the barbarian and upon perpetual spring, except through a catastrophe: the effect of a strictly unpredictable force within the system of the world. That is why the anthropological attribute of indolence must correspond to the geo-logical principle of inertia.

As the catastrophe of disturbance and seasonal differentiation could not be logically produced from within an inert system, one must imagine the unimaginable: a little push entirely exterior to Nature. This apparently "arbitrary"[60] explanation responds to a profound necessity and thus reconciles many exigencies. Negativity, the origin of evil, of society, of articulation, comes *from without*. Presence is surprised by what threatens it. On the other hand it is imperative that this exteriority of evil be nothing or nearly nothing. The little push, the "slight movement" produces a revolution out of nothing. It suffices that the force of the person who touched the axis of the globe with his finger should be exterior to the globe. A nearly nonexistent force is a nearly infinite force when it is strictly alien to the system it sets going. The system offers it no resistance; for antagonistic forces play only within a globe. The slight push is almighty because it shifts the globe in the void. The origin of evil or of history is thus nothing or nearly nothing. Thus is explained the anonymity of Him who inclined the axis of the world with his finger. It is *perhaps not God,* since Divine Providence, of which Rousseau speaks so often, could not have wished the catastrophe and had no need of chance and the void in order to act. But *it is perhaps God* in as much as the force of evil was nothing and supposes no real efficiency. *It is probably* God since His eloquence and His power are at once infinite and encounter no commensurate resistance. Infinite power: the finger that tips a world. Eloquence infinite because silent: a movement of the finger is enough for God to move the world. Divine action conforms to the model of the most eloquent sign, that, for example, which obsesses the *Confessions* and the *Essay*. In both texts, the example of the mute sign is the "simple movement of the finger," the "little sign of the finger,"[61] a "movement of the wand."

Finger or wand is here a metaphor. Not that it designates another thing. It concerns God. God has no hand, he needs no organ. Organic differentiation is the property and the misfortune of man. Here the silent movement does not even replace an elocution. God has no need of a mouth to speak, nor of articulating the voice. The *Fragment* on climates is here more emphatic than the *Essay*:

If the ecliptic had been confused with the equator, perhaps there never would have been the emigration of peoples, and each man, not being able to support a climate other than his native one, would never have left it. To tip the axis of the world with a finger or to say to man: Cover the world and be sociable, was the same thing for Him who needed neither hand to move nor voice to speak (p. 531).

It *certainly concerns God*, for the genealogy of evil is also a theodicy. The catastrophic origin of societies and languages at the same time permitted the actualization of the potential faculties that slept inside man. Only a fortuitous cause could actualize natural powers which did not carry within themselves a sufficient motivation for awakening to their own end. Teleology is in a certain way external; it is this that the catastrophic form of archeology signifies. So much so that between the finger giving movement out of nothing and that auto-affection of imagination which, as we have seen, *awakens* itself out of nothing and then awakens all other potentialities, there is an essential affinity. Imagination is within Nature and yet nothing in Nature can explain its awakening. The supplement to Nature is within Nature as its play. Who will ever say if the lack within nature is *within* nature, if the catastrophe by which Nature *is separated from itself* is still natural? A natural catastrophe conforms to laws in order to overthrow the law.

There is something catastrophic in the movement that brings about the emergence from the state of nature and in the awakening of the imagination which actualizes the natural faculties and essentially actualizes perfectibility. This is a proposition of the *Essay* whose placing or philosophical design is found at the end of the first part of the *Discourse*:

> Having proved that the inequality of mankind is hardly felt, and that its influence is next to nothing in a state of nature, I must next show its origin and trace its progress in the successive developments of the human mind. Having shown that human *perfectibility*, the social virtues, and the other faculties which natural man potentially possessed, could never develop of themselves, but must require the fortuitous concurrence of many foreign causes that might never arise, and without which he would have remained for ever in his primitive condition, I must now collect and consider the different accidents which may have improved the human understanding while depraving the species, and made man wicked while making him sociable; so as to bring him and the world from that distant period to the point at which we now behold them (p. 162) [p. 190].

What we have called external teleology allows the stabilization of a sort of discourse on method: the question of origin involves neither event nor structure; it escapes the simple alternatives of fact and right, of history and essence. The passage from one structure to the other—from the state of nature to that of society for example—cannot be explained by any structural analysis: an external, irrational, catastrophic factum must burst in. Chance is not part of the system. And when history is incapable of determining this fact or facts of this order, philosophy must, by a sort of free and mythic invention, produce factual hypotheses playing the same role, explaining the coming into being of a new structure. It would thus be abusive to reserve facts for history and right or structure for philosophy. So simplistic a dichotomy is intolerable to a form of the question of origin which requires the intervention of "very slight causes" whose "power" is "surprising."

> This will be a sufficient analogy for my not dwelling on the manner in which the lapse of time compensates for the little probability in the events; on the surprising power of trivial causes, when their action is constant; on the impossibility, on the one hand, of destroying certain hypotheses, though on the other we cannot give them the certainty of known matters of fact; on its being within the province of history, when two facts are given as real, and have to be connected by a series of intermediate facts, which are unknown or supposed to be so, to

supply such facts as may connect them; and on its being in the province of philosophy when history is silent, to determine similar facts to serve the same end; and, lastly, on the influence of similarity, which, in the case of events, reduces the facts to a much smaller number of different classes than is commonly imagined. It is enough for me to offer these hints to the consideration of my judges, and to have so arranged that the general reader has no need to consider them at all (pp. 162–63) [pp. 190–91].

The passage from the state of the nature to the state of language and society, the advent of supplementarity, remains then outside the grasp of the simple alternative of genesis and structure, of fact and principle, of historical and philosophical reason. Rousseau explains the supplement in terms of a negativity perfectly exterior to the system it comes to overturn, intervening in it therefore in the manner of an unforeseeable factum, of a null and infinite force, of a natural catastrophe that is neither in nor out of Nature and remains nonrational as the origin of reason must (and not simply irrational like an opacity within the system of rationality). The graphic of supplementarity is irreducible to logic, primarily because it comprehends logic as one of its *cases* and may alone produce its origin. Therefore the catastrophe of supplementarity, as that which procured for Jean-Jacques the "dangerous supplement" and the "fatal advantage" is quite—in the words of the *Confessions*—"inconceivable [to reason]." The possibility of reason, of language, of society, the *supplementary possibility, is inconceivable to reason.* The revolution that gave birth to it cannot be understood according to the patterns of rational necessity. The second *Discourse* speaks of the "fatal accident"; Rousseau is in the process of evoking the budding—barbaric—society between the state of nature and the state of society. It is the moment of the "perpetual spring" of the *Essay*, "the most happy and durable epoch" of the *Discourse*.

The more we reflect on it, the more we shall find that this state was the least subject to revolutions, and altogether the very best man could experience; so that he can have departed from it only through some fatal accident, which, for the public good, should never have happened (p. 171) [pp. 198–99].

What should never have happened had to come to pass. Between these two modalities is therefore inscribed the necessity of non-necessity, the fatality of a cruel game. The supplement can only respond to the nonlogical logic of a game. That game is the play of the world. The world had to be able to play freely on its axis in order that a simple movement of the finger could make it turn upon itself. It is because there was play in the movement of the globe that a force almost nonexistent could, *all at once*, by a silent gesture, give its good or ill fortune to society, history, language, time, relationship to the other, to death, etc. The consequent "luck" and evil of writing will carry with them the sense of play. But Rousseau does not *affirm* it. He resigns himself to it, he retains its symptoms in the regulated contradictions of his discourse, he accepts it and refuses it but does not affirm it. He who tipped the axis of the globe could have been a player God, unknowingly risking the best and the worst at the same time. But he is everywhere else determined as providence. By this last gesture and by all that it commands in Rousseau's thought, meaning is put out of play. As in all onto-theological metaphysics, as already in Plato. And the condemnation of art, each time that it is univocal, clearly testifies to it.

If societies are born in catastrophe, it means that they are born by accident. Rousseau naturalizes the Biblical accident: he makes a natural accident of the Fall. But by the same token, he transforms the throw of dice, the luck or checkmating of a player God, into a culpable Fall. Between the accidents of nature and social evil, there is a complicity that, moreover, manifests Divine Providence. Society is created only to repair the accidents of nature. Floods, earthquakes, volcanic eruptions, and conflagrations no doubt terrified savages but then made them come together "to recoup their common losses." "[These are] the instruments Providence uses to force people to reunite" [*Essay*, p. 40]. The formation of societies played a compensatory role in the general economy of the world. Born of catastrophe, society appeases unfettered Nature. It must in its turn have that regulatory role without which the catastrophe would have been mortal. The catastrophe itself follows an economy. It is *contained*. "Since societies have been established, these great accidents have ceased, or have become less frequent. It seems that is bound to be true even now. The same evils that once united separated people would now tend to separate those who are united"[62] (Chap. 9) [p. 40].

Human war has the effect of reducing the war of natural elements. This economy clearly shows that the degradation that came out of the catastrophe must be—as we have elsewhere verified—compensated for, limited, regularized, by a supplementary operation whose pattern we have outlined. "Otherwise I do not see how the system could be kept standing and equilibrium be maintained. In the two types of order, the greater species will finally absorb the lesser. The entire earth would soon be covered with nothing but trees and ferocious beasts, and finally all would perish" [*Essay*, p. 43]. There follows an admirable description of man's work where "the hand" holds back the degradation of nature and "retards this progress."

The catastrophe opens the play of the supplement because it inscribes local difference. After the unity of "perpetual spring," it causes a duality of principles to follow: the polarity and opposition of places (North and South), the revolution of seasons which regularly repeats the catastrophe;[63] in some ways it makes place and climate change then and there, and finally produces the alternation of hot and cold, water and fire.

Language and society institute themselves following the supplementary relationship of two principles or series of significations (North/winter/cold/need/ articulation; South/summer/warmth/passion/accentuation).

In the North, in winter, when it is cold, need creates convention.

Forced to provide for winter, people living under such conditions have to establish some sort of convention among themselves in order to help each other. When the rigors of frigid weather make it impossible to get about, boredom tends to unite them as much as need: the Lapps, buried in ice, and the Eskimos, the most savage of people, huddle all winter in their caverns, and then in summer do not even know each other any more. Give them somewhat greater development and enlightenment, and there you have them united forever. [*Essay*, pp. 40–41]

Fire is a substitute for natural warmth, and the men of the North must assemble around a hearth. Not only for the cooking of meat—and man in Rousseau's eyes is the only animal capable at the same time of speaking, living in society, and cooking what he eats—but for dancing and loving.

Neither the stomach nor the intestines of man are made to digest raw meat, nor does it usually suit his taste. With the possible single exception of the Eskimos, of whom I have just spoken, even savages cook their meat. To the necessary use of fire for cooking is joined the pleasure it gives to the eye and the warmth so comforting to the body. The sight of the flames, from which animals flee, is attractive to man. People gather around a common hearth where they feast and dance; the gentle bonds of habit tend imperceptibly to draw man closer to his own kind. And on this simple hearth burns the sacred fire that provokes in the depths of the heart the first feeling of humanity [ibid.].

In the South, the movement is inverse, it no longer leads from need to passion but from passion to need. And the supplement is not the warmth of the hearth but the coolness of the water hole:

In warm countries, unevenly distributed springs and rivers are even more necessary rallying agents than other such factors, since people are less able to do without water than fire. The barbarians especially, living off their herds, need common watering places. . . . The flowing of waters can retard the society of people inhabiting well-irrigated places [ibid.].

This movement is no doubt the inverse of the preceding, but it would be wrong to conclude that there is a symmetry. The privilege of the South is declared. To the structure of reversibility that we have just described, Rousseau assigns an absolute and fixed beginning: "the human race, born in warm lands." Reversibility is superimposed upon the simplicity of the origin. The warm countries are closer to the "perpetual spring" of the Golden Age. They are more in accord with the initial inertia. Passion there is closer to the origin, water is more in touch than fire both with the first need and with the first passion.

More in touch with the first need because "people are less able to do without water than fire"; and more in touch with the first passion, that is to say with love, because its "first fires" arise out of "the pure crystal of the fountains." Thus the original language and society, as they arose in warm countries, are absolutely pure. They are described closest to that ineffable limit where society is formed without having begun its degradation; where language is instituted but still remains pure song, a language of pure accentuation, a sort of neume. It is no longer animal since it expresses passion, but it is not completely conventional since it evades articulation. The origin of this society is not a contract, it does not happen through treaties, conventions, laws, diplomats, and *representatives*. It is a *festival* [*fête*]. It consumes itself in *presence*. There is certainly an experience of time, but a time of pure presence, giving rise neither to calculation, nor reflection, nor yet comparison: "Happy age when nothing marked the hours."[64] It is the time of the *Reveries*. Time also without differance: it leaves no interval, authorizes no detour between desire and pleasure: "Pleasure and desire mingled and were felt together."

Let us read this page, no doubt the most beautiful in the *Essay*. It is never quoted, as it should be every time the "transparence of the crystal"[65] is evoked.

> . . . in the arid places where water could be had only from wells, people had to rejoin one another to sink the wells, or at least to agree upon their use. Such must have been the origin of societies and languages in warm countries.
> That is where the first ties were formed among families; there were the first rendezvous of the two sexes. Girls would come to seek water for the household, young men would come to water their herds. There eyes, accustomed to the same sights since infancy, began to see with increased pleasure. The heart is moved by these novel objects; an unknown attraction renders it less savage; it feels pleasure at not being alone. Imperceptibly, water becomes more necesasry. The livestock become thirsty more often. One would arrive in haste and leave with regret. In that happy age when nothing marked the hours, nothing would oblige one to count them; the only measure of time would be the alternation of amusement and boredom. Under old oaks, conquerors of the years, an ardent youth will gradually lose its ferocity. Little by little they become less shy with each other. In trying to make oneself understood, one learns to explain oneself. There too, the original festivals developed. Feet skipped with joy, earnest gestures no longer sufficed, the voice accompanied them in impassioned accents; pleasure and desire mingled and were felt together. There at last was the true cradle of nations: from the pure crystal of the fountains flowed the first fires of love [pp. 44–45].

Let us not forget: what Rousseau describes here is neither the eve of society nor society already formed but the movement of a birth, the continuous advent of *presence*. One must give an active and dynamic meaning to this word. It is presence at work, in the process of presenting itself. This presence is not a state but the becoming-present of presence. None of the oppositions of determined predicates can be applied clearly to what, between the state of nature and the state of society, is not a state but a passage which should have continued and lasted like the present of the *Reveries*. It is already society, passion, language, time, but it is not yet servitude, preference, articulation, measure, and interval. Supplementarity is possible but nothing has yet come into play. Rousseau's festival excludes play. The moment of the festival is the moment of pure continuity, of in-differance between the time of desire and the time of pleasure. Before the festival, in the state of pure nature, there is no *experience* of the continuous; after the festival the experience of the *discontinuous* begins; the festival is the model of the continuous experience. All that we can fix in the conceptual oppositions is therefore society formed on the morrow of the festival. And these oppositions will first suppose the fundamental opposition of the continuous and the discontinuous, of the original festival to the organization of society, of the dance to law.

What follows the festival? The age of the supplement, of articulation, of signs, of representatives. That is the age of the prohibition of incest. Before the festival, there was no incest because there was no prohibition of incest and no society. After the festival there is no more incest because it is forbidden. Rousseau declares this, and we are going to read it. But since he says nothing about what happens in that place during the festival, nor in what the in-differance between desire and pleasure consists, we may, at least if we wish to, complete this description of the "first festivals" and lift the interdiction that still weighs on it.

Before the festival:

What then! Before that time did men spring from the earth? Did generations succeed each other without any union of the sexes, and without anyone being understood? No: there were families, but there were no nations. There were domestic, but not popular, languages. There were marriages but there was no love at all. Each family was self-sufficient and perpetuated itself exclusively by inbreeding. Children of the same parents grew up together and gradually they found ways of expressing themselves to each other: the sexes became obvious with age; natural inclination sufficed to unite them. Instinct held the place of passion; habit held the place of preference. They became husband and wife without ceasing to be brother and sister.

This nonprohibition is interrupted *after the festival*. If we have paid attention to another lacuna, to be sure very common, we shall be very little surprised by the omission of incest in the evocation of the festival: describing the nonprohibition, Rousseau does not mention the mother at all, only the sister.[66] And in a note called forth by the word "sister" Rousseau explains with some embarrassment that the prohibition of incest had to follow the festival, and be born of the act of birth of human society, and thus put upon it the seal of a *sacred* law:

The first men would have had to marry their sisters. In the simplicity of primitive customs, this practice would easily perpetuate itself as long as families remained isolated, and *even after the reunion of the most ancient peoples. But the law that prohibits it is no less sacred for its human institution.* Those who see it only in terms of the bond it forms among families, fail to see its most important aspect. Given the intimacy that domestic life is bound to establish between the two sexes, from the moment such *a sacred law ceased to appeal to the heart* and mind there would be no more integrity among men and the most terrifying practices would soon bring about the destruction of mankind (italics added) [pp. 45–46, n. 9].

In general, Rousseau gives a sacred and holy character only to the natural voice that speaks to the heart, to the natural law, which alone is inscribed in the heart. There is *only one* institution, *only one* fundamental convention that is sacred in his eyes: it is, as *The Social Contract* tells us, the social order itself, the right of law, the convention that serves as foundation for all conventions: "the social order is a sacred right which is the basis of all other rights. Nevertheless, this right does not come from nature, and must therefore be founded on conventions" (*Social Contract*, Bk. I, chap. I., p. 352).

Does this not justify us in placing the prohibition of incest, the law sacred among all, on the level of that fundamental institution, of that social order which supports and legitimizes all others? The function of the prohibition of incest is neither named nor expounded in *The Social Contract* but its place is marked as a blank there. Recognizing the family as the only "natural" society, Rousseau specifies that it cannot maintain itself beyond biological urgencies, except "by convention." Now between the family as natural society and the organization of civil society, there are relationships of analogy and corresponding image: "the ruler corresponds to the father, and the people to the children; and all, being born free and equal, alienate their liberty only for their own advantage" [*Social Contract*, p. 4]. One element alone breaks this analogical rapport: the political father no longer loves his children, the element of the law sets him apart. The first convention, which transformed the biological family into a society of institution, has thus displaced the figure of the father. But as the political father must, in spite of his separation and in spite of the abstraction of the law he incarnates, give himself pleasure, a new investment is necessary. It will have the form of the supplement: "The whole difference is that, in the family, the love of the father for his children repays him for the care he takes of them, while, in the State, the pleasure of commanding takes the place of [*supplée*] the love which the chief cannot have for the peoples under him" (p. 352) [p. 4].

One can therefore separate with difficulty the prohibition of incest (sacred law, the *Essay* says) from the "social order," "sacred right which is the basis for all other rights." If that holy law belongs to the very order of the social contract, why is it not *named* in the *exposition* of *The Social Contract*? Why does it only appear in a footnote in an unpublished *Essay*?

Everything in fact permits us to respect the coherence of Rousseau's theoretical discourse by reinscribing the prohibition of incest in this place. If it is called sacred although instituted, it is because, although instituted, it is universal. It is the universal order of culture. And Rousseau *consecrates* convention only on one condition: that one might universalize it and consider it, even if it were the artifice of artifices, as a quasi-natural law conforming to nature. That is exactly the case with this prohibition. It is also the case of the order of that first and *unique* convention, of that first unanimity to which, the *Contract* tells us "we must always go back" (p. 359) [p. 10] for understanding the possibility of law. The origin of laws must be a law.

In the note to the *Essay* this law is obviously not justified. It must not be explained by social circulation and the economy of kinship laws, by "the bond it forms among families." All this supposes the interdict but does not take it into account. What must make us turn away from incest is described in terms where morality ("terrifying practices") and a sort of biological economy of the species ("the destruction of mankind") mingle and are confused. Beside the fact that these two arguments are heterogeneous if not contradictory (it is the argument of the kettle that Freud recalls in *The Interpretation of Dreams*),* neither of the two is intrinsically pertinent to the argument: the morality that condemns incest is constituted from the interdict, the former has its origin in the latter; and the biological or natural argument is ipso facto annulled by what we are told of the Golden Age which preceded the interdict: generation followed generation. "Even after the reunion of the most ancient peoples," "this practice continued without ill-eflect": this fact, which ought to limit the universality of the sacred law, does not stop Rousseau.

Society, language, history, articulation, in a word supplementarity, are born at the same time as the prohibition of incest. That last is the hinge [*brisure*] between nature and culture. This statement does not name the mother in Rousseau's text. But it shows her place all the better. The age of the signs of institution, the epoch of the conventional relationships between the representer and its represented belongs to the time of this interdict.

* *GW* II–III, 125; *SE* IV. 119–20.

The natural woman (nature, mother, or if one wishes, sister), is a represented or a signified replaced and supplanted, in desire, that is to say in social passion, beyond need. She is in fact the only represented, the only signified whose replacement by its signifier Rousseau prescribes, thus exalting the sanctity of the interdict. Not only does he accept but he commands that, *for once*, one comply with the sacred obligation of the sign, to the holy necessity of the representer. "As a general rule—" one reads in *Emile*, "never substitute the symbol for the thing signified, unless it is *impossible to show the thing itself*; for the child's attention is so taken up with the symbol that he will forget what it signifies" (pp. 189–90; italics added) [p. 133].

Here, then, it is impossible to show the thing, but this impossibility is not natural. Rousseau himself says so; it is moreover not simply one element of culture among others, since it is a sacred and universal interdict. It is the element of culture itself, the undeclared origin of passion, of society, of languages: the first supplementarity which permits the substitution in general of a signifier for the signified, of signifiers for other signifiers, which subsequently makes for a discourse on the difference between words and things. So dangerous is this supplementarity that one can only show it indirectly, by means of the examples of certain effects derived from it. One can neither show it, nor name it as such, but only indicate it, by a silent movement of the finger.

The displacing of the relationship with the mother, with nature, with being as the fundamental signified, such indeed is the origin of society and languages. But can one speak of origins after that? Is the concept of origin, or of the fundamental signified, anything but a function, indispensable but situated, inscribed, within the system of signification inaugurated by the interdict? Within the play of suplementarity, one will always be able to relate the substitutes to their signified, this last will be yet another signifier. The fundamental signified, the meaning of the being represented, even less the thing itself, will never be given us in person, outside the sign or outside play. Even that which we say, name, describe as the prohibition of incest does not escape play. There is a point in the system where the signifier can no longer be replaced by its signified, so that in consequence no signifier can be so replaced, purely and simply. For the point of nonreplacement is also the point of orientation for the entire system of signification, the point where the fundamental signified is promised as the terminal-point of all references and conceals itself as that which would destroy at one blow the entire system of signs. It is at once spoken and forbidden by all signs. Language is neither prohibition nor transgression, it couples the two endlessly. That point does not exist, it is always elusive or, what comes to the same thing, always already inscribed in what it ought to escape or ought to have escaped, according to our indestructible and mortal desire.

This point is reflected in the festival, in the water hole [*point*] around which "feet skipped with joy" when "pleasure and desire mingled and were felt together." The festival *itself* would be incest *itself* if some such thing—*itself*—could *take place*; if, by taking place, incest were not to confirm the prohibition: before the prohibition, it is not incest; forbidden, it cannot become incest except through the recognition of the prohibition. We are always short of or beyond the limit of the festival, of the origin of society, of that present within which simultaneously the interdict is (would be) given with the transgression: that which passes (comes to pass) always and (yet) never *properly* takes place. It is always *as if* I had committed incest.

This *birth of society* is therefore not a passage, it is a point, a pure, fictive and unstable, ungraspable limit. One crosses it in attaining it. In it society is broached and is deferred from itself. Beginning, it begins to decay. The South passes into its own North. Transcending need, passion engenders new needs which in turn corrupt it. Post-originary degradation is analogous to pre-originary repetition. Articulation, substituting itself for passion, restores the order of need. The treaty takes the place of love. Hardly attempted, the dance degenerates. The festival becomes war. And already at the water hole:

The barbarians especially, living off their herds, need common watering places. And we learn from the history of the earliest times that, in effect, this is where both their treaties and their disputes originated.*

* See Genesis XXI, for an example of each, between Abraham and Abimilech, concerning the Well of Oath. [*Essay*, pp. 41–42]

The water hole is at the frontier of passion and need, culture and the earth. The purity of the water reflects the fires of love; it is "the pure crystal of the fountains;" but water is not only the transparency of the heart, it is also its freshness: the body—the body of nature, of the herds and their barbaric shepherd—*needs* it in its dryness: "People are less able to do without water than fire."

If culture is thus broached within its point of origin, then it is not possible to recognize any linear order, whether logical or chronological. In this broaching, what is initiated is already corrupted, thus returning to a place before the origin. Speech lets itself be heard and understood in the South only through articulation, through chilling itself in order to express need anew. It then returns to the North or, what comes to the same thing, to the south of the South. The morrow of the festival resembles the eve of the festival infallibly and the point of occurrence of the dance is only the ungraspable limit of their difference. The South and the North are not territories but abstract places that appear only to relate to each other in terms of each other. Language, passion, society, are neither of the North nor of the South. They are the movement of supplementarity by which the poles substitute each other *by turn*: by which accent is broached within articulation, is deferred through spacing. Local difference is nothing but the differance between desire and pleasure. It does not, then, concern only the diversity of languages, it is not only a criterion of linguistic classification, it is the origin of languages. Rousseau does not declare it, but we have seen that he describes it.

From here on, I shall constantly reconfirm that writing is the other name of this differance.

4

From/Of the Supplement to the Source: The Theory of Writing

Let us close the angle and penetrate within the text to the place where writing is named and analyzed for itself, inscribed within theory and placed in historical perspective. Chapters 5 "On Script," and 6 "Whether It Is Likely that Homer Knew How to Write," perhaps a little artificially separated, are among the longest in the *Essay*, in any case the longest after the chapter on the formation of southern languages. I have already called attention to the alterations in the chapter on Homer: now it is a matter of reconstituting or maintaining the coherence of the theory against a fact which seems to threaten it. If the song, the poem, the epic are incompatible with writing, if writing threatens them with death, how do we explain the coexistence of the two ages? And that Homer knew how to write, at any rate that he knew writing, as the episode of Bellerophon[1] in the *Iliad* seems to testify? Rousseau takes note of the fact but "stubborn in [my] paradoxes," he describes himself as tempted to accuse the "compilers of Homer." Did they not write that history of writing after the fact, introducing it violently into poems that "for a long time . . . were written only in men's memories?" "What is more, there are few traces of the art in the remainder of the *Iliad*. But I venture to suggest that the whole *Odyssey* is just a tissue of inanities and stupidities that would be dissolved by changing a letter or two. Instead, the poem is made reasonable and fairly continuous, by presuming that these heroes did not know how to write. Had the *Iliad* been written, it would have been sung much less."

Thus a thesis without which the entire theory of language would founder had to be saved at all costs. The sign of obstinacy which I have just quoted shows it well: these chapters on writing are a decisive moment of the *Essay*. In addition they introduce one of those rare themes which, treated in the *Essay*, are absent in the second *Discourse*; as themes articulated into an organized theory, absent, in fact, from all other texts.

Why did Rousseau never finish or publish a theory of writing? Because he judged himself a bad linguist, as he says in the draft of the preface? Because the theory of writing is rigorously dependent upon the theory of language developed in the *Essay*? And if it were not so, would not this argument, reasonably assumed, be all the more significant? Or further, is it because the *Essay* was supposed to be an appendix to the second *Discourse*? Or because Rousseau, as he says in *Emile*, is "ashamed' 'to speak of the non-sense that is writing? Why shame? What might one have invested in the signification of writing in order to be ashamed to speak of it? to write of it? to write it? And why is it nonsense, this operation in which one recognizes at the same time, notably in the *Essay*, such dangerous and mortal powers?

At any rate the importance of these two chapters, the obstinate effort to consolidate a theory, the laborious ruse to disqualify the interest in writing, are signs that one may not neglect. Such is the situation of writing within the history of metaphysics: a debased, lateralized, repressed, displaced theme, yet exercising a permanent and obsessive pressure from the place where it remains held in check. A feared writing must be cancelled because it erases the presence of the self-same [*propre*] within speech.

The Originary Metaphor

This situation is reflected in the placing of the chapter "On Script" in the *Essay*. How does Rousseau in fact construct this theory of writing with the help of borrowed elements? He does it after describing the origin of languages. It is the question of a supplement at the origin of languages. This supplement lays bare an additive substitution, a supplement of speech. It is inserted at the point where language begins to be articulated, is born, that is, from falling short of itself, when its accent or intonation, marking origin and passion within it, is effaced under that *other* mark of origin which is articulation. According to Rousseau, the history of writing is indeed that of articulation. The becoming-language of the cry is the movement by which spoken plenitude begins to become what it is through losing itself, hollowing itself out, breaking itself, articulating itself. The cry vocalizes itself by beginning to efface vocalic speech. It is indeed at the moment when it is a question of explaining this originary effacement of what, *properly* speaking, constitutes the spoken of speaking, that is to say the vocalic accent, that Rousseau introduces his chapter on writing. One must deal with the consonant—belonging to the North—and with writing at the same time. "On Script" must first—in its first paragraph—evoke the *obliteration* of the accent or intonation by consonantal articulation: *effacement* and *substitution* at the same time. We should reread that introduction here:

Anyone who studies the history and progress of the tongues will see that the more the words become monotonous, the more the consonants multiply; that, as accents fall into disuse and quantities are neutralized, they are replaced [*on supplée*] by grammatical combinations and new articulations. But only the pressure of time brings these changes about. To the degree that needs multiply, that affairs become complicated, that light is shed [knowledge is increased], language changes its character. It becomes more regular and less passionate. It substitutes ideas for feelings. It no longer speaks to the heart but to reason. For that very reason, accent diminishes, articulation increases. Language becomes more exact and clearer, but more prolix, duller and colder. This progression seems to me entirely natural. Another way of comparing languages and determining their relative antiquity is to consider their script, and reason inversely from the degree of perfection of this art. The cruder the writing, the more ancient the language.

The progress of writing is thus a natural progress. And it is a progress of reason. Progress as regression is the growth of reason as writing. Why is that dangerous progress *natural*? No doubt because it is *necessary*. But also because necessity operates within language and society, according to ways and powers that belong to the state of pure *nature*. A pattern that we have already encountered: it is need and not passion that substitutes light for heat, clarity for desire, precision for strength, ideas for sentiment, reason for heart, articulation for accent. The natural, that which was inferior and anterior to language, acts within language *after the fact*, operates there after the origin, and provokes decadence or regression. It then becomes the posterior seizing the superior and dragging it toward the inferior. Such would be the strange time, the indescribable diagram of writing, the unrepresentable movement of its forces and its menaces.

In what consists the *precision* and the *exactitude* of language, that lodging of writing? Above all in *literalness* [*propriété*]. A precise and exact language should be absolutely univocal and literal [*propre*]: nonmetaphorical. The language is written, and pro-regresses, to the extent that it masters or effaces the figure in itself.

Effaces, that is, its origin. For language is originarily metaphorical. According to Rousseau it derives this from its mother, passion. Metaphor is the characteristic that relates language to its origin. Writing would then be the obliteration of this characteristic, the "maternal characteristics" (cf. above, pp. 285, 199–200). It is therefore here that we must discuss "That the first language had to be figurative" (Chap. 3), a proposition that is explicit only in the *Essay*:

> As man's first motives for speaking were of the passions, his first expressions were tropes. Figurative language was the first to be born. Proper meaning was discovered last. One calls things by their true name only when one sees them in their true form. At first only poetry was spoken; there was no hint of reasoning until much later [p. 12].

Epic or lyric, story or song, archaic speech is necessarily poetic. Poetry, the first literary form, is metaphorical in essence. Rousseau belongs therefore—he could not be otherwise, and to make note of it is more than banal

—to the tradition which determines literary writing in terms of the speech present in the story or song; literary literality would be a supplementary accessory fixing or coagulating the poem, representing the metaphor. The literary object would have no specificity; at the most that of an unhappy negative of the poetic. In spite of what I have said about literary urgency as he lived it, Rousseau is at ease within this tradition. All that one might call literary modernity tries on the contrary to mark literary specificity against subjugation to the poetic, that is to say to the metaphoric, to what Rousseau himself analyses as spontaneous language. If there is a literary originality, which is by no means a simple certainty, it must free itself if not from the metaphor, which tradition too has judged reducible, at least from the savage spontaneity of the figure as it appears in nonliterary language. This modern protestation can be triumphant or, in Kafka's manner, denuded of all illusion, despairing, and no doubt more lucid: literature, which lives by being outside of itself, within the figures of a language which is primarily not its own, would die as well through a reentry into itself by way of the nonmetaphor. "From a letter: 'During this dreary winter I warm myself by it.' Metaphors are one among many things which make me despair of writing [*Schreiben*]. Writing's lack of independence of the world, its dependence on the maid who tends the fire, on the cat warming itself by the stove; it is even dependent on the poor old human being warming himself by the stove. All these are independent activities ruled by their own laws; only writing is helpless, cannot live in itself, is a joke and a despair" (Kafka, *Journal*, 6 November 1921).*

"That the First Language Had To Be Figurative:" although this proposition was not peculiar to Rousseau, although he might have encountered it in Vico,[2] although he must not only but surely have read it in Condillac who must not only but surely have taken it from Warburton, we must emphasize the originality of the *Essay*.

"I was, perhaps, the first who discovered his abilities," says Rousseau of Condillac, remembering their "tête-à-tête" at the moment that the latter was "engaged upon his 'Essay sur l'Origine des connaissances humaines'" (*Confessions*, p. 347) [pp. 356–57]. Rousseau is closer to Condillac than to Warburton. *The Essay on Hieroglyphics* is certainly governed by the theme of a language originarily figurative and it inspired, among other articles of the *Encyclopaedia*, that on the metaphor, one of the richest. But unlike Vico, Condillac,[3] and Rousseau, Warburton thinks that the originary metaphor does not come from "the warmth of a Poetic Fancy, as is commonly supposed." "The Metaphor arose as evidently from the *Rusticity of Conception*"[4] [Warburton, II: 147]. If the first metaphor is not poetic, it is

* *Tagebücher* 1910–23, ed. Max Brod (New York, 1948–49), pp. 550–551; *The Diaries of Franz Kafka* 1914–29 (New York, 1949), vol. 2, pp. 200–1.

because it is not sung but acted out. According to Warburton, one passes through a continuous transition from a language of action to a language of speech. That will also be Condillac's thesis. Rousseau is therefore the only one to indicate an absolute break between the language of action or the language of need, and speech or the language of passion. Without criticizing Condillac directly on this point, Rousseau opposes him after a fashion. For Condillac, "speech succeeding the language of action, retained its character. This new method of communicatiing our thoughts could not be imagined without imitating the first. In order then to supply the place of violent contorsions of the body, the voice was raised and depressed by very sensible intervals" (II,I,11,Sec. 13) [pp. 179–80]. This analogy and continuity are incompatible with Rousseau's theses about the formation of languages and local differences. For both Condillac and Rousseau the North certainly inclines toward precision, exactitude, and rationality. But for opposite reasons: for Rousseau the distance from the origin increases the influence of the language of action, for Condillac it reduces it, since for him everything begins through the language of action being continued within speech: "Precision of style was much sooner received among the northern nations. In consequence of their cold and phlegmatic constitutions, they were readier to part with any thing that resembled the mode of speaking by action. Every where else the influence of this manner of communicating their thoughts subsisted a long time. Even now, in the southern parts of Asia, pleonasms are considered as an elegance of speech." Sec. 67. "Style was originally poetical" (p. 149) [p. 228].

Condillac's position is more difficult to maintain. He must reconcile a poetic origin (Rousseau) and a practical origin (Warburton). Through the weaving of these difficulties and differences, Rousseau's intention becomes precise. History goes toward the North as it parts from the origin. But whereas for Condillac this distancing follows a simple, straight, and continuous line, for Rousseau it leads to a place before the origin, toward the nonmetaphoric, the language of needs and the language of action.

In spite of all his borrowings, all his convergences, the system of the *Essay* thus remains original. In spite of all difficulties, the caesura between the gesture and the spoken word, between need and passion, is maintained there:

> It seems then that need dictated the first gestures, while the passions wrung forth the first words. By pursuing the course of the facts with these distinctions we may be able to see the question of the origin of language in an entirely new light. The genius of oriental languages, the oldest known, absolutely refutes the assumption of a didactic progression in their development. These languages are not at all systematic or rational. They are vital and figurative. The language of the first men is represented to us as the tongues of geometers, but we see that they were the tongues of poets [p. 11].

The distinction between need and passion is justified in the last instance only by the concept of "pure nature." The functional necessity of this limit-concept and of this juridical fiction also appears from this point of view. For the essential predicate of the state of pure nature is *dispersion;* and culture is always the effect of reconcilement, of proximity, of self-same [*propre*] presence. Need, which manifests itself *in fact before or after passion,* maintains, prolongs, or repeats the original dispersion. As such, and to the extent that it is not born out of an anterior passion that modifies it, it is the pure force of dispersion.

And so it had to be. One does not begin by reasoning, but by feeling. It is suggested that men invented speech to express their needs: an opinion which seems to me untenable. The natural effect of the first needs was to separate men, and not to reunite them. It must have been that way, because the species spread out and the earth was promptly populated. Otherwise mankind would have been crammed into a small area of the world, and the rest would have remained uninhabited [p. 11].

If "all of this is not true without qualification," it is because need, structurally anterior to passion, can always in fact succeed it. But is it only a question of fact, of an empirical eventuality? If the principle of dispersion remains active, is it an accident or a residue? In fact, need is necessary to explain the eve of society, what precedes its *constitution,* but it is indispensable in accounting for the *extension* of society. Without need, the force of presence and attraction would play freely, constitution would be an absolute concentration. One would understand how society resists dispersion, one would no longer be able to explain how it distributes and differentiates itself within space. The extension of society, which can in fact lead to the dislocation of the "assembled people," does not contribute any the less to the *organization,* the differentiation, and the organic division of the social body. In *The Social Contract,* the ideal dimensions of the city, which must be neither too small nor too large, require a certain extension and a certain distance among citizens. Dispersion, as the law of spacing, is therefore at once pure nature, the principle of society's life and the principle of society's death. Thus, although the metaphoric origin of language can be analyzed as the transcendence of need by passion, the principle of dispersion is not alien to it.

In fact Rousseau cannot, as Warburton and Condillac do, allege the continuity of the language of sounds and the language of action which kept us back in "crude conceptions." He has to explain everything in terms of the structure of passion and affectivity. He laboriously helps himself out of the difficulty through a short cut that is very dense and complex under the surface. What is his point of departure in that second paragraph of the third chapter?

Not the difficulty of accounting for metaphor by passion; for him that is self-evident; but the difficulty of making the idea—in effect surprising—of a primitively figurative language acceptable. For do not *good* sense and good *rhetoric*, which agree in considering the metaphor a displacement of style, require that one proceed from the literal [*propre*] meaning in order to constitute and define the figure? Is not the figure a transference of the literal sense? a transport? Did the theoreticians of rhetoric known by Rousseau not define it thus? Is it not the definition given by the *Encyclopaedia*?[5]

To repeat the first springing forth of metaphor, Rousseau does not begin with either good sense or rhetoric. He does not permit himself the use of literal meaning. And, situating himself in a place anterior to theory and common sense, which allow the constituted possibility of what they wish to deduce, he must show us how either common sense or stylistic science is possible. Such is at least his project and the original aim of his psycholinguistics of passions. But in spite of his intention and all appearance to the contrary, he also *starts*, as we shall see, *from the literal meaning. And he does so because the literal* [*le propre*] *must be both at the origin and at the end.* In a word, he restores to the *expression of emotions* a literalness whose loss he accepts, from the very origin, in the *designation of objects*.

Here is the difficulty and the principle of solution:

However, I feel the reader stopping me at this point to ask how an expression can be figurative before it has a proper meaning, since the figure consists only of a transference of meaning. I agree with that. But, in order to understand what I mean, it is necessary to substitute the idea that the passion presents to us for the word that we transpose. For one only transposes words because one also transposes ideas. Otherwise figurative language would signify nothing [pp. 12–13].

Metaphor must therefore be understood as the process of the idea or meaning (of the signified, if one wishes) before being understood as the play of signifiers. The idea is the signified meaning, that which the word expresses. But it is also a sign of the thing, a representation of the object within my mind. Finally, this representation of the object, signifying the object and signified by the word or by the linguistic signifier in general, may also indirectly signify an affect or a passion. It is in this play of the representative idea (which is signifier or signified according to the particular relationship) that Rousseau lodges his explanation. Before it allows itself to be caught by verbal signs, metaphor is the relation between signifier and signified within the order of ideas and things, according to what links the idea with that of which it is the idea, that is to say, of which it is already the representative sign. Then, the literal or proper meaning will be the relationship of the idea to the affect that it *expresses*. And it is the *inadequation of the designation* (metaphor) which *properly expresses* the passion. If fear makes me see giants where there are only men, the signifier—as the idea of the object—will be metaphoric, but the signifier of my passion will be literal. And if I then say "I see giants," that false designation will be a literal expression of my fear. For in fact I see giants and there is a sure truth there, that of a sensible cogito, analogous to what Descartes analyzes in the *Regulae*: phenomenologically, the proposition "I see yellow" is unexceptionable, error becomes possible only in the judgment "the world is yellow."[6]

Nevertheless, what we interpret as literal expression in the perception and designation of giants, remains a metaphor that is preceded by nothing either in experience or in language. Since speech does not pass through reference to an object, the fact that "giant" is literal as sign of fear not only does not prevent, but on the contrary implies, that it should be nonliteral or metaphoric as sign of the object. It cannot be the idea-sign of the passion without presenting itself as the idea-sign of the presumed cause of that passion, opening an exchange with the outside. This opening allows the passage to a savage metaphor. No literal meaning precedes it. No rhetor watches over it.

We must therefore come back to the subjective affect, substitute the phenomenological order of passions for the objective order of designations, expression for indication, in order to understand the emergence of metaphor, and the savage possibility of transference. To the objection that the literal meaning is prior, Rousseau responds with an example:

> Upon meeting others, a savage man will initially be frightened. Because of his fear he sees the others as bigger and stronger than himself. He calls them *giants*. After many experiences, he recognizes that these so-called giants are neither bigger nor stronger than he. Their stature does not approach the idea he had initially attached to the word giant. So he invents another name common to them and to him, such as the name *man*, for example, and leaves *giant* to the false object that had impressed him during his illusion. That is how the figurative word is born before the literal word, when our gaze is held in passionate fascination; and how it is that the first idea it conveys to us is not that of the truth. What I have said of words and names presents no difficulty relative to the forms of phrases. The illusory image presented by passion is the first to appear, and the language that corresponded to it was also the first invented. It subsequently became metaphorical when the enlightened spirit, recognizing its first error, used the expressions only with those passions that had produced them [pp. 12–13].

1. The *Essay* thus describes at the same time the advent of the metaphor and its "cold" recapture within rhetoric. One cannot, then, speak of metaphor as a figure of style, as technique or procedure of language, except by a sort of analogy, a sort of return and repetition of the discourse; then one deliberately passes through the initial displacement, that which expressed the passion literally. Or rather the representer of the passion: it is not fear itself that the word *giant* expresses literally—and a new distinction

is necessary which would infiltrate as far as the literalness [*propre*] of expression—but "the idea that the passion presents to us" [*Essay*, p. 13]. The idea "giant" is at once the literal sign of the representer of the passion, the metaphoric sign of the object (man) and the metaphoric sign of the affect (fear). That sign is metaphoric because it is *false* with regard to the object; it is metaphoric because it is *indirect* with regard to the affect: it is the sign of a sign, it expresses emotion only through another sign, through the representer of fear, namely through the *false* sign. It represents the affect literally only through representing a false representer.

Subsequently, the rhetor or the writer can reproduce and calculate this operation. The interval of this repetition separates savagery from civility; it separates them within the history of the metaphor. Naturally, this savagery and this civility interrelate within the condition of society opened by passion and the primitive figures. The "enlightened spirit," the cold clarity of reason, turned toward the North and dragging the corpse of the origin, can, having recognized "its first error," handle metaphors as such, with reference to what it knows to be their true and literal meaning. In the south of language, the impassioned spirit was caught within metaphor: the poet relating to the world only in the style of nonliterality. The reasoner, the writer-calculator, and the grammarian, knowingly and coldly organize the effects of the nonliteralness of style. But one must also turn these relationships inside out; the poet has a relationship of truth and literalness with that which he expresses, he keeps himself as close as possible to his passion. Lacking the truth of the object, he speaks himself fully and reports authentically the origin of his speech. The rhetor accedes to objective truth, denounces error, deals with the passions, but all by virtue of having lost the living truth of the origin.

Thus, even while apparently affirming that the original language was figurative, Rousseau upholds the literal [*propre*]: as *arche* and as *telos*. At the origin, since the first idea of passion, its first representer, is literally expressed. In the end, because the enlightened spirit stabilizes the literal meaning. He does it by a process of knowledge and *in terms of truth*. One will have remarked that in the last analysis, it is also in these terms that Rousseau treats the problem. He is situated there by an entire naive philosophy of the idea-sign.

2. Does the example of fear come by chance? Does not the metaphoric origin of language lead us necessarily to a situation of threat, distress, and dereliction, to an archaic solitude, to the anguish of dispersion? Absolute fear would then be the first encounter of the other as *other*: as other than I and as other than itself. I can answer the threat of the other as other (than I) only by transforming it into another (than itself), through altering it in my imagination, my fear, or my desire. "Upon meeting others, a savage men will *initially* be frightened." Fear would thus be the first pas-

sion, the mistaken face of pity of which we spoke above. Pity is the force of reconciliation and presence. Fear would still be turned toward the immediately anterior situation of pure nature as dispersion; the other is *first* encountered at a distance, separation and fear must be overcome so that he may be approached as a fellow-being. From a distance, he is immense, like a master and a threatening force. It is the experience of the small and silent [*infans*] man. He begins to speak only out of these deforming and naturally magnifying perceptions.[7] And as the force of dispersion is never reduced, the source of fear always compounds with its contrary.

The acknowledged influence of Condillac also makes us think that the example of fear is not fortuitous. According to *An Essay on the Origin of Human Knowledge*, anguish and repetition are the double root of language.

As for the language of action. The fact that language was given to man by God does not forbid a search into its natural origin by a philosophic fiction which teaches the essence of what was thus received. It does not suffice "for a philosopher to say a thing was effected by extraordinary means." It is "incumbent upon him to explain how it could have happened according to the ordinary course of nature" [pp. 170–71]. It is the hypothesis of the two children left in the desert after the Flood, "before they understood the use of any sign"[8] [p. 169]. These two children began to speak only in a moment of fear: to ask for help. But language does not begin in pure anguish or rather anguish signifies itself only through repetition.

It is held between perception and reflection and is here called imitation. Let us italicize:

> Thus by instinct alone they asked and gave each other assistance. I say *by instinct alone*; for as yet there was no room for reflection. One of them did not say to himself, *I must make such particular motions to render him sensible of my want, and to induce him to relieve me*: nor the other, *I see by his motions that he wants such a thing, and I will let him have the enjoyment* [*jouissance*] *of it*: but they both acted in consequence of the want which pressed them most. . . . For example, he who saw a place in which he had been *frightened*, *mimicked* those cries and movements which were the signs of fear, in order to warn the other not to expose himself to the same danger.[9]

3. The work which produces the common noun supposes, like all work, the *chilling* and *displacement* of passion. One can substitute the adequate common noun (*man*) for the noun *giant* only after the appeasement of fear and the recognition of error. With this work the number and extension of common nouns (names) multiply. Here the *Essay* is in close accord with the second *Discourse*: the first substantives were not common but proper

nouns or names. The absolutely literal [*propre*] is at the origin: one sign to a thing, one representer per passion. It is the moment when the lexical element is as much the more extended as knowledge is limited.[10] But that is true only of categoremes, a fact that ought to raise more than one logical and linguistic difficulty. For the substantive as proper name is not quite the first state of the language. It does not stand alone within the language. It already represents an articulation and a "division of discourse." Not that, in Vico's manner, Rousseau makes the noun be born almost at the end, after onomatopoeia, interjections, first names, pronouns, articles, but before verbs. The noun cannot appear without the verb. After a first step, during which discourse is undivided, each word having "the sense of a whole proposition," the noun is born at the same time as the verb. It is the first internal rupture of the proposition that opens discourse. There are no nouns that are not proper, no verbal modes but the infinitive, no tense but the present: "When they began to distinguish subject and attribute, and noun and verb, which was itself no common effort of genius, substantives were at first only so many proper names; the present infinitive[11] was the only tense of verbs; and the very idea of adjectives must have been developed with great difficulty; for every adjective is an abstract idea, and abstractions are painful and unnatural operations" (p. 149) [*Discourse*, p. 177].

This correlation of the proper noun and of the infinitive present is important for us. One thus leaves the present and the proper in the same movement: that which—distinguishing the subject from subject with verb—and later distinguishing it from the subject with its attribute—substitutes for the proper noun the common noun and the pronoun—personal or relative—trains the classification within a system of differences and substitutes the tenses for the impersonal present of the infinitive.

Before this differentiation, the moment of languages "ignorant . . . of the division of discourse" [*Discourse*, p. 77] corresponds to that state suspended between the state of nature and the state of society: an epoch of natural languages, of the neume, of the time of the Isle of St. Pierre, of the festival around the water hole. Between prelanguage and the linguistic catastrophe instituting the division of discourse, Rousseau attempts to recapture a sort of happy pause, the instantaneity of a full language, the image stabilizing what was no more than a point of pure passage: a language without discourse, a speech without sentence, without syntax, without parts, without grammar, a language of pure effusion, beyond the cry, but short of the hinge [*brisure*] that articulates and at the same time disarticulates the immediate unity of meaning, within which the being of the subject distinguishes itself neither from its act nor from its attributes. It is the moment when there are words ("the words first made use of by mankind")—which do not yet function as they do "in languages already formed" and in which men "first gave every single word the sense of a whole proposition" [*Discourse*, p. 177]. But language cannot be truly born except by the disruption and fracture of that happy plenitude, in the very instant that this instantaneity is wrested from its fictive immediacy and put back into movement. It serves as an absolute reference point for him who wishes to measure and describe difference within discourse. One cannot do it without referring to the limit, always already crossed, of an undivided language, where the proper-infinitive-present is so welded to itself that it cannot even appear in the opposition of the proper noun and the verb in the infinitive present.

Language in its entirety, then, plunges into that breach between the proper and the common nouns (leading to pronoun and adjective), between the infinitive present and the multiplicity of modes and tenses. All language will substitute itself for that living self-presence of the proper, which, as language, already supplanted things in themselves. Language *adds itself* to presence and supplants it, defers it within the indestructible desire to rejoin it.

Articulation is the dangerous supplement of fictive instantaneity and of the good speech: of full pleasure [*jouissance*], for presence is always determined as pleasure by Rousseau. The present is always the present of a pleasure; and pleasure is always a receiving of presence. What dislocates presence introduces differance and delay, spacing between desire and pleasure. Articulated language, knowledge and work, the anxious research of learning, are nothing but the spacing between two pleasures. "We desire knowledge only because we wish to enjoy" (Second *Discourse*, p. 143 [p. 171]). And in *The Art of Enjoyment*, that aphorism which speaks the symbolic restitution of the presence supplied in the past of the verb: "Saying to myself, I enjoyed, I still enjoy."[12] The great project of *The Confessions*, was it not also to "enjoy [once more] . . . when I desire it" (p. 585) [p. 607]?

The History and System of Scripts

The verb "to supplant" or "to compensate for" [*suppléer*] defines the act of writing adequately. It is the first and the last word of the chapter "On Script." We have read its opening paragraph. Here are the last lines:

> Words [*voix*], not sounds [*sons*], are written. Yet, in an inflected language, these are the sounds, the accents, and all sorts of modulations that are the main source of energy for a language, and that make a given phrase, otherwise quite ordinary, *proper only to the place where it is*. The means used *to overcome* [*suppléer*] this weakness tend to make written language rather elaborately prolix;

and many books written in discourse will enervate the language. To say everything as one would write it would be merely to read aloud (italics added) [p. 22].

If supplementarity is a necessarily indefinite process, writing is the supplement par excellence since it marks the point where the supplement proposes itself as supplement of supplement, sign of sign, *taking the place of* a speech already significant: it displaces the *proper place* of the sentence, the unique time of the sentence pronounced *hic et nunc* by an irreplaceable subject, and in return enervates the voice. It marks the place of the initial doubling.

Between these two paragraphs: (1) A very brief analysis of the diverse structures and the general growth of writing; (2) starting from the premises of that typology and of that history, a long reflection on alphabetic writing and an appreciation of the meaning and value of writing in general.

Here again, in spite of massive borrowings, history and typology remain most singular.

Warburton and Condillac propose the diagram of an economic, technical, and purely objective rationality. The economic imperative must be understood here in the restrictive sense of economies *to be made*: of *abbreviation*. Writing *reduces* the dimensions of presence in its sign. The *miniature* is not reserved to illuminated capitals; it is, understood in its derivative sense, the very form of writing. The history of writing would then follow the continuous and linear progress of the techniques of abbreviation. The systems of script would derive from one another without essential modification of the fundamental structure and according to a homogeneous and monogenetic process. One script would not replace another except to gain more space and time. If one believes the project of "the General History of Script" proposed by Condillac,[13] writing does not have a different origin from that of speech: need and distance. Thus it continues the language of action. But it is at the moment that the social *distance*, which had led gesture to speech, increases to the point of becoming *absence*, that writing becomes necessary. (This becoming-absence of distance is not interpreted as a rupture by Condillac but described as the consequence of a continuous increase.) From then on, writing has the function of reaching *subjects* who are not only distant but outside of the entire field of vision and beyond earshot.

Why *subjects*? Why should writing be another name for the constitution of *subjects* and, so to speak, of *constitution* itself? of a subject, that is to say of an individual held responsible (for) himself in front of a law and by the same token subject to that law?

Under the name of writing, Condillac thinks readily of the possibility of such a subject, and of the law mastering its absence. When the field of society extends to the point of absence, of the invisible, the inaudible, and the immemorable, when the local community is dislocated to the point where individuals no longer appear to one another, become capable of being imperceptible, the age of writing begins.

> . . . laws and public transactions, together with every thing that deserved the attention of mankind, were multiplied to such a degree, that memory was too weak for so heavy a burden; and human societies increased in such a manner, that the promulgation of the laws could not, without difficulty, reach the ears of every individual. In order therefore to instruct the people, they were obliged to have recourse to some new method. Then it was that writing was invented: what progress it made I shall presently state (II. i. Sec. 73) [p. 232].
> When mankind had once acquired the art of communicating their conceptions by sounds, they began to feel the necessity of inventing new signs proper for perpetuating them, and for making them known to absent persons (Sec. 127) [p. 273].

Since the operation of writing reproduces that of speech here, the first *graphie* will reflect the first speech: figure and image. It will be pictographic. Again a paraphrase of Warburton:

> Their imaginations then represented nothing more to them than those same images, which they had already expressed by gestures and words, and which from the very beginning had rendered language figurative and metaphorical. The most natural way therefore was to delineate the images of things. To express the idea of a man or of a horse, they represented the form of each of these animals; so that the first essay towards writing was a mere picture.[14]

Like the first word, the first pictogram is therefore an image, both in the sense of imitative representation and of metaphoric displacement. The interval between the thing itself and its reproduction, however faithful, is traversed only by transference. The first sign is determined as an image. The idea has an essential relationship to the sign, the representative substitute of sensation. Imagination supplements attention which supplements perception. Attention may have for "first effect" "to make those perceptions which are occasioned by their objects to continue still in the mind, when those objects are removed" (I, ii, Sec. 17) [p. 38]. Imagination permits "the representation of an object in terms of a sign, by its simple name, for example." The theory of the sensible origin of ideas in general, the theory of signs and of metaphoric language which commands almost all eighteenth-century thought, here exhibits its Cartesian critique of rationalism against an intact theological and metaphysical base. It is the original sin, functioning as did the Flood in the previous examples, which makes possible and necessary the sensationalist criticism of innate ideas, the recourse to learning through signs or metaphors, speech or writing, the system of signs (accidental, natural, arbitrary). "Whenever therefore I happen to say, *that we have no ideas but what come from the senses,* it must be remembered, that I speak only of the state into which we are fallen by sin. This proposition applied to the soul before the fall, or after its separation from the body, would be absolutely false. . . . I confine myself therefore, in the following work, to the present state of humanity" (I, i, 8, p .10) [p. 18].

It is thus, as with Malebranche, for example, the very concept of experience which remains dependent on the idea of original sin. There is one law there: the notion of experience, even when one would like to use it to destroy metaphysics or speculation, continues to be, in one or another point of its functioning, fundamentally inscribed within onto-theology: at least by the value of *presence*, whose implication it can never reduce by itself. Experience is always the relationship with a plenitude, whether it be sensory simplicity or the infinite presence of God. Even up to Hegel and Husserl, one could show, for this very reason, the complicity of a certain sensationalism and of a certain theology. The onto-theological idea of sensibility or experience, the opposition of passivity and activity, constitute a profound homogeneity, hidden under the diversity of metaphysical systems. Within that idea, absence and the sign always seem to make an apparent, provisional, and derivative notch in the system of first and last presence. They are thought as accidents and not as conditions of the desired presence. The sign is always a sign of the Fall. Absence always relates to distancing from God.

In order to escape the closure of this system, it is not enough to get rid of the "theological" hypothesis or obligation. If he denies himself the theological facilities of Condillac when he looks for the natural origin of society, speech, and writing, Rousseau makes the substitutive concepts of nature or origin play an analogous role. How can we believe that the theme of the Fall is absent from this discourse? How especially when we see the disappearing finger of God appear exactly when the so-called natural catastrophe comes about? The differences between Rousseau and Condillac will always be contained within the same closure. One cannot state the problem of the model of the Fall (Platonic or Judaeo-Christian) except within this common closure.[15]

The first writing is thus a painted image. Not that painting had served as writing, as miniature. The two were at first intermingled: a closed and mute system within which speech had as yet no right of entry and which was shielded from all other symbolic investment. There, one had nothing but a pure reflection of object or action. "It is in all probability to the necessity of thus delineating our thoughts that the art of painting owes its original; and this necessity has doubtless contributed to preserve the language of action, as the easiest to represent by the pencil" (Sec. 128) [p. 274].

This natural writing is thus the only universal writing. The diversity of scripts appears from the moment the threshold of pure pictography is crossed. That would be a simple origin. Condillac, following Warburton in this, engenders or rather deduces all other types and all other stages of writing out of this natural system.[16] Linear progres will always be that of condensation, and of purely quantitative condensation. More precisely, it will concern an objective quantity: natural volume and space. To this profound law are submitted all displacements and all graphic condensations that only avoid it in appearance.

From this point of view, pictography, the primary method that employs one sign per thing, is the least economical. This squandering of signs is American: "Notwithstanding the inconveniences arising from this method, the most civilized nations in America were incapable of inventing a better. The savages of Canada have no other" (Sec. 129) [p. 274]. The superiority of hieroglyphic script—"picture and character"—depends on the fact that "only a single figure [is used] to signify several things" [pp. 275, 274]. Which supposes that there might be—it is the function of the pictographic limit—something like a unique sign for a unique thing, a supposition contradictory to the very concept and operation of the sign. To determine the first sign in this way, to found or deduce the entire system of signs with reference to a sign which does not belong to that system, is to reduce signification to presence. The sign from then on is nothing but a disposing of presences in the library. The advantage of hieroglyphs—one sign for many things—is reduced to the economy of libraries. That is what the "more ingenious" Egyptians understood. They "were the first who made use of a shorter method which is known by the name of hieroglyphics." "The inconveniency arising from the enormous bulk of volumes, induced them to make use of only a single figure to signify several things." The forms of displacement and condensation differentiating the Egyptian system are comprehended within this economic concept and conform to the "nature of the thing" (to the nature of things) which it thus suffices to "consult." Three degrees or three moments: the part for the whole (two hands, a shield, and a bow for a battle in curiologic hieroglyphs); the instrument—real or metaphorical—for the thing (an eye for God's knowledge, a sword for the tyrant); finally an analogous thing, in its totality, for the thing itself (a serpent and the medley of its spots for the starry heavens) in tropical hieroglyphics.

According to Warburton, it was already for economic reasons that cursive or demotic hieroglyphics were substituted for hieroglyphics properly speaking or for sacred writing. *Philosophy* is the name of what precipitates this movement: economic corruption which desacralizes through abridging and effacing the signifier for the benefit of the signified:

But it is now Time to speak of an Alteration, which this Change of the Subject and Manner of Expression made in the DELINEATION of *Hieroglyphic*

Figures. Hitherto the Animal or Thing representing was drawn out *graphically*; but when the Study of Philosophy (which had occasioned *Symbolic Writing*) had inclined their Learned to write much, and variously, that exact Manner of Delineation would be as well too tedious as too voluminous; they therefore by degrees perfected another Character, which we may call the *Running Hand* of Hieroglyphics, resembling the *Chinese* Characters, which being at first formed only by the Outlines of each *Figure*, became at length a kind of *Marks*. One natural Effect that this *Running-Hand Character* would, in Time, produce, we must not here omit to speak of; it was this, that its use would take off much of the Attention from the *Symbol*, and fix it on the *Thing signified* by it; by which means the Study of *Symbolic* Writing would be much abbreviated, there being then little to do, but to remember the *Power* of the *Symbolic Mark*; whereas before, the Properties of the Thing or Animal, used as a *Symbol*, were to be learnt: In a Word, it would reduce this Writing to the present State of the Chinese. (I: 139–40) [Warburton, p. 115]

This effacement of the signifier led by degrees to the alphabet (cf. pp. 125–26) [pp. 109–11]. This is also Condillac's conclusion (Sec. 134).

It is therefore the history of knowledge—of philosophy—which, tending to multiply books, pushes toward formalization, abbreviation, algebra. By the same movement, separating itself from the origin, the signifier is hollowed and desacralized, "demotized," and universalized. The history of writing, like the history of science, would circulate between the two epochs of universal writing, between two simplicities, between two forms of transparence and univocity: an absolute pictography doubling the totality of the natural entity in an unrestrained consumption of signifiers, and an absolutely formal *graphie* reducing the signifying expense to almost nothing. There would be no history of writing and of knowledge—one might simply say no history at all—except between these two poles. And if history is not thinkable except between these two limits, one cannot disqualify the mythologies of universal script—pictography or algebra—without suspecting the concept of history itself. If one has always thought the contrary, opposing history to the transparence of true language, it was no doubt through a blindness toward the archeological or eschatological limits, starting from which the concept of history was formed.

Science—what Warburton and Condillac call philosophy here—the *epistémè* and evenutally self-knowledge, consciousness, would therefore be the movement of idealization: an algebrizing, de-poetizing formalization whose operation is to repress—in order to master it better—the charged signifier or the linked hieroglyph. That this movement makes it necessary to pass through the logocentric stage is only an apparent paradox; the privilege of the logos is that of phonetic writing, of a writing provisionally more economical, more algebraic, by reason of a certain condition of knowledge. The epoch of logocentrism is a moment of the global effacement of the signifier: one then believes one is protecting and exalting speech, one is only fascinated by a figure of the *technè*. By the same token, one scorns (phonetic) writing because it has the advantage of assuring greater mastery in being effaced: in translating an (oral) signifier in the best possible way for a more universal and more convenient time; phonic auto-affection, dispensing with all "exterior" recourses, permits, at a certain epoch of the history of the world and of what one calls man, the greatest possible mastery, the greatest possible self-presence of life, the greatest possible liberty. It is this history (as epoch: epoch not of history but as history) which is closed at the same time as the form of being of the world that is called knowledge. The concept of history is therefore the concept of philosophy and of the *epistémè*. Even if it was only belatedly imposed upon what is called the history of philosophy, it was invoked there since the beginning of that adventure. It is in a sense unheard of until now—all idealist, or conventionally Hegelian follies of an analogous appearance notwithstanding—that history is the history of philosophy. Or if one prefers, here Hegel's formula must be taken literally: history is nothing but the history of philosophy, absolute knowledge is fulfilled. What exceeds this closure *is nothing*: neither the presence of being, nor meaning, neither history nor philosophy; but another thing which has no name, which announces itself within the thought of this closure and guides our writing here. A writing within which philosophy is inscribed as a place within a text which it does not command. Philosophy is, within writing, nothing but this movement of writing as effacement of the signifier and the desire of presence restored, of being, signified in its brilliance and its glory. The evolution and properly philosophic economy of writing go therefore in the direction of the effacing of the signifier, whether it take the form of forgetting or repression. Whether opposed or associated, these two last concepts are equally inadequate. At any rate, forgetfulness, if one understands it as the effacement of the power of retention by *finitude*, is the very possibility of repression. And repression, that without which dissimulation would have no *meaning*. The concept of repression is thus, at least as much as that of forgetting, the product of a philosophy (of meaning).

Whatever it might be, the movement of the retreat of the signifier, the perfecting of writing, would free attention and consciousness (knowledge and self-knowledge as idealization of the mastered object) for the presence of the signified. The latter is all the more available because it is ideal. And the value of truth in general, which always implies the *presence* of the signified (*aletheia* or *adequatio*), far from dominating this movement and allowing it to be thought, is only one of its epochs, however privileged. A European epoch within the growth of the sign; and even, as Nietzsche, who wrenches Warburton's proposition from its environment and its metaphysical security, would say: of the *abbreviation of signs.* (So that, let it be said in parenthesis, in wishing to restore a *truth* and an originary or fundamental *ontology* in the thought of Nietzsche, one risks misunderstanding, perhaps at the expense of everything else, the axial intention of his concept of interpretation.)

Repeating Warburton's and Condillac's statement outside its closure, one may say that the history of philosophy is the history of prose; or rather of the becoming-prose of the world. Philosophy is the invention of prose. Philosophy speaks prose, less in excluding the poet from the city than in writing. In necessarily writing that philosophy in which the philosopher has long believed, not knowing what he was doing, and not knowing that a most convenient writing permitted him to do it, and that by rights he could have been satisfied to speak it.

In his chapter on the "Origin of Poetry," Condillac calls it a *fact*: "At length a philosopher, incapable of bending to the rules of poetry, was the first who ventured to write in prose" (Sec. 67) [p. 229]. He is writing of "Pherecydes of the Isle of Scyres . . . , the first we know of who wrote in prose." Writing in the colloquial sense is by itself prosaic. It is prose. (On that point too Rousseau is different from Condillac.) When writing appears, one no longer needs rhythm and *rhyme* whose function is, according to Condillac, to engrave meaning within memory (ibid.). Before writing, poetry would in some way be a spontaneous engraving, a writing before the fact. Intolerant of poetry, philosophy would have taken writing to be a fact.

It is difficult to *appreciate* what separates Rousseau from Warburton and Condillac here, and to determine the *value of the rupture. On the one hand,* Rousseau seems to refine the models which he borrows; genetic derivation is no longer linear or causal. He is more attentive to the *structures* of the systems of writing in their relationship to social or economic systems and to the figures of passion. The appearance of forms of writing is relatively independent of the rhythms of the history of languages. The models of explication are in appearance less theological. The economy of writing refers to motivations other than those of need and action, understood in a homogeneous, simplistic, and objectivistic sense. But *on the other hand,* he neutralizes what is irreducibly *economic* in the system of Warburton and Condillac. And we know how the ruses of theological reason work within his discourse.

Let us approach his text. To the technical and economic imperatives of objective space, Rousseau's explication makes only one concession. It is in order discreetly to correct Warburton's and Condillac's simplism.

It is a matter of *writing by furrows.* The furrow is the line, as the ploughman traces it: the road—*via rupta*—broken by the ploughshare. The furrow of agriculture, we remind ourselves, opens nature to culture (cultivation). And one also knows that writing is born with agriculture which happens only with sedentarization.

How does the ploughman proceed?

Economically. Arrived at the end of the furrow, he does not return to the point of departure. He turns ox and plough around. And proceeds in the opposite direction. Saving of time, space, and energy. Improvement of efficiency and reduction of working time. Writing by the *turning of the ox —boustrophedon*—writing by furrows was a movement in linear and phonographic script.[17] At the end of the line travelled from left to right, one resumes from right to left. Why was it abandoned at a given moment by the Greeks, for example? Why did the economy of the writer [*scripteur*] break with that of the ploughman? Why is the space of the one not the space of the other? If space were "objective," geometric, ideal, no difference in economy would be possible between the two systems of incision.

But the space of geometric objectivity is an object or an ideal signified produced at a moment of writing. Before it, there is no homogeneous space, submitted to one and the same type of technique and economy. Before it, space orders itself wholly for the habitation and inscription in itself of the body "proper." There still are factors of heterogeneity inside a space to which one and the same "proper" body relates, and therefore there are different, indeed incompatible, economic imperatives, among which one must choose and among which sacrifices and an organization of hierarchies become necessary. Thus, for example, the surface of the page, the expanse of parchment or any other receptive substance distributes itself differently according to whether it is a matter of writing or reading. An original economy is prescribed each time. In the first case, and during an entire technological era, it had to order itself according to the system of the hand. In the second case, and during the same epoch, to the system of the eye. In both cases, it is a matter of a linear and oriented path, the orientation of which is not indifferent and reversible in a homogeneous milieu. In a word, it is more convenient to read than to write by furrows. The visual economy of reading obeys a law analogous to that of agriculture. The same thing is not true of the manual economy of writing and the latter was predominant during a specific era and period of the great phonographic-linear epoch. The fashion outlives the conditions of its necessity: it continued till the age of printing. Our writing and our reading are still largely determined by the movement of the hand. The printing press has not yet liberated the organization of the surface from its immediate servitude to the manual gesture, and to the tool of writing.

Rousseau, therefore, was already astonished:

> At first they [the Greeks] adopted not only the characters of the Phoenicians, but also the direction of their lines from right to left. Later it occurred to them to proceed as the plowman, that is, writing alternately from left to right and right to left. Finally, they wrote according to our present practice of starting

each line from left to right. This development is quite natural. Writing in the furrow fashion is undoubtedly the most comfortable to read. I am even surprised that it did not become the established practice with printing; but, being difficult to write manually, it had to be abandoned as manuscripts multiplied. [*Essay*, p. 20]

The space of writing is thus not an originarily *intelligible* space. It begins however to *become* so from the origin, that is to say from the moment when writing, like all the work of signs, produces repetition and therefore ideality in that space. If one calls reading that moment which comes directly to double the originary writing, one may say that the space of pure reading is always already *intelligible*, that of pure writing always still *sensible*. Provisionally, we understand these words inside metaphysics. But the impossibility of separating writing and reading purely and simply disqualifies this opposition from the beginning of the game. Maintaining it for convenience, let us nevertheless say that the space of writing is purely sensible, in the sense that Kant intended: space irreducibly oriented within which the left does not recover the right. One must also take into account the prevalence of one direction over the other within the movement. For here it is the question of an operation, not just of a perception. The two sides are never symmetrical from the point of view of the aptitude or simply the activity of the body proper.

Thus the "return of the ox" is less suitable for writing than reading. Between these two economic prescriptions the solution will be a labile compromise which will leave residues, entail inequalities of development and useless expenses. Compromise, if one wishes, between the eye and the hand. During the age of this transaction, one does not only write, one reads a little blindly, guided by the order of the hand.

Should one still recall everything that such an economic necessity made possible?

This compromise is already very derivative, a late arrival, if one remembers that it prevails only at a moment when a certain type of writing, itself charged with history, was already practiced: linear phonography. The system of speech, of hearing-oneself-speak, auto-affection that seems to suspend all borrowing of signifiers from the world and thus to render itself universal and transparent to the signified, the *phonè* which seems to guide the hand, was never able to precede its system nor, in its very essence, to be alien to it. It could only represent itself as order and predominance of a temporal linearity by *seeing* itself or rather *handling* itself, within its own self-reading. *It is not enough to say that the eye or the hands speak. Already, within its own representation, the voice is seen and maintained.* The concept of linear temporality is only one *way* of speech. This form of successivity is in return imposed upon the *phonè*, upon consciousness and upon preconsciousness from a certain determined space of its inscription.

For the voice is always already invested, undone [*sollicitée*], required, and marked in its essence by a certain spatiality.[18]

When I say a form is *imposed*, I obviously do not think of any classical model of causality. The question, so often asked, of knowing if one writes as one speaks or speaks as one writes, if one reads as one writes or conversely, refers in its banality to an historical or prehistoric depth more hidden than is generally suspected. Finally, if one notes that the place of writing is linked, as Rousseau had intuited, to the nature of social space, to the perceptive and dynamic organization of the technical, religious, economic and other such spaces, one realizes the difficulty of a transcendental question on space. A new transcendental aesthetic must let itself be guided not only by mathematical idealities but by the possibility of inscriptions in general, not befalling an already constituted space as a contingent accident but producing the spatiality of space. Indeed we say of inscription *in general*, in order to make it quite clear that it is not simply the notation of a prepared speech representing itself, but inscription within speech and inscription as *habitation* always already situated. Such a questioning, in spite of its reference to a form of fundamental passivity, ought no longer to call itself a transcendental *aesthetic*, neither in the Kantian, nor in the Husserlian, sense of those words. A transcendental question on space concerns the prehistoric and precultural level of spatio-temporal experience which furnishes a unitary and universal ground for all subjectivity, and all culture, this side of empirical diversity, as well as the orientations proper to their spaces and their times. Now if one lets oneself be guided by inscription as habitation in general, the Husserlian radicalization of the Kantian question is indispensible but insufficient. We know that Husserl reproached Kant for having allowed himself to be guided in his question by ideal objects already constituted into a science (geometry or mechanics). To a constituted ideal space a subjectivity constituted (into faculties) corresponded naturally. And from my present point of view, there is much to say on the concept of the *line* which so often intervenes in the Kantian critique. (Time, the form of all sensible phenomena, internal *and* external, seems to dominate space, the form of external sensible phenomena; but it is a time that one may always represent by a line and the "refutation of idealism" will reverse that order.) The Husserlian project not only put all objective space of science within parentheses, it had to articulate aesthetics upon a transcendental kinesthetics. Nevertheless, in spite of the Kantian revolution and the discovery of *pure* sensibility (free of all reference to sensation), to the extent that the concept of sensibility (as pure passivity) and its contrary will continue to dominate such questions, they will remain imprisoned in metaphysics. If the space-time that we inhabit is *a priori* the space-time of the trace, there is neither pure activity nor pure passivity. This pair of concepts—and we know that Husserl erased one with the other constantly—belongs to the myth of the origin of an uninhabited world, of a world alien to the trace: pure presence of the pure present, that one may either call purity of life or purity of death: determination of being which has always superintended not only theological and metaphysical but also transcendental questions, whether conceived in terms of scholastic theology or in a Kantian and post-Kantian sense. The Husserlian project of a transcendental aesthetics, of a restoration of the "logos of the aesthetic world" (*Formal and Transcendental Logic*)* remains subjected to the instance of the *living present*, as to the universal and absolute form of experience. It is by what complicates this privilege and escapes it that we are opened to the space of inscription.

Breaking with linear genesis and describing the correlations among systems of script, social structures, and the figures of passion, Rousseau opens his questions in the direction that I have indicated.

Three states of man in society: three systems of writing, three forms of social organization, three types of passion. "These three ways of writing correspond almost exactly to three different stages according to which one can consider men gathered into a nation" [*Essay*, p. 16]. Among these three manners, there are no doubt differences of "crudity" and "antiquity." But in as much as they can assure a chronological and linear localization, they interest Rousseau but little. Many systems may coexist, a cruder system may appear after a more refined system.

Here too all begins with painting. That is to say with savagery: "The primitive way of writing was not to represent sounds, but objects themselves." Is this painting satisfied with reproducing the thing? Does it correspond to that universal proto-writing that redoubles nature without any displacement? Here the first complication is introduced. In effect Rousseau distinguishes between two pictographies. One proceeds *directly* and the other *allegorically*, "whether directly as with the Mexicans, or by allegorical imagery, as previously the Egyptians did" [p. 17]. And when he links them thus: "This stage corresponds to passionate language, and already supposes some society and some needs to which the passions have given birth," he doe not designate the sole "Egyptian" or "allegorical" state with any verisimilitude. Without which it would be necessary to conclude that a writing—direct pictography—could have existed in a society without passion, which is contrary to the premises of the *Essay*. On the other hand, how should one imagine a direct, proper, unallegorical painting in a state of passion? That too is contrary to the premises.

One cannot overcome this alternative without reinstating something unsaid: pure representation without metaphoric displacement, the purely reflecting kind of painting, is the first figure. In it the thing most faith-

* Op. cit., "Schlusswort," p. 297, Eng. tr. "Conclusion," pp. 291–92.

fully represented is already no longer properly present. The project of repeating the thing already corresponds to a social passion and therefore requires a metaphoricity, an elementary transference. One transports the thing within its double (that is to say already within an ideality) for an other, and the perfect representation is always already other than what it doubles and re-presents. Allegory begins there. "Direct" painting is already allegoric and impassioned. That is why there is no *true* writing. The duplication of the thing in the painting, and already in the brilliance of the phenomenon where it is present, guarded and regarded, maintained, however slightly, facing the regard and under the regard, opens appearance as the absence of the thing in its self-sameness [*propre*] and its truth. There is never a painting of the thing itself and first of all because there is no thing itself. If we suppose that writing had a primitive and pictorial stage, it would emphasize this absence, this evil, or this resource which forever shapes and undermines the truth of the phenomenon; produces it and of course substitutes it. The original possibility of the image is the supplement; which adds itself without adding anything to fill an emptiness which, within fullness, begs to be replaced. Writing as painting is thus at once the *evil* and the *remedy* within the *phainesthai* or the *eidos*. Plato already said that the art or technique (*technè*) of writing was a *pharmakon* (drug or tincture, salutary or maleficent). And the disquieting part of writing had already been experienced in its resemblance to painting. Writing is *like* painting, like the *zoographeme*, which is itself determined (cf. *Cratylus*, 430–32) within a problematic of *mimesis*; resemblance is troubling: "I cannot help feeling, Phaedrus, that writing is unfortunately like painting" (*zoographia*) (275d). Here painting—zoography—betrays being and speech, words and things themselves because it freezes them. Its offshoots seem to be living things but when one questions them, they no longer respond. Zoography has brought death. The same goes for writing. No one, and certainly not the father, is there when one questions. Rousseau would approve without reservations. Writing carries death. One could play on this: writing as zoography as that painting of the living which stabilizes animality, is, according to Rousseau, the writing of savages. Who are also, as we know, only hunters: men of the *zoogreia*, of the capture of the living. Writing would indeed be the pictorial representation of the hunted beast: magical capture and murder.

Another difficulty in this concept of proto-writing: no recourse to convention is made there. The latter appears only in the "second way": moment of barbarism and of the ideogram. The hunter paints beings, the shepherd already inscribes languages: "The second way is to represent words and propositions by conventional characters. That can be done only when the language is completely formed and an entire people is united by common laws; for this already presupposes a twofold convention. Such is the writing of the Chinese; it truly represents sounds and speaks to the eyes" [*Essay*, p. 17].

One may conclude from this that, in the first state, metaphor did not give rise to any convention. Allegory was still a savage production. There was no need of institutions to represent beings themselves and metaphor here was the transition between nature and institution. Then the proto-writing which did not paint language but painted things could make shift with a language, therefore with a society which was not at all "completely formed." This first stage is always that unstable limit of birth: one has left "pure nature" but one has not completely reached the state of society. The Mexicans and the Egyptians would have the right, according to Rousseau, to only "some society."

The second manner paints sounds but without splitting up words and propositions. It would thus be ideo-phonographic. Each signifier would refer to a phonic totality and a conceptual synthesis, to a complex and global unity of sense and sound. One has not yet attained purely phonographic writing (of the alphabetic types, for example) in which the visible signifier refers to a phonic unity which in itself has no sense.

It is perhaps for this reason that the ideo-phonogram presupposes a "twofold convention:" that which links the grapheme to its phonematic signified, and that which links this phonematic signified, as a signifier, to its signified sense, to its concept, if one wishes. But in that context, "twofold convention" might also mean—it is less probable—something else: linguistic *and* social convention. ("That can be done only when the language is completely formed and an entire people is united by common laws.") One does not need institutional laws for being understood through the paintings of things and of natural beings, but one needs them for stabilizing the rules of the painting of sounds and of the unity of words and ideas.

However, Rousseau calls "barbaric" the nations capable of these "common laws" and this "twofold convention." The use of the concept of barbarity in the *Essay* is very disconcerting. Often (in Chapters 4 and 9) Rousseau makes it function in a perfectly deliberate, rigorous, and systematic way: three states of society, three languages, three scripts (savage/barbaric/civil; hunter/shepherd/ploughman; pictography/ideo-phonography/analytical phonography). Yet elsewhere, an apparently looser use of the word (certainly of the word "barbarity" if not of "barbaric") designates again a state of dispersion, whether it be of pure nature or of domestic structure. Note 2 of Chapter 9 calls "savages" those whose barbarity is subsequently described: "Apply these ideas to primitive men and you will see the reason for their barbarity. . . . These barbaric times were a golden age, not because men were united, but because they were separated. . . . Scattered over the vast wilderness of the world, men would relapse into the stupid barbarism in which they would be if they were born of the earth" [*Essay*, pp. 33, 36]. Domestic-barbaric society had no language. Familial idiom is not a language. "Living almost without society, widely scattered, hardly speaking at all, how could they write?" Is not this sentence in flagrant contradiction with the attribution, in Chapter 4, of a script and even of a twofold convention to barbaric peoples?

No commentary can, it seems, efface this contradiction. An interpretation may attempt it. It would consist, uncovering a profound level of literality while neutralizing another one more superficial, of searching then within Rousseau's text for the right to isolate relatively the structure of the graphic system from the structure of the social system. Although the social and graphic types correspond ideally and by analogy, a society of the civil type may have *in fact* a writing of the barbaric type. Although barbarians hardly speak and do not write, one finds the characteristics of a certain writing within barbarity. In saying thus that "the depicting of objects is appropriate to a savage people; signs of words and of propositions, to a barbaric people, and the alphabet to civilized peoples [*peuples policés*]" [*Essay*, p. 17], one does not contravene the structural principle, rather one confirms it. In our society, where the civil type has appeared, the elements of pictographic writing would be savage, the ideo-phonographic elements barbaric. And who would deny the presence of all these elements in our practice of writing?

For even while maintaining the principle of structural analogy, Rousseau insists nonetheless on preserving the relative independence of social, linguistic, and graphic structures. He will say it further on: "The art of writing does not at all depend upon that of speaking. It derives from needs of a different kind which develop earlier or later according to circumstances entirely independent of the duration of the people, and which might never have occurred in very old nations" [p. 19].

The *fact* of the appearance of writing is therefore not necessary. And it is this empirical contingency which allows the putting in parenthesis of the fact in structural or eidetic analysis. That a structure whose internal organization and essential necessity we know should appear in fact here or there, sooner or later, is, as I have noted elsewhere, the condition and the limit of a structural analysis as such and in its proper moment. In its proper instance, attention to the internal specificity of the organization always leaves to chance the passage from one structure to another. This chance may be thought, as it is here the case, negatively as catastrophe, or affirmatively as play. This structuralist limit and power has an ethico-metaphysical convenience. Writing in general, as the emergence of a new system of inscription, is a supplement of which one would wish to learn only the *additive* aspect (it *happens unexpectedly, at a stroke* [*sur-venu d'un coup*], into the bargain) and the *noxious* influence (arrives *ill-advisedly, in addi-*

tion [*mal-venu, en plus*], from the exterior, when nothing in the conditions of its past made it necessary). Not to attribute any necessity to its historical appearance is at once to ignore the appeal of substitution and to think evil as a surprising, exterior, irrational, accidental and therefore effaceable addition.

The Alphabet and Absolute Representation

Thus graphics and politics refer to one another according to complex laws. They must thus both clothe the form of reason as a process of degradation which, between two universalities and from catastrophe to catastrophe, *should* return to a total reappropriation of presence. *Should* [*devrait*]: it is the mode and tense of a teleological and eschatological anticipation that superintends Rousseau's entire discourse. Thinking differance and supplementarity in this mode and tense, Rousseau wishes to announce them from the horizon of their final effacement.

In this sense, in the order of writing as in the order of the city, as long as the absolute reappropriation of man[19] in his presence is not accomplished, the worst is simultaneously the best. The furthest in the time of lost presence is closest to the time of presence regained.

Hence the third condition: civil man and alphabetic writing. It is here that, in the most conspicuous and grave manner, law supplements nature and writing speech. In one case as in the other, the supplement is representation. We recall the fragment on *Pronunciation*:

> Languages are made to be spoken, writing is nothing but a *supplement* of speech. . . . The analysis of thought is made through speech, and the analysis of speech through writing; speech *represents* thought through conventional signs, and writing represents speech in the same way; thus the art of writing is nothing but a mediated *representation* of thought, at least in the case of vocalic languages, the only ones that we use.

The movement of supplementary representation approaches the origin as it distances itself from it. Total alienation is the total reappropriation of self-presence. Alphabetic writing, representing a representer, supplement of a supplement, increases the *power* of representation. In losing a little more presence, it restores it a little bit better. More purely phonographic than the writing of the second condition, it is more apt to fade before the voice, more apt to let the voice be. Within the political order—total alienation, that which develops, as *The Social Contract* says, "without reserve"—"we gain the exact equivalent of what we lose, as well as an added power to conserve what we already have" (Bk. I, p. 361) [p. 181]. On condition, of course, that the emergence out of the anterior state—at the limit, from the state of pure nature—does not make it fall back, as is always possible, short of the origin, and consequently if "the misuse of the new conditions still, at times, degrades him [the human being] to a point below that from which he has emerged" (p. 364) [p. 185].

Unreserved alienation is thus unreserved representation. It wrenches presence absolutely from itself and absolutely re-presents it to itself. Since evil always has the form of representative alienation, of representation in its dispossessing aspect, all Rousseau's thought is in one sense a critique of representation, as much in the linguistic as in the political sense. But at the same time—and here the entire history of metaphysics is reflected—this critique depends upon the naivete of representation. It supposes at once that representation follows a first presence and restores a final presence. One does not ask how much of presence and how much of representation are found within presence. In criticizing representation as the loss of presence, in expecting a reappropriation of presence from it, in making it an accident or a means, one situates oneself within the self-evidence of the distinction between presentation and representation, within the *effect* of this fission. One criticizes the sign by placing oneself within the self-evidence and the effect of the difference between signified and signifier. That is to say, without thinking (quite like those later critics who, from within the same *effect*, reverse the pattern, and oppose a logic of the representer to the logic of the represented) of the productive movement of the effect of difference: the strange graphic of differance.

It is therefore not at all surprising that the third condition (civil society and alphabet) should be described according to the patterns that are as much those of *The Social Contract* as those of the *Letter to d'Alembert*.

Praise of the "assembled people" at the festival or at the political forum is always a critique of representation. The legitimizing instance, in the city as in language—speech or writing—and in the arts, is the representer present in person: source of legitimacy and sacred origin. Perversity consists precisely in sacralizing the representer or the signifier. Sovereignty is presence, and the delight in [*jouissance*] presence. "The moment the people is legitimately assembled as a sovereign body, the jurisdiction of the government wholly lapses, the executive power is suspended, and the person of the meanest citizen is as sacred and inviolable as that of the first magistrate; for in the presence of the person represented, representatives no longer exist" (*Social Contract*, pp. 427–29 [p. 76].

In all the orders, the possibility of the representer befalls represented presence as evil befalls good, or history befalls origin. The signifier-representer is the catastrophe. Therefore it is always "new" in itself, in whatever epoch it might appear. It is the essence of modernity. "The idea of representation is modern," is a proposition which must be extended beyond the limits that Rousseau assigns it (p. 430) [p. 78]. Political liberty is full only at the moment when the power of the representer is suspended and given back to the represented: "In any case, the moment a people allows itself to be represented, it is no longer free: it no longer exists" (p. 431) [p. 80].

It is necessary, then, to reach the point where the source is held within itself, where it returns or reascends toward itself in the inalienable immediacy of self-possession [*jouissance de soi*], in the moment of the impossible representation, in its sovereignty. In the political order, that source is determined as will: "Sovereignty, for the same reason as makes it inalienable, cannot be represented; it lies essentially in the general will, and will does not admit of representation: it is either the same, or other; there is no intermediate possibility" (p. 429) [p. 78]. ". . . The Sovereign, who is no less than a collective being, cannot be represented except by himself: the power indeed may be transmitted, but not the will" (p. 368) [p. 20].

As corruptive principle, the representative is not the represented but only the representer of the represented; it is not the same as itself. As representer, it is not simply the other of the represented. The evil of the representer or of the supplement of presence is neither the same nor the other. It intervenes at the moment of differance, when the sovereign will delegates itself, and when, in consequence, law is written. Now the general will risks becoming a transmitted power, a particular will, preference, inequality. The decree, that is to say writing, can be substituted for the law; in the decrees representing particular wills, "the general will becomes mute" (*Social Contract*, p. 438) [p. 86]. The system of the social contract, which founds itself on the existence of a moment anterior to writing and representation, can, however, not avoid allowing itself to be threatened by the letter. That is why, obliged to have recourse to representation, "the body politic, as well as the human body, begins to die as soon as it is born, and carries in itself the causes of its destruction" (p. 424 [p. 73] Chapter 11 of Bk. III, "Of the Death of the Body Politic," opens all the developments of representation). Writing is the origin of inequality.[20] It is the moment when the *general will* which cannot err by itself, gives way to *judgment*, which can draw it into "the seductive influences of individual wills" (p. 380) [p. 31]. One must therefore separate legislative sovereignty from the power of *drawing up* laws. "When Lycurgus gave laws to his country, he began by resigning the throne." "He, therefore, who draws up the laws has, or should have, no right of legislation, and the people cannot, even if it wishes, deprive itself of this incommunicable right" (pp. 382–83) [pp.32–33]. It is therefore absolutely necessary that the general will express itself through *voices* without proxy. It "makes law" when it *declares* itself in the voice of the "body of the people" where it is indivisible; otherwise it is divided into particular wills, acts of magistracy, decrees (p. 369) [p. 21].

But the catastrophe that interrupted the state of nature opens the movement of distancing which brings closer; perfect representation should represent perfectly. It restores presence and effaces itself as absolute representation. This movement is necessary.[21] The telos of the image is it own imperceptibility. When the perfect image ceases to be other than the thing, it respects the thing and restores originary presence. Indefinite cycle: represented source of representation, the origin of the image can in turn represent its representers, replace its substitutes, supply its supplements. Folded, returning to itself, representing itself, sovereign, presence is then—and barely—only the supplement of a supplement. It is thus that the *Discourse on Political Economy* defines "the general will, the *source and supplement* of all laws, [which] should be consulted whenever they fail" (p. 250; italics added) [p. 242].* Is not the order of pure law, which gives back to the people their liberty and to presence its sovereignty, always the supplement of a natural order somewhere deficient? When the supplement accomplishes its office and fills the lack, there is no harm done. The abyss is the chasm which can remain open between the lapse of Nature and *the delay of the supplement*: "The time of man's most shameful lawlessness and greatest misery was when, new passions having smothered natural sentiments, human understanding had not yet made sufficient progress to substitute maxims of sagacity for natural impulses."[22] The play of the supplement is indefinite. References refer to references. The general will, that "celestial voice" (*Discourse on Political Economy*, p. 248) [p. 240] is therefore the supplement of nature. But when, by a return of catastrophe, society is degraded, nature can substitute itself for its supplement. It is then a bad nature, "it is under these circumstances that the voice of duty no longer speaks in men's hearts, and their rulers are obliged to *substitute* the cry of terror, or the lure of an apparent *interest*" (p. 253; italics added) [p. 245].

This play of the supplement, the always open possibility of a catastrophic regression and the annulment of progress, recalls not only Vico's *ricorsi*. Conjugated with what we have called geometric regression, it makes history escape an infinite teleology of the Hegelian type. In a certain way, considering that history can always interrupt its own progress, (and must even progress in regression), (re)turn behind itself; Rousseau does not make "the work of death," the play of difference and the operation of negativity, serve in the dialectical accomplishment of truth within the horizon of parousia. But all these propositions may be inverted. This finitism of Rousseau emerges also on the basis of a providentialist theology. Interpreting itself, it effaces itself on another level as it reduces the historic and negative to the accidental. It too is thought within the horizon of an infinite restitution of presence, and so on. In the closed field of metaphysics, what

* I have used the corresponding passages from Cole (op. cit.), and placed references with brackets.

I outline here as an indefinite exchange of "Rousseauist" and "Hegelian" positions (one might take many other examples) obeys the laws inscribed within all the concepts that I have just recalled. It is possible to formalize these laws and indeed they are formalized.

What I have just noted within the political order is applicable also to the graphic order.

Access to phonetic writing constitutes at once a supplementary degree of representativity and a total revolution in the structure of representation. Direct or hieroglyphic pictography represents the thing or the signified. The ideo-phonogram already represents a mixture of signifier and signified. It already paints language. It is the moment located by all historians of writing as the birth of phoneticization, through, for example, the picture puzzle [*rebus à transfert*];[23] a sign representing a thing named in its concept ceases to refer to the concept and keeps only the value of a phonic signifier. Its signified is no longer anything but a phoneme deprived by itself of all meaning. But before this decomposition and in spite of the "twofold convention," representation is reproduction; it repeats the signifying and signified masses en bloc and without analysis. This synthetic character of representation is the pictographic residue of the ideo-phonogram that "paints voices." Phonetic writing works to reduce it. Instead of using signifiers immediately related to a conceptual signified, it uses, through the analysis of sounds, signifiers that are in some way nonsignifying. Letters, which have no meaning by themselves, signify only the elementary phonic signifiers that make sense only when they are put together according to certain rules.

Analysis substituting painting and pushed to insignificance, such is the rationality proper to the alphabet and to civil society. Absolute anonymity of the representer and absolute loss of the selfsame [*le propre*]. The culture of the alphabet and the appearance of civilized man [*l'homme policé*] correspond to the age of the ploughman. And let us not forget that agriculture presupposes industry. But then, how can we explain the allusion to the trader who is in fact never named in the classification of the three conditions and thus seems to have no appropriate era?

> The third [way of writing] is to break down the speaking voice into a given number of elementary parts, either vocal or articulate [vowels or consonants], with which one can form all the words and syllables imaginable. This way of writing, which is ours, must have been invented by commercial peoples who, in traveling to various countries, had to speak various languages, which would have impelled them to invent characters that could be common to all of them. This is not exactly to depict speech, but to analyze it [p. 17].

The trader invents a system of graphic signs which in its principle is no longer attached to a particular language. This writing may in principle inscribe all languages in general. It gains in universality, it favors trade and makes communication "with other people who [speak] other languages" [p. 17] easier. But it is perfectly enslaved to language in general the moment it liberates itself from all particular languages. It is, in its principle, a universal phonetic writing. Its neutral transparence allows each language its proper form and its liberty. Alphabetic writing concerns itself only with pure representers. It is a system of signifiers where the signifieds are signifiers: phonemes. The circulation of signs is infinitely facilitated. Alphabetic writing is the mutest possible, for it does not speak any language immediately. But, alien to the voice, it is more faithful to it and represents it better.

This independence with regard to the empirical diversity of oral languages confirms a certain autonomy of the growth of writing. Writing may not only be born earlier or later, independently of the "duration of the people," slowly or at one stroke;[24] in addition, it implies no linguistic derivation. This is truer of the alphabet, bound to no particular language, than of other systems. One may thus borrow graphic signs, make them safely emigrate outside of their culture and their language of origin. "But though the Greek alphabet derives from the Phoenoecian, it does not follow at all that the Greek language derives from the Phoenoecian" [p. 20].

This movement of analytic abstraction in the circulation of arbitrary signs is quite parallel to that within which money is constituted. Money replaces things by their signs, not only within a society but from one culture to another, or from one economic organization to another. That is why the alphabet is commercial, a trader. It must be understood within the monetary moment of economic rationality. The critical description of money is the faithful reflection of the discourse on writing. In both cases an anonymous supplement is substituted for the thing. Just as the concept retains only the comparable element of diverse things, just as money gives the "common measure"[25] to incommensurable objects in order to constitute them into merchandise, so alphabetic writing transcribes heterogeneous signifieds within a system of arbitrary and common signifiers: the living languages. It thus opens an aggression against the life that it makes circulate. If "the sign has led to the neglect of the thing signified," as *Emile*[26] says speaking of money, then the forgetfulness of things is greatest in the usage of those perfectly abstract and arbitrary signs that are money and phonetic writing.

Following the same graphic, the alphabet introduces a supplementary degree of representativity which marks the progress of analytic rationality. This time, the element brought to light is a pure signifier (purely arbitrary), in itself nonsignifying. This nonsignification is the negative, abstract, and formal aspect of universality or rationality. The value of such a writing is therefore ambiguous. There was a natural universality of a sort in the most archaic degree of writing: painting, as much as the alphabet, is not tied to any determined language. Capable of reproducing all sensible being, it is a sort of universal writing. But its liberty with reference to languages is due not to the distance which separates painting from its model but to the imitative proximity which binds them. Under a universal appearance, painting would thus be perfectly empirical, multiple, and changeful like the sensory units that it represents outside of any code. By contrast, the ideal universality of phonetic writing is due to its infinite distance with respect to the sound (the primary signified of that writing which marks it arbitrarily) and to the meaning signified by the spoken word. Between these two poles, universality is lost. I say between these two poles since, as I have confirmed, pure pictography and pure phonography are two ideas of reason. Ideas of pure presence: in the first case, presence of the represented thing in its perfect imitation, and in the second, the self-presence of speech itself. In both cases, the signifier tends to be effaced in the presence of the signified.

This ambiguity characterizes the evaluation that all metaphysics has imposed upon its own writing since Plato. Rousseau's text belongs to this history, articulating one of its remarkable epochs. More rational, more exact, more precise, more clear, the writing of the voice corresponds to a more efficient civil order. But in so far as it effaces itself better than another before the possible presence of the voice, it represents it better and permits it to be absent with the smallest loss. Faithful servant of speech, it is preferred to writings used by other societies, but as a slave is preferred to a barbarian, fearing it at the same time as a machine of death.

For its rationality distances it from passion and song, that is to say from the living origin of language. It progresses with the consonant. Corresponding to a better organization of social institutions, it also gives the means of more easily doing without the sovereign presence of the assembled people. It tends to restore natural dispersion. Writing naturalizes culture. It is that precultural force which is at work as articulation within culture, working to efface a difference which it has opened. Political rationality—the rationality of fact, and not the rationality whose principle *The Social Contract* describes—favors writing and dispersion at the same time and in the same movement.

The propagation of writing, the teaching of its rules, the production of its instruments and objects, are considered by Rousseau to be an enterprise of political enslavement. That is what one also reads in *Tristes Tropiques*. Certain governments are interested in having languages muzzled, thus ensuring that one no longer speak to the soverign people. The abuse of writing is a political abuse. The latter is rather the "reason" of the former:

language, perfecting itself in books, is corrupted in discourse. It is clearer when one writes, duller when one speaks, syntax is purified and harmony is lost, French becomes more philosophic and less eloquent day by day, soon it will be good only for reading and all its value will be in libraries.
The reason for this abuse lies, as I have submited elsewhere [in the last chapter of the *Essay*], in the form that governments have taken and which results in our having nothing to say to others except the least interesting things in the world and things that they care least to understand: sermons, academic discourses. Fragment on Pronunciation (pp. 1249–50)

Political decentralization, dispersion, and decentering of sovereignty calls, paradoxically, for the existence of a capital, a center of usurpation and of substitution. In opposition to the autarchic cities of Antiquity, which were their own centers and conversed in the living voice, the modern capital is always a monopoly of writing. It commands by written laws, decrees, and literature. Such is Paris's role as Rousseau sees it in the text on *Pronunciation*. Let us not forget that *The Social Contract* judged the exercise of the sovereignty of a people and the existence of a capital incompatible. And as in the case of representatives, if it was impossible not to have recourse to them, it was at least necessary to remedy that evil by changing them often. Which amounts to recharging writing with the living voice: "Nevertheless, if the State cannot be reduced to the right limits, there remains still one resource; this is, to allow no capital, to make the seat of government move from town to town, and to assemble by turn in each the Provincial Estates of the country"[27] (p. 427)· [p. 76]. The instance of writing must be effaced to the point where a sovereign people *must not even write to itself*, its assemblies must meet spontaneously, without "any formal summons" [p. 75]. Which implies—and that is a writing that Rousseau does not wish to read—that there were "fixed and periodic" assemblies that "cannot be abrogated or prorogued," and therefore a "marked day [*jour marqué*]." That mark had to be made orally since the moment the possibility of writing were introduced into the operation, it would insinuate usurpation into the body of society. But is not a mark, wherever it is produced, the possibility of writing?

The Theorem and the Theater

The history of the voice and its writing is comprehended between two mute writings, between two poles of universality relating to each other as the natural and the artificial: the pictogram and algebra. The relationship of natural to artificial or arbitrary is itself subject to the law of "extremes" which "touch one another." And if Rousseau suspects alphabetic writing without condemning it absolutely, it is because there are worse.

It is structurally but the next to the last step of that history. Its artifice has a limit. Unbound to any particular language, it yet refers to the *phonè* or language in general. As phonetic writing, it keeps an essential relationship to the presence of a speaking subject *in general*, to a transcendental locutor, to the voice as the self-presence of a life which hears itself speak. In that sense, phonetic writing is not absolute evil. It is not the letter of death. Nevertheless, it announces death. To the extent that that writing progresses with consonantic chilling, it allows the anticipation of the'ice, speech degree zero: the disappearance of the vowel, the writing of a dead language. The consonant, which is easier to write than the vowel, initiates this end of speech in the universal writing, in algebra:

It would be easy to construct a language consisting solely of consonants, which could be written clearly but not spoken. Algebra has something of such a language. When the orthography of a language is clearer than its pronunciation, this is a sign that it is written more than it is spoken. This may have been true of the scholarly language of the Egyptians; as is the case for us with the dead languages. In those burdened with useless consonants, writing seems to have preceded speech: and who would doubt that such is the case with Polish? [*Essay*], Chap. 7 [p. 28]

The universal characteristic, writing become purely conventional through having broken all links with the spoken language—such then would be absolute evil. With the *Logic of Port-Royal*, Locke's *Essay*, Malebranche, and Descartes, Leibniz was one of Rousseau's primary philosophic readings.[28] He is not cited in the *Essay* but in the fragment on *Pronunciation*. With as much suspicion as the "art of Raymond Lully" in *Emile* (p. 575) [p. 425].

Languages are made to be spoken, writing serves only as supplement to speech; if there are some languages that are only written, and that one cannot speak, belonging only to the sciences, it would be of no use in civil life. Such is algebra, such was no doubt the universal language that Leibniz looked for. It would probably have been more useful to a Metaphysician than to an Artisan (p. 1249).

The universal writing of science would thus be absolute alienation. The autonomy of the representer becomes absurd: it has attained its limit and broken with all representeds, with all living origin, with all living present. In it supplementarity is accomplished, that is to say emptied. The supplement, which is neither simply the signifier nor simply the representer, does not take the place of a signified or a represented, as is prescribed by the concepts of signification or representation or by the syntax of the words "signifier" or "representer." The supplement comes in the place of a lapse, a nonsignified or a nonrepresented, a nonpresence. There is no present before it, it is not preceding by anything but itself, that is to say by another supplement. The supplement is always the supplement of a supplement. One wishes to go back *from the supplement to the source*: one must recognize that there is *a supplement at the source.*

Thus it is always already algebraic. In its writing, the visble signifier, has always already begun to seperate itself from speech and to supplant it. The nonphonetic and universal writing of science is also in that sense a *theorem.* It is enough to look in order to calculate. As Leibniz said, "*ad vocem referri non est necesse.*"

Through that silent and mortal glance the complicities of science and politics are exchanged: more precisely of modern political science. "The letter killeth" (*Emile*, p. 226) [p. 159].

Where should one search, in the city, for that lost unity of glance and speech? In what *space* can one again *listen to himself*? Can the theater, which unites spectacle and discourse, not take up where the unanimous assembly left off? "For a long time now one speaks in public only through books, and if one says something in person to the public that interests it, it is in the theater" (*Pronunciation*, p. 1250).

But the theater itself is shaped and undermined by the profound evil of representation. It is that corruption itself. For the stage is not threatened by anything but itself. Theatrical representation, in the sense of exposition, of production, of that which is placed out there (that which the German *Darstellung* translates) is contaminated by supplementary re-presentation. The latter is inscribed in the structure of representation, in the space of the stage. Let us not be mistaken, what Rousseau criticizes in the last analysis is not the content of the spectacle, the sense *represented* by it, although that *too* he criticizes: it is re-presentation itself. Exactly as within the political order, the menace has the shape of the representative.

In fact, after having evoked the misdeeds of the theater considered in the content of what it stages, in its *represented*, the *Letter to d'Alembert* incriminates representation and the *representer*: "Beyond these effects of the theatre, which are relative to what is *performed* [*representées*], there are others *no less necessary* which relate directly to the *stage* and to the *persons who perform* [*representants*]; and it is to them that the previously mentioned Genevans attribute the taste for luxury, adornment, and dissipation, whose introduction among us they rightly fear."[29] Immorality, then, attaches, to the very status of the representer (performer). Vice is his natural bent. It is normal that he who has taken up representation as a profession should have a taste for external and artificial signifiers, and for the perverse use of signs. Luxury, fine clothes, and dissipation are not signifiers incidentally coming about here and there, they are the crimes of the signifier or the representer itself.

Double consequence:

1. There are two sorts of public persons, two men of spectacle: on the one hand the orator or preacher, on the other the actor. The former represents himself, in him the representer and the represented are one. But the actor is born out of the rift between the representer and the represented. Like the alphabetic signifier, like the letter, the actor himself is not inspired or animated by any particular language. He signifies nothing. He hardly lives, he lends his voice. It is a mouthpiece. Of course the difference between the orator or preacher and the actor presupposes that the former does his duty, says what he has to say. If they do not assume ethical responsibility for their word, they become actors, hardly even actors, for the latter make a duty of saying what they do not think:

> The orator and the preacher, it could be said, make use of their persons as does the actor. The difference is, however, very great. When the orator appears in public, it is to speak and not to show himself off; he *represents only himself*: he fills only his own proper role, speaks only in his own name, says, or ought to say, only what he thinks; *the man and the role being the same* [being] [*étant le même être*], he is *in his place*; he is in the situation of any citizen who fulfils the functions of his estate. But an actor on the stage, displaying other sentiments than his own, saying only what he is made to say, *often representing a chimerical being*, annihilates himself, as it were, and is lost in his hero. And, in this forgetting of the man, if something remains of him, it is used as the plaything of the spectators (p. 187; italics added) [pp. 80–81].

It is the best possible situation: the actor accepts the role and loves what he incarnates. The situation may be still worse. "What shall I say of those who seem to be afraid of having too much merit as they are and who degrade themselves to the point of playing characters whom they would be quite distressed to resemble?" [p. 81].

The identity of the representer and the represented may be accomplished in two ways. The better way: by the effacement of the representer and the personal presence of the represented (the orator, the preacher); or the worse way: it is not illustrated by the actor alone (representer emptied of what he represents) but by a certain society, that of the worldly Parisians who have, in order to find themselves there, alienated themselves in a certain theater, theater of a theater, play representing the comedy of that society. "It is nevertheless solely for these people that theatrical entertainments are made. They are represented by fictitious characters in the middle of the theater, and show themselves in real ones on each side; they are at once persons of the drama on the stage, and comedians in the boxes" (*La Nouvelle Héloise*, p. 252).* This total alienation of the represented within

* *Eloisa: or, A Series of Original Letters*, collected and published by Mr. J. J. Rousseau, Citizen of Geneva, translated from the French, 2d edition (London, 1761), 2: 60.

the representer is the negative aspect of the social pact. In both cases, the represented is reappropriated when he is lost without reserve in his representation. In what terms should the elusive difference which separates the positive from the negative aspect, the authentic social pact from a forever-perverted theater, from a *theatrical* society, be defined?

2. The signifier is the death of the festival. The innocence of the public spectacle, the good festival, the dance around the water hole, would open a theater without representation. Or rather a stage without a show: without *theater*, with nothing to see. Visibility—a moment ago the theorem, here the theatre—is always that which, separating it from itself, breaches [*entame*] the living voice.

But what is a stage which presents nothing to the sight? It is the place where the spectator, presenting himself as spectacle, will no longer be either seer [*voyant*] or voyeur, will efface within himself the difference between the actor and the spectator, the represented and the representer, the object seen and the seeing subject. With that difference, an entire series of oppositions will deconstitute themselves one by one. Presence will be full, not as an object which is *present* to be seen, to give itself to intuition as an empirical unit or as an *eidos* holding itself *in front of* or *up against*; it will be full as the intimacy of a self-presence, as the consciousness or the sentiment of self-proximity, of self-sameness [*propriété*]. That public festival will therefore have a form analogous to the electoral meetings of a free and legiferant assembled people: the representative differance will be effaced in the self-presence of sovereignty. "The exaltation of the collective festival has the same structure as the general will of *The Social Contract*. The description of *public joy* gives us the lyrical aspect of the general will: it is the aspect that it assumes in its Sunday best."[30] The text is well known. It recalls the evocation of the festival in the *Essay*. Let us reread it in order to recognize the desire of making *representation* disappear, with all the meanings that converge in that word: delay and delegation, repetition of a present in its sign or its concept, the proposition or opposition of a show, an object to be seen:

> What! Ought there to be no entertainments in a republic? On the contrary, there ought to be many. It is in republics that they were born, it is in their bosom that they are seen to flourish with a truly festive air. [*Letter to d'Alembert*, p. 125]

These innocent spectacles will take place outdoors and they will have nothing "effeminate" or "mercenary" about them. The sign, money, ruse, passivity, and servility will be excluded from them. No one will use anyone, no one will be an object for anyone. There will no longer be, after a certain fashion, anything to see:

But what then will be the objects of these entertainments? What will be shown in them? Nothing, if you please. With liberty, wherever abundance reigns, well-being also reigns. Plant a stake crowned with flowers in the middle of a square; gather the people together there, and you will have a festival. Do better yet; let the spectators become an entertainment to themselves; make them actors themselves; do it so that each sees and loves himself in the others so that all will be better united. *Letter to M. d'Alembert*, pp. 224–25 [p. 126]

We must note that this festival without object is also a festival without sacrifice, without expense, and without play. Above all without masks.[31] It has no outside although it takes place out of doors. It maintains itself in a purely interior relation to itself. "So that each sees and loves himself in the others." In a certain way, it is confined and sheltered, whereas the hall of the theater, wrenched away from itself by the games and detours of representation, diverted from itself and torn by differance, multiplies the outside in itself. There are many *games* [*jeux*] within the public festival but no *play* [*jeu*] at all, if one understands by that singular number the substitution of contents, the exchange of presences and absences, chance and absolute risk. That festival represses the relationship with death; what was not necessarily implied in the description of the enclosed theatre. These analyses can turn in both directions.

At any rate, play is so much absent from the festival that the dance is admitted as the initiation into marriage and is contained within the closure of the ball. Such is at least the interpretation to which Rousseau submits, to fix it carefully, the meaning of his text on the festival. One could make him say quite a different thing. And Rousseau's text must constantly be considered as a complex and many-leveled structure; in it, certain propositions may be read as interpretations of other propositions that we are, up to a certain point and with certain precautions, free to read otherwise. Rousseau says A, then for reasons that we must determine, he interprets A into B. A, which was already an interpretation, is reinterpreted into B. After taking cognizance of it, we may, without leaving Rousseau's text, isolate A from its interpretation into B, and discover possibilities and resources there that indeed belong to Rousseau's text, but were not produced or exploited by him, which, for equally legible motives, he *preferred to cut short* by a gesture neither witting nor unwitting. In his description of the festival, for example, there are propositions which could very well have been interpreted in the sense of Antonin Artaud's[32] theater of cruelty or of the festival and sovereignty of which Georges Bataille has proposed the concepts. But these propositions are interpreted otherwise by Rousseau himself, who transforms play into games and the dance into a ball, expense into presence.

What ball are we speaking of here? To understand that, one must first understand the praise of the open air. The open air is undoubtedly Nature and in that respect it must lead Rousseau's thoughts in a thousand ways, through all the themes of pedagogy, promenade, botany, and so on. But more precisely, the open air is the element of the voice, the liberty of a breath that nothing breaks into pieces. A voice that can make itself heard in the open air is a free voice, a clear voice that the northern principle has not yet muzzled with consonants, not yet broken, articulated, compartmentalized, and which can reach the interlocutor immediately. The open air is frankness, the absence of evasions, of representative mediations among living spoken words. It is the element of the Greek city, "the great concern" of which was "its liberty." The north limits the possibilities of the open air: "Your severer climates add to your needs; for half the year your public squares are uninhabitable; *the flatness of your languages unfits them for being heard in the open air*; you sacrifice more for profit than for liberty, and fear slavery less than poverty" (*The Social Contract*, p. 431) [p. 79; italics added]. Once again the northern influence is pernicious. But a northern man must live like a northerner. To adopt or adapt southern customs in the North is pure folly and worse servitude (ibid.). One must therefore find substitutes in the North or in winter. The winter substitute of the festival is our dance for young brides-to-be. Rousseau recommends the practice: unequivocally and as he himself says, without scruple; and what he says of winter illuminates after a fashion what he might have said of summer.

Winter, a time consecrated to the private association of friends, is less appropriate to public festivals. There is, however, one sort concerning which I wish there were not so many scrupulous doubts raised, that is, the balls for young marriageable persons. I have never understood why people are so worried about dancing and the gatherings it occasions, as if there were something worse about dancing than singing, as if these amusements were not both equally an inspiration of nature, as if it were a crime for those who are destined to be united to be merry together in a decent recreation. Man and woman were formed for one another. God wants them to fulfill their destiny, and certainly the first and holiest of all the bonds of society is marriage.[33]

One should comment word by word on the long and edifying discourse that follows. A hinge articulates the entire argument: the full daylight of presence avoids the dangerous supplement. One must allow pleasures to "a lively and frolicsome youth" to avoid their "substituting more dangerous ones" and to prevent "private meetings adroitly concerted [from] tak[ing] the place of public gatherings." "Innocent joy is likely to evaporate in the full light of day; but vice is a friend of shadows" (*Letter to M. d'Alembert*, p. 227) [p. 129]. Furthermore, the nudity that presents the body itself is less dangerous than the recourse to sartorial signifiers, to the northern supplement, to "artful dress": the latter is not "less dangerous than an absolute nudity the habit of which would soon turn the first effects into indifference and perhaps distaste." "Is it not known that statues and paintings only offend the eyes when a mixture of clothing renders the nudity obscene? The immediate power of the senses is weak and limited; it is through the intermediary of the imagination that they make their greatest ravages; it is the business of the imagination to irritate the desires" (p. 232) [p. 134]. It will have been noticed that representation—the picture—rather than perception, is chosen to illustrate the danger of the supplement whose efficiency is the imagination. And it will then be noticed that, in a note inserted into the heart of this praise of marriage, anticipating the errors of posterity, Rousseau makes only one exception to his denials:

It is something amusing for me to imagine the judgments that many will make of my tastes on the basic of my writings. On the basis of this one they will not fail to say: "that man is crazy about dancing"; it bores me to watch dancing; "he cannot bear the drama"; I love the drama passionately; "he has an aversion to women"; on that score I shall be only too easily vindicated (p. 229) [p. 131n].

Thus the North, winter, death, imagination, representation, the irritation of desires—this entire series of supplementary significations—does not designate a natural place or fixed terms: rather a periodicity. Seasons. In the order of time, or rather like time itself, they speak the movement by which the presence of the present separates from itself, supplants itself, replaces itself by absenting itself, produces itself in self-substitution. It is this that the metaphysics of presence as self-proximity wishes to efface by giving a privileged position to a sort of absolute now, the *life* of the present, the living present. The coldness of representation not only breaks self-presence but also the originarity of the present as the absolute form of temporality.

This metaphysics of presence constantly reappears and is resumed in Rousseau's text whenever the fatality of the supplement seems to limit it. It is always necessary to add a supplement of presence to the presence that is concealed. "The great remedy to the miseries of this world" is "absorption into the present moment," says Rousseau in *The Solitaries*. The present is originary, that is to say the determination of origin always has the form of presence. Birth is the birth (of) presence. Before it there is no presence; and from the moment that presence, holding or announcing itself to itself, breaches its plenitude and starts the chain of its history, death's work has begun. Birth in general is written as Rousseau describes his own: "I cost my mother her life; and my birth was the first of my misfortunes" (*Confessions*, p. 7) [p. 5]. Every time that Rousseau tries to recapture an essence (in the form of an origin, a right, an ideal limit), he always leads us back to a point of full presence. He is less interested in the present, in the being-present, than in the presence of the present, in its essence as it appears to itself and is retained in itself. Essence is presence. As life, that is as self-presence, it is birth. And just as the present goes out of itself only to return to itself, a rebirth is possible which, furthermore, is the only thing that permits all the repetitions of origin. Rousseau's discourse and questions are possible only in the anticipation of a rebirth or a reactivation of the origin. Rebirth, resurrection, or reawakening always appropriate to themselves, in their fugitive immediacy, the plenitude of presence returning to itself.

That return to the presence of the origin is produced after each catastrophe, at least in so far as it *reverses* the order of life without destroying it. After a divine finger had *turned* the order of the world *over* [*renversé*] by inclining the axis of the globe on the axis of the universe and had thus willed that "men [be] sociable," the festival around the water hole was possible and pleasure was immediately present to desire. After a "great Danish dog" had *knocked* Jean-Jacques *over* [*renversé*] in the second *Promenade*; when after "the fall" which had *precipitated* him ("my head was thrown down lower than my feet") it was first necesasry to *recount* to him the "accident" that he had not been able to experience; when he explains to us what happened at the moment when, he says twice, "I came to myself," "I came back to consciousness,"—it is indeed awakening as re-awakening to pure presence that he describes, always according to the same model: not anticipation, not memory, not comparison, not distinction, not articulation, not situation. Imagination, memory, and signs are effaced. All landmarks on the physical or psychical landscape are natural.

The state in which I found myself in that instant was too singular not to make a description of it here.

The night was coming on. I perceived the sky, some stars, and a little grass. This first sensation was a delicious moment. I did not feel anything except through them. I was born in that instant to life, and it seemed to me that I filled with my light existence all the objects which I perceived. Entirely given up to the present moment, I did not remember anything; I had no distinct notion of my individuality, not the least idea of what had happened to me; I did not know who I was nor where I was; I felt neither evil nor fear, nor trouble.

And, as around the water hole, and on the Isle of St. Pierre, the enjoyment [*jouissance*] of pure presence is that of a certain flow. Presence being born. Origin of life, blood's resemblance to water. Rousseau continues:

I saw my blood flowing as I might have looked at a brooklet, without dreaming even that this blood in any way belonged to me. I felt in the whole of my being a ravishing calm, to which, each time that I think of it, I find nothing comparable in the whole action of known pleasures (p. 1005) [p. 49].

Are there other or more archetypal pleasures? This pleasure, which is the only pleasure, is at the same time properly *unimaginable*. Such is the paradox of the imagination: it alone arouses or irritates desire but also it alone, and for the same reason, in the same movement, extends beyond or divides presence. Rousseau would like to separate the awakening to presence from the operation of imagination; he always presses on toward that impossible limit. For the awakening of presence projects or rejects us immediately outside of presence where we are "led . . . by that living interest, foresightful and all-providing [*prévoyant et pourvoyant*], which . . . always throws us far from the present, and which does not exist for natural man" (*Dialogues*).[34] Function of representation, imagination is also the temporalizing function, the excess of the present and the economy of what exceeds presence. There is no unique and full present (but is there presence then?) except in the imagination's sleep: "The sleeping imagination does not know at all how to extend its being into two different times" (*Emile*, p. 69). When it appears, signs, fiduciary values [legal tender and trusts], and letters emerge, and they are worse than death.

> How many merchants lament in Paris over some misfortune in India! . . . There is a healthy, cheerful, strong, and vigorous man; it does me good to see him. . . . A letter comes by post. . . . [He] falls into a swoon. When he comes to himself he weeps, laments, and groans, he tears his hair, and his shrieks re-echo through the air. You would say he was in convulsions. Fool, what harm has this bit of paper done you? What limb has it torn away? . . . We no longer live in our own place, we live outside it. What does it profit me to live in such fear of death, when all that makes life worth living remains? (*Emile*, pp. 67–68) [p. 47]

Rousseau himself articulates this chain of significations (essence, origin, presence, birth, rebirth) on the classical metaphysics of the entity as *energy*, encompassing the relationships between being and time in terms of the now as being in action (*energeia*):

> Delivered from the disquietude of hope, and *sure of thus gradually losing that of desire*, seeing that the past was no longer anything to me, I undertook to put myself completely in the situation of a man who begins to live. I told myself that in fact *we were always beginning, and that there was no other link in our existence but a succession of present moments of which the first is always that which is in action*. We are born and die every moment of our life.

It follows—but it is a *liaison* that Rousseau works very hard to elide—that the very essence of presence, if it must always be repeated within another presence, opens originarily, within presence itself, the structure of representation. And if essence *is* presence, there is no essence of presence nor presence of essence. There is a play of representation and eliding that liaison or that consequence, Rousseau places play out of play: he eludes, which is another way of playing, or rather, as the dictionaries say, of playing (with). What is thus eluded is the fact that representation does not suddenly encroach upon presence; it inhabits it as the very condition of its experience, of desire, and of enjoyment [*jouissance*]. The intertior doubling of presence, its halving, makes it appear as such, that is to say, concealing enjoyment in frustration, makes it disappear as such. Placing representation outside, which means placing the outside outside, Rousseau would like to make of the supplement of presence a pure and simple addition, a contingence: thus wishing to elude what, in the interior of presence, calls forth the substitute, and is constituted only in that appeal, and in its trace.

Thence the letter. Writing is the evil of representative repetition, the double that opens desire and contemplates and binds [*re-garde*] enjoyment. Literary writing, the traces of the *Confessions*, speak that doubling of presence. Rousseau condemns the evil of writing and looks for a haven within writing. It repeats enjoyment symbolically. And just as enjoyment has never been present except in a certain repetition, so writing, recalling enjoyment, gives it as well. Rousseau eludes its admission but not the pleasure. We recall those texts ("Saying to myself I have rejoiced, I rejoice again. . . ." "I rejoice again in a pleasure that no longer is." . . . "Incessantly occupied with the thought of my past happiness, I recall it, so to speak, chew the cud of it to such an extent that, when I desire it, I am able to enjoy it over again") [p. 607]. Writing *represents* (in every sense of the word) enjoyment. It plays enjoyment, renders it present and absent. It is play. And it is because it is also the good fortune of enjoyment repeated that Rousseau practices it while condemning it: "I shall set down in writing those ['delightful contemplations'] which may still come to me: each time that I reread them will give me new pleasure" (*Reveries*, p. 999) [p. 38].

This entire digression was necessary in order to mark well that, unless some extrinsic desire is invested in it, Leibniz's universal characteristic represents the very death of enjoyment. It leads the representer to the limit of its excess. Phonetic writing, however abstract and arbitrary, retained some relationship with the presence of the represented voice, to its possible presence in general and therefore to that of a certain passion. A writing that breaks with the *phonè* radically is perhaps the most rational and effective of scientific machines; it no longer responds to any desire or rather *it signifies its death to desire*. It was what already operated within speech as writing and machine. It is the representer in its pure state, without the represented, or without the order of the represented naturally linked to it. That is why this pure conventionality ceases, being pure, to be of any use within "civil life," which always mingles nature and convention. The perfection of convention here touches its opposite extreme, it is death and the perfect alienation of the instrument of civil order. The telos of the alienation of writing has in Rousseau's eyes the form of scientific or technical writing, wherever it can act, that is to say even outside of the areas reserved for "science" or "technology." It is not by chance that in mythology, the Egyptian in particular, the god of sciences and technologies is also the god of writing; and that it is he (Thoth, Theuth, Teuthus or his Greek homologue Hermes, god of the ruse, of trade, and of thieves) whom Rousseau incriminates in the *Discourse on the Arts and Sciences.* (Plato had already denounced his invention of writing at the end of the *Phaedrus.*):

> An ancient tradition passed out of Egypt into Greece, that some god, who was an enemy to the repose of mankind, was the inventor of the sciences.* . . . In fact, whether we turn to the annals of the world, or supplement with philosophical investigations the uncertain chronicles of history, we shall not find for human knowledge an origin answering to the idea we are pleased to entertain of it at present. . . . Their evil origin is indeed, but too plainly reproduced in their objects. [Cole, op. cit., p. 131.]

* It is easy to see the allegory in the fable of Prometheus: and it does not appear that the Greeks, who chained him to the Caucasus, had a better opinion of him than the Egyptians had of their god Teuthus (p. 12).

The Supplement of (at) the Origin

In the last pages of the chapter "On Script," the critique, the appreciative presentation, and the history of writing, *declares* the absolute exteriority of writing but *describes* the interiority of the principle of writing to language. The sickness of the outside (which comes from the outside but also draws outside, thus equally, or inversely, the sickness of the homeland, a homesickness, so to speak) is in the heart of the living word, as its principle of effacement and its relationship to its own death. In other words, it does not suffice to show, it is in fact not a question of showing, the interiority of what Rousseau would have believed exterior; rather to speculate upon the power of exteriority as constitutive of interiority: of speech, of signified meaning, of the present as such; in the sense in which I said, a moment ago, that the representative mortal doubling-halving constituted the living present, without adding itself to presence; or rather constituted it, paradoxically, by being added to it. The question is of an originary supplement, if this absurd expression may be risked, totally unacceptable as it is within classical logic. Rather the supplement of origin: which supplements the failing origin and which is yet not derived; this supplement is, as one says of a spare part [*une pièce*], of the original make [*d'origine*] [or a document, establishing the origin.]

Thus one takes into account that the absolute *alterity* of writing might nevertheless affect living speech, from the outside, within its inside: *alter it* [for the worse]. Even as it has an independent history, as we have seen, and in spite of the inequalities of development, the play of structural correlations, writing marks the history of speech. Although it is born out of "needs of a different kind" and "according to circumstances entirely independent of the duration of the people," although these needs might "never have occurred," the irruption of this absolute contingency determined the interior of an essential history and affected the interior unity of a life, *literally infected* it. It is the strange essence of the supplement not to have essentiality: it may always not have taken place. Moreover, literally, it has never taken place: it is never present, here and now. If it were, it would not be what it is, a supplement, taking and keeping the place of the other. What alters for the worse the living nerve of language ("Writing, which would seem to crystallize language, is precisely what alters it; it changes not the words but the spirit of language . . .") has therefore above all not taken place. Less than nothing and yet, to judge by its effects, much more than nothing. The supplement is neither a presence nor an absence. No ontology can think its operation.

As Saussure will do, so does Rousseau wish at once to maintain the exteriority of the system of writing and the maleficent efficiency with which one singles out its symptoms on the body of the language. But am I saying anything else? Yes, in as much as I show the interiority of exteriority, which amounts to annulling the ethical qualification and to thinking of writing beyond good and evil; yes above all, in as much as we designate the impossibility of formulating the movement of supplementarity within the classical logos, within the logic of identity, within ontology, within the opposition of presence and absence, positive and negative, and even within dialectics, if at least one determines it, as spiritualistic or materialistic metaphysics has always done, within the horizon of presence and reappropriation. Of course the *designation* of that impossibility escapes the language of metaphysics only by a hairsbreadth. For the rest, it must borrow its resources from the logic it deconstructs. And by doing so, find its very foothold there.

One can no longer see disease in substitution when one sees that the substitute is substituted for a substitute. Is that not what the *Essay describes*? "[Writing substitutes] exactitude for expressiveness." Expression is the expression of affect, of the passion at the origin of language, of a speech that was first substituted for song, marked by *tone* and *force*. Tone and force signify the *present voice*: they are anterior to the concept, they are singular, they are, moreover, attached to vowels, the vocalic and not the consonantic element of language. The force of expression amounts only to vocalic sounds, when the subject is there in person to utter his passion. When the subject is no longer there, force, intonation, and accent are lost in the concept. Then one writes, one "substitutes" in vain "accentual marks" for "accent," one bows to the generality of the law: "In writing, one is forced to use all the words according to their conventional meaning. But in speaking, one varies the meanings by varying one's tone of voice, determining them as one pleases. Being less constrained to clarity, one can be more forceful. And it is not possible for a language that is written to retain its vitality as long as one that is only spoken" [*Essay*, pp. 21–22].

Thus writing is always atonal. The place of the subject is there taken by another, it is concealed. The spoken sentence, which is valuable only once and remains "proper only to the place where it is," loses its place and its proper meaning as soon as it is written down. "The means used to overcome [*suppléer*] this weakness tend to stretch out written language and make it elaborately prolix; and many books written in discourse will enervate speech itself."

But if Rousseau could say that "words [*voix*], not sounds [*sons*], are written," it is because words are distinguished from sounds exactly by what permits writing—consonants and articulation. The latter replace only themselves. Articulation, which replaces accent, is the origin of languages. Altering [for the worse] through writing is an originary exteriority. It is the origin of language. Rousseau describes it without declaring it. Clandestinely.

A speech without consonantic principle, what for Rousseau would be a speech sheltered from all writing, would not be speech;[35] it would hold itself at the fictive limit of the inarticulate and purely natural cry. Conversely, a speech of pure consonants and pure articulation would become pure writing, algebra, or dead language. The death of speech is therefore the horizon and origin of language. But an origin and a horizon which do not hold themselves at its exterior borders. As always, death, which is neither a present to come nor a present past, shapes the interior of speech, as its trace, its reserve, its interior and exterior differance: as its supplement.

But Rousseau could not think this writing, that takes place *before* and *within* speech. To the extent that he belonged to the metaphysics of presence, he *dreamed* of the simple exteriority of death to life, evil to good, representation to presence, signifier to signified, representer to represented, mask to face, writing to speech. But all such oppositions are irreducibly rooted in that metaphysics. Using them, one can only operate by reversals, that is to say by confirmations. The supplement is none of these terms. It is especially not more a signifier than a signified, a representer than a presence, a writing than a speech. None of the terms of this series can, being comprehended within it, dominate the economy of differance or supplementarity. Rousseau's *dream* consisted of making the supplement enter metaphysics by force.

But what does that mean? The opposition of dream to wakefulness, is not that a representation of metaphysics as well? And what should dream or writing be if, as we know now, one may dream while writing? And if the scene of dream is always a scene of writing? At the bottom of a page of *Emile*, after having once more cautioned us against books, writing, signs ("What is the use of inscribing on their brains a list of symbols which mean nothing for them?"), after having opposed the "tracing" of these artificial signs to the "indelible characters" of the Book of Nature, Rousseau adds a note: ". . . the dreams of a bad night are given to us as philosophy. You will say I too am a dreamer; I admit it, but I do what others fail to do, I give my dreams as dreams, and leave the reader to discover whether there is anything in them which may prove useful to those who are awake" [p. 76].

Notes

Translator's Preface

1. For Derrida's interest in his own Jewish tradition, see "Edmond Jabès et la question du livre," and "Ellipse," both in *L'écriture et la différence* (hereafter cited in the text as *ED*), (Paris, 1967), pp. 99–116, 429–36, and, of course, *Glas*. At the end of "Ellipse" he signs as he quotes Jabès—"Reb Dérissa." The few provocative remarks in response to Gérard Kaleka's questions after Derrida's paper "La question du style" (*Nietzsche aujourd'hui?* [Paris, 1973], 1: 289; hereafter cited as *QS*), can provide ideas for the development of an entire thematics of the Jew.

2. For an account of the *Tel Quel* group, see Mary Caws, "Tel Quel: Text and Revolution," *Diacritics* 3, i (Spring 1973): 2–8.

3. Edmund Husserl, *L'origine de la géométrie*, tr. Jacques Derrida (Paris, 1962). Jacques Derrida, *La Voix et le phénomène: introduction au problème du signe dans la phénoménologie de Husserl* (hereafter cited in the text as *VP*), (Paris, 1967); translated as *Speech and Phenomena* (hereafter cited in the text as *SP*) by David B. Allison (Evanston, 1973). *L'écriture et la différence* (Paris, 1967). *De la grammatologie* (Paris, 1967) (hereafter cited simply by page numbers in the text, page references to the French followed by references to the present edition in bold-face type). *La dissémination* (Paris, 1972) (hereafter cited as *Dis*). *Marges de la philosophie* (Paris, 1972) (hereafter cited as *MP*). *Positions* (Paris, 1972) (hereafter cited as *Pos* F;) parts of this book have been translated in *Diacritics* 2, iv (Winter 1972): 6–14 (hereafter cited in the text as *Pos* E I) and 3, i (Spring 1973): 33–46 (hereafter cited in the text as *Pos* E II). "L'archéologie du frivole," in Condillac, *Essai sur l'origine des connaissances humaines*, (Paris, 1973). Finally, *Glas* (Paris, 1974).

Four important essays that are as yet uncollected are "Le parergon," *Digraphe* 2: 21–57, "La Question du style," op. cit., "Le Facteur de la vérité, *Poétique* 21 (1975): 96–147 (soon to appear in translation in *Yale French Studies*), and "Le sens de la coupure pure: Le parergon II," *Digraphe* 3, 1976.

4. Jean Hyppolite, "Structure du langage philosophique d'après la 'Préface' de la 'Phénoménologie de l'esprit' de Hegel," *The Languages of Criticism and the Sciences of Man: the Structuralist Controversy* (hereafter cited in the text as *SC*), Richard Macksey and Eugenio Donato, eds. (Baltimore, 1970), p. 337. Translated in the same volume as "The Structure of Philosophic Language According to the 'Preface' to Hegel's *Phenomenology of the Mind*." The passage cited is on p. 159.

5. Georg Wilhelm Friedrich Hegel, *Phänomenologie des Geistes*, Suhrkamp edition (Frankfurt am Main, 1970), p. 37; *The Phenomenology of the Mind*, tr. J. B. Baillie, Harper Torchbooks edition (New York, 1967) p. 94. My general policy in quoting from English translations has been to modify the English when it seems less than faithful to the original. I have included references to both the original and the English, and generally included the original passage in the text when I have modified the translation.

6. Hegel, p. 65; Baillie, pp. 127–28.

7. Hegel, p. 22; Baillie, p. 79.

8. See "La dissémination," *Dis*, II. x. "Les greffes, retour au surjet," pp. 395–98, and pp. lxv–lxvi of this Preface.

9. Marcel Proust, "La fugitive," *A la recherche du temps perdu*, Pléiade edition (Paris, 1954), 3: 489; *The Sweet Cheat Gone*, tr. C. K. Scott Moncrieff, Vintage Books edition (New York, 1970), p. 54, italics mine.

10. Hegel, p. 35; Baillie, p. 92.

11. Stéphane Mallarmé, "Le Livre, instrument spirituel," *Quant au Livre*, *Oeuvres*

complètes, Pléiade edition (Paris, 1945), p. 381; *Mallarmé*, tr. Anthony Hartley (Baltimore), p. 194.

12. Martin Heidegger, *The Question of Being*, tr. William Kluback and Jean T. Wilde, bilingual edition (New York, 1958), hereafter cited in the text as *QB*.

13. Because it overlooks the invisible erasure, the usual superficial criticism of Derrida goes as follows: he says he is questioning the value of "truth" and "logic," yet he uses logic to demonstrate the truth of his own arguments! (A characteristic example would be Lionel Abel, "Jacques Derrida: His *'Difference'* with Metaphysics," *Salmagundi* 25 [Winter, 1974]: 3–21.) The point is, of course, that the predicament of having to use resources of the heritage that one questions is the *overt* concern of Derrida's work, and as such is prepared for, as I shall show, by the fundamental questionings of Nietzsche, Freud, and Heidegger.

14. "La différance," *Bulletin de la société française de philosophie* 62, iii (1968): 103. This remark occurs in the discussion following the lecture and is neither reprinted in *MP* nor translated in *SP*.

15. Claude Lévi-Strauss, *La Pensée sauvage* (Paris, 1962); translated as *The Savage Mind* (Chicago, 1966).

16. Ibid., Eng. tr., p. 17.

17. Ibid., pp. 44 f.; Eng. tr., pp. 16 f.

18. Here Derrida's often implicit Freudianism surfaces. The history of metaphysics, like a dream-neurosis-psychosis, is constituted by distortion. Metaphor and metonymy are rhetorical translations of "condensation" and "displacement," two major techniques, as Freud pointed out, of dream-distortion (see also page xlvi).

19. Marx is conspicuous here by his absence. Derrida's detachment from Marxist texts is often a ground for dissatisfaction among younger French and American intellectuals—some of the Tel Quel group, Felix Guattari, Fredric Jameson. I believe there is a simple enough explanation for this detachment. Derrida's method of deconstructive reading is laboriously textual. As a young philosopher he has coped with specifically "philosophical" texts. Catching the Freudian avant-garde of the fifties and sixties, he has coped, and is coping, with the texts of Freud. His interest now, for reasons I discuss on page lxxii, is going toward "literary" texts. In general, the literature of Marxism is so thoroughly schematized that for him to direct the same painstaking attention to the texts of Marx and Marxism will require a good stretch of time. In answer to a question of Jean-Louis Houdebine, Derrida presents a long and interesting answer which, for my purposes, can be summed up as follows: Marx, and his intertextuality with Hegel, Engels, Lenin, Mao, et alia, are still to be submitted to the protocol of reading. See *Pos* F 82 f., *Pos* E II 33 f. The distinctions between super- and infrastructures must be reexamined. The textuality of "economic" structures (in a narrow sense) must be opened up to a more general concept of economy. . . . A remote prospectus may be glimpsed in *MP*, pp. 257–58n, "White Mythology," tr. F. C. T. Moore, *NLH* VI. i. autumn, 1974, pp. 14–16, and "Economimesis," *Mimesis: desarticulations* (Paris, 1975).

20. "Über Wahrheit und Lüge im aussermoralischen Sinne," *Werke* (hereafter cited in the text as *NW*), ed. Giorgio Colli and Mazzino Montinari (Berlin and New York, 1973), vol. III, part 2, p. 370; "On Truth and Falsity in their Ultramoral Sense" (hereafter cited as *TF*), *The Complete Works of Friedrich Nietzsche*, ed. Oscar Levy (New York, 1964), 2: 174.

21. "Der Wille zur Macht," Books 1 & 2 *Nietzsche's Werke* (Leipzig, 1911), part 2, vol. 15 (herafter cited as *WM* 1), p. 448; *Will to Power*, tr. Walter Kaufmann (hereafter cited in the text as *WP*), (Vintage Books, 1968), p. 227.

22. "Der Wille zur Macht," Book 3 & 4, *Nietzsche's Werke* (Leipzig, 1911), part 2, vol. 16, p. 20 (hereafter cited in the text as *WM* 2); *WP* 273.

23. "Die fröhliche Wissenschaft," *NW* V. ii, 146; *The Gay Science*, tr. Walter Kaufmann (hereafter cited in the text as *GS*) (Vintage Books, 1974), p. 168.

24. Phillippe Lacoue-Labarthe, "La dissimulation: Nietzsche, la question de l'art et la 'littérature,' " *Nietzsche aujourd'hui?* (Paris, 1973), 2: 12.

25. "Zur Genealogie der Moral," *NW* VI. ii, 330. "The Genealogy of Morals" (here-

after cited in the text as *GM*), *On the Genealogy of Morals and Ecce Homo*, tr. Walter Kaufmann (Vintage Books, 1969), p. 77.

26. *MP*, 270–71; "White Mythology," tr. F. C. T. Moore, pp. 26–27.

27. For a discussion of the use of the *stigmè* in Aristotle see Derrida, "Ousia et grammè: note sur une note de *Sein und Zeit*," *MP*, pp. 44 f., translated as " 'Ousia and Grammè': A Note to a Footnote in *Being and Time*," by Edward S. Casey, *Phenomenology in Perception*, ed. F. J. Smith (The Hague, 1970), pp. 63 f.

28. "Vom Nutzen und Nachtheil der Historie für das Leben," *NW* III. i, 320; "The Use and Abuse of History" (hereafter cited in the text as *UA*), *The Complete Works of Friedrich Nietzsche*, ed. Oscar Lévy, vol. 5, p. 89.

29. Sigmund Freud, "Jenseits des Lustprinzips," *Gesammelte Werke* (hereafter cited in the text as GW) (Frankfurt am Main and London, 1940), 13: 46 f.; "Beyond the Pleasure Principle," *The Standard Edition of the Complete Psychological Works of Sigmund Freud* (hereafter cited in the text as *SE*), ed. James Strachey (London, 1959), 18: 44 f.

30. *MP* 163; "The Ends of Man" (hereafter cited in the text as *EM*), tr. Edouard Morot-Sir, Wesley C. Piersol, Hubert L. Dreyfus, and Barbara Reid, *Philosophical and Phenomenological Research* 30 (1969): 57.

31. "Ecce Homo," *Nietzsche's Werke* (Leipzig, 1911), part 2, vol. 15, p. 47, "Ecce Homo," *On the Genealogy of Morals, and Ecce Homo* op. cit., p. 258.

32. *NW* VI. ii, 137; *Beyond Good and Evil*, tr. R. J. Hollingdale (Harmondsworth and Baltimore, 1973), p. 113.

33. "Ecce Homo," op. cit., pp. 96–97; English tr., p. 306. The problem is, of course, not only the complicity between yes and no but also that between saying and doing, and being. For an analysis of the relationship between knowing and doing in Nietzsche, see Paul de Man, "Action and Identity in Nietzsche," forthcoming in *Yale French Studies*. I should mention here that, in a more restricted way, Jean-Michel Rey has noted the need to "erase" certain conceptual master-words in Nietzsche (*L'enjeu des signes: lecture de Nietzsche* [Paris, 1971], pp. 52–53).

34. Martin Heidegger, *Kant und das Problem der Metaphysik* (Frankfurt am Main, 1951), pp. 210–11 (hereafter cited in the text as *KPM* G); *Kant and the Problem of Metaphysics*, tr. James S. Churchill (Bloomington and London, 1962), pp. 241–42, (hereafter cited in the text as *KPM* E). Rey notes the incongruence between Nietzsche and Heidegger in passing, op. cit., p. 91 n.

35. Martin Heidegger, *Nietzsche* (Pfullingen, 1961), (hereafter cited in the text as *HN*), 1: 463–64. Translations are my own.

36. This very condensed remark by Paul de Man will give a hint of the gravity of the problem: " 'Only as an *aesthetic phenomenon* is existence and the world forever *justified*,' . . . the famous quotation, twice repeated in *The Birth of Tragedy* should not be taken too serenely, for it is an indictment of existence rather than a panegyric of art," "Genesis and Genealogy in Nietzsche's *The Birth of Tragedy*," *Diacritics* II, iv (Winter 1972): 50.

37. *Götzendämmerung: oder wie man mit dem Hammer philosophirt*, *NW* VI. iii, 74; *Twilight of the Idols and The Anti-Christ*, tr. R. J. Hollingdale (Harmondsworth, 1968), pp. 40–41.

38. *NW* V. ii, 291; *GS* 317. This Nietzschean passage might be related to Derrida's comments on Lévi-Strauss's play with the Nambikwara girls on p. 167 (p. 114) of the *Grammatology*.

39. For a lucid account of this reinscription, see Jean Laplanche et J.-B. Pontalis, "Fantasme originaire, fantasmes des origines, origine du fantasme," *Les temps modernes* 19, ccxv (1964): 1833–68; translated as "Fantasy and the Origins of Sexuality," *The International Journal of Psychoanalysis* 49, i (1968): 1–18.

40. For "the woman's point of view" on psychoanalysis see Luce Irigaray, *Speculum: de l'autre femme* (Paris, 1974). I am grateful to Michael Ryan for suggesting this line of inquiry.

41. I refer the reader to *QS*, pp. 280 f. Derrida's play on Nietzsche's "I have forgotten my umbrella" should be read in full.

42. Edmund Husserl, *Cartesianische Meditationen und Pariser Vorträge*, ed. S. Strasser (The Hague, 1950), pp. 70–71; *Cartesian Meditations*, tr. Dorion Cairns (The Hague, 1973), p. 32. See also *Formale und transzendentale Logik*, part II, chapter 6, Husserliana, Nijhoff edition (1974), 17: 239–73. *Formal and Transcendental Logic*, tr. Dorion Cairns (The Hague, 1969), pp. 232–66.

43. *ED* 315; "Freud and the Scene of Writing," tr. Jeffrey Mehlman, Yale French Studies 48 (*French Freud: Structural Studies in Psychoanalysis*; hereafter cited in the text as FF) (1972), p. 93.

44. Anthony Wilden, "Lacan and the Discourse of the Other," *The Language of the Self: the Function of Language in Psychoanalysis* by Jacques Lacan, tr. Anthony Wilden (Baltimore and London, 1968), p. 91.

45. Of a good many examples, I shall cite one: "The 'lacunae' to which you alluded, and do me the justice of believing this, are explicitly calculated to mark the loci of a theoretical elaboration . . ." (*Pos F* 85, *Pos E* II 33). An example of the defense of "my master's mastery" is to be found even in Paul de Man's brilliant essay "The Rhetoric of Blindness: Jacques Derrida's Reading of Rousseau" (*Blindness and Insight: Essays in the Rhetoric of Contemporary Criticism* [New York, 1971]): "Rousseau was not deluded and said what he meant to say. . . . Instead of having Rousseau deconstruct his critics, we have Derrida deconstructing a pseudo-Rousseau by means of insights that could have been gained from the 'real' Rousseau" (pp. 135, 139–40). Yet, as we read Derrida's own pages on Lévi-Strauss and Rousseau (part 2, chapter 1, *Of Grammatology*), we sense the same claim being made for Rousseau over Lévi-Strauss: both have given writing short shrift, yet Rousseau's *text*, if not Rousseau, had *known* that simply to do so would have been merely symptomatic. The value of mastery, of knowledge, of control, even of having got there first, persists, however vestigially. The "subject" of knowledge then becomes the text. "[The critic's] use may be no more than to identify an act of deconstruction which has always already, in each case differently, been performed by the text on itself" (J. Hillis Miller, "Deconstructing the Deconstructers," *Diacritics* V, ii [Summer 1975]: 31). This value-in-mastery too is perhaps a "metaphysical" axiom that criticism, at the limit, cannot avoid. For those who are "aware" that this battle cannot be won, there is some measure of comfort in being able to recognize that a *text*, even when assigned control, is never sovereign, always ridden by the absence of the subject, always offering a "lack" that the reader must fill, as well as the materials with which to begin to fill it.

46. See Jacques Lacan, "L'instance de la lettre dans l'inconscient ou la raison depuis Freud," *Ecrits* (Paris, 1966): 493–528; "The Insistence of the Letter in the Unconscious," tr. Jan Miel, *Structuralism*, ed. Jacques Ehrmann, Anchor Books (New York, 1970), pp. 94–137.

47. Martin Heidegger, *Sein und Zeit* (Tübingen, Niemeyer edition, 1960), pp. 22, 24; *Being and Time*, tr. John Macquarrie and Edward Robinson (New York and Evanston, 1962), pp. 44, 46.

48. de Man, *Blindness and Insight*, op. cit., p. 140.

49. *Sein u. Zeit*, pp. 24, 23; *Being and Time*, pp. 46, 45.

50. Eng. tr. (op. cit.), p. 89.

51. Ibid., pp. 17, 39.

52. Martin Heidegger, "Der Spruch des Anaximander," *Holzwege* (Frankfurt am Main, 1950): 296–343.

53. *Origine de la géometrie*, op. cit., p. 171.

54. *Cartesianische Meditationen*, p. 60; *Cartesian Meditations*, p. 20. It is a common error to equate the phenomenological reduction, "putting out of play," and the *sous rature*, "putting under erasure," (see, e.g., Fredric Jameson, *The Prison-House of Language: A Critical Account of Structuralism and Russian Formalism* [Princeton, 1972], p. 216). The distinction is simple: The gesture of bracketing implies "not this but that," preserving a bipolarity as well as a hierarchy of empirical impurity and phenomenological purity; the gesture of *sous rature* implies "both this *and* that" as well as "neither this nor that" undoing the opposition and the hierarchy between the legible and the erased.

55. Roland Barthes, *Essais critiques* (Paris, 1964), p. 216; *Critical Essays*, tr. Richard

Howard (Evanston, 1972), p. 216. For the purposes of this brief discussion of "Structuralism," I focus somewhat on Roland Barthes because, in Jonathan Culler's words, structuralism may be taken to be "the name of a particular intellectual movement centered around the work of a few major figures, among whom the chief, in the field of literary studies, is Roland Barthes" (*Structuralist Poetics* [London, 1975]), p. 3.

56. See, for example, *Russian Formalist Criticism*, tr. Lee T. Lemon and Marion J. Reis (Lincoln, 1965), and Krystyna Pomorska, *Russian Formalist Theory and Its Poetic Ambiance* (The Hague, 1968).

57. Vladimir Propp, *Morfologia Skazki*, second edition (Moscow, 1949); translated by Laurence Scott as *Morphology of the Folktale* (Indiana, 1958).

58. Ferdinand de Saussure, *Cours de linguistique générale* (Paris, 1931), p. 99; *A Course in General Linguistics*, tr. Wade Baskin (New York, 1959), p. 67.

59. Claude Lévi-Strauss, "Introduction," in *Sociologie et anthropologie* by Marcel Mauss (Paris, 1950), p. 49; quoted in *ED* 424.

60. Claude Lévi-Strauss, *L'Anthropologie structurale* (Paris, 1958), pp. 39–41; *Structural Anthropology*, tr. Claire Jacobson and Brooke Grunfest Schoepf, Anchor Books edition (New York, 1967), pp. 31, 32.

61. In "*Les Chats* de Charles Baudelaire," L'Homme II (1962), pp. 5–21 (translated as "Charles Baudelaire's 'Les Chats'," by F. M. de George; *The Structuralists from Marx to Lévi-Strauss*, eds. Richard T. and Fernande M. de George [Garden City, 1972], pp. 125–46), Lévi-Strauss and Jakobson have worked together on a literary text. The piece itself is perhaps not as impressive as the more general fruit of this conjunction.

62. Barthes, *Essais critiques*, p, 214; *Critical Essays*, pp. 214–15.

63. Ibid., p. 215.

64. Barthes, *Essais critiques*, p. 210; *Critical Essays*, p. 209.

65. *Cours; Course*, p. 118.

66. Barthes, *Essais critiques*, p, 213; *Critical Essays*, p. 213.

67. In an otherwise interesting discussion, "La structure, le sujet, la trace" ("La philosophie entre l'avant et l'après du structuralisme," *Qu'est-ce-que le Structuralisme?*, eds. Oswald Ducrot, Tzvetan Todorov, Dan Sperber, Moustafa Safouan, François Wahl [Paris, 1968], pp. 390–441), it is typically this question of the *sous rature* that François Wahl must treat very lightly as a precaution almost automatically taken for granted within all responsible structuralist practice. The discussion is, in general, not unsympathetic to Derrida. In the long run, however, it is not touched by Derrida, whose version of structuralism is put "in its place" as a "contamination of the properly structural gesture by the ontological, psychological, and transcendental determinations of phenomenology" (p. 419). Derrida's reactions to formulations such as these would be a variation on his response to Elisabeth Roudinesco.

68. Barthes, *Essais critiques*, p. 218; *Critical Essays*, p. 219.

69. Ibid., p. 218. In *Révolution du langage poétique* (Paris, 1974), Julia Kristeva attempts to neutralize signification and go beyond it into a study of the flexible and contingent positioning of subject and object that we come to call "signification." In "Sémiotique et symbolique," the opening section, she would appropriate into structuralism "the functioning of writing, of the trace, and the grammè that Jacques Derrida has introduced in his critique of phenomenology" (p. 40). When she writes "my concern is therefore not the operating and producing consciousness, but rather the producible consciousness" (p. 35 n.), we might think we hear an echo of Derrida's "there is no constituting subjectivity" (*VP* 94, *SP* 85 n.). But Derrida's next sentence is: "The very concept of constitution itself must be deconstructed." And Kristeva, as is evident from the quotation above, does not deconstruct or undo the concept of "production," but rather works within it to say of consciousness—not producing but producible. Aware of the importance of the ground of precomprehended questions, she proposes the thought of the *chora* (a Platonic term), designating "a non-expressive totality constituted by . . . drives [*pulsions*] and their *stases* into a motility as full of movement as it is regulated" (p. 23). The thought of the *chora*, a play of the movement and rest of forces, ". . . a delaying as well as one of the possible realizations of the death instinct" (p. 27 n.), "not a transcendental signifier but that which opens signification" (p. 46), does indeed seem

close to Derrida's vocabulary. But in fact that thought rests on a set of hierarchized oppositions, is defined always as anterior rather than posterior, pre- rather than post-verbal, pre- rather than postfigurative. It is an ambitious and valuable book, but it does not articulate or perform the "sous rature." It is not surprising, then, that Kristeva uses her long-standing dyad—the *génotexte* and the *phénotexte*—when she reads individual poems, reverting to the recognizable scientistic structuralist idiom, closing the book with a confidently compartmentalized "Synoptic Table" arranged under "Lautréamont," "Mallarmé," "Political Events and the Social Situation," "Scientific Events-Discoveries," and "French Colonialist Expansion"—material for those general laws that differance would not countenance.

70. Paris, 1961; *Madness and Civilization: A History of Insanity in the Age of Reason*, tr. Richard Howard, Plume Book edition (New York, Toronto, and London, 1971).

71. Ibid., p. ii, xi.

72. Ibid.

73. An early and vitriolic expression of this is to be found in "La chose freudienne," *Écrits* (Paris, 1966): 401–36 (hereafter cited in the text as *Ec*).

74. *Scilicet* I (Paris, 1968), (hereafter cited in the text as *Sc*), p. 47.

75. For example, Lacan's "delightful play of homonyms" (*Pos* F 115, *Pos* E II 43) in "La chose freudienne" (*Ec*, pp. 420–23) is discounted by Derrida as an ellipse that allows Lacan to escape responsibility!

76. *Les Séminaires de Jacques Lacan*, Livre XI, *Les Quatre concepts fondamentaux de la psychanalyse* (Paris, 1973), p. 132.

77. Ibid., p. 137.

78. This paper was presented at the Johns Hopkins University as early as 1966. Later Derrida will come to distrust such terms as "the totality of an era."

79. Jeffrey Mehlman relates this project—the desire that word be one with meaning—with Narcissus's desire to be one with his image, and with the child's narcissistic desire to be one with the mother in his *Structural Study of Autobiography: Proust, Leiris, Sartre, Lévi-Strauss* (Ithaca, London, 1974). I am indebted to Michael Ryan for an illuminating discussion of the relationship between such a narcissism and Derrida's project of "unbalancing" the equation. In "La dissémination" (*Dis* pp. 322–407), Derrida presents the structure of the square with an open (yet presupposed) fourth side—Ryan relates this to the forever active triangularity of the oedipal position, which intervenes to resolve the unfulfilled narcissistic desire for self-enclosure (review forthcoming, in *Diacritics*, of Mehlman's book.) For a somewhat restricted yet interesting discussion of Derrida's tetrapolarity (logic of the open square, rather than the Hegelian triplicity or circularity, and rather than the longed-for narcissistic self-enclosed dyad) see Robert Greer Cohn, "Nodes," I, *Diacritics* 4, i (Spring 1974): 39.

80. See J. Hillis Miller, "The Geneva School: the Criticism of Marcel Raymond, Albert Béguin, Georges Poulet, Jean Rousset, Jean-Pierre Richard, and Jean Starobinski," *Modern French Criticism: From Proust and Valéry to Structuralism*, ed. John K. Simon (Chicago and London, 1972), pp. 277–310. For descriptions specifically of Maurice Blanchot and Georges Poulet, see de Man, "Impersonality in the Criticism of Maurice Blanchot," "The Literary Self as Origin: the Work of Georges Poulet," *Blindness and Insight*, op. cit., pp. 60–78, 79–101. Paul Ricoeur's *Le Conflit des interprétations: essais d'herméneutique* (Paris, 1969) (*The Conflict of Interpretations: Essays in Hermeneutics*, tr. Don Ihde [Evanston, 1974]) should be of particular interest to readers of this book, since Ricoeur delivers hermeneutic interpretations of several texts that Derrida deconstructs. A most influential German text on hermeneutics is Hans-Georg Gadamer's *Wahrheit und Methode: Grundzüge einer philosophischen Hermeneutik*, second edition (Tübingen, 1965), English translation forthcoming from Seabury Press, New York.

81. Derrida refers to Gregory Bateson's theory of schizophrenia. See, for example, "Toward a Theory of Schizophrenia," and "Double Bind, 1969," *Steps to an Ecology of Mind*, Ballantine Books edition (New York, 1972), pp. 201–27, 271–78.

82. *Critique*, 223 (December 1965): 1017–42 (hereafter cited in the text as *Crit* I); and 224 (January 1966): 23–53 (hereafter cited in the text as *Crit* II).

83. "Die endliche und unendliche Analyse," *GW* XVI: 59–99; *SE* XXIII: 209–53.
84. For a cogent discussion of the problems relating to these two words as used by Derrida, see "White Mythology" 5.
85. For a cogent discussion of translation and intertextuality, see Jeffrey Mehlman, "Portnoy in Paris," *Diacritics* 2, iv (Winter 1972): 21.

Preface

1. It may be read as an essay published in the review *Critique* (December 1965–January 1966). Three important publications provided me the opportunity: Madeleine V.-David, *Le débat sur les écritures et l'hieroglyphe aux xvii° et xviii° siècles* (1965) (*DE*); André Leroi-Gourhan, *Le geste et la parole* (1965) (*GP*); *L'écriture et la psychologie des peuples* (Proceedings of a Colloquium, 1963) (*EP*).

Exergue

1. Cf. for example, the notions of "secondary elaboration" or "symbolism of second intention" in Edmond Ortigues, *Le discours et le symbole* (Aubier, 1962) pp. 62 and 171. "Mathematical symbolism is a convention of writing, a scriptural symbolism. It is only by an abuse of vocabulary or by analogy that one speaks of a 'mathematical language.' Algorithm is actually a 'characteristics,' it is composed of written characters. It does not speak, except through the intermediary of a language which furnishes not only the phonetic expression of the characters, but also the formulation of axioms permitting the determination of the value of these characters. It is true that at a pinch one could decipher unknown characters, but that always supposes an acquired knowledge, a thought already formed by the usage of speech. Therefore, in all hypothesis, mathematical symbolism is the fruit of a secondary elaboration, supposing preliminarily the usage of discourse and the possibility of conceiving explicit conventions. It is nevertheless true that mathematical algorithm will express the formal laws of symbolization, of syntactic structures, independent of particular means of expression." On these problems, cf. also Gilles Gaston Granger, *Pensée formelle et sciences de l'homme* (Paris, 1960), pp. 38 f. and particularly pp. 43 and 50 f. (on the "Reversal of Relationships between the Spoken Language and Writing").
2. All works on the history of writing devote space to the problem of the introduction of phonetic writing in the cultures that did not practice it previously. Cf. e.g., *EP*, pp. 44 f. or "La reforme de l'écriture chinoise," *Linguistique, Recherches internationales à la lumière du marxisme* 7 (May–June 1958).
3. Here I do not merely mean those "theological prejudices" which, at an identifiable time and place, inflected or repressed the theory of the written sign in the seventeenth and eighteenth centuries. I shall speak of them later in connection with Madeleine V.-David's book. These prejudices are nothing but the most clearsighted and best circumscribed, historically determined manifestation of a constitutive and permanent presupposition essential to the history of the West, therefore to metaphysics in its entirety, even when it professes to be atheist.
4. *Grammatology*: "A treatise upon Letters, upon the alphabet, syllabation, reading, and writing," Littré. To my knowledge and in our time, this word has only been used by I. J. Gelb to designate the project of a modern science in *A Study of Writing: The Foundations of Grammatology* [Chicago], 1952 (the subtitle disappears in the 1963 edition). In spite of a concern for systematic or simplified classification, and in spite of the controversial hypotheses on the monogenesis or polygenesis of scripts, this book follows the classical model of histories of writing.

Part I: Chapter 1

1. To speak of a primary writing here does not amount to affirming a chronological priority of fact. That debate is well-known; is writing, as affirmed, for example, by

Metchaninov and Marr, then Loukotka, "anterior to phonetic language?" (A conclusion assumed by the first edition of the Great Soviet Encyclopedia, later contradicted by Stalin. On this debate, cf. V. Istrine, "Langue et écriture," *Linguistique*, op. cit., pp. 35, 60. This debate also forms around the theses advanced by P. van Ginneken. On the discussion of these propositions, cf. James Février, *Histoire de l'écriture* [Payot, 1948–59], pp. 5 f.). I shall try to show below why the terms and premises of such a debate are suspicious.

2. I shall deal with this problem more directly in *La voix et le phénomène* (Paris, 1967) [*Speech and Phenomenon*, op. cit.].

3. Wiener, for example, while abandoning "semantics," and the opposition, judged by him as too crude and too general, between animate and inanimate etc., nevertheless continues to use expressions like "organs of sense," "motor organs," etc. to qualify the parts of the machine.

4. Cf., e.g., *EP*, pp. 126, 148, 355, etc. From another point of view, cf. Roman Jakobson, *Essais de linguistique générale* (tr. fr. [Nicolas Ruwet, Paris, 1963], p. 116) [Jakobson and Morris Halle, *Fundamentals of Language* (the Hague, 1956), p. 16].

5. This is shown by Pierre Aubenque (*Le problème de l'être chez Aristotle* [Paris, 1966], pp. 106 f.). In the course of a provocative analysis, to which I am here indebted, Aubenque remarks: "In other texts, to be sure, Aristotle designates as symbol the relationship between language and things: 'It is not possible to bring the things themselves to the discussion, but, instead of things, we can use their names as symbols.' The intermediary constituted by the mental experience is here suppressed or at least neglected, but this suppression is legitimate, since, mental experiences behaving like things, things can be substitued for them immediately. On the other hand, one cannot by any means substitute names for things" (pp. 107–08).

6. Roman Jakobson, *Essais de linguistique générale*, tr. fr., p. 162 ["The Phonemic and Grammatical Aspects of Language in their Interrelations," *Proceedings of the Sixth International Congress of Linguistics* (Paris, 1949), p. 6]. On this problem, on the tradition of the concept of the sign, and on the originality of Saussure's contribution within this continuity, cf. Ortigues, op. cit., pp. 54 f.

7. Cited by Emmanuel Levinas, in *Difficile liberté* [Paris, 1963], p. 44.

8. I attempt to develop this theme elsewhere (*Speech and Phenomena*).

9. This does not, by simple inversion, mean that the signifier is fundamental or primary. The "primacy" or "priority" of the signifier would be an expression untenable and absurd to formulate illogically within the very logic that it would legitimately destroy. The signifier will never by rights precede the signified, in which case it would no longer be a signifier and the "signifying" signifier would no longer have a possible signified. The thought that is announced in this impossible formula without being successfully contained therein should therefore be stated in another way; it will clearly be impossible to do so without putting the very idea of the sign into suspicion, the "sign-of" which will always remain attached to what is here put in question. At the limit therefore, that thought would destroy the entire conceptuality organized around the concept of the sign (signifier and signified, expression and content, and so on).

10. Postface to *Was ist Metaphysik?* [Frankfurt am Main, 1960], p. 46. The insistence of the voice also dominates the analysis of *Gewissen* [conscience] in *Sein und Zeit* (pp. 267 f.) [pp. 312 f.].

11. Cf. *Das Wesen der Sprache* ["The Nature of Language"], and *Das Wort* ["Words"], in *Unterwegs zur Sprache* [Pfüllingen], 1959 [*On the Way to Language*, tr. Peter D. Hertz (New York, 1971)].

12. [Martin Heidegger, *Einführung in die Metaphysik* (Tübingen, 1953) translated as *An Introduction to Metaphysics* by Ralp Manheim (New Haven, 1959).] Tr. French Gilbert Kahn [Paris, 1967], p. 50.

13. *Introduction à la métaphysique*, tr. fr. p. 103 [*Einführung* p. 70; *Introduction*, p. 92]. "All this points in the direction of what we encountered when we characterized the Greek experience and interpretation of being. If we retain the usual interpretation of being, the word 'being' takes its meaning from the unity and determinateness of the horizon which guided our understanding. In short: we understand the verbal substantive

'Sein' through the infinitive, which in turn is related to the 'is' and its diversity that we have described. The definite and particular verb form 'is,' the *third person singular of the present indicative*, has here a pre-eminent rank. We understand 'being' not in regard to the 'thou art,' 'you are,' 'I am,' or 'they would be,' though all of these, just as much as 'is,' represent verbal inflections of 'to be.' . . . And involuntarily, almost as though nothing else were possible, we explain the infinitive 'to be' to ourselves through the 'is.'

"Accordingly, 'being' has the meaning indicated above, recalling the Greek view of the essence of being, hence a determinateness which has not just dropped on us accidentally from somewhere but has dominated our historical being-there since antiquity. At one stroke our search for the definition of the meaning of the word 'being' becomes explicitly what it is, namely a reflection on the source of our hidden history." I should, of course, cite the entire analysis that concludes with these words.

14. *dem Statarischen*, an old German word that one has hitherto been tempted to translate as "immobile" or "static" (see [Jean] Gibelin, [tr. *Leçons sur la philosophie de la religion* (Paris, 1959),] pp. 255–57.

15. "La parole soufflée," *ED.*

Part I: Chapter 2

1. *Diogène* 51, 1965, [p. 54]. [Parallel English, French, and Spanish editions of this journal are published simultaneously. My references are to the English *Diogenes*.] André Martinet alludes to the "courage" which would formerly have been "needed" to "foresee that the term 'word' itself might have to be put aside if . . . researches showed that this term could not be given a universally applicable definition" (p. 39) [p. 39]. "Semiology, as revealed by recent studies, has no need of the word" (p. 40) [p. 39]. . . . "Grammarians and linguists have long known that the analysis of utterances can be pursued beyond the word without going into phonetics, that is, ending with segments of speech, such as syllables or phonemes, which have nothing to do with meaning" (p. 41) [p. 40]. "We are touching here on what renders the notion of the word so suspect to all true linguists. They cannot accept traditional writing without verifying first whether it reproduces faithfully the true structure of the language which it is supposed to record" (p. 48) [p. 48]. In conclusion Martinet proposes the replacement "in linguistic practice" of the notion of word by that of "syntagm," any "group of several minimal signs" that will be called "monemes."

2. Let us extend our quotation to bring out the tone and the affect of these theoretical propositions. Saussure *puts the blame on* writing: "Another result is that the less writing represents what it is supposed to represent, the stronger the tendency to use it as a basis becomes. Grammarians never fail to draw attention to the written form. Psychologically, the tendency is easily explained, but its consequences are annoying. Free use of the words 'pronounce' and 'pronunciation' sanctions the abuse and reverses the real, legitimate relationship between writing and language. Whoever says that a certain letter must be pronounced a certain way is mistaking the written image of a sound for the sound itself. For French *oi* to be pronounced *wa*, this spelling would have to exist independently; actually *wa* is written *oi*." Instead of meditating upon this strange proposition, the *possibility* of such a text ("actually *wa* is written *oi*"), Saussure argues: "To attribute the oddity to an exceptional pronunciation of *o* and *i* is also misleading, for this implies that language depends on its written form and that certain liberties may be taken in writing, as if the graphic symbols were the norm" (p. 52) [p. 30].

3. Manuscript included in the *Pléiade* edition under the title *Prononciation* (11, p. 1248). Its composition is placed circa 1761 (cf. editors' note in the *Pléiade*). The sentence that I have just cited is the last one of the fragment as published in the *Pléiade*. It does not appear in the comparable edition of the same group of notes by [M. G.] Streckeisen-Moultou, under the title of "Fragment d'un Essai sur les langues" and "Notes détachées sur le même sujet," in *Oeuvres et correspondances inédites de J. J. Rousseau* ([Paris], 1861), p. 295.

4. Text presented by Jean Starobinski in "Les anagrammes de Ferdinand de Saussure:

textes inédits," *Mercure de France* (February 1964), [vol. 350; now published as *Les mots sous les mots: les anagrammes de Ferdinand de Saussure*, ed. Starobinski (Paris, 1971)].

5. Rousseau is seemingly more cautious in the fragment on *Pronunciation*: "Thought is analyzed by speech, speech by writing; speech represents thought by conventional signs, and writing represents speech in the same way; thus the art of writing is nothing but a mediated representation of thought, *at least in the vocalic languages, the only ones that we use*" (p. 1249; italics added). Only seemingly, for even if, unlike Saussure, Rousseau here forbids himself to speak *in general* of the entire system, the notions of mediacy and of "vocalic languages" leave the enigma intact. I shall be obliged to return to this.

6. Cf. *L'origine de la géométrie*, 1962.

7. "The signifier aspect of the system of language can consist only of rules according to which the phonic aspect of the act of speech is ordered," [N. S.] Troubetzkoy, *Principes de phonologie*, tr. fr. [J. Cantineau (Paris, 1949); *Principles of Phonology*, tr. Christiane A. M. Baltaxe (Berkeley and Los Angeles, 1969)], p. 2. It is in the "Phonologie et phonétique" of Jakobson and Halle (the first part of *Fundamentals of Language*, collected and translated in *Essais de linguistique générale* [tr. Nicolas Ruwet (Paris, 1963)], p. 103) that the phonologistic strand of the Saussurian project seems to be most systematically and most rigorously defended, notably against Hjelmslev's "algebraic" point of view.

8. Page 101. Beyond the scruples formulated by Saussure himself, an entire system of intralinguistic criticism can be opposed to the thesis of the "arbitrariness of the sign." Cf. Jakobson, "A la recherche de l'essence du langage," [Quest for the Essence of Language,"] *Diogène*, 51, and Martinet, *La linguistique synchronique* [Paris 1965], p. 34. But these criticisms do not interfere—and, besides, do not pretend to interfere—with Saussure's profound intention directed at the discontinuity and immotivation proper to the structure if not the origin of the sign.

9. *Elements of Logic*, Bk. II, [*Collected Papers*, ed. Charles Hartshorne and Paul Weiss (Cambridge, Mass., 1931–58), vol. 2], p. 169, paragraph 302.

10. I justify the translation of *bedeuten* by *vouloir-dire* [meaning, literally "wish-to-say"] in *La voix et le phénomène*.

11. *The Philosophy of Peirce: Selected Writings*, [ed. Justus Buchler (New York and London, 1940)], ch. 7, p. 99.

12. Page 93. Let us recall that Lambert opposes phenomenology to aletheiology.

13. *Elements of Logic*, Bk. I, 2, p. 302.

14. These Heideggerian themes obviously refer back to Nietzsche (cf. *La chose* [1950], tr. fr. in *Essais et conférences* [tr. André Préau (Paris, 1958)], p. 214 ["Das Ding," *Vorträge und Aufsätze* (Pfüllingen, 1954)], *Le principe de raison* (1955–56), tr. fr. [André Préau, Paris, 1962] pp. 240 f. [*Der Satz vom Grund* (Pfüllingen, 1957)]. Such themes are presented also in Eugen Fink (*Le jeu comme symbole du monde* [*Spiel als Weltsymbol* (Stuttgart] 1960), and, in France, in Kostas Axelos, *Vers la pensée planétaire* ([Paris], 1964), and *Einführung in ein künftiges Denken* [*:über Marx und Heidegger* (Tübingen], 1966).

15. *Communications*, 4 (1964), p. 2.

16. "The conceptual side of value is made up solely of relations and differences with respect to the other terms of language, and the same can be said of its material side. The important thing in the word is not the sound alone but the phonic differences that make it possible to distinguish this word from all others, for differences carry signification. . . . A segment of language can never in the final analysis be based on anything except its noncoincidence with the rest" (p. 163) [pp. 117–18].

17. "Since an identical state of affairs is observable in writing, another system of signs, we shall use writing to draw some comparisons that will clarify the whole issue. In fact:

"1) The signs used in writing are arbitrary; there is no connection, for example, between the letter *t* and the sound that it designates.

"2) The value of letters is purely negative and differential. The same person can write *t*, for instances, in different ways: *t* & t. The only requirement is that the sign for *t* not be confused in his script with the signs used for *l*, *d*, etc.

"3) Values in writing function only through reciprocal opposition within a fixed system that consists of a set number of letters. This third characteristic, though not identical to the second, is closely related to it, for both depend on the first. Since the graphic sign is arbitrary, its form matters little or rather matters only within the limitations imposed by the system.

"4) The means by which the sign is produced is completely unimportant, for it does not affect the system (this also follows from characteristic 1). Whether I make the letters in white or black, raised or engraved, with pen or chisel—all this is of no importance with respect to their signification" (pp. 165–66) [pp. 119–20].

18. "*Arbitrary* and *differential* are two correlative qualities" (p. 163) [p. 118].

19. This literal fidelity is expressed:

1. In the critical exposition of Hjelmslev's attempt ("Au sujet des fondements de la théorie linguistique de L. Hjelmslev," *Bulletin de la Société Linguistique de Paris*, vol. 42, p. 40): "Hjelmslev is perfectly consistent with himself when he declares that a written text has for the linguist exactly the same value as a spoken text, since the choice of the substance is not important. He refuses even to admit that the spoken substance is primitive and the written substance derived. It seems as if it would suffice to make him notice that, but for certain pathological exceptions, all human beings speak, but few know how to write, or that children know how to speak long before they learn how to write. *I shall therefore not press the point*" (italics added).

2. In the *Eléments de linguistique générale* [(Paris, 1961); *Elements of General Linguistics*, tr. Elisabeth Palmer (London, 1964)], where all the chapters on the vocal character of language pick up the words and arguments of Chapter VI of the *Course*: "[One learns to speak before learning to read:] reading comes as a reflection of spoken usage: *the reverse is never true*" (italics added. This proposition seems to me to be thoroughly debatable, even on the level of that common experience which has the force of law within this argument.) Martinet concludes: "The study of writing is a discipline distinct from linguistics proper, although practically speaking it is one of its dependencies. Thus the linguist in principle operates without regard for written forms" (p. 11) [p. 17]. We see how the concepts of *dependency* and *abstraction* function: writing and its science are alien but not independent; which does not stop them from being, conversely, immanent but not essential. Just enough "outside" not to affect the integrity of the language *itself*, in its pure original self-identity, in its property; just enough "inside" not to have the right to any practical or epistemological independence. And vice versa.

3. In "The Word" (already cited): ". . . it is from speech that one should always start in order to understand the real nature of human language" (p. 53) [p. 54].

4. And finally and above all in "La double articulation du langage," *La linguistique synchronique*, pp. 8 f. and 18 f.

20. "On the Principles of Phonematics" (1955), *Proceedings of the Second International Congress of Phonetic Sciences*, p. 51.

21. Louis Hjelmslev and H. J. Uldall, *Etudes de linguistique structurale organisées au sein du Cercle linguistique de Copenhague* (Bulletin 11, 35, pp. 13 f.).

22. "Langue et parole" (1943), *Essais linguistiques* [Copenhagen, 1959], p. 77.

23. *Omkring sprogteoriens grundlaeggelse*, Copenhagen (1943), pp. 91–93 (translated as *Prolegomena to A Theory of Language*, [by Francis J. Whitfield (2nd edition, Baltimore, 1961)] pp. 103–04.

Cf. also "La stratification du langage" (1954), *Essais linguistiques* (*Travaux du Cercle linguistique de Copenhague*, XII [1959]). The project and the terminology of a *graphematics*, science of the substance of graphic expression, are there presented (p. 41). The complexity of the proposed algebra aims to remedy the fact that, from the point of view of the distinction between form and substance, "Saussure's terminology can lead to confusion" (p. 48). Hjelmslev demonstrates how "one and the same form of expression can be manifested by diverse substances: phonic, graphic, flag-signals, etc." (p. 49).

24. "Speech and Writing," 1938, *Acta Linguistica* 4 (1944): 11 f. Uldall refers also to

a study by Dr. Joseph Vachek, "Zum Problem der geschriebenen Sprache" (*Travaux du Cercle linguistique de Prague* 8, 1939) in order to indicate "the difference between the phonologic and glosseamtic points of view."

Cf. also Eli Fischer-Jorgensen, "Remarques sur les principes de l'analyse phonémique," *Recherches structurales*, 1949 (*Travaux du Cercle linguistique de Prague*, vol. 5, pp. 231. f.); Bertha Siertsema, A *Study of Glossematics* ([The Hague] 1955), (especially ch. VI), and Hennings Spang-Hanssen, "Glossematics," *Trends in European and Amercan Linguistics*, 1930–60 [ed. Christine Mohrmann (Utrecht,] 1961), pp. 147 f.

25. And already, in a very programmatic manner, in the *Prolegomena* (English translation, pp. 114–15). Cf. also Adolf Stender-Petersen, "Esquisse d'une théorie structurale de la littérature," and Stevan Johanson, "La notion de signe dans la glossématique et dans l'esthétique," *Travaux du Cercle linguistique de Copenhague* 5 (1949).

26. *Omkring*, p. 9 (*Prolegomena*, p. 8).

27. Page 14. Which does not prevent Hjelmslev from "venturing to call" his directing principle an "empirical principle" (p. 12, English translation, p. 11). "But," he adds, "we are willing to abandon the name if espistemological investigation shows it to be inappropriate. From our point of view this is merely a question of terminology, which does not affect the maintenance of the principle." This is only one example of the terminological conventionalism of a system, which, in borrowing all its concepts from the history of the metaphysics that it would hold at a distance (form/substance, context/expression, etc.), believes it can neutralize its entire historical burden by means of some declaration of intention, a preface or quotation marks.

28. As for this critique of the concept of origin in general (empirical and/or transcendental) we have elsewhere attempted to indicate the schema of an argument (Introduction to Husserl's *L'origine de la géométrie*, p. 60).

29. Op. cit., p. 111. Hjelmslev formulates the same reservations: "It is curious that linguistics, so long on guard against any suspicion of 'psychologism,' seems here, even if only to a certain extent and in very cautious proportions, to be on its way back to Saussure's 'accoustic image,' and equally to 'concept,' as long as that word is interpreted in strict conformity with the doctrine that I have just elaborated, in short to recognize, with however many necessary reservations, that, with the two aspects of the linguistic sign, one is in the presence of the 'purely psychological phenomenon' (*Course*, p. 28) [p. 11]. But it is rather a partial coincidence of nomenclatures than a real analogy. The terms introduced by Saussure, and the interpretations given in the *Course*, have been abandoned because they can be equivocal, and it is better not to make the same mistakes again. I too hesitate when I ask myself how much the researches advocated here may be considered as belonging to the psychological order: the reason being that psychology seems to be a discipline whose definition still leaves much to be desired" ("La stratification du langage" *Essais linguistiques* [1954], p. 56). Hjelmslev, posing the same problem, already evoked those "numerous nuances that the Genevan master could be fully aware of, but which he did not find it useful to insist upon; the motives behind this attitude naturally escapes us" (p. 76).

30. I have attempted a reading of Freud from this point of view ("Freud et la scène de l'écriture," *L'écriture et la différence*). It sets forth the relationship between the concept of the trace and the structure of "a-retardation" which I mention above.

31. This theme inhabits more than one mythological system. Among many other examples, Thoth, the Egyptian god of writing evoked in *Phaedrus*, inventor of the technical ruse, the analogue of Hermes, also performed essential functions in funeral rites. When the opportunity offered, he was the conductor of the dead. He inscribed the accounts before the Last Judgment. He also occupied the function of the secretary/substitute who usurped first place; of the king, the father, the sun, of their eye. For example: "As a general rule, Horus' eye became the lunar eye. The moon, like everything that touched the astral world, intrigued the Egyptians greatly. According to one legend, the moon was created by the Sun-god to replace itself at night: it was Thoth whom Rê designated for the exercise of this high function of substitution. Another myth tried to explain the vicissitudes of the moon by a periodic battle whose protagonists were Horus and Seth. During the combat, Horus' eye was wrenched out, but Seth, finally

vanquished, was obliged to return to his victorious opponent the eye that he had lifted; according to another version, the eye returned on its own, or was brought back by Thoth. Whatever the case might have been, Horus received his eye back joyfully, and put it back in its place after purifying it. The Egyptians called that eye *oudjat*, 'the healthy one.' We shall see that the *oudjat* eye played a considerable role in the funerary religion, in the Osirian legend, and in the sacrificial ceremony. This legend . . . later received a solar counterpart: it was said that the universal master, at the origin of the world, was seen, for some unknown reason, to be without an eye. He charged Shou and Tefnout to bring it back. The absence of the two messengers lasted so long that Rê was obliged to replace the unfaithful eye. The eye, when it was brought back by Shou and Tefnout, became very angry (a), seeing that its place had been taken. In appeasement, Rê transformed it into the serpent-uraeus and placed it on his forehead as the symbol of his power; furthermore, he charged it to defend him against his enemies. (a) The eye shed tears (*rémyt*) from which men were born (*rémet*); the mythic origin of men clearly rests upon a simple wordplay" (Jacques Vandier, *La religion égyptienne*, P.U.F. [Paris, 1944], pp. 39–40). This myth of substitution can be related to the story of the eye in Rousseau (cf. below, p. 212, 148–49).

32. "Linguistique et théorie de la communication," (op. cit., pp. 87–88) [p. 245].

33. Cf. particularly "La trace de l'autre," *Tidjschrift voor filosofie* (September 1963), and my essay "Violence et métaphysique: Essai sur la pensée d'Emmanuel Levinas," *L'écriture et la différence*.

34. I take the liberty of referring to a forthcoming essay, "Ousia et Grammè, note sur une note de *Sein und Zeit*."

35. Page 103 [p. 70]. See also everything concerning "homogeneous time," (pp. 64 f.) [pp. 38 f.].

36. Op. cit., p. 106. Cf. also the *Diogène* article already cited.

37. *Mercure de France* (February 1964): 254. Presenting this text, Starobinski evokes the musical model and concludes: "This reading is developed according to another *tempo* (and in another time); at the very limit, one leaves the time of 'consecutivity' proper to habitual language." One could of course say "proper to the habitual concept" of time and of language.

38. I have chosen to demonstrate the necessity of this "deconstruction" by privileging the Saussurian references, not only because Saussure still dominates contemporary linguistics and semiology; it is also because he seems to me to hold himself at the limit: at the same time within the metaphysics that must be deconstructed and beyond the concept of the sign (signifier/signified) which he still uses. But Saussure's scruples, his interminable hesitations, particularly in the matter of the difference between the two "aspects" of the sign and in the matter of "arbitrariness," are better realized through reading Robert Godel's *Les sources manuscrites du cours de linguistique générale* ([Geneva], 1957) pp. 190 f. Suffice it to say here that it is not impossible that the literality of the *Course*, to which we have indeed had to refer, should one day appear very suspect in the light of unpublished material now being prepared for publication. I am thinking particularly of the *Anagrams* [now published, see note 4]. Up to what point is Saussure responsible for the *Course* as it was edited and published after his death? It is not a new question. Need we specify that, *here at least*, we cannot consider it to be pertinent? Unless my project has been fundamentally misunderstood, it should be clear by now that, caring very little about Ferdinand de Saussure's *very* thought *itself*, I have interested myself in a *text* whose literality has played a well-known role since 1915, operating within a system of readings, influences, misunderstandings, borrowings, refutations, etc. What I could read—and equally what I could not read—under the title of *A Course in General Linguistics* seemed important to the point of excluding all hidden and "true" intentions of Ferdinand de Saussure. If one were to discover that this text hid another text—and there will never by anything but texts—and hid it in a determined sense, the reading that I have just proposed would not be invalidated, at least for that particular reason. Quite the contrary. Besides, at the very end of their first "Preface," the editors of the *Course* themselves foresee this situation.

Part I: Chapter 3

1. On the empirical difficulties of a research into empirical origins, cf. M. Cohen, *La grande invention de l'écriture* ([Paris], 1958), Book I, pp. 3 f. With *L'histoire de l'écriture*, by J. G. Février (1948–59), it is in France the most important work on the general history of writing. Madeleine V.-David has studied them in *Critique* [157] (June 1960).

2. Madeleine V.-David proposes a particular explanation for it. "It is certain that, in nineteenth-century thought, a gap is produced following the too exclusive apology for the facts of language (begun by Herder). Paradoxically, the century of the great decipherings made a tabula rasa of the long preparation for those decipherings, by parading the century's disaffection from the problem of signs. . . . Thus a gap remains to be filled, a continuity to be reestablished. . . . One can do no better than to indicate . . . the Leibnizian texts which deal, often conjointly, with the facts of Chinese and the projects for a universal writing, and the multiple positions possible for writing and for the spoken. . . . But perhaps we do not suffer only from the blindness of the nineteenth century with regard to signs. Undoubtedly the fact that we are 'alphabetic' writers also conspires strongly in hiding from us such essential aspects of the activity of writing" (Discussion, *EP*, pp. 352–53).

3. She has done it particularly in *Les dieux et le destin en Babylonie* (P.U.F., 1949); (cf. especially the last chapter on "The Reign of Writing") and in many articles in the *Revue philosophique*, the *Bulletin de la société linguistique de Paris*, in *Critique*, in the *Journal de psychologie* and in the *Journal asiatique*. Madeleine V.-David was the disciple and translator of B. Hrozny.

4. *DE*, pp. 34 f.

5. The group that was called the "Jesuits of Canton" applied themselves to discovering the presence of occidental (Judaeo-Christian and Egyptian) influences within Chinese writing. Cf. V. Pinot, *La chine et la formation de l'esprit philosophique en France* (1640–1740) ([Paris], 1932), and *DE*, pp. 59 f.

6. Athanase Kircher, *Polygraphia nova et universalis et combinatoria arte detecta* [Rome, 1663]. John Wilkins, *An Essay Towards a Real Character and a Philosophical Language* ([London], 1668).

7. Letter to Mersenne, 20 November 1629 [*Descartes: Philosophical Letters*, tr. Anthony Kenny (Oxford, 1970), pp. 9 f.]. Cf. also Louis Couturat and Léopold Léau, *Histoire de la langue universelle* [Paris, 1903], pp. 10 f.

8. Supra p. 57, 38–39.

9. I would like to restore the context of this quotation: "I believe, however, that it would be possible to devise a further system to enable one to make up the primitive words and their symbols in such a language so that it could be learnt very quickly. Order is what it needed: all the thoughts which can come into the human mind must be arranged in an order like the natural order of the numbers. In a single day one can learn to name every one of the infinite series of numbers, and thus to write infinitely many different words in an unknown language. The same could be done for all the other words necessary to express all the other things which fall within the purview of the human mind. If this secret were discovered I am sure that the language would soon spread throughout the world. Many people would willingly spend five or six days in learning how to make themselves understood by the whole human race.

"But I do not think that your author has thought of this. There is nothing in all his propositions to suggest it, and in any case the discovery of such a language depends upon the true philosophy. For without that philosophy it is impossible to number and order all the thoughts of men or even to separate them out into clear and simple thoughts, which in my opinion is the great secret for acquiring true scientific knowledge. If someone were to explain correctly what are the simple ideas in the human imagination out of which all human thoughts are compounded, and if his explanation were generally received, I would dare to hope for a universal language very easy to learn, to speak, and to write. The greatest advantage of such a language would be the assistance it would give to men's judgment, representing matters so clearly that it would be almost impossible to go wrong. As it is, almost all our words have confused meanings, and men's minds are so accustomed to them that there is hardly anything which they can perfectly understand.

"I think it is possible to invent such a language" [*Philosophical Letters*, pp. 5–6].

10. *Opuscules et fragments inédits de Leibniz*, ed. Couturat, [Paris, 1903], pp. 27–28.

11. Cf. Yvon Belaval, *Leibniz critique de Descartes* [Paris, 1960], especially pp. 181 f.

12. *Opuscules et fragments inédits de Leibniz* (Couturat), pp. 98–99.

13. Cf. Couturat, *Histoire de la langue universelle* [Paris, 1903], pp. 1–28. Belaval, op. cit., pp. 181 f. and *DE*, chap. IV.

14. Cf., for example, among many other texts, *Monadology* 1 to 3 and 51. It is beside the point both of our project and of the possibilities of our demonstrating from internal evidence the link between the characteristic and Leibniz's infinitist theology. For that it would be necessary to go through and exhaust the entire content of the project. I refer on this point to works already cited. Like Leibniz when he wishes to recall in a letter the link between the existence of God and the possibility of a universal script, I shall say here that "it is a proposition that [we] cannot demonstrate properly without explaining the foundations of the characteristic at length. . . . But at present, suffice it to remark that the foundation of my characteristic is also the demonstration of the existence of God, for simple thoughts are the elements of the characteristic, and simple forms are the source of things. Now I maintain that all simple forms are compatible among themselves. It is a proposition that I cannot demonstrate properly without explaining the foundations of the characteristic at length. But if it is granted, then it follows that the nature of God which holds absolutely all simple forms, is possible. Now we have proved above, that God is, provided He is possible. Therefore He exists. Which had to be demonstrated." (Letter to the Princess Elizabeth, 1678) There is an essential connection between the possibility of the *ontological argument* and that of the Characteristic.

15. Cf. *DE*, chap. IV.

16. *Nouveaux essais* [*sur l'entendement humain* (Amsterdam, 1765); translated as *New Essays Concerning Human Understanding*, by Alfred Gideon Langley (New York and London, 1896)], III, II, § I. In 1661, Dalgarno published the work entitled *Ars signorum, vulgo character universalis et lingua philosophica* (London, 1661). On Wilkins cf. supra, Couturat, op. cit., and *DE*, passim. A script or a language of pure institution and of pure arbitrariness cannot have been invented, as a *system*, except all at once. It is this that, before Duclos, Rousseau, and Lévi-Strauss (cf. infra), Leibniz deems probable: "Thus it was the opinion of Golius, a celebrated mathematician and great linguist, that their language is artificial, *i.e.* had been invented all at once by some clever man in order to establish verbal intercourse between the large number of different nations inhabiting this great country which we call China, although this language may now be found altered by long use" (III. I. § 1).

17. *Die philosophische Schriften*, ed. C. I. Gerhardt, [Berlin, 1875–90] Book VII, p. 25; and *DE*, p. 67. On all these problems, cf. also R. F. Merkel, "Leibniz und China," *Leibniz zu seinem 300 Geburtstag* [1646–1946], [ed. E. Hochstetter (Berlin, 1946–]52). On the letters exchanged with Father Bouvet on the subject of Chinese thought and script, cf. pp. 18–20 and [Jean] Baruzi, *Leibniz* ([Paris], 1909), pp. 156–65.

18. *DE*, chap. III.

19. *DE*, pp. 43–44.

20. *Prodromus*, p. 260, cited and translated by Drioton (cf. *DE*, p. 46). On the polygraphic project of Athanase Kircher, cf. *Polygraphia nova et universalis ex combinatoria arte delecta*, 1663. On his relationships with Lully, Becher, Dalgarno, Wilkins, Leibniz, cf. *DE*, pp. 61 f.

21. *Réflexions sur les principles généraux de l'art d'écrire et en particulier sur les fondements de l'écriture chinoise*, 1718, p. 629. Cf. also *L'Essai sur la chronologie générale de l'Ecriture*, which deals with "Judaic history," "an abstraction of the religious respect inspired by the Bible" (*DE*, pp. 80 f.).

22. [This number was omitted from the French edition by mistake. The omission is carried in this translation to keep the note numbers consistent with the original.]

23 [*sic*]. *Essai sur les hiéroglyphes des Egyptiens, où l'on voit l'Origine et le Progrès du Langage et de l'Ecriture, l'Antiquité des Hiéroglyphes Scientifiques, et des Remarques sur la Chronologie et la première Ecriture des Chinois* ([Paris] 1744). It is the title of the French translation of a portion [Vol. II, Book IV, sec. iv] of [Bishop William Warburton,] *The Divine Legation of Moses* [:Demonstrated, on the Principles of a Religious Deist, from the Omission of the Doctrine of a Future State of Reward and Punishment in the Jewish Dispensation, London,] (1737–41). I examine below the influence of this work on Condillac, Rousseau, and the collaborators of the *Encyclopaedia*.

24. *DE*, pp. 126–31.

25. Ernst Doblhofer, [*Zeichen und Wunder: die Entzifferung verschollener Schriften und Sprachen* (Berlin, 1957); [translated by Monique Bittebierre as] *Le déchiffrement des écritures* ([Grenoble], 1959), and *EP*, p. 352.

26. Op cit., p. 2 [p. 110]. Madeleine V.-David criticizes this instrumentalism in the works already cited. Instrumentalism, whose metaphysical dependence one could not exaggerate, also often inspires the linguistic definition of the essence of language, assimilated into a function, and, what is more significant, into a function exterior to its content or its agent. This is always implied by the concept of the utensil. Thus André Martinet accepts responsibility for and develops at length the definition of language as "instrument," "tool," etc., whereas the "metaphoric" nature of this definition, recognized by the author, ought to have made it problematic and to have renewed the question of instrumentality, of the meaning of functioning, and of the functioning of meaning. (Cf. *Eléménts de linguistique générale*, pp. 12–14, 25 [pp. 18–20, 29].)

27. Cf., for example, Cohen, op. cit., p. 6.

28. Cf. *GP* II pp. 12 f., 23 f., 262 f.

29. I, p. 119 f.

30. Page 161 f.

31. Page 183. I refer also to *L'Eloge de la main* by Henri Focillon [Paris, 1964] and to Jean Brun's book, *La main et l'esprit* [P.U.F., 1963]. In a totally different context, we have elsewhere specified the *epoch* of writing as the suspension of *being-upright* ("Force et signification" and "La parole soufflée" in *L'écriture et la différence*).

32. Bk. I, chap. IV. In particular, the author shows there that "the emergence of writing no more develops out of a graphic nothingness than does the emergence of agriculture without the intervention of anterior states" (p. 278); and that "ideography is anterior to pictography" (p. 280).

33. Certain remarks of Leroi-Gourhan on "the loss of multi-dimensional symbolic thought" and on the thought that "separates itself from linearized language" can perhaps be interpreted thus.

34. Cf. *EP*, pp. 138–39; *GP* I, pp. 238–50. "The development of the first cities not only corresponds to the appearance of the technician of fire but . . . writing is born at the same time as metallurgy. Here too, it is not a coincidence . . ." (I, p. 252). "It is at the moment when agrarian capitalism begins to establish itself that the means of stabilizing it in written balance accounts appears and it is also at the moment when social hierarchization is affirmed that writing constructs its first genealogists" (p. 253). "The appearance of writing is not fortuitous; after millennia of maturation in the systems of mythographic representation the linear notation of thought emerges at the same time as metal and slavery (see chapter VI). Its content is not fortuitous" (II, p. 67; cf. also pp. 161–62).

Although it is now much better known and described, this structural solidarity, particularly between capitalization and writing, has long been known: among many others, by Rousseau, Court de Gebelin, Engels, etc.

35. Linear writing has therefore indeed "constituted, during many millennia, independently of its role as conserver of the collective memory, by its unfolding in one dimension alone, the instrument of analysis out of which grew philosophic and scientific thought. The conservation of thought can now be conceived otherwise than in terms of books which will only for a short time keep the advantage of their rapid manageability. A vast 'tape-library' with an electronic selection system will in the near future show preselected and instantaneously retrieved information. Reading will still retain its im-

portance for some centuries to come, in spite of its perceptible regression for most men, but writing [understood in the sense of linear inscription] seems likely to disappear rapidly, replaced by automatic dictaphones. Should one see in this a sort of restoration of the state anterior to the phonetic confiscation of the hand? I should rather think that it is here a question of an aspect of the general phenomenon of manual regression (see p. 60) and of a new 'liberation.' As to the long-term consequences in terms of the forms of reasoning, and a return to diffuse and multidimensional thought, they cannot be now foreseen. Scientific thought is rather hampered by the necessity of drawing itself out in typographical channels and it is certain that if some procedure would permit the presentation of books in such a way that the materials of the different chapters are presented simultaneously in all their aspects, authors and their users would find a considerable advantage. It is absolutely certain that if scientific reasoning has clearly nothing to lose with the disappearance of writing, philosophy and literature will definitely see their forms evolve. This is not particularly regrettable since printing will conserve the curiously archaic forms of thought that men will have used during the period of alphabetic graphism; as to the new forms, they will be to the old ones as steel to flint, not only a sharper but a more flexible instrument. Writing will pass into the infrastructure without altering the functioning of intelligence, as a transition which will have some centuries of primacy" (GP, II, pp. 261–62. See also EP, *Conclusion*).

36. The "XXIIe Semaine de synthèse," a colloquium whose contents were collected in *L'écriture et la psychologie des peuples*, was placed under the rubric of this remark of Marcel Cohen's ("La grande invention de l'écriture et son evolution"). But at each moment the rich suggestions made during the colloquium point beyond the graphological project. Mr. Cohen himself recognizes the difficulty and the premature character of such a task: "We can obviously not begin to deal with the graphology of peoples; it would be too delicate, too difficult. But we can express the idea that it is not only because of technical reasons that there are differences, there may be something else" (p. 342).

37. Text of 1923, collected in the *Essais de psychanalyse*, tr. fr., pp. 95 f. I shall quote a few lines: "For Fritz, when he was *writing*, the lines meant roads and the letters ride on motor-bicycles—on the pen—upon them. For instance, 'i' and 'e' ride together on a motor-bicycle that is usually driven by the 'i' and they love one another with a tenderness quite unknown in the real world. Because they always ride with one another they become so alike that there is hardly any difference between them, for the beginning and the end—he was talking of the small Latin alphabet—of 'i' and 'e' are the same, only in the middle the 'i' has a little stroke and the 'e' has a little hole. Concerning the Gothic letters 'i' and 'e,' he explained that they also ride on a motor-bicycle, and that it is only a difference like another make of bicycle that the 'e' has a little box instead of the hole in the Latin 'e.' The 'i's are skillful, distinguished and clever, have many pointed weapons, and live in caves, between which, however, there are also mountains, gardens and harbours. They represent the penis, and their path coitus. On the other hand, the 'l's are represented as stupid, clumsy, lazy and dirty. They live in caves under the earth. In 'L'-town dirt and paper gather in the streets, in the little 'filthy' houses they mix with water a dyestuff bought in 'I'-land and drink and sell this as wine. They cannot walk properly and cannot dig because they hold the spade upside down, etc. It became evident that the l's represented faeces. Numerous phantasies were concerned with other letters also. Thus, instead of the double 's,' he always wrote only one, until a phantasy afforded the explanation and solution of this inhibition. The one 's' was himself, the other his father. They were to embark together on a motor-boat, for the pen was also a boat, the copy-book a lake. The 's' that was himself got into the boat that belonged to the other 's' and sailed away in it quickly upon the lake. This was the reason why he did not write the two 's's' together. His frequent use of ordinary 's' in place of a long one proved to be determined by the fact that the part of the long 's' that was thus left out was for him as though one were to take away a person's nose.' This mistake proved to be determined by the castration-father and disappeared after this interpretation." I cannot cite here all the analogous examples that Melanie Klein analyzes. Let us read the following passage, of a more general value: "With Ernst as well as with Fritz I could observe that the inhibition in respect of writing and reading, that is,

the basis for all further school activity, proceeded from the letter 'i,' which, with its simple 'up and down,' is indeed the foundation of all writing (Note [Klein's footnote]: At a meeting of the Berlin P. A. Society, Herr Rohr dealt in some detail with the Chinese script and its interpretation on a psychoanalytic basis. In the subsequent discussion I pointed out that the earlier picture-script, which underlies our script too, is still active in the phantasies of every individual child, so that the various strokes dots, etc., of our present script would only be simplifications, achieved as a result of condensation, displacement and other mechanisms familiar to us from dreams and neuroses, of the earlier pictures whose traces, however, would be demonstrable in the individual.) The sexual-symbolic meaning of a penholder is apparent in these examples. . . . It can be observed how the sexual-symbolic meaning of the penholder merges into the act of writing that the latter discharges. In the same way the libidinal significance of reading is derived from the symbolic cathexis of the book and the eye. In this there are at work, of course, also other determinants afforded by the component-instincts, such as 'peeping' in reading, and exhibitionistic, aggressive sadistic tendencies in writing; at the root of the sexual-symbolic meaning of the penholder lay probably originally that of the weapon and the hand. Corresponding with this too the activity of reading is a more passive, that of writing a more active, one, and for the inhibitions of one or the other of them the various fixations on the pregenital stages of organization are also significant" (tr. fr. [Marguerite Derrida (Paris, 1967)], p. 98) [English original, "The Role of the School in the Libidinal Development of the Child," *Contributions to Psycho-Analysis*: 1921–1945 (London, 1948), pp. 73–74, 75–76]. Cf. also [Julian de] Ajuriaguerra, [Françoise] Coumes, [Anne] Denner, Lavonde-Monod, [Roger] Perron, [Mira] Stamback, *L'écriture de l'enfant* [Neuchatel-Paris], 1964).

38. Cf. Husserl, *L'Origine de la géometrie*.

39. "*L'écriture cunéiforme et la civilisation mésopotamienne*," *EP*, pp. 74 f.

40. Alfred Métraux, "*Les primitifs, signaux et symboles, pictogrammes et protoécriture*." One example among many others of what Métraux calls "attempt at phoneticism": "Thus, the Cheyenne chief called 'tortoise-following-his-female' will be represented by a person with two tortoises above him. 'Little-man' will be identified by the silhouette of a child outlined above his head. This expression of proper names hardly raises problems when it is a question of concrete things, but it puts the imagination of the scribe to a hard test if he has to render abstract ideas through pictography. To transcribe the name of a person called 'highway,' an Oglagla Indian had recourse to the following symbolic combination: strokes parallel to footprints make us think of 'road,' a bird painted close to it evokes the rapidity which is evidently one of the attributes of 'good routes.' It is clear that only those who already know the names corresponding to these symbols can decipher them. On that count, these designs will have a mnemotechnic value. As another example, let us take the proper name 'Good-Weasel.' From the animal's mouth, drawn in a realistic fashion, emerge two wavy lines that ordinarily symbolize the flow of words. This sign being used for 'good discourses,' it is supposed that the reader will only retain the adjective and forget the idea of discourse" (*EP*, pp. 10–11).

41. *EP*, p. 12.

42. *EP*, p. 16. Here Métraux schematically summarizes the results of [Thomas] Barthel's *Grundlagen zur Entzifferung der Osterinselschrift* [Hamburg, 1958].

43. Gernet, "La Chine, Aspects et fonctions psychologiques de l'écritures," in *EP*, pp. 32 and 38. Italics added. Cf. also Granet, *La pensée chinoise* ([Paris], 1950), chap. 1.

44. Questioning by turns the logico-grammatical structures of the West (and first Aristotle's list of categories), showing that no correct description of Chinese writing can tolerate it, Fenollosa recalled that Chinese poetry was essentially a script. He remarked, for example: "Should we pass formally into the study of Chinese poetry, . . . we should beware of English [*occidental*] grammar, its hard parts of speech, and its lazy satisfaction with nouns and adjectives. We should seek and at least bear in mind the verbal undertone of each noun. We should avoid the 'is' and bring in a wealth of neglected English verbs. Most of the existing translations violate all of these rules. The development of the normal transitive sentence rests upon the fact that one action in nature promotes another; thus the agent and the object are secretly verbs. For example,

our sentence, 'Reading promotes writing,' would be expressed in Chinese by three full verbs. Such a form is the equivalent of three expanded clauses and can be drawn out into adjectival, participial, infinitive, relative or conditional members. One of many possible examples is, 'If one reads it teaches him how to write.' Another is, 'One who reads becomes one who writes.' But in the first condensed form a Chinese would write, 'Read promote write.' " "L'écriture chinoise considerée comme art poétique," tr. fr., *Mesures* (Oct. 1937), no. 4, p. 135 [English original, "The Chinese Written Character as A Medium for Poetry," included in Ezra Pound, *Instigations* (New York, n.d.), pp. 383–84].

45. Naturally we cannot think of describing here the infinite mass of factual content that we name in this paragraph. In an indicative and preliminary way, I cite the following works, all with important bibliographies: James Février, Marcel Granet, Marcel Cohen, Madeleine V.-David, op. cit. Cf. also Alfred Métraux, article cited, *EP*, p. 19 (see the comments of Germaine Dierterlen, p. 19 and Marcel Cohen, p. 27); Jacques Gernet, article cited, pp. 29, 33, 37, 38, 43; Jean Sainte Fare Garnot, "Les hieroglyphes, l'évolution des écritures égyptiennes" *EP*, pp. 57, 68, 70; René Labat, article cited, pp. 77, 78, 82, 83; Olivier Masson "La civilisation égéenne," "Les écritures crétoises et mycéniennes," *EP*, p. 99. Emmanuel Laroche, "L'Asie mineure, les Hittites, peuple à double écriture," *EP*, pp. 105–11, 113. Maxime Rodinson, "Les sémites et l'alphabet," "Les écritures sudarabiques et éthiopéennes," *EP*, pp. 136–45. Jean Filliozat, "Les écritures indiennes," "Le monde indien et son système graphique," *EP*, p. 148. Henri Lévy-Bruhl, "L'écriture et le droit," *EP*, pp. 325–33. See also *EP*, "Confrontations et conclusions," pp. 335 f.

Part II: Chapter 1

1. In *Structural Anthropology*. Cf. also "Introduction a l'oeuvre de Marcel Mauss," (op. cit.), p. 35.

2. It is especially *Tristes Tropiques*, all through that "Writing Lesson" (chap. 18) whose theoretical substance is to be found also in the second of the "Entretiens avec Claude Lévi-Strauss," G. Charbonnier, "Primitifs et civilisés," [*Les lettres nouvelles* 10 (1961), pp. 24–33; translated as *Conversations with Claude Lévi-Strauss*, by John and Doreen Weightman (London, 1969), pp. 21–31]. It is also *Structural Anthropology* ("Problems of Method and Teaching," particularly in the chapter speaking of the "criterion of authenticity," p. 400 [p. 363]). Finally, less directly, *The Savage Mind*, the part seductively entitled "Time Recaptured."

3. *The Savage Mind*, p. 327 [p. 247], cf. also p. 169 [p. 127].

4. "Jean-Jacques Rousseau, fondateur des sciences de l'homme," p. 240. It deals with a lecture included in the volume *Jean-Jacques Rousseau*—La Baconnière—1962. A theme dear to Merleau-Ponty is recognizable here: the work of anthropology *realizes* the imaginary variation in search of the essential invariant.

5. The idea of an originarily figurative language was pretty widespread at this time; it is to be found particularly in Warburton and in Condillac, whose influence on Rousseau is massive in this area. As for Vico: Bernard Gagnebin and Marcel Raymond have asked in connection with the *Essay on the Origin of Languages*, if Rousseau had not read the *Scienza Nuova* when he was Montaigu's secretary in Venice. But if Rousseau and Vico both affirm the metaphoric nature of primitive languages, Vico alone attributes to them this divine origin, also the theme of disagreement between Condillac and Rousseau. Moreover, Vico is one of the rare believers, if not the only believer, in the contemporaneity of origin between writing and speech: "Philologists [Derrida's version would incorrectly read "philosophers"] have believed that among the nations languages first came into being and then letters; whereas . . . letters and languages were born twins and proceeded apace through all their three stages" (*Scienza Nuova* 3, I) [*The New Science of Giambattista Vico*, tr. Thomas Goddard Bergin and Max Harold Fisch (Ithaca, 1968), p. 21]. Cassirer does not hesitate to affirm that Rousseau has "summarized" in the *Essay* Vico's theories on Language (*Philosophie der symbolischen*

Formen [(Berlin, 1923–29; translated as *The Philosophy of Symbolic Form*, by Ralph Manheim (New Haven, 1953)], I, I, 4).

6. "What we have here are thus two extreme types of proper name between which there are a whole series of intermediate cases. At one extreme, the name is an identifying mark which, by the application of a rule, establishes that the individual who is *named* is a member of a preordained class (a social group in a system of groups, a status by birth in a system of statuses). At the other extreme, the name is a free creation on the part of the individual who *gives the name* and expresses a transitory and subjective state of his own by means of the person he names. But can one be said to be really naming in either case? The choice seems only to be between identifying someone else by assigning him to a class or, under cover of giving him a name, identifying oneself through him. One therefore never names: one classifies someone else if the name is given to him in virtue of his characteristics and one classifies oneself if, in the belief that one need not follow a rule, one names someone else 'freely,' that is, in virtue of characteristics of one's own. And most commonly one does both at once" (p. 240) [p. 181]. Cf. also "The Individual as A Species" and "Time Recaptured" (chapters 7 and 8): "In every system, therefore, proper names represent the quanta of *signification* below which one no longer does anything but point. This brings us to the root of the parallel mistakes committed by Peirce and by Russell, the former's in defining proper names as 'indices' and the latter's in believing that he had discovered the logical model of proper names in demonstrative pronouns. This amounts in effect to allowing that the act of naming belongs to a continuum in which there is an imperceptible passage from the act of signifying to that of pointing. I hope that I have succeeded in showing that this passage is in fact discontinuous although each culture fixes its thresholds differently. The natural sciences put theirs on the level of species, varieties or subvarieties as the case may be. So terms of different degrees of generality will be regarded each time as proper names" (pp. 285–86) [p. 215].

Radicalizing this intention, it should perhaps be asked if it is any longer legitimate to refer to the pre-nominal "property" of pure "monstration"—pointing at—if pure indication, as the zero degree of language, as "sensible certitude," is not a myth always already effaced by the play of difference. It should perhaps be said of indication "proper" what Lévi-Strauss says of proper names: "At the lower end there is no external limit to the system either, since it succeeds in treating the qualitative diversity of natural species as the symbolic material of an order, and its progress towards the concrete, particular and individual is not even arrested by the obstacle of personal appellations: even proper names can serve as trems for a classification" (p. 288) [p. 218] (cf. also p. 242) [pp. 182–83].

7. [Pp. 269–70]. Since we read Rousseau in the transparence of the texts, why not slide under this scene that other taken out of a *Promenade* (9)? In spelling out all its elements one by one and minutely, I shall be less attentive to the opposition of term to term than to the rigorous symmetry of such an opposition. Everything happens as if Rousseau had developed the reassuring positive whose impression Lévi-Strauss gives us in the negative. Here is the scene: "But, soon weary of emptying my purse to make people crush each other, I left the good company and went to walk alone in the fair. The variety of the objects there amused me for a long time. I perceived among others five or six boys from Savoy, around a small girl who had still on her tray a dozen meagre apples, which she was anxious to get rid of; the Savoyards, on their side, would have gladly freed her of them; but they had only two or three pence among them all, and that was not much to make a great breach among the apples. This tray was for them the garden of the Hesperides; and the young girl was the dragon who guarded it. This comedy amused me for a long time; I finally created a climax by paying for the apples from the young girl and distributing them among the small boys. I had then one of the finest spectacles that can flatter a man's heart, that of seeing joy united with the innocence of youth, spreading everywhere about me. For the spectators themselves, in seeing it, partook of it, and I, who shared at such cheap expense this happiness, had in addition the joy of feeling that it was my work" (*Pléiade*, I, pp. 1092–93; [*The Reveries of a Solitary*, tr. John Gould Fletcher (New York, 1927), pp. 184–85]).

8. Of that word and that concept which, as I had suggested at the outset, has sense only within the logocentric closure and the metaphysics of presence. When it does not imply the possibility of an intuitive or judicative *adequation*, it nevertheless continues in *aletheia* to privilege the instance of a vision filled and satisfied by presence. It is the same reason that prevents the thought of writing to be simply contained within a science, indeed an epistemological circle. It can have neither that ambition nor that modesty.

9. A situation difficult to describe in Rousseauist terms, the professed absence of writing complicating things yet further: *The Essay on the Origin of Languages* would perhaps give the name "savagery" to the state of society and writing described by Lévi-Strauss: "These three ways of writing correspond almost exactly to three different stages according to which one can consider men gathered into a nation. The depicting of objects is appropriate to a savage people; signs of words and of propositions, to a barbaric people, and the alphabet to civilized peoples [*peuples policés*]" [p. 17].

10. "If the West has produced anthropologists, it is because it was so tormented by remorse" ("A Little Glass of Rum," *Tristes Tropiques*, chap. 38) [(p. 449) [p. 388]].

11. What one may read between the lines of the second *Disource*: "It is reason that engenders self-love, and reflection that confirms it: it is reason which turns man back upon himself, and divides him from everything that disturbs or afflicts him. It is philosophy that isolates him, and it is through philosophy that he says in secret, at the sight of the misfortunes of others: 'Perish if you will, I am secure' " (p. 60) [p. 184].

12. [*Jean-Jacques Rousseau*,] p. 245. Italics author's.

13. *Tristes Tropiques*, chap. 18. With respect to Diderot, let us note in passing that the severity of his judgment on writing and the book does not in any way yield to Rousseau. The article "book" [*livre*] which he wrote for the *Encyclopédie* is a most violent indictment.

14. *Tristes Tropiques*, chap. 6. "How I Became an Anthropologist."

15. In the Geneva lecture [see n. 4] Lévi-Strauss believes he can simply oppose Rousseau to the philosophies that take their "point of departure in the cogito" (p. 242).

16. Particularly in the *Conversations* with Georges Charbonnier which adds nothing to the theoretical substance of the "Writing Lesson."

17. This letter was never published by *Nouvelle critique*. It may be found in *Structural Anthropology*, p. 365 [pp. 340–41].

18. *Tristes Tropiques*, chap. 40: "In its own awy, and on its own level, each of them corresponds to a truth. Between Marxist criticism which sets Man free from his first chains, and Buddhist criticism, which completes that liberation, there is neither opposition nor contradiction. (The Marxist teaches that the apparent significance of Man's condition will vanish the moment he agrees to enlarge the object that he has under consideration.) Marxism and Buddhism are doing the same thing, but at different levels" (p. 476) [p. 395].

19. On this theme of chance, present in *Race et histoire* [published in French and English (*Race and History*) Paris, 1952] and in *The Savage Mind*, cf. above all the *Conversations*, pp. 28–29 [pp. 24–26]; in developing at length the image of the gambler at the roulette wheel, Lévi-Strauss explains that the complex combination that constitutes Western civilization, with its type of historicity, determined by the use of writing, could very well have developed at the beginning of humanity, it could have developed very much later, it developed at this moment, "there is no reason why this should be so, it just is. However, you may say: 'That is not very satisfactory.' " This chance is soon after determined as the "acquisition of writing." This is an hypothesis that Lévi-Strauss admittedly does not abide by but of which he says "we should begin by considering it as a possibility." Even if it does not imply a belief in chance (cf. *The Savage Mind*, pp. 22 and 291 [pp. 13–14 and 220]), a certain structuralism must invoke it in order to inter-relate the absolute specificities of structural totalities. We shall see how this necessity is also imposed on Rousseau.

20. It concerns only a small subgroup which is followed by the anthropologist only in its nomadic period. This subgroup has a sedentary life as well. In the introduction to the thesis one will find: "It is unnecessary to emphasize that this is not an exhaustive study of Nambikwara life and society. We were able to share the life of the natives only during

the nomadic period, and that alone would suffice to limit the range of our investigation. A voyage undertaken during the sedentary period would no doubt bring essential pieces of information and would correct the whole view. We hope one day to be able to undertake it" (p. 3). Is this limitation, which seems to have been definitive, not particularly significant with respect to the question of writing, which is clearly linked more intimately than most things and in an essential way, with the phenomenon of sedentarity?

21. *De l'origine du langage, Oeuvres complètes* [Paris, 1848], Bk. VIII, p. 90. The continuation of the text, that I cannot quote here, is most instructive if one is interested in the origin and function of the word "barbarian" and other related words.

22. "La chine, aspects et fonctions psychologiques de l'écriture," *EP*, p. 33.

23. "For thousands of years, after all, and still today in a great part of the world, writing has existed as an institution in societies in which the vast majority of people are quite unable to write. The villages where I stayed in the Chittagong hills in Pakistan [now Bangladesh] are populated by illiterates; yet each village has a scribe who fulfills his function for the benefit both of individual citizens and of the village as a whole. They all know what writing is and, if need be, *can* write: but they do it from outside as if it were a mediator, foreign to themselves, with which they communicate by an oral process. But the scribe is rarely a functionary or an employee of the group as a whole; his knowledge is a source of power—so much so, in fact, that the functions of scribe and usurer are often united in the same human being. This is not merely because the usurer needs to be able to read and write to carry on his trade, but because he has thus a twofold *empire over* his fellows" (p. 342) [pp. 290–91].

24. *Histoire et ethnologie* (*Revue de metaphysique et de morale*, [LIV, iii & iv,] 1949, [pp. 363–91] and *Structural Anthropology*, p. 33 [pp. 25–26]): "The anthropologist is above all interested in unwritten data, not so much because the peoples he studies are incapable of writing, but because that with which he is principally concerned differs from everything men ordinarily think of recording on stone or on paper."

25. Recalling, in "A Little Glass of Rum," that "In the neolithic age, Man had already made most of the inventions which are indispensable to his security. We have seen why writing need not be included among these," Lévi-Strauss remarks that man in earlier times was certainly "no more free than he is today." "But it was his humanness alone which kept him enslaved. As he had only a very restricted control over Nature, he was protected, and to a certain degree emancipated, by the protective cushion of his dreams" (p. 452) [p. 390]. Cf. also the theme of the "neolithic paradox" in *The Savage Mind*, p. 22 [p. 13].

26. However, "the scientific mind," Lévi-Strauss writes, "does not so much provide the right answers as ask the right questions" (*The Raw and the Cooked*, p. 15) [p. 7].

27. "Facilitate," "favor," "reinforce," such are the words chosen to describe the operation of writing. Is that not to forbid every essential and rigorous determination of principle?

28. Cf., for example, Leroi-Gourhan, *Le geste et la parole*. Cf. also *EP*.

29. Many propositions of this type are to be found in Valéry.

30. *Esprit* [XXXI, cccxxii] (November 1963), p. 652. Cf. also *The Raw and the Cooked*, p. 35 [p. 26].

Part II: Chapter 2

1. *La transparence et l'obstacle* [Paris, 1958] p. 154. Naturally, I can only cite Rousseau's interpreters to indicate borrowings or to circumscribe a debate. But it goes without saying that every reader of Rousseau is guided by the admirable edition of the *Oeuvres complètes* now in progress at the "Bibliothèques de la Pléiade," and by the masterful work of Messrs. [François] Bouchardy, [Pierre] Burgelin, [Jean-Daniel] Candaux, [Robert] Derathé, [Jean] Fabre, [Michel] Foucault, [Bernard] Gagnebin, [Henri] Gouhier, [Bernard] Groethuysen, [Bernard] Guyon, [Robert] Osmont, [Georges] Poulet, [Marcel] Raymond, [Sven] Stelling-Michaud and, here especially, Jean Starobinski.

2. Edition Garnier, p. 17. My references are to the *Oeuvres complètes* (Pléiade edi-

tion) only in cases where the text has been published in one of the three volumes that have currently appeared. Other works will be cited from the Garnier editions. Of the *Essay on the Origin of Languages*, which we cite from the 1817 Bélin edition, I indicate, for the sake of convenience, only the numbers of the chapters.

3. *Rêveries*. Septième Promenade (*Pléiade* I, pp. 1066–67 [pp. 144–45]. Italics added. It may be objected that the animal represents a natural life even more animated than the plant, but one can only deal with it dead. "The study of animals is nothing without anatomy" (p. 1068) [p. 146].

4. Ibid. Without looking for a principle of reading there, I refer, out of curiosity and from among many other possible examples, to what Karl Abraham says of the Cyclops, of the fear of being blind, of the eye, of the sun, of masturbation etc. in *Oeuvres complètes*, tr. Ilse Barande [and E. Grin (Payot, 1965)] II, pp. 18 f. Let us recall that in a sequence of Egyptian mythology, Seth, helper of Thoth (god of writing here considered as a brother of Osiris), kills Osiris by trickery (cf. Vandier, op. cit., p. 46). Writing, auxiliary and suppletory, kills the father and light in the same gesture (Cf. supra, p. 101, **328–29 n. 31**).

5. " 'Little one' was my name; 'Mama' was hers; and we always remained 'Little one' and 'Mama,' even when advancing years had almost obliterated the difference between us. I find that these two names give a wonderfully good idea of the tone of our intercourse, of the simplicity of our manners, and, above all, of the mutual relation of our hearts. For me she was the tenderest of mothers, who never sought her own pleasure, but always what was best for me; and if sensuality entered at all into her attachment for me, it did not alter its character, but only rendered it more enchanting, and intoxicated me with the delight of having a young and pretty mamma whom it was delightful to me to caress—I say caress in the strictest sense of the word, for it never occurred to her to be sparing of kisses and the tenderest caresses of a mother, and it certainly never entered my mind to abuse them. It will be objected that, in the end, we had relations of a different character; I admit it, but I must wait a little—I cannot say all at once" (p. 106) [p. 109]. Let us add this sentence from Georges Bataille: "I am myself the 'little one,' I have only a hidden place" (*Le petit* [2d edition (Paris, 1963), p. 9]).

6. This passage is often cited, but has it ever been analyzed for itself? The Pléiade editors of the *Confessions*, Gagnebin and Raymond, are no doubt right in being cautious, as they are, systematically and inevitbaly, of what they call psychiatry (note p. 1281. This same note checks off very usefully all the texts where Rousseau recalls his "follies" or "extravagances.") But this caution is not legitimate, it seems to me, except to the extent that it concerns the abuse—which has hitherto no doubt been confounded with the use—of psychoanalytic reading, and where it does not prescribe the duplication of the usual commentary which has rendered this kind of text most often unreadable. We must distinguish here between, on the one hand, the often hasty and careless, but often also enlightening, analyses by Dr. René Laforgue ("Etude sur J.-J. Rousseau," in *Revue française de psychanalyse*, I, ii [1927], pp. 370 f.; and *Psychopathologie de l'échec* [1944], [Paris], pp. 114 f.), which moreover do not consider the texts I have just cited, and, on the other hand, an interpretation which would take into more rigorous account, at least in principle, the teachings of psychoanalysis. That is one of the directions in which Jean Starobinski's fine and careful analyses are engaged. Thus, in *L'oeil vivant*, the sentence that has given us pause is reinscribed within an entire series of examples of analogous substitution, borrowed mostly from the *Nouvelle Héloise*; this one for example, among other "erotic fetishes": "All the parts of your scattered dress present to my ardent imagination those of your body that they conceal. This delicate headdress which sets off the large blond curls which it pretends to cover; this happy bodice shawl against which at least once I shall not have to complain; this elegant and simple gown which displays so well the taste of the wearer; these dainty slippers that a supple foot fills so easily; this corset so slender which touches and embraces . . . what an enchanting form . . . in front two gentle curves . . . oh voluptuous sight . . . the whalebone has yielded to the force of the impression . . . delicious imprints, let me kiss you a thousand times!" (p. 147 [tr. Judith H. McDowell (University Park and London, 1968), pp. 122–23].

But do the singularity of these substitutions and the articulation of these displacements hold the attention of the interpreter? I wonder if, too concerned with reacting against a reductionist, causalist, dissociative psychology, Starobinski does not in general give too much credit to a totalitarian psychoanalysis of the phenomenological or existentialist style. Such a psychoanalysis, diffusing sexuality in the totality of behavior, perhaps risks blurring the cleavages, the differences, the displacements, the fixations of all sorts that structure that totality. Do the place or the places of sexuality not disappear in the analysis of global behavior, as Starobinski recommends: "Erotic behavior is not a fragmentary given; it is the manifestation of a total individual, and it is as such that it ought to be analyzed. Whether it is to neglect it or to make it a privileged subject of study, one cannot limit exhibitionism to the sexual 'sphere': the entire personality is revealed there, with some of its fundamental 'existential choices.'" (*La transparence et l'obstacle*, pp. 210–11. A note refers us to the *Phénoménologie de la perception* of [Maurice] Merleau-Ponty [(Paris, 1945); *Phenomenology of Perception*, tr. Colin Smith (New York, 1965)]). And does one not, in this way, risk determining the pathological in a very classic manner, as "excess" thought within "existential" categories: "In the perspective of a global analysis, it will appear that certain primary givens of consciousness constitute at the same time the source of Rousseau's speculative thought, and the source of his follly. But these given-sources are not morbid by themselves. It is only because they are lived in an excessive manner, that the malady declares itself and is developed. . . . The morbid development will realize the caricatural placing in evidence of a fundamental 'existential' question that consciousness was not able to dominate" (p. 253).

7. Page 165 [p. 171].

8. In these celebrated pages of the first Book of the *Confessions*, Rousseau compares the first experiences of reading ("secret and ill-chosen reading") to the first discoveries of auto-eroticism. Not that the "filthy and licentious [books]" encouraged him in it. Quite the contrary. "Chance aided my modest disposition so well, that I was more than thirty years old before I set eyes upon any of those dangerous books which a fine lady finds inconvenient because they can only be read with one hand" (p. 40) [p. 40]. Without these "dangerous books," Jean-Jacques gives himself to other dangers. The continuation of the paragraph which closes thus is well known: "It is sufficient for me to have defined the origin and first cause of a propensity which has modified all my passions, and which, restraining them by means of themselves, has always made me slow to act, owing to my excessive impetuosity in desire" (p. 41) [p. 41]. The intention and the letter of this passage should be related to another page of the *Confessions* (p. 444 [p. 459]. Cf. also the editors' note), and to the page from which I quote these lines: "for I have always had a fancy for reading while eating, if I am alone; it supplies the want of society. I devour alternately a page and a morsel. It seems as if my book were dining with me" (p. 269) [p. 278].

9. See editors' note, p. 1569. [The English translation includes the sentence quoted in the Pléiade note on p. 617.]

10. [*Correspondance générale de J.-J. Rousseau* (Paris, 1934), vol. 19, p. 242, vol. 20, p. 122, the latter actually addressed to M. de Sartine, Lieutenant-general of police.]. See also the *Confessions* (p. 109, editors' note).

11. Pages 331–32 [pp. 340–41] (italics added), Starobinski (*La transparence et l'obstacle*, p. 221) and the editors of the *Confessions* (p. 332, n.1) justly relate the use of the word "supplement" to what is made of it on p. 109 [p. 111] ("dangerous means of assisting it" [a literal translation would be "dangerous supplement"]).

Part II: Chapter 3

1. Cf. *La voix et le phénomène*.

2. Here it would be appropriate to quote extensively from *Vom Wesen des Grundes* [Halle, 1931; translated into French as "Ce qui fait l'être-essentiel d'un fondement ou 'raison,'" by Henry Corbin, in *Qu'est-ce que la métaphysique* (Paris, 1951)] and *Vom*

Wesen der Wahrheit [(Frankfurt, 1943); translated into English as "Of the Essence of Truth" by R. F. C. Hull and Adam Crick in *Existence and Being* (London, 1949); and into French as *De l'essence de la verité*, by Alphonse de Waelhens and Walter Biemel (Louvain/Paris, 1948)], particularly everything relating to the notions of *Polis, Agathon*, and *Aletheia*.

3. I shall refer to the following editions: *Grammaire générale et raisonnée de Port-Royal, par* Arnaud *et* Lancelot; *Précédée d'un Essai sur l'origine et les progrès de la Langue française*, par M. Petitot, et suivi par le *Commentaire* de M. Duclos, auquel on a ajouté des notes. Perlet AN XI.-1803.

4. Page 396. The most precise echo of this text is found, outside of the *Essay*, in the notes grouped in the *Pléiade* edition under the title *Prononciation* (vol. 2, p. 1248) and in the Streckeisen-Moultou edition (op. cit.), under the title *Fragment d'un Essai sur les langues*. In his essay Rousseau connects the degradation of morals, the corruption of pronunciation, and the progress of writing. He even cites the examples of corruptions whose occurrence he had the dubious privilege of witnessing, and which are caused by a "fault of pronunciation in the organ, or in the intonation, or in the habit." "Words whose change in pronunciation I have witnessed: Charolois [Sharolwa]—Charolès [Sharolay], secret [sucray]—segret [sugray], presécuter—[perzcuter], etc." All these matters are also to be found in the abbé Du Bos, *Réflexions critiques sur la poésie et sur la peinture* (1719) [*Critical Reflections on Poetry, Painting, and Music*; with An Inquiry into the Rise and Progress of the Theatrical Entertainments of the Ancients, tr. Thomas Nugent (London, 1748)].

5. Page 397.

6. Page 421. "It is a people in a body that makes a language. It is by the convergence of an infinity of needs, ideas, and physical and moral causes, varied and combined through a succession of centuries, without the possibility of identifying the periods of change, alterations, or progress. Often caprice decides; sometimes it is the subtlest metaphysics, which eludes the reflection and knowledge of even those who are their authors. . . . Writing (I speak of the writing of sounds) was not born through a slow and imperceptible progression: it was many a century before it was born; but it was born all at once, like light."

7. *Pléiade* edition (vol. 1, p. 560, n. 3).

8. *Le rationalisme de Rousseau* (1948), pp. 17–18. *Rousseau et la science politique de son temps* (1950), p. 146.

9. *Political Writings*, I: 10. Cf. also [Charles William] Hendel, *Jean-Jacques Rousseau, Moralist* (London and New York, 1934), vol. 1, pp. 66 f.

10. Cf., infra p. 227 [p. 194].

11. I have already cited Derathé's note. Cf. also Starobinski, *Pléiade* edition, vol. 3, p. 154, n. 2.

12. He is referring to Mandeville. See Starobinski's note in the *Pléiade* edition of the *Discourse*, to which I refer here (vol. 3, p. 154; Italics added.)

13. Italics added. The examples chosen by Rousseau are not insignificant: "Not to mention the tenderness of mothers for their offspring and the perils they encounter to save them from danger, it is well known that horses show a reluctance to trample on living bodies. One animal never passes by the dead body of another of its species without being disturbed: there are even some which give their fellows a sort of burial; while the mournful lowings of the cattle when they enter the slaughter-house show the impressions made on them by the horrible spectacle which meets them. We find, with pleasure, the author of *The Fable of the Bees* obliged to own that man is a compassionate and sensible being, and laying aside his cold subtlety of style, in the example he gives, to present us with the pathetic description of a man who, from a place of confinement, is compelled to behold a wild beast tear a child from the arms of its mother, grinding its tender limbs with its murderous teeth, and tearing its palpitating entrails with its claws. What horrid agitation must not the eye-witness of such a scene experience, although he would not be personally concerned! What anxiety would he not suffer at not being able to give any assistance to the fainting mother and the dying infant! Such is the pure emotion of nature, prior to all kinds of reflection!"

14. I ask if one may, like Derathé, oppose the doctrine of *Emile* to that of the Second *Discourse* on this point ("In *Emile* pity becomes a sentiment derived from the love of self whereas the second *Discourse* would set these two principles against each other" *Le rationalisme de J.-J. Rousseau*, pp. 99–100).

15. It is known that Rousseau had projected writing an entire work on the role of women in history. It seems that for him the question was as much of restoring an historical truth (the importance of woman's role, which the history of man has deliberately dissimulated) as of recalling the occasionally pernicious character of that role, through making "some observations on great men who have allowed themselves to be governed by women. Themistocles, Antony, etc. Fulvia, Antony's wife, provoked war because she was not loved by Caesar." (Cf. *Sur les femmes* and *Essai sur les évènements importants dont les femmes ont été la cause secrète. Pléiade*, vol. 2, pp. 1254–57.)

16. [Derrida's references to this text are to the Garnier edition. I have quoted the corresponding passages from *Politics and the Arts: Letter to M. d'Alembert on the Theatre*, tr. Allan Bloom (Glencoe, Illinois, 1960), and have placed page references within brackets.] Garnier edition, p. 204 [pp. 100–01]. One should also read note 1 in its entirety; there the author is surprised that "such pleasantry, of which one sees sufficient application, has been taken at face value by Frenchmen of spirit."

17. Second *Discourse*, p. 159. On the subject of the relationship of these themes to the opposed or related themes of Voltaire, Buffon, or Pufendorf, see the notes in the *Pléiade* edition, pp. 158–59.

18. *Letter to M. d'Alembert*, pp. 206–07 [pp. 103–04]. See also the note on p. 206 [p. 103]. It begins thus: "Women, in general, do not like any art, know nothing about any, and have no genius." "In the union of the sexes . . . the man should be strong and active; the woman should be weak and passive" (*Emile*, p. 446) [p. 322].

Is it not remarkable that Nietzsche, sharing completely this conception of femininity, of the degradation of culture, and of the genealogy of morals as servitude to the slave, should have hated Rousseau? Is it not remarkable that he thought Rousseau an eminent representative of the slave morality? Is it not remarkable that he should have seen precisely in pity the true subversion of culture and the form of servitude of the masters?

There is much to say along this line. It will lead us in particular to a comparison of the Rousseauist and Nietzschean models of femininity; domination or seduction is equally feared, whether it takes, alternatively or simultaneously, the form of cloying sweetness, or of destructive or devouring fury. It would be a mistake to interpret these models as *simple* affirmations of virility. Perhaps Novalis saw more profoundly and beyond what Rousseau himself calls at the beginning of *The Confessions* (p. 12) [p. 10] his "character so effeminate." "Rousseau's *philosophèmes* are, absolutely speaking, a feminine philosophy or a theory of femininity" (*Encyclopédie*, tr. M. de Gandillac, Edition de Minuit, p. 361).

19. Cf. Derathé, *Le rationalisme de Rousseau*, most especially pp. 30 f.

20. Derathé recalls that "Durkheim is . . . the first to have indicated the importance of this notion of potential faculty in Rousseau." *Le rationalisme de Rousseau*, p. 13. Cf. [Emile] Durkehim, "Le Contrat social, histoire du livre," *Revue de métaphysique et du morale*, xxv, i & ii, (Jan.–Feb. 1918), pp. 1–23, 129–61. Most of Rousseau's systematic contradictions would be resolved by bringing into play this concept of a potential faculty which operates as a solder at every point of rupture, and primarily at the points where society breaks—and articulates itself—with Nature. Cf. Derathé, *Rousseau et la science politique de son temps*, p. 148. It is remarkable that this theme of *potentiality* should be so often misunderstood, wherever it crops up. This misunderstanding is at the center of the problematics of innate ideas, and of Locke's relationship with Leibniz, or Leibniz's with Descartes.

21. Naturally, this argument is marked by a reflection that would associate Kant and Rousseau differently from the chapter on morality. The entire chain that makes possible the communication of the movement of temporalization and the schematism of imagination, pure sensibility and the auto-affection of the present by itself, all that

Heidegger's reading has strongly repeated in *Kant and the Problem of Metaphysics* could, by way of a carefully staked out path, lead us back on to Rousseauist ground.

22. The *Essay* allows us to believe as little in original war as in the Golden Age. From these two points of view, the *Essay* matches the great Rousseauist theses. In the Geneva manuscript (the first version of *The Social Contract*, dating from 1756), Rousseau writes that "the golden age was always a condition alien to the human race."

23. Pages 153–54 [pp. 181–82; Cole's note: Justin, *Hist.* ii, 2. So much more does the ignorance of vice profit the one sort than the knowledge of virtue the other.] Cf. also p. 152 and the fragment on *L'état de nature*: "As long as men retained their first innocence, they needed no guide other than the voice of Nature; as long as they did not become evil, they were dispensed from being good" ([Pléiade, vol. 3,] p. 476).

24. The textual unity of this doctrine of pity is confirmed once again if these four passages are placed side by side: "Although pity is native to the human heart, it would remain eternally quiescent unless it were activated by imagination. How are we moved to pity? By getting outside ourselves and identifying with a being who suffers. We suffer only as much as we believe him to suffer. It is not in ourselves, but in him that we suffer" (*Essay*) [p. 32].

"So pity is born, the first relative sentiment which touches the human heart according to the order of nature. To become sensitive and pitiful the child must know that he has fellow-creatures who suffer as he has suffered, who feel the pains he has felt, and others which he can form some idea of, being capable of feeling them himself. Indeed, how can we let ourselves be stirred by pity unless we go beyond ourselves, and identify ourselves with the suffering animal, by leaving, so to speak, our own nature and taking his. We only suffer so far as we suppose he suffers; the suffering is not ours but his. So no one becomes sensitive till his imagination is aroused and begins to carry him outside himself" (*Emile*, p. 261) [p. 184].

"It is clear that such transport supposes a great deal of acquired knowledge. How am I to imagine ills of which I have no idea? How would I suffer in seeing another suffer, if I know not what he is suffering, if I am ignorant of what he and I have in common. He who has never been reflective is incapable of being malicious and vindictive. He who imagines nothing is aware only of himself; he is isolated in the midst of mankind" (*Essay*) [p. 32].

"To show the means by which he may be kept in the path of nature is to show plainly enough how he might stray from that path. So long as his consciousness is confined to himself there is no morality in his actions; it is only when it begins to extend beyond himself that he forms first the sentiments and then the ideas of good and ill, which make him indeed a man, and an integral part of his species" (*Emile*, p. 257) [p. 181].

25. Cf. notes 3 and 4 of the Pléiade edition of *Confessions*, p. 560.

26. [Pierre Maurice Masson], "Questions de chronologie rousseauiste," *Annales* [*de le société*] *Jean-Jacques Rousseau*, IX (1913): 37.

27. [Alfred Victor Espinas], "Le 'système' de Jean-Jacques Rousseau," *Revue* [*Internationale*] *de l'enseignement* [XXX (October 15, November 15], 1895).

28. That was also the conclusion of H. Baudouin (*La vie et les oeuvres de Jean-Jacques Rousseau* [Paris, 1891]). The page he devotes to the *Essay* shows how Rousseau, and notably the *Essay*, might then have normally been read, and allows us to measure the distance to be covered: "Between the *Discourse on the Sciences* and the *Discourse on Inequality*, one must place *The Essay on the Origin of Languages*. Rousseau also gave it the title of Essay on the *Principle of Melody*. In fact in it he deals equally with language and music; which does not stop him from speaking a great deal about society and its origins. . . . The date of its composition is not perfectly clear; but the context indicates it sufficiently. Even the passages therein where Rousseau speaks of the pernicious role of the arts and sciences show that his opinions were already decided on this point: it is well-known that he was yet hesitant at the time of composition of his discourse. He therefore could have written the *Essay* only at a later date. On the other hand, it is easy to see that on the question of society he had not yet formed those radical ideas which he professed in his book on Inequality. (The quotation from the *Lettre sur les spectacles* in

a note to Chapter 1 is not a serious enough objection. Nothing is simpler, in fact, than a note added after the event.) Such as it is, the *Essay* offers a curious enough mixture of truth and falsehood, caution and audacity. The method is constantly hypothetical, there are no proofs, the social doctrines are at the very least mediocre. Often one would believe one were reading the *Inequality*: same style, same turn of phrase, same investigative procedures, same sequences of reasoning and ideas. But in the midst of all this, there is such caution in the conclusions, such a respect for Holy Writ and tradition, such a faith in Providence, such a horror of the materialist philosophers, that one finds oneself disarmed, as it were. In sum then, Rousseau has created a transitional work here, which presages evil, rather than producing it fully. The good that he placed there might have led him to saner ideas, if he had known how to make use of it; unhappily enough he placed there the germs of those errors which he developed in his later works. A memorable example of the care that one must take in order somehow to orient his talent and life well, and what sort of route a principle, pushed to its extreme consequences by an extremist logic, would carve out" (vol. I, pp. 323–34).

29. "L'unité de la pensée de Jean-Jacques Rousseau," *Annales*, VIII (1912): 1.

30. "This is how Rousseau's work appears to me: very diverse, tumultuous, agitated by all sorts of fluctuations, and yet, beginning from a certain moment, continuous and constant in its spirit, in its successive directions. . . ." And opposing *the writer or the man*, "dreamer and timid," to the work which "lives with an independent life," moving by "its intrinsic properties" and "quite charged with revolutionary explosives," leading equally to "anarchy," and "social despotism," Lanson concludes: "We must not try to hide this contrast of man and work, which may even be called contradiction; for that is Rousseau himself." Is it still necessary to specify that what interests us in Rousseau, and here in Lanson, is the obstinate veiling of this "critical" unveiling of the "contradiction" between the man and the work? Allowing us the concession of a certain internal contradiction, what is hidden from us under this "Rousseau himself?" Where and when is one assured that there would have to be something that fits the proposition "that is Rousseau himself?"

31. That was Lanson's opinion as well and he finally came to agree with Masson.

32. "Note, in particular, that the long note to Chapter 7 was added and that the entire Chapter 6 ['Whether It Is Likely That Homer Knew How to Write'] was considerably revised. In the first draft, Rousseau thought it very probable that Homer did not know writing (pp. 29–30 of the manuscript). Rereading his text, he struck out that passage and added in the margin: 'N. B. This is a stupidity that one must avoid, since the story of Bellerophon, in the *Iliad* itself, proves that the art of writing was in use in the author's time, but this would not prevent his work from being more sung than written'" (Masson's Note. The examination of the manuscript seemed less fruitful to me than Masson seems to think).

33. "I am publishing the final text at which Rousseau seems provisionally to have stopped, for the Preface remains unfinished. . . . This Preface had already been published by A. Jansens, in his *J.-J. Rousseau als Musiker* (Berlin 1884), pp. 472–73, but with many lacunae and faults of reading which characterize most of his publications of texts" (Extract from Masson's notes).

34. Here is a passage that relates to the distinction between animal and human languages, which the *Essay* equates with the distinction between non-perfectibility and perfectibility: "That single distinction would seem to be far-reaching. It is said to be explicable by organic differences. I would be curious to see such an explanation" (end of Chapter I) [p. 10].

35. Is it useful to indicate here that we find the same problematics of example and a literally identical formulation in *The Critique of Practical Reason*, certainly, but above all in the *Metaphysische Anfangsgründe der Tugendlehre* (1797) [translated as *The Principles of Virtue: Part II of The Metaphysics of Morals*, by James Ellington (New York, 1964)], which distinguishes between the example as the particular case of a practical rule (*Exempel*) and the example as the particular instance of the purely "theoretical presentation of a concept (*Beispiel*)" (§52 [p. 148]), and in the notes to *Uber*

Pedagogik [translated as *The Educational Theory of Immanuel Kant*, by Edward Franklin Buchner (Philadelphia, 1908)], published in 1803?

36. "Mons. Rameau, insisting absolutely, in his system, that all our harmony should be drawn from nature, has had recourse, for this purpose, to another experience of his own invention. . . . But first, the experience is false. . . . Though we should suppose the truth of this experience, this would be very far from removing the difficulties. If, as Mons. Rameau pretends, the whole of harmony is derived from the resonance of a sonorous body, it does not then derive from it the single vibrations of a sonorous body which does not resound. In effect, it is a strange theory to derive from what does not resound, the principles of harmony; and it is strange in physic, to make a sonorous body vibrate and not resound, as if the sound itself was at all different from the air, shaken by these vibrations" [pp. 343–44].

37. Cf., for example, *The Confessions*, p. 334 [pp. 343–44].

38. "When we reflect, that of all the people of the earth, who all have a music and an air, the Europeans are the only ones who have a harmony and concords, and who find this mixture agreeable; when we reflect, that the world has continued so many years, without, amongst the cultivation of the beaux arts throughout mankind in general, any one's having known this harmony; that no animal, no bird, no being in nature, produces any other concord than the unison, no other music than melody; that the eastern languages, so sonorous, so musical; that the Greek air, so delicate, so sensible, exercised with so much art, have never guided these voluptuous people, fond of our harmony, that without it, their music had such prodigious effects, that with it, ours is so weak; that lastly, if it was reserved for the northern nations, whose rough and brutal organs are more touched with the eclat and noise of the voice, than with sweetness of the accent, and the melody of the inflections, to make this vast discovery, and to give it as a foundation of all the rules in art: When I say, we pay attention to the whole of this, it is very difficult not to suspect that all our harmony is but a gothic and barbarous invention, which we should never have followed if we had been more sensible of the true beauties of art, and of music truly natural. Mons. Rameau, however, pretends that harmony is the source of the greatest beauties in music; but this opinion has been contradicted by facts and reason.—By facts, because all the great effects of music have ceased, and it has lost all its energy and force since the invention of the counter point; to which I add, that beauties purely harmonic, are ingenious beauties, which please only persons versed in the art; whereas the true beauties of music, being those of nature, are, and ought to be, equally sensible to every man, whether learned or ignorant.

"By reason, because harmony furnishes no imitation by which music, forming images, or expressing sentiments, may be raised to the dramatic or imitative genus, which is the most noble part of art, and the only one energetic. Every thing that expresses only the physic of sounds, being greatly bounded in the pleasure which it gives us, and having very little power over the human heart" (*Dictionary*) [pp. 191–92].

Let us note in passing that Rousseau admits to two things that he elsewhere denies: 1. That the beauties of music are natural; 2. that there is an animal song, a song merely melodic, to be sure, but consequently absolutely pure. Thus the meaning and function of the contradiction within the handling of the concepts of nature and animality are confirmed: music, for example, does not become what it is—human—and does not transgress animality except through what threatens it with death: harmony.

39. Chapter 13, "On Melody," is almost entirely given over to painting. We must cite this remarkable page in extenso. Now more than ever, it is possible to comment on its irony in more than one sense: "Imagine a country in which no one has any idea of drawing, but where many people who spend their lives combining and mixing various shades of color are considered to excel at painting. Those people would regard our painting precisely as we consider Greek music. If they heard of the emotions aroused in us by beautiful paintings, the spell of a pathetic scene, their scholars would rush into a ponderous investigation of the material, comparing their colors to ours, determining whether our green is more delicate or our red more brilliant. They would try to find out which color combinations drew tears, which could arouse anger. The Burettes of that

country would examine just a few tattered scraps of our paintings. Then they would ask with surprise what is so remarkable about such coloring.

"And, if a start were made in a neighboring country toward the development of line and stroke, an incipient drawing, some still imperfect figure, it would all be treated as merely capricious, baroque daubing. And, for the sake of taste, one would cling to this simple style, which really expresses nothing, but brilliantly produces beautiful nuances, big slabs of color, long series of gradually shaded hues, without a hint of drawing.

"Finally, the power of progress would lead to experiments with the prism. And immediately some famous artist would base a beautiful system on it. Gentlemen, he will tell you, true philosophy requires that things be traced to physical causes. Behold the analysis of light; behold the primary colors; observe their relations, their proportions. These are the true principles of the pleasure that painting gives you. All this mysterious talk of drawing, representation, figure, is just the charlatanry of French painters who think that by their imitations they can produce I know not what stirrings of the spirit, while it is known that nothing is involved by sensation. You hear of the marvels of their pictures; but look at my colors" [pp. 53–54].

And Rousseau prolongs yet further the imaginary discourse of this foreigner who is in fact nothing other than the correspondent—foreigner and theoretician of painting—of a French musician and musicographer, Rameau's analogue. "French painters, he would continue, may have seen a rainbow. Nature may have given them some taste for nuance, some sense of color. But I have revealed to you the great and true principles of art. I say of art! of all the arts, gentlemen, and of all the sciences. The analysis of colors, the calculation of prismatic refractions, give you the only exact relations in nature, the rule of all relations. And everything in the universe is nothing but relations. Thus one knows everything when one knows how to paint; one knows everything when one knows how to match colors.

"What are we to say to a painter sufficiently devoid of feeling and taste to think like that, stupidly restricting the pleasurable character of his art to its mere mechanics? What shall we say of a musician, similarly quite prejudiced, who considers harmony the sole source of the great effect of music. Let us consign the first to housepainting and condemn the other to doing French opera" [p. 55].

40. It is in that passage of the first book which explains how "in this manner I learnt to covet in silence, to dissemble, to lie, and, lastly, to steal" (p. 32) [p. 30]. For various reasons the following passage, coming a little before the above, appears to me to be worth rereading at this point: "The trade in itself was not disagreeable to me: I had a decided taste for drawing; the handling of a graving-tool amused me; and as the claims upon the skill of a watchmaker's engraver were limited. I hoped to attain perfection. I should, perhaps, have done so, had not my master's brutality and excessive restraint disgusted me with my work. I stole some of my working hours to devote to similar occupations, but which had for me the charm of freedom. I engraved medals for an order of knighthood for myself and my companions. My master surprised me at this contraband occupation, and gave me a sound thrashing, declaring that I was training for a coiner, because our medals bore the arms of the Republic. I can swear that I had no idea at all of bad, and only a very faint one of good, money. I knew better how the Roman *As* was made than our three-sou pieces" [p. 30].

41. The closest reference here leads to Condillac. Cf. the chapter "On the Origin of Poetry," in *An Essay on the Origin of Human Knowledge* (1756).

42. This fragment, the manuscript of which is lost, was published in 1861 by Streckeisen-Moultou. It is reprinted in the Pléiade edition of the *Political Fragments* (vol. III, p. 529), under the title "L'influence des climats sur la civilisation."

43. Rousseau adds in a note: "Turkish is a northern tongue" [p. 49 n. 1].

44. The word "*suppléer*" [to compensate] appears also in the text on *Pronunciation* in connection with accent (p. 1249).

45. Cf. also the *Projet concernant de nouveaux signes pour la musique* (1742), the *Dissertation sur la musique moderne* (1743), *Emile*, p. 162 [p. 114] (the entire development that begins with "You may perhaps suppose that as I am in no hurry to teach

Emile to read and write, I shall not want to teach him to read music"), and J. Starobinski, *La transparence et l'obstacle*, pp. 177 f.

46. With regard to the oratorical intonation which "modifies the very substance of discourse, without perceptibly altering prosodic accent," Duclos concludes: "In writing we mark interrogation and surprise; but how many movements of the soul, and consequently how many oratorical inflections, do we possess, that have no written signs, and that only intelligence and sentiment may make us grasp! Such are the inflections that mark anger, scorn, irony, etc., etc." (p. 416).

47. Cf. Derathé, *Rousseau et la science politique de son temps*, p. 175.

48. Jean Mosconi shows that the state of pure Nature is not absent from the *Essay* and that the "age of 'huts' has . . . in the two texts, nothing comparable," "Analyse et genèse: regards sur la théorie du devenir de l'entendement au XVIIIe siècle," *Cahiers pour l'analyse*, 4, [Sept.–Oct., 1966]: 75.

49. In its elements at least, this argument does not belong to Rousseau. It owes a great deal particularly to Condillac's *Essay on the Origin of Human Knowledge* (the first section on "The Origin and Progress of Language"). Through Condillac, we are also brought back to Warburton (op. cit.). Probably also to the *Réflexions critiques sur la poésie et la peinture* of the abbé Du Bos ([Paris,] 1719) notably to Chapter 35 on the origin of languages, and to the *Rhétorique* [*ou l'Art de Pârler*, third edition (Paris, 1688)] of Father Lamy who is cited elsewhere in the *Essay*. On these problems, we refer to the *Pléiade* edition of the second *Discourse* by J. Starobinski (especially to p. 151, n. 1) and to his fine analysis of the theme of the sign in *La transparence et l'obstacle* (pp. 169 f.).

50. With regard to the "natural language" of the child: "To the language of intonation [*voix*] is added the no less forcible language of gesture. The child uses, not its weak hands, but its face" (*Emile*, p. 45; italics added) [p. 32].

51. "Psychonanalysis will tell us that in dreams dumbness is a common representation of death" (Freud, "The Theme of the Three Caskets," [*SE* XII, 295; GW X, 24–37]. Rousseau too says in the *Reveries* that silence "offers us an image of death" (p. 1047).

52. One finds all these examples once again, and presented in related terms, in Book 4 of *Emile*. It is a praise of the economy of speech in the eloquence of antiquity: "The most startling speeches were expressed not in words but in signs; they were not uttered but shown. A thing beheld by the eyes kindles the imagination, stirs the curiosity, and keeps the mind on the alert for what we are about to say, and often enough the thing tells the whole story. Thrasybulus and Tarquin cutting off the heads of the poppies, Alexander placing his seal on the lips of his favourite, Diogenes marching before Zeno, do not these speak more plainly than if they had uttered long orations? What flow of words could have expressed the ideas as clearly?" (p. 400) [p. 287].

53. This story, which all great works on writing recall, comes to us from Clement of Alexandria and Herodotus. Rousseau had perhaps read it in Warburton's *The Essay on Hieroglyphs*: "The story is told by *Clemens Alexandrinus* in these Words: *It is said that* Idanthura, *a King of the* Scythians, *as* Pherecydes Syrius *relates it, when ready to oppose* Darius, *who had passed the* Ister, *sent the* Persian *a Symbol instead of Letters, namely, a Mouse, a Frog, a Bird, a Dart and a Plow.* Thus this Message being to supply both *Speech and Writing* the Purport of it was, we see, expressed by a Composition of *Action* and *Picture*" [p. 87]. Warburton recalls Herodotus's interpretation (I.IV): "Darius believed that the Scythians wanted to tell him through this enigma that they presented him earth and water, and submitted to him. The mouse signified the earth to those in the know; the toad signified water; the bird could be compared to the horse; and by the arrows was meant that they were denuding themselves of their power. But Gobrias, one of those who destroyed the Magi, gave another interpretation: 'If instead of fleeing like birds, you hide yourself in the earth or water, like mice and toads, you will perish by *these* arrows.' For Herodotus, in place of one barb, counts five arrows and says nothing of the plough, etc. . . . I believed I would please the reader by adding this commentary of Herodotus to Pherecydes' text" (pp. 63–65) [my edition of

The Divine Legation of Moses lacked the footnote cited by Derrida, the translation above is mine].

54. Cf. *Speech and Phenomena* [op. cit.].

55. We shall content ourselves with referring to the notes and bibliographies given by the makers of the *Pléiade* edition of the *Reveries* (pp. 1045 f.).

56. *Discourse*: "The invention of the other arts must therefore have been necessary to compel mankind to apply themselves to agriculture" (p. 173) [pp. 200–01]. *Essay*: "The first men were hunters or shepherds, and not tillers of the soil; herdsmen, not men of the fields. Before the ownership of it was divided, no one thought to cultivate land. Agriculture is an art that requires tools" (Chapter IX) [p. 33].

57. *An Essay on the Origin of Human Knowledge* (II:I. "Of the Origin and Progress of Language." A. Colin edition, p. 111 [pp. 169–70]).

58. Although it further sharpens the break between the state of pure Nature and the state of budding society, the *Discourse* multiplies quite a few allusions to "the inconceivable pains and the infinite space of time that the first invention of languages must have cost" (p. 146) [p. 174], to "the rapidity of time," to the "almost insensible progress of things in their beginnings"; "for the slower the events were in their succession, the more rapidly may they be described" (p. 167) [p. 195]. A remark that Voltaire found "ridiculous." See editor's note in the Pléiade edition.

59. Rousseau is more specific in a note: "It is not possible to determine the precise degree of man's natural indolence. It is said that he lives only to sleep, to vegetate, to rest. Only with difficulty can he resolve to bestir himself enough to avoid dying of starvation. Nothing sustains the love of so many savages for their mode of life as does this delicious indolence. The feelings that make man restless, foresighted, and active arise only in society. To do nothing is the primary and the strongest passion of man after that of self-preservation. If one looks carefully, he will see that, just as among ourselves, it is in order to achieve repose that everyone works. It is laziness that even makes us hard-working" [pp. 38–39, n. 4].

60. Derathé has qualified it thus (*Rousseau et la science . . .*, p. 180).

61. Cf. Starobinksi, *La transparence et l'obstacle*, pp. 190–91.

62. If the force of dispersion can appear before and after the catastrophe, if the catastrophe reunites men at the time of its appearance but disperses them anew by its persistence, the coherence of the theory of need, under its apparent contradictions, is explained. Before the catastrophe, need draws men apart; during the catastrophe, it brings them together. "The earth nourishes men; but when their initial needs have dispersed them, other needs arise which reunite them, and it is only then that they speak, and that they have any incentive to speak. In order to avoid contradicting myself, I must be allowed time to explain myself" [*Essay*, p. 39].

63. *Essays*: "The cycles of the seasons are another more general and permanent cause that is bound to produce the same effect in the climates subject to this variety" [p. 40]. *Fragment* on climates: "A different diversity that multiplies and combines the preceding is that of the seasons. Their succession, containing several climates alternately within a single one, accustoms men who live there to their diverse impressions, and renders them capable of traveling and living in all countries of which the temperature is felt in theirs" (p. 531).

64. This description of the festival should be compared to that in the *Letter to d'Alembert* and, more specifically as far as time is concerned, to that in *Emile*. "We will be our own servants in order to be our own masters. Time will fly unheeded" [p. 318]. A very brief passage will lead us to the understanding that these two notations are not juxtaposed: the possibility of the "comparison," in the sense given to that concept by Rousseau, is the common root of temporal difference (which permits the measurement of time and throws us outside of the present) and of the difference or lack of symmetry between master and man.

65. Cf. Raymond, "Introduction," *Les Rêveries* [*du promeneur solitaire* (Geneva, 1967), pp. 7–52] and the chapter that Starobinski devotes to "La transparence du cristal" in *La transparence et l'obstacle*, p. 317. Rousseau is never cited in [Gaston] Bachelard's

L'eau et les rêves [*Water and Dreams*, tr. Edith Rogers Farrell, dissertation, University of Iowa, 1965].

66. As long as incest is permitted, there is no incest, to be sure, but there is also no amorous passion. Sexual relationships limit themselves to the reproductive needs; or they do not exist at all: this is the situation of the child as given in *Emile*. But would Rousseau say the same thing about the child's relationship with his mother as he says here about his relationship with his sister? It is true that the mother is quite absent from *Emile*: "The child brought up in accordance with his age is alone. He knows no attachment but that of habit, he loves his sister like his watch, and his friend like his dog. He is unconscious of his sex and his species; men and women are alike unknown" (p. 256) [p. 180].

Part II: Chapter 4

1. "It has often occurred to me in skeptical moments not only that Homer knew how to write, but that he wrote in the manner of his time. I am very sorry if this doubt is formally contradicted by the story of Bellerophon in the *Iliad*" [p. 23]. Subsequently engaged in denying the significance, that is to say the authenticity, of the Bellerophon episode, Rousseau pays no attention to its meaning: that the only piece of writing in Homer was a letter of death. Bellerophon unwittingly carried on himself the inscription of his own death sentence. Within an infinite chain of representations, desire carries death via the detour of writing. "Beautiful Anteia the wife of Proitos was stricken/With [illicit] passion to lie in love with him [Bellerophon, Glaucus' son]." Unsucccessful, she threatens her husband: "Would you be killed, O Proitos? Then murder Bellerophontes/ Who tried to lie with me in love, though I was unwilling." The king, representing Anteia's desire, dare not kill with his own hands. He does dare to write, and deferring murder, he traces with his hand "in a folding tablet" in "murderous symbols" (*thymophthora*—["*passion-wasting*"]) [the passages from the *Iliad* are taken from the Richmond Lattimore translation (Chicago, 1951), p. 157.] He sends Bellerophon to Lycea, charging him with these "fatal signs." Reading this message, illegible to Bellerophon, Proitos's father-in-law, reigning at Lycea, will understand that it speaks of putting the carrier of these "symbols" to death. In his turn, he defers the murder, sends Bellerophon to risk death through killing the invincible Chimaera or the famous Solymes, and lays ambushes for him. To no end. He finishes by giving him his daughter. Later, Bellerophon is no longer loved by the gods and he goes alone, wandering "the plain of Aleios, eating his heart out, skulking aside from the trodden track of humanity" (Lattimore, pp. 157–58).

2. Vico says that he understood the origin of languages at the moment when, after many difficulties, it appeared to him that the first nations "were nations of poets; by the same principles, we first identified the true origin of languages" (*Scienza Nuova*, I: 174). The distinction among three languages would correspond, *mutatis mutandis*, to Rousseau's schema; the second language, which marks the appearance of both speech and metaphor, would, strictly speaking, be the moment of origin, when the poetic song is not yet broken into articulation and convention. Let us compare: "Three kinds of language were spoken which compose the vocabulary of this Science: (1) that of the time of the families when gentile men were newly received into humanity. This, we shall find, was a mute language of signs and physical objects having natural relations to the ideas they wished to express. (2) That spoken by means of heroic emblems, or similitudes, comparisons, images, metaphors, and natural descriptions, which make up the great body of the heroic language which was spoken at the time the heroes reigned. (3) Human language using words agreed upon by the people, a language of which they are absolute lords" (3, 1, p. 32) [Bergin, op. cit., p. 18]. Elsewhere: "That first language . . . was not a language in accord with the nature of the things it dealt with . . . but was a fantastic speech making use of physical substances endowed with life and most of them imagined to be divine" (3, 1, p. 163) [pp. 114–15]. "We find that the principle of these

origins both of languages and of letters lies in the fact that the early gentile peoples, by a demonstrated necessity of nature, were poets who spoke in poetic characters. This discovery, which is the master key of this Science, has cost us the persistent research of almost all our literary life" (3, *Idea of the Work*, I: 28–29) [p. 19]. "Men vent great passions by breaking into song, . . . that . . . they were inexpressive save under the impulse of violent passions—[lead to the conjecture that] their first languages must have been formed in singing" (3, I: 95 [J.-B. Vico, *Oeuvres choisies*], tr. [J.] Chaix-Ruy [Paris, 1946]) [p. 69]. "All that has been reasoned out seems clearly to confute the common error of the grammarians, who say that *prose speech came first and speech in verse afterward*. And within *the origins of poetry*, as they have here been disclosed, we have found *the origins of languages and letters*" (Book II, *Poetic Wisdom*, Chap. V, § 5, [*Oeuvres choisies de Vico*,] tr. [J.] Michelet [(Paris, 1893–99), vol. 27,] (p. 430) [p. 142]. For Vico, as for Rousseau, the progress of language follows the progress of articulation. Thus, language suffers a fall and humanizes itself through the loss of its poetry and its divine character: "The language of the gods was almost entirely mute, only very slightly articulate; the language of the heroes, an equal mixture of articulate and mute, . . . the language of men, almost entirely articulate and only very slightly mute" (3, I: 178, tr. Chaix-Ruy) [p. 134].

3. Condillac recognized the convergence of his and Warburton's thoughts, rather than his debt to the latter. Yet this convergence, as we shall immediately see, is not complete: "This section was near finished, when I happened to light on an essay on hieroglyphics, extracted from the second volume of Dr. Warburton's Divine Legation of Moses; a work equally distinguished for strength of reasoning and variety of erudition. With pleasure I found that this author's notions and mine coincided, in supposing that language must, from its first beginning, have been very figurative and metaphysical. My own reflections had led me to observe, that writing at first could be no more than a simple picture; but I had not as yet made any attempt to discover by what progress mankind arrived at the invention of letters, and it seemed difficult to me to succeed in the inquiry. The task has been exceedingly well executed by Dr. Warburton, of whom the greatest part of this chapter has been borrowed" (Chap. 13, "Of Writing," § 127, p. 177) [p. 273 n.].

4. Page 195. "This way of *Speaking* by *Simile*, we may conceive to answer to the *Chinese Marks* or Characters in *Writing*; and as from such Marks proceeded the abbreviated Method of *Alphabetic Letters*, so from the *Similitude*, to make Language still more expedite and elegant, came the METAPHOR; which is indeed but a *Similitude* in little: For Men so conversant in matter still wanted sensible Images to convey abstract Ideas" (*Essai sur les hiéroglyphes*, T.I, pp. 85–86) [p. 94]. "This, and not the Warmth of a Poetic Fancy, as is commonly supposed, was the true Original of figurative Expression. We see it even at this Day in the Style of the *American* Barbarians, tho' of the coldest and most flegmatic Complexions. . . . Their *Phlegm* could only make their Stile *concise*, not take away the *Figures*: and the Conjunction of these different Characters in it, shews plainly that Metaphors were from Necessity, not Choice. . . . Thus we see it has ever been the way of Man, both in *Speech* and *Writing*, as well as in *Clothes* and *Habitations*, to turn his Wants and Necessities into Parade and Ornament" (pp. 195–97) [pp. 147–48].

5. METAPHORE, S. F. (gram.). "M. du Marsais says that it is a figure by which the proper signification of a noun (I would prefer to say *a word*) is carried over, so to speak, to another signification which is not appropriate to it except by virtue of a comparison which is in the mind. A word taken in its *metaphoric* sense loses its proper signification, and acquires a new one that presents itself to the mind only by the comparison undertaken between the proper meaning of the word and what one compares it to: for example, when one says that falsehood often decks itself in the colors of truth." And after long quotations from Marsais: "I have sometimes heard M. du Marsais reproached for being a little prolix; and I realize that it is possible, for example, to give fewer examples of *metaphor*, and to develop them less extensively; but who has no wish at all for such a happy prolixity? The author of a dictionary of language cannot read this article

on the metaphor without being struck by the astonishing exactitude of our grammarian in distinguishing the proper meaning from a figurative one, and in assigning to one the foundation of the other."

6. On this point, Rousseau's doctrine is most Cartesian. It is itself interpreted as a justification of Nature. The senses, which are natural, never deceive us. On the contrary, it is our judgment that misleads us and plays Nature false. "Nature never deceives us; we deceive ourselves"—a passage from *Emile* (p. 237) [p. 166] which the autograph manuscript replaces with the following: "I say it is impossible for our senses to deceive us because it is always true that we feel what we feel." The Epicureans are praised for having recognized this but criticized for having maintained that "the judgments that we made about our sensations were never false." "We sense our sensations, but we do not sense our judgments."

7. Here again we are reminded of a Viconean text: "The poetic characters, in which the essence of the fables consists, were born of the need of a nature incapable of abstracting forms and properties from subjects. Consequently they must have been the manner of thinking of entire peoples, who had been placed under this natural necessity in the times of their greatest barbarism. It is an eternal property of the fables always to magnify the ideas of particulars. On this there is a fine passage in Aristotle's *Ethics* in which he remarks that men of limited ideas erect every particular into a maxim. The reason must be that the human mind, which is indefinite, being constricted by the vigor of the senses, cannot otherwise express its almost divine nature than by thus magnifying particulars in imagination. It is perhaps on this account that in both the Greek and the Latin poets the images of gods and heroes always appear larger than those of men, and that in the returned barbarian times the paintings particularly of the Eternal Father, of Jesus Christ and of the Virgin Mary are exceedingly large" (*Scienza Nuova*, 3, II: 18, tr. Chaix-Ruy) [p. 279].

8. II.I, pp. 111–12 [pp. 168, 171]. This is also Warburton's procedure in the remarkable paragraphs that he devotes to the "Origin and Progress of Language" (I: 48 f.) [pp. 81 f.]. Thus: "In judging only from the nature of things, and without the surer aid of revelation, one should be apt to embrace the opinion of Diodorus Siculus (lib.ii) and Vitruvius (lib.ii, cap.I) that the first men lived for some time in woods and caves, after the manner of beasts, uttering only confused and indistinct sounds, till, associating for mutual assistance, they came, by degrees, to use such as were articulate, for the arbitrary signs or marks, mutually agreed on, of those ideas in the mind of the speaker, which he wanted to communicate to others. Hence the diversity of languages; for it is agreed on all hands that speech is not innate." And yet, "nothing being more evident from scripture, than that language had a different original. God, we there find, taught the first man religion; and can we think he would not, at the same time, teach him language?" [Condillac, p. 170].

9. II.I. 2, 3, p. 113 [pp. 172–73]. We have italicized only "frightened" and "mimicked." The same examples are reconsidered in the chapter on "The Origin of Poetry:" "For example, in the mode of speaking by action, to give an idea of a person that had been frightened, they had no other way than to mimic the cries and natural signs of fear" (§ 66, p. 148) [pp. 227–28].

10. "Every object at first received a particular name without regard to genus or species, which these primitive originators were not in a position to distinguish; . . . so that, the narrower the limits of their knowledge of things, the more copious their dictionary must have been. . . . Add to this, that general ideas cannot be introduced into the mind without the assistance of words, nor can the understanding seize them except by means of propositions. This is one of the reasons why animals cannot form such ideas or ever acquire that capacity for self-improvement [*perfectibilité*] which depends on them. . . . We must then make use of [. . .] language [*parler*] in order to form general ideas. For no sooner does the imagination cease to operate than the understanding proceeds only by the help of words. If then the first inventors of speech could give names only to ideas they already had, it follows that the first substantives could be nothing more than proper names" (pp. 149–50. See also the editor's notes) [pp. 177–78].

11. "The present of the infinitive" (edition of 1782).

12. Vol. I, p. 1174.

13. See Chapter 13 ("On Script") and especially § 134 of the *Essay*.

14. II, I, Chap. 13 [pp. 273–74]. See the corresponding pages in Warburton (I: 5) [p. 67] which take into account what Condillac does not—the "mutual influences" which speech and writing exercise upon each other. "To explain this mutual Influence in the Manner it deserves, would require a just Volume" (p. 202) [*Warburton*, p. 150]. (On the impossibility of a purely figurative script, cf. Duclos op. cit., p. 421.)

15. H. Gouhier broaches it systematically and in depth (*Nature et Histoire dans la pensée de Jean-Jacques Rousseau. Annales J.-J. Rousseau*, vol. 33 [1953–55])—To the question of the Judaeo-Christian model he replies—"Yes and no." (p. 30).

16. As for this monogeneticism and the economic rationality of this genealogy, Condillac's prudence has limits, although the *Traité des systèms* (1749) is careful enough (Chap. 17): "If all the characters in use since the origin of history could have come down to us with a key which would explain them, we would disentangle this progress in a sensible manner. With those that are extant, however, we can develop this system, if not in all its detail, at least sufficiently so as to assure us of the generation of the different types of script. M. Warburton's work is a proof of this" (Cf. DE, p. 101).

17. On the problem of boustrophedon writing, cf. J. Février and M. Cohen, op. cit. And on the relationships among writing, the via rupta, and incest, cf. "Freud et la scène de l'écriture" in *L'écriture et la différence* [FF (op. cit.)].

18. On these questions and their subsequent development, I take the liberty of referring once again to *Speech and Phenomenon* (op. cit.).

19. This final reappropriation of presence is most often named by Rousseau as an anthropological telos: "Let man appropriate everything to himself; but what is important for him to appropriate is man himself" (Manuscript of *Emile*). But as usual this anthropologism essentially comes to terms with a theology.

20. Other examples of the mistrust that everything operating through writing in social and political life inspired in Rousseau:—In Venice: "Here one is dealing with an invisible government and always in writing, which requires great circumspection." 2. —"In popular estimation the Platonic Institution stands for all that is fanciful and unreal. For my own part I should have thought the system of Lycurgus far more fanciful [chimérique] had he merely committed it to writing" (*Emile*, p. 10) [p. 8] J. de Maistre will say: "What is most essential is never written down and can in fact not be written down without exposing the state."

21. This is the reason why Rousseau admits the necessity of representation even while deploring it. See the *Considérations sur le gouvernement de Pologne* [*The Government of Poland*, tr. Willmoore Kendall (New York, 1972)]; there he proposes a very rapid turnover of representatives in order to make their "seduction more costly and more difficult," which is to be related to the rule formulated by the *Contract*, according to which "often should the Sovereign show himself" (p. 426) [p. 75]; cf. also Derathé, *Rousseau et la science politique de son temps* (pp. 277 f.).

What logic does Rousseau obey when he thus justifies the necessity of a representation that he simultaneously condemns? Precisely the logic of representation; the more it aggravates its disease, the more representative it becomes, representation restores what it takes away: the presence of the represented. A logic according to which one must force oneself "to draw from the disease itself its own remedy" (Fragment on *L'état de nature*, p. 479) and according to which, at the end of its movement, convention rejoins Nature, servitude liberty, etc. ("What then? Is liberty maintained only by the help of slavery? It may be so. Extremes meet." *The Social Contract*, p. 431 [p. 79]).

22. *De l'état de nature*, [*Pléiade*, vol. 3], p. 478. Cf. also, *Emile*, p. 70 [p. 49].

23. On the rebus, cf. supra, p. 136 [p. 90]. Vico who also distinguishes among three conditions or steps of writing, gives as one example, among others, of primitive writing (ideographic or hieroglyphic, "born spontaneously" and "not drawing its origins from conventions at all") the "rebus of Picardy" [p. 128]. "The second form of script is equally and completely spontaneous: it is a symbolic or emblematically heroic script" (coats of arms, blazonry, "mute comparisons which Homer calls *semata*, the signs in

which the heroes wrote" [p. 129]). "The third form of writing: alphabetic script" (*Science nouvelle*, 3, 1, pp. 61–62, 181–82, 194, tr. Chaix-Ruy).

24. This is Duclos's thesis: "Writing (I speak of the writing of sounds) was not born like language through a slow and imperceptible progression: many centuries passed before it was born; but it was born all at once, like light." After having retraced the history of pre-alphabetic scripts, Duclos appeals to that "stroke of genius" among languages: "Such is Chinese writing today, corresponding to ideas rather than to sounds; such are with us the signs of algebra and Arabic numerals. Writing was in that condition, with no relationship with today's writing, when a happy and profound genius sensed that discourse, however varied and extended in terms of ideas, is yet composed of only a few sounds, and the point was merely to give each of the latter a representative character. If one reflects upon this, one will see that this art, once conceived, must have been formed almost simultaneously; and it is this that exalts the glory of the inventor. . . . It was much easier to count all the sounds of a language, than to discover that they could be counted. One was a stroke of genius, the other a simple result of attention" (op. cit., pp. 421–23).

25. *Emile*, p. 218 [pp. 152–53]. There Rousseau presents a theory of the origin of money, its necessity, and its danger.

26. Ibid. In the *Fragments politiques* also, one will read: "Gold and silver, being nothing more than representative signs of the material for which they have been exchanged, have properly speaking no absolute value." "Since money has no real value by itself, it takes a value by tacit convention in every country where it is in use . . ." (p. 520) and in the *Government of Poland*: "Money, in the last analysis, is not wealth, but merely the sign for wealth; and what you must multiply is not the sign but rather the represented thing" (p. 1008) [p. 73]. It is precisely at the opening of Chapter 15 on "Deputies or Representatives" that *The Social Contract* (Bk. III) condemns money as the power of servitude: "Make gifts of money, you will not be long without chains" [p. 77].

Cf. also Starobinski, *La transparence et l'obstacle*, pp. 129 f. and the editors' note 3 on p. 37 of vol. I of the Pléiade edition of the *Confessions*.

27. Cf. also the *Projet de constitution pour la Corse*, pp. 911–12.

28. *Confessions*, p. 237 [p. 245].

29. Garnier edition, p. 168 [p. 57]. Italics added.

30. Starobinski, *La transparence*, p. 119. I refer also to the entire chapter devoted to the fête (p. 114), which Starobinski opposes to the theatre as a "*world of transparence*" to a "*world of opacity*."

31. It is well-known that Rousseau ruthlessly denounced the mask, from the *Letter to M. d'Alembert* to the *Nouvelle Héloise*. One of the tasks of pedagogy consists precisely in neutralizing the effects of masks upon children. For let us not forget, "all children are afraid of masks" (*Emile*, p. 43) [p. 30]. The condemnation of writing is also, as if self-evidently, an ambiguous condemnation of the mask.

32. Among other analogies, by this distrust, with regard to the spoken text, of Corneille and Racine who were nothing but "talkers" even though, "imitating the English," they must sometimes "place the stage itself within representation" (*La Nouvelle Héloise*, p. 253) [*Eloisa* II., p. 62]. But surely these reconciliations must be effected with the greatest caution. The context sometimes places an infinite distance between two identical propositions.

33. Page 226 [pp. 127–28]. One will relate to this the following passage from *Emile*: "but when spring returns, the snow will melt and the marriage will remain; you must reckon for all seasons" (p. 570) [p. 411].

34. Cf. also *Emile*, pp. 66–69 [pp. 46–48].

35. Rousseau dreams of an unarticulated language, but he describes the origin of languages as the passage from the cry to articualtion. The consonant which for him goes hand in hand with articulation, is the becoming-language of sound, the becoming-phonetic of natural sonority. It is the consonant that gives the possibility of a linguistic pertinence to sound, by inscribing it within an opposition. Jakobson has shown, against current prejudices, that "in the acquisition of language, the first vocalic opposition is

posterior to the first consonantal oppositions; there is thus a stage when the consonants already fulfill a distinctive function, whereas the unique vowel yet serves only as stress to the consonant and as material for expressive variations. Thus we see the consonants acquiring phonemic value before vowels" ("Les lois phoniques du langage enfantin et leur place dans la phonologie générale," *Selected Writings* [The Hague, 1962], I: 325).